The World's Biggest Corporation
in the Global Economy

Wal*Mart World

Stanley D. Brunn, Editor

Routledge
Taylor & Francis Group
New York   London

Routledge is an imprint of the
Taylor & Francis Group, an informa business

Routledge
Taylor & Francis Group
270 Madison Avenue
New York, NY 10016

Routledge
Taylor & Francis Group
2 Park Square
Milton Park, Abingdon
Oxon OX14 4RN

© 2006 by Taylor & Francis Group, LLC
Routledge is an imprint of Taylor & Francis Group, an Informa business

Printed in the United States of America on acid-free paper
10 9 8 7 6 5 4 3 2 1

International Standard Book Number-10: 0-415-95137-2 (Softcover) 0-415-95136-4 (Hardcover)
International Standard Book Number-13: 978-0-415-95137-1 (Softcover) 978-0-415-95136-4 (Hardcover)

Library of Congress Cataloging-in-Publication Data

Wal-Mart world : the world's biggest corporation in the global economy / edited by Stanley D. Brunn.
    p. cm.
  Includes bibliographical references and index.
  ISBN 0-415-95136-4 (hb) -- ISBN 0-415-95137-2 (pb)
    1. Wal-Mart (Firm)--Management. 2. International business enterprises--Management. 3. International economic relations. I. Brunn, Stanley D.

HF5429.215.U6W36 2006
381'.14906573--dc22
                                                      2006001774

Visit the Taylor & Francis Web site at
http://www.taylorandfrancis.com

and the Routledge Web site at
http://www.routledge-ny.com

Dedication

For all those who empower victims of twenty-first-century injustices in premodern, modern, and postmodern worlds

Contents

Part IV   Culture, Communities, and Conflicts

Part V   Globalization

Introduction

In February 2004 I was invited to participate in an interdisciplinary conference at the University of California, Riverside, entitled "Globalization in World Systems: Mapping Change over Time." Attending this three-day National Science Foundation-funded conclave were junior and senior scholars from a number of social, behavioral, and policy sciences, including anthropology, economics, geography, political science, and sociology. Paper and panel sessions were devoted to a wide range of topics, including international finance, labor regulations, urbanization, governance, development, the applications of geographical information systems (GIS), and social network theory. The regional impacts of globalization on individuals, economies, institutions, and communities were highlighted during the formal and informal discussions, as was the emergence of antiglobalization and global justice movements. The major objective of this conference was to provide opportunities for those attending to discuss current research directions in their fields and to ferret out possibilities for individual and team research. By the end of the second day, I noted that the single major international corporation most mentioned in prepared papers, question-and-answer sessions, and panels was Wal-Mart. Others mentioned included McDonald's, Exxon, IBM, and KFC. While only a few of the papers were specifically devoted to finance, labor, and logistics issues involving Wal-Mart (the world's largest retail chain, with nearly 3,500 stores in the United States), it became apparent that, as social and policy scientists interested in labor, community, marketing, and organizational issues, we should examine more closely this Arkansas-based global retail giant.

In the conference's final session, I suggested that it seemed propitious for an edited volume to be devoted to various facets of this corporation's past, present, and future, including its "footprint" on U.S. cities, towns, and neighborhoods, and also its successes and failures in other countries. The contributors to such a volume could and would come from various disciplines and perspectives, including those from outside the United States. I identified a number of prospective authors at this Riverside conference who expressed interest in contributing to such a volume. The need for the volume became further evident when I participated in a small international and interdisciplinary conference, "Gated Communities," sponsored by the University of New Orleans, also in February 2004, and in a one-day meeting in March of that year sponsored by the Center for Work, Labor, and Democracy, the Humanities Center, and the Women's Center at the University of California, Santa Barbara. The title of this conference was "Wal-Mart: Template for 21st Century Capitalism." This was, to my knowledge, the first major interdisciplinary conference specifically devoted to Wal-Mart's world—economic clout, corporate culture, financial networks, labor issues, and community relations. I identified scholars at both the New Orleans and Santa Barbara conferences who wished to contribute to an edited volume.

Once I returned to the University of Kentucky from Santa Barbara, I prepared a prospectus for an edited volume on Wal-Mart, a prospectus that listed nearly thirty individuals who expressed interest in preparing original chapters. One of my specific aims was to ensure that the contributors included a wide-ranging group of scholars who would address a broad array of topics about the corporation. I wanted the chapters to appeal to colleagues in their own disciplines, but also to interdisciplinary, transdisciplinary, and international audiences. It seems to me that chapters dealing with the company's origins, financial history, labor relations, health care, supply chains, advertising, and marketing would be of interest to readers in the trade market as well as scholars and students. I sought authors who could write about Wal-Mart histories and experiences in countries and regions outside the United States, including those who worked outside North America. This international and interdisciplinary perspective seems especially important as we witness Wal-Mart's growth and expansion in Europe, Asia, and Latin America, albeit with varying degrees of success.

Authors contributing to this volume were given relatively free rein with respect to what approach and methodology they chose to employ. As social and policy scientists, we are used to and familiar with various perspectives and conceptual frameworks when writing about a corporation's structure, marketing and advertising, gender and labor relations, and community relations. In short, any volume that includes varying interpretations and insights is considered a strength by those in the social sciences. As editor, I placed no personal or philosophical litmus tests on the content of chapters. The result of this inclusiveness is that the volume, in my estimation, represents some of the best current thinking and research about this retail colossus, written by some of our brightest and most creative junior and senior scholars in geography, retailing, marketing, sociology, community relations, women's studies, and popular culture. This mix of authors is absolutely imperative in presenting state-of-the-art thinking and discussion about any major corporation. We also expect there will be views both supportive and critical of Wal-Mart's positions on a wide range of social, economic, and policy issues.

I am very pleased with the twenty-five chapters in this volume and with the forty-two authors, nearly half of whom are women. The mix includes graduate students and senior scholars from the United States, Mexico, United Kingdom, Germany, and China. Almost all of those I identified early on and invited to contribute a chapter came through. A few did not because of other pressing research commitments. Only a few prospective authors I contacted expressed some apprehension about contributing a chapter in a volume that they perceived or thought would be harshly or unfairly critical of the corporation. I am grateful to friends who suggested other authors who might fill in important lacunae about this corporation's operations in the United States and elsewhere. And I will not forget the handful of authors (they know who they are) who came through at the last minute with quality, important, and substantial contributions. There are twenty-six different universities represented among the authors. This mix of authors and universities attests to the transdisciplinary and international interests scholars have in studying this global retailing giant.

The result of the past eighteen months is a volume in which the academic community can take much pride. I believe it is the first interdisciplinary and international treatment of Wal-Mart in which a half dozen major issues are addressed. These include its early financing, labor and gender relations, views from popular culture critics, marketing and retailing, logistics chains, community relations, and operations in the United States, United Kingdom, Germany, Japan, China, and Mexico. Mention is made of successes and setbacks elsewhere, including South America, Southeast Asia, and Asia. While other books on Wal-Mart have appeared that focus on labor history issues and the corporation's images, this volume stands alone at this point in offering a comprehensive treatment of a larger number of related topics. The importance and immensity of Wal-Mart on the global scale is highlighted in various ways in the ensuing chapters. Suffice it to say that the number of hits for Wal-Mart in the Google search engine in late October 2005 was nearly 37 million, more entries than in the same database for Geneva, Vienna, Madrid, or Istanbul.

Organization

The volume is organized into five parts, each of which addresses a specific theme. Part I, "Wal-Mart and the World," includes three chapters. Peter Hugill looks at major transnational and international corporations throughout history, and places Wal-Mart's recent expansion into a global systems context. Matthew Zook and Mark Graham develop the "Wal-Mart nation" concept and present a cartographic essay that examines the location of stores throughout the United States and Canada and their densities and distributions near major interstates and selected metropolitan areas. The third chapter takes a look at Wal-Mart's global reach. Steve Burt and Leigh Sparks, two scholars who have published previously on this corporation, investigate the corporation's global reach, including countries where it has been more and less successful.

Part II, "Early Years and Store Location," also contains three chapters. William Graves investigates the source of early capital to finance this corporation; he concludes that investment came primarily from northeastern and midwestern states. Dennis Lord specifically looks at Wal-Mart's grocery retail successes in major metropolitan areas. Holly Barcus develops the concept of "Wal-Mart-scapes" and applies it to small towns and rural areas of northern Wisconsin. Her story is familiar to many residents in rural and small-town America.

In Part III, "Organizational Culture," the themes invoke Wal-Mart's culture and the major worker and supplier issues the company faces. Jane Dunnett and Stephen Arnold present an interesting, not always flattering view of the corporation's image. Ellen Rosen examines in greater detail some of the major issues faced by women who work for this retailing colossus. Jennifer Bair and Sam Bernstein zero in on Wal-Mart's recent history of labor relations with workers and suppliers. Finally, Lea VanderVelde meticulously looks into the company's legal history and concerns in the United States.

Part IV, "Culture, Communities, and Conflicts," contains six chapters, which cover a rather wide range of topics. Inasmuch as images are an important part of any major corporation's place in the marketplace and consumer mind-set, it only makes sense that Wal-Mart's images be subject to scrutiny. Stephen Arnold and colleagues, including authors from Germany and China, look at the images and wording used on Wal-Mart fliers. Barney Warf and Thomas Chapman develop a "cathedrals of consumption" concept; they look at what Wal-Mart's successes in the marketplace tell us about American consumerism. Ben Smith takes a slightly different angle on Wal-Mart's images, specifically how the company has been portrayed in a recent Hollywood movie, *Where the Heart Is*, and on a television sitcom, *King of the Hill*. The next chapter, by Alecia Brettschneider and Fred Shelley, takes a closer look at Wal-Mart's advertising budgets and compares them to the budgets of other large discount stores, and also examines what kind of community relations and contributions the corporation makes. Community relations have been a focus of renewed attention by this corporation. The final two papers in this part look at different perspectives on the Wal-Mart community. Fred Shelley, Adrienne Proffer, and Lisa DeChano compare the distribution of Wal-Mart stores to "red and blue states" and conclude, not too surprisingly, that there is a positive relationship between recent presidential voting in "red" states and Wal-Mart stores. A local controversial issue involving a Wal-Mart store is the theme of the chapter by Margath Walker, David Walker, and Yanga Villagómez Velázquez. They discuss local resistance to a recently opened Wal-Mart store near the historical and sacred site of Teotihuacán, Mexico.

Globalization is the focus of Wal-Mart's operations in Part V. These nine chapters address histories, successes, failures, and problems the corporation has experienced in various countries. Edna Bonacich and Jake Wilson investigate Wal-Mart's logistics operations, which are among the reasons the corporation has been successful in moving merchandise from manufacturers to its stores. They focus in particular on the China and southern California connections. Steve Burt and Leigh Sparks, who in Chapter 3 looked at Wal-Mart's global network, here consider the corporation's mixed record in the United Kingdom. Susan Christopherson then discusses Germany, another country where Wal-Mart has not enjoyed overwhelming success. Yuko Aoyama and Guido Schwarz compare Wal-Mart's recent retail histories in Germany and Japan, both countries where the company faces challenges from national firms. The next three chapters are devoted specifically to China, the country that is Wal-Mart's major supplier and where it has enjoyed much success, although not without problems. Shuguang Wang and Yongchang Zhang investigate some of the difficulties the company had entering China's consumer landscape. Lucia Lo, Lu Wang, and Wei Li examine the specific successes Wal-Mart is enjoying in Shenzhen. And Chris Webster focuses on the supermarket concept in China's retailing history. The final two chapters in this part look at Wal-Mart in Mexico. James Biles focuses on Wal-Mart's successes and problems vis-à-vis food retailing, while Chris Tilly looks into retailing, but also worker and wage issues.

This volume is meant for several readers. First and foremost, it could be used by those in the social, policy, and behavioral sciences who examine corporation history, logistics, labor relations, market expansion, international initiatives, corporate law, popular culture, and community relations. These are also topics discussed in intermediate and advanced classes in corporate history, business administration, economic development, sociology of work, worker and corporate culture, labor law, relations between the state and the private sector, big-box retailing, globalization, and economic geography. Second, it could be used in reading groups and book clubs in which members with various backgrounds and interests discuss timely national and international issues. Wal-Mart would certainly seem to qualify as a topic for those readers. Third, individual chapters could be read, discussed, and assigned in classes or seminar or study groups. Even though the contents have some formal structure, one could read the chapters in different sequences. For example, some may choose to read the chapters in Part I last.

Where We Go from Here

After reading and rereading these chapters, I remain convinced, as I was in early 2004, that there is still little we know about the corporation, including its impacts on individuals, communities, economies, and consumers in the United States and elsewhere, and what it says about its successes and popularity among a certain consumer clientele, American popular culture, and the cultures of globalization. We do know much more about certain facets, as many of these authors have written cutting-edge papers that will interest scholars in their own disciplines and beyond. Each chapter and bibliography (the references are among the major strengths of this volume) suggests a number of topics awaiting the curious and investigative eye of the sociologist, economist, anthropologist, political scientist, photojournalist, media critic (visual, print, and sound), human and environmental geographer, and those in women's studies, international law, and corporate organizational behavior. Let me suggest a number of topics that might be addressed in future investigations; they are not listed in any priority.

First, we need to know more about the specific economic impacts of Wal-Mart's operations on local retailers and consumers in rural America, not only places on the fringes of metropolitan areas but also places where the populations are declining. These impacts might examine the "magnet" effects a superstore has on adjacent real estate, traffic patterns, and community relations.

The investors and stockholders of Wal-Mart and also the networks of corporate executives merit investigation. Do most of the stockholders come from the South, Midwest, East Coast, or West Coast? Are they in areas and regions where the store is most economically successful? What kind of interlocking executive networks are there with Wal-Mart's top brass and other corporations, and with political and nonpolitical organizations? What is the nature and extent of Wal-Mart's linkages with corporate and nonprofit boards in Europe and Asia? Answers to these questions will provide further insights into the regional preferences (if any) for Wal-Mart stock and also the company's international networks.

What are the impacts of Wal-Mart on northwest Arkansas and the University of Arkansas? The corporation plays major roles in this region and the university, including construction of corporate offices and homes for business executives as well as provision of large endowments for the university's business school and fine arts and athletic programs. There are also impacts on Sunday store hours and liquor sales. What influence does the corporation have on small-town and city planning and zoning boards and school boards in Arkansas and elsewhere?

Fourth, what can Wal-Mart teach other companies and local and state governments about responding to megadisasters? Since the company has a strong and effective business logistics network, it was able to provide supplies to its stores immediately after destructive hurricanes in the United States in September and October 2005. Could Wal-Mart's response model be adapted to natural disasters in other regions where it operates stores?

The economic impacts of Wal-Mart on existing towns outside the United States, particularly in China, Japan, and Mexico and where expansion is occurring, merit study. Are the issues of land use and land use conflicts, worker issues (pay, gender, working conditions, etc.), community relations, and marketing the same in Asian as in European and North American contexts?

What does the "Wal-Martization of the United States" say about America's popular culture and consumer tastes, whether for music, videos, clothing, or purchase of non-U.S.-made products? What images of the corporation are appearing in television dramas, in poetry and short stories, in cartoons, and even as backgrounds for candidates running for local and national political offices? I have also heard that Wal-Mart's annual stockholder meetings have elements of a festive circus, religious revival, and national political convention simultaneously. I wonder what these energizing events say about the company's image, regional roots, stockholders, philosophy, and also American popular culture.

Seventh, an investigation of the music Wal-Mart plays in its stores, which I understand is decided in Bentonville, would be fascinating. Who decides what music is played when and where? What kinds of regional variations exist? Are selections the same for a store in rural Georgia as rural Iowa? Suburban Washington, D.C., and suburban Los Angeles? Do English-language lyrics dominate? What music is played in stores outside the United States? What kinds of music produce high and low sales volumes on specific products? What music is deemed appropriate for holiday seasons, cold and hot days, and weekdays? Must one camp out in stores to learn about Wal-Mart's music selection?

Eighth, what kinds of corporate philanthropy does the company practice in urban and rural areas outside the United States? Do the corporation and its workers (associates and executives) express concern about environmental quality issues, literacy programs, or the living conditions of the poor? What kind of volunteer efforts are most and least successful?

What are the major legal controversies the company is dealing with outside the United States? Are employee issues of gender, race, and age discrimination paramount? Or are land use siting, store acquisition, worker unions, and worker health benefits more important? How is Wal-Mart changing international corporate retail law? How has it worked within the confines of Chinese and Japanese law to accomplish its goals?

How important are environmental and preservation issues in store location in the United States and elsewhere? Are these issues important only in selected regions of the United States or other countries? How has Wal-Mart confronted such issues considering that local and state regulations may welcome or inhibit construction in inner-city, suburban, or rural areas? Does it promote its "environmental and preservation messages" in store expansion proposals outside the United States, and with what success?

What controversial land use issues challenge Wal-Mart in rural and urban areas of Europe, Asia, Latin America, and potentially Australia and Africa? How does the company address local conflicts that may have a religious or spiritual base (as we observe in the Mexican case discussed in this volume) or the exporting and potential opposition of American consumer preferences, values, and products? And how does its southern small-town worldview and "Every Day Low Prices" message play in large cities and rural markets in the developed world?

Twelfth, and last, what is Wal-Mart's foreign policy? Considering its colossal strength in global retailing and expansion of stores, one might argue it plays a major role in U.S. foreign policy decisions regarding China, for example, and potentially other places where growth is sought. Suppliers, quotas, preferential treatment, and labor issues would seem to be topics of importance to Wal-Mart, whether one is studying its global worldview or its national views. Just as Sam Walton had a distinct view about the corporation's place in the rural South, so do his successors have a distinct view about internationalizing the company. Lobbying and contributions to political parties and individuals both in the United States and elsewhere might be a part of such inquiries.

I remain enthusiastic, as many of the authors do, about the prospect of continued study into Wal-Mart's operations, legal controversies, and community outreach efforts. Certainly there are ample opportunities for the enterprising social and policy scientist and the engaging journalist to study this corporation in small towns, large suburbs, and inner cities in the United States and abroad. I can envisage those wishing to study the corporation from "inside the store" as well as in the community and beyond. All scales of inquiry are welcome in the scholarly community. Only in this way will we be able to place our findings of Wal-Mart into our previous investigations into other megacorporations, such as Standard Oil, General Motors, Ford, Exxon, and Microsoft.

Acknowledgments

Finally, I want to acknowledge in particular the assistance of three individuals. First, I want to thank David McBride, Senior Editor at Routledge/Taylor & Francis for his encouragement throughout this project. He was excited about this volume when I first spoke with him; his support has been unwavering, and for that I, and all the authors, are deeply appreciative. Second, I want to thank Amy Rodriguez, Project Editor, for her steady hand in the copy editing and processing stages; it has been enjoyable working with her. Third, I want to thank Donna Gilbreath, University of Kentucky, for her cheerfulness, steady hand, and critical editorial and graphic eyes in preparing all manuscripts per Routledge style. She worked diligently on these tasks, including incorporating last-minute additions and corrections from nearly all authors and from the editor. Her professionalism is much appreciated. Fourth, I want to thank Christian Munoz for designing a most attractive and appealing book cover, which conveys multiple meanings about this corporation's global reach. Others who also played minor roles in seeing this effort come to pass, including through personal conversations and e-mail exchanges, include Dick Gilbreath, director of the Department of Geography's Cartography Laboratory at the University of Kentucky, Don Janelle, Karl Raitz, Holly Barcus, Don Zeigler, Jim Johnson, Matt Zook, Deborah Dixon, Leo Zoon, Tom Graff, and also Mike Goodchild, Jane Brooks, Richard Applebaum, Emily Corbato, and Nelson Lichtenstein.

Stanley D. Brunn
Lexington, Kentucky

Part I

Wal-Mart and the World

1

The Geostrategy of Global Business: Wal-Mart and Its Historical Forbears

Peter J. Hugill

Introduction

In 2004, Jon Talton, a reporter for the *Arizona Republic,* noted that the previous year, "*The Los Angeles Times* reported: 'Wal-Mart's decisions influence wages and working conditions across a wide swath of the world economy. ... Its business is so vital to developing countries that some send emissaries to the corporate headquarters in Bentonville, Ark., almost as if Wal-Mart were a sovereign nation'" (Talton 2004). Certainly Wal-Mart's annual income as the modern world's wealthiest corporation is well above the gross domestic product (GDP) of most sovereign states. With sales of $256.3 billion in 2003, Wal-Mart would have ranked twentieth, just above Austria. Talton concludes his piece by stating that Wal-Mart "is something new, a global economic superpower operating beyond the reach of fair competition, empowered workers or even national governments" (Talton 2004).

Since Wal-Mart makes few statements of purpose, it is hard to judge its behavior as a "global economic superpower" except on the basis of its performance, although when dealing with a firm, that seems entirely appropriate. Nevertheless, two significant historical-geographical facts stand out about Wal-Mart that help explain its behavior: (1) its geographical roots are in the small towns of the American South and West, regions well known for their dislike of planning and zoning, regulation, and unions, as well as for low wages, which has certainly helped promote Wal-Mart's obsessive "low price" policy; and (2) almost all the firm's international growth and success has been achieved since the end of the Cold War, in a period in which the world economy has been totally dominated by the return to global liberalism and the ideals of free trade. At one level this second fact is similar to the first: the ideals of global liberalism include free entry to the marketplace and unrestrained global wage competition. Judged by its performance, Wal-Mart's geostrategy is based on the fact of the return to a genuinely global world economy after the end of the Cold War, in which one country in particular, China, has sought to improve its relative position by offering itself as a major source of cheap labor.

The First "Global Economic Superpowers"

The historical geographer in me notes that firms such as Wal-Mart are, despite the press comments cited in the first paragraph of this chapter, not at all new or out of the ordinary. Trading companies such as the Hanseatic League operated well "beyond the reach of ... national governments" and dominated European trade for several centuries from the start of the second millennium (Hugill 1993: 50–51). Much more significantly, in the first round of expansions of the European world economy after the year 1431, two economic superpowers would emerge, operating even further "beyond the reach of fair competition, empowered workers or ... national governments" than the Hanseatic League had ever dreamed. Both were based in the emerging nation-states of the early 1600s. The first would become as powerful as any state on the planet, rule a "sovereign nation," and eventually have to be brought to heel by the state in which it was embedded. This was the British East India Company, founded in 1600 to establish trade with the Spice Islands of the Indonesian archipelago. The second was the Dutch Verenigde Oostindische Compagnie (VOC), founded in 1602 for the same purpose. Both quickly expanded into something much more, establishing major footholds on the Indian subcontinent in the early 1600s to acquire the cotton textiles they needed to persuade the inhabitants of the Spice Islands to part with their nutmeg, cloves, cinnamon, and pepper. This Indian textile trade quickly assumed much greater importance than the spice trade, especially for the British East India Company (Irwin 1955, 1956, 1957). French attempts to copy these British and Dutch companies were much less successful. During the Seven Years' War (1756–1763; called the French and Indian War in American history) the British East India Company, operating as a sovereign nation well beyond British control, though acting generally in British interests, used its huge private armies to wrest control of the Indian subcontinent from the French.

Before the emergence of the territorially bounded nation-state (a complex process that cannot be said to have gotten under way until the Peace of Westphalia ended the Thirty Years' War in 1648, and which was not completed until the emergence of the "New Nationalism" in the late 1800s), such private economic superpowers were a normal part of the geopolitical process as Europeans reached out to the rest of the world and, as many claim, began to exploit it. Only powerful states could control powerful firms.

Although for these eighteenth-century firms we lack the accurate financial data that we now have for the present day, which allows us to calculate national accounts, we can be sure that in its heyday the British East India Company ranked well above twentieth as a global power. It cannot be measured as simply as we can today measure the strength of a firm such as Wal-Mart, by expressing its sales as a percentage of GDP. Much of the economic return to Britain from the East India Company actually came from the private activities of its employees, who were paid extremely poor wages, speculated very heavily on the side, and returned, or hoped to return, to Britain with large private fortunes (Furber 1976: 227). Nearly all the output of economies before the Industrial Revolution of the late 1700s was agricultural, thus a product primarily of the natural endowment of land, soil, and climate. Nearly all the output of a modern economy is in industry and services, thus a product of capital and labor.

Chaudhuri's monumental econometric analysis of the East India Company between 1660 and 1760 indicates that the annual official receipts for the period 1710–45 averaged just over £1.5 million per year (Chaudhuri 1978: 438). This would have represented $188 million per year in 1990, the 1990 dollar being the baseline used by Maddison for long-run international comparisons (Maddison 1995: 164–79). The vast majority of this GDP was, however, generated in the agricultural sector, not in the trade or manufacturing that dominate a modern economy and that typified the activities of the East India Company, which in the mid-1700s would have dominated that sector. The East India Company also offered long-term returns that modern companies only dream of, although risks were clearly very much higher.

Because it was Parliament that granted the East India Company its monopoly on trade to the East within Britain, and because of the East India Company's increasingly central importance to the British economy of the period, it was involved from its very inception with both parliamentary and City of London politics. Many stockholders of the East India Company were wealthy, and they combined their forces and seats to protect their interests against a Parliament that was always seeking ways to increase the share of the company's revenue that it took for providing it with its monopoly (Sutherland 1952: 17–19, 86, 411–12).

> Beginning with a representation of 60 members [out of a total of 558] in July 1784, the East India membership increased by August 1802 to 95 [by which time the Act of Union with Ireland had increased Parliament to 658] and in October 1806 achieved a maximum of 103.... between 1830 and 1834 it fell from 62 to 45. (Philips 1961: 299)

These members were notorious for having little to do with British party politics of the period, although because of "the openly expressed dislike of the Whigs for the Company as a commercial body ... they worked more cheerfully and easily under a Tory Government" (Philips 1961: 300). They always, however, worked first and foremost for the good of the East India Company.

The Economic World Orders of Liberalism and Protectionism

Global economic superpowers such as the British East India Company and the VOC were so strong because they had first developed in a world of weak nation-states bounded primarily by free trade, thus part of an economic world order of global liberalism. Beginning in 1641, the British attempted to limit Dutch global liberalism with the Navigation Acts, which challenged the control of the emerging world economy that the Dutch had come to enjoy using their version of free trade, *mare liberum*, or "free seas." By the early 1800s, however, with the publication of David Ricardo's landmark work on free trade and the adoption of his ideas by Adam Smith, the British state had embraced global liberalism, and the British-dominated world economy that emerged after the Congress of Vienna of 1815 was defined almost entirely by these values. This bedrock British belief in free trade was, however, brought into question after the middle of the nineteenth century, first by the American adoption of high tariffs in 1862, then by the German shift in 1878. Thereafter, the world economy slipped increasingly into the protectionist world order, beginning a halting return to global liberalism only when the Bretton Woods conference of 1944 imposed American economic hegemony. Even so, from 1944 through 1989 a significant fraction of the world economy, a Communist bloc dominated by Russia and China, remained outside the pull of global liberalism, and a complete return did not come until the end of the Cold War and the fall of the Berlin Wall.

In this chapter, Wal-Mart, which established its first store outside America in Mexico in 1991, is compared with three earlier American multinational firms: Woolworth's, Ford, and General Motors. All three of these rose to prominence during the period of the protectionist world order and within a heavily protected domestic economy. It is important to bear in mind that the economic world order in which Wal-Mart has grown to prominence is one marked, since the end of the Cold War, by a virtually complete return to global liberalism. The current period is therefore much more like the liberal economic world order of the early 1600s or the early 1800s than the world order of the period of protectionism, which extended from 1862 to 1944 and to a lesser extent through 1989.

Geostrategy and Geopolitics

Geostrategy, like its parent term, *geopolitics,* is an ill-defined, flexible, misused concept, but there are clear archetypes for each term, based on the type of state employing the concept in question. Geostrategy is pursued almost entirely by trading states, which by definition are states heavily committed to global liberalism. I argue here that it is also pursued by the firms embedded in those states. Geopolitics is pursued by territorial states, which may or may not have any commitment to global liberalism and which have often used protectionist economic policies to distance themselves from a world economy dominated by the trading states (Hugill 2005). The geopolitics of the territorial state is "classic" geopolitics, first conceived by Ratzel in the late 1800s and defined most strongly by the work of Halford Mackinder (1902, 1904, 1919) in his attempt to understand and perhaps arrest the decline of British power as the protectionist world order developed. In keeping with Britain's role as the principal trading state in the world economy of the early 1900s, Mackinder, as his principal biographer notes, preferred the term *geostrategy* to *geopolitics* (Blouet 2005, personal communication).

At its most malignant, the geopolitics of the territorial state informed the work of German geopolitician Karl Haushofer and found its most thorough expression in his journal, *Zeitschrift für Geopolitik.* The geopolitics of the territorial state aimed to dominate the world economy by controlling vast swaths of earth space both for the military geographic advantages it gave and for the resources contained in that earth space. Mackinder argued, in his famous dictum of 1919, that if any one state came to control the heartland region of central Eurasia, it would come to control the "world-island" of Eurasia and Africa, and ultimately the entire world (Mackinder 1919: 150). By the 1930s, Haushofer's geopolitical ideas called for a world made up of three major pan-regions—one German, one Japanese, and one American—each pan-region extending from pole to pole in order to ensure access to needed agricultural resources grown in a wide variety of climatic zones as well as to the minerals contained in such a vast area (Whittlesey 1943).

In the inception and development of these ideas about the geopolitics of the territorial state, one central idea stood out. Mackinder's original formulation of geopolitics in 1904 was concerned with the possible emergence of a world state, in which he asked the geographer's question: "Where is the likely seat of power of such a state?" (Blouet 1987: 117–18). His famous answer was, as embodied in the title of his famous article, at "the geographical pivot of history," a concept he redefined in his 1919 book as "the Heartland," a region that would be most easily controlled by either Russia or Germany. Whereas in 1904 it was not clear whether Russia or Germany would be the greater problem, by 1919 Mackinder naturally leaned toward the conclusion that the trouble lay with Germany.

Karl Haushofer, Mackinder's greatest intellectual disciple, used the Heartland concept in the 1920s to inform the geopolitics of the Third Reich. As Blouet notes, despite Haushofer's partial influence on Hitler through Haushofer's student Rudolf Hess, Hitler fortunately resisted the main lesson he ought to have learned from Haushofer and Mackinder, which was not to pursue the geostrategy of a maritime trading state at the same time as he pursued the geopolitics of the territorial state (Blouet 2005: 3). Haushofer's main influence on Nazi geopolitics was troublesome enough, but it lay elsewhere, in his use of personal connections with Japan to forge the Axis alliance with that country almost independently of Hitler (Hayes 2004). With the defeat of the Axis in 1945, geopolitics was quickly retired (*buried* might be a better term) until such American realists as Henry Kissinger and Zbigniew Brzezinski resurrected it at the height of the Cold War to help deal with the Soviet Union. In any case, Mackinder's classic formulation was never forgotten. As Yale political scientist Nicholas Spykman put it so cogently in 1942, a "Russian state from the Urals to the North Sea can be no improvement on a German state from the North Sea to the Urals" (Spykman 1942: 460). American policy throughout the Cold War was to resist a Russian-dominated heartland just as strongly as it had been to resist a German-dominated one earlier.

America's foreign policy discourse in the early twenty-first century continues to use the term *geopolitics,* but it does so loosely, occasionally, and inaccurately (Taylor and Flint 2000: 50–51). The intellectual wing of the neoconservative camp is currently dominated by Robert Kagan's argument in his 2003 book, emerging out of a paper in *Foreign Affairs* by William Kristol and Robert Kagan in 1996, that America is hegemonic and can pursue pretty much whatever geopolitical designs it pleases. The neoliberal group, headed by such individuals as Charles Kupchan (2003), argues that America's period of unipolarity will be brief and that American global dominance, like all global dominances, will erode, so its geopolitical designs should be more careful and consultative. Yet America in the current period of the world economy, one of a return to unabashed global liberalism, is a trading state, not a territorial one, and our behavior in the international arena is far better termed *geostrategy* than *geopolitics.*

Geostrategy does, however, exist in the popular consciousness as the association of state behavior in the international arena with the economic advantage of the state and the firms considered central to the state in that international arena. The geostrategies people associate with such multinational firms are encapsulated, for example, in the oft-stated belief that in the Iraqi war that began in 2003 American concerns were with oil more than with the people of Iraq, and that favored firms such as Halliburton profited mightily from their links to Vice President Dick Cheney, a former Halliburton executive. In this popular discourse, the economic and political interests of states and multinational firms intertwine. For example, in 1952, the former president of General Motors, Charles Erwin Wilson, was asked if, as Secretary of Defense, he could make a decision that would run counter to GM's interests; he said that he could but was not able to conceive of such a situation, because "… for years I thought what was good for our country was good for General Motors, and vice versa." The difference did not exist. Wilson's quote certainly implies equality of geostrategic interest between firm and state, and Wilson, like Cheney, served both.

The Geostrategies of American Multinationals: From Woolworth's to Wal-Mart

The geostrategies of three earlier American multinational firms are well worth examining to better understand the successes and failures of Wal-Mart's geostrategy in today's world economy: that of an earlier American retail giant, Woolworth's, and those of the two major American automobile companies, Ford and General Motors.

Woolworth's is clearly the case most comparable to that of Wal-Mart, since it was a retail discounter of substantial proportions with, at its height, considerable international investment. However, even at its height Woolworth's accounted for a much smaller share of GDP than is accounted for today by Wal-Mart: in 1929 Woolworth's sales reached $300 million, which was 0.33 percent of an American nonfarm GDP of $92.9 billion (Woolworth 1954: 35). In the 1930s the farm component of GDP, which distorts national income comparisons since it largely reflects natural endowments rather than labor and capital, still exceeded 10 percent. In 2003 Wal-Mart, with sales of $256.3 billion, accounted for just over 2.3 percent of a nonfarm GDP of some $10,700 billion. Agriculture now accounts for under 1 percent of American GDP. Woolworth's is important because it pioneered American retailing abroad and can be reasonably described as America's first multinational corporation, though it was very closely followed by Ford. In 1890 Frank W. Woolworth, whose first American five-and-ten-cent store had opened in 1879, visited Europe, noting in his diary on a trip to London that "I think a good penny and six pence store run by a live Yankee would create a sensation here" (quoted in Winkler 1940: 84).

In fact, Woolworth would hold off for nearly twenty years on any British investment, perhaps put off by the depression of the 1890s and in turn attracted by the boom of the Edwardian era (1901–10). In any case, Woolworth's decision to enter the British market in 1909 was driven simply by the desire to access one of the world's most lucrative retail markets, since at the time British economic policies still aggressively favored global liberalism. When in 1909 Woolworth set up his first British store, he aimed it at the threepence-and-sixpence market so successfully that his British chain "was to become actually more lucrative than his American chain of stores." By 1938 the British stores were generating "approximately one-third of the company's profit flow" from only 27 percent of its stores (766 out of 2,866 in five countries). Those 766 British stores also had a market value in 1938 of $465 million, compared with a market value for 2,018 stores in America, Canada, and Cuba of only $446 million (Winkler 1940: 161, 240–41). Some of this market value was lost by the destruction of British stores, all of which were located in downtown shopping areas, in German bombing raids during World War II. Allied bombing raids, causing massive destruction of German cities and the virtual collapse of the German economy in 1945 effectively destroyed Woolworth's investment in that country.

Ford's pioneering foray into multinationalism, its decision to assemble its vehicles in Britain in 1913, was also simply a rational business decision, in this case to reduce transportation costs on fully assembled vehicles (Wilkins and Hill 1964: 46). Shipping Model T's as kits of parts and assembling them locally was simply more profitable than shipping them built because the kits took up so much less space in transport vessels. In the 1920s Ford's decision to manufacture entire vehicles in Britain for the European and British Empire markets at a huge, purpose-built, integrated production facility designed for easy import of raw materials and export of finished goods, located on the Thames estuary east of London at Dagenham, came from the same impulse. The Ford factory in Japan was established after the Tokyo earthquake of 1926 to assemble vehicles from kits and reduce transport costs, not to avoid Japanese tariffs. Ford did, however, establish a major new factory at Köln in Germany when German tariffs tightened in the early 1930s (Hugill 1988).

To an extent, General Motors followed Ford's lead in the 1920s, although GM came to value the German market more highly than that of Britain and bought European producers (such as Opel in Germany and Vauxhall in Britain) for their production facilities and the engineering skills of their existing labor force rather than building greenfield factories, as Ford chose to do. Before succeeding with Opel, GM had tried hard to buy a major British or French producer, its suit being rejected by Austin, Morris, and Citroën (Sloan 1964: 316–28), so the decision to concentrate in Germany was not driven by German tariffs. Following the 1926 Tokyo earthquake, GM, like Ford, established assembly and sale subsidiaries in Japan. The increasing militarization of the Japanese economy, itself a form of protection, would, however, drive both GM and Ford out of Japan in the late 1930s, as the army favored Japanese start-up firms such as Toyota and Datsun. Even so, both Ford and GM influenced the development of Japanese automobiles, Toyota leaning heavily on GM technology to begin with (Hugill 1988).

Both Ford and GM became major presences in the world economy that developed after 1944, as the West returned to global liberalism in the Cold War period. Ford, with its huge, integrated plant at Dagenham in Britain and a smaller production facility at Köln in Germany, emerged from the war relatively unscathed and with a much better-developed product line in the European market than GM. At the end of the war, the Russians removed the production line for GM's excellent and innovative small car, the 1939 Opel Kadett, from Germany as war reparations (Hugill 1988). In the 1950s GM was struggling in Europe relative to Ford and would not develop an effective small car for the European market until the Opel Kadett A series of 1962, which was introduced into Britain as the Vauxhall Viva HA the following year (Norbye 1992: 6; Dymock 1999: 156). Ford was, however, much better at this, having been very successful at designing cars for the market segment the Kadett/Viva was aimed at since 1935 (Allen 1986: 15) and losing little of its European productive capacity in World War II.

By 1962 total Ford sales were $8.1 billion (Wilkins and Hill 1964: 443). American GDP for that year was $585.6 billion, of which some 6 percent was farm income. Ford sales thus accounted for some 1.47 percent of nonfarm GDP for 1962. Of those sales, 26.7 percent were foreign sales, a figure that was increasing steadily as Europe recovered from World War II and experienced mass adoption of the automobile from the early 1960s on. GM's total domestic and foreign sales for 1962 were $16.8 billion (Sloan 1964: 214, 313), which accounted for 3.05 percent of nonfarm GDP, a larger share than Wal-Mart's today. In terms of the percentage of the company's sales accounted for by its international efforts, Wal-Mart's 2003 "international sales made up 18.5 percent of the $256.3 billion Wal-Mart took in last year" (Hays 2004). GM's non–North American sales for 1962 accounted for 12.8 percent of revenue, less than half that of Ford because of its slower recovery in the European market. Woolworth's at its height had a much higher percentage of its sales internationally. Much of the income of the British East India Company and the VOC was, of course, international.

Retail versus Industrial Multinationals

The geostrategy of a purely retail multinational firm such as Woolworth's or Wal-Mart must be viewed as very different from that of a Ford or GM. Capital costs for design and manufacture are so high for automobiles that firms must sell their wares in numerous markets to remain profitable. Capital costs for retail firms are very much lower, and the intense control of costs by Wal-Mart, as well as by such predecessors as Woolworth's, is legendary. Because companies such as Ford and GM grew in an earlier period, one dominated by protectionist thinking about the nature of largely national markets, neither could assume open access to raw materials, production facilities, and consumers. They thus had to invest heavily in the first two, particularly in production facilities, often in highly protected economies, if they were to reach consumers in those economies.

Despite the return of global liberalism, Wal-Mart's geostrategy has been thus far predictable on the basis of the behavior of earlier American multinationals. Like Woolworth's, Ford, and GM, it has focused on Britain, Canada, Germany, and Latin America. Like Ford and GM, it has made an unsuccessful foray into Japan. Woolworth's had stores in Cuba, GM built cars in Argentina, and Ford constructed plants in Mexico, in part to avoid local tariffs and in part because labor is cheaper in those countries. Neither Ford nor GM developed specific vehicles for the Latin American market the way they did in Europe. Wal-Mart's purchase of the Mexican chain of Cifra stores has given it a very successful presence in Mexico. Unlike all three of its predecessors, Wal-Mart has also entered China, with many commentators suggesting this is because it sources many of its goods in that country. GM has now followed Wal-Mart's example and is manufacturing vehicles in China. The GM China Web site (www.gmchina.com) currently claims GM has the highest sales of any Chinese automobile producer. At the end of the Cold War, China began to enter the world economy as a source of cheap labor and thus cheap manufactured goods. This was predictable. In his trip to Europe in 1890 Frank Woolworth had paid particular attention to Germany as a source of cheap labor and cheap manufactured goods. At the time, Germany was a rising economic power seeking to challenge British global hegemony. Before World War I Woolworth's sourced many of its cheap manufactured goods in Germany, and the company returned after the war to establish a retail presence there. Wal-Mart has pursued similar policies in China, and many Americans now see China as the next likely challenger to American global hegemony.

Germany was a cheap place in which to manufacture in the late 1800s because it lacked the labor unions of Britain or the high wages of America. In 1890 Frank Woolworth explained the production (in a small German town called Lanscha) of Christmas tree ornaments for his stores in terms that could just as easily be used today by critics of Wal-Mart's supply chain:

> Tree ornaments are made out of blown glass, and the quicksilver is put inside afterwards. They are made by the very poorest class there is in Europe and we were obliged to go into their dirty hovels to see what we could see. One place we went into we found a man and a woman in one room with six small children, the youngest not over eight years old.... It was the dirtiest and worst smelling place I was ever in. (quoted in Winkler 1940: 89)

Mercury poisoning must have been a constant risk for such workers, and the use of such young children had been outlawed in economies such as Britain since the reforms of the 1830s. In 2005 Wal-Mart was nominated for the Public Eye Award for "labour rights abuses in ... [its] garment supply chain ... [at] three Wal-Mart supply factories where workers must undergo strip searches" (www.evb.ch/en/p339.htm). Perhaps the one difference is that public criticism of Woolworth's for abusive labor practices in the early 1900s seems to have been almost nonexistent, whereas today Wal-Mart has become a lightning rod for attacks on its abuses of labor.

Wal-Mart's success abroad seems to parallel somewhat that of Woolworth's, whose stores in Britain, Canada, and Germany were all successful, however little the German stores were able to contribute to the profits of the American company after the rise of the Nazis. However, rather than building its stores from scratch, Wal-Mart's success in retailing abroad has, unlike that of Woolworth's, come primarily from the acquisition of preexisting local chains. Some of these acquisitions have been effective, some not. Perhaps the most significant difference, however, is that in Britain, where both Woolworth's and Wal-Mart have had their greatest financial successes, many British consumers believe that Woolworth's, which still has a major retail presence in Britain, is a British rather than American firm. Most British consumers continue to believe that Wal-Mart's subsidiary there, Asda, is a British company.

In three foreign locations, Wal-Mart has been successful. In Mexico, the first location into which Wal-Mart ventured outside the United States, Wal-Mart acquired the Cifra chain of supermarkets. It now has 708 stores there. In 1994, in Canada, Wal-Mart bought out the chain of 122 Woolco stores that had been Woolworth's attempt to compete with an earlier discount competitor, Kmart. Wal-Mart now has 261 stores in Canada, so the Woolco acquisition forms an important part of that base. In 1999 Wal-Mart acquired the 229 stores of an already successful British supermarket chain, Asda. It now has 293 stores in Britain.

Increasing competition in America from such firms as Target and Costco has encouraged Wal-Mart to continue its global expansion. As well as its stores in Britain, Canada, and Mexico, Wal-Mart has established a presence in Argentina, Brazil, China,

Germany, Hong Kong, Indonesia, Japan, Puerto Rico, and South Korea. "[A]s efforts to block Wal-Mart in the continental United States continue, Wal-Mart desperately needs to be able to be successful in South America and southern Asia," noted retail consultant Burt Flickinger III (quoted in Hays 2004). In more than half these countries—Argentina, Brazil, Germany, Hong Kong, Indonesia, and Japan—Wal-Mart's attempts to expand have been failures.

> In Canada, Britain and Mexico, Wal-Mart's sole foreign triumphs, it has won largely by default, filling a void created by the weak Canadian players T. Eaton Co. and Hudson's Bay Co. and Britain's J. Sainsbury, and in Mexico through acquiring its largest retailer. Global retailers Carrefour and Britain's Tesco PLC are another story, making life miserable for Wal-Mart in its South American markets with price wars and battles for the most lucrative store locations. Wal-Mart has already quit Hong Kong and Indonesia due to adverse market conditions and merchandise foul-ups, and its South Korean stores lack traffic for being located too distant from major cities. (Olive 2004)

Where there is effective retail competition and tough labor laws, such as in Japan and Germany, Wal-Mart has been a weak player. Even in Britain, where Asda continues to be very successful, Tesco remains the largest grocery retailer. Tesco has one-third of all grocery sales and is a highly effective competitor (http://news.bbc.co.uk/1/hi/business/4618061.stm). Even the formerly ailing Sainsbury's chain is rebounding. In 2003 Asda overtook Sainsbury's as Britain's second-largest grocery chain (http://news.bbc.co.uk/1/hi/business/3112689.stm). In 2004 Sainsbury's profits dipped sharply, but the company report shows a sharp increase in profits for 2005 on slightly lowered volume (www.j-sainsbury.co.uk/ar05/index.asp?pageid=64).

Unlike Woolworth's, much of Wal-Mart's foreign success has come through appearing *not* to be Wal-Mart. Although the company trades as Wal-Mart in Canada and China, in most other places it has bought other retail chains whose names it still uses. In Britain, for example, although Asda's corporate logo describes the chain as "part of the Wal-Mart family," many British consumers are simply unaware that Wal-Mart owns Asda. Some Asda stores identify themselves with a small Wal-Mart logo, some do not: the three I happened to drive past in June 2005 in areas as far apart as Cornwall, Essex, and Yorkshire did not.

Multinational Adaptations to Local Markets

Much of Wal-Mart's rather variable global success thus far seems to stem from its corporate roots in small-town, essentially southern, America: "behind the Wal-Mart mystique is a firm that spent three decades achieving a near monopoly in small town America. Outside that stronghold, the going is rougher" (Olive 2004). Comparison with the earlier American multinationals is instructive. Woolworth's, Ford, and GM all became successful in the international arena by adapting carefully to local markets, either by adopting local habits or by developing special product lines to suit local needs, neither of which Wal-Mart has done. Soon after it was founded in 1909 "the 'mother' store [of British Woolworth's] started serving afternoon tea in its second-floor 'Refreshment Room.' It served it free for a very long time, then at fixed, very low price, for excellent tea. The practice suited amazed consumers fine" (Nichols

1973: 73). Faced with such adaptive and pro-British behavior, many British customers began to perceive Woolworth's as a British store.

Ford and GM also both adapted quickly to the specialized automobile needs of Europe and Japan, designing cars specifically to meet the infrastructural needs of those markets for lighter, more compact, more fuel-efficient vehicles.

So far, other than stocking locally popular goods, special local adaptations by Wal-Mart have been limited. Wal-Mart has experimented with "singles night shopping" in some of its German stores (*Wall Street Journal*, November 9, 2004) and built its first "green" store in Vancouver, British Columbia, as a way of getting zoning permission from the city council (*Vancouver Sun*, February 3, 2005). Under substantial local competitive and regulatory pressure Wal-Mart has actually had to close stores in both Germany and Canada, citing union problems in both countries and restrictive opening laws in Germany (*Financial Times of London*, May 24, 2004; *M&M Planet Retail*, August 6, 2004; *Wall Street Journal*, November 9, 2004; *Retail Bulletin*, March 14, 2005). Wal-Mart has so far closed only a single store in America (in Hearne, Texas), citing a very high rate of loss to theft by employees and customers, although substantial improvements to State Highway 6 also made it far easier for customers from Hearne to reach the Super Wal-Mart in nearby Bryan and many Hearne residents work in Bryan and its neighbor city, College Station. Wal-Mart's attempts to move into Hong Kong and Indonesia both failed. The move into Indonesia in 1996 ended in failure in 1997 when customers "turned up their noses at the brightly lighted, highly organized stores … and because no haggling was permitted considered them overpriced" (Hays 2004). In 2005 Wal-Mart began, with encouragement from the Indian government, to source material more seriously in India (www.rediff.com/money/2004/jun/03bpol.htm). The move into India seems to be because the Chinese economy is cooling down at the same time as costs there are rising (www.indiadaily.com/editorial/08-19g-04.asp). Even so, the Indian government has refused Wal-Mart permission to establish a retail sales chain in India (*Planet Retail*, November 3, 2004).

Conclusions

Effectively, Wal-Mart's international financial success has been limited thus far to procuring cheap goods in China and its acquisition of already profitable chains of stores elsewhere. The financial contributions of the Canadian and Mexican stores are less clear than those of the profitable Asda chain in Britain, and some Canadian stores have closed. Although Wal-Mart's international program makes good geostrategic sense, it is neither new nor inspired. There are two reasons for this. First, given that Wal-Mart's corporate culture developed in the relatively unzoned, unregulated, "right-to-work" states of the American South, the company has had problems expanding into zoned, regulated, and unionized places elsewhere in America and internationally. Second, although Wal-Mart has often simply bought chains of stores in other countries and retained the identity of those chains, it has so far made little effort to present itself outside America as anything but an American firm, and where it has done that it has often been poorly received. Where it has been most successful abroad, it is, with few exceptions, simply doing business as a local company trading largely under local names. The logic of global liberalism suggests that all this is perfectly normal and reasonable, although ironically it has not allowed Wal-Mart the success in global markets enjoyed by such predecessors as the British East India Company, the VOC, Woolworth's, Ford, and GM, the last three of which flourished in a much less liberal economic environment and which, perhaps because of that, made very specific efforts to adapt to local cultural values through careful marketing and product design in a way that Wal-Mart has not.

Acknowledgment

I thank Lori Taylor, a colleague at the Bush School, for her comments on how to more accurately represent the share of national accounts earned by firms in times past. Any errors in interpretation are of my creation, not hers.

2

Wal-Mart Nation: Mapping the Reach of a Retail Colossus

Matthew A. Zook and Mark Graham

While debates surrounding Wal-Mart are contentious and their impact contested (see Stone 1995; Peterson and McGee 2000; Beaver 2005; Basker 2005), Wal-Mart is undeniably an enormously influential actor at the local and global levels. Founded in 1962 in northern Arkansas, Wal-Mart has become a ubiquitous component of the American landscape and for the past fifteen years has steadily expanded its retailing operations around the world. In many ways it has gone beyond the status of corporation and mimics the scale and influence of a nation, albeit one based on consumption rather than political identity. This chapter takes measure of this retail colossus through an analysis of its size and geographical reach, with particular attention to Wal-Mart's regional and local distribution within the United States.

The Size of Operations

In 2002 Wal-Mart surpassed Exxon Mobil to become the world's largest corporation (based on sales), a distinction it has held every year since then (Hjelt 2002; Gunyon 2005). This manifests in $285.2 billion of sales for the fiscal year ending January 31, 2005 (Wal-Mart 2005b). Although 2005 gross domestic product (GDP) figures are not yet available as of this writing, as of 2004 Wal-Mart sales were larger than the GDP of all but the twenty-three largest countries in the world—bigger than Saudi Arabia, Norway, and Poland (International Monetary Fund 2005).[1]

While the United States has long been (and remains) the center of Wal-Mart's operations, the company has an increasingly strong global presence. This can be observed not only in its international trade figures (Flint 2004 reports that Wal-Mart is China's eighth-largest trading partner, ahead of Russia and the United Kingdom) but also in the expansion of its retailing operations. As Table 2.1 outlines, Wal-Mart has retail operations in nine other countries (and Puerto Rico), although none are as extensive as those in the United States. Nevertheless, 19.7 percent of all Wal-Mart's sales currently take place outside of the United States, and this percentage is growing (Wal-Mart 2005b).[2]

The size of Wal-Mart is also evident in both its number of consumers (138 million customers per week visit Wal-Mart stores worldwide) (Wal-Mart 2005a), and the size

TABLE 2.1   Wal-Mart's Global Operations and Employment

Country	Date Started	Number of Stores*	Number of Employees	How Acquired
U.S.	1962	3,772	1,260,000	
Mexico	1991	708	112,000	Joint venture
Puerto Rico	1992	54	17,000	Greenfield
Canada	1994	261	60,000	Acquisition
Argentina	1995	12	4,000	Greenfield
Brazil	1995	142	28,000	Greenfield
Indonesia	1996			Licensing agreement (divested)
China	1996	48	20,000	Joint venture
Germany	1997	88	11,000	Acquisition
South Korea	1998	16	3,600	Acquisition
United Kingdom	1999	293	150,000	Acquisition
Japan	2002	405	35,000	Acquisition
Total		5,800	1,700,600	

Source: Wal-Mart 2005a.* Stores include units run under Wal-Mart brand and stores owned by companies in which Wal-Mart has a substantial share of ownership.

of its labor force (the 1.7 million employees of Wal-Mart is *more* than the populations of Estonia and Iceland combined). This labor force also makes it the world's largest employer with the exception of governments (Gunyon 2005). Finally, the square footage of all Wal-Mart stores in the United States *alone* is equivalent to the island of Bermuda (Table 2.2). Thus, by any number of measures including income, sphere of operations, population size, and territory, Wal-Mart ranks on par with many countries and in some cases, such as annual income, is larger than most.

Wal-Mart's parity with nations echoes Edwards's discussion of the emergence of "corporate nations" in his analysis of the geopolitical implications surrounding the spread of information technologies. He defines a corporate nation as "an entity less

TABLE 2.2   Distribution of U.S. Wal-Mart Stores by Retail Division, September 2005

Retail Division	Description	Average Size (square feet)	Number of Locations
Wal-Mart	General merchandise	100,000	1,258
Wal-Mart Supercenter	General merchandise and groceries	187,000	1,866
Neighborhood Market	Smaller stores emphasizing convenience and speed	43,000	95
Sam's Club	Warehouse club aimed at small businesses and individuals	128,000	553
Total			3,772

Source: Average store size is based on Reuters 2005.

concerned with geographic space and more concerned about connecting with individuals as consumers of information ... a transnational entity, spreading a global information context that overrides local contexts whenever possible" (2001: 308). Although Edwards focuses on the information technology sector rather than retailing, his emphasis on consumers and the global overriding the local resonates strongly with the contours of Wal-Mart's operations. While not a nation-state in the classical sense, Wal-Mart is nevertheless a central actor in the development of local and national economies, cultures, and politics around the world.

In the case of the United States, this centrality is in large part due to Wal-Mart's decidedly distinctive business model compared with other top global corporations. Its status as a retailer is incongruous with the energy, manufacturing, and finance companies that share the top rankings. This, in turn, colors its unique impact on the economic and physical landscape of the United States. Rather than having large clusters of employment and operations in a relatively small number of regions (although centers and headquarters such as Bentonville, Arkansas, are evident), Wal-Mart's operations are extremely diffused over geographic space. Thus, corporate policies and practices do not simply affect a few places of clustered employment but have the potential to reverberate throughout the country, creating the Wal-Mart consumer nation.

Data Mapping

In order to understand the geographic reach of Wal-Mart's retail operations in North America, store location data are analyzed via a series of dot and choropleth maps. [Because these maps are restricted by the size, format, and color requirements of this book, versions are also freely available online at www.zook.info/Wal-Mart for non-commercial use and distribution.]

The data on U.S. store locations come from Wal-Mart's store locator function on its Web site (www.walmart.com/cservice/ca_storefinder.gsp) and include store number, type of Wal-Mart store, address, city, state, and zip code. For example, a search on zip code 40506 (the location of the University of Kentucky) reveals that the closest Wal-Mart is store number 2783, located at 500 West New Circle Road in Lexington, Kentucky. Identical location information for Sam's Clubs in the United States was gathered from the store locator at the Sam's Club Web site (www.samsclub.com). A summary of the data used in this analysis is presented in Table 2.2. Unless otherwise indicated, the analysis presented in this chapter aggregates Wal-Mart stores from all divisions into its figures and maps.

Data for stores in Canada and Mexico were collected from www.walmartcanada.ca and www.walmartmexico.com.mx. Other international retail location data (for Germany, Brazil, etc.) were also collected but are not included here. All data were gathered during the middle of September 2005. The address data for U.S. stores were geocoded to decimal latitude and longitude coordinates and imported into ArcInfo 9.0 for analysis. Canadian and Mexican store data were aggregated to the province/state level for mapping.

Locating the Wal-Mart Nation within the Nation-State

Numerous scholars have outlined the diffusion of Wal-Mart (see Holmes 2005 and Basker 2005 for a series of temporal maps), but the basic contour is summarized by Graff and Ashton (1994). They note that Wal-Mart has a growth strategy that is primarily focused on small-town locations, and they map out three temporal phases of growth: Arkansas, regional, and all areas of the United States. To their analysis we wish to add a fourth phase of growth: *globally.* This diffusion pattern can be seen, even without time series data, in the per capita figures of Wal-Mart by Canadian, Mexican, and U.S. province or state.

As Barnes and colleagues (1996) and Graff (1998) document, Wal-Mart's central and southern roots and later expansion to the coasts are still very much in evidence in terms of per capita figures. For example, Arkansas and Oklahoma have a Wal-Mart location for approximately every 30,000 people, while the ratios for California and New York are almost 200,000 people per Wal-Mart (using 2004 population estimates from the U.S. Census).

The density patterns within Mexico and Canada are shown in Figure 2.1. They also tell a temporal story, as entry into these national markets did not take place until the early 1990s. The low populations of these areas produce density values similar to the Southeast despite much later entry into these markets. Although the less populated provinces of Saskatchewan, Manitoba, Prince Edward Island, New Brunswick, and Nova Scotia show high Wal-Mart densities, this is primarily a function of

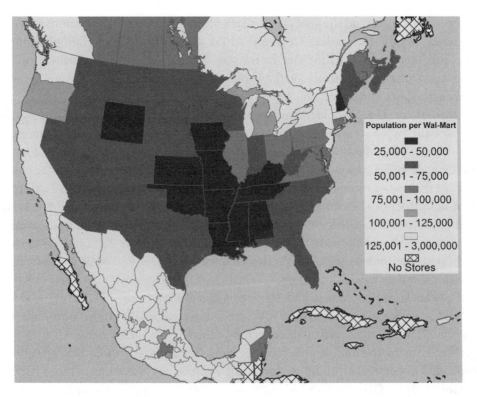

Figure 2.1   Wal-Mart density in the U.S., Canada, and Mexico, by province or state.

a small denominator. Despite their low per capita figures, the most populated prov-inces, Ontario and Quebec, also have the largest number of Wal-Marts, 86 and 46, respectively.

Mexico likewise shows much lower Wal-Mart densities than found in the United States when analyzed at the state level. While high densities exist, most notably in the Mexico City region, they remain significantly lower than U.S. figures. Note that the data in Figure 2.1 only include 409 Wal-Mart stores rather than the 708 listed in Table 2.1. This is because the remainder of Wal-Mart's Mexican locations are restau-rant operations rather than retail outlets.

Ubiquitous Locations

The concentration of Wal-Mart is also readily apparent in Figure 2.2, which displays all 3,792 U.S. Wal-Mart stores by location and type of retail operation. At this scale the distribution is closely correlated with population: the populous Northeast has an extremely dense concentration, while the sparsely settled Great Plains and Southwest have a much more dispersed pattern. While the state densities outlined in Figure 2.1 indicate there is significant variation within Wal-Mart densities, one should not be surprised that Wal-Mart's role as a retailer has led it to establish operations near population centers.

This close relation to population is clear when the area around Wal-Mart locations is "buffered." Buffering is simply a GIS technique in which a circle is drawn around a point to create a catchment area. While this as-the-crow-flies approach abstracts from the reality of actual travel patterns (determined by road networks, traffic, and

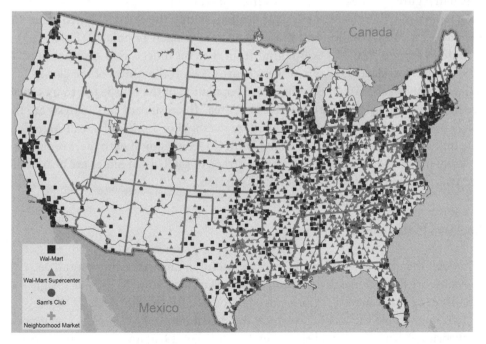

Figure 2.2   Wal-Mart stores in the U.S., by retail division.

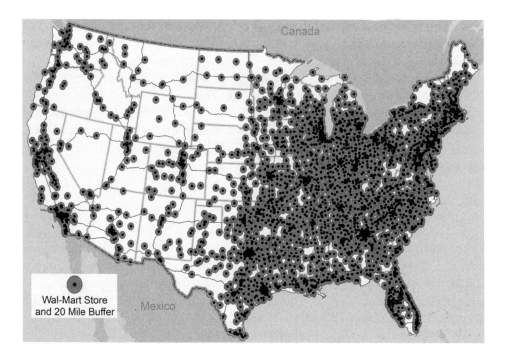

Figure 2.3   Areas within 20 miles of a Wal-Mart store in the U.S.

personal preference), it does provide a useful measure of proximity between two spatially distributed variables, in this case Wal-Mart locations and population.

While the results of this buffering are unsurprising given the distribution illustrated in Figure 2.2, the geographic coverage of Wal-Mart's system of stores is remarkable. Simply put, there are few physical locations within the eastern United States that fall outside a 20-mile buffer, and those that do are sparsely populated (Figure 2.3).

Buffers around Wal-Marts (ranging from 5 to 60 miles) were overlaid on 2000 U.S. census tract data (available at www.census.gov). If the center of the census tract fell within the Wal-Mart buffer, the entire population of the census tract was considered to be within this particular catchment area. The results of this analysis are that *fully 60 percent of the entire U.S. population lives within 5 miles of a Wal-Mart location and 96 percent are within 20 miles.* With the exception of extremely remote and sparsely populated locations, almost all citizens of the United States are also within the Wal-Mart nation's catchment of consumption.

Regional Distributions

Although the maps at the national level are useful in understanding overall patterns, they obscure the regional distribution of Wal-Mart locations. To provide insight for a smaller geographic area, a regional map is provided for the Midwest.

It is remarkable the extent to which the distribution of Wal-Marts corresponds to theories of central place advanced by Lösch (1954, 1975) and Christaller (1966) as much as fifty years ago. (This is particularly clear in the midwestern region, in which

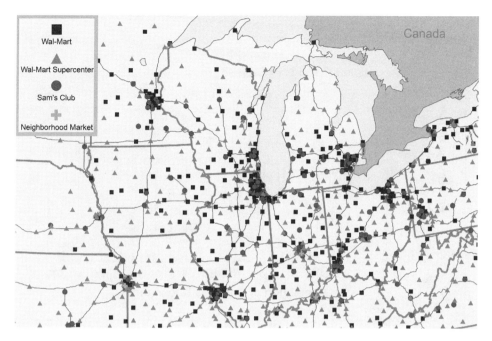

Figure 2.4   Wal-Mart stores in the midwestern U.S.

it is possible to distinguish individual store locations; see Figure 2.4.) Central place theory focuses on local (and monopolistic) markets as the means through which urban spatial structures are developed, and posits an evenly distributed honeycomb urban system. While it is beyond the scope of this chapter to consider the relevance of these theories to Wal-Mart, the combination of its size, ubiquitous distribution, and reach into local retail markets provides Wal-Mart with a degree of influence unmatched in history or the modern era.

Wal-Mart in Local Context

This level of influence is particularly relevant when coupled with the decidedly rural focus of Wal-Mart locations. Not only are there regional differences in the total and relative number of Wal-Mart stores, but there are also significant differences in their locations between urban and rural counties. Figure 2.5 illustrates the distribution of Wal-Mart stores by county population contrasted with the number of people within each population range. If Wal-Mart stores were perfectly correlated to the number of people within a county, one would see an even distribution of stores and population.

Figure 2.5, however, clearly shows that a higher percentage of people than Wal-Marts are in heavily populated counties, while in sparsely populated counties the opposite can be observed: a higher proportion of Wal-Marts per population. So even though Wal-Mart is a ubiquitous feature of the American economic landscape, the corporation tends to locate more stores in smaller and more rural counties than it does in urban ones. These smaller locations by definition have smaller economies and retail outlets, making the location of a Wal-Mart there disproportionately more significant

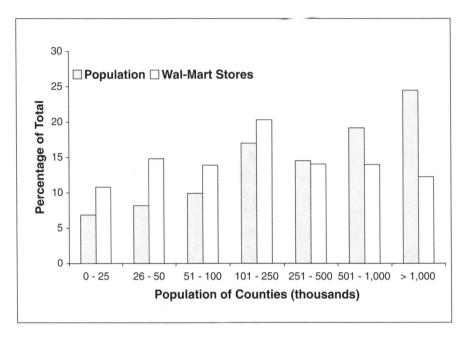

Figure 2.5   Relationship between population and Wal-Mart.

in terms of retail competition, jobs, wages, and workplace regimes than it is in more populous locations.

Few institutions outside federal and state governments have a similar potential for such ubiquitous and localized impacts. Its presence in rural America has been shown to fundamentally affect many segments of local economies. Wal-Mart has, for example, been found to significantly and negatively affect small retailers (Peterson and McGee 2000; Stone 1995). These effects do not appear to be a short-term phenomenon (Peterson and McGee 2000). And even though the entry of Wal-Mart into a region correlates to a small positive increase in local retail employment, this is counterbalanced by a drop in wholesale employment and a reduction in the number of small retail establishments (Basker 2005). While this chapter is not the venue for a detailed analysis of the specific local effects of Wal-Mart, it does argue that the ubiquitous nature of the corporation throughout the country (and more specifically in rural counties) means that its impacts, both positive and negative, are widely felt.

One commonly cited example is the claim that Wal-Mart locates its stores on the fringes of urban areas as a means to lessen its tax burdens (Anon. 2004). Likewise, factors such as land cost and availability can also be seen to affect location decisions (Holmes 2005). Unfortunately, the data available to this analysis are insufficient to address this question in a satisfactory manner. Measurement error in both the geocoding of Wal-Mart locations (a minor yet not entirely resolved concern) and more importantly in city boundary location data (a much larger concern tied to the timing of city boundary changes and the location of Wal-Mart stores as well as a multitude of tax policies across states and localities) prevents presenting a summary table on the frequency of Wal-Mart locations within or outside tax boundaries.

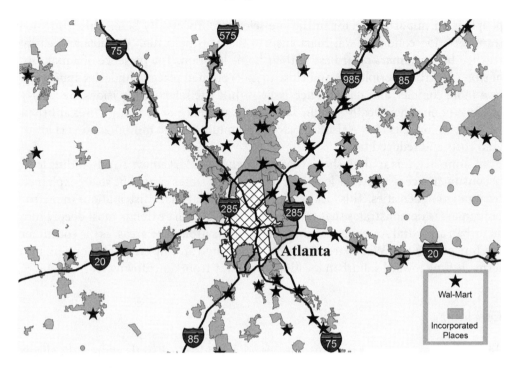

Figure 2.6   Wal-Mart Stores in the Atlanta metropolitan area.

It is possible, however, to note that 49 percent of Wal-Mart locations are within 500 meters of a city boundary, and an impressive 18 percent of stores are within 100 meters of a city boundary.[3] While the reasons for locating a store on the fringe may lie in a locally specific combination of tax reduction and land cost, these statistics indicate that Wal-Mart stores tend toward urban peripheries.

This trend is readily illustrated in Figure 2.6. Atlanta is surrounded by a ring of Wal-Mart sites. Many of these stores are located within a short distance of interstate highways (notably I-20 and I-75), making them relatively accessible to large parts of the metropolitan area as well as travelers. In addition to being sited on the periphery of Atlanta proper, Wal-Marts are situated on the fringes of most incorporated places within the metropolitan area. Furthermore, a significant number of stores do not even fall within the boundaries of an incorporated place.

Similar trends are evident in Omaha, Washington/Baltimore, and Pittsburgh.[4] In Omaha, one likewise sees a ring of stores at the city periphery, with some locations outside incorporated political spaces altogether. In the Washington/Baltimore area, peripheral location patterns and clustering close to interstate highways can again be observed. In Pittsburgh, store proximities to interstate highways are less apparent, but the ring of Wal-Marts around the city is unmistakable.

While maps of Atlanta, Omaha, Washington/Baltimore, and Pittsburgh provide no explanations for the specific locational strategies of Wal-Mart, a number of tentative conclusions can nonetheless be drawn. The many instances of Wal-Mart stores adjacent to interstate highways suggest that relative accessibility to large numbers of people is an important factor in the site selection process. By being close to major transportation conduits, Wal-Mart ensures that it is both highly visible and easily reached by consumers regardless of their home location. The presence of a majority of stores in urban peripheries and close to incorporated place boundaries appears to be a more complex and multifaceted issue. While site selection decisions are clearly contingent on other locally specific factors, the presence of so many stores at urban peripheries suggests that Wal-Mart places a premium on cost minimization via lower land costs and reduced taxes.

In summary, this analysis shows that although Wal-Mart enjoys an astounding level of consumer accessibility, the locations of Wal-Mart stores cannot be solely explained by population densities. This local-scale analysis of Wal-Mart distributions in metropolitan areas demonstrates that the presence of Wal-Mart extends most deeply into suburban and rural America. This indirectly affects urbanized areas, as the consumer catchment area of a Wal-Mart strengthens the long-running trend of shopping patterns shifting toward suburban locations and away from downtown areas.

Conclusions

The cartographic analysis presented here is not intended to directly address the effects and impacts of Wal-Mart on the United States; rather, the goal is to document its simultaneous national and local reach—constituting a "corporate nation" within the nation. Wal-Mart's far-flung network of retail outlets ensures that Wal-Mart interacts with and has an impact on virtually every locality within the United States. In effect, it is engendering a nation of Wal-Mart-based consumption within the bounds of political nationalism, a decidedly dynamic and contested process (see Stone 1995; Peterson and McGee 2000; Basker 2005; Anon. 2004). This analysis provides an overview of one snapshot in time, but future research on the specifics of localities and the contours of change is essential in understanding the development of the "Wal-Mart nation."

Furthermore, as outlined by the rest of the chapters in this volume, Wal-Mart serves as the dominant competitor within retailing, but more importantly is seen as an organizational model to emulate. While other companies (e.g., Ford, Toyota, Dell) have served similar functions in the past, their operations largely had been limited to a few production and research and development locations rather than the thousands of Wal-Mart locations outlined here. Future research should focus on how the propagation of Wal-Mart's organizational and business systems as a "best practices" model impacts firm location decisions and localities. In the same way as the adoption of just-in-time manufacturing systems changed the economic landscape of firms and interfirm transactions, the impact of Wal-Mart's business strategies (including location practices) could be significantly magnified as other companies emulate them. In short, the prominence of the Wal-Mart consumption nation in this particular time and space is likely to inspire and shape the formation of other corporate nations and the economic and social foundations of the United States itself.

Notes

1. This status has also translated into immense fortunes held by the Walton family. Sam Walton's widow, Helen, and four children, S. Robson, John, Jim, and Alice, each have an estimated net worth of approximately $18 billion apiece, or a combined net worth of $90 billion (Kroll and Goldman 2005).
2. This expansion, however, is not unproblematic. Both Aoyama and Schwartz (2006) and Gerhard and Hahn (2005) note that Wal-Mart faces considerable challenges in replicating its U.S.-based model of retailing and labor relations in other countries.
3. The incorporated place boundaries were obtained from the U.S. Census Bureau and are part of the 2000 Census data set. A fuller description of the data can be obtained at www.census.gov/geo/www/cob/pl_metadata.html.
4. The selection of these particular cities is not designed to be in any way fully representative of Wal-Mart location strategies in urban areas. Rather, they were chosen to visually highlight the statistical data relating to urban boundaries presented above.

3

Wal-Mart's World

Steve Burt and Leigh Sparks

Prologue

April 2001: the Global Retailing Conference at the Center for Retailing and Consumer Sciences at the University of Arizona. The keynote speaker is John Menzer, president and CEO of the international division of Wal-Mart. He tells the audience about the success of Wal-Mart and focuses, country by country, on the developments so far and the plans for future expansion of the international division. China is the star of the show. Slides of Wal-Mart shops in Argentina, Brazil, Canada, Korea, Mexico, and the United Kingdom demonstrate Wal-Mart's reach and success. But there's something missing. The first questioner spots it: where did Germany go? Cue nervous laughter.

Introduction

Wal-Mart does not like to get it wrong, not that in retailing terms it often has. After all, Wal-Mart reached the landmark of $1 billion annual sales in 1979, then achieved $1 billion sales in a week in 1993 before making $1 billion in sales *in a day* in 2001. But there is no doubt that Germany is a blot on Wal-Mart's world. Perhaps the company really would like to airbrush it away. Yet Germany is not the only country where Wal-Mart has been less than successful. In the mid-1990s Wal-Mart withdrew from Indonesia and Hong Kong. These are seldom referred to now. Brazil and Argentina have been slow to develop, and Korea remains unimpressive. In the United States, Wal-Mart has come under so much scrutiny and criticism over its environmental impact, effect on communities, and labor and business practices (see Mattera and Purinto 2004; Dube and Jacobs 2004; Goetz and Swaminathan 2004; Featherstone 2004) that in January 2005 it launched its own Web site, www.walmartfacts.com, as a counterbalance.

Wal-Mart's world is not as perfectly successful as some would have us believe. Resistance to Wal-Mart's spread across the United States is mounting (for a case study see Porter and Mirsk 2002). Internationally, although it has huge international buying and logistics operations to supply its stores in the United States and elsewhere, it has expanded store operations in only a small number of countries. Wal-Mart is not as international in outlet terms as other retailers (such as Carrefour and Delhaize, or Benetton and the Body Shop). Wal-Mart's world is narrower than this. While it has built considerable international scale ($56.3 billion in sales in 2004), the international contributions to Wal-Mart's business remain below 20 percent of sales. Due to its enormous size and perceived impact however, retailers and others fear Wal-Mart in many parts of the globe (see Hallsworth 1999; Hallsworth and Evers 2002). Rarely a day goes by without another rumor linking Wal-Mart with expansion or takeovers into another country. As we write it is Turkey; last week it was Russia, and before that Italy and India. Wal-Mart casts a big shadow.

This chapter analyzes Wal-Mart's internationalization and is divided into four main sections. First, the chapter examines business reasons behind the growth of Wal-Mart in the United States. Second, it reviews Wal-Mart's internationalization activities. Third, the success or failure of the market entries is evaluated in light of these key business drivers ("the Wal-Mart model"). Finally, it draws conclusions about the future state of Wal-Mart's world.

What Makes Wal-Mart Special?

Wal-Mart is the world's largest retailer. It reported sales in the financial year ending January 31, 2005 of $285 billion, operated more than 5,300 stores, employed more than 1.5 million associates, and made more than $17 billion in operating profit. The company was incorporated in 1969, although the founders, the Waltons, had been involved in retailing since 1946. Until 1962, the focus was on general-merchandise stores, but it then switched to discount stores. Wholesale clubs (Sam's Clubs) were added beginning in 1982, and supercenters (a general-merchandise/supermarket combination) from 1988. Expansion in the United States has been phenomenally rapid (Graff and Ashton 1993; Graff 1998), and Wal-Mart has a fearsome and well-deserved reputation for effective and successful retailing (Arnold 1998). The current strategy in the United States is to develop supercenters rather than the non-food-based discount stores, continue to develop Sam's Clubs, and to slowly roll out smaller food-based Neighborhood Markets. Food and grocery products have become the main drivers of sales growth for the company (Franklin 2001). As of January 2005, Wal-Mart in the United States operates 1,713 supercenters, 1,353 discount stores, 85 Neighborhood Markets, and 551 Sam's Clubs, comprising over 530 million square feet of floor space. In 2004 it *added* a net 38.7 million square feet of space in the United States. Wal-Mart is a massive business, operationally a phenomenon, and its speed of growth has been remarkable.

The scale and commercial success of Wal-Mart and its speed of growth, together with its form and impact of operations, have attracted a tremendous amount of research, general interest, and controversy. In January 2005, an Internet search produced over 26 million hits on Wal-Mart. There are thousands of institutional and investment analyst reports. A cottage industry in books about the company has arisen (see Ortega 1998; Quinn 1996; Slater 2003; Trimble 1990; Vance and Scott 1992; Walton 1992).

In a previous analysis (Burt and Sparks 2001) we summarized the driving factors behind Wal-Mart's growth in the United States as being an interdependent mix of culture, supply systems, cost and price control, innovation, and market destabilization.

Culture

Wal-Mart still remains fundamentally true to Sam Walton's creation. This is reflected in how "associates" are treated and rewarded and in how the customer is valued by the company. With an overriding emphasis on increasing sales volume through low (or lowest) prices, the corporate culture is predicated on perceived customer values rather than supplier or competitor niceties. Associates are motivated and driven to provide interpersonal service to customers. Their rewards are long-term through stock options rather than short-term through pay levels. The driving force is to build a bigger and better Wal-Mart through a consistent company culture that puts meeting customer needs above most, if not all, other things.

The most visible sign of this to the customer is the dress and demeanor of the staff. All staff members, from "greeters" to managers, are dressed similarly and are intended to be customer-friendly, although some may describe this as "aggressive hospitality." The inculcation of this culture and approach takes a number of forms (Dunnett and Arnold 1999), the most visible perhaps being the motivational Wal-Mart cheer and the "quasi-religious" annual meetings (Schneider 1998; Aggarwal 2001).

Wal-Mart portrays its culture as "small-town America." Arnold, Kozinets, and Handelman (2001) emphasize Wal-Mart's symbolic and community acts that reinforce this perception and the ways in which Wal-Mart connects itself symbolically to the dominant ideologies of American life (frugality, family, religion, neighborhood, community, and patriotism). The use of associates and customers in advertisements is part of the folksiness (and cuts costs). Schneider (1998), however, demonstrates how associates often bear the brunt of the service delivery and the costs of "customer heroics" and charity events.

Supply Systems

Wal-Mart places considerable emphasis on efficiency in logistics and on the supply chain in order to control costs and achieve high levels of product availability. Wal-Mart has considerable experience in centralized distribution (the company claims that in the United States only 12 percent of gross store space is non-sales-related, with 84 percent of product distributed centrally) and of the use of contract logistics specialists. Extensive communications systems allow sales-driven replenishment. Wal-Mart's insistence on suppliers using its bespoke "Retail Link" technology-based supply-chain toolbox enhances the efficiency of its distribution and supply systems. Technology use and data collection and dissemination in the supply chain as a whole are fundamental, and the scale of the company's information systems and databases is legendary ("greater than the Pentagon"). The company prides itself on its in-stock position despite the large number of stock keeping units (SKUs) held (at least 90,000 in a typical supercenter, of which at least 10,000 are in food).

The supply system includes developments in vendor merchandising with leading manufacturers nominated as "channel captains." Typically such "captains" are the dominant multinational manufacturers (e.g., Procter and Gamble), and there are tight working relationships—including extensive information sharing—between these key partners and Wal-Mart. This has been extended with recent expansion in the "own-brand" provision in Wal-Mart. The requirements on suppliers in cost terms and their need to adhere to Wal-Mart's practices are considerable. Bloom and Perry (2001) suggest that suppliers with relationships with Wal-Mart do well where they have large market shares. However, suppliers in markets with a more even market share distribution or where they are not the leading supplier do not perform as well when they have Wal-Mart as a customer. It would seem that the supplier base is reducing within product categories as a consequence, and also in reaction to the continuous need to evaluate SKU performance and to introduce new merchandise. Wal-Mart is keen to try to ensure that it is each supplier's most profitable customer, so as to "get their attention."

Cost and Price Control

Wal-Mart is synonymous with low prices. It operates on the basis of "everyday low prices" (EDLP). With this approach, the customer comes to trust that the prices are the lowest around and will not change erratically under frequent promotional activity (high-low pricing). Such an approach demands a low-cost operation in order to provide low pricing. EDLP provides costs and productivity benefits through the removal of disruptions or disturbances in the supply chain and shop floor activities and through the simplification of flows of goods and information. EDLP requires that the operation be efficient and effective and that no unnecessary costs be incurred by anyone associated with the business. Cost control is therefore of critical importance, allied to a determination to offer the lowest price possible and to focus on reducing prices for the customer. In many cases, known-value items (KVIs) are sold at or below cost (Hawker 1996; Boudreaux 1996; Boyd 1997) and store managers have the power to locally match or beat competitors' prices. Suppliers do not give up ownership of their goods until they are sold to the customer, improving Wal-Mart's cash flow and shrinkage figures, and at the same time focusing suppliers' attention on customers, stocking levels, and supply systems.

Wal-Mart rigorously pursues this lowest-price position (or perception) in the market, though this does not mean it is the lowest-price retailer on every item. Some of this emphasis on prices and costs is also seen in the stores, which are functional, as is the head office. Space is used intensively, and Wal-Mart stores, despite their large size, feel more densely merchandised than do competitor or comparator stores. An average supercenter is now more than 187,000 square feet, compared to 98,000 square feet for a discount store. Between 1990 and 2005 the average size of a Wal-Mart store in the United States (excluding Sam's Clubs) rose from approximately 66,000 to 146,000 square feet.

Prices are kept low through tight cost control and the large product volumes bought and sold. Pressure is exerted on local governments, employees, and suppliers to get the best deal possible for Wal-Mart. Suppliers are "encouraged" to offer the lowest possible price and to search for ways to continuously reduce this price. Such pressure includes Wal-Mart staff working in supplier companies to seek ways of reducing costs. Vendor agreements are tough and penalties for noncompliance are believed to be severe. Subsidies for store development and operations are considerable (Mattera and Purinton 2004). Wages are low, with limited benefits (Featherstone 2004). Unions are discouraged (Ortega 1999).

Innovation

The foregoing three issues are all fundamental tenets of the businesses that derive from Sam Walton and have his hallmark of providing the best deal (i.e., lowest price) for the customer. It would be wrong, however, to suggest a direct and unchanging lineage for the business and its stores from the 1950s to the present day. As David Glass (CEO until January 2000) indicated, Wal-Mart is keen to be at the forefront of new ideas for customers (Udell and Pettijohn 1991). Wal-Mart has reinvented itself on a number of occasions and continues to demonstrate the capacity to both reinvent and experiment, but also to learn from these and other activities. Thus, store formats have not been static and are the result of considerable experimentation followed by a single-minded focus on the chosen format, but enhanced additionally through a continuous improvement strategy. Supercenters did not arrive fully formed one Arkansas morning but are rather the product of extensive testing, development, and learning. This learning continues with new formats such as the smaller (35,000–60,000 square feet) food-focused Neighborhood Markets, the "Urban 99" downsized supercenter, and the relaunched Internet transactional site (www.walmart.com) (IGD 2004). Other trial formats, including Save Mor, Dot Discount Drugs, and Bud's Discount City, have not been pursued (IGD 2003). Operationally, Wal-Mart's current insistence on developing radio-frequency identification (RFID) in the supply chain offers it productivity enhancement potential but also transforms the RFID market globally.

Market Destabilization

The Wal-Mart focus on cost control, volume sales, and low prices is critically important. For many consumers, however, it has been suggested that price is but one of the factors influencing store choice, and that in many markets it is by no means the most important. Typically, convenience, range, and quality are measures that may be seen as more important. Wal-Mart, however, has appeared basically unconcerned by the state of the market. Wal-Mart's argument is that its offer will, over time, make its impact on consumers and that the offer is so good that consumers will in turn reevaluate their store choice and thus their reasons behind it. Everyone loves a bargain, the company claims, and if the price differentials and the breadth of choice offered by Wal-Mart are so great, then consumers may elect not to go anywhere else. In this regard Wal-Mart supercenters aim to capture more of a shopper's basket than Wal-Mart discount stores by raising the number of trips and basket size.

The evidence from market tracking studies (e.g., Arnold, Handelman, and Tigert 1998; Seiders and Tigert 2000) appears unambiguous. Studies of market entry in American and Canadian markets have shown an apparent initial lack of concern by consumers over price, as well as low-level starting points for market share and awareness of consumers for Wal-Mart. Time changes the pattern quite drastically, however. Price steadily becomes more important in consumers' eyes, and Wal-Mart's market share, volume, and awareness climb steeply. Wal-Mart's offer transforms the decision-making process of an entire market, changes the key competitive dynamics, and thus requires competitors to have strong market positions to compete.

There appear to be short-term and long-term effects of this destabilization. The low-price effect is felt initially through selective price cuts, but this does not necessarily lead to real declines immediately in competitive businesses. However, the continuation of EDLP pressure over a number of years appears to have quite considerable impacts. It is the *sustained* nature of the price reductions, volume and store growth, and reinvestment in margin reduction that destabilizes the market. There is a relentless logic to the process once this "Wal-Mart model" is fully introduced and working properly.

Wal-Mart's impact on competitors is thus considerable, as is its impact on communities. By emphasizing very large stores in smaller (initially rural) markets, Wal-Mart's dominance of communities has been massive (Vias 2004). Concern over Wal-Mart's impact on smaller stores and towns, as well as competitors, has been a recurring theme (see McCune 1994; Stone 1995; Barnes et al. 1996; McGee 1996; Arnold and Luthra 2000; Brennan and Lundsten 2000; Davidson and Rummel 2000; Peterson and McGee 2000; Seiders and Tigert 2000; Khanna and Tice 2000; Hicks and Wilburn 2001). It is not just the impact on market entry. Wal-Mart's innovation in formats means that land and sites are simply another disposable asset. In December 2004 Wal-Mart Realty had almost 25 million square feet of surplus floor space in almost 360 "dark" stores.

This impact on communities, existing retailing, market characteristics, and levels (for example, wage rates, price perceptions, and local governance) has been increasingly resisted (see Halebsky 2004; Porter and Mirsk 2002; Norman 1999, 2004; www.sprawl-busters.com). However, there are alternative viewpoints. Wal-Mart has become more proactive in putting its position forward (Hemphill 2005), running newspaper advertisements (starting January 2005) about its activities, and setting up a Web site (www.walmartfacts.com). The very success of Wal-Mart implies that its prices, range, and overall shopping offer consistently attract consumers. Wal-Mart is undoubtedly popular with many consumers. Its efficiency has been identified as the major productivity driver for the United States economy (McKinsey 2002). Its low prices have reduced consumer inflation and brought many products within range of previously underserved consumers. Wal-Mart may also be a job creator (Basker 2005).

The Internationalization of Wal-Mart

By 1991, Wal-Mart was the world's largest retailer, had considerable expansion plans within the United States, and was introducing its new format, the supercenter. Like many leading North American retailers, however, it had not opened stores outside its home country. This was in stark contrast to many of the leading European retailers, which had crossed borders within Europe and elsewhere (e.g., South America) from an early stage. These differing approaches derive in part from differing sizes of national markets. Wal-Mart's comparative insularity began to change in 1991, however, and by 2005 it had internationalized its store operations into twelve countries (refer to Table 2.1).

There are a number of ways in which this internationalization process could be described, but perhaps the most convincing is to divide it into three phases. In the first phase, which essentially predates the formal establishment in 1993 of Wal-Mart's international division, entry to adjacent markets was undertaken. The organizational method varied: joint venture in Mexico, subsidiary in Puerto Rico, takeover in Canada. In Mexico and Puerto Rico the expansion plan was based on organic growth. In Canada the purchase of an established chain provided a market position and store base that could be developed.

The second phase was essentially a world markets focus for the international division under the leadership of Bob Martin. In this phase, a variety of markets were entered (Hong Kong, Brazil, Argentina, China, Indonesia, Germany, and Korea) using various methods and approaches and developing different formats, though concentrating on supercenters. All seemed to involve putting a toe in the water in each country rather than establishing a dominant position. It is hard to avoid a sense that this effort was essentially haphazard flag planting.

In the third phase a more considered approach was developed mainly under John Menzer. The new approach is more financially focused and results-oriented, and there is a focus on strategic planning and performance. Since 1999 the only new markets entered have been the United Kingdom and Japan, and in both instances the approach has been to take over a large retailer and seek to convert its operations to the Wal-Mart model.

Phase One: Initial Market Entries

Viewing the internationalization in this three-phase way begins to help us understand some of the outcomes that have been achieved (refer to Table 2.1). The phase one initial market entries can be seen as successes, albeit at different scales. Mexico is one of the three major international markets for Wal-Mart (sales in 2003 of $10.65 billion), though success did take quite a few years to occur, only really coming after the shareholding in Cifra was increased (at some cost). Wal-Mart de Mexico runs a very wide range of formats deriving from the Cifra business, most of which are not seen elsewhere. Puerto Rico is a small and less important market, though here again takeover in the market (controversial and legally challenged) has been needed to get a dominant position. Canada has been a major success story and Wal-Mart is a dominant retailer in the markets in Canada in which it trades, though as yet the supercenter format has not been used (Simmons and Graff 1998; Evans and Barbiero 1999; Burt and Sparks 2001; Simmons 2001). These three adjacent markets (North American Free Trade Agreement in reality) have been strong performers for Wal-Mart.

Phase Two: World Market Focus

The flag-planting phase, however, is somewhat different in its outcomes. None of the seven markets entered during this time can be said to be an unqualified success. Market withdrawal has occurred from two countries (Indonesia and Hong Kong), the South American position in Brazil and Argentina is not strong, Germany is a major trauma (Christopherson 2001; Knorr and Arndt 2003), and Korea has been slow to develop (Choi 2003). China is the brightest country in this batch, but even here there are problems to overcome (Wang 2003; Au-Yeung 2003; Jinglun 2003). There seem to be a number of common and interrelated reasons why these situations have not gone as well as Wal-Mart might have wished.

First, in none of these markets was there a convincing or dominant entry position taken. In each case the entry was essentially small-scale or even new start-up. Organic growth was seen to be the way to develop. Some were joint ventures with local partners, but this did not protect against failure (e.g., Hong Kong, Indonesia). The largest entry was into Germany, but even here the combined size of both companies purchased did not give a strong market position. In each case these forays stimulated the local competition and/or generated a more competitive situation to which Wal-Mart was insufficiently large at the local level to react effectively. In some cases (e.g., Korea, Brazil, and Argentina) the competition included some international retailers that had been in the market for some time (e.g., Carrefour and Ahold) or which entered in a stronger or more aggressive fashion than Wal-Mart (e.g., Tesco).

Second, the business model that Wal-Mart wished to import to these countries was not easily transferred in some cases. The EDLP proposition depends on being able to demonstrate that Wal-Mart is the lowest-priced retailer in the market. This in turn depends on the low-cost orientation and supply system of the operation working correctly. Scale is an important part of this, as is a strong and efficient supply base and supply chain and the ability to harness technological advantages such as Retail Link. Even in an advanced country such as Germany, however, the supply system was constructed very differently than Wal-Mart expected, and it has struggled to recreate the supply chain it is used to and would prefer to operate. Logistics issues also loom large in China (Huffman 2003), as they have in Korea (Han et al. 2002), Brazil (da Rocha and Dib 2002), and Argentina.

Third, there were operational mistakes in some countries, which meant that the basic proposition did not do what it promised. For example, supply chain difficulties meant that product availability was low, and this began to erode customers' perceptions of the business (Argentina and Brazil). In Indonesia, the style of retailing was too "Western" for the market at that stage. In Korea, Wal-Mart faced supply chain problems as well as stores that appeared to be in the wrong locations and had the wrong products for the target market (Han et al. 2002; Upbin 2004). In Brazil there were additional problems with the store merchandise mix, supplier relationships, and the availability of credit (da Rocha and Dib 2002; Kotabe, de Godoy, and Salzstein 1997). Wal-Mart relied on its price, range, and availability of "pulling power" to destabilize these markets, but the offer actually put in front of consumers was often insufficient to meet their expectations. In some markets EDLP itself was not readily understood initially or accepted by consumers, or indeed by Wal-Mart's business partners or even local-country managers.

Finally, Wal-Mart was in some places constrained by the prevailing business and regulatory regimes in the country. In Germany the established competition was such that demonstrating price leadership was difficult, made even more so by regulations (Knorr and Arndt 2003). Labor is more unionized than elsewhere, and the process of co-determination at various levels is more prevalent (Berggoetz and Laue 2004). The market is structured and organized differently than in the United States, and restrictions on opening hours, wage rates, supplier relationships, layoff payments and processes, and below-cost selling have all impacted and constrained Wal-Mart's performance (Christopherson 2001; Christopherson and Lillie 2005; Fernie and Arnold 2002; Knorr and Arndt 2003). Wal-Mart has been unable to remake the market in the image it requires. In China there have been major restrictions on the organizational model that could be adopted (number of stores, store locations, technology versus labor costs) and in how and from where products are sourced (Huffman 2003; Upbin 2004).

These operational and regulatory issues are not, of course, restricted solely to the countries that were entered by Wal-Mart in this second internationalization phase. Additionally, in most of these countries economic crises affected development possibilities, as with Mexico in the early 1990s, Indonesia and Hong Kong in the mid-1990s, and Brazil and Argentina at the turn of the century. However, given Wal-Mart's previous easier and successful entry in adjacent countries, the toe-in-the-water style of market entry in these cases, and perhaps a degree of retail arrogance, Wal-Mart faced real difficulties. Wal-Mart was simply not large or dominant enough locally to change the market (consumer and supplier) quickly enough to suit its operational practices and desired positioning. As such, the accumulation of issues has constrained these market entries. Some have been exited (Indonesia and Hong Kong) and others are basically static (Argentina, Korea, and Germany, about which decisions will have to be made in due course), while two are seeing investment (Brazil and China), though scale and profitability remain low. In Brazil an opportunistic purchase of Bompreço from Ahold in 2004 has increased the scale of the business but extended the operation into new areas of the country. Whether this is a good long-term fit remains to be seen. In China, development has been steady and Wal-Mart is clearly positioning itself to become a major player in this transforming market. It faces competition from local and international businesses, as well as an unfamiliar operating environment, but the potential is considerable. Perhaps in China there was no other way to enter, given the economic and governmental situation of the country and legal restrictions at the time (Jinglun 2003).

Phase Three: Strategic Vision

The third internationalization phase has seen far less development, but arguably it is more significant. The purchase of ASDA in 1999 was a major coup (Arnold and Fernie 1999, 2000; Burt and Sparks 2001; Hallsworth and Clarke 2001; Fernie and Arnold 2002). The United Kingdom has become the most important international market for Wal-Mart (46 percent or $26 billion in sales in 2004). In buying ASDA, Wal-Mart was purchasing a strong business in a good position, one that had modeled itself on Wal-Mart in many respects (Burt and Sparks 2001). ASDA has overtaken Sainsbury for second place in the U.K. grocery market. In 2004, however, the Competition Commission blocked ASDA Wal-Mart from taking over Safeway (which ranked fourth in the United Kingdom) and thus closely challenging the dominant market leader, Tesco (Burt and Sparks 2003).

The second entry in this more planned phase has been to Japan. Here, a longer-term market entry strategy has been used, but essentially Wal-Mart is now in control of Seiyu and is transforming it into a Japanese version of Wal-Mart. Full control will come formally by 2007 if the agreed fixed-price warrants are implemented (a learning point from problems Wal-Mart had in getting control at an acceptable price in Mexico), as seems likely from the announcement in early 2005 that Seiyu was to become a Wal-Mart subsidiary. While Seiyu is not as "Wal-Mart-ready" as was ASDA, it is a large business in Japan. Even now, however, Wal-Mart is looking to see if it can also gain some of the sites likely to be available from the reconstruction of Daiei. Scale in Japan will be important, though there are still difficulties to be confronted with developing the supply chain and customer demands and perceptions as in EDLP (Deloitte 2003).

In summary, the internationalization process at Wal-Mart has therefore been somewhat mixed in outcome, for a variety of reasons. Despite this, however, the international division has become increasingly more important to Wal-Mart (Figure 3.1). The proportion of sales from the international division has risen to almost 20 percent of the total, and while not as strong in operating income terms (17 percent), this also has been increasing. Almost 30 percent of the stores and 20 percent of the floor space are now outside the United States. Growth in the United States business has been strongly consistent for the last decade (Figure 3.2) but has been outperformed by growth in the international division. Some of the international growth is by acquisition, but like-for-like growth has also been strong. In the four years to 2005, international store numbers rose by over 50 percent and floor space by 78 percent. Despite the performance shown in Figure 3.1 and Figure 3.2, Wal-Mart has publicly stated even higher goals for the international division—one-third of sales and profit growth to come from this source. This suggests that the larger markets with strong growth prospects are likely to be the main focus (with strategic acquisitions necessary to help achieve this goal), or new country entries where market leadership can be purchased.

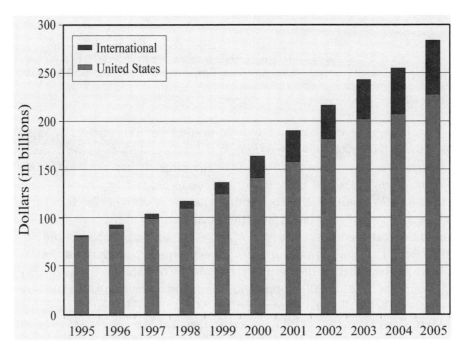

Figure 3.1   Wal-Mart's U.S. and international sales, 1995–2005. *Source:* Wal-Mart 10-K reports to the SEC (www.sec.gov).

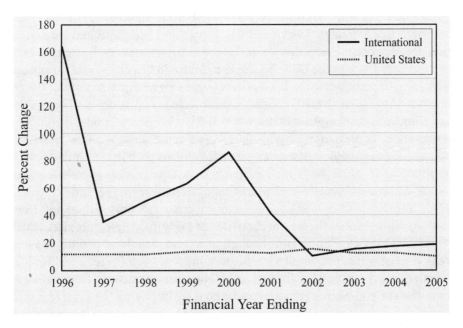

Figure 3.2   Wal-Mart sales growth rates, 1996–2005. *Note:* The growth rate for Wal-Mart in the United States in 2004 is calculated after the disposal of McLane. *Source:* Wal-Mart 10-K reports to the SEC (www.sec.gov).

Discussion

> If it were a country, Wal-Mart would be the 21st largest economy in the world—ranked just
> behind Taiwan and ahead of Austria. If its rivals wished to eclipse it in sales terms, then an
> unlikely alliance of Carrefour, Metro, Ahold and Kroger would be required. If all its employ-
> ees resigned overnight, it could fill its vacancies by hiring Iceland and Estonia. (M&M Planet
> Retail 2004)

Wal-Mart is huge. Its international division would be an internationally significant
retail business if operated in its own right. Wal-Mart's ambitions in the United States
and internationally are clear and dramatically large. It has achieved substantial
growth in recent years and intends to continue to expand in this way. This scale
generates fear (Whysall 2002). This fear occurs at many different levels of the supply
structure. Large retailers wonder how they will compete. Small retailers and local
communities fear the impact of a Wal-Mart on their own livelihoods and on community fabric. Distributors and suppliers are concerned about their businesses after
Wal-Mart arrives, whether they supply the company or not. Some consumers resent
the change from "traditional" shopping locations and outlet forms. Yet fear is not the
only reaction (Whysall 2002). Some suppliers thrive through their relationship with
Wal-Mart. Consumers benefit from low prices that Wal-Mart offers. Many employees
appear satisfied and motivated.

Wal-Mart destabilizes local and national markets and businesses and forces consolidation, whether directly by entry (agreed mergers in China), indirectly by fear
(Promodes/Carrefour protective merger in France), or competitively (copying of the
business model and consolidation in the United States) (Wrigley 2002). Competition
becomes focused among the largest retailers (Colla and Dupuis 2002) or transnational
corporations (see Wrigley 2000; Coe 2004; Currah and Wrigley 2004). Such destabilization does not occur everywhere, nor does it occur without reactions from existing
retailers such as Tesco in the United Kingdom, Metro in Germany, and various supermarkets in California, as well as from others (e.g., labor and government in Germany,
suppliers in Argentina, Brazil, Germany, and Korea, regulatory authorities in the
United Kingdom). The implementation of Wal-Mart's business model is contested.

Resistance or contestation of Wal-Mart's development is not a new phenomenon
(Benoit and Davies 1996). Resistance takes many forms both in the United States and
internationally. In some cases the resistance may slow or stop expansion, whereas
elsewhere Wal-Mart succeeds. Wal-Mart's expansion in recent years and its published
plans for future store development suggest it succeeds more often than not. In many
parts of the United States there is local resistance to planned new stores (see Halebsky
2004) on a case-by-case basis and through local and state land zoning procedures.
There is activist resistance about specific developments (see Porter and Mirsk 2002)
and about the very nature of Wal-Mart itself (Norman 1999, 2004). Complaints about
the true costs of Wal-Mart's activities and who is really paying the costs of low prices
for American consumers (sweatshops, labor, United States manufacturing jobs, local
communities, government subsidies) (see Mattera and Purinto 2004; Dube and Jacobs
2004; Goetz and Swaminathan 2004; Featherstone 2004) are allied to concerns about
the moral guardianship or "censorship" that Wal-Mart exerts (Jacques et al. 2003;
Fox 2005). Wal-Mart has been forced to defend its practices, most notably in terms

of sexual discrimination (www.walmartfacts.com; www.walmartclass.com) and the employment of illegal labor. Wal-Mart's scale in the United States and its dominance of the market, as well as its operating practices—which some argue are a new variant of capitalism and risk sharing (see Christopherson 2001)—make it ripe to be challenged. This does not, however, indicate that Wal-Mart has "had its day" (O'Higgins and Weigel 2002).

At the international retail level there are at least two levels of resistance to Wal-Mart. One level (based on the cultures of resistance that apply in the United States) is focused on a concern that the market will develop as in the United States and that this is inappropriate, for example, in Germany. A second level arises from the battleground with existing and other international retailers. Local businesses are forced to react to Wal-Mart's entry, whether they are suppliers or retailers. Common cause can be made, and in some instances government and other regulatory agencies can intervene to make Wal-Mart's development less rapid. In a number of countries, however, Wal-Mart is but one international retailer. As Wal-Mart expands away from the United States it has to confront and compete with some strong international retailers. It faces Tesco in Korea, Japan, and the United Kingdom. In Brazil, Argentina, Japan, China, and Korea, Carrefour is a competitor. Metro confronts it in Germany, China, United Kingdom, and Japan. While Ahold has been forced to withdraw from much of its international retail activities (see Wrigley and Currah 2003), and Carrefour and Tesco are rationalizing their market entries (in the case of Taiwan and Slovakia/Czech Republic by swapping assets between the two companies), the competition faced by Wal-Mart is considerable.

A further way of looking at the impacts and effectiveness of Wal-Mart's internationalization is through consideration of the driving factors for Wal-Mart as a business, which was outlined earlier.

Wal-Mart has sought to introduce its distinct corporate culture wherever it has internationalized. However, this has not been possible in all situations, and there has been resistance to aspects of the culture in a number of countries, particularly Germany. Wal-Mart's culture and its links to the dominant ideologies in the United States may not apply elsewhere. To work successfully, culture has to be developed and believed rather than imposed. While corporate success will aid this process, corporate struggle, as in many countries where Wal-Mart has expanded, will breed resistance. In some other countries (such as China), there is initial evidence that the "quasi-religious" corporate culture is finding associate acceptance (DSN Retailing Today 2004). There have also been business cultural difficulties with joint venture partners, which resulted in Wal-Mart ending the ventures.

The supply system that Wal-Mart seeks to operate is a technology-rich, centrally controlled model that requires adherence by stores, suppliers, and logistics specialists. It also needs critical mass to work effectively. For Wal-Mart this area has perhaps caused it the biggest problem. The supplier and logistics infrastructure may not exist in some countries, and attempts to build it may be both slow and resisted. Suppliers may not wish to give up such control (as in Argentina). As a result, chaotic outcomes have occurred, with lack of product supply and availability problems. Wal-Mart is attempting to circumvent this by developing its global relationships with particular suppliers and utilizing them both directly and indirectly through "own branding."

In 2002 Wal-Mart reorganized and internalized its global procurement. It has more than fifty-five "elite" suppliers and twenty-one sourcing offices worldwide, and it sources products from more than sixty-five countries (IGD 2004). The sheer scale of sourcing from China ($18 billion per annum) dwarfs other countries, but Brazil ($800 million) and Korea ($500 million) are not insignificant in this regard. Such imports are leverage in Wal-Mart's ongoing entry efforts in these countries and also function to help reorder the supplier base to better suit Wal-Mart's needs. With the global penetration of Wal-Mart in supplier/sourcing terms being far greater than its current retail (shop) presence, this activity may help inform the country knowledge and the government and supplier contact base for future international retail expansion (as indeed has recently happened in Central America).

Cost control allowing price leadership is the fundamental tenet of Wal-Mart and is its key factor in successful expansion. If the model does not work fully, price leadership may be more difficult to demonstrate. The constant search for cost reduction has led Wal-Mart into various difficulties as the extent of its reliance on low-cost suppliers, low wage rates, labor practices, other operating practices, and demands for subsidies have been questioned. Where its power cannot be fully brought to bear, Wal-Mart struggles to make economic inroads into the market and to compete successfully. Much, therefore, depends on government willingness to see low prices in stores and to modernize retail facilities and supply practices, irrespective of any impact on existing businesses or existing practices. In China this may be the way forward, but in Germany the reconfiguration has been resisted at a number of levels.

Wal-Mart is an innovator, or more strictly perhaps a learner (see Currah and Wrigley 2004). Previous business practices have been challenged. It has learned from entry errors in Mexico and applied them in entry to Japan. Learning from ASDA in the United Kingdom about food, fashion, and retail branding has been applied elsewhere (e.g., the George clothing brand is now in Wal-Mart in eight countries). The "arrogance" or "hubris" of Wal-Mart internationally in the mid-1990s has perhaps been replaced with a willingness to accept different practices (Knorr and Arndt 2003). Supercenters across the world have different merchandise mixes and balances, are of different shapes, levels, and site types, and recognize and embrace local brand strengths. Operational practices from one country are transferred to another, as with "retailtainment" from Korea to China. Talented management and ideas as well as formats are being placed where they can enhance the business and meet market demands (Currah and Wrigley 2004). The Todo Dia stores in Brazil are based on Wal-Mex's Bodega format, and Neighborhood Markets are being trialed in China. Far from being a monolithic imposition, Wal-Mart is now trying to adapt to the challenges in different countries, but always within a desire to implement its business model.

This learning is perhaps illustrated by Wal-Mart's market destabilization practices. Destabilization seems to succeed when Wal-Mart's model and power can be fully used, as in Canada. If this cannot be done, then resistance can be mobilized and impacts reduced. Market scale is thus one key to destabilization, combined with the ability to operate supply systems and other practices that complete the EDLP model. This is not possible where market entry is small-scale or slow, or where barriers are entrenched in legislation or can be built easily. Sectoral competitiveness is probably enhanced, however, whatever the situation, as existing retailers and suppliers recognize the real or potential threat. This is seen by reactions in the United States with wage rate reductions and strikes in California supermarkets and internationally in the strengthened international activities of Wal-Mart's international competitors.

This consideration of the effectiveness of the internationalization of the key components of the Wal-Mart model also highlights a number of broader issues. There has been considerable debate in the business literature over what constitutes retail internationalization. In particular, Dawson (1994) has argued that internationalization is more than just the opening of retail outlets. Geographers have also argued that there has, in the past, been an excessive concentration on descriptions of which companies have gone where, without broader considerations of the processes involved (see Wrigley 2000). Such arguments have increasingly focused on the impacts and interrelationships in internationalization (see Dawson 2003; Coe 2004). Many of these issues have been included in the discussion above. In particular, the analysis illustrates the three interrelated relationship aspects emphasized by Currah and Wrigley (2004). Interfirm relationships with suppliers and market agencies are well noted. Extrafirm relationships with localities and countries have also been a focus of aspects of Wal-Mart's internationalization (e.g., in the United Kingdom and China). Perhaps less obvious, but of increasing importance, are the intrafirm relationships by which Wal-Mart decides investment priorities. Decisions about where and how to invest for the best returns are increasingly important given the breadth of opportunities available both in the United States and internationally, differential returns on investment, and the resistance encountered in building the Wal-Mart model in different situations.

Conclusions

This chapter has considered Wal-Mart's internationalization. The scale of internationalization is impressive. Wal-Mart is an increasingly global presence in both sourcing and retailing. Yet it is a retail success in relatively few international markets. The failures have been concerning, even embarrassing, but they have also proved educational. Other retailers have had their failures as well, so Wal-Mart is no different in this regard. Wal-Mart can afford to spend time trying to construct the market in its image in different countries; other companies may not be able to be as patient. However, even Wal-Mart's pockets and patience can run dry, as Wal-Mart has to grow and succeed in order to drive its stock price upward; this is a touchstone for many investors and employees (through share options and holdings).

So what happens next? Wal-Mart is under pressure over some of its practices in the United States. Such pressure can affect consumers' and others' perceptions, both locally and internationally. Perhaps some practices will have to be altered, probably at some expense, and both in the United States and in other countries. There are different operating approaches by other international retailers on which to draw (see Colla and Dupuis 2002; Christopherson and Lillie 2003).

On the retail front, the United States will see Wal-Mart take further strides into new areas geographically (e.g., California) and in product terms (e.g., the emphasis on food). Internationally, Wal-Mart has successful businesses in Mexico, Canada, and the United Kingdom. However, it has to decide whether it is worth persevering with some or all of its flag-planting experiments. Recent expansion in Brazil suggests it remains interested there, but is this true of Argentina, Korea, or even Germany? Here it may be that further purchases, if possible, to increase scale are needed. Alternatively, divestment, as symbolically problematic as this would be for Wal-Mart, may have to be contemplated. China and Japan would seem to be the foci for major investment, though each market has challenges to overcome.

Then there are new markets. If international growth is to hit its targets, then there have to be some new developments in addition to growth in existing markets. The largest international market globally in this respect is probably India, though this is dependent on market opening and deregulation. It is perhaps surprising that Wal-Mart has not entered Eastern Europe. In this regard it is well behind many of the leading European retailers such as Tesco, Carrefour, and Metro, which have built significant store portfolios, though opportunities still remain, as for example in Russia. Shakeouts in Eastern European markets such as Poland may provide opportunities. Elsewhere, South Africa (often overlooked) might be possible given language and development potential.

There is a question over how to approach such market opportunities. Recent internationalization has involved substantial acquisitions, and it would seem that this offers the most promising potential. However, are the right companies up for sale at the right price? While Wal-Mart has deep pockets, it does not want to overpay, and others may wish to block its entry or expansion. The alternative organic growth model of China may be utilized in some cases, where no dominant player exists, but requires government willingness and cooperation to open up markets and to change regulatory regimes. This requires careful preparation and effort at the political level. Wal-Mart has demonstrated its capabilities in this regard.

Wal-Mart is not infallible. Nor is it an "evil empire." Wal-Mart's world is riven with contradictions. It is, however, a company that has been used to getting its own way (eventually). Despite the trauma of Germany, Lee Scott, CEO of Wal-Mart, has recently said that he could not think of any country in Europe that Wal-Mart would not want to be in over the long course of time. Replace Europe with the world and you might be nearer the truth. One day Wal-Mart may well be larger internationally than in the United States.

Postscript

In late September 2005, Wal-Mart announced the purchase for an undisclosed sum of Ahold's 33 percent stake in CARHCO. This is its second purchase from Ahold as the Dutch company attempts to remedy its financial problems (Wrigley and Currah 2003). CARHCO (sales in 2004 of $2 billion) owns an 86 percent stake in La Fragua, a discount store, supermarket, and hypermarket company in Guatemala, with a presence as well in El Salvador and Honduras. CARHCO, among other operations, fully owns CSU, a discount store, supermarket, and hypermarket operator in Costa Rica, Nicaragua, and Honduras. As of August 2005, CARHCO operated a total of 363 stores—120 in Guatemala, 57 in El Salvador, 32 in Honduras, 124 in Costa Rica, and 30 in Nicaragua—with market leadership in the first three of these countries. The new Central America Free Trade Agreement (CAFTA) comes into force in January 2006. It is perhaps significant that Wal-Mart has done well in countries that are signatories to NAFTA. It may also be looking to any future Free Trade Area of the Americas (FTAA).

Wal-Mart agreed to purchase additional interests in CARHCO and move to majority ownership. This was achieved in March 2006. Then the company was also renamed Wal-Mart Central America. Wal-Mart imports more than $350 million of products (mainly clothing) from these countries, as well as many other goods from suppliers with factories and farms in the region. The strategic purchase provides market leadership and an opportunity to link with its strength in Mexico and to a lesser extent with its positions in Brazil and Argentina. It seems possible that further acquisitions in Central and South America will occur, with current thinking focusing on Chile and Argentina.

In May 2006, and as presaged by this chapter, Wal-Mart withdrew from Korea, selling its 16 stores to the market leader Shinsegae Co. for $882 m (subject to Korean regulator approval). It thus followed Carrefour in exiting this market. The Wal-Mart press release commented:

> As we continue to focus our efforts where we can have the greatest impact on our growth strategy, it became increasingly clear that in South Korea's current environment it would be difficult for us to reach the scale desired.

Now that one such major exit has been made and the symbolic bridge of divestment crossed, it might be expected that a concentration strategy for investment will become even more clear.

Part II

Early Years and Store Location

4

Discounting Northern Capital: Financing the World's Largest Retailer from the Periphery

William Graves

The southern United States has long been peripheral to the remainder of the nation's economy. The historical absence of natural resources, poorly articulated transportation networks, and the lack of sustained immigration created a condition of chronic poverty in most parts of the South. This absence of capital has compounded the region's disadvantages and has discouraged the development of an entrepreneurial culture. The South's economic handicaps forced regional economic development policy to focus on attracting branch plant facilities to create jobs, attract capital, and bring entrepreneurial skills to the region. This dependence upon outside human and financial capital has reinforced the region's peripheral status, since profits generated by externally owned facilities were extracted from the South and managers were typically trained outside the region. Indeed, the historical poverty and current economic development strategy have widened the economic gulf separating the South from the remainder of the United States.

While there are a handful of examples of modern southern entrepreneurship (Coca-Cola, Bank of America, Home Depot), the rare economic successes are confined to the region's largest cities. One of the few exceptions to the South's metropolitan-centered growth is Wal-Mart of Bentonville, Arkansas. Under Sam Walton's leadership, the firm has brought billions of dollars in capital into the southern economy from global investment markets. This reversal of normal capital flows required overcoming the region's poverty, its risk-averse culture, and its isolation from capital markets, conditions that have stunted entrepreneurship throughout the South since the Civil War. Overcoming these impediments is an achievement that is frequently obscured by the company's pervasive global reach and aggressive competitive stance. However, Wal-Mart's success can serve as a model to other entrepreneurs in the region. The purpose of this chapter is to view the evolution of Wal-Mart through the lens of southern economic history. By doing so one can not only see how Sam Walton overcame impediments to southern entrepreneurship but also measure the extent of Wal-Mart's impact on the region and identify strategies for promoting additional entrepreneurship within the region.

Capital Availability in the South

Southern poverty is attributed to a variety of forces—its culture, history, contentious race relations, environment, etc.—but economic historians generally return to capital starvation as the primary explanation for the region's stunted postbellum development (Carlton and Coclanis 1989). While it is assumed that the causal mechanisms behind these disparities have been rectified, evidence suggests that the peripheral status of the South continues in modern investment markets.[1] The southern share of the nation's equity investment is well below the region's share of population. If Wal-Mart's contribution to a region's capital supply is hypothetically removed from the accounts of capital flow, the South would have attracted less of the nation's investment in 2004 than it did in 1970.

From a neoclassical perspective, the South's capital shortage is a result of an absence of investment opportunities. The expectations of perfect capital mobility mandate that investment will flow out of areas that lack investment opportunities and into areas with firms that promise higher returns. However, such market efficiency is not supported by a growing array of research (Thaler 1993) in which disadvantaged regions have repeatedly been shown to be underserved by capital markets regardless of the quality of their investment opportunities (Green 1995; Bodenman 2000; Graves 2003). These inefficiencies are attributed to an absence of social networks used to transmit tacit knowledge (e.g., information related to a firm's management skill, innovative potential, market positioning, expansion strategy, etc.) embodied in firms that investors rely upon as a fundamental part of their decision making (Zook 2004). The absence of personal connections between investors and investment targets has been repeatedly shown to impact the capital supply of entire regions (Zook 2002; Graves 2002; Carlton and Coclanis 1989). The majority of American investors are concentrated in the northeastern United States, specifically New York. The contentious historical relationship between the Northeast and the South, combined with a paucity of investment opportunities, has maintained the discontinuities between northern investors and southern entrepreneurs. Even after modern transport linkages into the South were developed, social networks between investors and targets failed to evolve. Empirical analysis of capital flows reveals that investors have reduced their interest (as reflected by company valuation) in rural southern firms since 1990. It was shown that these reduced valuations were not a reflection of the quality of the individual businesses but rather an indication that investors had refocused their attention on firms that were less remote (Graves 2002).

While the significance of tacit knowledge transfer to the flow of capital is not disputed, its importance to investors is dependent upon the nature of their investment targets. As risk of firm failure increases, the need for personal contact between investor and target also increases. This situation makes it paramount for technology-oriented firms to remain close to investors (Lundegaard 1999; Zook 2002), while it is expected that less sophisticated firms (e.g., retailers) can maintain looser contacts between management and investors. The relatively unsophisticated nature of Walton's retail operation should have facilitated its competition for distant capital. However, Walton's retail model of lean inventory coupled with a dedicated distribution and communications network was unusual for retailers of the era, and Wal-Mart represented a significant technological advance within the sector. The benefits of these advances were not immediately apparent outside the region, in part because of the separation between investors and the firm. Conversely, the costs of this new retail model were readily apparent to investors since the expenses of the system appeared on the firm's balance sheet (Walton 1992). The disadvantages of Wal-Mart's isolation were compounded by the inability of distant investors to quickly recognize the benefits of Walton's new business model.

The View of Wal-Mart from Wall Street

Walton financed the early expansion of Wal-Mart by borrowing from family, selling equity to store managers, and obtaining bank loans that leveraged existing revenue streams. This piecemeal approach to finance consumed growing amounts of Walton's energy and limited the ability of the firm to move into risky, primarily urban markets (Vance and Scott 1994). While such internally financed expansion was the norm for most retailers in the early stages of growth, Walton understood that the success of his discount retail model required a more rapid expansion in order to strengthen his bargaining position with suppliers (Graff and Ashton 1993). An additional difficulty presented by Walton's business model was that this volume of purchases required substantial warehouse space and a well-articulated distribution system connecting warehouses and stores. Urban retailers such as Kmart and Dayton Hudson (now Target) could subcontract these services (thus reducing capital expenditures), but no distributor or trucking company was willing to service Wal-Mart's isolated, small-town network of stores (Vance and Scott 1994). Walton was forced to construct his own distribution facilities, fleet of trucks, and satellite communications network in order to maximize the supplier discounts required by his business model. Substantial expenses such as these required more capital than ongoing store operations could provide and were atypical of the retail industry. Banks were reluctant to loan money to fund the construction of the unusual distribution network or new stores that required such a costly network.

The combination of isolated, small-town locations coupled with the expense of a wholly owned distribution system made Wal-Mart appear unattractive to distant investors (Graff and Ashton 1993) and required Wal-Mart to constrain its expansion in order to minimize its consumption of capital (Meyer and Brown 1979; Vance and Scott 1992). Unfortunately, the substantial capital needs of the nascent retailer became so great that Walton saw the stock market as the only opportunity to finance the firm's continued growth (Walton 1992).

Wal-Mart's growing capital needs forced the firm to offer equity to the public in the early 1970s. However, Wal-Mart's southern regional base and preference for small-town locations made the company's virtues invisible to Wall Street. The prominence of Wal-Mart's competition compounded the problems of isolation from capital. Sears, the nation's largest retailer until the 1990s, and Kmart, the undisputed king of discount retail, were viewed as superior and less risky investments and presented what appeared to be an insurmountable obstacle to Wal-Mart's expansion into attractive urban markets. The combination of Wal-Mart's physical and cultural distance from

Wall Street, its unorthodox business model, and its formative competition rendered its capital acquisition prospects bleak. It appeared in the 1960s and early 1970s that Wal-Mart would share the fate of most southern firms—a capital shortage would fatally stunt the development of the company.

Despite the obstacles, Walton recognized that the sale of equity in a public offering (IPO) was the only means of financing the firm's ambitious growth. The considerable expense of filing the required paperwork combined with the need to continue to finance the chain's growth forced him to venture outside his home region to obtain a short-term loan. Walton again expressed frustration at the reluctance of northern investors to finance his business model. Ultimately, Walton was forced to sacrifice equity to secure a bridge loan to sustain the company before its IPO (Walton 1992). Fortunately, the difficulties produced by Wal-Mart's isolation were mitigated by the coincidental presence of Stephens, Inc., one of the nation's largest investment banks outside the Northeast, in Little Rock, Arkansas. The presence of a semilocal investment banker that could underwrite and market Wal-Mart's IPO was considered vital to the offering's success (Walton 1992).

Wal-Mart went public in the spring of 1970. The firm was valued at $21.5 million (one ten-thousandth of its 2005 market value). The proceeds of the stock sale were used to pay off short-term debt, acquire inventory and fixtures for store expansion, and fund construction of the firm's first distribution center. According to Walton, the IPO was successful in ending Wal-Mart's chronic capital shortage: "Going public really turned the company loose to grow, and it took a huge load off me.... . The company has rolled along on its own and financed itself" (Walton 1992: 99). The infusion of capital from the IPO required Walton to sell only 23 percent of the company's shares, preserving Walton's control of the limited number of shares available to trade, and reducing the attractiveness of the stock to institutional investors (Vance and Scott 1994).

It was frequently suggested that few local investors were interested in purchasing shares in the early stages of Wal-Mart's evolution. Walton suggested that local familiarity with his modest history discouraged the purchase of shares (Walton 1992). Unfortunately, local interest was commonly used as a litmus test for outside investors (Carlton and Coclanis 1989). This lack of local interest, combined with the firm's isolation and innovative business model, required the cultivation of extraregional investors in order to sustain capital flows into the firm. One strategy was to conduct elaborate annual shareholder meetings in Bentonville, which provided an opportunity to communicate relevant tacit knowledge about the firm to current and potential investors. Investors were escorted by company managers for tours of stores, distribution facilities, and corporate headquarters in order to acquaint them with the firm's culture and prospects. Entertainment such as square dances and rafting with company representatives was provided to further acquaint investors with the company culture. Walton admitted the necessity of such an expensive and time-consuming strategy: "The values and approach of most retailers were entirely different from what this crazy bunch in Arkansas was doing, and we wanted them to see it for themselves" (Walton 1992: 101).

Based on his firm's valuation relative to his direct competition, Walton's promotion of his firm was quite successful. Wal-Mart's price-to-earnings ratio was roughly

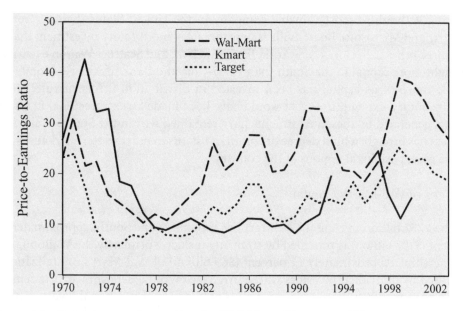

Figure 4.1   Price-to-earnings ratios for Wal-Mart, Kmart, and Target.

the same as that of Dayton Hudson (now known as Target) and marginally less than Kmart's at the time of the firm's IPO (Figure 4.1). Walton suggests that Wal-Mart's valuation would have been higher in its early stages of growth if it were not for the pessimism of distant securities analysts about the firm's future growth prospects. Wal-Mart did not face direct competition from Kmart or Target or operate in any large metro areas until 1977. This discounting of the firm's growth prospects frustrated Walton: "We were having a heck of a time convincing Wall Street to stick with us. A lot of people didn't think we could stand up to real competition" (Walton 1992: 194). Over time, Wal-Mart's isolation and small-town markets became an asset, as U.S. urban areas suffered from a glut of retail competition in the late 1970s and early 1980s. Simultaneously, Wal-Mart reached the critical mass necessary to justify its considerable investments in its distribution system, and it was now considered to be the most efficient of the discount retailers. As the fortunes of Kmart and Target declined due to their saturated markets, and Wal-Mart's efficiency became increasingly evident to investors, Walton's firm became the most valuable discount retailer in terms of market capitalization. Wal-Mart's meteoric rise further fueled the company's expansion, and the firm gained the leverage necessary to extract better terms from suppliers. The end result of these events was that Wall Street was finally forced to confront its historical geographic biases. Wal-Mart's annual growth rate of 36 percent during the 1980s made the firm an irresistible target for capital.

Wall Street's ambivalence toward Wal-Mart continued into the mid-1990s. Securities analysts considered the firm to be overvalued given the limited growth prospects associated with its omnipresence and the continued prominence of Kmart and Target (Walton 1992). As investors watched Wal-Mart's steady expansion occur concurrently with the economic collapse of direct competitor Kmart as well as indirect competitors such as Toys "R" Us, Wall Street rewarded the firm's unparalleled efficiency. By February 2005 Wal-Mart had a market capitalization of $257 billion, making it the third most valuable company in the United States (behind General Electric and Microsoft). Bentonville is now the site of more equity investment than all but three other U.S. cities (New York, San Francisco, and Seattle). Walton eventually brought more capital to the South than Coca-Cola and Bank of America combined. While much of its capital has been invested in distribution infrastructure, stores, and inventory, expenditures that would have been made by extraregional firms, the profits generated by these investments have remained within the South. Wal-Mart's success has brought a high degree of command status to northwestern Arkansas, one of the most peripheral regions of the country.

Sources of Wal-Mart's Capital

Of the $257 billion in capital Wal-Mart has brought to the South, approximately 40 percent ($102 billion) is provided by company insiders (primarily the Walton family partnership). Approximately 25 percent ($65 billion) of Wal-Mart's capitalization is provided by individual investors whose origins cannot be determined. The remaining 35 percent ($90 billion) of investment is provided by institutional investors. Conventional views of capital availability suggest investors prefer nearby firms to more distant ones. Walton was forced to actively solicit investment from outside the region in order to overcome the absence of significant supplies of local capital. Consistent with expectations of the tacit-knowledge literature, the amount of institutional ownership in Wal-Mart is significantly lower than its competition. However, the low rates of institutional ownership do not correspond to low company valuations (see Figure 4.1). In Wal-Mart's case, institutional disinterest does not appear to result in depressed price-to-earnings ratios. Walton's entrepreneurial strategies may provide an explanation of this unusual situation as the family's high rate of insider ownership after the IPO reduced the firm's liquidity and thus inflated its valuation in the absence of institutional interest.

The roster of institutional investors in Wal-Mart today suggests that geography no longer plays a role in attracting capital (Table 4.1). It appears that Wal-Mart's success, visibility, and skilled management have overcome the disadvantages of its peripheral southern location. While access to international capital markets is de rigueur for a global retailer, the sources of corporate investment shown in Table 4.1 are truly remarkable for a company once regarded as the "courtier to the hillbillies" (Vance and Scott 1992: 237). Wal-Mart has attracted capital from New York, California, Britain, and Germany, an indirect transfer of capital from the core of the global economy into what was once the least developed portion of the American economic periphery. The opportunity to control extraregional capital is rare within the South. Command of these resources presents development opportunities that would not be available in the absence of Wal-Mart's success.

Conclusions

The culture and poverty of the South have long discouraged entrepreneurship. While a growing acceptance of risk taking has recently emerged in the urban portions of

TABLE 4.1   Ten Largest Institutional Investors in Wal-Mart, September 30, 2004

Rank	Institution	Location	Investment (in thousands)	Percent of Total Wal-Mart Capitalization
1	Barclays Bank	California	$6,802,468	3.03%
2	Vanguard Group	Pennsylvania	$6,637,051	2.95%
3	State Street Corp.	Massachusetts	$5,851,491	2.60%
4	FMR Corp.	Massachusetts	$5,065,889	2.25%
5	Northern Trust Corp.	Illinois	$2,622,881	1.17%
6	Deutsche Bank	Germany	$2,350,052	1.05%
7	Mellon Bank	Pennsylvania	$2,139,192	0.95%
8	AXA	France	$1,776,104	0.79%
9	Capital Research	California	$1,473,919	0.66%
10	JP Morgan Chase	New York	$1,388,784	0.62%

Source: Vickers Investment Research.

the South, endogenous corporate growth has been almost entirely absent from the region's smaller towns. The lack of entrepreneurship has forced policy makers in the South to attract branch plants by promoting the region's low costs. The dependent (and mobile) nature of these jobs has depressed local wages and accelerated the drainage of local capital; this has created jobs but has widened the divide between the peripheral rural South and the remainder of the nation in terms of wages, entrepreneurship, and supply of capital (see Lyson 1989; Hartshorn and Walcott 2000). While it was hoped that a process of industrial succession would spawn locally owned firms from the branch plants and eventually create knowledge- and technology-oriented companies, examples of such diffusionary development have been rare in the South (Johnson 1997).

Wal-Mart's evolution within northwestern Arkansas is an aberration in the economic and cultural context of the South. Sam Walton created the world's largest retailer by leveraging the few advantages associated with the region's remoteness (e.g., a lack of competition). Wal-Mart's claim to being the youngest retailer to exceed $1 billion in sales is more remarkable considering the financial constraints behind the firm's expansion. Wal-Mart's success presents one of the few examples of southern entrepreneurial success, and as such, Wal-Mart has partially reversed the exodus of capital from the region. Without Wal-Mart, the southern retail environment would have likely become dependent upon externally owned chains, a retail structure where profits generated by retailers would be extracted from the region. Wal-Mart's presence has created an innovation complex focused on discount retail in a region that was previously without command status. While the net benefit of Wal-Mart to the region and nation has been debated elsewhere in this volume, this chapter presents Wal-Mart and the efforts of Sam Walton as vital to the economic viability of its home region, and by extension the South as a whole.

An aspect of Wal-Mart's growth that has not been addressed in depth is Walton's decision to remain in Arkansas. Walton stated in his biography that his family's preference to remain in the area was the sole factor in the headquarters location decision (Walton

1992). While the simplicity of this explanation is appealing, it is extraordinarily dismissive of the additional risk this decision entailed—a less isolated headquarters location certainly would have facilitated the firm's growth. Walton clearly valued his understanding of the southern customer base and the relative absence of competition within his home region. Walton was able to leverage the region's clear disadvantages into a strong competitive niche, one that was unlikely to be disturbed by well-funded competitors. Walton had become one of the region's few entrepreneurs to find success despite the region's poverty and isolation.

If Wal-Mart were not successful, erosion of capital from the South would have continued (Graves 2002). Unfortunately, Wal-Mart's success likely precludes the spin-off of most related retail firms for competitive reasons. The creation of non-retail spin-offs remains unlikely due to the necessity of strong linkages between investors and firms that are more sophisticated than retail. However, Walton's strategy does offer a model for development of southern firms. Sam Walton was able to overcome the biases of northern capital sources by combining a business plan that addresses the weaknesses of a remote market with the active cultivation of the social networks that channel investment from outside the region. In addition, Walton's strategy demonstrates how some of the disadvantages of the South (its poverty) can be levered into advantages to firm creation (lack of competition). Wal-Mart provides an example of a highly innovative and efficient firm within a region not known for its innovative or organizational capacity. The firm has created a "new normal" for the retailing industry, since it required retailers to adopt similar efficiencies or they would be starved of investment. The fact that a firm headquartered in the peripheral South acts as such a role model is truly remarkable.

Acknowledgment

This research was supported, in part, with funds provided by the University of North Carolina at Charlotte.

Note

1. The South is defined using the U.S. Census Bureau designation, which includes the following states: Alabama, Arkansas, Delaware, Florida, Georgia, Kentucky, Louisiana, Maryland, Mississippi, North Carolina, Oklahoma, South Carolina, Tennessee, Texas, Virginia, and West Virginia.

5

Wal-Mart Supercenter Market Share of Grocery Retailing in U.S. Metropolitan Areas

J. Dennis Lord

Introduction

In the late 1980s, Wal-Mart began to build a new retail-format store known as the Wal-Mart Supercenter. This new format included both a discount department store and a grocery store under one roof, with the grocery store function accounting for about 30 percent of the floor space in the approximately 180,000-square-foot store. As Wal-Mart continued to build the supercenters in the 1990s, these new stores often served to replace the chain's nearby existing discount stores. In the ten years from 1991 to 2001, the number of supercenters increased from only 10 to more than 1,000 (Wrigley 2002). By early 2004, the number of supercenters had reached 1,471, with stores in all but six states. Wal-Mart's foray into grocery retailing via the supercenter format and its rapid expansion of this format throughout the 1990s and into the new millennium understandably raised concerns among many conventional supermarket chains relating to the potential adverse effect of Wal-Mart's presence on their market shares in the grocery retailing sector (Franklin 2001). Advantages of name identity, large stores, low prices, and cross-shopping opportunities have contributed to Wal-Mart's significant market share capture in grocery retailing through its supercenter format.

Wal-Mart's presence in grocery retailing reached two milestones in 2003–2004. First, in 2003 it passed Kroger as the largest grocery chain in the United States in terms of market share. The top 10 firms in grocery sales in 2004 were Wal-Mart, Kroger, Costco, Safeway, Albertsons, Sam's Club, Ahold USA (Bi-Lo, Bruno's), Publix, Delhaize America (Food Lion), and Winn-Dixie (Trade Dimensions International 2004b). Wal-Mart Supercenters hold a substantial lead over second-place Kroger ($66.7 billion versus $53.8 billion, respectively). Wal-Mart's growing dominance in food sales is even greater when sales from its warehouse club format, Sam's Club, and its conventional supermarket chain, Neighborhood Market, are also counted. In fact, Sam's Club is the sixth largest firm in grocery sales nationally. The combined sales of Wal-Mart Supercenters, Sam's, and Neighborhood Market more than doubled the sales volume of second-place Kroger.

A second milestone for Wal-Mart was reached in 2003–2004 when for the first time it became the market share leader in several metropolitan-area markets. The combined metropolitan statistical areas (MSAs) of Dallas and Fort Worth provide an example of Wal-Mart's ascendancy to the position of leading market share grocery retailer in individual MSA markets (Halkias 2004). This was the first top 10 market (gauged in terms of population size) where Wal-Mart had become the market share leader. Between 2003 and 2004, it passed Albertsons, which had just under a 20 percent market share in the two combined MSAs. By 2004, Wal-Mart's market share had reached 22.1 percent in these markets, while Albertsons had experienced some slippage in its market share. Wal-Mart reached this position by taking market share from major players in the market (including Albertsons) as well as smaller firms. In Tampa, where Wal-Mart is still behind the market leader, Publix, it has taken significant market share from other grocery retailers such as Kash n' Karry, Winn-Dixie, and Albertsons (Albright 2003).

The geographical expansion of the supercenter has followed a similar pattern to that of Wal-Mart's conventional discount store, namely, a neighborhood diffusion pattern outward from the headquarters location of Wal-Mart in Arkansas over time, and a greater concentration of stores in non-metropolitan markets compared to metropolitan markets (Graff and Ashton 1994; Graff 1998). This pattern of "storing market areas" can be seen at the state level by examining the number of supercenters relative to the population of the state. States with the largest number of supercenters per million population are the ones most proximate to Arkansas, and states with a substantial proportion of rural population (*Frontline* 2004). The five leading states on this measure in 2004 were Arkansas (17.7 supercenters per million population), Mississippi (16.0), Wyoming (14.0), Alabama (13.1), and Oklahoma (12.9). Among metropolitan areas, supercenters have been most concentrated in moderate-size markets. Of the 1,471 supercenters in operation at the beginning of 2004, only one-third (490) of these stores were located in the nation's 100 largest metropolitan areas (Trade Dimensions International 2004b). In fact, supercenters were present in only 68 of the 100 largest metropolitan markets. Similar to the pattern noted above for states, metropolitan areas with the highest presence of supercenters (stores per million population) were areas most proximate to Wal-Mart headquarters in northwest Arkansas. The correlation between supercenters per million population and distance from Bentonville was -.62. The five leading MSAs in Wal-Mart Supercenter presence included Birmingham (15.0 supercenters per million population), Little Rock (12.8), Oklahoma City (11.6), Tulsa (11.4), and Baton Rouge (11.2). Wal-Mart had 5 or fewer supercenter stores in almost half (33) of these 68 markets, and had more than 10 stores in only 15 of these markets. The number of supercenter stores in each of these markets has been limited by the relatively high population threshold for the supercenter compared to that for stores of a conventional supermarket chain, which might operate more than 30 stores in a given metropolitan area. Even so, Wal-Mart is more national in its grocery retailing presence than conventional supermarket chains, which in the past have operated primarily as regional chains. Only recently has this latter situation begun to change as mergers and acquisitions among some of these firms have allowed them to become more national in their geographic presence. In fact, this merger and acquisition activity, which has generated more buying power and other scale efficiencies for these conventional supermarket retailers, may be due in part to the competitive threat posed by the growing presence of Wal-Mart in the grocery retailing sector (Wrigley 2002).

The aim of this chapter is to examine Wal-Mart's market strength in grocery retailing across U.S. metropolitan markets, specifically focusing on the 100 largest metropolitan areas because of data availability. The purpose here is to identify the variability in Wal-Mart's market share and market share per store in grocery sales across metropolitan markets, and to identify factors that explain this variation. This work extends the previous research of Franklin (2001) on Wal-Mart Supercenter market share by using more recent data and including a measure of market presence as a predictor of market share. The present study also examines an alternative measure of market performance, market share per store, and identifies correlates of its variability. Market share and market share per store data are for the year 2004.

Variables and Methods

Data on the market strength of Wal-Mart Supercenters in grocery retailing were obtained from *Market Scope,* a leading source for data on market share in the grocery retailing sector (Trade Dimensions International 2004b). This source provides data on the number of stores and market share for grocery retailers in the 100 largest U.S. metropolitan areas and for other large market geographies. Two measures were used to gauge market strength: market share in supermarket sales and market share per store. Wal-Mart's market strength in the 68 markets in which it has a presence was expected to be affected by several factors. It is widely accepted that a firm's market share, measured as share of sales, should be related to its market effort. The latter can be measured in various ways, including the firm's share of the total stores in the market or its number of stores in the market relative to the size of the market, that is, its level of market presence. An increase in market effort should lead to a corresponding increase in market share. Research on the market-share/share-of-stores relationship indicates that this relationship may not be linear, but instead may be an S-shaped curve as a firm adds additional stores in a market (Lilien and Rao 1976; Lilien and Kotler 1983; Mahajan, Sharma, and Kerin 1988). Researchers have suggested that initially the addition of stores in a market area results in increasing returns to market share, but as stores continue to be added, the relationship eventually switches to one of decreasing returns to market share, thereby resulting in the familiar S-shaped curve. This study uses Wal-Mart's market presence, measured as the number of Wal-Mart Supercenter stores per million population in the metropolitan area, as a predictor of the firm's market share, with the expectation of a strong positive relationship. This empirical investigation will determine if the relationship is linear or S-shaped in form. It is expected that market presence will be negatively related to market share per store, as more stores relative to the population in the market may dilute market share on a per-store basis.

Additional factors that are investigated for their possible relationship to market share and market share per store variation across U.S. metropolitan areas include the population size and income level of these markets. Both variables were used in a previous study by Franklin (2001). Wal-Mart's reverse hierarchical diffusion pattern of geographic expansion is well documented—it expanded first to small markets and only later to larger ones (that is, its expansion has been one of diffusing up, rather than down, the urban or metropolitan hierarchy over time). This pattern not only was characteristic of the traditional Wal-Mart discount department stores but also has been followed in the expansion of the supercenter format (Graff and Ashton 1994; Graff 1998). Therefore, Wal-Mart Supercenters may have generated a larger market share in smaller metropolitan markets than in larger ones. No doubt some of this difference simply reflects a difference in the market presence of supercenters by market size and will be captured by the market presence variable noted above. Whether there is still any effect of market size remaining once the level of market presence is considered remains to be seen. One or only a few supercenter stores would be more effective in serving a smaller metropolitan market than a larger one because of greater customer convenience. Therefore, it is expected that population size of the metropolitan area will be negatively related to market share and market share per store. Population size of the metropolitan area for the year 2002 is used as the measure (U.S. Census Bureau 2003). Franklin (2001) did not find population size to be a statistically significant variable in his model of Wal-Mart Supercenter market share in grocery sales.

Because of its low-price image, Wal-Mart may exert stronger drawing power from low- and modest-income consumers than from the higher-income population. If this is the case, Wal-Mart's sales performance may be strongest in lower-income metropolitan areas. It is expected, therefore, that market share and market share per store will be negatively related to the income level of the metropolitan area. Per capita personal income in the year 2002 is used as the income measure (BEA 2004). Franklin (2001) found income level to have a statistically significant negative effect on Wal-Mart market share.

Results

Wal-Mart Supercenter market share in the year 2004 averaged 14.9 percent across the 68 metropolitan areas, varying from a low of 0.6 percent in Newark, NJ to a high of 40.7 percent in El Paso. A market share of 5 percent has been used as a benchmark by antitrust authorities for indicating that a firm has a significant presence in a market. Using this benchmark figure, Wal-Mart had a significant presence in 48 of the 68 markets. Over time, as Wal-Mart has aggressively expanded its supercenter store format, it has grown market share. For example, in 1999 its market share in 54 of the 100 largest population markets where it had a presence averaged only 4.8 percent, and exceeded 5 percent in only 19 of these 54 markets (Franklin 2001). The firm's market share is highest in those markets most proximate to its home base in Arkansas, consisting primarily of southeastern and southwestern U.S. metropolitan areas. The leading market share metropolitan areas, in addition to El Paso (40.7 percent), were Tulsa (35.4 percent), Oklahoma City (35.1 percent), Baton Rouge (34.3 percent), and Colorado Springs (34.1 percent). This pattern likely reflects the geographic expansion of Wal-Mart outward from its home base over time. Because of the rapid expansion of the supercenter format in recent years and its success in attracting grocery shoppers, Wal-Mart has now become the leading grocery retailer in some metropolitan markets and is challenging for the position of leading market share firm in many others. Between 2000 and 2004, Wal-Mart's market share has grown rapidly in many of its top markets: from 5.9 percent to 40.7 percent in El Paso, 11.5 percent to 35.4 percent in Tulsa, and 9.5 percent to 35.1 percent in Oklahoma City. There was an especially large increase in Wal-Mart's share of supermarket sales in its leading markets between 2003 and 2004, an increase that appears out of proportion to the increase in the number of supercenters in these markets. Perhaps some of this increase was due to the poor economy, especially in lower-income MSAs, which may have caused shoppers to become more price-conscious and therefore to gravitate to a chain with a low-price image, such as Wal-Mart.

An alternative measure indicating the strength of a retailer in a market is the market share obtained per store. The mean value for Wal-Mart Supercenters in these 68 MSA markets in 2004 was 2.59 percent and ranged from 0.50 to 7.65 percent. This mean value is much higher than for conventional supermarket chains, whose market share per store often does not exceed 1.00 percent in the highly competitive metropolitan markets. The higher market share per store for Wal-Mart Supercenters no doubt is due to more grocery retailing floor space than the typical supermarket, the attraction of low prices, and the additional consumer draw exerted by the general merchandise component of the supercenter store. The mean market share per store value of 2.59 percent is considerably higher than the value of 1.97 only one year earlier, indicating that the firm grew market share well beyond the rate of new store expansion in these markets.

Correlation coefficients between the dependent and independent variables show that, as expected, both population size and income level of the metropolitan area have negative (although modest) correlations with market share, -.34 and -.39, respectively. Therefore, Wal-Mart Supercenter market share appears to be highest in small, lower-income metropolitan markets. These two independent variables are also moderately correlated with each other (+.46). The market presence measure, Wal-Mart Supercenter stores per million population, has a very strong positive correlation with market share (+.94). A closer examination of this relationship using a scatter plot reveals that it is linear rather than the S-shaped curve that some researchers have suggested may describe the relationship between market share and market effort. Thus Wal-Mart appears to gain market share in a linear manner with its increased market presence. Perhaps Wal-Mart has not yet stored markets to a level that would result in diminishing returns to market share. The firm had more than 10 stores in only 15 of the 68 metropolitan markets in 2004. The market presence measure also shows modest negative correlations with both population and per capita income. The second measure of market strength, market share per store, has moderate negative correlations with population size and income level, with values of -.64 and -.54, respectively. Similar to the market share relationship, market share per store is highest in smaller-population and lower-income metropolitan areas. Contrary to expectations, market share per store did not have a negative correlation with market presence, but rather exhibited a weak positive association.

The results from the multiple regression analysis are not surprising given the results noted above regarding the pattern of simple correlations. The market presence measure dominates the market share model, capturing most of the explained variance as revealed by its relative large beta coefficient and statistical significance level. As Wal-Mart has increased its market presence, it has received a corresponding increase in its market share. Despite the dominant effect of market presence on market share, per capita income also is statistically significant, has the expected sign (negative), and adds slightly to the explanation of market share variation. Although the population measure had a similar level of simple correlation with market share, as did per capita income, it is not significant in the model and therefore does not add to the explanation of the variation in market share. Population was correlated with both market presence and per capita income, and with these latter two variables in the model, population size was not able to add further to the explanation of variation in market share. Even though the strong positive skewness of the population variable suggests a log transformation would be in order, use of the transformed measure did not alter the results. Due to the strength of the market presence measure, the R square (coefficient of determination) of the model is a very high value of .92. If the regression model is run excluding the market presence measure, both population and per capita income are significant and have negative coefficients, but the R-square value is only .17.

An alternative measure used for examining the market strength of Wal-Mart Supercenters is market share per store. A multiple regression with this measure as the dependent variable and market presence, the log of population, and per capita income as the independent variables produced an R-square value of .75. Both log of population and per capita income were statistically significant, with the former being the stronger predictor as indicated by its much larger beta coefficient. Both variables were negatively related to market share per store, indicating that market share capture on a per store basis is highest in smaller, lower income metropolitan areas. Even when the log value for population is used, the relationship with market share per store is still nonlinear. By also using the log value of market share per store in the regression model, the R-square value improves to .87. The market presence measure was not statistically significant in either model and did not add to the explanation of the variation in market share per store across large U.S. metropolitan areas. Thus, no evidence was found that market share per store is increased or reduced as Wal-Mart expands its market presence in these metropolitan areas.

Conclusions

Wal-Mart entered food retailing in the late 1980s with the introduction of the supercenter format, and since then the firm has steadily grown market share in the grocery sector. Although its impact and presence have been greatest in non-metropolitan markets and in smaller metropolitan areas, by 2004 it had entered 68 of the 100 largest U.S. metropolitan markets with its superstore format and had an average market share of 14.9 percent in these markets. In 33 of these 68 markets, its market share was substantial, exceeding 15 percent. The analysis reveals that the variation in Wal-Mart's market share in grocery retailing across U.S. metropolitan markets largely reflects the variation in its level of market presence, measured as the number of Wal-Mart Superstores per million population. A secondary factor that has some effect also on the firm's market share is the income level of the metropolitan area, with Wal-Mart having a higher market share in lower-income areas. Wal-Mart's rapid growth of the supercenter format and its pull of shoppers away from other grocery chains have enabled it to become the largest supermarket retailer in the United States. It has also recently become the leading market share firm in supermarket sales in several metropolitan areas. Despite the fact that Wal-Mart is currently the leading grocery retailer in only a limited number of metropolitan markets, its continued rapid growth, competitive success, and past history suggest that this list of metropolitan markets is likely to grow substantially over the next several years.

6

Wal-Mart-scapes in Rural and Small-Town America

Holly R. Barcus

> Although the commodification of rural landscapes and cultures has the potential to contribute to population and economic growth, it can also lead to a process of overdevelopment [that] has the capacity to undermine the very attributes which made the countryside attractive, such as idealized farming landscapes, picturesque country towns, and scenic natural environments.

> Tonts and Greive 2002: 58

> Indeed, we might speculate that the extent to which villages maintain their traditional material shape and appearance is in inverse proportion to the amount of social change that has taken place.

> Murdoch and Marsden 1994: vi

Background

The American rural landscape of the late twentieth century is an evolving and dynamic environment that is increasingly embedded in the global economy. Rapid economic change at state and national levels has left many rural areas struggling to find their own economic niche in order to maintain a rapidly aging and declining population base. Despite the drastic but varied economic, social, and cultural changes taking place, there remains a strong attachment to the idealized notion of "rural" as place.

> Rural life has long been associated with an uncomplicated, innocent, more genuine society in which "traditional values" persist and lives are more real. Pastimes, friendships, family relations and even employment are seen as somehow more honest and authentic, unencumbered with the false and insincere trappings of city life or with their associated dubious values. (Little and Austin 1996: 102)

This idealization neglects many of the realities of rural communities that often include largely invisible and marginalized populations with high rates of poverty and limited access to health care and basic social services (Furuseth 1998). This conflict between rural reality and the rural idyll is clearly evidenced by the battles waged against the opening or expansion of a Wal-Mart store in a rural community or small town that has a strong sense of place collectively valued by residents.

The battle to keep Wal-Mart out of rural towns is partly a battle of ideologies and partly one of economics. To some, Wal-Mart embodies the worst characteristics of globalization, including endless corporate greed, low wages, sweatshops, and homogeneous landscapes (for example, McCourt et al. 2004; Miller 2004; Wisconsin Sierra Club 2004). To others, Wal-Mart represents an opportunity to consume goods from a global market economy characterized by low-cost, high-quality consumer products. Wal-Mart has come to symbolize the decline of small-town mom-and-pop stores and the hollowing out of Main Street, particularly since "rural" is portrayed and often idealized by such popular images as those painted by artist Norman Rockwell. Galston and Baehler (1995: 4) suggest that at the heart of the dilemma are two competing tensions inherent in rural development in the United States: the "conflict between market- and place-oriented development" and the failure of American culture to value "place" over growth and change.

This chapter approaches the conflicts created by Wal-Mart in rural places from three perspectives. The first discussion highlights the importance of how society collectively views rural places, and more specifically, the social construction of rural and the rural idyll and how these conceptualizations of rural environments enhance our understanding of the debate about Wal-Mart in rural places. The second section provides a general overview of controversies that surround Wal-Mart stores in rural communities. Last, the experiences of two rural Wisconsin towns are drawn on to provide insight into these debates.

The Importance of "Rural" in Understanding Opposition to Wal-Mart in Rural Communities

The social valuation of rural places based on their existence as entities to be preserved in a particular historical or economic state conflicts with the needs of rural residents for greater accessibility to consumer goods and services, many of which are unavailable to them in places distant from an urban center. There are two important cultural conflicts that seem to underlie the controversies surrounding Wal-Mart in rural places: (1) the contradiction between rural realities and the popular rural idyll, and (2) the importance of mass markets and mass consumption in the United States, which contrasts with an imaginative view of rural people as producers and consumers of local goods and services. In order to fully understand the opposition to Wal-Mart, we must first investigate the cultural importance of "rural" to Americans and the tensions that are created when this more traditional view meets contemporary societal norms.

In America, "rural" has come to symbolize small-town values and pastoral landscapes at the heart of which is a thriving downtown market area. "Rural," however, has many different meanings, and rural areas are not homogeneous landscapes or cultures (Ilbery 1998). What constitutes a rural place has been widely debated in geography and the social sciences, and numerous definitions and indices of rural have been proposed (see, for example, ERS 2003; Halfacree 1993; Murdoch and Marsden 1994). The value and desirability of rural places is also evidenced by strong residential preferences for rural and rural-like places, which are associated with characteristics such as improved quality of life, lower crime rates (security), and a sense of community (Fuguitt and Zuiches 1975). These perspectives are particularly important to understanding why Wal-Mart faces such intense opposition in rural places. For example, Murdoch and Marsden (1994) suggest that one type of rural area is the "contested countryside" (one of four types of rural areas defined by the authors), a place in which newcomers increasingly oppose development deemed acceptable and desirable by local residents, preferring instead to maintain the countryside in its idyllic form. In rural areas with high amenity ratings (for example, scenic mountain or coastal locations), conflicts between different groups such as residents versus non- or new residents are increasingly common (Tonts and Greive 2002).

The stereotyping of rural places as warm and friendly and urban places as cold and impersonal (Jakle 1999) underscores the important attachment that Americans have to rural places. This attachment extends to the visible landscape. Indeed, the reproduction of rural-like places has become an important component in modern upscale residential development strategies. As Bascom (2001) points out, places such as Disney's Celebration, a newly developed community replicating small-town Main Street through building and design codes, are examples of the importance associated with rural-like places. Even more salient is the idea of rural commodification or the marketing of rural places based on their rural appeal (Mitchell 1998). This can include the promotion of a particular place based on its utility for hiking, biking, and seasonal tourism, or the creation and elaborate development of heritage villages (Tonts and Greive 2002). This social construction of rural places also includes generic assumptions about how rural places and people interact and what they are perceived to represent. This process of promoting and selling rural places based on their rural characteristics may ultimately lead to increased conflict and the destruction of the rural idyll (Mitchell 1998; Tonts and Greive 2002).

These definitions of rural and the collective attachment to idealized rural places neglects the realities of many rural places. The past fifty years in America witnessed rapid economic and social change in rural towns and communities. Population decline accompanied the restructuring of agriculture, the growth and then decline of manufacturing, and the more recent growth of rural amenity areas (Galston and Baehler 1995; Johnson 1999). Most rural areas struggle to attract growth opportunities and many have turned to corporate farming, garbage dumps, or toxic chemical storage to create a few jobs and generate taxes (Furuseth 1992). In addition to accepting noxious or less desirable facilities, rural towns are also likely to give incentives to companies to locate in their area, despite the negative implications of hosting such facilities. Rural communities see these new enterprises as one type of economic development opportunity. Economic growth strategies embraced by other rural communities include self-promotion as retirement destinations (Rowles and Watkins 1993) or as desirable destinations for natural amenity seekers (Rudzitis 1999). Others embark on downtown revitalization strategies to encourage tourism and investment by re-creating the quintessential rural downtown.

Why does the introduction of a Wal-Mart in a rural community incite such intense controversy? One possibility is that a Wal-Mart conflicts sharply with the idealized image of rural space and place. The typical landscape surrounding a rural Wal-Mart is characterized by a massive, brightly colored building surrounded by acres of asphalt and generally set outside of the immediate downtown shopping area. In an urban setting this is the norm, and few people notice Wal-Mart among the other big-box retailers, but in rural areas this type of development is quite distinctive, although not unique to Wal-Mart. This argument, however, suggests incorrectly that Wal-Marts are universally unwanted in rural places. Wal-Mart represents a second, and important, American pastime: shopping, an activity that took on great importance in the latter part of the twentieth century. The significance of shopping and the associated pleasure of mass consumption form an important aspect of American life, one that is readily identifiable through the sheer volume of space dedicated to this activity in the form of shopping malls (Goss 1993). Shopping malls have become a source of entertainment as well as a place of consumption. For the rural consumer, Wal-Mart presents the opportunity to participate in a shopping experience similar to that of a mall and relatively close to home. Wal-Mart is an example of a mass culture in which shopping is now done for pleasure rather than necessity (Mokhiber and Weissman 1998). For rural youth and college students, the late hours of Wal-Mart stores also provide a place to "hang out." "From scavenger hunts and aisle football to a relay race limbo under the shopping-cart stand, college students around the country—particularly in rural areas—have found Wal-Mart's endless aisles and 24-hour operations to be perfect for middle-of-the-night romps" (Zimmerman and Stevens 2005: A1). This tension between the idealized rural and modern consumption-oriented lifestyles provides an important backdrop to the very divisive battles that are waged in rural areas when Wal-Mart comes to town.

Where Is Wal-Mart?

Looming on the horizon, a distinctive red, white, and blue monolith surrounded by a sea of asphalt, Wal-Mart stands as a stark reminder of globalization and mass markets and their influence on rural land use and small-town economies. Beginning in 1962 with the opening of the first store in Rogers, Arkansas, Wal-Marts have sprung up across rural America. Fifty-six percent of the more than 3,000 counties located in the lower 48 states have at least one Wal-Mart (Figure 6.1). Large concentrations of counties with Wal-Marts dominate the Southeast, especially in the states immediately surrounding Arkansas. Graff and Ashton (1994) note that Wal-Mart, unlike its competitors, initially focused expansion efforts on small towns in adjacent states with access to its first warehouse in Bentonville, Arkansas. During the second and third phases of expansion, identified by the authors as 1975–1984 and 1985–1989, respectively, Wal-Mart continued to expand into southeastern states and a few metropolitan areas, and then, during the third phase, nationwide. Across four consecutive four-year periods from 1970 to 1989, the percentage of new stores in counties with populations of less than 100,000 dropped from 96 to 64 percent. In 1990, 55 percent of the new store openings occurred in such counties (Graff and Ashton 1993: Table 1).

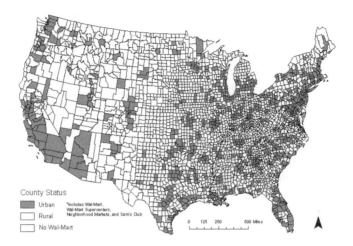

Figure 6.1   Urban and rural counties in the U.S. with Wal-Mart stores, 2005.

In a later article, Graff (1998) suggests that Wal-Mart may use its new supercenter retail format to replace older Wal-Mart discount stores, many of which are located in rural areas.

Of the counties with a Wal-Mart, 54 percent are rural (defined as Codes 4–9 on the Urban-Rural Continuum) (ERS 2003). However, when we look at the proportion of all Wal-Mart stores in the United States, only 32 percent are located in rural places. Fully 68 percent of stores are located in urban areas. This suggests that many urban counties have multiple stores. For example, 77 percent of the stores in Texas and 90 percent of Florida stores are in counties classified as urban. About 30 percent of the stores in Vermont, Wyoming, and Nebraska are urban.

Figure 6.1 illustrates the widespread distribution of Wal-Mart stores in the United States. The eastern half of the United States is saturated with Wal-Marts—few counties are without at least one store. Georgia and Virginia appear to have the most counties without stores. There are only four stores in Vermont, six in Rhode Island, and seven in Delaware. Texas tops the list with over 375 locations, followed distantly by Florida with 191. The median number of Wal-Mart stores per state is about 60. Eastern states appear to have the greatest spatial coverage of stores, but further west the density of stores, like that of population, becomes much less clustered, and large Wal-Mart-free areas are evident. Most stores are located in close proximity to interstate or U.S. highways.

Wal-Mart and Small Towns

Communities become divided around the possible opening of a new store in their midst, and the controversy often pits neighbors against each other in the struggle to keep a Wal-Mart store out (Peled 2001). The communities that band together are not limited in their geographic proximity to each other, since many have turned to the Internet to generate support and share news and strategies. For example, on Wal-Mart

Watch's Web site, communities from places as far apart as Rehoboth Beach, Delaware, and Tijeras, New Mexico, share their stories and anti-Wal-Mart strategies with other communities (Wal-Mart Watch 2005). These Web sites, as well as organizations such as the Sierra Club and Smart Growth, offer reasons why Wal-Mart is not good for rural America (Wal-Mart Watch 2005; Hulsey and Burg 2005). The list of hidden costs is long and has very little to do with what is sold at each big-box retailer. Hidden costs include increased traffic congestion; loss of trees, open space, and farmland; displaced small businesses; substitution of jobs that support families with low-paying jobs that do not; air and water pollution; dying downtowns with vacant buildings; abandoned shopping centers; a degraded sense of community; and sprawl (Beaumont and Tucker 2002: 7; Wisconsin Sierra Club 2005).

Economic Implications for Small Towns

From an economic perspective, Wal-Mart is criticized for "infiltrating small-town America" while offering an extremely large variety of consumer goods at very low prices (McCune 1994). Critics argue that this strategy undermines the ability of small, locally owned businesses to compete, forcing many to close. The closing of small businesses ultimately results in less consumer choice because large retailers such as Wal-Mart, who carry an extensive array of goods, often stock a limited variety of any specific product, thereby leaving the consumer with less choice overall (McCune 1994). With fewer locally owned businesses, money spent on goods no longer stays within the community but rather is funneled back to the corporate headquarters of the retail chain. In a study conducted in Austin, Texas, one consultant found that smaller, locally owned retail establishments generate greater economic activity for the local area than do chain retailers because the smaller retailers keep profits within the local economy, support local artisans and producers, and spend a greater proportion of total revenue on local labor (Civic Economics 2002).

Another criticism is the trading of jobs in locally owned businesses for lower-paying jobs at Wal-Mart. In a study of California Wal-Mart workers, Dube and Jacobs (2004) found that Wal-Mart employees earn about 31 percent less than employees of other large retailers and are more likely to rely on public health and social services than employees of other large retailers. The authors concluded that Wal-Mart employees cost taxpayers in California $86 million annually in health and related social assistance. Representative George Miller argues that "whether the issue is basic organizing rights of workers, or wages, or health benefits, or working conditions, or trade policy—Wal-Mart has come to represent the lowest common denominator in the treatment of working people" (Miller 2004).

The controversy surrounding the opening of a Wal-Mart store is generally focused on the town in which the store will be located, but one study points out that a new Wal-Mart store has repercussions for surrounding towns as well. In a multiyear study of the effects of Wal-Mart on small towns (population 5,000–30,000) in Iowa, Stone (1995: 61) found that towns that attracted a Wal-Mart had greater than average sales and a geographically broader customer base, but these same towns saw sales decline to levels lower than before Wal-Mart after the first few years. While Wal-Mart towns attracted a sizable increase in sales initially, the biggest losers were small towns in close proximity, which had significant sales loss (up to 47 percent) when a Wal-Mart opened within 20 miles. Stone also outlines the "saturation effect" that occurs when a new Wal-Mart store is located within about 20 miles of an existing Wal-Mart, thereby reducing the trade area and sales of the original store. Stone concludes with an assessment of state level shopping habits of consumers arguing that when a large mass merchandiser, such as Wal-Mart, opens in town, consumers shift from purchasing goods from multiple retailers to buying the majority of goods from mass merchandisers (Stone 1995).

Cultural and Visual Impacts of Wal-Mart

The economic pitfalls of Wal-Mart are compounded by visual changes in the landscape of a small town. Critics argue that since many Main Street businesses close following the opening of a big-box store such as Wal-Mart and these closings result in vacant retail space, Main Street becomes an area of empty storefronts (for example, Beaumont and Tucker 2002; Civic Economics 2002). Visually, Main Street is no longer an attractive and desirable place to spend time or to shop, and the town loses both local businesses and a visual and emotional sense of vitality once created by the downtown area. The emotional loss of downtown is further exacerbated by its replacement: the development of a retail location distant from the downtown area in which a large "cinderblock box" is dropped on a parcel of land and surrounded by acres of asphalt. From a cultural perspective, the town has lost a visual reminder of its history, the accessible, pedestrian-scale community center, and the unique identity of the small town (McCourt et al. 2004).

Wal-Mart stores have a distinctive design that contrasts sharply with the typical pastiche of rural building styles. To reduce the visual impacts of big-box stores, some communities have started to propose and implement design standards. Evanston, Wyoming, limits retail stores to 30,000 square feet and requires large stores to build structures that blend well with the existing architectural styles of the town (Beaumont and Tucker 2002). Cape Cod, Massachusetts, prohibits strip mall developments, restricts the placement of parking lots, and strictly regulates where big-box stores can locate (Beaumont and Tucker 2002).

The next section evaluates the landscape characteristics of two towns in rural Wisconsin, focusing specifically on the Main Street and Wal-Mart built environments and the contradictions of each landscape in the broader community design.

Landscape Contradictions of Two Rural Wisconsin Towns

The first Wal-Mart in Wisconsin opened in 1985 and quickly grew to 87 Wal-Mart locations by January 2005, including 36 supercenters, 38 discount stores, 11 Sam's Clubs, and 2 distribution centers (Wal-Mart Stores 2005). As of October 2004, 26,248

Figure 6.2   Wal-Mart Supercenter in the rural town of Hayward, Minnesota.

people were employed by Wal-Mart. Wal-Mart and Wal-Mart Supercenters continued to expand in northern Wisconsin through 2003 and were joined by other big-box retailers including Target, Menards, and Home Depot. The growth of these retailers resulted in the closing of several grocery stores across the state (Hanson 2003). Most counties in Wisconsin have at least one Wal-Mart store, and most counties without a Wal-Mart are located in the northern regions of the state.

Hayward and Ashland are two small towns in the northern tier of Wisconsin counties. Both are a modest three-to-four-hour drive from the Minneapolis–St. Paul metropolitan area, and in both towns Wal-Mart coexists with small but vibrant downtown shopping areas frequented by increasing waves of summer tourists. Hayward, in Sawyer County, is home to the American Birkebeiner international cross-country ski race and has become a destination for outdoor enthusiasts and second-home buyers. With hundreds of miles of skiing and biking trails in addition to the ubiquitous lakes of northern Wisconsin, Hayward is ideally situated as a tourist destination. Ashland is located on the south shore of Lake Superior, boasts a small college and hospital, and is functionally a regional center for this area. Ashland's past is wedded to Great Lakes shipping, forestry, and mineral extraction, and while it is the economic center of the area, it competes with the town of Bayfield, named the "Best Little Town in the Midwest," for tourism and tourist dollars (Solomon 1997). Both Hayward and Ashland emerged as tourist destinations during the 1990s and had engaged in a Wal-Mart controversy between 2003 and 2005. They represent different types of rural growth patterns, with Hayward boasting a population of 2,129 in 2000 (up 12 percent from 1990), and Ashland having lost population (8695 in 1990 and 8620 in 2000). Both communities became more racially and ethnically diverse between 1990 and 2000.

Hayward, Wisconsin

In Hayward, the first indication that Wal-Mart was arriving appeared in the *Sawyer County Record* in January 2001, with an article titled "Is Wal-Mart Coming to Hayward?" Between January 2001 and February 2002, sixteen articles and letters to the editor followed, and were equally divided between those opposed to locating a Wal-Mart in Hayward and those supporting it. Two articles clearly opposed Wal-Mart, two supported it, and three reported mixed reactions to the potential change (Benton 2002; Clute 2001; Hagan 2001; Morand 2001a, 2001c, 2001f; Speich 2001; Stockinger 2001). Six articles provided general information such as opening dates and permits and land purchases, and two articles specifically addressed strategies that local retailers might employ to remain competitive (Baily 2002; Boettcher 2002; Morand 2001b, 2001e, 2001g; Pedersen 2002). Businesses were concerned that Wal-Mart would offer higher wages than local merchants, lure customers away with lower prices, and create a community eyesore that did not conform to the "north woods" theme of the community (Morand 2001d). Others expressed optimism about Wal-Mart drawing more people into Hayward, especially people who would otherwise bypass Hayward for the next closest Wal-Mart, in Rice Lake (Morand 2001a). Hayward's main business corridor, Main Street, markets itself as a unique place to shop, and business owners reportedly did not see Wal-Mart as a threat to their niches.

The 107,356-square-foot Wal-Mart Supercenter in Hayward opened on February 20, 2002 (Boettcher 2002), to a crowd of 3,000 shoppers (Pedersen 2002). The total number of shoppers far exceeded the town's 2,129 residents. In 1998, Hayward had 94 retail establishments, the two largest of which employed 100–249 people (U.S. Census Bureau 2000b). Seventeen establishments employed 10 or more people. By 2002, the number of retail stores remained stable at 94, but 20 had more than 10 employees, and one establishment had grown to employ 250–499 people. Although the 2004 data have not been released as of this writing, at least one business, the Winter Co-op, was on the verge of closing in late 2002. One letter to the editor suggested that while increased competition from Wal-Mart likely played a role in the closing, the failure of management to act proactively was also an important factor (Benton 2002).

Ashland, Wisconsin

In Ashland, the controversy was a bit different, focusing on expansion of an existing "regular" Wal-Mart discount store into a new Wal-Mart Supercenter. In September 2004, Wal-Mart announced its intention to open a new supercenter in Ashland, expanding from the existing store's 71,000 square feet to 176,000 square feet. The new store will include a grocery store, a tire and lube center, and a lawn and garden center (Broman 2004a). Although the first Wal-Mart in Ashland opened in 1991 following a heated controversy to keep the retailer out of Ashland (Broman 2004a), there has been less debate about the new supercenter. A small group of expansion opponents began organizing in December 2004 (Broman 2004c), and one motel owner, located across the street from Wal-Mart, had her proposal to build an eight-foot fence to block noise and light from the Wal-Mart denied by the Ashland Planning Commission because it conflicted with the city's comprehensive plan (Broman 2004b). These are the only two indications of opposition to the new store. In late 2004 an online forum posed the question "What do you think about the prospect of a Super Wal-Mart coming to Ashland?" (Forum 2004). Fifty-five percent of 525 votes were cast for "It's about time," 8 percent for "It's no big deal either way," 2 percent for "More discussion needed," 6 percent for "Regular Wal-Mart is enough," and 29 percent for "It will hurt small businesses." Clearly opinions are divided, but the majority of respondents were in favor of the new store. While the poll is not scientific, it does underscore an interesting division of community opinions related to Wal-Mart. Minutes from the city council meetings between September 2004 and January 2005 did not include any discussion of the new supercenter. As of February 2005, there was no evidence of significant or widespread opposition to the supercenter.

Wal-Mart-scapes and Small-Town Downtowns

The visual landscape of each of these two towns is strongly influenced by their geographic location. The Hayward landscape is heavily wooded with lots of small lakes, while Ashland is located on the south shore of Lake Superior, with picturesque Chequamegon Bay as a focal point. Main Street (also known as Highway 2) in Ashland is located several blocks from Lake Superior and is the main thoroughfare through the area, running from Duluth, Minnesota, to Ironwood, Michigan, and functioning as a major east-west transportation corridor. During the summer, the sidewalks are lined with flags, colorful awnings, and sidewalk sales. Ashland's Main Street is dominated by historic brownstone buildings interspersed with 1970s-era infill development. Businesses located along this busy two-lane road with on-street parking are characteristic of many downtown areas that were once a hub of commercial activity. Businesses include a small J. C. Penney store, Army-Navy Surplus, Oien's Furniture, and a growing number of boutique and craft stores. The local brewery (relocated from the historic train depot to the fringe area of downtown) and an increasingly popular food co-op, bakery, and coffeehouse are also within walking distance. The historic and still vibrant county courthouse, surrounded by large well-kept lawns and trees, occupies an entire block of the downtown area. For tourists unaware of the history of the town, a mural of townspeople in historical costumes is painted along a side street near the courthouse as a reminder of Ashland's history; it depicts loggers and fishermen alongside Native Americans and frontier women. These are clear invitations to embrace or at least acknowledge the history of the town.

Standing in stark contrast on the other end of town, easily accessible from Highway 2 and located on the edge of the city, Wal-Mart occupies a vast area surrounded by parking lots. This Wal-Mart is blue and red, not yet a supercenter, and is always busy, although the parking lot is rarely full. A visual survey of the vehicle license plates in the parking lot suggests that most shoppers reside in Wisconsin, although there are a few vehicles from Minnesota and Michigan. Unlike the downtown area, there are no sidewalks leading to Wal-Mart, and the external environment, with its dilapidated parking lot and overgrown landscaping, invites escape, if only to the inside of Wal-Mart.

Main Street in Hayward, as compared to Main Street in Ashland, is clearly court-ing tourists. Ashland has both tourist shops and stores catering to a local clientele. Hayward is clearly focused on the tourist, with specialty shops such as a pet boutique, candy stores, a historic bakery and cheese shop, and an outdoors store. There is an immediate and forced sense of place re-created. This area of Hayward resembles a summer fair, with approximately three blocks of shops, eateries, and souvenir stores, and competition for parking significant enough to overflow into the surrounding neighborhoods on a busy Saturday as tourists clamor for a close parking spot. Hay-ward's appeal to tourists is not limited to this one area, although it is certainly a focal point. Located across the main thoroughfare is the Chamber of Commerce, appropriately housed in a large north-woods-style cabin, and the headquarters of the American Birkebeiner. Much like in downtown Ashland, there are important visual cues to the culture and heritage of the local community. Many souvenir shops sell T-shirts and cabin accessories that embrace the north woods theme. The street is lined with old-fashioned streetlights and hanging flower baskets; buildings hug the sidewalk, allowing easy window-shopping. Hayward presents a much more contrived and separate nostalgic shopping environment clearly directed first to the tourist and second to the resident. Cars, trucks, and SUVs line the streets, with most bearing Wisconsin, Minnesota, or Illinois license plates. On this particular day there is also one from Iowa and two from Nebraska. As a tourist spot, the downtown area draws people who are staying in the local area as well as those passing through to points further north. While the streets of this downtown are packed with people in the sum-mer, few pedestrians are found anywhere else in town.

Located about half a mile from the downtown area is the new Wal-Mart. It is beige and green and located off the main route through town. Much like in Ashland, the landscape conflicts sharply with that of the old downtown. Wal-Mart is accessed by a four-lane road and is surrounded by expansive parking lots with a thin strip of grass and trees as the only barrier. The majority of vehicles are from Wisconsin, although a few other border states are represented. Adjacent to Wal-Mart is a new Slumberland, another big-box store anchoring the opposite end of the parking lot. Unlike in Ashland, the area still looks clean and freshly developed. The visual impact is not as drastic, but the contrast with the downtown is stark. The downtown area provides pedestrian-friendly walkways and access to stores, and although the streets are always busy, on-street parking provides a comfortable, leisurely environment; in contrast, the Wal-Mart parking lot is uninviting and discourages any form of non-vehicular travel.

Hayward and Ashland Discussion

There are clear differences between the landscapes of the modern consumer and the tourist, but these landscapes and their associated commercial activities seem to be coexisting through the physical and visual separation of two developments. In both towns, Wal-Mart is located away from the downtown area and is not visible from the Main Street locations. In order to patronize the Wal-Mart it is necessary to drive an automobile, since the store is not accessible by sidewalk. These landscape contradictions reflect the divided nature of rural development strategies during the late 1990s and early 2000. There is a desire to preserve the historic downtown areas as a symbol of local history and heritage, but these stores cannot meet the everyday needs of local residents. They are designed to appeal to tourists specifically and to local residents seeking specialty goods and services. In Hayward, this division between tourist shops and shops for daily living existed before the Wal-Mart store opened; in Ashland, the downtown functions as a hybrid for local residents and tourists, with the stores along Main Street eclectic and much less focused on tourism. The importance of maintaining businesses on Main Street in both communities appears tied to a collective community desire to preserve community heritage and traditions through the preservation of the idyllic rural downtown Main Street. But in both cases, the majority of stores in these areas could not meet the needs of the town population. For example, there is no grocery store on either Main Street, and although there is a small hardware store in Hayward, its target customers are not contractors but rather weekenders seeking to make aesthetic changes to their cabins.

It is surprising that so little debate has been initiated in opposition to the new or expanded Wal-Marts in each town. One possible explanation is the geographic location of Ashland and Hayward. Both communities are well outside the commuting range of larger towns or cities. By highway, Ashland is about two hours from Duluth, and Hayward is also distant from any large employment center. This lack of access to the resources of larger communities requires residents to shop and find entertainment within close proximity rather than to supplement a limited array of locally available goods with those purchased in larger places. A short article by 1,000 Friends of Wisconsin, a group promoting responsible community planning, states: "The presence of a Wal-Mart indicates a disinvestment in a community's downtown, sprawling growth in the urban fringe, and potential environmental hazards. Furthermore, the ability to keep a Wal-Mart out of a town shows a community's ability to rally to protect its local identity and economy" (Friends of Wisconsin 2005). The separation of retail environments suggests a clearly defined distinction between the roles of big-box retailers and community heritage environments—an allusion to the competing desires for cultural preservation and mass consumption.

The economic, social, and environmental impacts of Wal-Mart on each of these communities are more difficult to ascertain. While Ashland has lost numerous businesses since the first Wal-Mart opened in 1991, its population has also declined and aged during that time, making it impossible to hold Wal-Mart responsible. In Hayward it is simply too early to tell what the long-term consequences of opening a Wal-Mart will be on local businesses.

Conclusions

It is clear from the literature that many rural communities object to having a Wal-Mart in their community; however, less well represented are those communities in which there is little opposition to the mass merchandiser. It is also clear that one aspect of the opposition is objection to the visual landscape that surrounds a typical Wal-Mart. In the Wisconsin towns of Hayward and Ashland, the Wal-Mart-scape is similar to that found in other places: a large, featureless cement structure surrounded by parking lots. Here, Wal-Mart and heritage landscapes have been separated, as have their respective target customers, and the two entities seem to coexist. This is not to minimize or overlook the economic and environmental issues that may be occurring in these towns because of Wal-Mart, but rather from a cultural and landscape perspective, these two towns have found balance between preserving the cultural heritage in the form of maintaining Main Street and also acknowledging the desire of some residents to engage in the rural version of America's increasingly popular pastime—shopping.

Part III

Organizational Culture

7

Falling Prices, Happy Faces: Organizational Culture at Wal-Mart

A. Jane Dunnett and Stephen J. Arnold

Introduction

As a graduate student in marketing and retail, to me, Jane Dunnett, a summer job as a Wal-Mart associate seemed like a golden opportunity to learn about my field of study from within the world's largest retailer. Tonight while working at Wal-Mart, I have an experience with a customer that tests my patience. I am puttering around the domestics department, tidying and cleaning as I go, when I decide to tackle a display of beach towels that we have on a freestanding module by the departmental telephone. The display always looks messy, partly because of the large quantity of merchandise on display, and partly because these oversized beach towels are too thick to keep folded in neat piles. Also, many of the towels were carried here by customers from other racks and simply left on this shelf. In order to sort the towels into their proper price categories, I find it necessary to run many of them by the departmental scanning gun, which takes additional time. Even though I realize that I am taking a lot of time for this one small area (nearly an hour spent sorting, folding, and stacking), I am very pleased with the result.

I can hardly believe my eyes when minutes later, a female customer comes by with a boy about twelve years old and starts going through the stack, towel after towel. The two of them reach into the stack, pull out a sample, shake it out to look at the design, and then throw it on the top of the pile to pull out another. When I come to my senses, I hurriedly ask them if I might be of any help, but they assure me they are just looking. I stand helplessly by and watch my work come apart before my eyes in a fraction of the time it took me to tidy it up. When they ask if there are any other beach towels, I amaze myself as I lead them around the aisle to another display set up in the main traffic area.

I leave them there and return to the first display to begin restoring my work, but the customer and her son soon rejoin me. She asks if all these towels are the same price, and I reply that they *were* all sorted and folded into identical price categories, but it is difficult to keep them that way because *some* customers pull them all apart and they get mixed up. I scan the towel she is holding to verify the price. She then

79

wants me to check the price on every other towel. I quickly decide that perhaps the best way for me to deal with this customer is not at all, and I move on to another area of the department. After all, we have other customers.

I reflected later about this episode. It seemed that while wearing the blue vest that designates a Wal-Mart associate (Figure 7.1), I gained another personality. My individual feelings were hidden beneath a cloak of customer service, just as my clothes were covered by the Wal-Mart vest with the words "How may I help YOU?" written across the front. I asked myself several questions. Why did I continue to serve this troublesome customer and provide her with the same level of service as I would any other customer? Why did I put aside my personal feelings of annoyance, disappointment, and frustration in seeing my work so callously pulled apart, to show these customers other merchandise that might better satisfy their needs? How is Wal-Mart's goal of outstanding customer service achieved and maintained? What methods are used to convey to so many employees the objective of serving customers *beyond* the customers' demanding expectations?

I had been taught in my Wal-Mart introductory training that it was important to put the good of the company ahead of my own individual feelings. I concluded that it was this training and other forms of socialization into the Wal-Mart culture that pushed me to provide the same service to all customers and prompted me to set aside personal disappointment for the benefit of the organization.

The recognition that organizational socialization and culture are such powerful forces led me to explore them further, resulting in this chapter, which has three primary objectives. First is to consider the way in which organizational culture encourages its members to adopt the goals of the organization as their own. Second is to outline the process by which organizational culture emphasizes the good of the group over the good of the individual. Third is to identify inconsistencies between practice and philosophy that may signify weaknesses in the protective armor, which if left unaddressed may weaken or destroy Wal-Mart's organizational culture.

In examining Wal-Mart, I will look at the sources of its culture, the artifacts and values that symbolize it, the processes by which it is passed on to new members, and the techniques by which it is strengthened and maintained. In keeping with the discussion by Arnold and Fischer (1994), this paper deals primarily with hermeneutic self-understanding, about what *we* as scholars and researchers believe about the behavior of organizations and people. Just as Hamper (1991) recounted his story of life on the assembly line at General Motors, I am relating my personal experiences as a retail salesclerk at Wal-Mart and sharing what I believe there is to be learned from this experience. It follows in the tradition of a number of ethnographies, including Miklas 1999, Schouten and McAlexander 1995, and Workman 1993.

Access to Wal-Mart

Wal-Mart has 6,400 stores and 1.8 million employees worldwide (Wal-Mart 2006). Sam Walton, the founder, opened his first Wal-Mart Discount City store in 1962. Wal-Mart became a public company in 1970, Sam's Clubs were rolled out in the 1980s, and supercenters came in the 1990s. Wal-Mart's sales from all of these formats totaled $312.4 billion for the fiscal year ending January 31, 2006 (Wal-Mart 2006). This volume makes Wal-Mart not only the world's largest retailer but also considerably larger than its nearest global competitor. It went international in the early 1990s and now has a presence in Argentina, Brazil, Canada, China, Germany, Korea, Mexico, Puerto Rico, and the United Kingdom.

With a desire to learn more about the world's largest retailer, I contacted Wal-Mart officials at the head office of its Canadian subsidiary to initiate the process of gaining access to the organization. Many phone calls, letters, and weeks later, I entered the company as a regular "peak-time" associate, which is the term used for part-time employees who work less than twenty-eight hours per week. I underwent the same training and socialization processes experienced by all new recruits as they become Wal-Mart associates, and was given the same responsibilities, scheduling, and benefits. Originally hired for a cashier position, I was paid $5.80 Canadian (U.S. equivalent $4.25) per hour. I worked at the same store for ten weeks and made notes in my personal journal after each shift.

Organizational Culture

People who work together necessarily spend a considerable amount of time together, often sharing significant events in their lives as well as their careers. This common experience may lead to a pervasive attitude throughout the company about the accepted behavior and "correct" responses to specific situations. Such shared behaviors and values indicate the culture of the organization. "Culture implies that human behavior is partially prescribed by a collectively created and sustained way of life that cannot be personality based because it is shared by diverse individuals" (Van Maanen and Barley 1985: 31). Culture molds a group together into one unit while at the same time distinguishing and separating it from other groups. Culture cannot be entirely separated from the people who make up the community or group, since it relies on them for its interpretation, adaptation, and propagation (Van Maanen and Barley 1985).

Sources of Organizational Culture

There are several ways culture may be created within an organization, including founder's vision, shared learning, and work environment. Wal-Mart represents a strong organizational culture, predominately derived from the model provided by its founder, Sam Walton (Walton 1992). Walton's values and priorities were conveyed to store managers and to all members of the organization through store policies, meetings, and eventually as shared experience. As employees recognized the strength of commitment from the founder, they were more willing to make a similar commitment themselves. In fact, many of the early managers became limited partners in the organization by investing their own funds to obtain a small percentage share in the store they were managing (Walton 1992). This partnership tradition continues today with profit-sharing programs and the opportunity for employees to purchase shares in the company at a discount. Therefore, use of the term *associates* for Wal-Mart employees accurately conveys the message of partners in the business.

As members of the group adopt the founder's vision and attitude as their own, and these beliefs are tested over time, shared learning occurs that develops the original beliefs into shared assumptions (Brown 1995; Schein 1990). While the group works together to solve problems in their day-to-day operations, they develop patterns of behavior that are encouraged by the company according to their success. At Wal-Mart, positive reinforcement through group meetings, "happy face" motivational posters, and a corporate commitment to the team works to promote such shared assumptions.

Organizational culture also develops from the environmental climate of this company. The "selling" environment of the retail industry, willingness to match competitors' prices, and pride in their "everyday low prices" are factors that influence the values of the group.

Portrayals of Organizational Culture

Culture is portrayed at three basic levels in an organization: its artifacts, values, and underlying assumptions (Schein 1990). At Wal-Mart, artifacts would include the physical setup of the stores, with their spacious interiors and uniform departmental structures, as well as the products found within the stores and advertised in promotional flyers and on television. A whistling happy face on television advertisements helps to convey a sense of fun and contributes to the informal, "down-home" atmosphere.

The dress code at Wal-Mart is casual, another artifact that helps to build the friendly atmosphere of approachable staff. The blue vests, which make staff highly recognizable to customers, and name tags that specify first names only further emphasize this accessibility. The front of my vest was inscribed with "How may I help YOU?" and "Wal-Mart/ALWAYS LOW PRICES. ALWAYS Wal-Mart. *Always*" (see Figure 7.1). In this manner, the front of the vest greets customers and offers the associate's help before a word is spoken. In addition, the corporate name tag, which is to be worn at all times, identifies the store as Wal-Mart and the associate by first name; the phrase "We Work for You. *Always*" printed under the associate's name reminds the customers that associates are there to serve the customers. Likely the phrase is a reminder for associates more often than for customers because the associates see this message most frequently, on both their own and their fellow associates' name tags.

The message on the back of the vest also deserves attention: "Wal-Mart: Our People Make the Difference" (see Figure 7.1). This statement of pride in work being conducted by associates provides a symbolic pat on the back, and perhaps a subtle vote of encouragement and appreciation for a difficult job done well.

Arriving a few minutes early to the store for my initial employment interview, I asked a Wal-Mart associate about the location of the office for the People Division. I was guided to a stairway at the back of the store and upstairs along a hallway lined with posters and slogans reminding employees of several things, such as the upcoming inventory days and the importance of customers. Many of the posters were quotations from Wal-Mart's founder, including a large poster at the top of the stairs with Sam Walton's picture and the words "Pride through Performance" written across the bottom. On the door at the foot of the stairs was another poster, which associates

Figure 7.1 Wal-Mart vest (left: front; right: back).

would see as they leave the locker/lunchroom area to go out onto the sales floor. It had a happy face saying, "Meet 'em & greet 'em!" There was also a slogan, "Remember the 10 foot rule," across the bottom of the poster, referring to the company rule that associates try to make customers feel welcome by smiling and speaking to everyone who comes within this distance.

The second way organizational culture is portrayed is through values. Values are determined in discussions with various members of the culture and through the activities and behavior of the group, based on mutually agreed-upon standards of acceptable performance. One of the basic values incorporated into the "Wal-Mart Way" is the idea of servant leadership (Walton 1992). The Christian roots of the organization's founder, and perhaps of the southern United States society from which the earliest organizational members were drawn, are evident in this concept. The original servant leader in Christianity, Jesus Christ, told His followers that whoever among them would desire to be great would first need to humble themselves as servants. The Wal-Mart organization believes in providing management/leadership that serves members by listening to their ideas, supporting their efforts, and encouraging their progress.

Finally, organizational culture is represented in the underlying assumptions of its members, those subtle understandings that influence the perceptions and behaviors of the group (Schein 1990). In describing the organizational culture of Wal-Mart stores, Walton recounted stories of the company cheer, Saturday morning meetings, and numerous promotional stunts, all undertaken with the intention of providing "fun for the customers and fun for the associates" (Walton 1992: 203).

Training and Socialization

Culture in an organization is passed on to new members in three stages: preselection, socialization, and incorporation/rejection (Brown 1995). Some preselection is carried out by the individuals themselves, who decide whether they should apply for a position based on their prior knowledge of a firm. The interview process carried out at Wal-Mart, as with most organizations, allows the firm an opportunity to choose candidates who would provide the best fit with existing members and culture.

Both formal and informal socialization processes commence after the individual is accepted as an employee, as they learn the accepted values and behaviors so they may function as part of the group. Orientation programs, trainee courses, and mentoring systems are examples of formal socialization, while informal methods rely mainly on trial and error with the aid of colleagues (Brown 1995). My experience as a new hire at Wal-Mart began with self-conducted, computer-based learning, covering the company's basic beliefs, policies on customer service, dress codes, shrinkage, health and safety issues, hazardous materials, and on-the-job training.

While Wal-Mart's formal training process is completed within the first few days of hire, the informal socialization of new members is ongoing. Such things as helpfulness of associates, willingness of others to answer questions, and an abundance of patience from those who have responsibility for "coaching" new associates all contributed to my learning. This informal process continues throughout an individual's organizational life as stories are shared, other members enter and exit, and the cultural community continually adapts to changing conditions.

The incorporation/rejection stage of learning about culture in the Wal-Mart organization coincides with the ninety-day new hire period. New associates are informed that the first ninety days are a trial period for *both* employee and employer "to determine whether we meet each other's employment expectations."

The preceding quotation comes from the Wal-Mart Canada Associate Handbook, which was given to me as a new employee. The handbook includes a brief company history, elaboration of the ten basic principles (derived from "the values our founder helped to instil in all of us"), and associate benefits, among other topics. Quotations from Sam Walton are printed beside a large red maple leaf on a red banner at the top of many of the handbook's pages.

Wal-Mart "Family" Organizational Culture

The term *associate,* used for all Wal-Mart employees, conveys the impression of equality among members and helps place a sense of value on all ideas and suggestions, regardless of the source. The use of first names builds the team idea among staff and aids the customers' perception of a friendly, family-style operation. With family, everyone uses first names. This is an exception to the more common practice in business of using names and titles to distinguish position within a company. Everyone with whom I spoke, from the regional personnel manager to store managers to new recruits, used first names only. This ritual is an attempt by Wal-Mart to eliminate the perception of rank and to indicate equality among staff.

One associate commented to me about the sharp contrast between Wal-Mart and the company that had owned the store before it was purchased by Wal-Mart. At break one day I was sitting with two other associates—Krista, in her mid-forties, and Gail, about twenty years old. Both associates were cashiers from the front checkouts. Krista was full-time, having worked at Woolco first, then for Wal-Mart after it bought Woolco, for a total of eighteen years, with some time off for children. Gail worked only during the summer because she was away at school for the rest of the year. This was her third summer at Wal-Mart, and she followed her sister, who worked here before that.

I mentioned to them that everything I'd heard about Wal-Mart in retail was so ... "Positive?" finished Krista. "Yeah, I guess so ... putting the customer first and being a great place to work. That sort of thing."

I asked what it is that makes Wal-Mart such a good example of a retail company. Krista, without any hesitation, replied: "Oh, it's the people! It's like family here."

I replied, "That's true, everyone's very friendly. It's the people you work with, then, so it's not really the organization?"

Krista responded: "Well, they [the organization] promote a family atmosphere. Like first names, even for management. It wasn't like that at Woolco. There it was Mr. this or Mr. that."

As an extension to this idea of first names within the organization, associates are encouraged to call the customers by name, if possible, when the customer is known or a cashier sees the name on a bank card or check.

Organizational Culture as Impetus for Member Solidarity

The integration that organizational culture provides to the group has the effect of promoting a common perception of problems, issues, and options, which in turn decreases conflict among members and simplifies the processes of coordination and control (Brown 1995). This role of culture, to encourage desired behaviors from the firm's members, may be more effective and far-reaching than any formal regulatory system the company could enact. In terms of associates dealing with customers, perhaps it is a feeling of "We're all in this together."

Many organizations credit the success of their organizational culture to having the right attitude among their workers. The degree to which an organization's culture will be successful in providing high-caliber service to its customers may depend on that culture's ability to motivate its members and gain commitment from them to serve the customers in that way. "Affective commitment" refers to emotional attachment and identification with the organization or group, and it is most closely related to behavior when that behavior is relevant to the area or group to which the commitment is directed (Meyer and Allen 1997). In this regard, organizations need to emphasize the commitment of employees to the *customers,* rather than to the organization itself, if the overall objective is to provide a higher level of customer service. Thus, the behavior of employees toward customers will improve as employees identify more with customers and build an emotional attachment to them, such as through the practice of referring to customers by name.

During discussion about a new computer-based learning module on sexual and other harassment, Lorna told a story about a male customer grabbing her by the arm as she passed him while carrying a mirror for an elderly customer. Lorna was a big, tall woman with a muscular build who was fond of telling stories about fights she'd had, so I half expected that she would have clobbered this guy. Instead, she said she simply told him very firmly that she was helping another customer right then but would return immediately to help him. He was in a nasty mood, and she had to insist that she would be back. She finished her story by saying that now she joked with that particular customer when he was in the store shopping. "He'll ask me if I'm busy and I'll say, 'That depends—what kind of a mood are you in?' He'll say, 'I'm in a pretty good mood today,' so I'll say, 'Then I'm not busy.'"

Lorna's story emphasizes the relationships employees sometimes build with customers. The most immediate feedback given to associates is through the customers, whether complimentary or critical. This adds to the image of the customer being the "boss," and might also facilitate the employee's sense of commitment being directed toward the customer rather than the store. As one associate commented: "I don't know what it is. People have a love affair with Wal-Mart. I guess as long as it lasts, we have a job." Goal congruence suggests that events that are good for the company will also be good for employees over the long term. Therefore, delivering the best possible value to customers in terms of quality, price, and service on every visit will provide the most benefit to the overall group.

Inconsistencies in Organizational Culture

I identified four practices that I believe are inconsistent with Wal-Mart's organizational culture. They relate to display practices, the role of the greeter, associate scheduling, and wage rate differentials.

Merchandising

The first practice inconsistent with Wal-Mart goals pertains to the beach towel story recounted earlier. Since normal customer behavior would dictate that goods be inspected before purchase, a display that would facilitate this examination, such as hanging racks rather than stacks of folded towels, would reduce employee frustration and promote more constructive customer/employee interaction. Such incidents emphasize the importance to organizations of reviewing even the most basic procedures on a periodic basis to ensure an appropriate fit between practice and culture.

"Welcome to Wal-Mart—Maybe"

A second inconsistency concerns the "aggressive hospitality" outlined in the Associate Handbook and exemplified by the People Greeter program. This unique element of Wal-Mart's organizational culture is a powerful device—the same person welcoming shoppers to the store every week tends to make even the biggest ware-house store format as personalized as the local neighborhood store. However, use of many different employees as greeters on a temporary basis defeats the idea of famil-iarity to the customers. As well, somewhere along the way, security checking was added to the greeter's role.

Dorothy gave me basic instructions on what was expected from the greeter when I took over from her at the end of her shift. She added that she hadn't been given any guidelines when she started the job, and I was grateful for her advice to get me started. She cautioned me that I should never check inside anyone's parcels when they enter the store, since that would be an invasion of privacy. Rather, I should ask the customers *if they would mind* if I put a sticker on any parcels they are bringing into the store. Some customers were used to this procedure and brought their parcels over to me for the sticker to be applied. Even when I was busy putting stickers on other customers' parcels, these customers would wait patiently to have their bags stickered before entering the store. Others were not as enthused about this process and would bypass me to avoid either a greeting or the sticker being applied to their parcel.

One woman, in about her mid-twenties, responded to my request to sticker her parcel from another mall store with the question "Why?" When I tried to explain that we just wanted to indicate that she had the merchandise with her when she came into the store, she haughtily replied, "Yes, you can, but it doesn't make the store look very good!"—at which point I apologetically attached a sticker to her shopping bag. Later a boy about twelve or thirteen years old snapped, "No," when I asked if I might put a sticker on his parcel. I thought he might have been trying to impress his two friends with his curt reply. Then a senior responded to my "Would you mind … ?" with a quick "Yes, I mind" as she walked past me into the store. This request to mark par-cels with stickers doesn't seem to fit very well with "Welcome to Wal-Mart"; in many cases, I just said hello to entering customers, then asked about the sticker.

This single role of people greeter has developed a dichotomy of purpose. The first role is the friendly associate who symbolically rolls out the red carpet for cus-tomers entering the store, ready to answer questions and offer directions. This role stands in stark contrast to the greeter's second role: abrupt security official who stops every shopper who has made a purchase at another store to tag their package upon entrance to Wal-Mart, thus figuratively "accusing" each one as a potential thief. Yet these activities have been combined, resulting in an awkward situation for both asso-ciate and customer.

Is This Equality?

A third inconsistency in the Wal-Mart organization occurs in the work scheduling of associates. Ruth had worked at Wal-Mart for two or three years as a peak-time associate, working mostly evenings and weekends. One summer she wanted to have a yard sale, she told me, but she didn't have a Saturday off until October and "by then it was too cold to have a yard sale." At the time we were discussing this situation (mid-August), she had worked the past eleven Saturdays in a row and was starting to work Sunday afternoons as well now that the store was opening on Sundays. This type of scheduling places extra pressure on associates who have family members with more traditional workdays where weekends are their leisure time. Though Ruth had been aware when she was hired that peak-time work would involve evenings and weekends, she was getting tired of never having a free weekend to spend with her family. She suggested that she wouldn't mind working three Saturdays out of four if the full-time associates could juggle their schedules to allow it.

Although the business is retail, with its accompanying long hours in evenings and weekends, the organization may benefit by distributing shifts in a more equitable fashion, rather than privileging full-time staff with all-weekday schedules and asking part-time employees to consistently work weekend shifts. The apparent "right" of some associates to keep so-called banker's hours while other dedicated and conscientious employees work every Saturday without exception brings to mind the barnyard commandments in George Orwell's *Animal Farm*. Originally the animals agreed to include the statement "All animals are equal." Later, when the pigs gained control of the farmyard, this was revised to state "All animals are equal but some animals are more equal than others."

It is inconsistent that a distinction should exist between associates based on the number of hours they work each week. Wal-Mart is an organization that has made a substantial effort to create a culture of equality among its members through use of first names and the term *associate* for all employees. This arbitrary creation of two classes of employees works against the uniformity of the team concept and could potentially destroy the organizational culture. While Wal-Mart takes measures to increase the commitment of its members through its family atmosphere and socialization processes, scheduling problems may result in some associates missing the beneficial effects of staff meetings, participatory decision making, and the Wal-Mart cheer. An appropriate solution might involve rotating schedules so that all associates participate in these activities occasionally, rather than the same associates every time.

Inconsistent Wage Rates

The final discrepancy observed between organizational policy and action was the difference in wage rates among positions. When I started with the organization as a cashier I was paid $5.80 per hour. This wage rate was later reduced to $5.60 per hour when I was moved to a department to gain a different perspective on the employee/ customer relationship. I was told this was a position of less responsibility, since I was no longer handling money for the organization. I was, however, more directly involved with serving customers in lengthier interactions and on a more personal level. This policy on wage rates seems to conflict with the philosophy that the customer is "number one" in terms of organizational priorities.

Initial Questions Revisited

Conformity, group pressure, and imitation are all indications of the effects of the actions and expectations of others on the individual. The principle of authority suggests that the appearance of authority is sufficient to influence the behavior of an individual (Cialdini 1993). In a retail environment with a strong emphasis on the importance of the customer and quality service, sales personnel may be more inclined to overlook rude and counterproductive behavior from potential clients than they would in their daily life outside work should they encounter this same conduct. Surrounded by posters, quotations, and other reminders, I considered Sam Walton's views and principles to be the authoritative voice while working at Wal-Mart. I strived for obedience to the organization's policies, regardless of how I responded outside the role of Wal-Mart associate. Through shared learning with the group and positive reinforcement by the company, many of my personal goals became aligned with the organization's goals, and I tried to provide the best possible shopping experience for each and every customer I encountered. For this reason, troublesome customers were given the same quality of service as any others (regardless of what they did to the beach towel display).

Respect for the individual is one of the three basic beliefs of Wal-Mart's value system, as noted in the associate handbook I was given. This belief incorporates the idea of servant leadership, which is the ability to lead people while taking care of their needs. This concept encouraged me to provide unreasonable customers with the same level of service I would show to any others, even if it meant overlooking my frustration at having my efforts undone. The Wal-Mart organization encourages the idea that managers and supervisors are always ready to guide and support associates. As I watched these people acting as servant leaders to me, never too busy to answer my questions or too important to help me with a problem, I imitated this behavior in serving customers.

The principle of social proof causes people to consider that a particular behavior is appropriate to the extent that others are observed carrying out that behavior (Cialdini 1993). The more people who have chosen a certain belief or action in a particular situation, the more determined one will be to make the same choice. In this way, then, the organizational culture emphasizes the greater good of the group over the good of an individual, while retaining respect for the individual as one of the company's primary values. All associates represent the Wal-Mart organization every time they step onto the sales floor wearing the blue vest that designates them as a member of the "team." It is this aspect of representing the organization and all its members that weighs on the associate's response to each customer and affects the way the associate delivers service. One's attitude and reply to every request, whether pleasant or unreasonable, reflects on each member of the organization. Awareness of this fact tempers employees' remarks.

Implications and Future Research

It is evident, then, that organizational culture impacts customer service through its influence on store employees. For this reason, Wal-Mart and similar organizations must be very self-conscious of the aspects of its culture that have built commitment within its membership and led to positive behavior toward customers. Through the company's strong obligation to the store "team," the use of first names, and reference to the term *associate* to denote equality and partnership, Wal-Mart has developed a cohesive service concept with a common goal. It would be devastating to this harmony to let conflicts emerge between the philosophy that has generated such an effective organizational culture and the day-to-day practices at the store level. Wal-Mart must attend to the weaknesses identified here, such as poor merchandise displays, awkward encounters between associates and consumers with the people-greeter/security-check program, divisive scheduling policies, and differentiating pay scales. In this way, they may avoid forces that would destroy the emotional attachment and identification with customers that has led to the associates' building affective commitment toward customers, or that would cause discord within the family of team members.

From this case study it becomes apparent that other organizations as well need to be constantly vigilant in examining their practices periodically in order to prevent inconsistencies that may work against their carefully constructed culture. For retailers who may copy Wal-Mart's practices without regard to the underlying philosophies, they should be aware that their actions may generate the wrong perceptions in the views of their customers or cause dissension among their sales staff.

Many benefits of the "team" concept and workforce equality are apparent in the experiences related above. However, it is crucial that this egalitarian approach be extended to every aspect of employee treatment, not held up for display when it is most convenient or advantageous for the company but then disregarded when wage rates or scheduling conflicts emerge.

Wal-Mart and other retailers should consider that their organizational culture socializes their employees in a certain way and leads them to expect certain behaviors from the company. This contributes to the development of a psychological contract between the organization and the employee, according to the beliefs and philosophies of the culture now adopted by the employee as their own. Robinson (1995) observed that violating the psychological contract will have a greater impact on workers' attitudes toward the company than perceptions of inequity, if equality was never addressed. If the organization breaks the psychological contract with an employee, trust is diminished and feelings of betrayal arise (Robinson 1995). An employer may tell its employees that all are equal, that decisions and opinions are valued, and that serving the customer is the number one priority of the organization. However, if it then creates a class system between full- and part-time employees through scheduling, or pays higher wage rates to employees who spend more time handling cash than serving customers, it should expect to suffer the consequences of decreased trust, satisfaction, and commitment from its employees.

Future research should consider this relationship between organizational culture and the psychological contract more directly. Also, differences between full-time and part-time employees deserve to be examined.

Acknowledgment

This research has been supported partially by a research grant awarded to S.J.A. by the Social Sciences and Humanities Research Council of Canada.

8

Wal-Mart: The New Retail Colossus

Ellen I. Rosen

Wal-Mart is the most highly rationalized, centralized retail chain in the world. Designed to run like an assembly line, and controlled from the top down, Wal-Mart's success is based on its ability to monitor, manage, coordinate, and control this enterprise directly from the company's home office in Bentonville, Arkansas.

Wal-Mart locates an inordinately high proportion of its management at company headquarters. Yet managers spend the major part of the week in their district or region and then report back to the company's main office at the end of the week, where they discuss the week's findings at a regular Saturday morning meeting they are required to attend (Walton 1992).

Wal-Mart's centralization is facilitated by use of new information technologies (Bendick 2003). Technology alone is not responsible for Wal-Mart's efficiencies; it is also the way in which the company has deployed the technology to centralize information flows. Because information flows directly from company headquarters to stores and distribution centers, and from stores and distribution centers directly to company headquarters, Wal-Mart's executives have an ability, virtually unequaled in any other company, to gain access to detailed information about each of its more than 3,500 U.S. stores on a daily basis.

Wal-Mart's success has led other companies to follow its lead—to more fully centralize their operations and to introduce new information technologies in their supply chains and store operations, efforts that have generated an increase in the productivity growth in the entire U.S. retail industry in the last decade or so (McKinsey and Co. 2002).

Wal-Mart's efficiencies extend to the way management treats employees. Human resources policies keep Wal-Mart functioning like a great machine. The company has a special "People Division" whose authority comes from the top of the management hierarchy and extends directly to each store.

In this chapter I will show that Wal-Mart's organizational structure and its human resources policies serve its operational goals, reducing costs and enhancing its profits. The existence of wage abuse, sex discrimination, and antiunion behaviors that the company is alleged to perpetrate on the state and national levels, however, is prefigured in the human resources practices that impact sales associates on a daily basis.

No doubt there are many Wal-Mart employees who like or at least are relatively satisfied with their jobs. Nevertheless, most Wal-Mart employees, both management and hourly workers, are impacted by the company's policies and practices. Pressure on people at higher levels is transmitted to those lower down the occupational ladder. Women are at the bottom of this ladder, representing 70 percent of all nonsupervisory workers at Wal-Mart. Employed at the lowest occupational levels, women earn the lowest wages and are the most serious victims of Wal-Mart's labor practices (Kim 2000).

Other retail employers often do many of the same things. Companies are routinely sued for sex discrimination. Attorneys claim that wage abuse is common among corporations today. Why, then, focus on Wal-Mart? The reason is that Wal-Mart's growth, size, and organizational strategies have made it the leader of the new global retail industry. The company's rapid expansion and tremendous profitability have allowed it a market power unequaled by any of its large corporate competitors, a power that is reshaping the nature of America's and the world's retail industry.

Wal-Mart's advantage starts with its advanced technology and the way it is used throughout the company's 3,500 U.S. stores. "Wal-Mart computers store and use sales data from every department in every store, payroll records for every employee, warehouse inventory levels, and a great deal more" on a daily basis (Ortega 1998).

When a customer buys a tube of toothpaste at any Wal-Mart store, an electronic record of that sale is made at the cash register. This record goes directly from the checkout counter to Wal-Mart's main computer at corporate headquarters in Bentonville, Arkansas, where the product is immediately reordered. Suppliers have access to this sales information and will replenish that toothpaste to the store in the same type and size. Store managers send daily sales, inventory, and personnel data to corporate headquarters via this information network. These data are analyzed and used to make plans for the future.

Unlike some discount stores that are its chief competitors today, Wal-Mart is a corporation dedicated almost exclusively to the building of standardized stores—first discount stores, then Sam's Clubs, supercenters, and Neighborhood Markets, all of which sell comparable merchandise.[1] Within each type of store, departments are laid out in the same place. Wal-Mart buys other retail stores only when they are already designed to fit the Wal-Mart format or can be redesigned in ways that serve Wal-Mart stores. Then they are incorporated into the traditional Wal-Mart format.

Human Resources Strategies

The down-home folksy image of Wal-Mart is not a fiction created by Madison Avenue to promote the company image. Wal-Mart's public persona is a direct outgrowth of Sam Walton's personal vision, developed as he came to maturity in the postwar rural South—a vision built on the values embedded in southern religion, idealized views of community and family, and the principles of hard work, frugality, and competitiveness.

Wal-Mart's human resources strategies have grown from this vision and now facilitate a fully institutionalized company culture that has value for labor discipline. These practices have been fully embedded in Wal-Mart's organizational hierarchy through the company's human resources department. Wal-Mart's People Division runs parallel to its operations hierarchy and originates at the home office in Bentonville.

Wal-Mart culture and personnel policies are central to Wal-Mart's main opera-tions and help the company operate like a fully coordinated machine. Their goal is to legitimate the need for workers to change tasks quickly and continually, in order to make workers more "productive" (i.e., to increase efficiencies and reduce costs). Wal-Mart culture is constantly reinforced through a comprehensive set of education and training programs required for all employees.

Personnel Policies

The main goal of Wal-Mart's operational and personnel policies is to ensure that employees identify with the company in order to allow management to maintain labor "flexibility." To do this it is also necessary to keep the stores union-free as a way to control operating costs. Human resources managers who are good at what they do are rewarded by promotion to operations (e.g., to district manager positions).

Workers at different levels of the corporate hierarchy get information from dif-ferent sources—store managers from a program called the Manager's Workbench, store personnel managers from the Pipeline and the intranet database, and hourly employees through computer-based learning modules, the company handbook, and recruitment orientations.

Wal-Mart follows a practice of deliberately understaffing its stores. Each store manager is asked to generate a budget for labor costs on a weekly and monthly basis. According to a former Wal-Mart store manager I spoke with, this budget must be calculated on the basis of store sales. For example, according to a manager I talked to, if stores increased their sales by 7 percent last year compared to the previous year, the goal was to save 0.1 percent of that increase during the next year. The wage bill for the next year could not be budgeted to exceed 6.9 percent of sales. Should sales increase over 10 percent, the managers are required to budget 0.2 percent of wage costs. Based on this estimate, each store manager must budget, on a monthly basis, how many hours to schedule workers. Yet, as one manager told me, a preferable budget would require calculation based on 9.8 percent of increased sales.

The store manager sends the projected budget to the district manager, the regional vice president, and the divisional vice president for approval. The store manager's compensation is based on the sales and profitability of the store. Central headquar-ters enforces this wage budget by giving bonuses and promotions to managers who increase their sales. Those who fail to do so, often through no fault of their own, may be demoted or fired. Subordinates, managers, and sales associates have very little control over the personnel resources they need to get their jobs done. Because of the required understaffing, there are never enough employees working enough hours to get all the work assigned to them done in the time officially available to do it.

Managers and assistant managers work sixty to eighty hours a week, a form of incentivized cooperation that is reinforced by careful training in the Wal-Mart culture, often done at company headquarters. Concomitantly, Wal-Mart's hourly employees are taught to be "flexible" in ways that allow Wal-Mart managers to deploy subordinates to different jobs and different departments throughout the store as they feel necessary. Hourly workers learn they have overly broad job descriptions; each associate is responsible for the whole store. Employees are educated to believe they are part of the "Wal-Mart family." Family and team members, of course, pitch in to do what has to be done for the good of the whole group. But, of course, no family fires its members, as Wal-Mart does, if they don't get their work done.

Inevitably, reality intrudes. Hourly employees complain that there are never enough people to do all the work that needs to be done in the time officially allotted. As Lydia, a department manager in the jewelry department, told me: "At Wal-Mart you are expected to do the work of three people."

Susan works in a Florida Wal-Mart. Her job is to stock freezers. She also answers the phone and helps customers. After 4 p.m. the department managers leave, so she is sometimes the only one—depending on staffing schedules in other departments—responsible for covering other departments as well as her own for shorter or longer periods of time. She is also sometimes paged to work the registers at the front of the store (for which she received training on a computer-based learning module). When the store's security officer told her that Health and Beauty Aids, a high-theft area, was not staffed properly, Susan made it clear that she could not stock the freezer, run the cash register, and monitor Health and Beauty Aids all at once.

It is hardly surprising that employees miss their lunch and work breaks. Management feels free to tell employees, "If you can't get the job done, we can always find someone who can." Shaming, harassment, and the threat of being fired promote compliance. Yet Wal-Mart has no grievance procedures for its employees.

Upon hire, Wal-Mart employees fill out an "availability sheet" indicating when they can work. If possible, employees are offered their preferred schedule. Wal-Mart managers, however, are free to cut hours at a moment's notice if sales decline, leaving workers, often unexpectedly, with less earnings than they have budgeted for. Based on sales, store managers also make decisions about schedule changes. Such changes adversely affect workers. For example, students may be scheduled to work hours when they are committed to being in class. Schedule changes can also be used as a way to encourage employees to quit if they are "uncooperative."

Insurance

Wal-Mart offers health insurance to workers. Employees pay about 30 percent of the costs. Many of the people I spoke with told me that the insurance is often inadequate and that they cannot afford the employee contribution on a Wal-Mart salary. The insurance has increasingly high deductibles and co-payments that do not cover the full cost of a variety of treatments. A new study done in California found that Wal-Mart encourages its low-income workers to avail themselves of state social services, particularly public health care benefits. In this way, taxpayers subsidize this wealthy corporation (Democratic Staff of the Committe on Education and Workforce 2004).

Other Wal-Mart labor practices raise questions about the company's commitment to its people. Several workers told me they were harassed on the job after suffering a serious accident or an illness. Many believe the harassment was an effort to encourage them to voluntarily quit. Barbara has worked in a Wal-Mart in a small town in Iowa for twelve years. She told me: "Last March I had to have surgery and at the time the doctors told me I would be out of work two weeks. Well, those two weeks turned into six weeks, and then I was diagnosed with diabetes." When she returned to work, Barbara was terminated on trumped-up charges. When she applied for unemployment insurance, she was denied benefits because she was "fired for cause." Retaining an attorney, she fought Wal-Mart's claim and won her case. The judge who presided made it clear that just cause had not been established for her termination.

Several other workers I interviewed also claimed they were fired on trumped-up charges. They believe Wal-Mart does this not only to avoid paying high levels of unemployment insurance but also to replace them with lower-wage workers—new employees not yet eligible for health insurance. Now the average waiting time at Wal-Mart is only a year, when for other retailers the waiting time is 2.8 months on the average.

Wal-Mart's labor practices also create financial incentives for illegitimate behavior. In many states Wal-Mart self-insures for worker's compensation and coverage for accidents that occur among employees and customers through a wholly owned subsidiary called Claims Management, Inc. (CMI). CMI has its main office in an old Wal-Mart store in Bentonville, Arkansas, where the company's headquarters are located, and its employees are paid by Wal-Mart. CMI employees and Wal-Mart workers allege that those who work on the job at CMI lack good training and that the agency makes a practice of denying legitimate claims (McCall 2002). Many workers who are hurt on the job, often due to dangerous conditions, must sue for compensation they should not have been denied. It is not clear whether Claims Management, Inc. is regulated, and if so, by which Arkansas state agency. Nor is it clear how Arkansas regulates its insurance industry.

Labor costs represent the overwhelming proportion of operating costs for all retailers. It is not clear that Wal-Mart pays lower hourly wages than many other retailers. Indeed, the company claims its wages are slightly higher than average wage rates in each labor market area where its stores are located. Lower wage costs can, of course, reduce a retailer's operating costs. But what makes Wal-Mart different from other retailers is its extremely high turnover rate, often described as about 70 percent a year. When new employees are hired, they start at the bottom of the wage scale. Low wages and poor treatment may be a cause of such high turnover.

Unionization

Many of these cost-saving employment practices allow Wal-Mart to control its workforce in ways that would not be possible in a unionized firm. In order to maintain its operating cost advantage, calculated as about 25 percent less than those of its competitors, Wal-Mart needs to sustain these labor practices and to remain union-free.

Wal-Mart's policy is to oppose unions and to fight efforts at unionization. To keep Wal-Mart nonunion, when employees are hired they are immediately shown an antiunion video. Wal-Mart managers are required to inform the People Division in Bentonville, Arkansas, about efforts to unionize. Then teams of labor specialists may be deployed from corporate headquarters to visit the stores, hold meetings with workers, and in general discourage them from signing union cards or encouraging others to do so. Store managers are often held accountable for the success of union organizing, and sometimes violate labor laws to stop it. Managers who are not successful at preventing union organizing have been demoted and transferred.

Wage Abuse

To date, there are lawsuits filed in twenty-eight states (in state and federal courts) around the country charging that Wal-Mart stores have violated the Fair Labor Standards Act and other state wage and hours laws by failing to pay their employees for hours worked, by failing to pay overtime, and by forcing employees to work without pay during legally required lunch and work breaks (Greenhouse 2002; McCall 2002).[2]

In the first of these suits that has come to trial, in 2002 a federal jury in Oregon found Wal-Mart guilty of forcing employees in Oregon to work unpaid overtime between 1994 and 1999. Carolyn, a plaintiff in this case and a former personnel manager at one of Wal-Mart's Oregon stores, said, "The first worst word at Wal-Mart was 'union.' The second worst word was 'overtime.'" Then she told me how she "fudged" employee hours. When an associate worked more than forty hours in a week, her supervisor would ask her to "delete the overtime." Managers tell their subordinates, either directly or indirectly, to "get the job done any way you can, but don't work off the clock." Yet if employees complain, they risk losing their jobs (McCall 2002).

Sex Discrimination

Over the years, Wal-Mart has been sued repeatedly for sexual harassment and pregnancy discrimination. In June 2001, Wal-Mart was hit with a nationwide class action sex discrimination suit. In 2001 a suit was filed in federal court in San Francisco on behalf of 46,000 of Wal-Mart's California employees. In April 2003 the plaintiffs petitioned the court to give this suit class action status. If the petition is granted, this lawsuit could become the largest sex discrimination suit ever filed against a private U.S. employer (Drogin 2003; Bielby 2003; Bendick 2003).

At Wal-Mart managers often make discretionary and arbitrary decisions about promotions and wage increases for sales associates, even within guidelines set by Bentonville. Few regulations are in place to monitor or enforce a manager's behavior or to hold a manager accountable for compliance with Title VII, which prohibits employment discrimination based on race, color, religion, sex, or national origin. Nor are there goals or timetables designed to prevent or correct potential sex discrimination. As a result, gender stereotypes, which abound, can easily lead to discriminatory behavior within an employment climate that is hostile to women.

Wal-Mart and Women Abroad

Despite its earlier "Buy American" campaign, today Wal-Mart is the largest importer of Chinese-made products in the world. In 2003 the company bought $15 billion worth of merchandise from several thousand Chinese factories. These goods are estimated to have generated more than 12 million jobs (Xinhua News Agency 2003). A search of U.S. Customs Service shipping records shows that between October 1999 and March 2000, 53 percent of Wal-Mart's imports worldwide came from China. In addition, 71 percent of toys sold in the United States come from China, and Wal-Mart now sells one out of five of the toys Americans buy (National Labor Committee 2003).

Workers in factories in China's export processing zones are most often teenage girls and young women who work in sweatshop conditions—thirteen to sixteen hours a day for 13 cents an hour, a wage well below the level of subsistence. In China's export processing toy factories there is no enforcement of health and safety rules and workers have no protective clothing. They inhale paint dust and handle glue, paint thinners, and other toxic solvents, while shop floor temperatures hover at 100 degrees.

Conclusions

Certainly sex segregation and sex discrimination are two of the reasons women suffer economically in retailing, as in other low-wage industries. Yet women suffer more at Wal-Mart than at other retail stores. One reason is that women are 65 percent of Wal-Mart's hourly wage workers, and so whatever the extent of wage abuse in Wal-Mart stores—whether it is being forced to work "off the clock" or by being denied overtime pay—women are more likely than men to suffer from it. In addition, there is more overt sex discrimination—both wage discrimination and a glass ceiling—at Wal-Mart (Bielby 2003; Bendick 2003).

In the retail food sector unionized women workers have a wage premium of about 33 percent over non-union women (Lovell, Song, and Shaw 2002). Hourly workers at Wal-Mart, both men and women, earn lower wages and benefits than workers in unionized firms. Insofar as Wal-Mart is alleged to use illegal tactics to prevent unionization, workers who have been thwarted in their organizing efforts have been deprived of benefits they otherwise might have gained.

Notes

1. For a time Sears also had a credit division, and Kmart owned and ran a variety of other store formats.
2. At Wal-Mart a full-time job is defined as twenty-eight hours or more per week. Hourly employees may be asked to work twelve more hours a week, for a total of forty, before they are legally entitled to overtime. Part-time workers, who make up the majority of Wal-Mart's staff, need not be paid overtime until they work more than forty hours.

9

Labor and the Wal-Mart Effect

Jennifer Bair and Sam Bernstein

Introduction

The yellow smiley face that is Wal-Mart's corporate logo appears in Wal-Mart's commercials, careening through store aisles to alert potential shoppers about various products for which Wal-Mart's already low prices will be further "rolled back." As corporate logos go, this generic smiley face is not much of a match for McDonald's golden arches or Happy Meal–toting clown. But as a symbol of American consumerism and the particular form of contemporary capitalism on which it rests, Wal-Mart has displaced McDonald's as the company most closely associated with U.S. political-economic and cultural power.

Wal-Mart's economic scale and global scope have made it a lightning rod for concerns ranging from the magnitude of the U.S. trade deficit with China to the destruction of mom-and-pop businesses. Among these concerns, Wal-Mart's labor issues are a particularly prominent and recurring theme in the large (and often critical) volume of press attention the company receives. Most discussions of Wal-Mart's employment practices focus on its retail workers (or associates, as they are called by the company) or the vast labor force in Asia employed by the many companies manufacturing goods for Wal-Mart. We, however, examine the broader implications of Wal-Mart's policies for workers and for the unions that represent them through a discussion of two recent events and the role Wal-Mart played in them.

Specifically, we are interested in how the 2002 lockout of the West Coast dockworkers and the 2003–2004 southern California grocery workers' strike can be understood in terms of the "Wal-Mart effect"—the impact the company has on American workers and labor movement in general.[1] While the scale and scope of Wal-Mart's global operations make it a formidable economic power in its own right, we want to underscore how Wal-Mart's practices shape the experience of workers *beyond* the organizational confines of its own retail empire. In our concluding section we examine recent developments in the American labor movement that reflect debates about how to confront Wal-Mart, both as the country's largest employer and as the standard bearer of an industrial relations model that sees no role, and little future, for unions.

Wal-Mart's Impact on Labor: Inspiring a Global Race to the Bottom?

Wal-Mart has come under attack of late from a wide variety of constituencies for its treatment of those who labor for the company. These include attacks by trade unions (Arndorfer 2003), women's rights organizations (Borda 2003), the U.S. Department of Citizenship and Immigration Services (Greenhouse 2005a), and author Barbara Ehrenreich (2001). These attacks have generated negative publicity, but the impact on the company's performance is ambiguous. Even as Wal-Mart continues to grow, registering a 10 percent increase in sales and a 13 percent increase in profits in 2004, its stock has remained more or less flat for several years. It is clear, however, that the recent deluge of criticism has put the company on the defensive. This is reflected in its decisions to hire a new public relations firm, to emphasize its financial support of various community organizations, to invite academics studying the company to present their research findings at a conference, and to inaugurate a Web site designed to counter what it contends is a lot of misinformation disseminated by ill-informed or self-interested critics (A. Bernstein 2005).

The gist of the criticism leveled at Wal-Mart by many of its detractors is that the company pursues and, through its influence as an economic power both at home and abroad, promulgates a low road to competitiveness. This strategy is based on sweating labor throughout a global supply chain that encompasses factory laborers in China and dockworkers on the West Coast of the United States, as well as greeters, cashiers, and stock clerks in the company's 5,000 stores worldwide. Wal-Mart's retail employees are the most visibly and directly affected by this strategy.

Researchers at the University of California, Berkeley's Labor Center studied use of social safety net programs by Wal-Mart workers to calculate the "hidden cost" of Wal-Mart jobs to the state's taxpayers. They found that Wal-Mart workers earn, on average, a third less than their counterparts employed by other large retailers. When compared with those counterparts, the families of Wal-Mart employees use an estimated 40 percent more publicly funded health care and 38 percent more food stamps and other kinds of public assistance (Dube and Jacobs 2004). The Berkeley study challenges Wal-Mart's claim that it can provide good jobs with good benefits to its employees while also providing "everyday low prices" to consumers. The study also represents one widely cited and influential effort to document the negative social and economic consequences arising from the company's pursuit of the lowest possible costs.

Wal-Mart's efforts to keep unions out of its stores have generated considerable animosity toward it on behalf of organized labor. In November 2004 the company bowed to pressure from Beijing and announced that its retail associates in China would be allowed to affiliate with the Communist Party–controlled All-China Federation of Trade Unions. This decision was interpreted by some as a watershed event, potentially signaling a change in the company's attitude toward unions (Barboza 2004). But less than six months later these hopes were dashed when Wal-Mart closed a Québec store whose workers had voted to affiliate with the Canadian branch of the United Food and Commercial Workers union and were attempting to negotiating a contract with Wal-Mart (Struck 2005). The more or less subtle union-busting that goes on in Wal-Mart stores is undoubtedly responsible for much of the considerable ill will between organized labor and the company's management. However, the increasing determination of labor leaders to target Wal-Mart and anger generated by the retailer's efforts to avoid (and defeat) organizing drives reflects anxiety about the broader implications of the company's operations both at home and abroad as much as anger generated by the retailer's efforts to avoid (and defeat when necessary) organizing drives targeting its own workers.

Not only Wal-Mart's direct employees are affected by its low-cost business strategy. There are at least two broad categories of workers who, though not employed or paid by Wal-Mart, are nevertheless impacted by what the company does: indirect workers and competitors' employees.

Indirect Workers

Indirect workers are employed by the various operations that constitute Wal-Mart's global supply chain. These include, for example, manufacture of household appliances, electronics, toys, clothes, and other items that end up on the shelves of Wal-Mart stores. Having abandoned the "buy American" policy it touted in the early 1990s, Wal-Mart is doing an increasing amount of its purchasing in China, where more than 5,000 of its 6,700 suppliers are located (Jingjing 2004). In 2003, $15 billion worth of goods were shipped from these suppliers to Wal-Mart. These goods accounted for more than 10 percent of total U.S. imports from China, an amount greater than China's exports to Russia or Great Britain (Lichtenstein 2005; Bonacich 2005).

The volume of Wal-Mart's purchasing in China has been increasing at a rate of 20 percent annually (Xinzhen 2005). Perhaps the best evidence of China's centrality to Wal-Mart's operations is the company's decision in 2000 to relocate the headquarters of its overseas sourcing operations, which employs 1,200 people worldwide, from Hong Kong to the south China city of Shenzhen (Jingjing 2004). Although Wal-Mart's growing procurement operations in China mean that many of these indirect employees are located in East Asia, this labor force extends across much of the global South. Large volumes of blue jeans Wal-Mart sells under its Route 66 label are made in the northern Mexico city of Torreón (Bair and Gereffi 2001). Wal-Mart's fastest-growing sourcing base is not China but India, where the company purchases clothing, furniture, and electronics. Operating out of a single sourcing office in Bangalore in 2005, Wal-Mart plans to open additional procurement centers in Delhi and Mumbai (Bhushan 2005).

Also in this first category of indirect Wal-Mart workers are those whose labor is subcontracted to Wal-Mart by third-party providers. An example is the 300-plus undocumented janitors employed by a company Wal-Mart hired to clean its stores. When several of these stores were raided by U.S. immigration authorities, the undocumented workers ended up at the center of a federal investigation, resulting in an $11 million settlement paid by Wal-Mart. This amount is "four times larger than any other single payment to the government in an illegal immigrant employment case" (Greenhouse 2005a).

Last, but not least in importance, this category includes those who work in transportation and logistics jobs that provide the infrastructure for Wal-Mart's global operations. Wal-Mart is regarded as an industry leader in the field of business logistics, as Edna Bonacich and Jake Wilson explain in their contribution to this volume. In managing its international supply chain, the company relies heavily on information technology, much of it in the form of real-time point-of-sale data that track where and what is being purchased. Given the enormous volume of goods the company procures from its global web of vendors, and the exacting standards Wal-Mart demands in terms of continual replenishment, this just-in-time model of retailing requires a smooth and constant flow of both information and merchandise between Wal-Mart and its suppliers (Tirschwell 2004). Intermediaries who handle these goods (such as the dockworkers that were at the center of one of the two labor conflicts discussed below) are critical for the success of Wal-Mart's strategy—to sell large volumes of low-priced goods procured from an international network of the world's most cost-competitive suppliers.

Competitors' Employees

Employees of Wal-Mart's competitors are the second category of workers who are forced to reckon with the discount giant and its influence. These employees' wages and working conditions are being benchmarked against their counterparts at Wal-Mart. The workers and the unions that represent them are among the most acutely concerned about the threat Wal-Mart poses—that the giant retailer is becoming, among other things, the new standard-bearer of industrial relations in America.

This is the perspective advocated by Nelson Lichtenstein (2005), who argues that Wal-Mart's sheer heft makes Sam Walton's Bentonville-based company a "template for twenty-first-century capitalism." According to this view, Wal-Mart provides the model to be emulated by other companies—just as General Motors did during the postwar decades of the Fordist expansion.[2] (Aglietta 1979; Marglin and Schor 1992). Will aspirants to Wal-Mart's success see its meteoric rise as the product of a competitive strategy that combines extensive offshore sourcing from low-wage countries with the cost savings provided by a poorly remunerated, largely feminized, and unorganized labor force at home? On the domestic front, is the inevitable outcome of the Wal-Mart juggernaut the continued erosion of unionized manufacturing jobs in the United States and a declining standard of living for wage earners? Internationally, will the widespread adoption of the Wal-Mart model ensure a race to the bottom that pits workers in China, Bangladesh, and El Salvador against each other, as countries seek to keep labor costs low in hopes of attracting orders from the retailers who represent their primary link to the global economy?

Of course this reading is an overly simplistic account of Wal-Mart's standard-setting influence. The retail giant's global sourcing program is not singularly responsible for the hollowing out of America's manufacturing sector. The decline of domestic industrial employment is an ongoing process spanning several decades, even if the pace of job losses in the manufacturing sector has increased in recent years. And attributing Wal-Mart's success solely to a low-wage, low-road strategy would ignore its status as an innovator in supply chain management. Nevertheless, concerns about the influence of Wal-Mart in wages, benefits, and working conditions in the U.S.

are not entirely unfounded, nor are concerns about the threat the company poses to American unions.

That Wal-Mart's reach extends beyond its own corporate structure to affect both categories of workers described above has been aptly demonstrated by two labor conflicts in California, which we discuss in the remainder of this chapter.

The West Coast Dockworkers: ILWU versus the Pacific Maritime Association

As is well known, the last several decades have been difficult ones for organized labor in the United States; private sector union density in 2005 was at a historic low of just under 8 percent. The weakening of American unions reflects a series of structural changes in the economy (epitomized by Wal-Mart's rise), which has entailed the loss of millions of manufacturing jobs. It also reflects a political environment that presents formidable obstacles to the organizing of new workers, leading at least some scholars to argue that "the future survival of a labor movement in the United States [is] a very real and serious question" (Fantasia and Voss 2004: 33).

Despite a tradition of radicalism and labor militancy atypical among American unions, the International Longshore and Warehouse Union (ILWU) has not escaped these pressures. The members of the ILWU that were locked out during an acrimonious contract battle in 2002 belong to the category of workers we referred to above as indirect employees of Wal-Mart—that is, workers whose labor connects them to Wal-Mart's global supply chain. In fact, given the increasing importance of the West Coast as the major gateway for shipments from Asia, the California dockworkers occupy a central node in the global supply chains of retailers. This is particularly true of Wal-Mart, whose status as an importer of merchandise and whose reliance on the intermodal transportation system that includes the West Coast ports is unrivaled.

While the ILWU remains relatively strong compared to many other unions, membership has declined over the past two and a half decades. This trend is particularly worrisome given that cargo volumes at the West Coast ports worked by the ILWU's constituency have increased 151 percent over the same period (Mongelluzzo 2005). Weakening the power of the ILWU has been a priority of the multinational ocean freight carriers on whose container ships $300 billion worth of imports enter the United States each year. In recent years, the industry association representing the steamship lines and port terminal operators (the Pacific Maritime Association, or PMA) has been joined in this effort by their powerful clients (importers such as Wal-Mart and Toyota), which formed their own group, the West Coast Waterfront Coalition (WCWC), in late 2000. In general, the existence of the WCWC is evidence of the growing importance retailers attribute to the logistical side of their businesses. Timing of its creation reflected their particular determination to play a role in contract negotiations with the ILWU scheduled for 2002. This constituted an unusual organizational effort in cross-sector employer solidarity vis-à-vis a remaining niche of trade union power.

In January 2002, six months before the ILWU's current contract was scheduled to expire, the union elected delegates to a bargaining committee to prepare for the upcoming negotiations. Maintaining excellent health care coverage was deemed a priority issue, as were increases in pension benefits and specific provisions giving the union a voice in the implementation of new technology on the docks. At the same time, the PMA made clear that it intended to use the contract negotiations to seek wage freezes and cuts in health care and pension benefits. In addition, the carriers wanted to introduce new technology that they argued would make operations more efficient, but which the union saw as a means for subcontracting and outsourcing union jobs to nonunion operations in open-shop states. Finally, in a move the ILWU viewed as part of a long-term strategy to weaken its power on the docks, the employers' association sought to negotiate individual contracts in place of the existing master contract that allows all West Coast dockworkers to bargain jointly. When negotiations began, the inability of the ILWU and PMA to reach a quick agreement became apparent, and the health care issue immediately emerged as a sticking point.

In July, as the existing contract's expiration date approached, the leadership of the ILWU decided in an unprecedented move to extend it, largely due to well-grounded (and, as it turned out, prescient) fears that the Bush administration would intervene on behalf of the employers if a work stoppage occurred.[3] According to union officials, the employers' association used the opportunity of the contract extension (which would have made any job actions by the ILWU illegal) to force a speed-up on the docks, occasioned by an increase in shipments from anxious importers concerned about the possibility of future disruptions. The PMA warned that any failure on the part of workers to handle these increased volumes would be interpreted as a deliberate slowdown and just cause for a lockout, which would, in turn, open the door for President Bush to invoke an eighty-day injunction against a strike under the Taft-Hartley Act.[4] In this respect, the employers appeared to have the support of the U.S. secretary for homeland security, Tom Ridge, who informed ILWU president Jim Spinosa that the administration could interpret a work stoppage on the docks as a threat to national security.

Union leaders maintained that the pace of work on the docks was becoming untenable, and when they declared a "work safely" campaign in late September, the PMA locked out the dockworkers, charging them with orchestrating an undeclared slowdown designed to paralyze the ports. President Bush, after initially proposing a thirty-day contract extension, intervened after ten days of the lockout amid growing concerns about its impact on the economy. His invocation of the Taft-Hartley Act forced the ports to reopen and compelled union members back to work during an eighty-day cooling-off period.

During this period, the PMA and ILWU carefully monitored each other and the enormous volumes of cargo that had accumulated in the ports and on the docks. The employers' association continued to warn the union about possible consequences of any actions (such as slowdowns) that could be interpreted as a violation of the Taft-Hartley injunction. Both sides were under political pressure to reach a settlement, and negotiations were by then being overseen by a government mediator. The breakthrough to the impasse came in the form of a framework regarding the implementation of new technology that was arguably so vague as to be agreeable to both sides. Though this agreement was announced in early November, the new six-year contract (one of the longest in the ILWU's history) was not ratified until the following month.

Union leadership hailed the outcome as a victory for the ILWU, pointing out that the new contract retained some of the best health care benefits in the country, included a 50 percent increase in pensions, and provided rather modest wage increases. Provisions of the contract regarding implementation of new technologies and their consequences for the work process were regarded as more controversial, however. Union jurisdiction (which was a major issue throughout the negotiations) was preserved in the new contract for any jobs immediately created or changed through the adoption of new technology, but the jurisdiction for similarly created jobs in the future will be decided by an arbitrator. The union did agree to cut at least 400 clerk positions, which were among the best-paid in the union.

The contract was ratified by 90 percent of union members who voted and can be considered a successful outcome (Coodin 2003). This was the position advanced by both ILWU president Jim Spinosa, who hailed it as "a landmark victory for longshore workers and their families," and Richard Trumka, AFL-CIO secretary-treasurer, who concluded that "the ILWU has negotiated a truly historic contract for its members." However, some within the labor movement expressed skepticism about this interpretation, especially when an editorial in the *Wall Street Journal* entitled "Taft-Hartley, Victorious" offered a similarly enthusiastic assessment of the conflict's denouement:

> By taking away the longshoremen union's bargaining chip—a stranglehold on the entire economy—and returning things to normal, the President made it that much harder for dockworkers to maintain their belligerent stance. The lockout had already proved a public-relations disaster, with Americans angry about footing the bill for $106,000-a-year dockworkers who refused to use handheld scanners. Even the labor movement had lost patience, one reason the more moderate AFL-CIO secretary-treasurer, Richard Trumka, parachuted into negotiations to take the Luddite longshoremen in hand. (*Wall Street Journal* 2005)

Some members of the union shared the view that negotiations were strongly impacted (in their view negatively) by Taft-Hartley, arguing that the conduct of the union's leadership reflected a fear of government intervention in the conflict (which, as it turned out, occurred anyway). One longtime union activist from Los Angeles who acknowledged that the contract battle was successful on the issues of health care, wages, and pensions nevertheless insisted that

> the real issues ... were job security and union jurisdiction—power on the waterfront. On that front, we lost in the short-term and, in the long-term, gave the balance of power to the bosses.... In the future, the door has been opened for the PMA to get everything it wanted this time around. (Personal interviews 2005)

While some workers expressed anger that the Taft-Hartley injunction represented "a gun to the head" of the union's negotiators, others felt that the lockout strategy clearly backfired for employers and that it helped turn public opinion against the PMA and WCWC. Since the work stoppage had been caused by an employer lockout and not a strike, the union was able to claim its members were the ones anxious to get the ports open again while lamenting management's intransigence (Bonacich 2005). Although from the PMA's perspective the new contract secures some of the hoped-for outcomes with regard to new technology, the employers did not achieve all the concessions it wanted in the new contract. And as for the ILWU, the union has recently announced that it is setting its sights on organizing warehouse workers.

The growing number of warehouse and distribution complexes on the West Coast, and particularly in southern California, is evidence of the logistics revolution being engineered by companies such as Wal-Mart. The inland location of these facilities and the demographics of the mostly immigrant workforces that are employed there present challenges for a union whose membership consists primarily of native-born (and today, mostly African American) dockworkers. But the decision to organize workers at other nodes of the intermodal freight transportation system is important to the future of the ILWU:

> Widespread use of cargo tracking and radio frequency identification systems represents the future of supply chain logistics, so the union must expand its knowledge of this technology from the marine terminal to warehouses at inland locations. (Mongelluzzo 2005)

Thus, the stage is being set for future battles between the ILWU and the WCWC. One of the huge warehouse complexes outside of Los Angeles that might well be targeted by the ILWU in a future organizing campaign is home to the distribution centers of several large retailers—among them Wal-Mart.[5]

Southern California Grocery Workers: UFCW versus the Supermarket Chains

The grocery strike that occurred in southern California, which began in November 2003 and extended into 2004, involved unionized supermarket employees that fit into the other broad category of workers impacted by Wal-Mart: those who work for its main competitors. Like the rest of the retail sector, the grocery industry has witnessed significant consolidation in recent decades, following a wave of mergers involving national chains. Five years ago, four companies claimed over half (55 percent) of the grocery retail market in the U.S.: Kroger, Albertsons, Safeway, and Ahold. Although these companies have remained highly profitable, their market share has nevertheless been eroded by Wal-Mart Supercenters (Candaele and Dreier 2003).

The supercenter concept dates from the mid-1990s, when Wal-Mart executives looking for a way to jump-start the company's growth during an uncharacteristically sluggish period wagered that the introduction of supermarkets within giant Wal-Mart stores would do the trick. The plan worked, and Wal-Mart quickly became a formidable presence in the grocery industry (Serwer, Bonamici, and Hajim 2005); by the end of 2002, Wal-Mart had surpassed Kroger as the largest grocery retailer in the United States (Callahan and Zimmerman 2003).

The contrast between Wal-Mart's nonunionized grocery operations and the leading national supermarket chains (whose workers are represented by the United Food and Commercial Workers, or UFCW) was not lost on industry analysts. They noted that Wal-Mart Supercenters were able to pay their workers 20–30 percent less in wages and benefits than their unionized counterparts. For national chains, the implication of Wal-Mart's success was clear: unionized grocers had to restructure their operations and dramatically reduce costs in order to compete with the supercenters. A Los Angeles Times article describing the UFCW's upcoming contract fight in California reported that the "supermarkets' negotiators will have a staunch, if invisible ally at the bargaining table: Wall Street stock analysts." One analyst quoted in the article opined that the struggle with the UFCW that resulted in a strike and lockout involving tens of thousands of grocery workers and cost the supermarkets involved $1 billion in lost sales was "one of the best investments food retailers could make" and "likely to pay off over a number of years" (Peltz 2003).

When negotiations between the supermarket chains and the UFCW began in fall 2003, it was evident that the supermarkets would seek major concessions from workers as the central plank of their efforts to cut costs and increase competitiveness vis-à-vis Wal-Mart. Their proposal included cuts in health care, wage freezes, and the establishment of a two-tier wage and benefits system. The UFCW understood the high stakes in what was shaping up to be a grueling struggle, particularly given the timing—the southern California contract fight would set the tone for negotiations that were soon to follow in the northern part of the state as well as in several cities throughout the Midwest. Although the union was prepared to accept some reductions in health care coverage, the two-tier system that the supermarkets wanted to introduce was regarded as unacceptable, and the UFCW announced that its members would strike on October 11, 2003. However, only one of the chains involved in the negotiations was struck by workers: Vons, which is owned by Safeway. Despite union requests to keep their stores open, Kroger and Albertson's locked out their workers the day after Vons employees walked off the job.

The significance of the strike became obvious early on, as UFCW members received substantial support from other unions, including the ILWU (which held stop-work meetings affecting the southern California ports) and the teachers union (which distributed food and medicine on the picket lines and paid for radio advertisements in support of the striking grocery workers). The AFL-CIO established a national strike fund, and business at the grocery stores appeared to be significantly affected, as large numbers of customers honored the pickets. In late November, the International Brotherhood of Teamsters announced that its members would also honor the picket lines and locked-out grocery workers at the supermarkets' distribution centers. This commitment and other acts of solidarity by members of various unions was widely noted by UFCW members as well as by outside observers (Shaiken 2003).

The UFCW strike was notable for the high levels of solidarity it generated; however, it was also characterized by some amount of uncertainty and confusion. Twenty days into the strike, the UFCW leadership decided to pull pickets at Ralphs, one of the Kroger-owned chains involved in the strike, claiming this would reward customers who had honored the picket lines by giving them a place to shop. Observers also speculated that the move was designed to weaken the solidarity of the employers, but it proved disheartening to some workers who had been locked out by Ralph's (Uthappa 2003).[6] Despite the widely reported announcement in November that Teamsters would not deliver to distribution centers picketed by grocery workers, UFCW officials called upon their members to abandon the picket lines at the centers in December, apparently under pressure from the Teamsters leadership. Some UFCW members refused to comply with this order, however, and continued to picket a distribution center in El Monte, California, for several additional weeks. The Teamsters who worked in this facility (which supplied the Vons supermarket chain) honored the picket lines as long as the defiant UFCW members were able to maintain them.

Officials from the UFCW argued that pulling pickets from the supermarkets' distribution centers shortly before negotiations between the two sides were due to begin in December was a "goodwill gesture." Little progress was made though throughout December or January, despite involvement of national labor leaders such as John Sweeney and Rich Trumpka of the AFL-CIO. As the strike extended into its fourth month, the union announced cuts in strike pay and medical coverage. On February 4, the UFCW leadership proposed that both sides submit to binding arbitration. The supermarket chains rejected this request, but the status of negotiations improved later that month when employers began giving ground on the issues of health care and pensions. Although the grocery chains continued to insist on a two-tier structure for the new contract, an agreement with the union was reached and workers voted to approve. After four and a half months, the strike ended during the weekend of February 28–29, 2004, when 59,000 UFCW members voted in favor of approving a new three-year contract.

The president of one of the UFCW locals involved in the dispute hailed its outcome as "a great deal because we were able to preserve affordable healthcare." The international president of the UFCW, Douglas Dority, who retired a few days after the contract vote, went so far as to claim that the grocery workers' struggle was "one of the must successful strikes in history" (LeDuff and Greenhouse 2004). However, the outcome of the UFCW strike was widely regarded as a defeat for labor. Although the contract was approved by an overwhelming majority of those who voted (86 percent), most observers agreed that this reflected exhaustion and weariness on the part of workers as opposed to enthusiasm for a contract that did not differ greatly in its terms from the employers' early proposals. The fact that the grocers prevailed in their demand for a two-tier structure in the new contract was interpreted as an ominous sign for UFCW members elsewhere whose contracts were set to expire. Some observers noted that if the southern California workers, who belong to the largest bargaining unit in the UFCW, could not win a four-month strike, prospects for other local or regional battles were bleak. The outcome of the strike, they argued, showed that what the UFCW needed was an opportunity to wage a coordinated, national battle. However there was no progress made in coordinating the contract expiration dates of the southern California locals with those in Seattle and the Bay Area that also signed new contracts in spring 2004.

Although Wal-Mart did not play a role in the UFCW strike analogous to its activities as part of the West Coast Waterfront Coalition during the ILWU lockout, it was, at least implicitly, a party to the conflict. The *threat* presented by Wal-Mart's plans to open forty supercenters in California framed the battle for both capital and labor despite the fact that at the time of the conflict not a single supercenter had opened in the state (Cleeland and Goldman 2003). As the regional head of public relations for Kroger admitted, "We had to plan for the future.... We had to make the unions understand that costs are soaring and that we will soon face serious competitive threats."

From the vantage point of the union, the Wal-Mart threat is equally obvious. When Wal-Mart announced plans to open a new store in Joliet, Illinois, members of the UFCW lobbied the city council to make Wal-Mart's further expansion in the city contingent on a demonstrated commitment to remain neutral in any organizing campaigns that occurred at the store once it opened. In explaining the importance of the UFCW's efforts to organize Wal-Mart outlets in Illinois, a spokesperson for the union observed that "Wal-Mart is essentially the third party at the bargaining table at every retailing negotiation in the country" (Arndorfer 2003). While UFCW president Rick Icaza criticized the supermarket chains for manipulating and exaggerating the threat posed by the arrival of supercenters in California in order to extract concessions from unionized workers, he nevertheless concluded that "the number one enemy has still got to be Wal-Mart" (Cleeland and Goldman 2003).

The protracted battle between the supermarket chains and the UFCW in southern California is a particularly illustrative example of what we referred to earlier as the Wal-Mart effect. Fears of the Wal-Mart effect may be based on an inflated estimation of the company's actual impact, as suggested by a Merrill Lynch study that found that there was less direct competition between supercenters and traditional supermarkets than commonly supposed. Yet analyses of this sort are likely to have little influence on the *perception* of Wal-Mart's importance because, in this sense, the Wal-Mart effect is more metaphorical than empirical. The attention Wal-Mart receives in the press and the anxiety it generates in some quarters reflect not merely its economic power as the world's largest retailer but perhaps also Wal-Mart's symbolic heft as a standard-setting company whose example other corporations disregard only at their own peril.[7]

The standards Wal-Mart is thought to be setting are generally low. For workers and their unions, Wal-Mart represents an employment and industrial relations model far removed from the Fordist consensus of the postwar period (in which General Motors set the standards: relatively stable employment, secure benefits, and rising wages in exchange for productivity increases and protracted periods of labor peace). With Wal-Mart being the standard-bearer of post-Fordist employment relations, it is difficult to imagine a role for organized labor that is analogous to the role played by the United Auto Workers in the decades after its hard-fought struggle for recognition in the mid-1930s. In this sense, the threat posed by the Wal-Martization of the economy is very real for American unions, and we now turn to the question of how organized labor is trying to respond to it.

Taking on Wal-Mart: The Challenge for Labor

As we noted in our discussion of the southern California grocery strike, UFCW members enjoyed the support of several other unions during the conflict—including the Service Employees International Union (SEIU) and the Teamsters. In fact, fears of the Wal-Mart effect may have contributed to the high levels of solidarity displayed by organized labor throughout much of the strike, which helps explain why workers in other industries were able to identify with the grocery workers' struggle. One Teamsters official who was quoted in a *Los Angeles Times* article about the conflict expressed his fear: "We're going to end up just like Wal-Mart workers. If we don't, as labor officials address this issue now, the future for our membership is dismal, very dismal" (Cleeland and Goldman 2003).

The Wal-Mart effect can be a force for labor solidarity, uniting workers who feel threatened by the diffusion of Wal-Mart's employment model. However, disagreements about how unions should respond to the Wal-Mart effect contributed to growing tensions, and eventually a split, within the American labor movement. On July 25, 2005, two of the country's largest unions announced they were leaving the AFL-CIO. The departure of the SEIU and the Teamsters cost the federation three million members and $20 million a year in lost dues (one-sixth of the AFL-CIO's annual budget). These two unions are members of a coalition, Change to Win, that was founded earlier the same year (largely at the urging of SEIU president Andy Stern) to advocate and pursue a program of reform within the AFL-CIO. The coalition's platform stressed the need for new strategies to halt and reverse the decline in the power of organized labor (including the consolidation of smaller unions into larger, preferably industry-wide unions) and an increase in the amount of resources allocated to support organizing. The July announcement that SEIU and the Teamsters would leave the federation transformed the Change to Win coalition from a dissident, reformist faction with the AFL-CIO to a separate, and some argued competing, organization.

In September 2005, the Change to Win coalition held its inaugural conference in St. Louis, Missouri. At the time of this founding convention, five of the seven unions in the Change to Win coalition had already left the AFL-CIO: SEIU, Teamsters, UNITE HERE (a merger of Union of Needletrades, Industrial, and Textile Employees and the Hotel Employees and Restaurant Employees International Union), the United Food and Commercial Workers Union, and the United Brotherhood of Carpenters and Joiners of America. Two other unions—the Laborers' International Union of North America and the United Farm Workers of America—are also part of the Change to Win federation, although as of September 2005 they had not officially withdrawn from the AFL-CIO. Together, these seven unions represent approximately 5.5 million workers, more than half the AFL-CIO's total of 9 million.

Pressures leading up to the split within the AFL-CIO and the departure of several of the federation's largest unions had been building for some time. The de facto leader of the reformist coalition, Andy Stern of SEIU, was particularly vocal about the need to expand organized labor's ranks. He argued that the AFL-CIO was spending too much time and money on electoral politics at the expense of organizing new members. Stern proposed that the AFL-CIO rebate half of the dues paid by individual unions to support organizing drives. This proposition was supported by several of the other unions that later joined SEIU in disaffiliating from the federation. Organizing new members is the central plank of the Change to Win coalition, and this principle is advocated most strongly by unions representing workers in the service, hospitality, and retail sectors. These include SEIU (1.8 million members working in health care, long-term care, public sector jobs, and property services including janitorial and security work), UNITE HERE (450,000 workers in apparel and textile manufacturing and service and hospitality jobs at hotels, restaurants, and casinos), and UFCW (1.4 million members in the United States and Canada, including workers in food retail, food processing, and health care). Rapid growth in the service sector of the American economy appears to be creating a propitious environment for these

organizing efforts. The Bureau of Labor Statistics projected that employment in services will increase 20 percent between 2002 and 2012, in contrast to a decline of 1 percent in manufacturing employment (BLS 2004). These trends are positive for unions
such as SEIU and UNITE HERE but worrisome for unions that represent workers in
traditional manufacturing industries including steel, autos, and textiles.

Employment trends seem auspicious for the organizing drive championed by
members of the Change to Win coalition, yet efforts to increase union density will
undoubtedly encounter obstacles as well. Chief among these obstacles is employer
opposition. While such resistance may be common, Wal-Mart has been particularly
zealous in its antiunion efforts. Antagonism (if not hostility) toward unions characterizes Wal-Mart's corporate culture, and this philosophical objection to organized
labor is buttressed by an array of pragmatic efforts designed to keep unions out.[8] In
Wal-Mart's case, the reality appears to match the rhetoric in terms of the company's
commitment to remaining union-free. We noted above that in 2005 Wal-Mart closed
one of two stores in Canada where workers succeeded in securing union certification,
leaving the fate of the second store uncertain. Closure of the Canadian Wal-Mart was
reminiscent of the company's decision to replace fresh meat with prepackaged meat
in all its stores after eleven meat cutters in Texas voted to join the UFCW in February
2000. Based on this history, it appears safe to assume that the company will continue
to demonstrate its opposition to unions in deed as well as word, and the extent of
Wal-Mart's commitment to preserving a union-free workplace makes membership
drives costly and uncertain for organizers as well as employees.

This fact is not lost on the leadership of the UFCW, the union that has been trying to organize workers at Wal-Mart stores in the United States and Canada. Along
with SEIU and UNITE HERE, the UFCW has strongly supported the principle that
more aggressive organizing campaigns are a prerequisite for reversing the decline
in labor's power. In the months leading up to their split from the AFL-CIO, these
unions called on the federation to significantly increase resources allocated to a new
Wal-Mart campaign that had been under discussion for some time. In a December
2004 interview, Chris Chafe, the political director of UNITE HERE, explained the
logic of this proposal.

> Wal-Mart is going to open a store every single day in 2005 somewhere in America, [but] we
> are not ready in the American labor movement to take them on at any level.... We don't
> have a corporate campaign taking place right now to make sure there's enough education,
> both in the workplace and in our communities, about the impact that Wal-Mart is having
> on the retail world ... in the industrial world. We don't have the capacity to run a media
> message that takes on this company. And most importantly, we have no effort right now, to
> organize the workers.... This could be the signature campaign that gives workers across this
> country a clear reason to feel like the labor movement, and the AFL-CIO, is actually stand-
> ing up for the standards of all workers. So, we believe that we should take $25 million a year
> out of the royalties from the union privilege credit card and put it directly into a firewalled
> account that's just about organizing Wal-Mart. (Goodman 2004)

Yet in the months that followed, the Wal-Mart campaigns launched by members
of the Change to Win coalition focused more on broad-based campaigns to edu-
cate consumers and build alliances between labor and community groups and less
on efforts to organize Wal-Mart's retail workers. At the founding convention of the

Change to Win coalition in September 2005, there was extensive discussion about the need to expand organizing efforts and focus on workers in industries, such as retail, whose jobs are difficult to offshore or outsource to lower-wage, nonunion workforces. Despite this expressed enthusiasm, the *Wall Street Journal*'s coverage of the meeting quoted Bruce Raynor, head of UNITE HERE, observing that "[t]o ask Wal-Mart employees to seek the right to organize now 'would be suicidal' because the company could respond by closing stores as it has previously" (Maher 2005). One close observer and critic of Wal-Mart is not alone in concluding that organized labor has "decided to give up for now on organizing the workers," opting instead for a strategy of mobilizing external pressure by educating and encouraging consumers to purchase nothing (or as little as possible) from the retailer until it changes its employment practices (Featherstone 2005).

In April 2005, the UFCW launched a campaign called "Wake Up Wal-Mart," which was being directed by a young staffer fresh from the campaign of aspiring Democratic presidential candidate Howard Dean (Murray 2005). Echoing the grassroots structure of that campaign and its heavy reliance on the Internet, Wake Up Wal-Mart uses e-mail to inform individuals who register on the site about events in and around local stores, including pickets and informational meetings (Joyce 2005). A second Change to Win union, SEIU, provided $1 million in seed money to launch another Internet-based corporate campaign called "Wal-Mart Watch" in April 2005. While similar to Wake Up Wal-Mart in terms of its strategy, Wal-Mart Watch is a coalition of various groups, including environmental and religious groups (such as the Sierra Club and Clergy and Laity United for Economic Justice) as well as organized labor. In addition to supplying a steady flow of press releases scrutinizing the company, Wal-Mart Watch sponsored a campaign called "Higher Expectations Week" in mid-November 2005. Planned to coincide with the beginning of the holiday shopping season, the event consisted of several coordinated "grassroots actions to raise awareness of the problems Wal-Mart causes for our society," according to Wal-Mart Watch's director (A. Bernstein 2005).

This switch in tactics (on the part of the UFCW and SEIU) to corporate campaigns such as Wake-Up Wal-Mart and Wal-Mart Watch must be understood in the context of organized labor's failure to secure a union presence at a single Wal-Mart store in the United States. Given the company's apparent willingness to close stores when unionization efforts do succeed (as suggested by the fate of the Wal-Mart in Jonquière, Québec), this strategy may represent organized labor's best bet for resisting the process of Wal-Martization that the corporation's critics fear. Corporate campaigns targeting Wal-Mart aim to damage the company's reputation as well as its bottom line, by enlisting consumers as key allies in the struggle to push Wal-Mart in the direction of policies more favorable to its employees. By improving wages, benefits, and working conditions at Wal-Mart stores, organized labor hopes to resist a process of Wal-Martization that could prove deleterious for union as well as nonunion workers.

But these efforts to transform Wal-Mart from outside would undoubtedly prove more effective if coupled with pressure on the corporation from within its own enormous workforce. Of course, it is equally obvious that Wal-Mart is particularly successful in resisting organizing efforts, as labor leaders correctly note. What remains unclear is whether the split within the AFL-CIO (which resulted, at least in part, from disagreements about how to confront the Wal-Mart effect) will infuse the American labor movement with new energy and focus or simply serve to weaken it further. In the weeks and months following the split, observers speculated on possible parallels between the departure of the Change to Win unions from the AFL-CIO and the creation of the Committee for Industrial Organization by dissident AFL leaders in the 1930s (which ushered in the most successful period of labor organizing in the country's history). Can the Change to Win coalition be for service sector employees what the CIO was to industrial workers? While corporate campaigns and community movements advocating reform of Wal-Mart's employment practices are a positive development, a revitalized labor movement is the best way to assure that the diffusion of the Wal-Mart model does not result in a downward harmonization that weakens the economic security and well-being of American workers.

Notes

1. Our discussion of the ILWU lockout and UFCW strike draws heavily on primary data collected by one of the authors, Sam Bernstein, who conducted interviews in 2004 with union officials, workers, and management representatives involved in both conflicts. While in this chapter we are particularly interested in the role Wal-Mart played in these struggles, see S. Bernstein 2005 for a more detailed analysis of the cases.
2. The contrast between GM and Wal-Mart as the leading employers (or template companies in Lichtenstein's terminology) of their respective eras has been widely noted, even by Wal-Mart's C.E.O., H. Lee Scott Jr., who acknowledged that some people "believe that Wal-Mart, because of our size, should play the role that General Motors played after World War II, and that is to establish the post-war middle class that the country is so proud of. The facts are that retailing doesn't perform that role in the economy as G.M. does or did. Retailing doesn't perform that role in any country in the world" (Greenhouse 2005b).
3. These concerns stemmed in part from the historical precedent of President Reagan's response to the air traffic controllers strike. As one union official put it, "We were potentially in the same position as the PATCO strikers in 1982 when the government just came in and crushed the strike."
4. Officially known as the Labor-Management Relations Act, the Taft-Hartley Act was passed by Congress in 1947 over the veto of President Harry Truman. It amended the 1935 Wagner Act (officially known as the National Labor Relations Act) to include a list of "unfair labor practices" including closed shops and secondary boycotts. It also allows the president to impose an eighty-day injunction against a strike (or, as in the case of the ILWU conflict, an employer lockout) that is deemed to threaten the nation's health and/or safety.
5. Some observers suggest that the port shutdown occasioned by the lockout, which left shippers deeply rattled, may lead to greater use of East Coast ports and a concomitant decline in the dominance of the West Coast (and particularly southern California ports). According to one logistics industry consultant, increasing volumes of goods routed through the Panama Canal "will likely lead to innovations such as distribution centers [DCs] located at off-shore container shipping hubs such as Freeport, Bahamas ... The key to these DCs is low-cost labor ... Strategically you can see growth in DCs offshore, where you can hold cargo and stage it for distribution into regional DCs" (Tirschwell 2004: 17).
6. This effort to weaken corporate solidarity was manifestly unsuccessful. On the basis of an agreement negotiated before the conflict began, the supermarket chains shared profits during the strike. This prompted California attorney general Bill Lockyer to file a lawsuit in February 2004 charging that the agreement violated antitrust law (Said 2004).
7. This is certainly not to suggest that all companies feel the isomorphic pressures of the Wal-Mart model. Even within the discount retail sector, the striking differences between Wal-Mart and Costco in terms of employment practices and labor relations have drawn attention (Holmes and Zellner 2004, Greenhouse 2005b).
8. Visitors to Wal-Mart's Web site are assured that the company does not oppose unions, but rather considers them irrelevant: "there is simply no need for a third party to come between our associates and their managers." Wal-Mart's strenuous efforts to defeat organizing drives strain the credibility of this professed laissez-faire attitude, however.

10

Wal-Mart as a Phenomenon in the Legal World: Matters of Scale, Scale Matters

Lea VanderVelde

During many time periods, economic, civic, and social laws (and lives) seem to be refit along the lines of the predominant private institution. In the nineteenth century, litigation over coal and railroad interests shaped the emerging law. From the 1950s to the 1970s, litigation over automotive and steel factories shaped the law. It follows, then, that this decade—perhaps this century—is the era of litigation over the super-retailer Wal-Mart.

Certainly other corporate entities stand out as exhibiting disproportionate influence in other arenas of government and law—for example, Haliburton in government contracts and the tobacco industry in maintaining lobbying efforts—but in terms of shaping the common law as a repeat player in the courts, Wal-Mart may be king.

It is theoretically well established that large firms can and do pursue legal strategies that shape the common law not only for themselves but also for all those that come after. Oliver Williamson suggested that active participation in law shaping, whether through lobbying or through litigation, is one of the hallmarks of the modern corporation.[1] Organized parties can undertake sustained campaigns of litigation.[2] For example, Mark Tushnet demonstrated how the NAACP utilized a legal strategy of picking the good cases to advance civil rights reform.[3] Centrally organized parties, whether for civil rights or self-interest, can more easily sustain litigation campaigns. Marc Galanter's powerful analysis "Why the 'Haves' Come Out Ahead" demonstrated that repeat players can have an influence on the rules of the legal system not only by aggressive lawyering.[4] In further work, Galanter has written, "Party capacity to litigate not only affects the outcome of individual cases, but shapes the judicial agenda."

Galanter's thesis indicates that in strategically playing for rules, certain actors (which he dubs repeat players) can unduly influence the public order to their advantage and in their image. Galanter demonstrated how by selecting which disputes to litigate and appeal and which cases to settle out, repeat players could selectively shift their litigation resources to nudge the law in a direction favorable to them because they could expect to reap the rewards over the long haul. One-shot players, by contrast, were always playing for keeps and fought to the finish whether or not they produced a precedent that generally harmed similarly situated players. "Unduly influence the public order" is my own phrase, and by it I mean they can influence rules to a degree and by a method that we would identify as not in pursuance of the social compact of equals, who agree to follow law because it is the fair result produced by a fair means of consent and agreement. Galanter's thesis rivals other explanations of the development of legal rules and the concomitant rise of corporate actors, provided by writers such as Willard Hurst. Hurst explains the rise of nineteenth-century corporations as the release of economic liberty and freedom.[5]

Today, few private actors have as much opportunity to engage the legal system as repeat players as does Wal-Mart. Factors of size indicate opportunities for influencing the legal system by playing for more favorable rules that then, in turn, govern other entities—rules that have been crafted upon the interests of the predominant player, Wal-Mart, as the norm.

Currently, Wal-Mart is not only a repeat player in one area of litigation but is most likely the largest repeat player in the nation on several distinct legal issues. This not only gives Wal-Mart a wider opportunity for legal influence on the judicial agenda but may give the megacorporation opportunities of an additional kind: to play off rules for advantage between different areas of law conventionally seen as self-contained. Thus, the question about Wal-Mart's influence is not only whether and the extent to which it plays for rules, as all repeat players are presumed to, but also whether, by virtue of its position as the largest repeat player, its influence becomes a phenomenon in itself. Can Wal-Mart, because of its huge size, play for rules and push the judicial agenda in ways that other repeat players cannot? When other corporate entities may need to band together to press for a rule change, Wal-Mart's size, strength, and long-term interest may give it the perseverance and preeminence to go it alone.[6] Because Wal-Mart not only is the largest corporate retailer but also has no close second, can it take positions on legal issues that only a predominant corporate influence could imagine in terms of ambition, endeavor, and follow-through? The tentative answer to the question, as this chapter suggests, is yes—although the chapter's secondary answer is that we cannot know for sure without considerably more inquiry, and possibly information from inside the company itself.

This chapter raises more questions than it answers. One cannot attempt to demonstrate the effect that Wal-Mart has had in shaping common law rules in the variety of legal areas in which it engages because of several limitations. More importantly, the proof of many of the theoretical suppositions in this chapter would require information from within the company that Wal-Mart has no interest in disclosing. Claims of intentional strategy require proof of intentional planning and execution beyond the evidence that is available to a researcher of litigation patterns. Without Wal-Mart's cooperation in releasing information, or some enforced transparency, the research tools that can be brought to bear upon this topic can only be the reasonable theoretical assumption that Wal-Mart strategizes for its self-interest and the evidence from the public record of litigation it has participated in. The assumption that a firm such as Wal-Mart strategizes for its self-interest is uncontroversial. It did not accidentally become the world force that it is. The public record of Wal-Mart litigation, Wal-Mart's imprint upon the law, is subject to considerable interpretation.

Information from Wal-Mart directors and litigation staff would be invaluable in considering how much influence Wal-Mart attempts to exert on common-law rule making. Much is made of occasional leaks of corporate memos that reveal intentionality of action. For example, on October 26, 2005, a leaked corporate memo from

Wal-Mart made news revealing a company directive to hire healthier people a day after it issued a press release announcing that it would begin offering some health benefits.[7] Other details in the leaked memo suggested a "concern that workers with seven years' seniority earn more than workers with one year's seniority, but are no more productive," thus possibly implying that the public relations campaign was a bait-and-switch—employees may be terminated before they can achieve the seniority to take advantage of the promised health benefit.[8] The point is that only with access to internal memos is it possible to prove an entity's intentions. Mapping an entity's stated intentions upon specific contexts and outcomes is the only definitive method of demonstrating an entity's influence.

Nonetheless, if it is supposed that repeat players such as Wal-Mart do exert undue influence on legal decision making, there may be reasons to legally require greater disclosure than corporate privacy currently permits. Laws that promote greater transparency of the influences on economic, civic, and social life always encourage good governance. Without greater access to Wal-Mart's decision making, it may take a century before the proof of Wal-Mart's influence could be revealed. Revelations may require that the principal persons involved are long dead and that economic means of production have evolved yet again so that existing entities no longer have an interest in concealing information. Thus, it is only after an entity has lost predominance on the public stage that its intentionality can be fully observed. For example, the most extraordinary information on the American Fur Company, operating under John Jacob Astor and others in the early nineteenth century, only came to light a hundred years later, when through the patient indexing labor of Grace Nute, the calendar of letters of the American Fur Company could be organized for reading.[9]

Thus, the aim here is much more modest: simply to explore the areas of Wal-Mart litigation available from the vast public record of the megacorporation's litigation and sketch the contours of that record, imagining a blueprint for gauging Wal-Mart's effect on the legal rules, which then come to control the legal lives of many other persons, artificial and natural, members of the nation and world.[10] There will be places in this chapter where I can only suggest the outline of further inquiry and suggest what sorts of information would be useful in testing various parts of the hypothesis.

The Public Record

In attempting to assay the dimensions of Wal-Mart's legal influence based on available sources, I tried several methodologies. By searching electronic legal databases it is possible to come up with numbers, though still difficult to divine their meaning. Searching for Wal-Mart as a party in a lawsuit produced 3,034 reported cases, not a small measure of presence as a litigator in the legal world.[11] More than half (1,590) of these reported cases were decided in state courts, with the remainder heard in federal courts. Since only a fraction of the cases brought are ever reported, these numbers suggest that many more lawsuits—perhaps twice as many or more—were filed but never appealed.[12] Refining the search shows Wal-Mart appears in court much more often as a defendant than as a plaintiff. This pattern holds true for most corporations and other so-called artificial persons.[13] Wal-Mart's opportunity to play for rules should then show up much more often at the appeals level than in the cases filed. Since Wal-Mart does not take the initiative in bringing suits against its employees and customers, it is only in the area of business competition where Wal-Mart can be seen as going on the litigation offensive by filing suits.

The simple fact of large numbers of cases in which Wal-Mart is the defendant may indicate breadth of exposure rather than magnitude of influence. After all, the existence of many more slip-and-fall accident cases against Wal-Mart may demonstrate rather impressively that Wal-Mart owns more stores, has more shopping square footage, and enjoys more customer traffic than other corporate entities (more, in fact, than any other corporate entity), making the number of slip-and-fall cases against them proportionate to the number against other retail corporations with less floor space and customer traffic. Wal-Mart can therefore be expected to have more tort victims on its premises, whether those slip-and-fall victims are customers or employees. Similarly, if Wal-Mart experiences more lawsuits brought by disgruntled, discharged employees, it stands to reason because Wal-Mart has more employees than any other private employer.[14] To assess an impact on the legal rules, numbers of lawsuits is surely one factor, but not the sole factor.

One additional method would be to compare the dimensions and nature of Wal-Mart's slip-and-fall litigation to some other retailers', say, those of Kmart. If Wal-Mart's accident case numbers are in proportion to Kmart's, one is tempted to conclude that scale may not matter. But such a conclusion would be too facile. There may be some significance to occupying the position as the overall largest defender against these suits, if only because of the framing effect of being the usual fact example that comes to mind in legal thinking.[15]

Large numbers of similar lawsuits against the same party can still influence legal rules by a means other than Galanter's repeat player thesis. The repetition of a particular type of case—for example, a customer slipping and falling on a spilled drink—can frame a norm in the legal consciousness against which other accidents are evaluated as more serious or less serious, parties as more culpable or less culpable. Thus, the subliminal influence of this framing effect can take place without any intention on the entity's part to influence legal rules.

Moreover, the fact that the largest corporate entity is a retailer, rather than a railroad or steelmaker, means that the foci of the median has changed. In the area of torts, for example, the predominant nature of employment accidents is more likely to be premises liability of an unskilled cashier scanner rather than the mechanical injury of a skilled worker, and the nature of wage shortcuts may more likely be assigning employees to work overtime without overtime pay, rather than the 1970s production equivalent of the speed-up of the assembly line. Similarly, with more customers trawling for values at Wal-Mart stores than walking through the public square, the focus of premises liability is spilled Icees on linoleum rather than cracked or snow-covered pavement on city sidewalks. The extraordinary uniformity of Wal-Mart stores together with their pervasiveness in American life has amplified the modal situation in each contextual topic of torts, the example I've drawn from. Imagine what it has done for contracts, criminal and constitutional protections of privacy, and real property land use law, to name a few.[16]

Numbers of lawsuits may also be influenced by factors of moral hazard.[17] If Wal-Mart is perceived as a deep pocket, as it surely is, more plaintiffs may attempt to sue Wal-Mart in hopes of recovery; however, one would not expect that factor to play much of a role in the public record of reported cases. The moral hazard effect—an increase in the number of marginal claims or nonmeritorious suits—does not necessarily produce an increased number of reported cases. One would expect motions to dismiss or adverse verdicts to weed out many of these suits, and trial court cases are rarely reported anyway. Moreover, recent empirical scholarship suggests that juries actually "find more frequently in favor of corporations, but where they do find corporations liable, they award higher damages than against other parties for comparable injuries." This is not so much "a deep pocket effect as an effect of jurors' estimation [that] corporations [are] equipped with greater capacity to foresee and prevent harm."[18]

The fact that more marginally meritorious plaintiffs sue may be matched by corporate litigation strategies, aimed at discouraging plaintiffs seeking deep pockets. A tough reputation for failing to settle accident claims may discourage marginal or frivolous cases from being brought, as they will not survive motions to dismiss. This is rumored to be the litigation strategy of the Disney Corporation.[19] A no-settlement policy discourages plaintiffs who are unlikely to go the distance of actually trying the case. Nonetheless, a no-settlement corporate policy of taking every case to trial should not result in any more reported cases, again because few trial court decisions are ever reported. To register as a data point in the reported cases column, there most likely had to be a disappointed party willing to appeal.

Since appeals can be brought on error of law or insufficiency of evidence to support a fact finding, not all appeals are situations where an appellant plays for rules. Unless the appeal is only to review "sufficiency of the evidence" supporting the trial court decision, most appeals should be seen as cases that play for rules.

Of the more than 3,000 reported cases in which Wal-Mart is a party, only 251 mention the term "sufficiency of evidence," though not necessarily as the case's exclusive basis of appeal. Presumably, then, most appeals turn on arguments over rules of law, and Wal-Mart, as the party more likely to be the repeat player, is likely to be the one playing for rules.

Another methodology that I tried is to sort the appeals by identification of amicus briefs filed. Sometimes an organized opposition can turn one-shot players (in Galanter's terminology) into repeat players. Wal-Mart was joined or opposed by a party seeking to be heard as an amicus in 59 reported cases, most at the highest level of appeal, the state or federal supreme court.[20] Some of the more interesting were the amicus brief of the Czech Republic in a case involving illegal immigrant workers in New Jersey, amicus curiae of the National Association of Chain Drug Stores and the Chamber of Commerce of the United States in drug-dispensing cases, the amicus curiae brief of the National Association of the Deaf in support of a deaf employee and several state attorney generals, agencies, and departments in a variety of worker's compensation, overtime, minimum wage, and tax cases. The shoe companies Reebok and Rockport joined as amici curiae in a suit against Wal-Mart brought by Nike. The National Employment Lawyers Association has submitted amicus briefs in support of several employee parties suing Wal-Mart, as has the Disability Rights Center.

The tort liability cases brought to state supreme courts seemed to routinely call out amicus briefs on both sides of the issue, from the plaintiffs' injury bar on one side and from the defense counsel's bar on the other.[21]

The presence of organized amici clearly illustrates that Wal-Mart is a player, playing for rules that these organizations find important for their constituencies. The presence of an organized amicus organization may counter some of a repeat player's influence, since by filing an amicus brief the organization is also attempting to influence the decision. But as amicus organizations are often limited by their funding and the actual one-shot player party's ability to decide how far to pursue the case, even well-funded amici cannot play for rules as effectively as a single integrated and supremely well-funded player such as Wal-Mart. What are the dimensions of its play? Is it a bigger player in the algebraic or exponential sense? Are its scales of magnitude, its economies of scale, relatively bigger or absolutely bigger for this largest of all retailers and employers? Can the predominantly large player play different kinds of games than other players?

Three Types of Rule-Influencing Appeals

Measures of Wal-Mart's significance as a key actor on the modern legal stage then should be visible in at least three ways. One is by identification of legal policies and issues being pressed and raised exclusively by Wal-Mart policies or practices. I call these Wal-Mart "signature cases." Again, since Wal-Mart is more often the defendant than the plaintiff, these are cases where Wal-Mart's practices must have "drawn the charge," so to speak. This Wal-Mart signature in litigation is more likely to impart legal rules when Wal-Mart seeks to establish or pursue a unique privilege. One example has been Wal-Mart's persistent policy over several years and across several states of monitoring dating behavior among its employees. In the past, Wal-Mart has insisted upon this employment policy privilege to a greater extent than other retail or commercial corporations. Another distinctive Wal-Mart signature example is its land use siting practices, although other big-box retailers, realizing the benefits of Wal-Mart's practices, have followed suit.

The second type of effect is where Wal-Mart presses for rules from which it will benefit, but the benefits of the rule redound to all corporations generally, or all retail corporations, or all discount retail corporations, whatever is the parallel class. I call these cases "parallel cases" since Wal-Mart's interests are aligned with those of parties in parallel situations, whether the nature of the parallel is as employers, insurers, land owners, or premises owners. Where Wal-Mart's position parallels the interests of others, we may see other corporate entities or business associations joining in the filing of amicus briefs.[22]

The signature category and the parallel category blend together. If Wal-Mart is successful in establishing the legitimacy of one of its signature policies—big-box siting, for example, or even the prerogative of monitoring employee dating behavior—one would expect other parallel players (Target, Kmart, and Best Buy) to follow Wal-Mart's pattern if it is profitable. The fact that a signature policy has come to be identified with Wal-Mart, or Wal-Martization, does not mean that other companies may not seek to emulate a new norm that is perceived as successful.[23]

A third category is the set of cases where Wal-Mart's interest in achieving the rule differs from that of parallel entities because its interest is in maintaining its relative position, particularly its leading competitive position. This set can be called "positional cases" because the effect of the rule is to secure the relative competitive position of Wal-Mart, the largest party with regard to the others. I did not examine these cases, but evidence should be found by looking at the many predatory pricing cases against Wal-Mart. I found no lawsuits in which Wal-Mart went head to head with other large retail discounters. Ironically, the situation of the predominant player in a competitive setting is that if Wal-Mart has managed to attain its dominant position under existing rules, it need not attempt to play for rules at all in order to maintain that position. Resisting rule change, or simply preserving the status quo, should stabilize its leading position, absent large market shifts.

Since other entities benefit from these gains achieved by Wal-Mart playing for rules, particularly in the parallel cases, one must consider free rider strategies. Smaller corporations may be less likely to take the financial risk in the short term to play for a rule, if other larger corporations, such as Wal-Mart, may be expected to benefit as well or benefit more. Thus, if Wal-Mart is seen as the entity most likely to benefit from a particular rule, or is perceived to benefit more, other entities may not play for a rule unless caught in a situation where they are forced to defend against a particularly large claim. There is little incentive for Wal-Mart to join as amicus, since repeat players need not fight others' parallel battles; their strategic advantage is the opportunity to wait for the best of the cases in which they are drawn into dispute.

What is the inverse? Does the free rider strategy affect Wal-Mart? Will Wal-Mart hold back as a free rider, waiting for others to pursue the advantageous rule? One would speculate that Wal-Mart's size would mean that it has more cases to choose among, and it could always underwrite playing for the rule because it can expect to benefit from the rule as soon as it is achieved, and carry those benefits over immediately, and repeatedly, in future applications to its gain. Hence, one tentative conclusion is that Wal-Mart can influence rules because it can speed the process of playing for rules by realizing an immediate and longer-term benefit from winning.

Moreover, what is the significance of win-loss records? Early studies of corporate players in the state supreme courts indicate

> that parties with greater resources—relatively speaking, the "haves"— generally fared better than those with fewer resources.[24] In match-ups between stronger and weaker parties, the stronger consistently and on a variety of different measures won an advantage averaging 5 percent.

The study concluded that "the more sharply party disparity can be delineated, the larger the net advantage of the stronger parties."[25] As for success in federal courts, the extent of advantage was found to be larger with each incremental increase in strength with respect to the strength of their opposing party.[26]

Does Wal-Mart win more often than litigants who are one-shot players? The theory would suggest so for several reasons. Does Wal-Mart win more contests with one-shot players than other litigants who are repeat players? Dunworth and Rogers compared the litigation of the largest corporations with that of all other parties in the federal courts for a twenty-year period. The largest corporations were more successful both as plaintiffs and as defendants: they won 79 percent of the federal cases in which they were plaintiffs, compared to 62 percent won by all other parties.[27] As defendants, the gap was even greater: the largest corporations won some 62 percent of the time, while other parties won only 33 percent of their cases. The largest businesses actually won a smaller percentage of their plaintiff cases than did other businesses but maintained their winning ways as defendants. Other businesses outperformed nonbusiness parties by a wide margin as plaintiffs and a more modest one as defendants. If scale is a factor, this would suggest that Wal-Mart would exceed the win-loss record of other large entities. It would be useful to have this type of appraisal of Wal-Mart's win record in both reported and unreported cases with those of other large corporations.

However, there may be a more tenuous relationship between cases won and rule change. Winning under a particular rule indicates that that rule is beneficial to the victor. Winning repeatedly under a rule can shore up precedent.[28] But beyond that, winning under a rule does not necessarily mean that the entity is having an impact on rule change or setting judicial agendas, just that rule is routinely being applied in cases involving that entity.

To assess the influence of Wal-Mart upon rules, I turned to another publicly accessible record, a search of the scholarly legal literature. If Wal-Mart is at the lead in effecting a new rule, some legal scholar or some law student concentrating on new developments in the law or changes in basic rules should have noticed it. In a search of the legal literature to October 1, 2005, Wal-Mart shows up on 5,186 different articles.[29] Limiting the search by repeated reference to Wal-Mart demonstrated that 248 articles utilized the name "Wal-Mart" more than fifteen times, 442 articles utilized it more than ten times, and 833 articles utilized the corporate name more than six times.

From this batch of articles, one can identify the clusters of categories of law in which Wal-Mart is identified by name as playing a significant role as a repeat player. I turn now to those features of Wal-Mart litigation that have generated scholarly commentary. The categories include land use and store siting battles; trade dress; employment policies that threatened employee privacy; employment discrimination claims based on race occasionally, gender more often, and disability very often; employee benefits, whether government-provided or obtained through private insurance; predatory pricing; unfair competition; intellectual property infringement cases; and even slip-and-fall rules.[30] In the elaboration of each Wal-Mart litigation context, I will consider whether the evidence suggests that Wal-Mart's influence is present as a signature, a parallel, or a positional player in the cases.

Wal-Mart as Neighbor: Land Use and Store Siting Battles

As a neighboring land use, Wal-Mart is perceived as the "equivalent of the 19th-century coal mine."[31] To combat the factory-like aesthetic of big-box retail stores and superstores, communities are increasingly requiring stores to modify their appearance in order to receive a building permit. In Evergreen, Colorado, for example, Wal-Mart added an oak portico, stone pillars, forest-green accents, and evergreen trees in park-ing lot medians to its otherwise ubiquitous red and dull blue-gray buildings.

The stores' appearance is not the only reason Wal-Mart is perceived as a nega-tive in a neighborhood. The corporation's siting strategy has guaranteed that it will run afoul of local land use provisions in small towns across the country. Instead of locating within the designated marketplace of small town squares and cross roads, Wal-Mart has consistently followed the big-box siting method of creating a substitute marketplace surrounded by acres of parking for its customers' use.[32] Hence, Wal-Mart rarely contributes to the scale of a common marketplace of multiple merchants offer-ing cross-competition for prices and qualities of goods. Once the consumer parks in the Wal-Mart parking lot, he or she is discouraged from strolling to other stores. The big-box parking lot design ensures that Wal-Mart is the shopper's one and only des-tination. The Wal-Mart layout means that foot traffic, impulse buying in other stores, comparison shopping, or personally examining competing goods is impossible with-out parking, driving, and reparking, a considerable inconvenience to consumers.

To the extent that city planning efforts are designed to facilitate pedestrian shop-ping with ease of comparison and purchase for a healthy, diversified business base, Wal-Mart's creation of an independently sited substitute market at driving distance from other merchants attempts to displace shopping from downtowns and shopping malls by providing a corporate island of only those choices purveyed by Wal-Mart.

Although many Wal-Mart siting decisions lead to litigation, Wal-Mart is less likely to show up as a party defendant because if Wal-Mart is given the necessary permits from the local or state government, the cases will be styled as a neighbor's case (neighbors versus government entity) or a competitor's case (such as Chamber of Commerce versus government entity).[33] These suits, though extremely significant in effecting the future of a town's land use control, do not show up in the case numbers where Wal-Mart is a party, though Wal-Mart's siting was the central factor perpe-trating the litigation. Hence the numbers of reported cases against Wal-Mart must actually be adjusted upward, since the cases between residents and the permitting authority do not customarily name Wal-Mart as a party.

The siting of a Wal-Mart outside a small town's central business district is a phenom-enon that will likely displace any future efforts by the town to engage in commercial land use regulation in the town because it will divert the commercial activity and mar-ketplace. A study by Kenneth E. Stone of Iowa State University demonstrated that the siting of a Wal-Mart effectively displaced other commercial entities that had previously occupied the central business district, although for a short period of time there were likely to be additional sales for merchants not directly competing with Wal-Mart.[34]

Communities that are rejecting Wal-Mart argue not only that it destroys down-towns and shuts out local stores but also that it makes sprawl and traffic worse, threat-ens employment and unions, and increases poverty rates. In Inglewood, California, voters in a referendum rejected Wal-Mart's proposal to build a new store in their small community despite a $1.5 million public relations campaign launched by the company.[35] In Dunkirk, Maryland, where a local ordinance limits stores to 75,000 square feet, Wal-Mart played to the limits by proposing a 74,998-square-foot store with a 22,689-square-foot garden.[36] Upland, California, and Biloxi, Mississippi, have been successful in preventing Wal-Mart from opening stores.[37] Vermont is at the forefront of shutting Wal-Mart out of developing in rural areas with a zoning statute targeted directly at big-box siting, growth, and urban sprawl.[38]

Siting a new Wal-Mart at some distance from the city center contributes to urban sprawl, which is "low-density development outside compact urban and village centers along highways and in rural countryside."[39] Sprawl has also been defined as "dispersed, auto-dependent development outside of compact urban and village centers, along highways, and in rural countrysides."[40] Although even New York City has been fighting big-box retailers, sprawl and Wal-Mart became a particular concern seen as threatening the destruction of picturesque, natural New England.[41]

In 1970, Vermont enacted Act 250 in an effort to regulate and control development and its ill effects.[42] The act was passed after a report by the Commission on Environmental Control noted concerns that economic growth might harm the state's fragile ecology. Desiring to protect Vermont's natural beauty, the National Trust for Historic Preservation named the *entire state* as one of America's Most Endangered Places. The National Trust is said to have been reacting to Wal-Mart's plans to "saturate the state" with seven superstores. Vermont's Act 250 was meant to promote "a shared cultural image of Vermont, a rugged pastoral ideal originally informed and shaped by farming and logging in a beautiful natural environment."[43] Act 250 reviews development projects of more than 10 acres for a range of criteria.[44]

The Vermont statute did not block all seven Wal-Mart superstores planned for the state, but it did foster litigation and a set of legal by-rules for regulating a big-box siting.[45] In St. Albans, for a time at least, Wal-Mart was effectively excluded. Wal-Mart sought to build on a piece of undeveloped land outside the community. Although Wal-Mart initially obtained a permit, it was later revoked on appeal as inconsistent with Act 250. Two civic organizations, the Vermont Natural Resources Council and Citizens for Downtown Preservation, argued that the growth impacts and costs of scattered development would be detrimental to the area.[46] Wal-Mart appealed, challenging the statute in *In re Wal-Mart*.[47]

The Vermont Supreme Court upheld the legitimacy of Act 250 and the revocation of Wal-Mart's land use permit, finding that the potential ill effects on local competitors and the municipal services cost to accommodate the sprawl should be considered. The splinter of issues in the case illustrates another feature of repeat player corporate strategy. When challenging a statute aimed at blocking a company move, it is in the company's interests to splinter a general rule into a myriad of subrules, any one of which will yield some sort of gain. Hence, in further evaluation of how Wal-Mart effects legal rules, inquiry must be directed at what constitutes a unit of rule or subrule. If a repeat player can chip away at a rule by splintering it and returning a second time for more sway, the influence of repeat players may be achieved over a series of related cases, rather than in any well selected one. If the repeat player is not faced with a complete and total defeat—and what court confronted by a multi-issue case is likely to rule against a party on every single issue?[48]—the repeat player can return in another case to attempt to pry open any remaining loopholes.

The Vermont court addressed only the growth impact issue, and since Wal-Mart failed to meet the protection criteria, the court never addressed whether the siting would also increase costs based on scattered development.[49] The court noted that the planning board must consider whether a proposed development would affect the financial capacity of the town and region to accommodate growth.[50] To make the growth determination, "the plain language of the statute requires the Board to consider the growth caused by the project (secondary growth), the anticipated costs to the town and region, and the financial capacity of the town and region to accommodate the growth." This determination was reached over Wal-Mart's argument that including secondary growth factors was unfair. Wal-Mart additionally argued that the growth assessment should include not commercial growth effects but only population growth. The court rejected both arguments.

Although Wal-Mart opponents were successful in upholding the statute and the revocation of Wal-Mart's first permit,[51] it may be that the statute only delayed sprawl.[52] St. Albans granted approval for a Wal-Mart store, Vermont's fifth and largest, on June 14, 2005. Wal-Mart had first attempted to develop the St. Albans site twelve years earlier.[53] Whereas other retailers and developers may have been effectively deterred by the Vermont growth control statute, Wal-Mart persevered for more than a decade at the same site. Scale may have played a role in the firm's willingness to persevere. The comparative information to establish such a possibility would be whether other retailers pursued development in such a single-minded manner in a particular area in the face of sustained community resistance.

Wal-Mart as an Employer

With 1.5 million employees, Wal-Mart is not only the world's largest corporation but also "the world's most sued corporation."[54] The range of employment-based cases have included discrimination, unjust termination, and a full range of employee suits over state- and federally mandated benefits such as worker's compensation and minimum wages.[55]

At Wal-Mart, every employee nationwide is sent to a central culture training program and required to attend daily meetings, which include briefings on the Wal-Mart culture and participation in a Wal-Mart cheer.[56] Although some large corporations have moved in the direction of toleration of employee independence and lifestyle, Wal-Mart seems to have maintained a more paternalistic attitude and company culture approach toward its employees as well as its products. One writer commented that when one speaks of God at Wal-Mart headquarters, one does so in hushed tones.[57]

Wal-Mart has been sued for race and gender discrimination,[58] usually arguing that due to its size, it is not centrally responsible and cannot monitor all the activity taking place in its 3,400 stores in the United States.[59] In attempting to spin liability off to its individual stores, Wal-Mart is taking the same approach that other corporations frequently do, "subcontracting away" liability or responsibility for potentially illegal practices. This can be an effective corporate strategy, whether the method is attained formally, through activity technically known as "subcontracting" (the actual hiring of so-called independent contractors to perform services for the company), or informally, by insisting that there is no corporate responsibility because its 3,400 stores are individually run.

Most recently, allegations of gender discrimination within the company and its use of illegal workers to clean its stores through subcontractors and denying employees their legal right to a lunch break have taken center stage. In October 2003, after a four-year investigation, federal immigration officials rounded up more than 250 undocumented immigrants working at sixty Wal-Mart stores in twenty-one states around the country.[60] Charges were dropped in these high-profile suits after Wal-Mart agreed to pay the government $11 million.[61] After the raid, one of the targeted employees explained that he worked 56 hours a week making $6.25 an hour, 363 nights a year (Christmas and New Year's Eve being the only exceptions).[62] A class-action wage-and-hour lawsuit against Wal-Mart based on information obtained through the federal raid is pending.[63] Following the October 2003 raids on Wal-Mart stores, nine undocumented aliens filed suit against the retail chain for violations of state and federal labor laws, including under RICO.[64] Clearly other employers are watching and interested in the outcome. Using the Wal-Mart raids as a cautionary note, one recent commentator advised: "Employers should never assume their liability is diminished simply because they lease employees."[65] Some maintain that employing illegal workers through its subcontracting arrangements has "helped Wal-Mart, its shareholders, and managers by reducing the company's costs. This, in turn, benefitted consumers because Wal-Mart consequently lowered its retail prices."[66]

Although Wal-Mart is not the only large corporate employer subject to discrimination charges, Wal-Mart is the player exposed to the single biggest gender discrimination claim in history. The class certification case currently working its way through the courts, if upheld, will expose Wal-Mart to the largest class ever of certified employee litigants.

The gender discrimination case is particularly important because two-thirds of Wal-Mart's employees are women.[67] Though Wal-Mart was named by *Fortune* magazine as one of the most admired companies in the United States, the National Organization for Women has named Wal-Mart a "Merchant of Shame" for its consistent gender discrimination.

Wal-Mart, which employs more women than any other company in the country, currently faces this class action in *Dukes v. Wal-Mart*.[68] Betty Dukes, who worked at a Wal-Mart in Pittsburgh, California, started a national campaign in 2001 to end Wal-Mart's discriminatory practices against women. After ten years of working for Wal-Mart, she had been repeatedly passed over for promotion and made $12.53 an hour. She was joined by five other women from stores in California, Texas, Florida, Illinois, and Ohio filing a complaint based on Title VII of the 1964 Civil Rights Act.[69] The plaintiffs claim that women employed in Wal-Mart stores are paid less than men in comparable positions, despite having higher performance ratings and greater seniority, and receive fewer promotions to in-store management positions than do men, and those who are promoted must wait longer than their male counterparts to advance. The women also complain of demeaning treatment of women in the company culture.[70]

The plaintiffs ask that Wal-Mart be ordered to reform its employment policies and practices and pay lost wages and punitive damages to all those women it has discriminated against. The *Dukes* cases argue that Wal-Mart's personnel policies allowed male managers to decide pay and promotions without oversight. This led women to be significantly disadvantaged as a group. In *Dukes*, plaintiffs argue there is a "glass ceiling/sticky floor" for employment opportunities at Wal-Mart in that women largely occupy lower-paying positions within the corporate structure (sticky floor) and find it difficult to be promoted (glass ceiling).[71]

The six women who filed the complaint against Wal-Mart have asked to represent a class of women. A class-action lawsuit allows a small number of plaintiffs to sue on behalf of a much larger group in a similar situation. For plaintiffs, it is a faster and less expensive way to seek redress while increasing the defendant's potential liability. Hence, class actions create leverage against large-scale defendants. The trial court ruled for the plaintiffs and certified what may become, if the decision is upheld on appeal, the largest civil rights class action ever against a private employer. The judge himself described the case as "historic in nature, dwarfing other employment discrimination cases that came before it."[72] Though the class certified may comprise 1.5 million women, the judge found enough commonalities among the women and the alleged discriminatory practices to try the case as a whole. The judge cited Wal-Mart's alleged failure to follow through with its diversity efforts as an issue common to all plaintiffs' claims of intentional discrimination.[73] As such, all women who have worked for Wal-Mart, including Sam's Club, at any time since December 26, 1998 (the limitation date for claims according to the civil rights legislation), will constitute the class.

A plaintiffs' attorney said: "We discovered Wal-Mart was subject to thousands of discrimination complaints, [but] it did not appear to us that Wal-Mart was changing its practices. It was settling, litigating, and not altering its personnel policies."[74] This pattern identified by plaintiffs' lawyers, if established, may suggest that Wal-Mart considered itself sufficiently immune to the pressure of repeated claims that it did not feel the need to strategize for rules.[75]

Wal-Mart, in turn, has used its size as its defense, arguing that its stores are individually run by managers who autonomously make hiring, pay, and promotion decisions. Wal-Mart argues that the decisions by thousands of managers at its stores are "highly individualized and cannot be tried in one fell swoop in a nationwide class action." Wal-Mart also argues that its 3,400 stores are independent businesses with independent management decisions for which the company as a whole should not be liable.

Broader corporate support coming to Wal-Mart's aid indicates that this is a parallel case. When the Ninth Circuit Court of Appeals heard Wal-Mart's appeal of the class certification order, several business groups, including the U.S. Chamber of Commerce, filed amicus briefs in support of Wal-Mart's position. In resisting the imposition of nationwide class action sex discrimination claims, Wal-Mart may simply be the leader on an issue of general business interest, rather than seeking some signature privilege. Many large chains would prefer a rule that precludes nationwide certification. If the court affirms the certification, Wal-Mart may settle out of court, as happens in most large discrimination cases. However, potential liability for Wal-Mart could reach $300 billion, and Wal-Mart has not been known to back away from a fight.

In response to these high-profile, multistate law suits, Wal-Mart has begun to change some of its oversight policies and employment practices.[76] It has also attempted to improve its image by buying full-page advertisements in more than one hundred newspapers across the county stating its opportunities and benefits package, and establishing a Web site "to set the facts straight."[77] The most dramatic attempt by

Wal-Mart to change directions for its employment policies was found in a recent press release of the creation of a "Corporate Compliance team." Some ascribe this change in corporate direction to legal pressure brought about by increasing litigation over Wal-Mart's employment policies.[78]

"According to the company, new software will ensure that workers are taking required breaks and not working 'off the clock'; a new job classification and pay structure will ensure pay equity; and managers' compensation will reflect in part their achievement of 'diversity goals.'"[79]

One commentator, Professor Cindy Estlund, asks the key question:

> What are we to make of Wal-Mart's vowing to reorganize itself into a model corporate citizen in its labor practices? Is this a superficial public relations gesture? A genuine and public-spirited embrace of corporate responsibility? Or perhaps simply a rational set of precautions against future accidents and attendant liability? Are these measures diversionary tactics to be exposed and discounted, or do they show the law working just as it should by inducing compliance?[80]

Again, Professor Estlund's question asks for evidence of intention. Professor Estlund concludes that these measures "bring the locus of enforcement of both rights and regulations inside the firm or under the firm's control. The internal compliance regimes of Wal-Mart ... must be seen ... as efforts not simply to comply with the law but to secure the legal advantages of self-regulation and to erect a partial shield against regulatory and judicial intervention."[81]

Unlike other big-box retailers, Wal-Mart has insisted on several prerogatives in its workforce policy that have not been sought by other retailers or other giant corporations. One particular employment policy that Wal-Mart has persisted in has been its assumption of a prerogative to regulate employee dating behavior. At one time Wal-Mart required that co-employees seek company permission to date, whether or not the employees were in a supervisory relationship.[82] Although other companies have adopted anti-fraternization policies between supervisors and subordinates, Wal-Mart's insistence on regulating dating activity between a wider group of co-workers was relatively singular. Wal-Mart has been sued numerous times for discharging employees because they had engaged in dating behavior without Wal-Mart's permission.[83] The fact that it often lost such suits did not seem to induce the company to relinquish its interest in its employees' dating choices.

The state of New York eventually enacted a statute banning the policy of employers discharging employees for their legal recreational activities. At the time many believed that the statute was aimed precisely at Wal-Mart's fraternization policy, especially when the state of New York sought to prosecute Wal-Mart under the act immediately after it went into effect. Quite surprisingly, when Wal-Mart appealed, the intermediate appellate court held that the definition of "recreational activities," for purposes of the statute, did not include dating relationships, and thus Wal-Mart's no-dating policy did not violate the statute.[84] Some have found this distinction nonsensical.[85] Why the State of New York never appealed the loss of the case against Wal-Mart to the highest court of New York is an unexplained mystery.[86] More recently, Wal-Mart has rewritten its fraternization policy along more conventional lines to bar dating between employees and their supervisors.

Race has played some role in Wal-Mart's supervisors' interest in employee dating. In *Deffenbaugh-Williams v. Wal-Mart Stores, Inc.*, the white plaintiff was harassed for dating a black man.[87] Her supervisor pursued "a series of pretextual disciplinary actions" against her that led to her ultimate termination on what the court found constituted "fabricated workplace-policy grounds."[88]

Deffenbaugh presented substantial evidence that Wal-Mart failed to respond effectively to her complaints about her supervisor's racial animus. Reviewing the evidence, the Fifth Circuit Court of Appeals upheld the jury finding that any Wal-Mart policy against discrimination was too poorly enforced to distinguish the company's actions from its supervisor's. Therefore, the Fifth Circuit reinstated the jury's punitive damages award, after remittitur, to $75,000.

Wal-Mart's interest in its employees' lives has drawn it into trouble for electronic eavesdropping. Wal-Mart was found to have illegally recorded the private conversations of four former employees, and was ordered to pay $40,000 in liquidated damages.[89]

Wal-Mart has the reputation of opposing labor organizations. Some commentators have called Wal-Mart the "reigning nemesis of organized labor and other employee advocates."[90] Wal-Mart has been described as resolutely antiunion, with "perhaps the most aggressive union-busting operation of any major U.S. corporation."[91]

As a result of defeating union organization at its stores, Wal-Mart has become the bastion of upholding the employment-at-will rule—the prerogative of firing an employee for no reason or any reason at all, unless the reason is illegal. As a result, Wal-Mart has drawn its share of discharge cases arguing the range of exceptions to the at-will rule.[92] With regard to the often raised claim of emotional distress for wrongful termination, the significance of Wal-Mart's victories may not simply be that the employees lose but that the way they lose creates expanded privileges for a large-scale employer such as Wal-Mart.

In *Wal-Mart Stores, Inc. v. Canchola*, for example, the Texas Supreme Court once again refused to recognize a claim for emotional distress in ordinary employment disputes.[93] Such a case hardly even merits note in the legal scholarship.[94] What is different here is the language that Wal-Mart won in winning what was a weak evidentiary case. The plaintiff alleged that Wal-Mart failed to conduct a full and fair investigation into the conduct that was the claimed basis of the termination. He claimed that the investigation was one-sided and inadequate and that the real reason for his termination was his age or disability.[95] The court held that it is not enough for an at-will employee to prove that the reasons given for his termination were false or ill-founded. The court wrote, "An at-will employer does not incur liability for *carelessly forming* its reasons for termination." This may be splitting hairs, but while the at-will doctrine maintains that an employer can fire any employee for any reason or no reason at all, it says nothing about carelessly forming reasons for termination. Particularly for Wal-Mart, a company so efficient in so many of its other processes, the court's language allows the retailer to enjoy the privilege of carelessness in following its own procedures.

In *Canchola*, the plaintiff alleged that he was fired because of his disability. Disability is emerging as an additional area of law where Wal-Mart lawyers are carving a niche.[96] A study of Wal-Mart's role in playing for rules under this new employee protection statute would prove very worthwhile.

Wal-Mart as a Place of Injury: Slip and Fall, Falling from Above

One source notes that Wal-Mart was sued 4,851 times in the year 2000 alone.[97] Claims against Wal-Mart typically involve injuries resulting from slips and falls and from falling merchandise. "Since 1987, about 30,000 falling-merchandise incidents resulting in injuries to customers have occurred at Wal-Mart."[98] Its large parking lots have been the sites of rapes and murders resulting from carjackings and abductions alleged to be due to inadequate security.[99]

Commentators have noted that the company aggressively fights most of these lawsuits even if it would be cheaper to settle the claim, and the company has been sanctioned repeatedly for "willfully frustrate[ing] discovery."[100] If this behavior is seen as permissible and successful, other corporate defendants may follow. Plaintiffs suing Wal-Mart often must fight over not only the merits of the case but also access to documents and other evidence they are entitled to in order to reach the merits. Large corporate defendants have vast resources that can be daunting to even the most sophisticated plaintiffs and their attorneys.[101]

According to an article in the bulletin of the Association of Trial Lawyers of America, "Wal-Mart ... [uses] several tactics to stall discovery and delay compensation for plaintiffs. The four most common strategies are burying important documents in subsidiary companies, enlisting outside counsel in order to assert attorney-client privilege, insisting that plaintiffs agree to confidentiality orders, and adopting document retention policies that allow evidence to be lost, modified, or destroyed."[102]

In one such case, *Wal-Mart Stores, Inc. v. Johnson,* a customer was injured when a Wal-Mart employee accidentally knocked decorative reindeer onto him.[103] After a report and investigation, the supervisor discarded her notes and Wal-Mart got rid of the reindeer. Six months later, when Johnson sued, he argued that it was Wal-Mart's fault that it was impossible at trial to determine whether the reindeer were papier-mâché and weighed five to eight ounces, as Wal-Mart insisted, or if they were made of wood and weighed up to ten pounds, as Johnson claimed. Based on Wal-Mart's failure to keep the reindeer, the court gave a spoliation instruction and entered a judgment against Wal-Mart for $76,000, which was affirmed on appeal.

Wal-Mart's pervasive use of security cameras in its stores mean that many injuries are captured on tape.[104] Security cameras have played an evidentiary role in several Wal-Mart cases. When the area has been recorded on security cameras, it is possible to track the spill as well as the slip and fall. Delay in receiving videotapes is a complaint of plaintiffs in discovery.

It's unclear whether the rules have been formed to Wal-Mart's advantage or to its disadvantage.[105] In many of these premises liability cases, Wal-Mart finds itself both aided and opposed by amicus briefs.[106] Much of the rule variability seems to turn on what sort of evidence is required to demonstrate whether Wal-Mart, as owner of the premises, was given constructive notice of a dangerous spill. Once the plaintiff establishes that he or she fell due to a substance, there are a variety of presumption rules in play in the various states.

In *Smith v. Wal-Mart Stores, Inc.,* the plaintiff slipped on a wet blue substance, later identified as a melted Icee, in the domestics department.[107] Not surprisingly, the plaintiff could stipulate neither who spilled the Icee nor how long it had been on the floor. The jury returned a verdict for the plaintiff, and the defendant appealed on the grounds that the plaintiff failed to show that the spill had been on the floor for a sufficient length of time for the defendant to be given constructive notice.

The Kentucky Supreme Court reinstated the jury's verdict on the grounds that the "[p]laintiff was entitled to the reasonable inference that because it was in liquid form when she slipped upon it, the Icee, which is normally found in semi-frozen state, remained on the floor for a sufficient period of time to allow the ice to melt." In effect, the court allowed the plaintiff to prove constructive notice through "circumstantial evidence that [showed that] the condition existed for a sufficient length of time prior to the injury so that in the exercise of ordinary care, [Wal-Mart] could have discovered it." In this rule change that went against Wal-Mart, some commentators see this decision as endorsing a strict liability standard counter to sixty years of precedent.[108] Others see the decision as finally ignoring the archaic traditional standard.[109]

In Texas, the issue of constructive notice to premises owners of unsafe conditions has been under review in a basically identical fact pattern.[110] In *Wal-Mart Stores, Inc. v. Reece*, Wal-Mart argued that the evidence was legally insufficient to conclude that the store had constructive notice of a "pizza-size" puddle of clear liquid near the snack bar that caused Lizzie Reece to slip and fall and injuring her knee so severely as to require surgery.[111] A Wal-Mart employee, who was responsible for keeping that area clear, was in line directly in front of Ms. Reece and walked right by the puddle. He was standing not far from Ms. Reece when she fell. Furthermore, the puddle was near the ice and drink machine, where there were known to be frequent spills. Although the jury found that Wal-Mart had had constructive notice, the Texas Supreme Court disagreed and held that this evidence was insufficient to provide constructive notice, reversing the trial court and ruling for Wal-Mart. The Texas case and the Kentucky case suggest that across the states there is no clear evidence that Wal-Mart is always successful in playing for rules.

Wal-Mart as a Competitor

Wal-Mart's record of predatory pricing and shaving corners in competition is legendary.[112] One legal expert has written:

> The pressure Wal-Mart places on suppliers is enormous. Wal-Mart requires its suppliers to drop prices annually by as much as 5%. There are different responses to this type of pressure. In some instances, Wal-Mart has driven its suppliers out of business.... Another common response is for a business to cannibalize itself. This cannibalization occurs when a business is forced to undercut its own products in other markets (often much more profitable markets) or give up markets in order to supply Wal-Mart. In other words, it is a zero-sum situation in which the change in business from a profitable market to Wal-Mart has no net gain to the supplier: it is pure loss. And the cost involved is borne solely by the business supplying Wal-Mart, not only through the cannibalization, but also in the cost of shifting production resources from one product to another. Businesses contract with Wal-Mart for different reasons, including being unable to compete, and not having sufficient or complete information as to how Wal-Mart deals with its suppliers. Interestingly, Wal-Mart's suppliers are not free to talk to the press about their experiences for fear of retaliation, or in their terms, "being in the penalty-box."[113]

Perhaps Wal-Mart's most well-known recent participation in commercial litigation is its U.S. Supreme Court victory in *Samara Brothers v. Wal-Mart*. The issue of trade dress is clearly an example of a rule change of significant advantage to Wal-Mart[114] and of interest to many, as shown by the numerous amici in the case.[115] Wal-Mart appears to have been playing for a rule in *Samara*. To lose to Samara could have left Wal-Mart exposed to suit for copying several lines of clothing products that regularly change with fashion trends. To win is to allow it to continue to produce low-cost copies of popular clothing styles.

In a rather short opinion, the court made a clean break from its previous cases. Gone was the deference to lower courts; gone was the acceptance of the judicial expansion of trademark law.

Wal-Mart contracted with one of its suppliers to buy a line of clothing that had been copied from Samara Brothers designs.[116] The plaintiff, Samara Brothers, Inc., designs and manufacturers children's clothing. Samara sued Wal-Mart and several other parties for violating its trade dress. Although all other parties settled with Samara, Wal-Mart did not, claiming that Samara's designs could not be legally protected as trade dress.[117] Wal-Mart went for the big win, and went forward alone after its similarly situated competitors settled out.

The U.S. Supreme Court granted certiorari on the question of "under what circumstances a product's design is distinctive and therefore protectable, in an action for infringement of unregistered trade dress."[118] Certiorari had been sought in several other product cases involving Wal-Mart, but the U.S. Supreme Court had declined to take the others.[119]

Wal-Mart won the day, but the decision left the state of the law somewhat confused.[120] The decision weakened trade dress as a protection for small producers whose products can be copied by large retailers, a profile that clearly fits Wal-Mart. Other commentators have noted that *Samara Brothers* lowers the protection for new entrants to the market and newer brands. The Supreme Court held that product design trade dress can almost never be inherently distinctive and that in order to obtain protection some proof that the item has a secondary meaning must be shown, a difficult condition to establish.[121] Clearly Wal-Mart won a rule that was beneficial to its mode of operation beyond the contours of the instant case.

Is the Sum Even Greater than the Parts?

It must be noted, however, that the whole may be much greater than the sum of the parts. The retail-distribution-industrial reconfiguration that is Wal-Mart may have a much greater effect than as simply the biggest repeat player in each of several legal areas that are frequently perceived in legal circles as distinctively different subjects (tort premises liability, employee privacy, wage protection and nondiscrimination, trade dress and intellectual property, land use siting, and more). Wal-Mart is not just the biggest repeat player in these areas but a principal hub in the legal system because it is simultaneously playing the dominant role in the variety of subject matter fields, whether for signature, parallel, or positional benefits. Not only can it trade off benefits among and between cases, but as a principal hub, it may be in a position to draw upon opportunities to trade off benefits between distinctive legal subject areas. With so little data in the public domain about Wal-Mart's inner workings, the point can best be made theoretically. One of the more interesting developments in network theory has been the development of studies of scale.[122] Scale-free networks have been found to explain why those with many connections tend to be so much more connected than the rest of us. In the case of Wal-Mart, for example, although I have grouped these rules by substantive area of law, they could equally have been ordered by rules over remedies, evidence, or judicial procedures. These areas may offer a hub player the opportunity to cross over subject areas in ways such as to play for rules on remittitur, a reduction of punitive damages, or security camera evidence, which when established in one substantive law area can carry over to others.

Clearly there is more to be studied here before the magnitude and dimensions of the largest repeat player in so many fields can be assessed.

Acknowledgments

I wish to thank Margaret Brinig, Ethan Stone, Michele Falkoff, Nancy Jones, and Geoff Herbon for their critiques of this essay.

Notes

1. Oliver E. Williamson, "The Modern Corporation: Origins, Evolution, Attributes," 19 J. Econ. Literature 1537 (1981).
2. Marc Galanter, "Planet of the APs: Reflections on the Scale of Law and Its Users," 53 Buff. L. Rev. 1369 (2006).
3. Mark V. Tushnet, *The NAACP's Legal Strategy against Segregated Education* (1987).
4. Marc Galanter, "Why the 'Haves' Come Out Ahead: Speculations on the Limits of Legal Change," 9 Law & Society Rev. 95 (1974).
5. James Willard Hurst, *The Growth of American Law: The Law Makers* 129–31, 140 (1950); Hurst, *Law and the Conditions of Freedom* 9–10 (1956) ("[P]revailing nineteenth century attitudes in fact made private property pre-eminently a dynamic, not a static institution").
6. Robert H. Frank and Philip J. Cook, *The Winner-Take-All Society* (1995); Stanley Bing, *Throwing the Elephant: Zen and the Art of Managing Up* (2003).
7. NEW YORK (Reuters)—"An internal memo sent to the Wal-Mart Stores Inc. board proposes numerous ways to hold down health care and benefits costs with less harm to the retailer's reputation, including hiring more part-time workers and discouraging unhealthy people from seeking jobs, the *New York Times* said Wednesday."
8. Article posted at http://www.nytimes.com/packages/pdf/business/26walmart/pdf.
9. Grace Nute, *Calendar of the American Fur Company's Papers*, Parts I and II (1944).
10. Other authors have coined the terms "Wal-Martization" and "the Wal-Mart effect," but not in the sense of the company's influence on legal rules. See, e.g., Randolph T. Holhut, "The Wal-Martization of the American Economy," 10 Am. Rep. (Sept. 2004).
11. All searches were performed on Westlaw between October 1 and October 31, 2005. Given the magnitude of these case lists, it is not possible to reproduce all the case names and article names here.
12. Galanter, "Planet of the Aps."
13. Ibid.
14. Wal-Mart is estimated to have 1.5 million employees. See the section "Wal-Mart as an Employer" later in this chapter.
15. Amos Tversky and Daniel Kahneman, "Rational Choice and the Framing of Decisions," 59 J. Bus. S251 (1986).

16. See, e.g., George Lefcoe, "The Regulation of Superstores: The Legality of Zoning Ordinances Emerging from the Skirmishes between Wal-Mart and the United Food and Commercial Workers Union," University of Southern California Law and Economics Working Paper Series, April 2005.

17. "Moral hazard" and "adverse selection" are often used interchangeably in the legal literature. Jennifer Brown and Ian Ayres have attempted to distinguish between the terms as follows: "Adverse selection is caused by hidden information that distorts the terms of a contract; because of adverse selection, for example, unhealthy people are more likely than healthy people to opt for life insurance." Moral hazard, on the other hand, "is caused by hidden conduct; because of moral hazard, insured people are more likely than uninsured people to take risks." Jennifer Gerarda Brown and Ian Ayres, "Economic Rationales for Mediation," 80 Va. L. Rev. 323 (1994).

18. Marc Galanter, "Planet of the Aps," at p. 24; Valerie P. Hans, "The Jury's Response to Business and Corporate Wrongdoing," 52 Law & Contemporary Problems 177 (1989); Robert J. MacCoun, "Differential Treatment of Corporate Defendants by Juries: An Examination of the 'Deep Pockets' Hypothesis," 30 Law & Society Rev. 121–61 (1996).

19. Conversation with Professor Ethan Stone of the Iowa Law School.

20. *Zavala v. Wal-Mart Stores, Inc.* 393 F. Supp. 2d 295 (D.N.J., Oct. 7, 2005) Thomas F. Reilly, Attorney General, Glenn S. Kaplan, Assistant Attorney General, Jesse M. Kaplan, Assistant Attorney General, and Timothy E. Moran, Assistant Attorney General, on the brief for the Commonwealth of Massachusetts and 19 other states, amici curiae. Kevin J. O'Connor, Jennifer L. Peterson, and La Follette Godfrey & Kahn, on the brief for the American Antitrust Institute, amicus curiae. Michael Stumo and Stumo & Milleron, LLC on the brief for the Organization for Competitive Markets and the Puerto Rico Farm Bureau, amici curiae.

21. See, e.g., *Shoup v. Wal-Mart Stores, Inc.,* 335 Or. 164, 61 P.3d 928 (Or., 2003), patron of retail store brought negligence action against store after store employee allegedly injured her by bumping into her and knocking her to the floor, amicus curiae Oregon Trial Lawyers Association, amicus curiae Oregon Association of Defense Counsel; *Tyrrell v. Wal-Mart Stores Inc.,* 97 N.Y.2d 650, 762 N.E.2d 921, 737 N.Y.S.2d 43 (2001), in a negligence action arising from a slip and fall where the trial court allowed into evidence a statement made by an unidentified employee of defendant, New York State Trial Lawyers Association, amicus curiae, Defense Association of New York, Inc., amicus curiae.

22. Amicus briefs were filed in fifty-nine of the cases in which Wal-Mart was a party.

23 Randolph T. Holhut, "The Wal-Martization of the American Economy," 10 Am. Rep. (Sept. 2004).

24. Galanter, "Planet of the Aps," describing the study by Wheeler, Cartwright, Kagan, and Friedman (see note 25).

25. Stanton Wheeler, Bliss Cartwright, Robert A. Kagan, and Lawrence M. Friedman, "Do the 'Haves' Come Out Ahead? Winning and Losing in State Supreme Courts, 1870–1970," 21 Law & Society Rev. 403 (1987).

26. In a study of the success of appellants before U.S. Courts of Appeals for the 4th, 7th, and 11th Circuits in 1986, Songer and Sheehan found "the success rates of appellants consistently increase with each incremental increase in their strength relative to the strength of the respondent." Donald R. Songer and Reginald S. Sheehan, "Who Wins on Appeal? Upperdogs and Underdogs in the United States Courts of Appeals," 36 American Journal of Political Science 235, TK (1992).

27. Terence Dunworth and Joel Rogers, "Corporations in Court: Big Business Litigation in U.S. Federal Courts, 1971–1991," 21 Law & Social Inquiry 497 (1996).

28. I have demonstrated how repeated rulings against actresses in cases involving negative specific performance had the effect of shoring up precedent for a rule reversal, in Lea VanderVelde, "The Gendered Origins of the Lumley Rule," 101 Yale L. J. 775 (1992).

29. All searches were performed on Westlaw between October 1 and October 31, 2005.

30. Westlaw indicates there are seventeen articles on slip-and-fall liability that cite Wal-Mart more than fifteen times. Seventeen articles citing Wal-Mart more than fifteen times dealt with falling merchandise. I have mentioned only about half of the subjects of litigation involving Wal-Mart. Insurance, financing, predatory pricing, and release of information to employee shareholders are additional areas in which Wal-Mart has and continues to play a role as litigant.

31. Sheryl McCarthy, "Keep Wal-Mart Out of the Neighborhood," Newsday, Feb. 14, 2005.

32. Big-box stores are "large, industrial style buildings that range from twenty thousand to over two hundred thousand square feet" and "resemble big boxes with wide entrances, high ceilings (and a staggering array of merchandise stacked almost to the ceiling), stark interior, warehouse-like appearances, surrounded by acres of concrete parking areas." Big-box stores "adhere to a fairly rigid design formula—at least 100,000 square feet of new, windowless, concrete block boxes—a plan they present to towns on a take-it-or-leave-it basis." Akila Sankar McConnell, "Making Wal-Mart Pretty: Trademarks and Aesthetic Restrictions on Big-Box Retailers," 53 Duke L. J. 1537, 1537 (2004); idem, quoting Stanley D. Abrams, "The Big Box Store: Regulating and Controlling Godzilla," ALI-ABA Course of Study: Land Use Institutes Planning, Regulation, Litigation, Eminent Domain, and Compensation 1103, 1105 (1995); Thomas Scheffey, "Fighting 'Sprawl-Mart,'" *Conn. L. Trib.*, Dec. 25, 1995, at 1.

33. Local opposition to new Wal-Mart siting is becoming much better organized. There are entire Web sites for neighbors seeking to learn how to resist a new Wal-Mart in their town, for example, www.wakeupwalmart. com/news/20050605-fwjs.html.

34. For a full listing of his work, see http://www.econ.iastate.edu/faculty/stone/VITA-KES.pdf. (last visited Nov. 6, 2004).

35. Liza Featherstone, "Wal-Mart's P.R. War," Salon.com, Aug. 2, 2005, available at www.salon. com/news/feature/2005/08/02/walmart/index_np.html?x.

36. Candace Page, "Mega-store Opponents Swap Best Strategies," Burlington Free Press, Mar. 12, 2005.

37. Featherstone, "Wal-Mart's P.R. War."

38. Richard C. Schragger, "The Anti–Chain Store Movement, Localist Ideology, and the Remnants of the Progressive Constitution, 1920–1940," 90 Iowa L. Rev. 1011, 1087 (2005).

39. John Ewing, director of the Vermont Forum on Sprawl, www.vtsprawl.org. See also William E. Roper and Elizabeth Humstone, "Wal-Mart in Vermont—The Case against Sprawl," 22 Vt. L. Rev. 755, 757 (1998).

40. Vermont Forum on Sprawl, "Learn about Sprawl/Smart Growth," "What Is Sprawl?" www.vtsprawl.org/ Learnabout/sprawl/whatissprawlmain.htm. For a complete explanation of the ill effects of sprawl, see James Murphy, "Vermont's Act 250 and the Problem of Sprawl," 9 Alb. L. Envtl. Outlook 205 (2004).

41. See Richard V. Francaviglia, *Main Street Revisited: Time, Space, and Image Building in Small-Town America* (1996).

42. Vt. Stat. Ann. tit. 10, 6086(a)(1)–(10) (2003).

43. Quoted in Sherry Keymer Dreisewerd, "Staving off the Pillage of the Village: Does *In re Wal-Mart Stores, Inc.* Offer Hope to Small Merchants Struggling for Economic Survival Against Box Retailers?" 54 Wash. U. J. Urb. & Contemp. L. 323 (1998).

44. Projects must be approved and receive a permit from one of nine district environmental commissions. Appeals are made to an Environmental Court and then to the Vermont Supreme Court. Projects are evaluated based on ten criteria that assess pollution, soil erosion, impact on scenic beauty, burden on local utilities and services and conformity with land use plans.

45. Wal-Mart opened a store in Williston in 1997.

46. Wal-Mart's permit was revoked on December 23, 1994.

47. 702 A.2d at 400.

48. One case where a state supreme court ruled against a repeat player on every single issue was *Amana Colonies v. Schantz Furniture.*

49. Wal-Mart claimed: (1) considering perceived adverse impacts on municipal tax revenues arising from Wal-Mart's competition in the regional market was irrelevant and speculative; (2) it should not be required to produce a study of secondary-growth impacts to satisfy several statutory criteria; (3) Criterion 9(A)'s considerations on the impact of growth should apply to commercial growth, not simply population growth; (4) its plan should not be considered "scattered development" under Criterion 9(H); (5) it should not be required, under Criterion 5 (traffic), to meet a lower level of congestion than is required by the Agency of Transportation; and (6) the proposed store would not unduly burden local municipalities' ability to provide municipal and educational services.

50. 10 V.S.A. § 6086(a)(9)(A).

51. It also forced Wal-Mart to alter its development plans in some areas. In Rutland, Wal-Mart remodeled a downtown store instead of building a new store in an undeveloped area. In Bennington, it simply remodeled its existing store rather than rebuild.

52. Two books have been published detailing the Wal-Mart opposition movement: Bill Quinn, *How Wal-Mart Is Destroying America (and the World)*, 3d ed. (2005) and Al Norman, *Slam-Dunking Wal-Mart! How You Can Stop Superstore Sprawl in Your Hometown* (1999).

53. In September 1993.

54. According to Professor Steven Ashby of the University of Indiana who teaches a course called "Wal-Mart Lee Ann Sandweiss, 'Big Box' Retail 101 (2004), at http://www.homepages.indiana.edu/040904/text/workweekBigBox.shtml.

55. Suits for worker's compensation have elicited amicus briefs by several entities. *Clark v. Wal-Mart,* 619 S.E.2d 491 (N.C., 2005), North Carolina Academy of Trial Lawyers, amicus curiae; *Alexander v. Wal-Mart Stores, Inc.,* 359 N.C. 403, 610 S.E.2d 374 (N.C., 2005), North Carolina Academy of Trial Lawyers, amicus curiae; *Wal-Mart Stores, Inc. v. Workers' Comp. Appeals Bd.,* 112 Cal.AppAth 1435, 5 Cal.Rptr.3d 822 (Cal.App. 4 Dist., Oct. 30, 2003), California Workers' Compensation Institute as amicus curiae for California Society of Industrial Medicine & Surgery, Inc., and California Psychiatric Association, Inc., as amici curiae; *Gettle v. Wal-Mart and National Union Fire Insurance Company, Insurance Carrier,* five affidavits attached to an amicus brief to the court, and statements by attorneys in hearings before a House of Representatives Subcommittee in 1985; *Crist v. Wal-Mart Stores, Inc.,* 489 U.S. 1090 (1989) *cert denied,* below 855 F.2d 1326, Texas Property and Casualty Insurance Guaranty Association brief as amicus curiae. *Injured workers of Kansas v. Franklin* 942 p.2d 591 (Kan 1997).

56. Tristin K. Green, *Work Culture and Discrimination,* 93 Cal. L. Rev. 623 (2005) at note 57. See *Dukes v. Wal-Mart Stores, Inc.,* 222 F.R.D. 137, 15153 (N.D. Cal. 2004) (describing employer efforts to instill a Wal-Mart "culture").

57. As one supplier put it, "When you speak to God in Bentonville, you speak in hushed tones." See Anthony Bianco et al., "Is Wal-Mart Too Powerful?" Bus. Wk., Oct. 6, 2003, at 100.

58. *Deffenbaugh-Williams v. Wal-Mart Stores, Inc.,* 188 F.3d 278 (5th Cir. 1999).

59. Declaration of Christine Webber Ex. 70 at 3–5, 12, 23.

60. "Wal-Mart Raids by U.S. Aimed at Illegal Aliens," *New York Times,* October 24, 2003, Friday, by Steven Greenhouse; National Desk Late Edition-Final, Section A, Page 1, Column 5, 1045 words.

61. Steven Greenhouse, "Wal-Mart to Pay U.S. $11 Million in Lawsuit on Illegal Workers," N.Y. Times, Mar. 19, 2005, at A1; Michael Barbaro, "Wal-Mart to Pay $11 Million," Washington Post, Mar. 19, 2005.

62. See Steven Greenhouse, "Cleaner at Wal-Mart Tells of Few Breaks and Low Pay," N.Y. Times, Oct. 25, 2003, at A10.

63. Steven Greenhouse, "3 Chains Agree in Suit Over Janitors' Wages and Hours," N.Y. Times, Dec. 7, 2004, at A18.

64. Sarah Paoletti, "Should Illegal Aliens Be Able to Sue U.S. Employers for Labor Racketeering? Yes," Insight on the News, Jan. 6, 2004, at 46 (discussing Wal-Mart raids and subsequent suit by illegal aliens). Detailed in Adam J. Homicz, "Private Enforcement of Immigration Law: Expanded Definitions under Rico and the Immigration and Nationality Act," 38 Suffolk U. L. Rev. 621 (2005).

65. Stephen J. Dunn and Karen B. Berkery, "Employee Leasing: The Risks for Lessees," 84 Mich. B. J. 22 (2005).

66. At least some of those involved in the underground economy in the United States recognize this effect on consumers. "Robert, a Czech who runs a Web site to attract Eastern Europeans to janitorial work, said … 'If they [Wal-Mart] hired Americans, it would take 10 of them to do the work done by five Czechs. This helps Wal-Mart keep its prices low." Steven Greenhouse, "Illegally in U.S., and Never a Day Off at Wal-Mart," N.Y. Times, Nov. 5, 2003, at A1. Detailed in Aristides Diaz-Pedrosa, "A Tale of Competing Policies: The Creation of Havens for Illegal Immigrants and the Black Market Economy in the European Union," 37 Cornell Int'l L.J. 431 (2004).

67. Liza Featherstone, *Selling Women Short: The Landmark Battle for Worker's Rights at Wal-Mart* (2004).

68. 222 F.R.D. 137 (N.D. Cal. 2004). The plaintiffs are represented by three public interest nonprofit groups and four private law firms.

69. Under Title VII it is "unlawful employment practice for an employer … to … discriminate against any individual with respect to … compensation, terms, conditions, or privileges of employment, because of such individual's … sex."

70. In addition to statistical evidence, 114 women who gave statements for the plaintiffs complain of various other discriminatory and stereotyping practices. Managers have repeatedly told women employees that men "need to be paid more than women because they have families to support." This is said to be a widespread practice among Wal-Mart stores in several states. A Women in Leadership group, disbanded by Wal-Mart in the mid-1990s, found that "stereotypes limit opportunities offered to women" because "men are viewed as replacements [while] women are viewed as support" and "aggressive women intimidate men." Some senior managers regularly refer to female employees as "little Janie Qs" and "girls," and some management meetings are held at Hooters or strip clubs. "Women are treated as second-class employees at Wal-Marts from Florida to Alaska. This is not just an isolated or local problem. Wal-Mart has known about this for years and has refused to act," says Brad Seligman, executive director of the Impact Fund.

71. The bulk of the evidence was the statistical record of Wal-Mart's hiring practices. The women presented "largely uncontested descriptive statistics which show that women working in Wal-Mart stores are paid less than men in every region, that pay disparities exist in most job categories, that the salary gap widens over time even for men and women hired into the same jobs at the same time, that women take longer to enter into management positions, and that the higher one looks in the organization, the lower the percentage of women." Among the specific complaints, the plaintiffs cite statistics that show women hold less than 10 percent of store manager positions, while they hold more than 70 percent of store hourly positions. Women are paid less than men with the same seniority in every major job category every year since 1997 "though the female employees on average have higher performance ratings and less turnover than men." Women were denied the training necessary to be promoted within the company, and when some complained of this unfair treatment, they were disciplined and forced to accept a pay cut. Those women who did eventually become store managers were continually called upon to work more hours and sacrifice weekends, vacation time, and holidays, while their male counterparts were not. Despite their performance, men hold 90 percent of store manager positions, 40 percent more than Wal-Mart's competitors. And Wal-Mart has only one woman among its top twenty officers. One study found that it took women twice as long to be promoted to assistant manager than men; it took women two additional years to be promoted to store manager than men; and female managers make about $15,000 less a year than men. Data from Richard Drogin, a statistician at California State University at Hayward.

    Maintaining individual cases would be expensive, especially for the plaintiffs who survive on a Wal-Mart salary and for the judicial system, which would be clogged with cases. Instead, the plaintiffs propose to unify complaints because "Wal-Mart stores are virtually identical in structure and job duties.... . There is a high emphasis on a common culture, which is the glue that holds the company together." It is Wal-Mart's common company culture, management training, and movement of supervisors between stores that plaintiffs claim justifies their suit against Wal-Mart for "company-wide discrimination."

72. This class action exceeds other class actions by a considerable margin. Though there has never been an employment discrimination class action of 1.5 million members, Microsoft was faced with a consumer class action of about a million members.

73. *Dukes v. Wal-Mart Stores, Inc.*, 222 F.R.D. 137 (N. D. Cal. 2004). Plaintiffs' co-counsel said, "Certification of this class shows that no employer, not even the world's largest employer, is above the law."

74. Quote of Joseph M. Sellers, co-counsel for plaintiffs.

75. Bing, *How to Throw an Elephant.*

76. At the annual shareholder meeting, chief executive H. Lee Scott Jr. said he would cut executive bonuses by up to 7.5 percent this year and 15 percent next year if the company does not promote women and minorities in proportion to the number applying for management positions. In April 2005, a slide presentation of Wal-Mart's changes was presented in which it was shown that women among the store's officials and managers rose from 35.06 percent in 2002 to 38.25 percent in 2004.

77. The URL is http://www.walmartfacts.com/keytopics/default.aspx.

78. "Frustrated by labor and community opposition to its expansion plans and battered by legal challenges under wage and hour laws, immigration laws, labor laws, and discrimination laws—including the certification of an unprecedented multi-million member class action—the firm has vowed to use its legendary organizational capabilities, along with new technology and compensation policies, to become "a corporate leader in employment practices." Cynthia Estlund, "Rebuilding the Law of the Workplace in an Era of Self-regulation," 105 *Colum. L. Rev.* 319 (2005).

79. News release, Wal-Mart, Inc., "Wal-Mart Details Progress Toward Becoming a Leader in Employment Practices" (June 4, 2004), at http://www.walmartstores.corn/wmstore/Wmstores/Mainnews.jsp?pagetype=news&template=NewsArticle.jsp&categoryOI D=8300&contentOI D=138 58&catID=null&year=2004. On growing community opposition, see Stephen Kinzer, "Wal-Mart's Big-City Plans Stall Again," N.Y. Times, May 6, 2004, at A27. For a discussion of wage and hour litigation against Wal-Mart, see Steven Greenhouse, "In-House Audit Says Wal-Mart Violated Labor Laws," N.Y. Times, Jan. 13, 2004, at A16. See generally Sanhita Sinha Roy, "Wal-Mart Shows a Pattern of Labor Violations," Augusta Chronicle, July 1, 2004, at A5 (mentioning five of the biggest recent lawsuits brought against Wal-Mart); Lewis L. Laska, Wal-Mart Litigation Project, at http://www.Wal-Martlitigation.com (last visited Nov. 19, 2004) (discussing past and pending actions, including labor-related litigation).

80. Estlund, "Rebuilding the Law of the Workplace."

81. Ibid. at 323.

82. Conversation with attorney Lois Cox, clinical professor, University of Iowa, who sued Wal-Mart in Iowa courts over such a policy. Despite an appeal to the intermediate court of appeal, the case remained unreported.

83. Law review articles on this topic include Jason Bosch, "None of Your Business (Interest): the Argument for Protecting All Employee Behavior with No Business Impact," 76 S. Cal. L. Rev. 639 (2003); Seth Howard Borden, "Love's Labor Law. Establishing a Uniform Interpretation of New York's 'Legal Recreational Activities' Law to Allow Employers to Enforce No-dating Policies," 62 Brook. L. Rev. 353 (1996), Jennifer L. Dean, "Employer Regulation of Employee Personal Relationships," 76 B.U. L. Rev. 1051 (1996); *Standeford v. Wal-Mart Stores, Inc.,* 1996 U.S. Dist. LEXIS 4645, at *7 (W.D. Mich., Mar. 4, 1996) (finding that firing a female customer service manager for violating the company's fraternization policy by having a sexual relationship with, and later marrying, a subordinate male employee did not prove disparate impact or enforcement of the policy against women), aff'd, 1997 U.S. App. LEXIS 13126 (6th Cir. June 2, 1997).

84. *State of New York v. Wal-Mart Stores Inc.,* 207 A.D.2d 150, 621 N.Y.S.2d 158 (1995).

85. Conversation with attorney Lois Cox, who represented litigants suing Wal-Mart under its no-dating policy.

86. However, in *Pasch v. Katz Media Corp.,* 1995 U.S. Dist. LEXIS 11153 (S.D.N.Y. Aug. 7, 1995), the federal district court declined to be bound by the intermediate state court's construction of the statute in Wal-Mart Stores and found "cohabitation" of employees a protected recreational activity. Recently, in another case the Second Circuit held that it was bound by the opinion of the intermediate-level New York state court. In *McCavitt v. Swiss Reinsurance Am. Corp.,* 237 F.3d 166 (2nd Cir. 2000), the Second Circuit interpreted the New York state recreational activities statute to not protect an employee who had an off-hours relationship with another employee, reasoning that an amorous relationship was not a "recreational activity" within the meaning of the statute. Earlier, a federal district court and a New York state intermediate appellate court disagreed as to whether dating is a protected "recreational activity" under New York law such that it would be unlawful for a company to fire an employee for violating a company prohibition of romantic relationships between a married employee and another employee other than his or her own spouse.

87. 188 F.3d 278 (5th Cir. 1999).

88. Id. at 280.

89. In *Desilets v. Wal-Mart Stores Inc.,* 171 F.3d 711 (1st Cir. 1999), the Court of Appeals for the First Circuit partially affirmed the award of liquidated damages against Wal-Mart for secretly recording conversations of night-shift employees, though it cut in half an $80,000 jury verdict. Two store managers at a New Hampshire Wal-Mart store admitted to using voice-activated tape recorders to secretly record and listen to the employees' conversations. Even though the plaintiffs claimed no actual damages, the jury awarded each plaintiff $20,000 in liquidated damages. The Court of Appeals reduced the award by half because it found liquidated damages were to be calculated based on the number of days the act was violated, not on the number of discrete violations occurring in a single day.

90. Estlund, "Rebuilding the Law of the Workplace."

91. Randolph T. Holhut, "The Wal-Martization of the American Economy," 10 Am. Rep. (Sept. 2004).

92. For example, in *Roberson v. Wal-Mart Stores, Inc.,* 44 P.3d 164 (Ariz. Ct. App. 2002), over a strong dissent, the court found that Wal-Mart's disclaimers in its job application and employee handbook overcame the argument that an implied-in-fact contract had been created.

93. 121 S.W.2d 735, 740 (Tex. 2003).

94. The plaintiff failed to provide good evidence of his claim and in this case, as generally, the court held that to justify a claim for emotional distress, the employer's conduct must be extreme and outrageous.

95. In *Canchola,* the plaintiff sued under the Texas Commission on Human Rights Act, claiming that his employment was unlawfully terminated because of his disability.

96. There are seventeen articles in the legal literature on Wal-Mart and employment disability alone.

97. Richard Willing, "Lawsuits Follow Growth Curve of Wal-Mart," *USA Today,* Aug. 14, 2001, at A1.

98. 37-JAN *Trial* 44 2001 Feature FALLING MERCHANDISE. Merchants know falling merchandise presents dangerous risks to unwary customers, and courts are holding them accountable. Jeffrey A. Hyman, Molly E. Homan, "Falling Merchandise," 37, Trial 44 (Jan. 2001).

99. Bruce Kramer and Elaine Sheng, "Busting Open the Big Box Premises Liability," 37 *Trial* 27 (2001).

100. *Osterhoudt v. Wal-Mart,* No. 86433 (N.Y. App. Div. July 2000). The court granted the plaintiff's motion for a mistrial when, after years of refusing to produce names of witnesses and copies of reports, statements, and documents regarding maintenance procedures in a slip-and-fall case, a Wal-Mart store manager turned over the requested documents for the first time at trial. See John Caher, "Justices Blast Wal-Mart's Late Discovery Reply," *N.Y.L.J.,* June 28, 2000.

101. Kramer and Sheng, "Busting Open the Big Box Premises Liability."

102. Subsidiary companies. Wal-Mart has a subsidiary, Claims Management, Inc., which it uses to manage, control, and track claims against the parent company. It functions as Wal-Mart's self-insurer, claims adjuster, and investigative agent: It 'works' the claim, taking statements and obtaining documents in the guise of pursuing settlement. When a plaintiff requests documents regarding prior litigation, Wal-Mart can claim it does not have them... .

"The court sanctioned the company for discovery abuse. GTFM, *Inc. v. Wal-Mart Stores, Inc.* No. 98 Civ. 7724 (RPP), 2000 WL 335558 (S.D.N.Y. Mar. 30, 2000); Attorney-client privilege. Some companies use outside counsel to help draft risk-management polices and procedures. When a plaintiff requests background information on the policies—such as memos, correspondence, and notes concerning the drafting of and basis for the policies—the company objects, claiming that these documents are protected by the attorney-client privilege and/or work product doctrines. Confidentiality orders. Wal-Mart ... also attempt[s] to thwart plaintiffs' discovery efforts by insisting that the parties enter into restrictive confidentiality orders.

"First, the company tries to contain the scope of discovery. When a plaintiff asks for companywide information about prior incidents, audits, surveys, legal claims, and so forth, the defendant contends that only information pertaining to the particular site involved in the case—whether it be a store, apartment complex, hospital, or other premises—is relevant. This is an attempt to isolate the plaintiff. It also delays the litigation, forcing him or her to file motions seeking disclosure of documents and to wait for hearing dates.

"Next, defendants often seek protective orders that prevent plaintiffs from disclosing information they obtain in discovery to anyone other than their attorneys and expert witnesses.

"Discovery rules permit parties to seek protective orders to shield them from 'annoyance, embarrassment, or oppression.' [T]he primary reason a defendant in a premises liability or other personal injury case seeks a protective order is to prevent plaintiffs from sharing information.

"Spoliation. In jurisdictions where courts have acknowledged the duty to preserve evidence that is potentially discoverable in pending or foreseeable litigation, intentional and negligent spoliation of evidence has been recognized as an independent tort."

Kramer and Sheng, "Busting Open the Big Box Premises Liability."

103. 106 S.W.3d 718, 720 (Tex. 2003).

104. *Richter v. Wal-Mart, Inc.*, not reported in S.W.3d, 2004 WL 1835928 (Tex.App.-San Antonio, Aug. 18, 2004); *Hodge v. Wal-Mart Stores, Inc.*, 360 F.3d 446 (4th Cir. 2004); *Harrison v. Wal-Mart Stores, Inc.*, 287 F.Supp.2d 847 (W.D.Tenn., Oct. 16, 2003); *Rushing v. Wal-Mart Stores, Inc.*, not reported in F.Supp.2d, 2002 WL 1397247 (W.D.Tenn., Jan. 2, 2002). See, e.g., *Gump v. Wal-Mart Stores, Inc.*, 93 Hawai'i 428, 5 P.3d 418 (Hawai'i App., Nov 17, 1999) (Gump and Wal-Mart agreed to exclude the security camera videotape).

105. *Lanier v. Wal-Mart Stores, Inc.*, 99 S.W.3d 431 (Ky. 2003); *Smith v. Wal-Mart Stores, Inc.; Wal-Mart Stores, Inc. v. Johnson; Gump v. Wal-Mart Stores, Inc.* , 93 Hawai'i 417, 5 P.3d 407 (2000); *Wal-Mart Stores, Inc. v. Reece; Smith v. Wal-Mart Stores, Inc.*, 253 F. 3d 700 (5th cir. 2001); *Wal-Mart Stores, Inc. v. Johnson,* 106 SW 3d 718 (Tex. 2003).

106. *Martino v. Wal-Mart Stores, Inc.*, 908 So.2d 342 (Fla., 2005); *Gribben v. Wal-Mart Stores, Inc.*, 824 N.E.2d 349 (Ind. 2005); *Lanier v. Wal-Mart Stores, Inc.*, 99 S.W.3d 431 (Ky., 2003), customer brought action; *Shoup v. Wal-Mart Stores, Inc.*, 335 Or. 164, 61 P.3d 928 (Or. 2003); *Tyrrell v. Wal-Mart Stores Inc.*, 97 N.Y.2d 650, 762 N.E.2d 921, 737 N.Y.S.2d 43 (2001); *Lake v. Wal-Mart Stores, Inc.*, 582 N.W.2d 231 (Minn., 1998); *Miller v. Wal-Mart Stores, Inc.*, 219 Wis.2d 250, 580 N.W.2d 233 (Wis. 1998); *Wal-Mart Stores, Inc. v. Gonzalez*, 968 S.W.2d 934, 41 Tex. Sup. Ct. J. 811 (1998); *White v. Wal-Mart Stores, Inc.*, 699 So.2d 1081 (La. 1997); *Werner v. Wal-Mart Stores, Inc.*, 116 N.M. 229, 861 P.2d 270 (N.M.App.1993).

107. 6 S.W.3d 849 (Ky. 1999).

108. D. Maurice Moore, "Watch Your Step: An Analysis of Premises Liability in the Wake of *Lanier v. Wal-Mart Stores, Inc.*," 43 Brandeis L.J. 283 (2004–05).

109. David A. Elder, "An End-of-Millennium Odyssey Through Tort Liability of Occupiers and Owners of Land," 28 N. Ky. L. Rev. 352 (2001).

110. *Wal-Mart Stores, Inc. v. Rosa,* 52 S.W.3d 842, 844 (Tex. App.—San Antonio 2001, pet. denied) (holding that employees' proximity to area where plaintiff fell did not tend to prove how long the condition had existed for purposes of charging constructive notice); *Wal-Mart Stores, Inc. v. Garcia,* 30 S.W.3d 19, 23 (Tex. App.—San Antonio 2000, no pet.) (noting proximity evidence as one reason that the premises owner should have known of the hazard).

111. *Wal-Mart Stores, Inc. v. Reece,* 81 S.W.3d 812 (Tex. 2002).

112. The case, *American Drugs, Inc. v. Wal-Mart Stores, Inc.*, 1993-2 Trade Cas. (CCH) 70,382 (Ark. Ch. Oct. 12, 1993), interprets the Arkansas Act to protect competitors, described in Michael L. Weiner, "State Bans On Below Cost Pricing Loss Leaders As Misleaders?" 8 Antitrust 2 (1994); Eric D. Placke, "*Culhane v. State* and the Battle of the Blue Light Specials: A Right to Receive Commercial Information While on Another's Property?" 39 Ark. L. Rev. 146 (1985); eleven articles on Wal-Mart and Cracker Barrel.

113. Benedict Sheehy, "Corporations and Social Costs: The Wal-Mart Case Study," 24 J.L. & Com. 1, 37 (2004), citing Charles Fishman, "The Wal-Mart You Don't Know," Fast Company 68 (Dec. 2003), at http://www.fastcompany.com/magazine/77/Wal-Mart.htmi.

114. The decision has spawned some fifteen articles.

115. 1999 WL 1045126 (Appellate Brief) Brief Amicus Curiae of Payless Shoesource, Inc. in support of petitioner (Nov. 18, 1999); 1999 WL 1045127 (Appellate Brief) Brief for the United States as Amicus Curiae Supporting Petitioner (Nov. 18, 1999); 1999 WL 1045132 (Appellate Brief) Brief for Amicus Curiae American Intellectual Property Law Association in Support of Neither Party.

116. Samara Brothers designs and manufactures children's clothing, specializing in spring and summer seersucker outfits. Samara's collection possessed such design elements as seersucker fabric, large collars, and full-cut one-piece bodies. Wal-Mart contracted with Judy-Philippine, Inc. to manufacture children's outfits that imitated the popular Samara children's line. Judy-Philippine's knockoffs were sold at several major retailers, including Wal-Mart, Kmart, Caldor, Hills, and Goody's.

117. A jury in the Southern District of New York found for Samara, and the other parties that Samara sued, except for Wal-Mart, settled. Wal-Mart moved for judgment as a matter of law, The district court denied the motion, the circuit court also denied the motion, and Wal-Mart appealed to the Supreme Court.

118. *Wal-Mart Stores, Inc. v. Samara Brothers, Inc.*, 520 U.S. 205 (2000).

119. *Nike, Inc. v. Wal-Mart Stores, Inc.*, 528 U.S. 946 (U.S. 1999)

120. *Samara Brothers* has generated considerable secondary literature.

121. Trade dress doctrine is a subset of trademark law and is protected by the Lanham Act, 15 U.S.C. § 125. Unregistered trade dress has long been protected by common law and statute. When early courts found liability for a defendant's use of trade dress they based their reasoning on "the theory that a competitor should not dress its product in the clothes of another." Trade dress law protects a product's packaging, or the design of the product itself. Packaging or design of the product need not be registered to be eligible for trademark protection. Although *Samara Brothers* verges upon implying that trade dress can never be inherently distinctive, such a statement would be counter to Supreme Court precedent. In *Two Pesos, Inc. v Taco Cabana, Inc.*, 505 U.S. 763 (1992), Justice White, writing for the majority, defined inherent distinctiveness and secondary meaning, which *Samara Brothers* makes no attempt to overrule. *Samara Brothers* notes that *Two Pesos* establishes that trade dress can be inherently distinctive. Justice Scalia preserves the precedent of *Two Pesos* by creating a new distinction between trade dress in a clothing line and trade dress in a restaurant. The opinion divides trade dress into three subsets: product packaging, product design, and some hard-to-define tertium quid. Product packaging can be inherently distinctive, but product design can almost never be inherently distinctive and must have secondary meaning in order to receive trade dress protection. The secondary meaning standard for product design discourages litigation and other anticompetitive problems that arose under *Two Pesos* allowing product design to be found to be inherently distinctive. The opinion says that the trade dress protected in *Two Pesos*—the restaurant's decor—was product packaging and not product design.

122. According to Barabasi, networks are governed by two laws: (1) growth—networks are assembled one node at a time, and (2) preferential attachment—new nodes prefer to attach to more connected hubs. Albert-Laszlo Barabasi, *Linked: How Everything Is Connected to Everything Else and What It Means* (2002). See also Steven Strogatz, *Sync: How Order Emerges from Chaos in the Universe, Nature, and Daily Life* (2003); Duncan J. Watts, *Six Degrees: The Science of a Connected Age* (2003); Duncan Watts, *Small Worlds: The Dynamics of Networks Between Order and Randomness* (2004); Mark Buchanan, *Nexus: Small Worlds and the Groundbreaking Science of Networks* (2002).

Part IV

Culture, Communities, and Conflicts

11

The Institutional Semiotics of Wal-Mart Flyers and Signage in the United States, United Kingdom, Germany, and China

Stephen J. Arnold, Nailin Bu, Ulrike Gerhard, Elke Pioch, and Zhengxin Sun

Introduction

Wal-Mart bestrides the globe like a colossus. It marks its entry into each country by attaching the ubiquitous "Wal-Mart" sign to most of its discount and hypermarket stores. Beyond the "Wal-Mart" sign, however, an interesting question is whether other elements of the retail strategy of the world's largest retailer are also similar across countries. Does Wal-Mart appeal to the same kind of shopper in each country? Is this retailer's message similar from market to market?[1]

In this chapter we use a study of institutional semiotics as a means to answer these questions, comparing flyers and signage from Wal-Mart stores in four countries: the United States, United Kingdom, Germany, and China, the last three different in language and culture to varying degrees from Wal-Mart's U.S. base. The study draws conclusions regarding Wal-Mart's adaptations to this wide variety of markets and how the success of its adaptations can shed light on its varying levels of success in different markets. Beyond its contribution to the deeper understanding of Wal-Mart, our motivation for this article is the desire to better understand the process of internationalization and why the same company can succeed in some markets and struggle in others.

Institutional Semiotics

From the perspective of institutional theory, organizations are embedded in a social environment, an organizational field that includes social actors such as retailers, consumers, suppliers, regulatory agencies, and competitors (DiMaggio and Powell 1983; Meyer and Rowan 1977). Within the organizational field, there are taken-for-granted social and cultural systems, also referred to as norms, that have been established by the social actors. These norms serve as guidelines for the different social actors on how to act within the organizational field.

In order for an organization to survive in its social environment, it has to conform to the institutional norms and legitimate itself in the eyes of other social actors (DiMaggio and Powell 1983; Meyer and Rowan 1977; Zucker 1987). Legitimation was defined by Suchman (1995: 574) as a "generalized perception or assumption that the actions of an entity are desirable, proper, or appropriate within some socially constructed system of norms, values, beliefs and definitions." Legitimation helps the organization to survive by acquiring the necessary resources.

In the process of internationalization, a retailer may encounter environmental norms that are different from those in the home market. The icons and signs used by the retailer can reveal how it acts in this situation to adhere to these new norms and thereby legitimate itself among new social actors. Since an organization's adherence to institutional norms can be both objective and symbolic, studying symbolic actions is important in understanding how organizations manage to gain legitimacy in the institutional environment (Meyer and Rowan 1977). Institutional semiotics is a fitting tool for this purpose (Arnold, Kozinets, and Handelman 2001).

In the context of the current study, the relevant institutional norms relate to task/economic norms, such as convenience, price, quality, selection, store environment, promotions, and service, as well as the cultural/societal norms of community, trustworthiness, and hedonism. These norms were derived from previous studies (e.g., Arnold 2003).

Semiotics can be generally defined as a study of "the ways people communicate with each other, consciously and unconsciously, through things such as language, visual images and music" (Lawes 2002: 253). It looks into how meanings can be extracted from different signs in communications. Saussure'sv approach states that signs, mainly linguistic signs, construct meaning with a pre-coded system. When signs are organized to form a message, the meaning is established according to the coding system.

Jakobsonian semiotics is a framework that follows the Saussurian tradition (Jacobson 1985). It directs the analysis of message decoding by asking structured questions that relate to the three elements involved in communication: Who is being addressed? Who is the sender? What are the mythologies? These questions lead to investigations of the characteristics of the people who will receive the message, such as socioeconomic status, age, gender, and lifestyle. It will also investigate the characteristics of the message sender, as well as the tone the sender uses in the message and the emotions conveyed to the receivers. An investigation of the message itself would focus on the consumer mythologies or stories that underpin the message elements.

Institutional theory then can be used to interpret the answers to the Jakobsonian questions by identifying the underlying norms. Arnold, Kozinets, and Handelman (2001) characterized this integration of Jakobsonian semiotics and institutional theory as "institutional semiotics" and used this approach to study a thirty-two-page Wal-Mart flyer printed in Stillwater, Oklahoma, in 1997. In doing so, they unmasked the Wal-Mart advertising to reveal the identities of its American speaker and the intended consumer recipient. Identification of various mythologies also revealed

Wal-Mart's adherence to certain institutional norms presumed to be important to American shoppers.

More specifically, the reader was determined to be a working- or middle-class American female between the ages of twenty-five and fifty-five whose main concern was her family and especially her children. In turn, the Wal-Mart speaker was revealed to be an ordinary, plainspoken person who might also be a friendly neighbor or even a trusted friend. The interpretation further identified the mythology of *Homo economicus*—adherence to the Puritan/Calvinist virtue of thrift through paying low prices and being a smart shopper.

The analysis also identified the mythology of family, emphasizing the institutional norms of caring, loyalty, and commitment. Furthermore, it revealed the mythology of America, which is characterized by the norms of antistatism, populism, egalitarianism, and especially patriotism. Finally, the mythologies of community and hometown pointed to an idealized small-town America where friends, family, and neighbors meet and socialize while shopping at their local, friendly Wal-Mart store.

In the next sections, flyers and signage created by Wal-Mart in the United Kingdom, Germany, and China are interpreted in a similar manner through the lens of institutional semiotics.

The Flyers and Signage

Advertising and promotion practices in the markets investigated here use different media, including Web sites, television advertising, flyers, and in-store signage. As the Arnold, Kozinets, and Handelman (2001) study used one randomly selected flyer, the same procedure was followed in the U.K. and German markets, thereby ensuring a consistent methodology. However, references are also made to other flyers from the same year, so that the proposed interpretations are relevant beyond the selected flyers.

In the United Kingdom, Wal-Mart's 1999 acquired subsidiary, ASDA, was issuing multipage, nonglossy flyers several times a year containing a wide range of products but sometimes concentrating on a particular seasonal event. The flyers are usually distributed to households as inserts in free local papers. Depending on the season, they are from four to thirty-two pages, with the Christmas issue being printed on glossy paper and assuming the format of a catalogue. The following analysis is based primarily on the 2004 Easter flyer but also makes references to a summer flyer, a special Halloween (October) edition, and the Christmas flyer.

In Germany, following Wal-Mart's 1997 acquisition of two hypermarket chains, weekly flyers are regularly issued. A flyer valid from November 15 to 20, 2004, was chosen for interpretation, supplemented by references to a Christmas flyer and to the five-year anniversary flyer celebrating Wal-Mart's entry into the German market.

Wal-Mart entered China in 1996, but at least in the Dalian market considered for this paper, no flyers were being published. In lieu, the semiotic analysis conducted in 2002 used signs and posters displayed in a Dalian Wal-Mart Supercenter. This supercenter was opened in 2000 and was named "the best new store" by Wal-Mart Stores, Inc. in 2001. It was also the most visited store in the world, according to the public relations department of Wal-Mart China. The signs and posters that were selected for analysis included slogans, decorations, pictures, and photographs. Despite this variety, the signage was still not as visually rich as the flyers.

Who Is Being Addressed?

The United Kingdom

Analysis of the U.K. ASDA flyers reveals an intended audience with specific characteristics. Members of the target audience appear to be primarily females who look after a family. Younger men, health-conscious consumers, those on a budget, and time-pressured individuals are also addressed. The general impression is that the addressee is an ordinary, price-conscious person who nevertheless enjoys little luxuries.

A first glimpse of this consumer can be gained in the Christmas catalogue, which depicts under the slogan "Gifts for her" a rather beautiful woman wearing a necklace, matching ear studs, and an embroidered dress. The text states, "Make her feel truly special this Christmas with stunning jewelry, chic fashions from George, sophisticated fragrances and a wonderful range of toiletries and beauty accessories." The woman looks similar to female models in middle-market (home-shopping) catalogues, making the reader aware that ASDA provides its female customers with products that extend the "supermarket" selection to personal items of adornment at the right price. At the same time it invites the male reader to take part in the shopping process.

The color schemes and selection of glasses in a beer, wine, and spirits display in the Easter flyer continue the appeal to females aspiring to something less ordinary in their shopping basket. For instance, slender, simple glasses finished off with a slice of orange immerse ice cubes in the light green of Absolut vodka mixed with Del Monte World Fruits juice (New Zealand kiwi fruit is shown). They contrast with the red/pink color scheme of Russian Stolichnaya vodka mixed with Ocean Spray cranberry juice drink. The whole page has a rather enticing and feminine feel to it, mostly evoked by the color scheme.

Younger men could also be attracted to experiment with the new drinks. The combination of displayed products leads the taste of the male reader by introducing exotic ideas (e.g., a "Breezer" is ideal with either tonic or lemonade, or a "Xuxu" mixes nicely with fresh strawberries and a touch of vodka).

At first glance, the opposite page, displaying beers, has clear male connotations created through advertising campaigns (e.g., Foster's, Carling, Stella Artois, and the multipacks). However, a closer examination reveals that the masculine feel to this page is moderated by the display of brands less strongly associated with the macho male (e.g., Grolsch and Heineken). These brands are displayed in nonstandard beer glasses and are reminiscent of younger people found at trendy pubs, bars, and restaurants.

Health-conscious consumers are addressed with the Good for You! product line, where fat content, calories, and ingredients appear clearly visible on the label. Even here, though, the potential to enjoy little luxuries shines through—for example, raspberry trifles at £1.18 per three-pack (125 grams) that apparently can be consumed without danger to either one's health or one's purse.

That the reader of these flyers is more time-pressured and most likely catering to a family is reflected in careful collages of food presented as whole meal serving suggestions: a roast leg of lamb is seasoned with rosemary, thyme, sage, and cloves, garnished with roasted garlic and onions, and served on a wooden board with Bird's Eye "steam fresh vegetables," chilled Chantenay carrots, and Aunt Bessie's roast potatoes. All vegetables are presented in simple white dishes, and two glasses of red wine are set out with the bottle discreetly in the background. All vegetables are already prepared and only the leg of lamb requires some effort. The female reader especially may appreciate these products because she likely works outside of the home and needs convenience and easy preparation.

The only flaw in the otherwise meticulously planned layout and product selection seems to be a tacky and cheap-looking container with ASDA chicken gravy granules sitting next to a stainless-steel-like gravy serving dish. However, it could also be argued that this cheap-looking item at the bottom of the page next to the rosé-filled "Smartprice" wineglasses communicates with the shopper on a budget. Fortunately, neither the rosé wine nor the container with gravy granules find their way onto the laden Easter table to betray the "classiness" of the meal.

Germany

While the U.K. flyers do not depict any consumers (except as models for garments and jewelry), the German Wal-Mart flyer portrays overwhelmingly young families. Almost all of the illustrations show either young mothers with a child, young women engaged in household tasks, or young couples or children alone. Excluding the children, all of the customers portrayed appear to be between twenty-five and forty years old. The older generation is absent, as there is not a single person in any flyer who appears older than forty-five or fifty.

One page shows a relatively large living room equipped with a comparatively small cupboard, two couches, and a couch table. A second couch table holds a television. Wineglasses are in the cupboard and candle holders are on the shelves, but the style is neither fancy nor luxurious. In fact, the furniture is standard-looking, not over stuffed, and more modern than traditional. It is all neatly arranged on a rather empty wooden floor. There is enough space for everybody, in contrast to a crowded family room. Overall, it suggests a standard, middle-income family with some taste.

Following the practice of U.S. flyers, customers are identified by their first names. This practice suggests a familiarity that is unusual in Germany, where even young adults of the same age use last names when talking with each other. A clear, modern, American style is being used.

The customer names given are quite common and neither extremely traditional nor extremely contemporary. Some have Anglophone touches such as Fiona, Denise, Sharien, or Steven, but most are popular German names such as Nina, Julia, Paul, Rasmus, Linda, Laura, and Lena. Typical is their shortness, consisting of only two syllables.

All the customers shown are white, presumably German. There is hardly any reference to a multicultural society. Books are absent from all rooms; in one, a woman reads a glossy magazine. In sum, the German flyer addresses an ordinary female consumer who has a young family.

China

As previously discussed, no flyers were available for analysis in China. Nonetheless, several properties of the intended audience are implied by Wal-Mart's China signage. First, it is clear Wal-Mart is targeting Chinese citizens, not expatriates who live and work in China, as all signs are written in Chinese except Wal-Mart's name. Posters in the store feature Chinese people in Wal-Mart uniforms. Two large characters meaning "China" have been assembled at one side of the cashier's counter.

Second, the Chinese Wal-Mart store seems to be addressing neither peasants nor the wealthy but instead working, middle-class urban residents who do not display extravagant tastes. The Wal-Mart store sign has a small panel attached to it that says "Foods, nonfoods, and clothes." Nothing fancy such as electronics or jewelry is mentioned here. The implication is that this store sells daily necessities for ordinary people and not luxury goods for the wealthy. Peasants in the surrounding villages would more likely patronize the local wet markets.

Summary

The element common to the U.K. and German flyers is an apparent attempt to reach the female shopper between twenty-five and forty-five years old. Children and babies are always present, although to a much greater degree in German flyers. Overall, age, gender, and stage in the family life cycle of U.K. and German shoppers are consistent with those portrayed in the U.S. flyer. The greatest difference is that, consistent with U.S. practice, individuals are named in the German flyers, whereas the models in the U.K. flyers are completely anonymous.

In China, the store signs do not depict customers, so their age and other demographic characteristics could not be determined. However, in emerging economies such as China, international retailers are at least initially of greater interest to more-educated and higher-income consumers (Cui and Liu 2001). Shoppers from this group have broader, worldlier knowledge and the income ability to investigate offerings of the retail entrants.

In contrast to the similar demographics, socioeconomic differences are apparent across the markets. Whereas U.S. advertising appears to be directed to working-class and middle-class consumers, German Wal-Mart communications are directly focused on a middle-class shopper. In contrast, the U.K. flyer does not primarily work with class definitions but focuses on lifestyle, which will be discussed in more detail below. The focus of the two European Wal-Marts differed in that the U.K. product mix reflected easy-to-prepare items for families/households in which both partners are employed outside the home, whereas there was no direct emphasis in the German and American flyers on products for time-poor customers.

Who Is the Speaker?

The United Kingdom

The U.K. ASDA speaker is a very ordinary but credible person who may come from any one of a number of walks of life. This individual is referred to as a "colleague," similar to the American practice of referring to a Wal-Mart employee as an "associate." Illustrated, for example, is Claire, a young woman with a smile who wears the ASDA shop floor uniform (a green polo shirt with a blue collar and sleeve trim). She appears as a friendly but ordinary person, attractive but not glamorous or beautiful. She has warm, smiling eyes.

Nav is a young man with a clean, friendly image, short hair, and smiling eyes and mouth, looking into the camera. His ethnic background is ambiguous—one can associate him with Pakistani, Indian, or mixed-race heritage.

Paul is probably in his thirties. He has a receding hairline, a clean image, and smiling eyes exuding friendliness. His strong-looking hands hold a bag of compost (ASDA brand). The impression given is that if Paul were your neighbor, you could ask him to look after your garden when you were on holiday, because he has gardening skills and knowledge.

Sharon faces the camera with a broad smile, showing her teeth. Her hair is neatly but simply arranged. Possibly in her thirties, she exudes confidence, competence, and friendliness. Sharon can probably advise you on your holiday needs.

In fact, every ASDA speaker is an advisor. The flyers relay the feeling that there are specialists at ASDA who have a clear sense of what is already available in your house. These characters "peep in," are familiar with consumers' needs and wants, and have the expert knowledge at hand to guide without being patronizing. For example, one ASDA advisor helps put together the Easter meal and suggests attractive ways to present food prepared largely from frozen and chilled products. Cooking accessories as well as crockery, glasses, cutlery, and paper dishes are offered alongside the food products.

The ASDA advisor also helps select a range of products that might entertain your children on sunny days. Presented in a garden setting, these products include paddling pools, inflatable toys, water pistols, a badminton set, bucket and spade, space hoppers, and popular children's books.

The U.K. speakers' name badges are usually clearly visible, which enhances their trustworthiness (a concept investigated in more detail later) and contrasts with the anonymity of the consumers. Trustworthiness is further enhanced through the naturalness of the color scheme. Prominent colors in the day-to-day flyers are green, blue, and yellow (Halloween and Christmas material use more seasonal colors, such as orange and gold). Green, the dominant color associated with ASDA, is reminiscent of the origins of the company (the original name was Associated Dairies) and reflects the pastures on which cows graze. The blue is found in the clear sky and yellow in the sun. These three colors would be used by a child painting images of spring (and summer) to conjure up unspoiled freshness and nature.

Although most food products in the flyers are anything but fresh and unspoiled (frozen, chilled, canned, ready-to-heat meals, etc.), the way they are presented within the color scheme gives them a halo effect of healthiness that elevates the retailer to a genuine and trustworthy food supplier. This effect is important in the current climate of food scares, obesity concerns, and other health-related issues and may also communicate strongly with the health conscious consumer identified earlier. In sum, the U.K. ASDA advisor is an ordinary, very friendly, trustworthy, reliable, credible, knowledgeable person.

Germany

The German flyers, like their U.K. and U.S. counterparts, also clearly display names of the Wal-Mart speakers, who are identified as *Mitarbeiterin* (associates) and who appear proud to be using their employer's products (e.g., a shaver or lipstick). Heike has chestnut-colored hair, lipstick that matches her hair color, and a bright but shy smile. Her moderate self-confidence and shyness create a likeable image. A customer would feel comfortable approaching her to ask for help, and she would understand the customer's concerns.

Verena, another co-worker, looks a little more "professional." She has shining blond hair falling on her shoulders and three new but cheap and childish hair clips holding it back. Her white teeth are framed by the color of her shiny lipstick. Since she is associated with hair products, she is allowed to be prettier than average. Her eyes are warm, but she is still like the girl next door, as underlined by her simple red T-shirt. Verena, too, is very approachable.

Fred is in the bathroom shaving in front of a very simple mirrored cupboard that is standard in every ordinary household. He looks like the reliable husband in his mid-forties who gets up every day to go to work and earn the family income. His reliability is stressed by his mustache, a traditional style that not many young men would wear in Germany today. Fred looks neat and refined but is not overly stylish. He is the typical neighbor across the street who also happens to be a Wal-Mart co-worker.

Beate is in her mid-forties. Her hair is short and she has a modern, practical haircut that does not take too much effort to style. She looks deeply and openly into the reader's eyes and can immediately be trusted as someone who can be approached with questions.

In the Christmas catalogue, Wal-Mart speaks through the voice of a secret Santa. The slogan "Hier werden Kinder-Wünsche wahr" (Here children's wishes come true) directly addresses children and their parents. This invisible voice takes the reader through the leaflet: "Geschenk-Hits für die Kleinen" (top gifts for the small ones), "Ein Spielplatz voller Geschenk-Ideen" (a playground full of gift ideas), and so on. Then the speaker uses a very young person's voice: "Hier fahren kids voll drauf ab" ("Cool for kids"), which is rather colloquial German and used by kids but not by mothers or teachers.

The message is that if one just relies on "Father Wal-Mart," concerns about Christmas gifts will disappear. The illustration additionally suggests that Wal-Mart, in the shape of the secret Santa, is directly addressing children's feelings and wishes and that the speaker understands them and wants to satisfy their every desire. Everybody, including children and their parents, will be more than satisfied. Everyone can just relax. The effect is to give the flyer a likeable, personal, and pleasant touch.

In sum, the German Wal-Mart speakers are neither glamorous nor fashionable but just ordinary and average. They are supported by a seasonal character who stresses the family orientation. Similar to the U.K. speaker, this individual is friendly, likeable, approachable, helpful, reliable, and trustworthy.

China

The tone used to communicate with the audience in China is quite friendly and plain. Similar to American flyers, the language is "simple to understand, busy, talkative, and direct" (Arnold, Kozinets, and Handelman 2001: 250). Store signs and slogans invite the shopper into the store and repeat again and again that associates are always ready and willing to help. In the store itself, there are several large posters that feature Wal-Mart employees. In these posters, workers are always smiling and their gestures encourage shoppers—a female worker arranging fruits, a male worker extending his arms for a handshake, or a food worker delivering an order. They all talk in the same voice: "We are happy to help you and we are ready."

One sign reads "We provide you friendly customer service, high-quality and high-value products, choice among large varieties." Another reads "100% satisfaction is guaranteed." Still another sign suggests "Wholeheartedly serve you" and hangs in every aisle of the store as well as appearing in many other places. All these signs use the respectful form of "you," consistent with the prevailing East Asian tradition of store clerks bowing deeply to their customers. As the speaker, Wal-Mart is a humble, respectful, and eager servant—always willing and ready to help.

Summary

The Wal-Mart voice is very consistent across the three international markets and imitates the communication strategies used in American flyers. As in the United States, the Wal-Mart speaker is revealed to be respectful, helpful, approachable, pleasant, warm, and friendly. The associates/colleagues/co-workers are neither glamorous nor fashionable but quite ordinary and plainspoken. They could easily be a friendly and helpful neighbor or even a reliable and trusted friend. Knowledge, credibility, trustworthiness, and competence in their specialty areas were also apparent, and the advice of the Wal-Mart associates could be accepted with confidence.

What Are the Mythologies?

In Jakobsonian semiotics, the speaker and spoken to are treated separately from the mythologies created through language, signs, and symbols. In practice, however, mythologies are shaped largely (though not exclusively) through the narrator and addressee. This feature will become particularly apparent in the mythologies that relate to cultural/societal institutional norms prevalent in each of the markets discussed here. In the following sections, mythologies related to economic institutional norms are first considered and then followed by those related to the cultural/societal norms. As will be seen, the latter norms are more varied across the markets.

The Mythology of Homo Economicus

The mythology of *Homo economicus* is evident in the U.K., German, and Chinese artifacts (flyers and signage) and follows the pattern set in Wal-Mart's domestic market. It presses home the "everyday low prices" message and thereby directly reflects the institutional norm that when shopping for frequently purchased products shoppers want to buy them at the lowest possible prices.

United Kingdom   ASDA uses an everyday low price (EDLP) strategy and communicates it clearly in all of its flyers. Page headings such as "A feast of Easter value" and "Party food at prices to celebrate" not only refer to the seasonality of the Easter flyer but also harness the price message, otherwise more directly advertised in other flyers as "Biggest ever price cuts with Rollback" or "Unbeatable prices."

The ASDA EDLP strategy is also supported by a sophisticated array of price labels, which invariably draw the reader's attention to the low-price strategy. A very common label is "Price rollback," which is signaled by a white square with rounded edges. A green and yellow stripe appears at the top of the label and has the rollback script superimposed (inclusive of the smiley face). In the white field, the old price is struck out in black and the new price printed in bold black figures. If the saving goes beyond a one-digit amount (e.g., "SAVE 21p") the old price is struck out in red, and the saving printed in white on a red stripe at the bottom of the square.

The label "That's ASDA Price" replays a slogan familiar to British consumers through a long-running television commercial. The consumer, usually a young to middle-aged female shopper, but at times also an associate, pats a rear trouser pocket. Clinking coins can be heard accompanied by the "That's ASDA Price" jingle. Visually, the slogan is portrayed on a white square containing at the top "That's" on a broad, slightly curved green stripe. Below the stripe is a chunky green downward-pointing arrow displaying "ASDA Price" and reminding the reader of the ASDA pressure on prices. The price is displayed again in bold black print.

The "Outstanding value" label is white lettering on a bright red background positioned on the right side of a red-and-white oblong. The left side of the oblong is white with red writing and states the price of a single bottle of a beer multipack ("Less than 42p per bottle!") or the price of one glass of an aptly named Smartprice set of four wineglasses ("only 22p per glass").

"! WOW !" is still another price label and is presented in white capital letters surrounded by two yellow exclamation marks. This text is set against a red background and sticks out of the white square price tag, seeming to astonish the reader with yet another price surprise.

Germany   German flyers similarly suggest that adhering to the norm of low prices is Wal-Mart's most important goal. The overall headline is "Wal-Mart. Die Preise bleiben unten. Immer!" This heading is directly carried over from the American flyers ("Wal*Mart. Always low prices. Always Wal*Mart. Always"). Although the style of the letters is different, the colors are the same—white on blue with "Always" in yellow. The effect is to put the Wal-Mart EDLP strategy in the headline of each flyer. With this message, Wal-Mart differentiates itself from other German retailers who instead conduct weekly sales.

Low prices are also clearly communicated in German flyers through use of a number of different price categories characterized by different colors and/or symbols: "Spar noch mehr" (Save even more) is primarily green with the bargain price and the regular price in bold black numbers on a white background. Underneath is the date after which this sale price will expire. "Sonderposten" (Special buy, running out of stock) is a yellow category. Underneath this label is the information that the price will continue as long the item is in stock (suggesting customers are running out of time to make the purchase). "Roll back" is in red and the *o* is a smiley. Again, the price is in bold black letters on a white background and underneath it is the date when the price was rolled back. "Immer Niedrigpreis" (Always low price) is a blue category. As blue is the overall color of Wal-Mart, it makes sense to use it for the "typical" prices, which are "always" low.

One remarkable table directly addresses the norm of *Homo economicus*. It is titled "Euro oder Teuro," alluding to the debate in Germany of perceived and actual price increases after the introduction of the euro in 2002. Consumers perceived that prices had gone up considerably, which was caused by the practices of several retailers who converted two deutsche marks into one euro. German consumers felt betrayed and reacted by refusing to buy. The table compares 2004 Wal-Mart prices in euros to prices in deutsche marks before the advent of the single currency. Eight items are selected (butter, milk, eggs, beer, coffee, toilet paper, toothpaste, and bananas), displaying the prices before and after the conversion of the old currency into euros, which resulted in a cumulative 9.4 percent cost reduction. This reduction compares favorably with those shown for six other stores (Aldi, Lidl, Plus, Extra, Norma, and Edeka).

One slogan states "Preisgarantie—Markenartikel woanders günstiger? Wir geben Ihnen den gleichen Preis" (Price guarantee—branded product cheaper elsewhere? We offer you the same price). This is an interesting statement because it implicitly acknowledges that another retailer may have lower prices. Wal-Mart would never make this statement in America because it would not entertain the possibility that another retailer has lower prices. The heritage of founder Sam Walton is that a Wal-Mart associate checks prices of frequently purchased goods at other retailers and then reduces the Wal-Mart price to match even if it is below cost. In Germany, below-cost pricing is illegal, and as competitors such as Aldi offer goods just above cost or at cost, Wal-Mart has not been able to achieve the image of the lowest-price store and to effectively communicate the mythology of *Homo economicus*.

China   Similar to the United States, United Kingdom, and Germany, the mythology of *Homo economicus* is well told in China. With symbols and phrases associated with different products, the Wal-Mart store demonstrates its adherence to the economic norm of low prices. For instance, the Wal-Mart has a large board at one entrance with detailed descriptions of six different signs. Except for one ("New items"), the other five are all related to saving money or getting more for less. "Special buy" lets customers know there is only a limited supply. "My recommendation" indicates that some of the store's managers believe the product to be of especially high value. "Wow, more value for the money" is self-explanatory.

The two most often seen signs in Wal-Mart are the blue "Wholeheartedly *save money for you*" and the red and yellow "*Giving back profit*—try as much as possible to save money for you." The italic type reflects Chinese characters on the sign in a larger font, which emphasizes the economic concepts of money and profit. All of these signs convey the same message to customers: "Wal-Mart is the right place to go. We like to save money, just as you do."

Besides the store decorations, Wal-Mart shopping bags also feature a smiley face that says "Everyday low prices." Since many Wal-Mart customers get to Wal-Mart by foot, bike, or bus, shopping bags are highly visible to the public. In this sense, they become moving mini-billboards that tell people about Wal-Mart—it has a low price and can save you money. Similarly, each receipt is printed with: "Everyday low price, from the beginning to the end."

The Mythology of Credibility

The need to establish credibility, although not overtly addressed in Wal-Mart's U.S. flyers, can be observed in all three of the international markets studied here. For example, headlines in the U.K. flyers claim that Wal-Mart is "Britain's lowest-priced supermarket" and "officially Britain's lowest-priced supermarket for the 7th year." The credibility of these claims is supported by references to an independent industry survey conducted by *The Grocer*, the country's leading trade magazine for food retailing. The layout and setup of an accompanying table also look very scientific, suggesting trustworthiness of the company.

In a similar manner, assertions regarding Wal-Mart's emphasis on low prices in the German flyers are supported by footnotes, similar to those found in a scholarly publication. In another instance, the believability of the low-price claim is supported by a miniature-format reprint of an article to this effect published previously in a local newspaper.

In China, credibility is also important, especially considering the prevalence of counterfeit products (Floum 1994) and false advertising (Peerenboom 1995). Two social norms in the Chinese society are attention to hierarchy and respect for authority—especially governmental authority (Fiske 1992; Ralston et al. 1993; Smith, Dugan, and Trompenaars 1996; Lodge and Vogel 1987). Thus, the Wal-Mart Supercenter in Dalian invokes the approval of government authority to establish its credibility. Many banners labeled "worry-free food" in the food section of the Dalian store are signed by Dalian city government officials. Also in the same store are many "100% satisfaction guaranteed" signs embedded in a round design in red, which resembles the traditional round red seal that serves as a symbol of official approval in China. The omnipresence of this sign in the store, such as on windows, walls, and cashiers' counters further strengthens the impression that Wal-Mart defers to government authority. This practice conforms to the Chinese cultural norm of respect for governmental authority and contrasts with the antistatist stance reflected in the Wal-Mart flyers in the United States.

To this point, the search for mythologies in flyers and signage has produced categories that are related to economic institutional norms. The remaining sections consider the societal/cultural norms, including the norms of family, community, patriotism and racial tolerance.

The Mythology of Family

The mythology of the family so strongly portrayed in Wal-Mart's U.S. advertising is found in all international markets. The most overt message is expressed in German Wal-Mart flyers, where most products are designed or put together in order to fit family demands. Pictures show mainly family members. A "cozy" household is reflected in "kuschelige Heimdecken" (cuddly blankets), fuzzy slippers, cozy fleece loungewear, terry-cloth pajamas, flannel shirts, and other items labeled as "100% cotton" or "soft touch" (evoking care for the family). This coziness is underlined by background shades of red, blue, and green, which start dark at one side and fade into lighter shades at the other corner of the page. Warm colors are also reflected in the products themselves.

Germany   The mythology of family is also represented in German flyers in a very traditional portrayal of mother and child at home with the father at work. This family consists of a young, good-looking mother who appears to have plenty of time to teach and talk to her children. If the children are at school, the mother can spend her free time wrapping gifts or writing cards bought at Wal-Mart. The smart and good-looking mothers shown here seem completely happy with doing domestic tasks.

The overall mythology clearly idealizes a content family life. Happy, relaxed mothers seem to live in a world free of work, stress, or crying children. In the German Wal-Mart world, women have time to concentrate on their offspring. They are not portrayed as bored housewives who never get out of their house (even though it is in their house where they are exclusively portrayed). For instance, Lena is sitting on a comfortable, big chair with her little daughter Marlena on her lap. They are reading a children's book together. Julia is happily watching her son Rasmus playing with a model railway. She looks relaxed, not stressed, and content with what she and her children are doing. It is the naturalness, the peacefulness, and the happiness being communicated that idealize family life. Having the mother and her children speak in the Wal-Mart flyer may persuade other consumers to try Wal-Mart for the sake of a peaceful family life.

Many children of customers are displayed in the flyers. They communicate feelings of happiness, contentment, and freedom from worries. Cute little Sophia with blond curls, blue eyes, and a pink shirt is riding a rocking horse that sits on a cozy wool carpet. She, like other children in these kinds of families, does not cause stress or chaos. They whisper: "Shop for us! Buy these products—or do you not want to make us happy?" It is hard to resist this call.

In the apparel section of the flyer are six good-looking teenagers wearing sporting gear. These teenagers are young, polite, well-educated, and dress well, play sports, and help their mother with chores. The male teenagers are clean-shaven except one who is demonstrating his week's growth of beard. They have no facial blemishes and display no signs of rebelling against the adult world even though they are in the midst of adolescence. This picture reflects the ideal family as well.

The happy-family message is further strengthened in the Christmas flyer, where Christmas symbolizes family life. Here, children are shown happily playing with their toys and presented in an orderly line according to their age, from baby Lily followed by Stella, Jan, Laura, Marie, Maximilian, Alexander, Johanna, and fourteen-year-old Alex.

This Christmas theme, symbolizing family life, is carefully introduced without being too dominant, as Christmas is still seven weeks away. Hints of Christmas are spread over almost every illustration—branches of a Christmas tree in the background of a room, a Christmas star decoration placed casually beside a table lamp, a fir branch lying on the floor behind a teddy bear in Laura's room, and two Christmas stars decorating the table in Maximilian and Alexander's room. These hidden signs subconsciously take the reader into the Christmas feeling, the joy of every family.

Men, however, are nearly absent in the Wal-Mart families. Adult men are shown either alone or with a female partner. No men are seen with children. The man's world seems to have nothing to do with family life except that he is earning the money to be able to purchase the products displayed.

Almost all male Wal-Mart employees displayed in the different flyers are either presenting clothes or technical equipment. No man is shown in a food section or among cleaning supplies, again supporting a traditional male-female division of labor. This traditional definition of gender roles is further perpetuated in games the children play. Boys are playing with model railways and cars while girls are huddling with their mothers and playing with their dolls.

The United Kingdom   The direct communication in the German flyers with women and children in a family context differs from the covert inferences of family life in the ASDA flyers in the United Kingdom. Here, the family meal, the children's paddling pool complete with toys, the school uniforms on happy-looking youngsters, and cute toddlers sporting children's wear all evoke family life without actually naming or displaying it. The closest illustration to a family scene is depicted in the Christmas catalogue, where two children clothed in fancy dress (a girl in an angel's outfit and another child in Spiderman pajamas) pose in front of a Christmas tree.

China   With the materials available for analysis in the China market, it was not possible to identify the mythology of family as it is presented in the U.S., German, or U.K. flyers. However, one of the commonly accepted institutional norms regulating Chinese interpersonal relationships is loosely related to the mythology of family. This norm is known as *renqing,* which is best translated as "humanized obligation," or interpersonal obligation with a sentimental touch (Chen 1995). Chinese people adhere to *renqing* through well-scripted social practices such as offering compliments, congratulations and condolences, and exchanging favors and gifts in appropriate forms and on suitable occasions (Hwang 1987; Yang 1994). The norm of *renqing* prescribes the obligations people owe to others with whom they are connected in some way. *Renqing* is not unlike the U.S. expression of the family mythology with terms such as *warmth, loyalty, commitment,* and *obligation.* The difference is that in the United States, loyalty and obligation are owed to nuclear family, but in China, such consideration is also extended to loosely defined "family," including extended family, neighbors, and friends.

At the Dalian Wal-Mart, two of the most visible signs have the words "for you," which makes the relationship between Wal-Mart and customers active and two-way. In store pictures, people are portrayed smiling and performing helping gestures, which create feelings of friendliness or neighborliness in contrast to an unconnected, mechanical-seeming store clerk.

There were also many small signs in the store that do not specifically address the store or products (e.g., "Leisure time in May" and "Happy summer holidays"). These smaller signs usually have bright colors and lovely scenes. Together with some balloons and ribbons hanging from the ceiling, they create a very busy atmosphere. This may fit the Chinese preference for being "hot and noisy" in family gatherings and celebrations.

The mythology of family has varying prominence in the German, U.K., and China Wal-Mart images, although they are all related to either the nuclear or extended family. In contrast, the American flyers broaden the understanding of family to include "the family of Wal-Mart associates." This image is evoked through the naming of all characters and an explanation of their interrelationships and job functions within Wal-Mart. It is a feature uniquely applied to the company's domestic market, linked to the cultural/societal norm of community, and more specifically captured in the mythology of community, discussed in the next section.

The Mythology of Community

Wal-Mart has always tried to build up its image as a community member in its domestic U.S. market. In a reflection of its small-town origins, it wishes to be perceived as a responsible member of the town or city in which it resides. Different social actors in the institutional environment (such as customers, citizens, and suppliers) all have votes in determining whether the store meets the community norms before they give it the support needed for survival. However, these norms do not stretch beyond the immediate community, as there are no references to fair trade, fair employment, ethical trading, environmental consciousness, and the like.

The same ideal was brought to China as well—to be a community member and participate in community improvement. To reflect this mythology, the Wal-Mart Supercenter in Dalian has signs in the store that are related to community involvement. Pictures with descriptions of Wal-Mart's support of education, protection of the environment, and disaster relief are hung above cashiers' counters. A donation box for Project Hope (a foundation to help Chinese children who cannot afford to pay for tuition, books, and school supplies) is installed at every cashier's counter.

In the German flyers, the community norm is addressed through a note on the last page informing the reader that the flyer is printed on 100 percent recycled paper. This obviously refers to the importance of environmental issues and recycling initiatives, in which Germany has taken a worldwide lead. However, this reference must bemuse German readers, as all retail and other commercial flyers are printed on recycled paper and consumers would not expect anything else. It thus feels that Wal-Mart is paying lip service to an important community norm, an observation supported by other Wal-Mart actions that contradict the environmental message. For example, Wal-Mart tries to appeal to the mythology of *Homo economicus* by advertising free (plastic) shopping bags. This action contrasts with that of other grocery stores, which for a long time have charged around €0,25 per bag because the bags are considered to contribute to environmental pollution. Furthermore, many retailers offer reusable cloth bags that are sometimes marketed as a special contribution to environmental awareness. In fact, the future of disposable plastic bags is under discussion in several European countries.

More generally, Wal-Mart does not appear to show any environmental consciousness in Germany. There is almost a complete absence of references to products that would be considered environmentally friendly (e.g., organic or healthy foods).

In the U.K. flyers, no direct or indirect reference to community can be detected, although the company is emphasizing community relations by supporting local as well as national charities and sponsoring, for example, local school activities (such as providing free use of a minivan for a year).

The mythology of community is closely linked to the mythologies of patriotism and racial tolerance, as shown in the next two sections.

The Mythology of Patriotism

Patriotism, loyalty and devotion to one's country were apparent in the U.S. flyer (flag displays, military heritage, "Made in the USA" signs) and were also apparent in the Chinese Wal-Mart store. In 2002, the Chinese soccer team got a chance to play in the World Cup tournament for the first time ever. The big victory sign between the characters that make up the name "China" and the soccer banners with messages "Cheers for soccer, cheers for China" are all indications of Wal-Mart's adherence to the patriotism norm. The color red, found in the Chinese flag, folklore, and religious shrines, meaning luck and happiness, is also the color of the Wal-Mart Supercenter sign and many other store signs.

With some exceptions, there are few signs of overt patriotism in Germany and the United Kingdom. In Germany, displays of patriotism are considered counterproductive given historical circumstances. Symbols of America are not very fashionable either, and so there are only very subtle hints to symbols of the United States. One example is a cartoon-like blue star with white arms and eyes and red hands and mouth. This mascot talks to the reader as it variously sits on top of sausages, pops up behind a computer screen, sends greetings from behind a package of prepared food, or has its thumbs up behind a case of beer. This mascot is recognized as symbolizing both the star in the "Wal*Mart" logo as well as the star in the American flag, but Wal-Mart minimizes and plays down what is otherwise a symbol of American patriotism. They make it cute, like a toy, reminding the reader only at the subconscious level of the "friendly" American nation. In this way, as the company speaks, the reader is guided through products without feeling dominated or led.

In the United Kingdom, a display of the Union Jack would not be unopposed in Edinburgh or Cardiff, hence overt patriotic symbols are avoided. The only potential for a patriotic interpretation in U.K. flyers is to make such a reading based upon the ubiquitous school uniforms found in the flyer illustrations, with their red, white, and blue color schemes.

The Mythology of Racial Tolerance

The presence of Nav, a member of an ethnic minority, in the U.K. ASDA flyer could suggest an attempt to adhere to a multicultural society's norm of racial tolerance. However, Nav is the only adult in the flyers who does not look white. There is a puzzling lack of people from different ethnic backgrounds, and the singular presence of Nav does not represent the racial diversity of the United Kingdom. Could Nav's appearance be tokenism, a subtle form of racism?

Nav is also standing in front of cleaning products (Dettol is clearly visible) in a two-page section of the flyer that advertises detergents and other household cleaning items. His position in the cleaning product section creates stereotypical links between ethnic minority groups and cleaning jobs. It is a rather odd combination, again either pointing to hidden racism or a faux pas that cannot be explained away.

The other adult models in the ASDA illustrations are white. Among the children, a cute little black girl stands out, and there is some racial diversity among the children in school uniforms. This racial balance is similar to the American Wal-Mart flyer, which portrays one black adult female and a couple of young black sisters. The curious element of the adult female is that she is seated below a white woman who has her hand on the black woman's shoulder.

The response by Wal-Mart to the mythology of racial tolerance in Germany is similar to that found in the United Kingdom. Almost all of the models/customers shown are white, presumably German. There is hardly any reference made to Germany's multicultural society. In all analyzed flyers there is only one picture with three girls/young women of mixed ethnic background: Marie seems to be Asian (while the name is not) and Luanda is of African heritage. They are wearing summer dresses. The other non-German person is nameless—he is of darker color and is advertising underwear. His muscular body contrasts with the ordinary people portrayed in other parts of the German flyer and in the American flyer as well, and he may be a professional model. This underlying ignorance of Germany's multiculturalism is both surprising and annoying.

Neither is racial diversity reflected in the Chinese Wal-Mart store signage. However, it does reflect the homogeneous nature of the Chinese population in the coastal region where Dalian is located.

Conclusions

The preceding analysis identified both similarities and differences across the four markets in the mythologies and associated institutional norms being expressed in Wal-Mart flyers and signage. It is not surprising that the mythology of *Homo economicus* is expressed in every market, as everyday low prices are Wal-Mart's raison d'être. Thus, the virtues of thrift and smart shopping are championed by Wal-Mart with its slogans about low prices and price rollbacks and its repetitive use of words such as *value, save, savings, cheap, cheaper, bargain, special, less, only, cuts, unbeatable, wow,* and *multi-buys* (e.g., "Any 3 for £2.50"). Also similar to the U.S. practice is the use of various low-price categories marked by differentiated typefaces, colors, and symbols.

Only in Wal-Mart's German flyers is there evidence that the mythology of *Homo economicus* could not be fully realized. On the contrary, the price guarantee statement found there is an implicit acknowledgment that another retailer might have lower prices.

Common to the United Kingdom, Germany, and China is Wal-Mart's use of credible outside sources to support its claim of being the cheapest or most reliable supermarket. This use of an outside testimonial is absent in Wal-Mart's domestic U.S. market, perhaps because of the long-standing reputation it has enjoyed for low prices. The specific outside sources used to create credibility, however, differ across the three foreign markets. Nongovernment sources and symbols, such as trade magazines, daily newspapers, scientific procedures, and icons, are invoked in the United Kingdom and German Wal-Mart flyers. In China, "worry-free food" Wal-Mart banners signed by the Dalian city government and "100% satisfaction guaranteed" signs resemble official red seals. These varying practices seem to reflect Wal-Mart's understanding of the differences across various institutional environments in what is perceived to be a credible source. In China, authorities are considered more credible and trustworthy. In Europe, scientific communities and experts are viewed by Wal-Mart to be credible sources.

The American mythology of family and associated norms of caring and commitment are apparent in German and Chinese Wal-Mart advertising. In the German market, like its U.S. counterpart, Wal-Mart uses a traditional gender role depiction, with mother and child interacting at home while the working father is absent. There are many happy and cute children and teens in these households. The idealized at-home American and German family life contrasts with the household represented in ASDA flyers in the United Kingdom, with busy parents who work outside the home. Interestingly, there is in fact a very insignificant difference among the three countries in women's labor force participation rate. Among women twenty-five to fifty-four years of age, in the United States 74 percent are employed, in the United Kingdom the figure is 73 percent, and 71 percent in Germany (*OECD Employment Outlook* 2002).

The China mythology of *renqing* is closest to the American mythology of family when the emphasis is upon obligation and loyalty. Common to these mythologies is the connectedness of individuals involved and its expression most often in family circumstances. Despite the multiracial character of American and U.K. Wal-Mart flyers, arguments could be made for a hidden racism in some of the illustrations in those flyers as well as in those from Germany.

While thrift norms expressed in the U.S. flyer are also present in its U.K. counterparts, the U.K. flyers also reflect the appearance of aspiration to upward mobility through display of style and sophistication at low cost. In U.K. flyers, outdoor furniture set with wine, cheese, and grapes invoke an association with stately homes and gardens. There is no evidence of such aspiration in American flyers. Differences in this respect seemingly contradict the commonly held notion that the United States is the embodiment of meritocracy and social mobility and the antithesis of the rigid class system of the Old World. However, there is growing evidence suggesting that the extent of class saliency and barriers to social mobility in the United States is no less than many other rich countries, including the United Kingdom and Germany (e.g., Solon 2004; Vanneman 1980).

American mythologies of patriotism and community displayed in Wal-Mart's domestic flyer are also quite apparent in China, where the Wal-Mart sign resembles China's red flag. In the store, signs give the message "Cheers for China" and advocate support of a foundation to help Chinese children with the costs of going to school.

In contrast to American flyers and the China signage, there is no overt mythology of patriotism in German and U.K. flyers. There is also no hint of community support or community involvement in these countries, nor is any hometown ideology communicated. Since patriotism has a very different meaning in the German society than in the United States, it would not be appropriate to show patriotic signs in stores or flyers. Hardly anybody would use the German flag or its colors—red, yellow, and black—for decoration, as it is simply not appropriate. In general, the only occasion when pride in Germany or in being German is shown is when quality needs to be emphasized (e.g., German cars, German technique). However, since high quality is not a special characteristic of Wal-Mart or Wal-Mart products, the flyers do not need to emphasize the German colors. In fact, the only hint of patriotism in German flyers is of American patriotism, in the playful use of the blue star mascot that evokes the American flag.

In the analysis it was apparent that the Wal-Mart speaker has a varying voice across the four markets studied: the United States, United Kingdom, Germany, and China. Actions taken to represent the mythologies of *Homo economicus* and family share a high degree of similarity, but those reflective of the mythologies of community and nation do not. Furthermore, there is some variance in the addressee of Wal-Mart's communications—the Wal-Mart flyers would suggest, for example, that British shoppers aspire to upward mobility and the Chinese respect power and authority. In other words, Wal-Mart is attempting to adapt its U.S.-grown competency to gain legitimacy in different countries with their different institutional environments.

Given the analysis presented above, Wal-Mart's advertising adaptation to the German market has been less thoughtful than that in the United Kingdom and China. In German Wal-Mart flyers there was an inappropriate identification of customers by their first names, an absence of any reference to Germany's multicultural society, an inability to imply it is the lowest-priced retailer, a failure to reflect the important German norm of quality and reliability, and paying only "lip service" to environmental consciousness.

Other studies also suggest that Wal-Mart is less successful in Germany as well (Fernie and Arnold 2002; Burt and Sparks 2001; Knorr and Arndt 2003).

As noted in the introduction, one motivation for this article was a desire to better understand the process of internationalization and why one same company can succeed in some markets and struggle in others. The answer is that even in markets with the same language and historical cultural affinity, there can be quite different institutional environments, not only between markets (e.g., the United States versus the United Kingdom) but also within them (e.g., England vs. Scotland vs. Wales vs. Northern Ireland). Furthermore, as Wal-Mart traverses languages and increasingly different cultures (from the United States to the United Kingdom, Germany, China, and elsewhere), the differences and challenges are multiplied, and no one individual or retailer can appreciate all the subtleties of these different environments. This reality suggests that the key to success in the international arena is to fully engage a multinational, multicultural team, as is demonstrated in the authorship of this article. Furthermore, the process of institutional semiotics appears to provide a helpful common language through which team members can engage in a productive discussion.

Note

1. The economic success of Wal-Mart in Germany compared with other retailers has been analyzed in Ulrike Gerhard and Barbara Hahn: Wal-Mart and Aldi: Two Retail Giants in Germany, *GeoJournal* (2005) 62: 15-26; Ulrike Gerhard and Steve Arnold (2006): Konsumentenverhalten im internationalen Vergleich. Ein Beitrag zur Institutionentheorie, *Berichte zur deutschen Landeskunde* 80, 2 (forthcoming) and an article by Elke Pioch on the economic success of retailers in Great Britain in the same journal.

12

Cathedrals of Consumption: A Political Phenomenology of Wal-Mart

Barney Warf and Thomas Chapman

> Our total objective should be to serve our customers every time they are in our store and make their shopping experience enjoyable. Remember, they are our guests.
>
> Sam Walton

Wal-Mart is more than the world's largest retail chain, more than a convenient place to buy cheap goods: it is also a site of consumerist culture, a locale in which commodities become embedded in human consciousness. Every week, 138 million shoppers visit Wal-Mart's 4,750 stores worldwide. In 2002, 82 percent of American households made at least one purchase at Wal-Mart (Bianco 2003). Four out of ten American women shop at Wal-Mart weekly (Featherstone 2002). The average American family spends $1,100 annually at Wal-Mart (Norman 1999). To understand Wal-Mart's popularity as America's favorite shopping destination, it is essential to understand consumers' views of the store and their motivations and experiences—how they worship at what Kowinski (1985) calls "cathedrals of consumption." Wal-Mart's style of presentation and accessibility meshes seamlessly into the exceptionally intense consumerism of American culture ("shop till you drop"), sustaining and deepening it, while the chain's global operations export this culture along with the goods they sell (Figure 12.1). Yet Wal-Mart is also a form of politics. With its roots in Arkansas dating back to 1945, Wal-Mart has long held to a deeply conservative corporate philosophy that is, among other things, religious and virulently antiunion (Vance and Scott 1992, 1994). However, Wal-Mart's politics are often subtle and difficult for shoppers to discern, which makes them all the more insidious and in urgent need of decoding.

This chapter offers an applied phenomenology of Wal-Mart. Phenomenology is an old and respected philosophical tradition, extending to such notables as Husserl and Heidegger, that is concerned with what it means to be human, the nature of human consciousness, the shape of human experience, and the ways people derive and give meaning to and from their environments. Phenomenologists emphasize that social reality is always and inescapably a lived experience for someone, and must necessarily be understood through the lens of human subjectivity. Departing from the notion of objectivity, phenomenology focuses on the question of human consciousness and interpretation. Within geography, this tradition has been largely concerned with the semiotics of place, the ways in which people give meanings to their everyday worlds, and the intangible qualities of particular areas. Human consciousness—in all its messy complexity—both is shaped by particular environments and in turn shapes those contexts; space and discourse are shot through with each other. Unlike much conventional phenomenology, the approach adopted here is explicitly political, that is, it is concerned with the ways in which human subjectivity is filled with power (Warf 1986). While this line of thought has often been interpreted as having little practical or pragmatic application, in fact it opens numerous avenues through which

Figure 12.1   Wal-Mart's world (reproduced with permission of artist Ron Zalme).

a topic such as Wal-Mart may be understood. Phenomenology provides an avenue to explore the significance of large retailers such as Wal-Mart in their clients' daily life worlds. This approach is quite different from conventional geographical accounts of the geography of Wal-Mart (Vance and Scott 1992, 1994; Graf 1994, 1998), which tend to be empiricist in nature.

The argument and evidence here are organized through the following sections. First, the chapter offers a background of major lines of thought concerned with the social significance and meaning of the commodity, including Marx's notion of commodity fetishism, Walter Benjamin's Arcades Project, Ritzer's process of McDonaldization, Baudrillard's simulacra, and contemporary applications to the study of shopping malls. Second, the chapter addresses the semiotics of Wal-Mart, drawing upon fieldwork and interviews to explicate the multiple meanings that the store has for the multitudes that pass through its doors. Third, it explores the reality behind Wal-Mart's imagery, including its advertising and ways of presenting itself to consumers with celebrity endorsements. Wal-Mart presents itself as a value-neutral, apolitical retail outlet. Yet upon deeper study, Wal-Mart's public image is carefully crafted, and its image management contains a deeply conservative politics that infiltrates consumers' impressions. Thus, far from simply being a store, Wal-Mart is also a moral universe external to the commodity.

The Commodity as a Bundle of Signs

Any journey into Wal-Mart brings to mind (at least to the critically informed observer) a variety of theoretical positions that can be used to interpret the complex meanings that swirl within the store's environs. Such an exercise, of course, is equally applicable to other sites of mass consumption such as shopping malls, fast-food outlets, grocery stores, and large franchised stores, although Wal-Mart's fame and scale generate a unique experience. The sterile, ahistorical view of neoclassical economists, in which customers maximize utility in the face of Wal-Mart's intimidating array of goods, offers one limited avenue into this question but fails to do justice to the rich semiotics and social dimensions of the store's culture. Drawing upon the work of numerous sociologists, historians, philosophers, and anthropologists, geographers have engaged in several lines of thought that suture commodities to their social and spatial origins. Rather than a simple act of utility maximization, as represented by neoclassical economics, this body of work points to shopping and consumption as social and spatial practices that emanate from, and in turn reinforce, existing structures of power, culture, and ideology.

One of the earliest and most influential interpretations of commodities came from Marx, who argued that social science must penetrate the veneer of outer appearances to reveal the social relations that lie beneath them. In this vein, Marx argued that commodities are not simply *things* but embodiments of social relations. Marx's discussion of commodity fetishism argued that the opaqueness by which market relations obscure relations among producers is functional for capitalism. Commodity fetishism abstracts commodities from their social context and (re)presents them as purely market-based phenomena. Marx (1976: 73, 75) argues that the social character of labor appears as an objective, given nature of products:

> The relations connecting the labour of one individual with that of the rest appear, not as direct social relations between individuals at work, but as what they really are, material relations between persons and social relations between things.... To [producers], their own social action takes the form of the action of objects, which rule the producers instead of being ruled by them.

In highly individualized societies such as the United States, much personal status is achieved through the consumption of commodities. Indeed, self-identity and even self-esteem are frequently linked to owning the "right" brands of goods. The exorbitant cost of Nike shoes, for example, serves to make this point. In such a context, it is the symbolic value of goods that is of primary importance. So naturalized has the culture of commodities become in American culture (especially) that it is often difficult for many people to think of the world in any other way. Class, for example, is typically conceived in terms of relations to consumption rather than relations to production.

In the same vein as the Frankfurt School, these issues were interpreted creatively by the cultural theorist Walter Benjamin, who extended historical materialism to include the bourgeois infatuation with the commodity (Buck-Morss 1989). Working in the highly charged and creative atmosphere of Paris and Berlin in the 1920s, Benjamin's Arcades Project examined the linkages between the urban environment, experience, history, and memory (Savage 2000), portraying cities as labyrinths in which individual subjectivity was swept aside by the tsunami of modernity and its impersonal relations, bureaucracies, and markets. Perception, Benjamin maintained, was itself historically specific. Commodities, in this reading, were far more than embodiments of labor power—they were visual aesthetics with powers above and beyond the narrow realm of the economic. He deconstructed commodity fetishism, revealing that commodities are distillations of signs as much as they are embodiments of use and exchange values. For example, he argued that objects possess specific "auras," or meanings that could not be readily replicated through mechanical reproduction such as photography, that is, an authenticity that mass production and consumption ignored or demolished. In Gregory's (1994: 231) words, Benjamin attempted to represent "the cultural landscape of nineteenth-century Paris (and, by extension, Europe) as a *phantasmagoria*" or painted lantern, that is, a projection of signs (cf. Cohen 1989). Benjamin's Arcades Project thus captured the "scopic regime" of modernity, the deep linkages between seeing (and knowing), on one hand, and money and the commodity, on the other. This step effectively opened up the analysis of consumption as social process, noting its mounting autonomy from production and the pervasive role of symbols in the construction and manipulation of consumer consciousness.

Ritzer's well-known book *The McDonaldization of Society* (2000) approaches mass production and consumption as extensions of Weber's theory of rationalization. In this reading, the capitalist division of labor creates an increasingly secular and efficient means of organizing people, goods, and information through markets and bureaucracies. Far from simply a means of making work more productive, rationalization becomes the overarching principle that guides all other spheres of activity, including entertainment, education, health care, and consumption. Central to this process is the drive to make all activities more scientific, streamlined, predictable, standardized, and impersonal, characteristics epitomized in McDonald's and the fast-food industry in general. In the calculus of McDonaldization, quantity matters more than quality, and uniformity and cost control loom as more significant than individuality or aesthetics. Wal-Mart, in this light, is simply an extended outcome of a much broader process with deep roots in the very structure of capitalism, particularly its more nakedly consumerist American variant.

Geographers have addressed issues of consumption and the semiotics of place in a variety of ways. Drawing on the inspirational work of Yi-Fu Tuan and the notion of sense of place (1976, 1977), early phenomenologists in the discipline, such as Relph (1976), distinguished between "authentic" and "inauthentic" senses of place. An authentic sense is "not mediated and distorted through a series of quite arbitrary social and intellectual fashions about how the experience should be, nor following stereotypical conventions" (Peet 1998: 50). Whereas the construction of an authentic sense of place takes time and effort, the processes of homogenization and alienation characteristic of mass production and consumption generate inauthentic senses of place that are not personally constructed but passively consumed. The growth of shopping malls, franchises, and other outlets of mass consumption contribute to the explosion of placelessness, which Relph defines as "the casual eradication of distinctive places and the making of standardized landscapes that results from insensitivity to the significance of place" (Relph 1976: preface).

Retail trade, a topic long dominated by empiricist approaches, has come into its own through the lens of political economy (e.g., Hallsworth 1992). By embedding this sector within wider circles of finance, investment, trade, and consumption, this literature notes the ways in which globalization has unleashed a tidal wave of cheap imports that has propelled the high rates of consumer spending in societies such as the United States, a phenomenon in which Wal-Mart lies at the very center. Moreover, this body of work has pointed to shopping as a multidimensional experience tied to dominant norms of status as defined through material possessions. Even within the generally conservative literature on consumer research, phenomenological methods have widened the understanding of shopping from a simple decision to choose among goods to include hitherto ignored sensory, aesthetic, and emotional dimensions of consumption (Holbrook and Hirschman 1982; Murray and Ozanne 1991; Thompson, Locander, and Pollio 1989, 1990). What one may call the "sensuous" nature of consumption thus includes the complex social and psychological motivations that underpin the urge to buy, including consumers' ego, sense of self, status definition, and alleged individuality that comes from the purchase of mass-produced commodities.

In similar fashion, but with more attention to the social and spatial relations that underlie consumption, there has emerged a literature on the geography of shopping malls. Goss (1993, 1999), for example, writes of megamalls such as the Mall of America in Bloomington, Minnesota, which has 520 stores, chapels, a roller coaster, an aquarium, and a rain forest. In this environment, fantasy, fun, and the commodity are merged into a seamless whole. Similarly, Hopkins (1990) describes the world's largest mall, West Edmonton Mall in Edmonton, Canada: completed in 1986, it employs 18,000 people in 600 stores, a fourth of the total retail space of the city, and boasts a water park, an aquarium, an ice skating rink, a mini-golf course, a roller coaster, 19 movie theaters, a 360-room hotel, and streets replicating the French Quarter of New Orleans.

These observations mesh well with the astute critique of contemporary capitalism offered by Baudrillard (1998), who paved new roads into the understanding of the postmodern political economy of signs. For Baudrillard, the mass media have made the sign more important than its referents, creating a world of simulacra, in which we can no longer distinguish between simulations and reality, between "true" and "false." Thus, pseudo-Irish bars are more "Irish" than the "real" Ireland. Baudrillard's dissection of Disney World and its "Main Street" reveals it to be just such a simulacrum, with Epcot offering stereotypical representations of various world cultures that for many people are more "real" than the countries they purport to represent. Disney World is at its heart a giant shopping mall, and for Baudrillard (1988), the United States is essentially Disney World writ large. Television carries this process of abstraction to new heights, reflecting and shaping the material world in complex and highly stylized ways.

More recently, geographers have generated a considerable literature on the spatiality of consumption and retailing (Fine 1995; Bell and Valentine 1997; Clarke 2000; Hartwick 2000; Clarke and Purvis 1994). This body of work, typically informed by political economy, traces the nature of global commodity chains (Gereffi and Korzeniewicz 1994), which link producers and buyers through complex, contingent lines of causality across multiple spatial scales. Such a perspective reveals consumption as being simultaneously an economic, cultural, psychological, and environmental act that reproduces both the most abstract space, the global economy, and the most intimate, the individual subject and body (Crewe and Lowe 1995; Valentine 1999).

Inside Wal-Mart's World of Signs

> Give me a W!
> Give me an A!
> Give me an L!
> Give me a squiggly!
> Give me an M!
> Give me an A!
> Give me an R!
> Give me a T!
> What's that spell?
> Wal-Mart!
> Whose Wal-Mart is it?
> My Wal-Mart!
> Who's number one?
> The customer! Always!
>
> —The Wal-Mart cheer

When people are in Wal-Mart, what do they experience? Clearly, Wal-Mart is not just a store but also a culture, a way of experiencing and representing the world. People's views of Wal-Mart, of course, will vary according to their social and economic status, age, gender, ethnicity, degree of religiosity, and other variables, indicating there is no single experience in Wal-Mart but a plethora of them. The Gale Group (2004), a consulting firm for Wal-Mart, identified four types of shoppers who frequent the store, including (1) "champions," or enthusiastic shoppers, (2) "enthusiasts," (3) "rejecters," who are reluctant, and (4) "conflicted" buyers, who have mixed feelings. Their survey also revealed that Wal-Mart is teenage shoppers' favorite destination. Regardless of the diversity of its clientele, the phenomenology of Wal-Mart—how its customers view it, what they experience inside—is hardly some random mixture of elements, but is carefully constructed to maximize the store's appeal and throughput of people.

These elements include the size and layout of stores, the physical and symbolic environments they contain. Like most retail chains, Wal-Mart is not known for its architectural novelty. As Quinn (2000: 26) puts it, "The master plan for Wal-Mart, wherever it goes, involves the 'box': the classic Wal-Mart square, prefab, ugly monstrosity of a building surrounded by asphalt parking lots as far as the eye can see." The average Wal-Mart Supercenter consists of a single-story structure averaging 181,300 square feet in size, although they range from 110,000 to 241,000 square feet (Simplicity.com 2005).

When Walter Benjamin conducted his Arcades Project in the 1920s, he sought to uncover the ways in which the commodity penetrated into the consciousness of buyers, charting the growth of bourgeois consciousness in the emerging malls and stores of early-twentieth-century Europe. Likewise, Wal-Mart offers an "Arcades" of a different sort, one that arises from the globalized hyperreality of postmodern capitalism. Within Wal-Mart, the customer is apt to be impressed, if not outright awed, by the sheer size. Ceilings tower over the multitude of goods, and the customer is dwarfed by the number of products he or she may purchase; the average Wal-Mart in the United States sells 75,000 different items (Owens 1996). Any observer even faintly aware of the productivity of capitalism must acknowledge the unprecedented extent to which Wal-Mart stores constitute a cornucopia unimaginable to most of the world's people. Wal-Mart stores are invariably spotless and well lit by row after row of fluorescent lights, with clear signs indicating major groups of commodities, sales, and services (Figure 12.2). Overhead speakers play Muzak, with frequent interruptions to announce "specials." Stores are a cacophony of colors and are physically comfortable—temperatures in all 3,500 U.S. outlets are controlled by Wal-Mart's headquarters in Bentonville (Greenhouse 2004). The layout of products in Wal-Mart stores, which is almost identical, involves careful product placement and merchandise mix (Vance and Scott 1992). At the entrance, customers are likely to see an array of conservative books, many emphasizing religious, especially biblical, themes.

Beyond the entrance lie miles of aisles designed to saturate the shopper with temptation. Many stores contain a McDonald's, video arcade, or kids' viewing center, which contribute to the overall carnivalesque atmosphere, one suitable for a family excursion. Having a place where the kids can entertain themselves while the parents shop is just part of Wal-Mart's appeal. Indeed, high school and college students often use Wal-Mart's size and late hours to play games such as scavenger hunts, aisle football, and A-Z "alphabet shopping" (Zimmerman and Stevens 2005). In some stores, Wal-Mart and Dubble Bubble gum co-host bubble-blowing contests (The Boxtank.com 2004). The Wal-Mart in Madison, Wisconsin, offers bingo for older folks at the McDonald's inside (dailycut.blogspot.com 2005), a form of recreation that stores

Figure 12.2   Two views inside Wal-Mart.

in New York State attempted to offer but were prohibited by law from doing so. In Korea, some Wal-Marts offer "guess the weight of the banana" contests (Wal-Mart Korea 2004). In Germany, Wal-Mart lures lonely customers with "singles shopping" in its ninety-one outlets, including "flirting points" around the store equipped with wines, cheeses, and chocolates (Bhatnagar 2005). Thus, Wal-Mart creates an inviting atmosphere that attracts clients whose primary motivation may be other than simply shopping: some people are there not just for the goods but because it is fun. Indeed, in Seattle, some Wal-Marts have invited RV enthusiasts to use empty parking lots as parks for recreational vehicles, creating instant communities. In this case, Wal-Mart commodifies not only public spaces but private ones too (The Boxtank 2004).

The sheer variety of goods available in the typical Wal-Mart facilitates one-stop shopping and thus time savings that are central to the store's appeal and success. For families pressed for time in the accelerated world of post-Fordist capitalism, this can be one of the store's most alluring features: Wal-Mart is not just cheap, it is efficient. Much of the store's efficiency reflects the economies of scale incurred when buying and selling in bulk; indeed, consumers must buy in large quantities in order for Wal-Mart to realize a competitive rate of profit. Most commodities are sold, therefore, in "family-size" quantities, some of which may be difficult for small households (including single adults) to store at home. Large sizes at low prices, however, can generate unintended problems.

> A gallon-sized jar of whole pickles is something to behold. The jar is the size of a small aquarium. The fat green pickles, floating in swampy juice, look reptilian, their shapes exaggerated by the glass. It weighs 12 pounds, too big to carry with one hand. The gallon jar of pickles is a display of abundance and excess; it is entrancing, and also vaguely unsettling. This is the product that Wal-Mart fell in love with: Vlasic's gallon jar of pickles. Wal-Mart priced it at $2.97—a year's supply of pickles for less than $3! ... Therein lies the basic conundrum of doing business with the world's largest retailer. By selling a gallon of kosher dills for less than most grocers sell a quart, Wal-Mart may have provided a service for its customers. But what did it do for Vlasic? The pickle maker had spent decades convincing customers that they should pay a premium for its brand. Now Wal-Mart was practically giving them away. And the fevered buying spree that resulted distorted every aspect of Vlasic's operations, from farm field to factory to financial statement. (Fishman 2003: 68)

Among other things, Wal-Mart is famous for its "greeters," overly friendly staff who welcome customers. Some customers enjoy the "hometown" atmosphere that this service ostensibly provides. Wal-Mart greeters and other staff are required by company policy to be fastidiously polite to the store's clients. One woman interviewed for this chapter noted that she *loved* Wal-Mart "because everyone is so friendly and polite." However, one cashier interviewed for this chapter noted that she "was only polite to everybody because they [the management] make me." Apparently the degree to which Wal-Mart's friendliness is contrived is lost upon some customers.

Wal-Mart's size works both for and against the firm. *Consumer Reports* found, for example, that 35 percent of the chain's customers disliked its overcrowding (Consumers Union 2002; Hajewski 2002). Some clients reported in interviews that they disdained the large crowds Wal-Mart must attract in order to generate the profits that sustain it. Another consumer noted that she liked the relative absence of salespeople compared to department stores, as it placed little pressure on her to buy. Stalk and

Lachenauer (2004) argue that Wal-Mart may be facing diseconomies of scale that discourage some clients:

> Customers are forced into a compromise when they shop at Wal-Mart. They usually have to travel a long distance to get to a store. They have to park in a large, crowded lot. They must roam through acres of retail space, through aisles designed to take them ever deeper into the store. Sales help is scarce and not always knowledgeable. The prices are dramatically low, but the experience is mediocre at best and unpleasant at worst. Some customers … refuse to shop at Wal-Mart because they don't enjoy the experience. Others refuse to shop there because they are opposed to Wal-Mart's effect on communities or dislike their labor practices.

James Cramer goes even further: "The stores are dowdy. The aisles are ugly. There's nothing exciting or different or even colorful at Wal-Mart. It feels almost Soviet in its selection and presentation" (Cramer 2004).

More than Cheap Stuff: The Politics of Wal-Mart's Imagery

Wal-Mart's obvious appeal to consumers is its low prices and the convenience offered by one-stop shopping, which allows buyers to purchase everything from condoms to condiments, goldfish to guns, and tampons to tires in one visit. Wal-Mart also offers a variety of specialty services, such as opticians, photo processing, jewelers, and pharmacies. The infinity of products Wal-Mart sells reveals the store as a center both of Fordist consumption and simultaneously of postmodern consumption, as it targets multiple niche markets, filling the need of every conceivable sociodemographic group. As Bianco (2003) notes, "At Wal-Mart, 'everyday low prices' is more than a slogan; it is the fundamental tenet of a cult masquerading as a company." Low prices, of course, reflect the chain's enormous economies of scale and its reliance upon cheap labor both to manufacture goods abroad and to sell them at home.

Although its customers come from a broad spectrum of social positions, the centrality of cheapness is most appealing to those with limited or modest incomes, who constitute the store's client base. In this sense, Wal-Mart made buying cheap goods respectable, allowing lower socioeconomic classes to feel that they have attained middle-class status. For example, Wal-Mart offers many brand-name goods at prices lower than may be found in other major retailers. The wide appeal of Disney products led the Walt Disney Corporation to form Disney Consumer Products, one of the largest licensers in the world, to assist Wal-Mart in acquiring and licensing Disney products. Disney Consumer Products has just one client: Wal-Mart (*Magical Mountain News* 2005). However, Wal-Mart simultaneously deploys strategies to appeal to middle-class consumers, who often value image and quality more than price.

Wal-Mart maintains a large information systems division, which employs 75,000 people, to track product deliveries in real time and to anticipate changes in the demand for specific goods. The retailer's 2005 annual report claims that its system's data storage capacity is 570 terabytes, more space than needed for all the fixed pages on the Internet (Wal-Mart 2005). The extent to which such geodemographic systems allow the chain to respond to contingencies is fascinating: when Hurricane Ivan was heading toward Florida's panhandle in 2004, the computer system anticipated a rise in demand for Kellogg's Strawberry Pop-Tarts, large quantities of which were then dispatched to the region.

Wal-Mart also offers "knockoffs," or inferior copies of well-known brands. Although it is illegal to pass off knockoffs as the real thing, Wal-Mart is not above doing so. In 1983, Nike charged Wal-Mart with trademark infringement, and did so again in 1996 for copying Nike's Air Mada shoe. In 1993, Florida's attorney general cited Wal-Mart for selling knockoff Seiko watches (Quinn 2000: 94). Not surprisingly, the firm does its best to conceal the social origins of its goods; indeed, "Wal-Mart refuses to disclose the specific source of imported goods to its customers—and there's no law to make them do it" (Quinn 2000: 92). Revealing the origins of its products is a matter of political expediency often tinged with hypocrisy: while Wal-Mart was engaging in a "Buy American" campaign in the 1990s, it simultaneously became China's sixth largest trading partner.

How much money does it take to convince people that you have "low everyday prices," or "we sell for less," or "the customer is boss"? As Table 12.1 reveals, Wal-Mart's advertising budget is a cottage industry in its own right. As Wal-Mart does not usually advertise in newspapers (Quinn 2000), most of these expenditures are for television advertisements. Wal-Mart knows its customers, and most of them are not big readers. While spending almost $2 million per day (overwhelmingly on television advertisements), Wal-Mart is increasing its expenditures to counter growing criticisms that it pays its workers very low wages (Katz 2005). In a scene reminiscent of presidential campaigns, Wal-Mart recently hired high-level campaign operatives from both political parties to establish a "war room" deep inside its headquarters in order to oppose these criticisms and to sell a new and improved image (Barbaro 2004).

Wal-Mart also offers its own in-store television network, the fifth largest in the United States (Noe 2005), with programming that reaches 133 million viewers a month, which "rivals the four major broadcast networks in audience reach" (French 2004). Wal-Mart TV, which started in 1998, includes products ads purchased by companies, which pay between $137,000 and $292,000 per commercial for a four-week period (Hays 2005). The average viewer watches Wal-Mart TV for seven minutes per visit. Because up to 70 percent of brand decisions are made inside the store, products advertised on the Wal-Mart TV Network see a "discernible lift" in sales. Occasionally, the network carries news, such as the invasion of Afghanistan. Broadcasts cannot be

TABLE 12.1   Wal-Mart's Advertising Expenditures, 2002–2005

Year	Total Advertising Expenditures	Expenditures per Day
2002	$618 million	$1.69 million
2003	$676 million	$1.82 million
2004*	$966 million	$2.23 million
2005	$1.4 billion	$3.83 million
4-year average	$915 million	$2.39 million

* Increase partially reflective of new accounting procedure, see above, p. 38.
Source: Wal-Mart 2005 Annual Report (available at   http://www.walmart-facts.com/docs1078wal-martannualreport20051053897253.pdf).

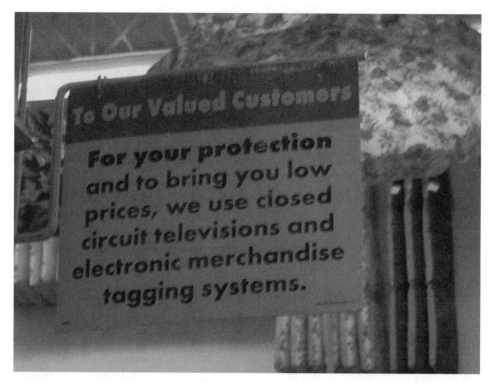

Figure 12.3   Wal-Mart sign warning customers of closed-circuit television.

switched off by store managers, only by company headquarters in Bentonville (Hays 2005). Wal-Marts are also laced with closed-circuit televisions that transform the store into a panopticon, able to monitor shoppers' every movement (Figure 12.3).

Wal-Mart is much too sophisticated a supplier to leave consumer preferences to consumers. Unlike textbook models of neoclassical economics, in which utility curves magically appear out of nowhere, Wal-Mart actively shapes its customers' preferences using a variety of strategies. Several important ones include the use of celebrity endorsements, ties to popular working-class events such as NASCAR races, and a censorship of material that reflects Wal-Mart's management's deeply conservative religious and political views.

Celebrity Endorsements

One tactic that Wal-Mart often employs is the use of celebrities to endorse its products, a tactic designed to impart respectability. For many consumers, celebrities exude an aura of sophistication that they may hope to acquire through imitation. For example, aging movie actress Lauren Hutton endorsed female hormone replacement therapy for the chain in a free video handed out at Wal-Mart stores. In the video, produced with an "educational grant" from pharmaceutical giant Wyeth-Ayerst, Hutton does not explicitly mention the product, Premarin, but claims that estrogen replacement gave her a new lease on life (including her sex life), and she scoffs at "natural alternatives" (Adams 2003). Similarly, Alicia Minshew, star of the soap opera *All My Children,* endorsed the fragrance Enchantment, which was named after a fictitious cosmetics company on the show (Zap2it 2004), a clear case of life imitating art. The idolization of celebrities thus serves to mobilize consumer consciousness by implying that Wal-Mart customers will enjoy the same aura of success, savoir-faire, and sophistication that surrounds the celebrities who endorse its goods.

During the mid-1990s, Kathie Lee Gifford, popular television talk show host and singer, established a line of children's clothing that was sold at over 2,100 Wal-Mart outlets. In 1996, the media exposed Dickensian working conditions in the factories producing that clothing line (Charette 1998). In Honduran and New York sweatshops, young women and girls were found toiling up to thirteen hours per day for minimum and subminimum wages to manufacture the garments that bear Gifford's name in Wal-Mart aisles. Gifford interpreted the exposé as nothing but character defamation. Gifford's husband, former professional football player and sports announcer Frank Gifford, fanned the flames by visiting the New York sweatshop that produced the goods, where he stuffed envelopes filled with three $100 bills into workers' hands.

Following intense public scrutiny, Kathie Lee Gifford promised that the twenty-eight plants that produced her clothing line would be subject to monitoring by independent human rights organizations. Instead, Wal-Mart insisted it had already established a system of independent monitoring. The company pointed to its 1992 Code of Conduct—a document that is superficially a great leap forward in corporate ethics. Without such a code, companies have little incentive to consider labor conditions when deciding where to manufacture their products. Ideally, the Code of Conduct would create a framework guiding Wal-Mart away from contractors that abuse and underpay employees. It would assure consumers who buy from Wal-Mart that they are not supporting the exploitation of young workers throughout the world. But behind Wal-Mart's Code of Conduct's glossy cover lurks a set of loose regulations, including an allowance for fourteen- and fifteen-year-old workers in factories producing goods sold in its stores. The code stipulates a series of independent inspections of company factories, but Wal-Mart officials themselves admitted that company buyers often perform these inspections. These lax rules help to explain why Wal-Mart has not taken substantial steps to change the conditions that brought Gifford so much negative attention. In its report *Made in China,* the National Labor Committee (2000) reveals that workers in the Liang Shi Handbag Factory in Dongguan City, Guangdong, China, earn as little as twelve cents an hour for sixty- to seventy-hour weeks producing Kathie Lee Gifford handbags. Even after it is adjusted to the local cost of living, this wage is barely enough to cover basic necessities. Worse, the factory has no fire exits, and workers have deductions taken from their wages for housing in cramped dormitories provided by the factory's owners. The National Labor Committee suspects there are at least ten factories of this kind producing Kathie Lee Gifford handbags in China. For obvious reasons, Wal-Mart has recently deemphasized the "Buy American" campaign that Sam Walton started in the 1980s to great promotional effect.

Wal-Mart and NASCAR

Wal-Mart and NASCAR have entered into a joint promotion program in the form of "Fan Days," featuring various "retailtainment" events such as racing radio-controlled stock cars in the toy department, handing out more than a million "Nascar Fan Guides" to shoppers, playing NASCAR trivia games in the store, and even posing in a photo booth with life-size cardboard cutouts of famous NASCAR drivers. Other corporate sponsors Including Coca-Cola, Kellogg, and Kingsford Charcoal are also participating in NASCAR events in Wal-Mart parking lots, such as riding in a race car simulator and getting up close to their favorite sponsor show cars. Wal-Mart is the largest seller of NASCAR licensed items in the country, offering more than 250 products. Wal-Mart is also the exclusive retailer of a DVD, *NASCAR 3D: The IMAX Experience*, which was the second highest grossing film documentary of 2004 (*Sports Business Journal* 2003; jayski.com/teams/nascar-sponsors.htm 2005).

Wal-Mart Censorship

Part of Wal-Mart's sales strategy is to project the image of its stores as "family" oriented. In this context, it is notoriously vigilant about "protecting" consumers from products the management deems offensive, a strategy in keeping with the conservative campaign to "protect family values" in the United States. For example, the world's largest music retailer refuses to sell any CD with a parental warning sticker:

> Wal-Mart will not stock music with parental guidance stickers. While Wal-Mart sets high standards, it would not be possible to eliminate every image, word or topic that an individual might find objectionable. And the goal is not to eliminate the need for parents to review the merchandise their children buy. The policy simply helps eliminate the most objectionable material from Wal-Mart's shelves. (PBS 2004)

Thus, the chain refuses to carry CDs with cover art or lyrics deemed overtly sexual or socially controversial, such as abortion or homosexuality. According to a 2004 PBS news report "Wal-Mart is the world's largest CD retailer, and in some regions the only place in town to purchase music (PBS 2004)". Subsequently, Wal-Mart's refusal to carry their products would seem to have dire consequences for recording artists. Because Wal-Mart accounts for about 10 percent of total U.S. music CD sales, most musicians and record companies will agree to create a "sanitized" version specifically for the chain. The construction of these "cleaned up" versions entails a variety of different possible modifications, including altering the cover art, "as John Cougar Mellencamp did when asked to airbrush out an angel and devil on one of his album covers" (PBS 2004). The PBS report goes on to state that other musicians have been asked to change their lyrics and song titles, such as the group Nirvana, who changed a song title from "Rape Me" to "Waif Me" specifically for the 'Wal-Mart' version of the song. Nirvana also altered the back-cover artwork for the album *In Utero* because Wal-Mart objected to its portrayal of fetuses. Another example is Sheryl Crow's release of her self-titled album, in which Wal-Mart objected to the lyric, "Watch our children as they kill each other with a gun they bought at Wal-Mart discount stores."

Crow refused to change the verse, so Wal-Mart refused to carry the album. Ultimately, "This type of censorship has become so common that it is often regarded as simply another stage of editing. Record labels are now acting preemptively, issuing two versions of the same album for their big name artists. Less well-known bands, however, are forced to offer "sanitized" albums out of the gate" (PBS 2004).

Wal-Mart has also implemented policies against literature it deems offensive, stripping men's magazines such as *Maxim* and *Stuff* from the store's racks along with gay publications including *The Advocate* and *Out*. It also obscures the covers of *Glamour, Redbook, Marie Claire, Cosmopolitan, Rolling Stone*, and *Vibe* with binders. Some magazines willingly send advance copies to Wal-Mart for their approval before publication, and will even alter cover artwork to avoid losing sales (PBS 2004). Although Jon Stewart's parody of a civics book, *America*, reached the top of the best-seller list, Wal-Mart's management declined to sell it in stores; however, it is available online at Wal-Mart's Web site (Hall 2004). Similarly, Wal-Mart refuses to sell comedian George Carlin's best-selling new book, *When Will Jesus Bring the Pork Chops?* because its cover makes fun of Leonardo da Vinci's *The Last Supper,* inserting the comedian in the scene next to an empty chair usually occupied by Jesus.

Wal-Mart's standards of offensiveness became an issue in 2004 when customers and civil rights groups complained about its Web site selling *The Protocols of the Learned Elders of Zion.* A notorious forgery that describes a vast Jewish conspiracy to rule the world, the *Protocols* has been a highly controversial product, widely denounced as a pernicious, racist fraud. Wal-Mart's Web site, however, described it differently, using endorsements lifted from the book's jacket: "If ... *The Protocols* are genuine (which can never be proven conclusively), it might cause some of us to keep a wary eye on world affairs" (Southern Poverty Law Center 2004). Similarly, the 1905 novel *The Clansman*, basis of the infamous film *Birth of a Nation*, a 1915 ode to white supremacy, is still available on Wal-Mart.com. The Wal-Mart Web site's 700,000-book inventory also included *The South Was Right!* by James and Walter Kennedy, founding members of the League of the South white supremacist group; Wal-Mart describes the book as the story of "how the South was an independent country invaded, captured, and still occupied by a vicious aggressor." Wal-Mart.com also carries books such as *Was Jefferson Davis Right?* which alleges the Confederate president "was innocent of all of the heinous allegations made against him" (Southern Poverty Law Center 2005). As Bianco (2003) puts it, "by most accounts, Wal-Mart's cultural gatekeeping has served to narrow the mainstream for entertainment offerings while imparting to it a rightward tilt."

Video games also appear to be subject to Wal-Mart's censorship. Twenty-five percent of all video games in the U.S. are sold through Wal-Mart, certainly enough for Wal-Mart to have a voice in shaping the content of customer purchases. In 2000, to make their product acceptable to Wal-Mart, makers of an action-strategy video game, *Giants: Citizen Kabuto,* changed the color of the characters' blood from red to green and dressed a formerly topless female character in a bikini. Wal-Mart managers often preview games to be sure that both packaging and content are acceptable before the product is published, and as noted above, video game publishers have been known to make adjustments—or even release special conservative versions—for sale at Wal-Mart.

In many communities, Wal-Mart's growth has come at the cost of smaller merchants, often located downtown. As the number of smaller markets in a given region declines, shoppers increasingly must travel farther from home and find their shopping restricted to merchandise that Wal-Mart chooses to sell. Wal-Mart's success thus allows it to impose its own moral vision over a growing number of clients. However, this hegemony is uneven over time and space, and does not go uncontested. As Wal-Mart expands beyond its rural southern and midwestern roots, imposing its morality on other communities will be difficult, particularly more liberal ones higher in the urban hierarchy. Bianco (2003) argues, "Wal-Mart will be hard pressed to continue censoring its product lines using the justification of customer preference. The market for profanity-laced hip-hop may be tiny in Bentonville, Arkansas, but it is big in Los Angeles. Overseas, the company does not presume to impose a small-town, Bible Belt moral agenda on shoppers." These comments help shed light on the difficulty Wal-Mart has experienced in attempting to penetrate into cities such as New York, Los Angeles, and Toronto.

Conclusions

On the surface, Wal-Mart presents itself to customers simply as a center of low prices, and is designed to make shopping appear simply as "fun" (i.e., without an overt political agenda). Understandably, this strategy has been highly successful. Yet social science is the art of penetrating surface appearances to uncover less obvious forces and structures. Behind Wal-Mart's façade of bland consumerism lurks a deeply conservative and religious political agenda, present since it began in Arkansas decades ago. Wal-Mart is much more than simply a supplier of goods in the sterile sense of neoclassical economics; it is also a model of neoliberal consumption, linking globalized commodity chains, low-wage labor, and bare-knuckled competition. Just as a home is so much more than a house, or a car is much more than simply a means of transportation, so too is Wal-Mart more than just a place to buy cheap goods. From the abstract spaces of the global economy to the intimate worlds of the self and the body, Wal-Mart comprises a world of signs and meanings that shape the views and behaviors of the countless hordes that shop there.

As this chapter has demonstrated, shopping in Wal-Mart entails a host of ideological assumptions and consequences, including the store's careful engineering of customer satisfaction, celebrity endorsements, alliances with NASCAR, in-store television, and "retailtainment" (a term Wal-Mart attempted but failed to copyright). Many people visit Wal-Mart not simply to buy things but to have a good time. Whereas intellectuals often fear or disdain the giant, many consumers love it. Yet hiding behind the façade of commodity fetishism lurks a distinct and deeply conservative politics, often religious in nature. Wal-Mart's politics emerge in terms of what it chooses or refuses to sell, its censorship of certain materials, the careful way it encourages people to "buy American" yet rely heavily on foreign imports. Wal-Mart is thus much more than a purely economic phenomenon. Social theory has delved deeply into the ways in which commodities structure consciousness, revealing Wal-Mart as a place of signs and meanings as well as a place of goods.

13

Visualizing Wal-Mart as Home: *Where the Heart Is* and *King of the Hill*

Benjamin Smith

For better or worse, the concept of "branding," which refers to the image, identity, and personality that particular companies or goods try to project as well as how the company or product is perceived by consumers, has become central to the functioning of contemporary corporate culture. Common wisdom is that having a strong brand is a key to success, and to have a strong brand means to have an image that evokes the highest possible utility, or that at least successfully connects (often tangentially) the product to desirable qualities or emotions. In the pantheon of branding a special place is reserved for "pioneering" brands that have become so stupendously successful in their field that their brand name becomes the generic name for the product category or, even better, their name transforms into the verb used to denote the use of that product: Xeroxing for photocopying, Rollerblading for in-line skating, Tivoing for digital video recording, and Hoovering for vacuuming (if you are British) are just a few. Apart from the hassle and expense of the legal maneuvering required to make sure the brand's trademark does not become nullified by generalized use, this complete domination/association is considered a good thing for business.

However, there are rare cases where a pioneering, highly successful company's name becomes a synonym not for the intended use of its product but instead for its nasty side effects. The Walt Disney Company has seen its name transformed into "Disneyfied" and "Disneyfication," words used to describe the simulation and sanitization of reality done in the name of making a product more palpable to the "average consumer." George Ritzer (Ritzer 1998, 2004) turned McDonald's into a verb that emphasized the de-skilling, routinizing, top-down nature of the contemporary service economy, just as Morgan Spurlock turned the company's slogan into a description of what literally happened to his body during the filming of his 2003 documentary, *Supersize Me,* in which he ate only McDonald's fare for thirty days. Coca-Cola, that brand so closely associated with Americana, has been modified to become "Coca-colonization," and from time to time, most notably in the Middle East, the company has faced boycotts due to U.S. foreign policy actions. So while market trailers such as Wendy's do not get to see their name transformed into a verb synonymous with getting an inexpensive meal quickly, neither do such names become synonymous with any particular social malady.

Wal-Mart has not quite reached the lofty status of verbdom. Yet there is no doubt that Wal-Mart is becoming associated with a slew of images far away from its domestic branding strategy as a down-home, power-to-the-salt-of-the-earth, all-American, pro-family community builder (see Arnold, Kozinets, and Handelman 2001). In many circles, especially academic ones, Wal-Mart is a veritable folk devil whose mention conjures up images of exploitive capitalism, unsustainability, the destruction of uniqueness, American blandness, suburban blight, and a disposable culture in a way that the mention of Target, which is no more social-justice-friendly but is infinitely more design-conscious, never could.[1] In fact, I myself am guilty of the "say Wal-Mart and say no more" style of shorthand. The following snippet comes from the scene-setting opening paragraph of a paper I presented on the selective use of Kentucky imagery by KFC founder Colonel Harland Sanders:

> The other museum dedicated to Sanders is located on the restored site of his original hotel and restaurant, which is in largely rural and poor Appalachian, Southeastern Kentucky, just outside of Corbin, a town of 8000 people. This museum/fully functional "modern" KFC restaurant sits several miles from the interstate interchange, past an abandoned Wal-Mart that is adjacent to a new, larger Wal-Mart, beyond a half dozen rundown antique stores. (Smith 2004)

This quote demonstrates the flexibility of Wal-Mart as a negative descriptor for those who are so inclined to use it that way—it can stand as symbol for both social blight (low-paying jobs, decline of rural areas) and aesthetic blight (as in ugly, uninteresting).

Of course, academics are not alone in turning Wal-Mart into a symbol for larger problems. To give one example, in October 2005, JibJab Media, which during the 2004 U.S. presidential campaign created a popular Internet cartoon set to the tune of Woody Guthrie's "This Land Is Your Land," released a fine polemical cartoon called "Oh, Big Box Mart," set to the tune of "Oh, Susannah" (JibJab 2005). Though the authors claimed in an October 14, 2005, interview on the *Your World with Neil Cavuto* show on Fox News (quoted in Melanie 2005) that the new cartoon was not about Wal-Mart especially but about the loss of American jobs to cheap labor overseas, the last line of the song reads, "Oh Big Box Mart, my paycheck reminds me, your everyday low prices have a price, they aren't free," which of course includes the famous Wal-Mart tag line.

Yet for all the criticism it has faced on both social justice and aesthetic grounds, Wal-Mart and its brand have proven remarkably resilient, continuing to dominate the U.S. retail sector and increasingly the global retail scene. The goal of this chapter is to better understand why this is so, that is, to understand why so many remain attached to Wal-Mart despite the frequent attacks. To do so, I will delve into the world of popular fiction and the discourse surrounding the corporation in order to contextualize the way in which attachment to the Wal-Mart brand takes place, notably in its relation to the concept of "home." I have chosen two works that focus both on Wal-Mart and the rural/exurban U.S. South, the context out of which the Bentonville retail giant grew: Billie Letts's 1995 novel *Where the Heart Is*, which in 2000 was turned into a motion picture, and the long-running animated series *King of the Hill*, where Wal-Mart's fictional stand-in is named Mega-Lo Mart. Both works are especially fruitful to focus on because both have been widely praised by critics and fans for their realistic portrayals of places and people, as opposed to the stock characters and outright negative portrayals of the region found in other fictional works such as *Deliverance* and *The Dukes of Hazzard*. By the conclusion of this chapter, I hope that Wal-Mart emerges not as some unassailable monolithic terror but rather as something with which the idea of "home" has developed a circular, dependent relationship that is not necessarily positive but which remains strong because of connections to other powerful ideas about locality and values.

"Reel" and "Real" Together

Before delving into the individual works, an interlude about my theoretical approach to popular culture is in order. Because I am a geographer, I am heavily influenced by the thought of other geographers on the topic (Aitken and Zonn 1994; Rose 2001). At the heart of this geographic approach to popular culture is a quest to understand the dynamic, mutually constructed, and ultimately inseparable relationship between "reel" fictionalized cultural landscapes and the "real" on-the-ground "tangible visible scene" (Lewis 1979) and how these foci together help produce effects of difference and inequality, such as racism and sexism (Lukinbeal 2004). Thus, as Dixon and Grimes (2004) note, in so doing I am shunning an approach of "bad dialectics" (Mitchell 2003) where the point of analysis is to show how, in the end, popular media is used to produce a "false" ideological image used to lull the proletariat into a stupor of not seeing the "real" source of their lower status. To avoid this type of dialectics does not mean a complete evacuation of a social justice position, just a commitment to a more complex explanation than top-down causality. An additional highlight of the "real"-and-"reel" approach is that to understand effects, one must pay attention to "audiencing," or the impact of the circulation of media images among viewers on the production of meaning (Bunnell 2004; Fiske 2000). This approach was easy to achieve here, because *Where the Heart Is* was an Oprah's Book Club selection, meaning a great deal of reader feedback about the novel and the subsequent movie is archived on the section of her Web site (www.oprah.com) devoted to the book club.

Where the Heart Is

> 'Cause home gives you something no other place can ... Home is where your history begins.... [And as] the late Brother Husband said, "Home is the place that'll catch you when you fall. And we *all* fall."

—Sister Husband, in *Where the Heart Is*

Published in 1995, *Where the Heart Is* is the story of Novalee Nation, a single, teenage mother from Tennessee who, due to a twist of fate and with the help of the friendly local characters, comes to build a life and home for herself in a small town in Oklahoma. The novel's plot is set in motion when Novalee is abandoned by her get-rich-quick-scheming boyfriend Willy Jack at a Wal-Mart in Sequoyah, Oklahoma, while the couple is en route to California. With only $7.77 remaining in her pocket, a baby due in two months, and no family (her mother abandoned her when she was seven),

friends, or transportation, she decides that sleeping in the Wal-Mart (which in this
era closes at 9 p.m.) overnight is her best (and really only) option. She continues this
way for two months, writing down in an IOU book everything she eats, wears, and
uses from Wal-Mart. Eventually, she goes into labor at the store while it is closed,
only to have her baby delivered and her life saved by the local librarian (and later
love interest), Forney. This event makes her a celebrity, brings a host of good and bad
people into her life, including Wal-Mart founder Sam Walton, who visits her in the
hospital, thanks her for the free advertising, gives her a $500 check, and says she can
have a job at Wal-Mart whenever she is ready. As the book progresses and a steady
stream of trials and tragedies beset the lives of her and her multicultural band of
friends, Novalee grows more independent and becomes a good employee, artist, parent, and friend who learns to always see the good in people and keep trying.

   Given the overall optimistic tone of the book, doing a "bad dialectics" analysis of
the film would be simple: Novalee's personal "quiet, noble determination," instead of
a revolutionary stance against the forces of patriarchy and capitalism, only sends a
message to readers not to look beneath the surface for larger patterns and not to seek
big changes. Even though no published book review nor reader comment on Oprah's
discussion board expressly mentioned "a failure to pay attention to dominating structures" as a shortcoming of the book, quite a few readers came to the related conclusion that the book, while well written, was ultimately lightweight, inconsequential
fare that was good only for a quick summer read and pick-me up. This is not to say
that a "bad dialectics" interpretation of the effect of the book on readers is entirely
without merit. In fact, several of the readers who posted comments on Oprah's discussion forum took this book as a confirmation of an individualist attitude toward
life: that people who work hard will always win in the end and that those who fail
probably deserve to because of personal, not societal, shortcomings. The following
posting serves as an example:

> The message this book gives ... is just the type of example we need in our society. Instead
> of blaming people for her situation, Novalee met it straight on and rose above it. Instead of
> repeating the cycle, she challenged herself to make herself different, better than what she
> learned as a child. It is truly inspiring and a book I plan on sharing with my daughter when
> she is capable of understanding its message. This book's message is something I think we can
> all use in our daily struggle of living in a world of blaming somebody else for our problems.

   Similarly, others take away from Novalee's tale the need for a Zen-like approach to
life; they feel that "you probably don't have it so bad, so don't worry" is the true lesson.
In other words, "don't let the system trouble you." According to one reader:

> I feel Billie Letts reminded us to remember the basic things in life and not to get wrapped up in
> the little daily things that get us down. Things can always get worse, the book reminds you. How
> many of us have really had it this bad? Most have not, but are far less happy than Novalee.

   However, this pseudo-Marxist reading, despite some merits, is far from the only
approach to Letts' work and the response to it, nor is it the most useful or fairest. For
starters, it misses what is truly unique about Letts' effort: the diversity and (somewhat
broadly drawn) detail with which Oklahoma native Letts paints a picture of life in
Wal-Mart's backyard. As the Oprah Web site described it, "*Where the Heart Is* puts a

human face on the look-alike trailer parks and malls of America's small towns." Letts touches on many (almost too many) issues affecting small-town women in America: teenage pregnancy, child abuse, lack of jobs. She also goes to pains to point out that even small towns in Oklahoma display cultural diversity. And as Letts states in the reading group guide at the end of her 2000 edition: "I suspect that the common perception on the coasts is still that the great middle is populated by Anglo ranchers and wheat farmers" (Letts 2000: 362). Moses Whitecotton, a professional photographer specializing in infant portraits, who is African American, acts as a father figure for Novalee; Benny Goodluck, a teenage Native American, is one of the first people to befriend Novalee on her arrival in town; and when she finally moves out of the Wal-Mart, she ends up living next door to the Ortiz family, who are immigrants from Mexico.

It is this diversity and these problems that led Letts to feel Wal-Mart was a natural choice as the linchpin of her story about making a home in Oklahoma:

> Many small towns in our part of the country have central meeting places, the social centers of towns—churches, high school gyms, football fields, and, increasingly so, the Wal-Mart store, which has changed not only Main Street, but the very rhythms and movements of these communities. So for my story, the Wal-Mart in Sequoyah, Oklahoma, was the most likely place for Novalee to encounter Sister Husband, a white woman, Moses Whitecotton, a black man, and Benny Goodluck, a Native American boy. (Letts 2000: 361–62)

In this and other statements in the reading group guide found at the back of her novel, one gets the sense that Letts clearly understands the racism, classism, and sexism that pervade many small towns (as well as large ones), and that one of the good aspects of Wal-Mart is that, unlike some small-town businesses of the past that would exclude African Americans or women, it admits everybody. In some ways Wal-Mart may be the retail version of the lowest common denominator, but that it is "common" is one of its strong suits.

Furthermore, Letts understands that part of Wal-Mart's appeal is that it opens formerly small places to a world of goods, making them accessible not just from a Sears catalog but in person just a short drive away. Indeed, unlike Target and Kmart, which started out in urban/suburban areas, Wal-Mart's original growth came from serving smaller towns other chains would not (Graff and Ashton 1994). As Letts puts it, the original impetus for her story came one day during a visit to Wal-Mart, during which she thought:

> Someone could probably live in there for weeks, months … years, maybe, without ever having to go outside. And just like that I came up with the idea of a girl hiding out in that store, living there, because she had nowhere else to go. (Letts 2000: 361)

And to Novalee, who, as the book points out numerous times, had "never lived in a home without wheels underneath it" and dreams of a "home firmly rooted to the ground" with "an outdoor table with an umbrella where she can drink chocolate milk," Wal-Mart must not have seemed "cheap." It offered a level of comfort to which Novalee, for most of her life, could only aspire. Indeed, while she lives at Wal-Mart, she often sits at its display plastic outdoor table with the umbrella, and eventually when she does get a house anchored to the ground, she buys one for herself. Thus, while the JibJab cartoon "Big Box Mart" includes the line "Big Box Mart is the place I go to buy all my crap," this sentiment does not reflect how many people in the United States and foreign markets feel about Wal-Mart. Rather, it is where they go to make their lives comfortable. As someone who grew up in a small town of around 2,000 people in Ohio, I can remember with excitement when the Super Kmart and Super Wal-Mart opened in our county seat, just as I thought my town had moved up in the world when our first fast-food restaurant, a Hardee's, opened. The Wal-Mart was open twenty-four hours a day, a big thrill to high school kids with nowhere outside of each other's houses to go on a weekend night.[2] In places such as Mexico, where I have visited Wal-Mart more times than I rightly should have, the store does not offer the lowest possible prices on many goods (especially when compared to local markets), and the southern/conservative tinge the stores in the United States have is far less noticeable. Instead, the Wal-Marts in Mexico project an air of American consumer plenty and focus on images of happy, middle-class families.

While Letts does shed light on the positive aspects of Wal-Mart in terms of community and worldliness, she does not shy away from some of the negative aspects, either. Within the first few pages after her abandonment at Wal-Mart, Novalee meets Moses in this scene:

> Back inside the store, Novalee stopped at a wooden porch swing displayed near the door. She ran her hand across the dark wood and thought of cool yellow porches and morning glories thick on white trellises. "Old man out on Stickel Creek makes porch swings out of hickory." She turned toward the voice and the big black man sitting on her bench. "Those won't last," he said. "Threads'll strip in that soft wood. You want a swing that'll last, go out on Stickel Creek." (Letts 2000: 22)

While there are clues throughout the book that what can be found in Wal-Mart may not be all that is needed for a good life, it is Moses who serves as the strongest antimaterialist force for Novalee. For example, while Moses, who is a professional photographer, uses a new, high-tech camera for his portrait work at Wal-Mart, he prefers an old, dual-lens Rollei for personal photograph taking. When Novalee inquires about the strange-looking camera, he insists that "they don't make them like this anymore," and as she learns more about Moses, she comes to appreciate the artistry of the Rollei, soon seeking out a Rollei of her own at garage sales (where she also buys other goods for herself and her baby). In addition, when Novalee builds a house of her own, she does so with labor and expertise gifted from her friends, including a stone fireplace built by Moses using rocks from a local creek. This happens in part because, despite inheriting $29,000 and the lot used for the building site, Novalee, who by that time in the story is fully employed by Wal-Mart, could not afford to pay people to help her build. But this also happens because Novalee has become part of a gift economy that includes most of her neighbors, in which exchanges of cooking, child care, and car rides are commonplace. Indeed, some of the respondents on Oprah's discussion forum indicated the antimaterialist message was one of the chief inspirational aspects of the book: that what is most important is family, friends, and strong community, not just the things you own.

Not only does Wal-Mart gradually become decentered from Novalee's material world, it becomes increasingly distant from the heart of her social world as well—not that it was ever that vibrant a heart. Novalee's arrival at Wal-Mart comes only a few pages into the story, and for the first few chapters it is her home: "the place that'll catch you when you fall," the place "that gives you something no place else does" (in this case food and shelter). Though she meets a few nice people there early on— Moses and Benny, as well as Sister Husband, whom she eventually lives with when she leaves Wal-Mart—by and large it is a place where her social world is empty and always precarious. This symbolically charged description comes from shortly after her abandonment:

> And little by little, as they went to lunch … sneaked a smoke … stocked more shelves, as clerks and stock boys and managers drifted by, they forgot the pregnant girl on the bench by the door, sitting under a red, white and blue banner that said MADE IN AMERICA. (Letts 2000: 17)

Though it is home, it is a home of cold comfort, of last resort. When Novalee first hides out in the Wal-Mart for the night, it makes her physically ill that she has no place else to go. She also finds the smallest hiding place she can (in a closet next to the water heater), because she feels more comfortable there. At first Novalee fears the sound of the wind and rain against the warehouse-like store, but soon she grows used to the "metallic" sound-scape. Though she reads popular magazines on pregnancy and has her pick of candy bars, Novalee's life there is fairly empty.

In contrast, it is the local library that provides an alternative space for Novalee to center her existence and where she begins to move beyond the Wal-Mart world. It is there she meets her love interest, Forney Hull, who, after having to drop out of college to care for his ill sister, became the town librarian. In the first scene Forney appears in, he quotes literature and demonstrates an extensive knowledge of animal and plant taxonomy, which overwhelms and intimidates Novalee. Over time Forney's stance toward her softens, and since Novalee makes almost daily visits to the library—the only place in town besides the park and Wal-Mart that is open to the public—and shows great enthusiasm for learning, it is not long before his curiosity causes him to follow Novalee (without her knowledge) and discover that she most likely lives in Wal-Mart. Once he learns this, Forney begins to care for her mental and physical well-being, developing long reading lists for her and being sure to have some type of healthy food "lying around" for her to eat every day. The library and the books in it come to be a place of knowledge, beyond the minimal material comfort offered by Wal-Mart. In a scene after the birth of her daughter:

> Novalee looked around her at a room filled with books. Books stacked in corners, standing on her dresser, crammed into her headboard, pushed into a bookcase. And in the library, Forney's library, there were more. More books … more stories … more poems. And suddenly, Novalee knew—knew what she hadn't known before. She wasn't who she had been. She would never again be who she was before. She was connected to those women she had read about…. Untouchables. Black women. Arab women. She was connected to them just as she had been to girls in seventh grade gym classes and to make-believe women named Brenda and to real ones named Lexie. (Letts 2000, 156–57)

Though the importance placed on books no doubt reflects the author's status as an English professor, it also conveys the idea that the small-town, hometown, all-American outlook of Wal-Mart is not sufficient for an extraordinary life. So throughout the book, the library and Forney as its representative become more and more the center of Novalee's life, pushing Wal-Mart further to the periphery, even though she continues to work there.

What is especially interesting is that this move away from Wal-Mart is something that really doesn't feature in the film version of *Where the Heart Is*. As noted by the *Wall Street Journal* in a blurb about the movie (Zimmerman 2000), Wal-Mart very rarely grants permission for its image to be used in film or television, so adjustments to the script were probably done to make the movie appear more in line with Wal-Mart's branding in order to secure its permission. For example, in the film, Moses never says the Wal-Mart swing is of questionable quality; Novalee, though she starts out with a Rollei, gets a high-end SLR once she becomes a wedding photographer.

An even larger discrepancy is that, in the book, after a tornado devastates Sequoyah, the Wal-Mart is severely damaged and the corporation decides to close down the store permanently, because the cost to rebuild would be too much. Though the corporation offers employees jobs at a supercenter that will soon be opening fifty miles away, few move to take the jobs, and only Novalee stays in Sequoyah and commutes to the new work site, because she feels obligated to Wal-Mart. This has to be devastating for the town, as the only other major places of employment mentioned in the book are a plastics factory and an IGA, and, as Letts hints, Wal-Mart's abandonment causes the loss of a social center as well.[3] However, none of this happens in the movie: the Wal-Mart never moves and, in fact, Forney and Novalee get married in the Wal-Mart in the final scene, something that does not happen in the book. There is no IGA in town in the movie; there is no nursery where Benny Goodluck and his family work (there is no Benny, even). Though in the film Novalee grows, she grows in coordination with Wal-Mart, not gradually away from it. If anything, this portrayal shows that Wal-Mart at least dislikes, and possibly fears, the book's fairly gentle antimaterialist message.

That being said, what is especially interesting, and telling, is Novalee's continued loyalty to Wal-Mart, even after the retailer moves out of her adopted hometown of Sequoyah and she moves beyond the world of goods they offer through her growing circle of friends. Though part of this likely comes from the fact that Sam Walton chose not to prosecute her for pilfering and trespassing but instead gave her money and a job, there is something deeper at work. When Sam Walton dies, Novalee cries, and it is not just because of his kindness; it is because Wal-Mart's story is like her story. It rose from the most unlikely of conditions, the poor rural South, to outperform better-funded chains that started elsewhere in the country. Despite the issues the author has with Wal-Mart, it remains on the inside of a clear moral geography Letts builds up throughout the novel. Almost all unsympathetic characters are people running from the rural South to less wholesome urban areas.[4] For example, Sister declares at one point that it is a good thing Novalee did not get to California, because "all the pricks" go to California, and that it might as well be called "Prick-afornia" (and as we all know, California has been the center of resistance to Wal-Mart in the United States). Similarly, we find out that Novalee's mother, who makes a brief appearance, had been heading to New Orleans looking for work, and again we are reminded of the advice of Sister, who noted, "Any woman on her way to New Orleans can't have too many Lamentations" (the Bible book) (Zimmerman 2000). Nashville, where Novalee's original boyfriend, Willy Jack, ends up, is similarly portrayed as a place of hustlers as well as decadent wealth. What Letts relates through her characters is an attitude I feel is probably a common one toward Wal-Mart in rural areas: though Wal-Mart acts as a less-than-ideal center of community life, it is still "on the inside," because it came to rural areas when no one else would and because it too came from a rural area. An attack on Wal-Mart, especially on the culture or aesthetics of Wal-Mart, is viewed as an attack on a whole set of perceived positive qualities of the region.

This metonymic extension helps to explain the overwhelmingly positive response to the book on Oprah's Web site and why the book, despite an ambiguous attitude toward Wal-Mart, was probably a public relations success for the company. Almost every poster to the message board, with maybe only 3 percent disagreeing, said this was (1) one of their favorite books, (2) the best book Oprah had picked (not at all depressing in any way), or (3) highly inspirational. Many liked how Novalee overcame repeated hardships that were thrown in her path, and that she was a strong woman, as they hoped to be. In a slight variant of that read, many teenage mothers, as well as a teacher who teaches at a special school for teenage mothers, noted how it not only inspired these young women to read but also, by portraying the life of someone much like themselves, showed them that there might be light at the end of the tunnel. Others noted, finally, that it portrayed small towns and their close-knit ties in a good light, one poster even noting, "Though we do not have a Wal-Mart in my town, I would like to believe we would have taken Novalee in." What all these posts had in common is that they saw part of themselves as they wanted to be in Novalee, in her friends, or in Sequoyah. Wal-Mart has been very successful in tapping into this metonymic chain based on strong womanhood in small towns, and it accounts for at least some of the store's appeal (Arnold, Kozinets, and Handelman 2001). To find proof of this, one need not look further than Oprah's message board, where several posters acknowledge that they will go visit a Wal-Mart soon just to meet people.

So to conclude, what Letts shows is that most people know that Wal-Mart, like many homes, is not perfect. While perhaps they rely on it too heavily (though not for everything) and it can ultimately leave them, for many, in a world they see largely as hostile, it remains firmly inside their moral geography.

King of the Hill

Mega Lo Mart now has propane and propane accessories at Mega Lo prices, and it *fuels* so good.

—Chuck Mangione, real-life trumpeter and fictional spokesperson for Mega Lo Mart[5]

King of the Hill, an animated series that began airing in 1997, is the product of Mike Judge, a resident of Austin, Texas, who is also well known for the cartoon series *Beavis and Butt-Head* and the corporate culture comedy classic *Office Space.* The show, which as of this writing has entered its tenth and final season, has been at the forefront of the emergence of adult-oriented, sitcom-style cartoons as a major television genre. The trend was begun in late 1989 by *The Simpsons* and includes other programs such as *South Park* and *Family Guy.* What all these shows have in common is that their comedy, in greater or lesser degrees, comes from social commentary and satirizing American life.

What makes *King of the Hill* different from its peers is that it is (mostly) realist in its approach. The series focuses on the Hill family (Hank, who sells propane and propane accessories, substitute teacher Peggy Hill, and aspiring comedian Bobby) and their neighbors in the fictional small city of Arlen, Texas. Comparatively little happens in the show that could not be done with live actors on real sets, forgoing one of the major advantages of animation as a medium.[6] In fact, its core cast of characters has become so well rounded and complex over the years that, despite the characters' rather unusual personality tics, the ultimate effect is that you actually believe these people could exist somewhere in the world (something very few dramas, let alone comedies, are able to achieve, even with runs as long as *King of the Hill*'s). Despite the many laughs had at the passions of the Hills and their neighbors, especially concerning their love of country, guns, the Dallas Cowboys (the town middle school is named after longtime Cowboys coach Tom Landry), beer, and their thoroughly unglamorous jobs, the laughs do not belittle the characters. Every single major character on the show, even quarrelsome neighbors Kahn and Minh, gruff grandfather Cotton, highly impressionable Luann, conspiracy theorist Dale, womanizer Boomhauer, and sad sack Bill, is shown to have redeeming qualities and an underlying sense of honor and dignity. In fact, in a recent article in the *New York Times Magazine* titled "'King of the Hill' Democrats?" the show gets praise from the governor of North Carolina as "only the second show that's a comedy about the South—this and 'Andy Griffith'—that doesn't make fun of Southerners" (Bai 2005).[7]

Arlen is portrayed as representative of towns/small cities/exurbs in Texas. Apart from the well-manicured lawns that are the pride of Arlen's families, there are two centers to town social life. The first is Arlen High School, where football reigns supreme, especially when the time comes to play the neighboring city and close rival McMaynerberry. Like in the town I grew up in, in Arlen adults still wear lettermen's jackets to games, and Hank is still known as a member of a team that almost won the state championship. The other town center is Mega Lo Mart, a clear Wal-Mart clone.

The treatment of Mega Lo Mart is not as gentle as Wal-Mart's in *Where the Heart Is*. Whereas in the Letts book and movie, employees are generally friendly and helpful, Mega Lo Mart employees are almost always uninformed teenagers, who, unlike Novalee, feel no loyalty to the store, one noting, "If I wasn't stealing so much beer from this place, I'd totally quit." Yet, like in *Where the Heart Is,* the store remains the center of town life. Apart from a grocery store that occasionally appears and Strickland Propane, where Hank works, almost all shopping done during the show is done at Mega Lo Mart. It also serves as a source of entertainment, such as in the episode where Peggy became obsessed with trying to guess the exact weight of an ice cream sundae at Mega Lo Mart in order to get the sundae for free. As in other aspects of the show, the people of Arlen are not judged for going to Mega Lo Mart; it is just something they do.

There are three episodes to which I want to draw attention because they focus on Mega Lo Mart in particular. The first of these episodes is "Mega Dale," from the seventh season of the series. In the episode, Hank's friend Dale, who is an exterminator, gets a prized contract to clear up a mysterious infestation at the Mega Lo Mart, but only because Hank recommended him. The evidence of the pests consists of lots of opened packages, droppings, and chewed-through wiring on the security system.

Dale determines, after eliminating rats and baboons, that it is likely a human causing the damage, and not just any human, but Mega Lo Mart spokesperson Chuck
Mangione. Hank, thinking that Dale is crazy, tries to stop Dale from doing any lasting damage to the Mega Lo Mart, or Hank's good name, by rushing off to the job
site with the intention of saving the day. After a series of events involving young
employees, Dale is proven right after all: it is Chuck Mangione who has been doing
all the damage, since he has been living in the Mega Lo Mart. The following exchange
occurs soon after Dale discovers Chuck:

> DALE: Chuck, I don't get it. What are you doing here? This is a long way from the *Merv Grif-
> fin Show*.
>
> CHUCK: When I signed a contract to be the Mega Lo Mart spokesman, I didn't read it care-
> fully. I have to be at every store opening, and they open 400 stores a year. I haven't had time to
> record, or tour, or give my old lady any slow sweet lovin' in years. So I disappeared to the last
> place they'd ever look for me. I've been living here rent-free, eating their Cheerios, playing
> their video games and trying on their underpants. Anything to stick it to the Man.
>
> DALE: You chewed through the security camera wires?
>
> CHUCK: It was necessary so I could come and go as I pleased.
>
> DALE: But what about the droppings? There were droppings all over the place!
>
> CHUCK MANGIONE: Make those Mega Lo chumps pick it up—they owe me.

So Chuck Mangione, like Novalee Nation, ends up at Mega Lo Mart because he has
nowhere else to go. Unlike Novalee, who is the ultimate Wal-Mart captive customer
who has no choice but to go there for the basic ingredients of survival, Chuck Mangione is the famously squeezed Wal-Mart supplier, out of whom is demanded an ever-
increasing supply at ever lower costs (with predictably horrible results for working
conditions and pay) and for whom there is no exit, because to not sell to Wal-Mart
is suicide. Thus, like other suppliers, Mangione is forced to take cold comfort in the
belly of the beast.

The second focus is a two-part episode that closed season two and began season
three, titled "Propane Boom/Death of a Propane Salesman." In the beginning of the
episode, Hank is sitting at home watching television when he sees the ad for Mega
Lo Mart, quoted at the beginning of this section, announcing that the store will now
be selling propane and propane accessories. This makes Hank furious. This is partly
because, to Hank, propane is a special product, not profane like the other stuff Mega
Lo Mart sells, and partly because Mega Lo Mart will sell it for lower prices than
Hank's employer, Strickland Propane, could ever hope to.

This causes Hank's world to start crumbling around him. Feeling betrayed, he
throws away the considerable amount of stuff that his family had bought from Mega
Lo Mart over the years. Further indignities follow at work, where the extremely
reserved Hank is forced to participate in Strickland Propane's new sales gimmick,
"service with a hug," for which he is forced to hug all the customers. Despite (or probably partly because of) this, Strickland decides to close Hank's branch of the retail
chain, because, despite Strickland service, customers will not pay "pennies more …
actually several hundred pennies more."

Hank, having been left with no other options, eventually takes a job selling propane at Mega Lo Mart, where he is lorded over and abused by high school students who do not have Hank's respect for propane. Ultimately, this lack of respect by one of the young workers leads to a propane explosion that annihilates the Mega Lo Mart. However, Hank was fingered as a likely culprit, because just before the explosion he had been about to lead a protest of older Mega Lo Mart workers whose prior jobs had been eliminated due to competition with the corporate giant.[8] Eventually he is cleared; Strickland Propane reopens because Mega Lo Mart will no longer sell the combustible gas for liability reasons, and Hank gets back his job, despite the experience having given him a temporary fear of propane, which, after his wife, Peggy, is his greatest love.

What is interesting, though, is that as the series goes on, Hank eventually forgets his animosity toward the corporate giant, and the Hills are seen shopping there again. In fact, in the "Mega Dale" episode cited earlier, Hank actually runs to rescue both the Mega Lo Mart as well as his own good name in the eyes of Mega Lo Mart. Here the theme of the inescapability of Wal-Mart comes into play again. Instead of being primarily a home builder, as it mostly is in *Where the Heart Is*, Mega Lo/Wal-Mart plays the role of home wrecker as well as home cornerstone. Though Mega Lo Mart had become a central part of Hank's home, it showed no loyalty, one of Hank's core values, only indifference toward him, and it destroyed his livelihood. After destroying him, it ends up as the only place Hank can go to for work, becoming even more necessary for home. Even though Hank eventually sees Mega Lo Mart temporarily destroyed, an event that causes him to fear propane, something at the core of his identity, in the end he finds himself back at the Mega Lo Mart, back to the source of indifference he once felt. So for Hank, Chuck, and Novalee, Wal-Mart is the inescapable home of last resort, "the place that'll catch you when you fall. And we *all* fall."[9]

Conclusions: Can the Circle Be Broken?

So, in the end, what type of conceptual purchase do *Where the Heart Is* and *King of the Hill* give us on Wal-Mart that we did not have before? For starters, they show that one must not confuse the cultural preferences, such as those enjoyed by the Hills and their neighbors, of people who shop at Wal-Mart with Wal-Mart as the target of opposition. There are countless real, strong, powerful, legitimate reasons to dislike Wal-Mart; these include unfair labor practices, which have led to a class action lawsuit by female Wal-Mart employees; the loss of domestic jobs from companies, such as Rubbermaid, that go overseas to keep costs low so they can sell to Wal-Mart at low prices (Buckley 2004); the working conditions in which people produce Wal-Mart's low-priced goods; its strategy of purposely opening many outlets in an area only to shut some down after the competition has been wrecked, leaving abandoned buildings and towns (Kaplan 2004); and many more. At the bottom of this list are aesthetic criteria, the design of the store building, and the facts that many products obliterate all known design principles and that it sells muu-muus and Christian books. Indeed, one of the things I find admirable about Wal-Mart is its aesthetics, especially its (likely far from altruistic) decision to use actual store employees, few of whom look like models, in its store ads. Remember, if you take away Method cleaners, Isaac Mizrahi–designed items, and glowing endorsements on David Letterman's show from Sarah Jessica Parker, then Target is the same beast, just smaller and wrapped in red instead of blue.[10] Among the big-box stores, only Costco stands out for actually paying its employees a decent wage.

Thus, if one is interested in attempting to battle the ill effects of Wal-Mart, one must understand that it is wrapped up in a metonymic chain that connects it to rural/exurban living, at least in the United States. Both *King of the Hill* and *Where the Heart Is*, which have won near universal praise for being rare, sensitive portrayals of regional conditions, feature Wal-Mart, or a proxy for it, as centerpieces of their stories. Both works show that the people in these places are not cold-hearted, that the characters are far from being duped and have a strong sense of right and wrong—even if some display an "us-versus-them" mentality. These characters, as well as the type of people they represent, know on some level Wal-Mart is hurting them, or at least that theirs is a dependent relationship. But they, though I should really say we, shop at Wal-Mart anyway. It carries styles of clothes and media the customers there want to buy (Wal-Mart's sophisticated tracking software makes sure of that), it offers low prices a large percentage of U.S. consumers can afford, and it also fits into a larger narrative that many ascribe to their own lives, a narrative about being simple, hardworking, and friendly. Thus, attacks on Wal-Mart often are seen as attacks by outsiders on everything that people hold dear. Wal-Mart has been very savvy to tap into this mythology (although its history has made it easy to do so), just as it also has been very good about attracting Hispanic customers to the store and about being a representative not of southern rural America but of American, family-oriented consumer plenty as it goes overseas.

So could anything break the connection, could anything push Wal-Mart away from the people who shop there and weaken it enough to make it more responsive to social justice concerns? Certainly it must be possible, though it would be difficult to do. After all, Wal-Mart already tears itself away from southernness when it goes abroad. That is because Wal-Mart's success is not derived just from its original cultural stance. Even if styles change and people desire to shop somewhere else, they will likely go somewhere else with all the same problems—or, more likely, Wal-Mart will adjust its marketing. In other words, consumerism as a phenomenon feeds Wal-Mart.

Here—borrowing a page from the article "'King of the Hill' Democrats?"—the key might be to adopt Wal-Mart's own discursive positioning in a campaign to undermine its influence. One could do worse than to work to make living wages and affordable health care coverage a "family value" and push for federal regulation to require all companies, not just Wal-Mart, to provide them. Since people feel forced to go to Wal-Mart as a social center, time might be wisely spent advocating for government funding for parks, community centers, and libraries near stores on traditional main streets—to create a center for one-stop shopping and entertainment on the scale of Wal-Mart—so that people feel like they have a choice. And, believe it or not, the constant deluge of bad publicity has forced Wal-Mart's hand. Just before the completion of this chapter, Wal-Mart announced a plan to fund women- and minority-owned enterprises, and also to more strictly monitor its suppliers for safe working conditions and progressive thinking—because "the retailer, not the suppliers, bears the brunt of the bad publicity" (Kabel 2005). Unlike a clothing manufacturer, Wal-Mart has to meet the customer face-to-face, and eventually it can lose face.

Notes

1. And here I am being a bit narrow: academics interested in supply chains, logistics, and management see Wal-Mart as a synonym for "got it together."
2. Perhaps what most thrilled me was that the Wal-Mart sold bulk packages of peppermint-flavored Breath-Savers, which, for reasons I no longer remember nor understand, were an addiction for me.
3. Though disaster closed this Wal-Mart, it is not uncommon for Wal-Mart to open stores in a lot of little towns in an area at once, driving all local competition out of business, and then, as had been the plan all along, closing down the least successful of the area outlets.
4. The notable exception is a Christian fundamentalist couple from Midnight, Mississippi, who think Novalee's baby was born in sin and is in need of saving. However, their harsh brand of Christianity is still put outside the confines of Sequoyah, where Sister Husband's more tolerant version is the only one that features.
5. All quotes from the show were found on www.geocities.com/arlen_texas/kothquotes.htm.
6. Indeed, one of the main characters of *Family Guy* is a dog named Brian who talks and walks on four legs, and South Park has included hundreds of characters and events that would be prohibitively expensive to stage with real persons.
7. I would add to this list *Designing Women* and possibly *Evening Shade,* both of which were semi-dramedies.
8. Ironically, the agitprop weapon of choice for Hank's protest group was the kazoo, "because they're portable, they're annoying, and Mega Lo Mart has them for three dollars a case."
9. It is also tempting to link the stories of Novalee and Chuck with the reports of cleaning crews being locked in Wal-Marts overnight, for whom Wal-Mart truly is an inescapable home.
10. In fact, I have always thought that protests and media campaigns against Target would be much more successful than against Wal-Mart, because Target's sales are much more dependent on its image.

14

Examining Wal-Mart's Relationships with Local Communities through Investigation of Advertising

Alecia M. Brettschneider and Fred M. Shelley

Introduction

Advertising is a critically important but often overlooked aspect of contemporary capitalism. Print and media advertisements are often the most important sources from which potential consumers obtain information about products, services, and prices. By viewing advertisements, consumers develop images of products and the corporations that produce and market them. The history of business is replete with examples of how successful advertising has enhanced (and how unsuccessful advertising has diminished) a company's success in marketing various products and creating its image.

During the 1980s and 1990s, Wal-Mart rose to a dominant position among retail chains in the United States and internationally (Graff and Ashton 1993). As the company expanded, Wal-Mart emphasized two key themes in its advertising: low prices and the importance of family and community. However, as Wal-Mart's prominence increased, many became critical of the company's alleged insensitivity to the needs and interests of the local communities in which their retail outlets are located (Swanson 2004; Burress 2004). Critics have pointed out that, relative to other corporations, Wal-Mart is only marginally involved in local community improvement projects, charities, and other community activities. Despite their advertised "we're all family" message, the perception that Wal-Mart has little interest in local community development has contributed to recent local antipathy toward Wal-Mart's expansion plans.

In this chapter, we examine Wal-Mart's recent advertising strategies and the demographic characteristics associated with these strategies. Understanding Wal-Mart's advertising activities and comparing them with advertising strategies of its major competitors is a key to assessing the validity of claims that Wal-Mart is insensitive to local concerns and charitable organizations. Thus, our purpose is to investigate the relationships among Wal-Mart's advertising and marketing efforts, community relationships, and image among consumers. After reviewing Wal-Mart's locational history, we examine the demographics of Wal-Mart's customer base and link them to the corporation's advertising activities. We then use this information as a base for understanding its perceived and actual relationship with charities and philanthropic organizations.

Retail Background

Wal-Mart's dramatic expansion has coincided with, and indeed contributed to, a changing retail landscape whose evolution is associated with dramatic changes in the urban structure of the U.S. population. Since World War II, suburban and exurban communities have grown much faster than central cities or rural areas. These changes have had considerable impact on the distribution of retail opportunities. Locally owned, downtown mom-and-pop stores have given way to strip malls, nucleus and outlet malls, and big-box retailers such as Wal-Mart. Retailers have followed the large numbers of more affluent Americans who have moved over the past half century from urban centers to suburbs. This movement is associated with the decline of manufacturing jobs in cities and an increase in business and service employment in suburban areas (Gong 1997).

In contrast to other large retail corporations, Wal-Mart did not initially focus on urban or suburban locations, nor did it adopt a strategy of relocation from the city to the suburb. Rather, Wal-Mart's initial growth occurred in nonmetropolitan areas such as Rogers, Arkansas, where the first Wal-Mart opened in 1962. Founder Sam Walton foresaw that increasingly affluent people in nonmetropolitan areas would take advantage of the opportunity to purchase urban goods and services at prices appreciably lower than those typical of locally owned nonmetropolitan retailers at the time. As Wal-Mart expanded, it was able to take advantage of economies of scale in reducing distribution costs, passing these savings on to consumers.

Large corporations such as Wal-Mart also benefited from the Consumer Goods Pricing Act of 1975 (Boyd 1997). The act facilitated the bargaining power of large retailers such as Wal-Mart because it allowed them to take advantage of volume purchasing at heavily discounted prices, thus reducing the cost to the customer. The act, therefore, favored large corporations, which expanded while small businesses struggled to survive in light of the competitive pricing and growth of major retailers.

Between 1962 and 1990, most of Wal-Mart's store openings occurred in counties with populations of less than 100,000, primarily in the South and Midwest (Graff and Ashton 1993). After passage of the Consumer Goods Pricing Act, Wal-Mart began to move into metropolitan areas, focusing particularly on places where Wal-Mart was able to take over when competitors encountered financial difficulty. Thus, the Consumer Goods Act facilitated Wal-Mart's takeover of already established competitor locations. During the late 1980s, Wal-Mart began to enter larger metropolitan areas, using a new and larger store format and carrying a more competitive and diverse product line (Graff 1998).

Many of Wal-Mart's critics have pointed out that Wal-Mart's expansion has driven smaller, less competitive local retailers out of business. As a large and expanding corporation, Wal-Mart has taken advantage of economies of scale in distribution, enabling it to sell goods at lower prices than its competitors. Thus, the presence of a Wal-Mart has had considerable impact on the retail structure of its host community. Wal-Mart's arrival results in lower consumer prices, but reduced competition. Vias (2004) suggested that retail survival in rural counties may only be possible through the decrease of retailers and an average increase in size of stores. Interestingly, Peterson and McGee (2000) found in small communities that larger retailers felt less of an impact from a new Wal-Mart than smaller retailers. As a result, small retailers in nonmetropolitan areas are most vulnerable to Wal-Mart's "geographically fortified" locational strategy, which emphasizes smaller communities (Speer 1994).

Critics of Wal-Mart's activities have also argued that Wal-Mart has less of a stake in the communities in which it operates than locally owned retailers have. Wal-Mart has been portrayed as concerned about profit margins in Bentonville and, therefore, insensitive to the needs of local communities and their residents. Many corporations establish foundations or charities. For example, Wendy's established the Dave Thomas Foundation for Adoption, a cause dear to founder Dave Thomas, who was himself adopted as a child. L.L. Bean partners with several nonprofit organizations to promote protection of rivers and waterways in the United States. Other corporations contribute to existing charities and philanthropic activities. Such contributions are often advertised to encourage customer preference and loyalty (Demko 1998; Blum 1999, 2000, 2001).

What are the linkages among Wal-Mart's locational strategies, consumer profiles, advertising activities, and corporate philanthropy? In this chapter, several sources of information and data were consulted to examine these relationships.

Wal-Mart's Locational Strategy and Advertising

As we have seen, a major strategy of Wal-Mart in its early years was to locate in counties with relatively small populations. By designing an efficient distribution system and through utilization of economies of scale, Walton was able to lower prices on many retail items relative to his competitors. As Wal-Mart expanded, it began to open stores in larger communities. In contrast, Target, Sears, J.C. Penney, and other prominent retailers expanded outward from metropolitan areas into suburbs and exurbs.

Wal-Mart's predominance in relatively less populated areas is evident from examining the populations of the counties in which its outlets are located. The advertising industry analyzes and monitors advertising expenditures and consumption at several levels, disaggregating counties into four categories, as diagrammed in Figure 14.1 (see also Figure 6.1). Counties in Category A contain the central cities of the twenty-five largest metropolitan areas in the United States. Counties in Category B have populations over 150,000 and are also part of the twenty-five largest metropolitan areas. Category C includes all counties that have a population over 35,000, and all counties adjacent to them. Category D includes all remaining counties.

Initially, most Wal-Marts were located in D counties. Later, Wal-Mart expanded into the small metropolitan areas represented by C counties. Only in more recent years has the corporation expanded into B and A counties. Since 1984, Wal-Mart has

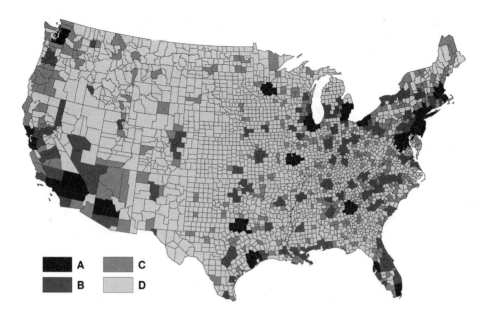

Figure 14.1   U.S. counties, by advertising industry category. A: County contains the central city of one of the 25 largest metropolitan areas in the United States (Chicago, for example); B: county has a population over 150,000 and is part of one of the 25 largest metropolitan statistical areas; C: county has a population greater than 35,000 or is adjacent to a county with >35,000; D: all other counties.

moved more aggressively into larger counties in categories A and B, but there remain substantial numbers of Wal-Marts in category D.

The preponderance of Wal-Marts in smaller communities is also evident from examining the demographics of Wal-Mart customers. In the early 1980s, Mediamark Research Inc. (MRI) began conducting national surveys intertwining demographics, product usage, and media consumption. MRI is highly regarded in the advertising industry and by media companies. More than 450 advertising agencies utilize MRI data, to which 90 of the top 100 subscribe.

The MRI survey is designed to ensure proper representation of different U.S. population variances. A sample of 50,000 individuals for the United States enables a statistically significant cross-tabulation between demographics and shopping behavior. Specifically, the demographics considered include gender, presence of children, marital status, education, employment, age, ethnicity, household size, income, and value of home. In addition, several geographic levels include region, marketing region, metropolitan area, and county size. For this chapter, shopping behavior is defined as having shopped within the past thirty days at a particular retailer.

In order to compare and contrast consumers' shopping behavior, MRI data are normalized by calculating indices. The base population for the study is the adult population, given the assumption that the adult population is responsible for a majority of household consumption and, therefore, decides where to consume. Each individual shopping behavior is defined as a dependent variable (variable of interest). The transformation to an index is accomplished by dividing the percentage target population by the percentage base population of the variable of interest.

This process is illustrated by comparing the relative tendency of men and women to shop at Wal-Mart. In one recent year, the total adult base population was estimated at 209,373,000. The adult base male population was 100,457,000 and the adult base female population was 108,916,000. Based on the survey results, it was estimated that 123,107,000 adults had shopped at Wal-Mart in the past thirty days. Of these shoppers, 56,019,000 were male and 67,087,000 were female. Thus, 58.8 percent of the adult population, including 55.8 percent of males and 61.6 percent of females, had shopped at Wal-Mart in the past thirty days. The final step in the transformation is to divide the percentage of the target population (male or female in this example) by the percentage of the base population of the variable of interest. Therefore, the male index is 95 ((55.8 ÷ 58.8) × 100), whereas the female index is 105 ((69.2 ÷ 58.8) × 100).

The calculation of the indices allows for a normalized analysis within and between variables of interest. In our example, it is apparent from the indices that in the past thirty days women (index of 105) were more likely to shop at Wal-Mart than men (index of 95). The more the index differs from 100, the more or less likely a particular population is to have shopped at Wal-Mart. Very high indices indicate a high likelihood of shopping at Wal-Mart, while low indices indicate a low likelihood of shopping at Wal-Mart. Advertisers pay particular attention to index values above 110, as these values indicate relatively high proportions of customers and represent attractive target populations. For example, a company finding a high index value for female shoppers would likely concentrate its advertising on products that are typically of more interest to women, such as clothing and accessories, rather than those typically of more interest to men, such as power tools and electronics. Likewise, the company might concentrate its advertising in places likely to be viewed by female consumers, for example, by advertising during soap operas and romantic comedies as opposed to sports broadcasts.

Analysis of MRI data indicates interesting differences between the demographics of Wal-Mart's customers and those of its major competitors including Sears, Target, and J.C. Penney. The index values for Wal-Mart shoppers living in B, C, and D counties were 110, 113, and 121 respectively, whereas the index value for A counties is less than 100. These values indicate that Wal-Mart shoppers are more likely to live in smaller communities relative to the general population. Target's consumers live in metropolitan statistical area cities and suburbs as well as A and B counties. Relatively few Sears consumers are found in D counties, reinforcing their status as an urban-oriented retail chain. In contrast, J.C. Penney consumers typically live in D counties. A disproportionate share of Wal-Mart customers live in the South. Target, Sears, and J.C. Penney consumers are more likely to live in the more highly urbanized north-central region.

Wal-Mart customers tend to range across the demographic spectrum. There is no particular age pattern of Wal-Mart consumers, since the values associated with each age category are very near 100. Target consumers, on the other hand, tend to be between the ages of twenty-five and forty-four, while Sears and J.C. Penney appear to attract older shoppers. The household income of typical Wal-Mart consumers is the lowest among the four retailers. Target consumers have the highest household income, while Sears and J.C. Penney consumers are between the two extremes. This pattern holds true for median home values as well.

Advertising

How are the demographics and locational profiles of retailers related to their advertising strategies? In order to address this question, we examine the advertising budgets for Wal-Mart along with Sears, Target, and J.C. Penney between 2000 and 2004. During this period, Wal-Mart increased its advertising expenditure by 25 percent. Among the four competitors, Sears spent the most on advertising throughout this period. Relative to the total volume of sales, Wal-Mart spends little on advertising compared to its major competitors.

The four companies vary with respect to the distribution of their expenditures among various advertising media including television, radio, newspapers, and magazines. Whereas all four use television as their primary medium of advertising, in Wal-Mart's case nearly 90 percent of its advertising is accomplished via television. This high percentage reflects the fact that television is the most efficient medium to reach mass audiences, whereas newspapers are more efficient at reaching local audiences. The local audiences in category C and D counties are small, reinforcing the efficiency of television as an advertising medium for companies such as Wal-Mart, whose locations tend to be concentrated in such places. Newspapers published in C and D counties, with their limited circulations, are thus not attractive to national retailers such as Wal-Mart.

A deeper look into Wal-Mart's advertising reveals yet another interesting trend. Television advertising includes four distinct categories: network television, spot television, syndicated television, and cable networks. Of these, only network television is solely national, and it is therefore the most cost-efficient for reaching mass audiences. Spot, syndicated, and cable television advertising are more economical for reaching select regions or market areas. Wal-Mart is progressively moving a majority of its advertising expenditure into network television. In the advertising industry, a transition from a local plan to a national plan indicates a strategy for reaching a mass audience in an attempt to sell the same image nationally. While national advertising is more cost-effective than local advertising, reliance on national advertising can reinforce an existing perception that the corporation is ignorant of or unconcerned about local circumstances.

Advertising attempts to relay a message to a specific audience, and the nature and content of the message varies according to the audience that the advertiser intends to reach. As we indicated earlier, Wal-Mart is modifying its advertising efforts toward a national audience. The content of this advertising effort has also changed. Advertisements produced by retail corporations are categorized on the basis of their content. Some advertisements focus on the corporation itself, while others focus on the specific products that the buyer can purchase. In 2000, roughly half of Wal-Mart's advertisements focused on the corporation and the remaining half focused on the products. By 2004, the percentage focusing on the corporation had increased to more than 60 percent, with only 37 percent referring to specific merchandise (CMR 2004).

Corporate Philanthropy

Wal-Mart's advertising is increasingly oriented to promoting the corporation as a responsible, effective, and caring corporate citizen. As part of this imaging, Wal-Mart's advertisements have begun to emphasize a philanthropic commitment. The web site, walmartfacts.com, emphasizes corporate responsibility. Web site users can access information on "Community Impact," and can also click on links to "Sustainability Diversity" and "Disaster Relief." As of May 2006 the sustainability link included statments such as "Using, encouraging, and investing in renewable energy is good for the environment and good for business." The message in this web site relates compassion and concern for the local community through ever-increasing contributions to charitable organizations. As we have seen, this is an increasing trend among major corporations that is designed to ensure loyalty among consumers.

Ironically, corporate donations to charity are outweighed by contributions from individuals. In 2003, corporate charity contributions were merely 6 percent of all funds contributed to charities, compared with bequests at 9 percent, foundations at 11 percent, and individuals at 74 percent (Giving USA 2004). These numbers are especially surprising considering the mass marketing efforts that tout companies' philanthropic efforts.

How do the four major retailers compare with respect to charitable contributions, as reported in the *Chronicle of Philanthropy*? Wal-Mart has been a larger donor in overall dollar amounts relative to Target, Sears, and J.C. Penney. This is to be expected considering that Wal-Mart is ranked number one in the Fortune 500 and therefore has a greater amount of profits to donate. If the corporations are compared on the basis of giving as a percentage of the previous year's pretax profits, however, Wal-Mart actually contributes a lower percentage of its pretax profits to charity relative to its rivals. Between 2000 and 2003, Target's range of contribution was 2.3 to 2.5 percent, that of Sears was 1.8 to 3.6 percent, and J.C. Penney's was 2.0 to 4.8 percent. Wal-Mart's percentage, in contrast, ranged from 1.2 to 1.7 percent. Thus, Wal-Mart's formal charitable contributions were low relative to other major retailers.

Wal-Mart's Web site contains a video library labeled "Community Involvement" (http://walmart.freedom.com). This channel contains links to video replays of twenty-two examples of Wal-Mart's involvement in community programs and activities. There are also links to the company's retail business, leadership, supplier networks, hurricane relief, career information, and company culture. This highlights local efforts to promote the company's visibility and philosophy, reinforcing Wal-Mart's efforts to represent itself as a solid corporate citizen.

Another example of Wal-Mart's community involvement is in its Acres for America campaign. In 2005, Wal-Mart's web site included a very colorful, attractive photo of an eagle soaring over a Grand Canyon–like desert landscape. The quote at the base of the photo read: "Mother Nature does her most stunning work when you give her some space."

Beneath this photo was the following quote from John Berry, executive director, National Fish and Wildlife Foundation:

> Wal-Mart is making history today toward protecting and preserving America's natural habitats. Wal-Mart's Acres for America program will conserve an acre of natural habitat for every acre of land Wal-Mart uses to develop facilities. That's every developed acre of land Wal-Mart owns today and will build on for years to come. Wal-Mart is helping protect our natural resources so you, your kids and your grandkids can enjoy more wildlife and more natural areas. Wal-Mart is the first company to tie its footprint to land conservation, and we are proud to partner with Wal-Mart to build this premier land stewardship model.

To the left of the quote was the insignia of the National Fish and Wildlife Foundation.

In recent years, Wal-Mart has attempted to restructure its corporate image by promoting itself as a corporation concerned about local welfare. Yet, as mentioned, the percentage of pretax profits that Wal-Mart donates to charities and other philanthropic organizations is small relative to its competitors. How does Wal-Mart reconcile this apparent disconnect, especially in light of its international prominence?

The answer to this question may lie in Wal-Mart's roots in the culture of the American South and Southwest. As the chapters by Hugill, Graves, and others in this volume illustrate, Wal-Mart is a product of the American Sunbelt during its boom years of the late twentieth century. The prevailing capitalistic ethic of the Sunbelt, as is well documented in many scholarly and journalistic accounts in recent years, is one of unrestrained individualism coupled with an aversion to big government and large-scale management. Wal-Mart's well-documented history of opposition to labor unions is very much consistent with this.

Sam Walton himself was a product of this philosophy. In his autobiography, Walton stated specifically that Wal-Mart is giving back to its host communities and contributing to individual welfare by saving residents money at Wal-Mart stores (Walton 1992: 239). He also discussed the "Bring It Home" advertising campaign, implemented in 1985 (Walton 1992: 241). Walton felt that this concerted effort to encourage American consumers to purchase American-made products over imports benefited the U.S. economy, and therefore he regarded this effort as a form of charity with the United States and Americans as the beneficiaries (Walton 1992: 244). Individual Americans, in turn, are encouraged to give back to their communities, but the impetus for such contributions is to come from the individual, not from the corporation. The individual is responsible for his or her own decisions about life, including whether to contribute to organizations intended to improve social, economic, spiritual, or environmental conditions.

This approach to charity is consistent with data concerning the geographic distribution of charitable giving by state. People in less urbanized states in the South and Midwest, including Arkansas, contribute substantially higher percentages of their cash incomes to charities (including churches and religious organizations) than do those in the North and West. Charity is seen as an individual rather than corporate responsibility.

This view also alleviates concerns among stockholders of some corporations who object to patterns of corporate donations. In recent years some stockholders have publicly voiced objection to the disbursement of corporate profits to organizations and causes that they oppose on political, religious, or other grounds. For example, some stockholders have objected to corporate donations to political parties and candidates whose campaigns they oppose. Other stockholders who are against legalized abortion have objected to their corporations' efforts to donate money to organizations such as Planned Parenthood that they regard as encouraging or at least tolerating legal abortion. On a local level, many Wal-Marts encourage their employees to contribute to local organizations, churches, and charities, and many match or augment individual contributions to such activities.

Conclusions

As Wal-Mart has grown and risen to national and international prominence, the corporation, along with individual Wal-Mart retail outlets, has been accused of insensitivity to and disinterest in local concerns. Wal-Mart has been criticized for ignoring local needs and declining to participate in local charitable and philanthropic efforts. Much of Wal-Mart's advertising takes place on network television and in other nationwide media. Given the magnitude of Wal-Mart's operations, such a strategy is cost-effective, but it leaves the corporation open to charges of insensitivity to local needs and concerns.

In recent years, Wal-Mart has begun to respond to these concerns about insensitivity by attempting to focus on its corporate image in its advertising. An increasing percentage of Wal-Mart's advertisements are focused on the company itself. Many emphasize relationships between the corporation and its employees, the local communities in which it does business, and the natural environment. Fewer advertisements are focused on specific types of merchandise available in Wal-Mart's stores. Relative to many corporations, however, Wal-Mart donates a fairly small percentage of its pretax profits to charities and philanthropic causes. The relatively modest charitable efforts associated with Wal-Mart may, however, be a reflection of the economic environment in which the corporation began and continues to operate: the idea that charity is an individual rather than a corporate responsibility is deeply ingrained in the economic culture of the rural South and Midwest, in which Wal-Mart originated and in which it continues to prosper.

15

Wal-Mart and Partisan Politics: From Agricultural Volatility to Red-State Culture

Fred M. Shelley, Adrienne M. Proffer, and Lisa DeChano

Introduction

Over the past decade, partisan politics in the United States have been closely and bitterly contested. The presidential elections of 2000 and 2004 were among the most evenly divided electoral contests in recent history. Much has been written about the political, economic, demographic, and cultural differences between "red" (Republican) and "blue" (Democratic) states and communities. Large central cities have become increasingly Democratic, while exurbs and many rural areas are trending Republican.

The current polarization of American politics has coincided with the national and global expansion of Wal-Mart. As Peter Hugill documents in his chapter in this volume, Wal-Mart's national and global expansion has coincided with, and indeed is linked to, the post–Cold War era of global liberalism. Many people, including business leaders and community residents, have opposed Wal-Mart's continued expansion for a variety of reasons. In October 2005, Wal-Mart announced plans to construct nearly 300 new retail outlets, in part on the grounds that the corporation "expects zoning laws to get tougher in the years to come" (CNNMoney 2005). Opponents of Wal-Mart's expansion have used local and national political forums in order to express and act upon their opposition. The politicization of Wal-Mart's expansion has meant that Wal-Mart itself is a subject of political debate. At the same time, Wal-Mart has also become more involved in both nonpartisan and partisan political issues.

In this chapter, we investigate the relationships between Wal-Mart's locational strategies and the results of recent partisan elections in the United States. We compare these relationships during Wal-Mart's early years with the situation today, demonstrating that the late 1980s and early 1990s marked the beginning of a fundamental shift in the relationship between Wal-Mart, its consumers and opponents, and the landscape of partisan politics in the United States.

The Early Period (1962–1990)

As is documented in detail in other chapters in this volume, Wal-Mart was founded in Rogers, Arkansas, by Sam Walton in 1962. During the 1960s and 1970s, Wal-Mart gradually opened additional outlets in small to medium-sized communities in the South and Middle West. Walton's basic philosophy was to make urban retail goods available to customers in nonmetropolitan areas at urban prices, which at the time were substantially lower than prices in rural areas. Walton took advantage of economies of scale and of effective, aggressive distribution methods to reduce prices of consumer goods, and he was able to pass these reduced costs on to consumers. Wal-Mart also provided customers with pharmacy, optical, automotive repair, banking, and photo services that had previously been provided by independently owned and operated small businesses. Wal-Mart's lower prices attracted large numbers of consumers who were able to buy services more cheaply. In many cases, Wal-Mart's success meant that many smaller, less efficient locally owned retailers were forced out of business.

Central place theory examines locations of retail outlets in communities of different sizes (Christaller 1966). The theory distinguishes between low-order and high-order central place functions. Low-order central place functions are retail outlets that sell low-order goods, characterized by low thresholds of demand (that is, a relatively low number of customers needed to keep a business thriving) and low ranges (the distance that a consumer is willing to travel to buy the good). High-order central place functions sell high-order goods, characterized by high thresholds and ranges. Thus groceries, T-shirts, gasoline, and other everyday consumer items are low-order items; automobiles, appliances, electronics, and jewelry are high-order goods.

Historically, central place theory was based on the premise that central places existed in order to provide retail services to surrounding rural hinterlands. The theory postulated that small communities contained only low-order central place functions, whereas larger communities would contain both low-order and high-order central place functions. The applicability of the theory to the actual location of retail outlets in the rural United States was documented in a variety of studies undertaken in the 1960s and 1970s (Berry and Horton 1970), which demonstrated that small communities indeed hosted mainly low-level central place functions. The customer base associated with these functions was assumed to consist primarily of local farmers and other residents of nearby rural areas.

In locating Wal-Marts during the corporation's early years, Walton concentrated on communities of this type—central places that served nearby agricultural hinterlands whose residents made up a goodly share of the local outlet's customer base. Of course, Wal-Marts were not located indiscriminately. Walton and his executives paid careful attention to the viability of local rural hinterlands. Areas with sparse and declining rural populations were bypassed in favor of those with more robust and expanding rural populations. This strategy is illustrated by Wal-Mart's expansion in Nebraska. The first Wal-Marts in Nebraska were located in the agricultural service communities of York, Fairbury, Kearney, Lexington, and Norfolk. Only later did Wal-Mart expand into the Lincoln and Omaha metropolitan areas, which today contain about half of the state's population. Many of the early Wal-Marts in Nebraska are located in communities characterized by little or no growth today.

Prior to the 1980s, Wal-Mart's strategy of locating retail outlets in communities that functioned as agricultural centers meant that Wal-Mart's locational pattern represented a reasonable approximation of the viability of agricultural communities in the United States (Shelley 1993). Thus the locational pattern of Wal-Marts in Nebraska is linked closely with the distribution of the state's rural population. There are few Wal-Marts in the sparsely populated Sand Hills region of northern and western Nebraska; most of the state's Wal-Marts are located in metropolitan areas, along Interstate 80, and in Corn Belt farming communities such as Fairbury, York, and Fremont in the southern and eastern portion of the state.

Agricultural service communities have a strong interest in maintaining agriculture as a mode of production. Thus, many Wal-Marts were located in regions characterized by a Jeffersonian view of agriculture—a view that conceptualizes farming not only as a business but as a way of life that is morally superior to lifestyles associated with living in the city.

The Jeffersonian viewpoint influenced and affected political debate in many nonmetropolitan areas in the United States during the 1960s, 1970, and 1980s. In Nebraska, for example, a statewide referendum was held on a proposed constitutional amendment that placed strict limitations on corporate ownership of farmland. "The amendment was most strongly supported in Corn Belt communities in rural southern and eastern Nebraska, places in which Wal-Mart symbolized the Jeffersonian view of agriculture as a sustainable, morally superior way of life were prevalent. Wal-Mart emphasized such communities in selecting locations in Nebraska and other agriculturally-oriented states" (Roberts, Ufkes, and Shelley 1990). This view also affected partisan politics during that period. Historically, voters in farming communities have tended disproportionately to vote in opposition to the party in power. This tendency dates back to the Populist era of the late nineteenth century, and reflects the economic relationship between agriculture and the national and global economy: when the national economy does well, farmers, as primary-sector producers, tend to suffer relative to urban dwellers (Hofstadter 1961).

In recent American history, at times when the farm vote was much more significant than is the case today, there have been strong backlashes against the party in power—for example, against Franklin D. Roosevelt and the Democrats in 1940, against the Republican Eisenhower administration in 1956, against the Republicans Nixon and Ford in 1972 and 1976, and against Carter and the Democrats in 1980 (Barone 1990). These backlashes were especially pronounced in counties with large, relatively stable farm populations. In Nebraska and Kansas, for example, the drop-off in Republican support between 1984 and 1988 was considerably greater than the national average in both states and was particularly high in rural communities containing Wal-Marts (Shelley 1993). The same phenomenon was noticed with respect to the third-party effort of Ross Perot in 1992: in Nebraska and Kansas, Perot exceeded his statewide percentages in a large majority of nonmetropolitan counties with between 5,000 and 30,000 residents, while he did worse than his statewide averages in metropolitan areas and in counties of less than 2,000 residents in both states. In general, Wal-Marts tended to be found in areas of political volatility prior to the early 1990s.

The Later Period (1990–Present)

The pattern evident prior to 1990 has broken down during the past fifteen years. The first three decades of Wal-Mart's expansion were characterized by emphasis on agricultural service communities, which were associated with Jeffersonian ideals. Today, Wal-Mart's locational strategies are much more closely associated with the red side of the contemporary red-blue polarization between Republicans and Democrats. Wal-Mart is no longer as concerned with locating in agricultural service centers; suburban and exurban locations, as well as locations outside the United States, have become more prominent.

Although Wal-Marts are found in every state, the ratio of Wal-Mart outlets to population varies considerably from state to state. The number of Wal-Marts per million state residents varies from more than 32 in Arkansas to less than 5 in New Jersey, New York, and California. Of the 2000 and 2004 elections, eighteen of the fifty states supported the Democrats in both 2000 and 2004; twenty-nine voted Republican in both elections, and the other three went Republican once and Democratic once. The eighteen states that went Democratic in both elections include the twelve states that have the fewest Wal-Marts per capita. Of the fifteen states with fewer than 10 Wal-Marts per million population, fourteen are blue states. In contrast, only one of the twenty states with more than 15 Wal-Marts per million population (Maine) is a blue state; seventeen are red, and the other two, Iowa and New Hampshire, went for each party in one of the two elections. The correlation between number of Wal-Marts per state and percentage of the popular vote cast for Republicans in 2004 was .59 ($R^2 = .35$), which is significant statistically at $p < .001$.

Similar patterns are evident in examining outcomes of elections for the U.S. Senate. In 2005, every state with two Republican senators had at least 11.4 Wal-Marts per million population. Of the thirty-two states with more than 11.4 Wal-Marts per million people, twenty had two Republican senators and only four had two Democratic senators. On the other hand, fifteen states have fewer than 10 Wal-Marts per million people. Of these, eleven send two Democrats to the Senate, three send one Democrat and one Republican, and the other (Vermont) is represented by one Democrat and one independent. On the average, Republican U.S. senators represent places with far more Wal-Marts per capita than do their Democratic colleagues. The relationship is not nearly as strong at the gubernatorial level, perhaps because local issues are generally more important in determining the outcome of gubernatorial races.

Combining support for Republican and Democratic presidential nominees, senators, and governors, we can define a "complete Republican state" as one that gave its electoral votes to Republican George W. Bush in 2000 and 2004 and that sends two Republican senators to Washington and has a Republican governor. Similarly, a "complete Democratic state" gave its electoral votes to Democratic nominees in 2000 and 2004, is represented by two Democratic senators, and has a Democratic governor. Based on this definition, there were eleven complete Republican states and six complete Democratic states in 2005. The eleven complete Republican states averaged 17.1 Wal-Marts per million residents; the six complete Democratic states averaged 8.0 Wal-Marts per million residents.

What has caused these changes? Why is Wal-Mart now so closely linked with areas of Republican strength? We postulate three major reasons for this change. These include the death of Sam Walton, the end of the Cold War, and the transition of U.S. politics from industrial politics to the postindustrial age. These factors have impacted the relationship between Wal-Mart and electoral politics since 1990. The continued restructuring of this relationship may continue to impact Wal-Mart in the years ahead.

During this period, Wal-Mart itself tended to stay out of the partisan political arena. Sam Walton made no secret of his personal dislike for partisan politics. Walton often "contributed to both sides in a political campaign, in case he needed a favor" (Albright 2005). Wal-Mart's board of directors included prominent Democrats and prominent Republicans. For example, Hillary Clinton, who in later years would become First Lady and then a Democratic senator from New York, served on the board while her husband was governor of Arkansas.

After Sam Walton died in 1992, however, his widow and four children inherited his fortune and about 40 percent of the company (Hopkins 2004). Since Sam Walton's death, the Walton family has become identified increasingly with conservative and Republican causes. In 2004, the Waltons gave more than $3 million to conservative causes and candidates. These gifts included a donation of more than $250,000 to the Republican Party of Florida, which is headed by the president's brother, Governor Jeb Bush. Sam's son John Walton, who was killed in an accident in 2005, was a major financial contributor to organizations supporting charter schools and school vouchers. These educational reform efforts are also associated primarily with the Republican Party.

Of course, the fact that the Walton family is increasingly associated with Republican causes is not sufficient to explain why Wal-Mart locations are concentrated in Republican-leaning areas. This concentration is also associated with subtle but meaningful transitions in American politics associated with the post–Cold War world. As other chapters in this volume document, Wal-Mart's global expansion has coincided with the large-scale globalization of the world economy that has taken place since the collapse of Communism in the former Soviet Union and Eastern Europe. The collapse of Communism has accelerated the pace of global production and distribution. Trade barriers have been reduced or eliminated, and the increasing speed and decreasing cost of global communication have made it easier and more cost-efficient to decentralize and globalize production and distribution of goods and services.

This globalization process is associated with a continued transformation of the American economy from industrial to postindustrial. In 1960, shortly before Wal-Mart came into existence, nearly 10 percent of American workers were farmers. This percentage was considerably higher in those southern and midwestern states in which Wal-Marts were first located. In addition, nearly 30 percent of American workers were employed in factories or in occupations associated with other aspects of industrial production. Thus, nearly 40 percent of the American workforce was associated with the primary or secondary sectors of the economy. Today, in contrast, the primary and secondary sectors of the economy employ well under 20 percent of American workers. More than 80 percent are employed in the tertiary service and quaternary (government) sectors, and this percentage continues to increase.

This transition has had a marked impact on American electoral politics. The "farm vote," which was so critical to election outcomes prior to the 1960s, is now insignificant. In industrialized areas, politics in the 1950s and 1960s were dominated by conflict between large industrial corporations and large labor unions such as the AFL-CIO, the Teamsters, and the United Auto Workers. Typically, corporations supported Republican candidates for president and other public offices, while labor union leaders and many rank-and-file members supported Democratic nominees. Labor favored increased government intervention to protect the interests of industrial workers, and thus it was supportive of programs promoting increased social security, high minimum wages, unemployment compensation, and similar economic policies.

During the 1970s and 1980s, however, many American-based corporations began to shut down or to move low-wage, low-skill labor operations overseas. By the mid-1980s, for example, nearly all of the steel mills that had been a major component of the economy of western Pennsylvania and northeastern Ohio had been shut down. Countries such as South Korea and Mexico replaced the United States as major steel producers. Areas dependent on heavy industry became identified as the "Rust Belt" and went into economic decline. On the other hand, those areas associated with the tertiary and quaternary sectors experienced rapid economic and population growth.

The impact of these differences is evident in Ohio, which was a critical state in the outcome of the 2004 election. Given how close the election was nationwide, the winner of the popular vote in Ohio would win a majority in the Electoral College. In his successful reelection campaign, Republican George W. Bush carried Ohio over his Democratic challenger, Senator John Kerry, by approximately 120,000 popular votes, securing his nationwide victory. Both candidates campaigned extensively in Ohio. In numerous speeches and campaign advertisements in Ohio, Kerry hammered on economic issues. He pointed out that Ohio, with its long history as a major industrial state, had lost more than 200,000 jobs during Bush's first term, and he blamed these job losses on the administration's economic policies. Thus, Kerry targeted those voters who were concerned about industrial job losses. On the other hand, Bush downplayed economic issues and emphasized foreign policy issues such as the war in Iraq and homeland security, along with issues associated with moral values.

On Election Day, Bush carried seventy-two of Ohio's eighty-eight counties. Kerry won most of northeastern Ohio, including the industrial cities of Cleveland, Akron, and Youngstown. He won Cuyahoga County, including Cleveland, by a two-to-one majority. However, Kerry's margins in Cleveland and other industrial areas of northeastern Ohio were overshadowed by Bush's strengths in less industrialized, more prosperous central and western Ohio. Bush carried the Columbus and Cincinnati metropolitan areas by substantial margins, losing the central cities only very narrowly and winning big in the suburbs of both these cities. These areas are much less dependent on heavy industry than is the case in northeastern Ohio. Significantly, these are also the parts of Ohio characterized by substantial population growth. Since

2000, counties in Ohio carried by Kerry lost a total of more than 14,000 residents; those won by Bush grew by an aggregate total of nearly 100,000 new residents.

The Ohio case parallels nationwide trends. During the 1990s, counties that were blue in 2004 experienced a population increase of about 5 percent; red counties grew by about 14 percent. In general, Americans are moving from blue to red places. In other words, places dominated by tertiary and quaternary sector employment—especially suburbs and exurbs—are growing much more rapidly than is the United States as a whole. It is these places, and no longer the farm communities that Sam Walton once emphasized in locating Wal-Marts in the corporation's early years, that now dominate Wal-Mart's sales throughout the country. These places have also emerged as major bastions of Republican support. The two fastest-growing counties in Ohio are Delaware County (exurban Columbus) and Warren County (exurban Cincinnati). Both grew by more than 50 percent in the 1990s, and Bush carried each in 2004 with two-thirds of the popular vote. These counties also reported the highest median per capita incomes in Ohio. Exurban communities such as these in Ohio and throughout the country are growing rapidly and contain larger and larger numbers of residents who appear to be identifying themselves with the Republican Party.

Wal-Mart's locational patterns in closely divided Ohio parallel a national trend. The seventy-two red counties of Ohio contain about 52 percent of the state's population, nearly 60 percent of the state's Wal-Marts. On the average, red counties contain more than 13.0 Wal-Marts per million people, as opposed to approximately 9.4 Wal-Marts per million in the more densely populated blue counties.

Two other trends should be noted. First, postindustrial politics are associated with a fundamental shift in the relationship between levels of formal education and partisan identification in the United States. During the heyday of industrial politics, there was generally a linear relationship between partisanship and education level. Persons with more formal education tended to hold professional, managerial, or technical jobs and were more likely to be Republicans. Labor union members, who typically did not attend or graduate from college, were more likely to be Democrats. Thus, high levels of formal education coincided with high levels of Republican support. As the U.S. economy has moved into its current postindustrial mode, this relationship has broken down. Instead, the relationship between formal education and partisanship is bipolar. Support for Democrats in 2004 was greatest among persons with both very low and very high levels of formal education, with Republican strength in between

TABLE 15.1 Relationship between Education Level and Presidential Support, 2004

Level of Education	% of Population	% for Bush	% for Kerry
Not high school graduate	4	49	50
High school graduate, no college	22	52	47
Some college, not college graduate	32	54	46
College graduate	26	52	46
Graduate education	16	44	55

Source: CNN exit polls, www.cnn.com/ELECTION/2004/pages/results/states/US/P/00/epolls.0.html

(Table 15.1). This relationship holds because of the relationship between educational requirements in professions such as education, law, medicine, and social work and support among practitioners in these fields for the Democrats. Educators, attorneys, physicians, and social workers are all in professions that are increasingly identified with support for activist domestic policy, which is in turn associated with support for the Democrats. On the other hand, Republican support is associated with the business community and other occupations that generally do not require practitioners to obtain graduate degrees.

A second trend involves the distribution of charitable contributions among individuals. The average percentage of income donated to charity per capita varies dramatically among the fifty states. According to the National Center for Charitable Statistics (2005), the average adjusted gross income reported on federal income tax returns in 2003 was $47,425, and the average person reported contributing $3,283 to charities and nonprofit organizations, including churches. Thus the ratio of charitable contributions to adjusted gross income across the United States was approximately 6.4 percent. Of the fifty states, seven reported charitable giving rates of more than 10 percent. These included Alabama, Arkansas, Mississippi, Oklahoma, Tennessee, Utah, and Wyoming. With the exception of Utah, these states—all seven of which went Republican in 2004 and 2000—also have lower per capita incomes than do many other states, and Wal-Mart's emphasis on low prices may therefore be more appealing to families in these states who are careful in managing their money.

In contrast, per capita church and charitable contributions are considerably lower in the Northeast and Pacific Coast regions. Areas with high levels of charitable contributions not only are associated with recent Republican support but also are more likely to be sympathetic to Republican policy emphasizing individual responsibility and faith-based initiatives as opposed to reliance on government to provide services. Thus, those areas most associated with Wal-Mart are areas more likely to be inhabited by cultural conservatives who contribute more to charity and who are more likely to support Republican nominees for the presidency and for other state and local offices.

Conclusions

The past fifteen years have been characterized by a dramatic shift in Wal-Mart's locational strategy. This shift has coincided with the death of founder Sam Walton, the end of the Cold War, and the transition of the United States and global economies from an industrial orientation to a postindustrial one. At the same time, Walton's heirs have become more identified with the Republican Party, while Wal-Mart's locations are more and more oriented to Republican-oriented places and regions.

Will this trend continue in the future? The Walton family is among the richest in the United States, but it made its money by selling goods and services to lower- and middle-income people attracted by their policy of maintaining low consumer prices. Historically, lower- and middle-income people were more likely to be Democrats, with Republican support more predominant at the upper end of the income continuum. Today, however, many high-income places have become oriented to the Democrats, while the red states tend to have relatively lower per capita incomes. Cultural issues are becoming more central to electoral outcomes in contemporary postindustrial society, and Wal-Mart has become associated with the cultural conservatism that is linked with the contemporary Republican Party. Many cultural conservatives believe that blue-state Democrats sneer at their values; such cultural conservatives are much more likely than their critics to shop at Wal-Mart.

This trend may be ephemeral or may be long-lasting. Throughout U.S. history, politicians have been on the lookout for wedge issues that will redivide the electorate. Key constituencies, many of whom are geographically concentrated in particular areas, are identified as critical to election outcomes. During the 1980s, Republicans were successful by attracting the votes of "Reagan Democrats," who remained liberal on economic issues but were drawn to the social and foreign policy conservatism expressed by Ronald Reagan and the Republicans. In the 1990s, Bill Clinton's electoral success was associated with his inroads into the normally Republican suburbs: so-called soccer moms expressed concern that Republicans would cut back education and social services.

Of course, Wal-Mart's customer base has long included, and surely continues to include, large numbers of farmers, Reagan Democrats, and soccer moms. What will be the key swing demographic group in 2008 and beyond, and to what extent will this demographic group be associated with large numbers of Wal-Mart consumers? To the extent that the Democrats succeed in making inroads into communities containing large numbers of suburban and exurban voters, especially in the current red states, the linkage between Wal-Mart and Republican support may begin to break down. However, a continued cultural division between blue-state intellectual elites and red-state middle-class voters will likely reinforce this ongoing relationship.

16

The Wal-Martification of Teotihuacán: Issues of Resistance and Cultural Heritage

Margath A. Walker, David Walker, Yanga Villagómez Velázquez

Introduction

In what has been labeled the "developing world," progress and development are often symbolically linked with consumption icons from the "first" or "developed" world. In Mexico, a country whose largest source of income is remittances sent by migrant workers laboring in the United States—surpassing revenues generated by the oil industry and tourism—small and medium-sized towns often positively perceive the construction of an international supermarket chain or the establishment of a transnational corporation as a constructive step on the road toward Western-style modernization. The sociospatial processes and impacts embedded in the embrace of such economic practices have been labeled in various ways, in line with those defining these phenomena. Characterizations include phrases such as "the power of commercialization," "globalization and its homogenizing effects," and "economic development" (Amin 2002; Castells 1989; Sassen 1996). Regardless of which conceptualization scholars choose, the reasons for the perceived benefits of "Wal-Martization" in Mexico cannot be isolated from the material realities of some of the economic and political shifts that have occurred during the last thirty years (Dezalay and Garth 2002). The arrival of transnational corporations has occurred in tandem with rapid and unfettered urban growth that has resulted in an urbanization rate of 80 percent, a figure higher than that of the United States (Barajas and Zamora 2002; Camp 1996; LaBotz 1995). The neoliberalization of Mexican political and economic life, which has strongly encouraged first-world consumption patterns, has also led to the decentralization of the Mexican government, effectively undoing the ties between municipal, state, and federal levels of government that were so strong during the seventy-year "perfect dictatorship" of the Institutional Revolutionary Party (Babb 2001; Middlebrook 2002). The complexities and idiosyncrasies touched on above are imbricated in the proliferation of Wal-Mart stores in Mexico and provide an informative lens through which to analyze how a seemingly sacred site such as the Pyramid of the Sun (Figure 16.1) can become a backdrop for a global mega-retailer.

Figure 16.1   Pyramid of the Sun.

In this chapter we briefly outline key moments in Wal-Mart's recent history across the globe, moving into the growth of Wal-Mart in Mexico by describing the company's aggressive takeover of homegrown supermarkets and retail stores. Mexican companies' attempts to compete with a transnational giant such as Wal-Mart are then discussed, followed by a detailed account of the "Wal-Martization" of Teotihuacán, one of Mexico's most sacred historical sites. In the next two sections, we provide an overview of perspectives from Mexican academics, commentators, and influential actors involved in the Wal-Mart debate, continuing on to an in-depth account of resistance to Wal-Mart construction in the area. We then present primary field research based on interviews done in Teotihuacán, a challenging and rewarding exercise considering issues of access, intense media scrutiny, and the local politics of community. We conclude with comments on some of the more recent occurrences in Teotihuacán and how current events interface with contemporary Mexican opinion.

Wal-Mart in Context

Wal-Mart has become a driving economic and political force in Mexico and has impacted the landscapes of small and medium-sized towns across the country. The transformative power of such an organization can best be understood by briefly profiling the company. For starters, Wal-Mart's gross earnings surpass the gross domestic product of Portugal, Norway, Switzerland, Poland, Turkey, and Saudi Arabia while practically matching the size of Belgium's economy of $247.6 billion in 2004 (Slater 2004; Wal-Mart 2000; Marrero Ruiz 2002). Currently the largest corporation in the world, with more than 7,000 locations worldwide, Wal-Mart is also the largest retailer in the United States, Canada, and Mexico (Soderquist 2005). It is believed that if it were a nation, Wal-Mart would be the 19th largest economy in the world. Big companies such as this often act as if they are nations unto themselves, and according to statistics compiled by the Institute for Policy Studies, fifty-two of the world's hundred largest economies are corporations, leading one analyst from the institute to claim that "we've given corporations more power than we reserve for ourselves" (Warren 2005: 34).

In Mexico, Wal-Mart employs more than 100,000 workers and controls 54 percent of the entire retail market, as it is the sole owner of the following supermarkets, department stores, and restaurants: El Porton, Ragazzi, Superama, Suburbia, Bodega Aurrerá, Vips, as well as the warehouse chain Sam's Club, and all Wal-Mart stores, making the conglomerate the leading employer in Mexico (Ribeira 2005). Employees are prohibited from organizing a union. When workers have attempted to organize, they have been fired and blacklisted (Bellinghausen 2004). The presence of Wal-Marts has negatively impacted local retailers and traditional markets in both major cities and smaller urban centers in part because they move in close to family-owned businesses and undersell the competition (Ribeira 2005). Controlling such a large percentage of the market allows Wal-Mart to wield considerable power over consumers, distributors, producers, and, as we shall see, Teotihuacán and Mexican politics (Ribeira 2005).

Mapping out the growth of Wal-Mart in Mexico necessitates a description of the Mexican national companies that were engulfed by the transnational corporation. Wal-Mart now controls the supermarket chains Aurrerá S.A. and Superama. Aurrerá opened its first store in Mexico City in 1958, making it one of the first U.S.-style supermarkets (Figure 16.2) in Mexico (Cano 2004), coinciding with the demands of

Figure 16.2   Wal-Mart store in Mexico.

the middle class, which was emerging during the import-substitution-fueled "Mexican miracle" (Camp 1989). The opening occurred during a period of changing consumption patterns among the middle class, spurred on by the end of the bracero program, whereby Mexican laborers were contracted to work in the United States; the program had begun in 1941 in order to fill the labor shortage that occurred during World War II (Herzog 1990). Upon returning to Mexico in the 1950s, they brought with them new ideals of consumption, creating a space for the emergence of Aurrerá, the success of which led to the creation of another Mexican-owned supermarket, Superama. During the 1960s, the demands of the still-growing middle class were met by other businesses that patterned themselves after U.S. models, such as Vips, a restaurant chain that opened in 1964. After several years of success, Aurrerá shifted its operations to warehouse-based retail in the form of Bodega Aurrerá, establishing a company called CIFRA S.A. to oversee operations. CIFRA gained control of both Aurrerá and Superama and began selling shares on the Mexican stock market in 1972 (Castillo Peraza 2000).

The first Wal-Mart unit in Mexico was a Sam's Club in Mexico City established in 1991, which was a joint venture with CIFRA. Wal-Mart acquired a controlling interest in CIFRA in 1997. As of 2000, *Vips* and *Suburbia* chains had been bought out, and the Wal-Mart Corporation had gained control of CIFRA, renaming it *Wal-Mart de Mexico S.A*, now a publicly traded company encompassing all of the formerly purchased companies (Lopez Reyes and Casco Alva 2002). With control of nearly half the retail market, in 2001 Wal-Mart renovated many of its stores around the country. Of interest is that Wal-Mart has not penetrated the consumer market in Monterrey, Nuevo Leon, in the north of the country. This industrial stronghold is home to several homegrown supermarket chains, including Soriana (Morais 2004).

More recently, Wal-Mart's quest to stay on top has met with struggles and challenges (Malkin 2004). Three Mexican domestic supermarket chains (or hypermarkets, as they are called in Mexico) won a battle against Wal-Mart stores when they received approval from Mexico's Federal Competition Commission to jointly purchase goods. The three companies, Controladora Comercial Mexicana, Organizacíon Soriana, and Grupo Gigante, formed a corporation called Sinergia, which will attempt to compete with the transnational company by increasing their mutual purchasing power (Castillo Mireles 2005). When the chief executive officers from Sinergia were confronted by critics who insisted that the success of Wal-Mart was the result of efficient marketing and state-of-the-art computer logistics, the president of Comercial Mexicana responded angrily, "I am fed up with hearing about Wal-Mart's efficiencies and logistics. The reality is that their efficiency is in the volumes they have and the way they squeeze suppliers" (Malkin 2004: 2), echoing frustrations heard from competitors of Wal-Mart in the United States.

Wal-Mart not only drives out domestic competition in the Mexican market but also aggressively attacks other foreign companies operating in Mexico. According to a May 13, 2005, interview with a PriceSmart executive who worked in Mexico and requested that his name not be used, Wal-Mart made it impossible to continue operations in Mexico. The company's strategy was to set up small stores in the state of Mexico with the goal of eventually opening megastores in larger urban locations. Each time PriceSmart chose a location to open one of its stores, Wal-Mart aggressively pursued opening stores in the same urban center, underselling PriceSmart and driving it out of the local market. This pattern continued until PriceSmart concluded that it could not compete with Wal-Mart, thus selling its share of the Mexican market to the competitor: Wal-Mart.

The Wal-Martification of Teotihuacán

In Mexico alone Wal-Mart has 671 stores in seventy-one urban centers (Marrero Ruiz 2002). Originally Wal-Mart mapped its stores onto the location of existing Aurrerá and CIFRA stores with strong customer bases in major urban areas such as Mexico City and Guadalajara. According to a study conducted by researchers in the geography department at the National Autonomous University of Mexico (UNAM), Wal-Mart then began to locate new stores in expanding areas of urban centers near major thoroughfares and new suburban-style developments (Marrero Ruiz 2002; López Reyes and Casco Alva 2002). As these markets became saturated, Wal-Mart looked to key sites in smaller urban centers that relied on clientele from the hinterland who came to shop on a weekly basis, a model upon which the establishment of the Teotihuacán store in the state of Mexico was based.

In order to understand how a Wal-Mart superstore could conceivably be constructed on a historical archaeological site that has been granted prestigious UNESCO recognition as a World Heritage Site requires a brief explication of the political events leading up to the decisions that allowed Wal-Mart to lease the property on Perimeter C of the Teotihuacán archaeological site, popularly known as the Temple of the Sun. Executive choices made by the National Institute of History and Anthropology (INAH) permitting such illegal construction are intertwined with the complex shifts in national politics leading up to the 2000 elections.

INAH is a federal-government-sponsored institution whose director is appointed by the president of Mexico. In 2000, President Vicente Fox appointed Sergio Raúl Arroyo as INAH's director, the first time a leader from the National Action Party (PAN) was selected for such a position. The PAN has historically been the center-conservative party, in opposition to the long-dominant Institutional Revolutionary Party (PRI), in power for seventy-one years prior to the PAN victory in 2000. Because neoliberal economic and political policies dominate the PAN's domestic agenda and the party's doctrine is well known for favoring big business, it was of little surprise to observers and longtime critics that the PAN-appointed director of INAH and the federal government worked closely with Wal-Mart to establish a Bodega Aurrerá warehouse store at Teotihuacán (interview with INAH employees, August 14, 2005; Salinas and Ramón 2004).

Part of the reason the PAN government and appointed INAH director facilitated Wal-Mart's establishment of a chain store in Teotihuacán is interlinked with the development ethos that has firmly gripped Mexico's domestic business elite, a sector of the country instrumental in guiding financial decisions (Dezalay and Garth 2002). Attracting foreign direct investment and promoting the appearance of economic stability are important goals for the country's current administration. Wal-Mart, with its material and symbolic connotations, encapsulates and reflects dominant hegemonic values at the heart of discussions regarding Mexico's position in an increasingly globalized world. For Fox, a former head of Coca-Cola for Mexico and the rest of Central America, the financial figures generated by Wal-Mart—Wal-Mart's gross earnings in Mexico in 2004 were $10.7 billion— resonate with a successful model of economic development. Critics of this development policy (Aridjis and Toledo 2004) accuse the administration of *malinchismo*,[1] as they are overtly privileging a foreign company (and, worse, a U.S. one) over domestic commerce.[2]

The construction of a Wal-Mart-owned store in Perimeter C of Teotihuacán's archaeological site has not followed an easily tracked linear trajectory, nor have associated events unfolded without controversy and debate. Such decisions and their effects have taken place within a politically charged context that has at times discursively pitted "tradition" against change, leading one Mexican critic to proclaim that the establishment of the Wal-Mart "is an affront to the culture and national traditions of the country. It is a demonstration of how transnationals do not value the independence and sovereignty of the country, while not respecting the historical and cultural significance of a site such as Teotihuacán. The fact that the Wal-Mart store's construction went through is witness to the policies of a government that have not sufficiently defended national traditions and culture" (Aridjis and Toledo 2004b: 56).

Counterhegemonic media outlets, including the left-leaning newspaper *La Jornada*, have been vocal in denouncing not only the decision to build but also the less-than-transparent processes at work within specific organizational frameworks (García Hernández 2004; Amador Tello and Vertiz 2004).

A cartoon by Rocha (Figure 16.3) appeared in *La Jornada* on October 5, 2005. It has President Vicente Fox asking the question: "If the conquistadors built churches on top of the pyramids, why not let those from Wal-Mart build a superstore on top of them?" This cartoon speaks to several different themes at work in the Mexican national imaginary. The first is that centers of consumption, such as Western-style malls, supermarkets, and multinationals including Wal-Mart, have become the postmodern temples of the Mexican populace, surpassing the importance of Catholic churches. Another interesting theme being evoked is ethnicity. President Fox's paternal grandfather was Irish and lived for a time in the United States before immigrating to Mexico; his mother is from the Basque region in Spain. In fact, if former president Carlos Salinas de Gortari had not changed the law allowing Mexicans whose parents were not born in Mexico to run for public office, Fox would not currently be president. The Mexican media is obsessed with Fox's background and consistently question his "Mexicanness." The cartoon can also be read as demonstrating Fox's sympathy to the Spaniards, who did indeed build churches atop pyramids, while simultaneously showing his empathy for the transnational corporation along with his inability or refusal to understand how such actions deface a national icon. In highlighting the *malinchista* or *vende patria* (one who sells the nation) tendencies of the current administration, the political cartoon is meant to emphasize the incredulousness of many Mexicans when confronted with the potential destruction of their history.

Figure 16.3 "If the conquistadors built churches on top of the pyramids, why not let those from Wal-Mart build a superstore on top of them?" (Reprinted with permission from *La Jornada*.)

Wheeling and Dealing across Scale

Three levels of government are involved in administering permits for construction of the Wal-Mart store. The first entity is INAH, operating at the federal level and responsible for making the property on Perimeter C available, and later authorizing construction of the megastore. The state government defined land use policies designating the area suitable for the Wal-Mart location. The municipal government authorized building permits for construction and promoted the project through legislative channels.

The area surrounding the Temple of the Sun at Teotihuacán is divided into what is known as three perimeters. Perimeter A is the central area where the Pyramid of the Sun and Moon are located, along with other aboveground ruins. This area first became protected in 1907. It is federal property and any alterations or new construction are strictly prohibited. Perimeter B is the area directly surrounding the pyramids. Within this space, according to federal law concerning monuments and archaeological zones as interpreted by union[3] members associated with INAH, "it is prohibited to construct any new buildings or add onto buildings that already exist, with the exception of edifices constructed by INAH that serve in the recovery or revitalization of the archaeological monuments found in the area" (Bravo et al. 2005). In Perimeter C, the same law concerning land use policy says that "new constructions will be allowed that do not negatively impact the preservation or integrity of the zone of archaeological monuments. Any construction must follow the plans and rules of the municipalities of Teotihuacán, and also follow the legal regulations of the state and federal government" (Bravo et al. 2005: 46). So how did Wal-Mart establish a store within Perimeter C of Teotihuacán? Does not such construction directly deface the integrity of the archaeological monuments?

According to information provided to the authors while they were in Mexico, in March 2004, Wal-Mart de Mexico S.A. requested a permit to open a Bodega Aurrerá on the property of Cruz de la Mission, in the subdivision of La Parroquia in the municipality of Teotihuacán, the exact location of which lies just at the edge of Perimeter C and the private property of resident Elda Pineda Alvarez. On May 19, 2004, the head of INAH in the state of Mexico, Maribel Miró Flaquer, authorized construction of the warehouse store, although the site is located just 500 meters from the Perimeter B section of an archaeological ruin called La Ventanilla, while also apparently ignoring the fact that there were archaeological ruins located in Perimeter C, where Wal-Mart had requested permission for construction (interview with Maribel Miró Flaquer, June 25, 2005; Amadar Tello and Vertiz 2004). Flaquer authorized construction on the basis of research conducted in 1984 by archaeologist Silvia Guitierez y Vera, stating that the site requested by Wal-Mart had no known archaeological vestiges in the subsoil and there was no possibility for future archaeological finds (interview with Maribel Miró Flaquer, June 25, 2005; Bravo et al. 2005).

According to interviews done on August 14, 2005, with members of the INAH workers' union who were employed at the federal offices prior to the administrative change in 2000, Flaquer's interpretation of the research may have been cursory at best and privileged the requests of the transnational corporation. Among the INAH unionized workers, it is well known that Perimeter C harbors archaeological ruins that remain unexcavated. INAH employees believe that the decision, based on twenty-year-old documents, is negligent and threatens precedents of honoring laws designed to protect historical monuments, which broadly fall under the rubric of property that is part of the "patrimony of the humanities and the nation" (Bravo et al. 2004). In conjunction with informal allegations of negligence and pandering to corporate powers, accusations include municipal government fraud in obtaining the building permits.

One of the interviews that we conducted for this chapter revealed yet another complication in building on Perimeter C. According to a municipal employee, part of the area where Wal-Mart sits is supposed to be designated strictly for agriculture, barring construction of commercial buildings. Thus this decision represents further disregard for the laws of Teotihuacán. Wal-Mart began construction of the warehouse store on August 4, 2004, just two months after receiving the necessary permits from INAH and the municipal government.

Resistance to Wal-Mart in Teotihuacán

There was immediate reaction and protest to the presence of Wal-Mart in Teotihuacán. The specter of a transnational corporation financed by U.S. capital subsequently resulted in a coalescing, however temporary, of diverse sectors of the Mexican population while also capturing the imagination of foreigners. A grassroots organization, Frente Civico en Defensa del Valle de Teotihuacán, led by Professor Emanuel

D'Herrera Arizcorreta, emerged, arguing in a flyer it distributed that the presence of Wal-Mart at a UNESCO World Heritage Site has "destroyed the archaeological patrimony, has violated the current laws regarding archaeological sites, and the presence of a transnational corporation at Teotihuacán gravely affects the symbolism that this archaeological zone represents for national identity." The Frente Civico has been active in organizing protests against both Wal-Mart and INAH and has had widespread success in obtaining national and international press coverage, for the most part due to its use of blockades, hunger strikes, and permanent protest sites at Teotihuacán, one in front of the entrance to the pyramids and another at the entrance to the Bodega Aurrerá parking lot. UNAM students have organized protests in tandem with the Frente Civico, leading marches to INAH headquarters and writing editorials critiquing Wal-Mart, U.S. capital investment, imperialism, and U.S.-style consumption patterns. Mexican intellectuals rallied together under the leadership of Homero Aridjis, a famous Mexico City–based poet and intellectual, and Francisco Toledo, a Oaxacan artist, activist, and critic of U.S. imperialism. Aridjis and Toledo wrote a letter condemning Wal-Mart, which they sent directly to the multinational corporation and President Vicente Fox and which was also published in *La Jornada* (Aridjis and Toledo 2004a). Sixty Mexican intellectuals endorsed and signed the document, including Carlos Monsiváis and Néstor Canclini, two globally recognized Mexican intellectuals. The Mexican press has been very vocal in critiquing Wal-Mart and the three levels of government involved in the case, placing the majority of the blame for the construction of the warehouse store on INAH. The media has been so active in following this case that one INAH employee stated in an interview on August 14, 2005, that "the press has practically become a protagonist in the Wal-Mart case, even though in reality it is not a contender. It has shown how the media can sway opinions and not always have all of the facts." The Frente Civico has been successful at incorporating local *ejidatarios*, or communal farmers, to protest the construction of the Bodega Aurrerá (Salinas Cesareo 2004). In fact, during the early phases of construction there were several incidences of *ejidatarios* who vandalized the construction site (Salinas Casares 2004). A more complicated read of some of the press accounts suggests that the foreign press, which has covered the events sporadically, has at times taken a romantic view of the actors involved in the struggle, whereby the noble Teotihuacanos are bracing themselves against the nebulous forces of capitalism and globalization. Web sites are full of opinion pieces by foreign intellectuals and activists concerned with the events at Teotihuacán.[4]

On the Ground in Teotihuacán

At the national and international scale, reactions to Wal-Mart's Bodega Aurrerá at Teotihuacán have been understood in terms of the deleterious effects of global capital systems and the kinds of development models they bring to bear on small and mid-size communities. Discourses from the press and public intellectuals are at times thinly veiled attempts to preserve national history and tradition while arguing that corporations such as Wal-Mart do not represent an unproblematic path for Mexico, in contrast to the rhetoric of government officials and many national and transnational business elites. However, much of the debate seems to beg two questions: (1) why would the municipal president and the chamber of commerce representatives in Teotihuacán work so closely with Wal-Mart to establish a store in the municipality, and (2) how do residents of the communities interpret Wal-Mart's presence?

A brief contextualization of Teotihuacán can facilitate an understanding of some of the socioeconomic conditions within the municipality. Like the majority of Mexican urban centers, the municipality of Teotihuacán has grown haphazardly over the last twenty-five years (Barajas and Zamora 2002; Davis 1994). Many of the 50,000 residents have moved to the municipality of Teotihucán to work in the tourism industry and the tertiary economies that have come up around this sector. Growth has occurred with little or no planning, and the urban landscape is dominated by "self-help housing," in which people take over lots, build homes, and then later negotiate with the municipal and state governments for land title and service (interview with Teothucán residents, Veronica Ortega, October 7, 2005; Norma Franchi, October 5, 2005; and Ignacio Kunz Bolaños, April 20, 2005).

"This is a poor municipality," offered Guillermo Rodriguez-Céspedes the municipal president of Teotihuacán in an interview on September 30, 2005. "The majority of the population lives off of the tourism generated by the pyramids or the poor farming that we have in the region. Why do these wealthy foreigners and people from Mexico City come here and tell us that we should not have a Wal-Mart in our town? The store will bring jobs and cheap goods that the people can afford to buy. The INAH and other government offices have not provided for the town, which grows more each year, so perhaps the Wal-Mart will help ease the poverty." This politician from Teotihuacán is echoing the official development policies of the current national administration. In his view, the invisible hand of the free market will lead to development and pull the country out of poverty.

Individuals who perhaps suffer the most from economic conditions are the *ambulantes* or street peddlers who are the mainstay of the Mexican informal economy in both small and large cities and who provide everything from household goods to foodstuffs. They also sell souvenirs to tourists who visit the pyramids (Cross 1998). "I for one am glad to see the Wal-Mart," commented one *ambulante* on September 22, 2005. "The store has already hired one of my children. There are too many of us selling souvenirs to the tourists; it is good to have another form of employment." (Interview with townspeople and vendors Sept. 22, 2005.) These testimonies coincide with the numerous public rallies organized by residents of Teotihuacán to support Wal-Mart's presence in the community, exemplified by the 2,100 Teotihuacanos who applied for the 185 positions available when the store opened (Cano 2004).

The owner of a fruit and vegetable store interviewed on September 22, 2005, was less comfortable with the presence of a Wal-Mart-owned store in Teotihuacán. "We will have to see. I have not yet been to the store to see what they sell. I am worried that they will have produce that they will sell cheaply and people will not come to me." (Interview with townspeople and vendors Sept. 22, 2005.) The vendor stated that he had not lost business since the store had made its debut in the town. Following the track record of Wal-Mart in other towns in both the United States and Mexico, it will only be a matter of time before the local stores begin to feel the pinch of the transnational's presence. For example, Mexican economic analysts report that for every two jobs that the Wal-Mart corporation creates, three jobs are lost in other sectors, creating a negative impact on the labor market in Mexico and perhaps eliminating employment for the more than one million Mexican workers who annually enter the workforce (OECD 2005).

The threat of loss of jobs and cultural heritage can result in violent reactions. Residents of Teotihuacán joined forces with members of Frente Civico and *ejidatarios* from Atenco, a town in the state of Mexico controlled by the radical Revolutionary Democratic Party. On a Sunday in December 2004 the group organized a march and rally against the presence of Wal-Mart that led to violence, demonstrating the intensity of sentiment against the transnational corporation. After conducting a ceremony inside the grounds of the Pyramid of the Sun, the 100 protesters began marching toward the Bodega Aurrerá to take over the warehouse store's facilities. Protesters wielding clubs and machetes were confronted by the municipal police, but after three police motorcycles were burned and one police car was destroyed, the municipal police retreated. Riot police were called upon and were eventually able to protect the warehouse store from the protesters (Salinas Cesareo 2004). The politics behind the Teotihuacano participation is not clear. There is some speculation that the *ejidatarios* were coerced by members of the Frente Civico to participate in the demonstration. Nevertheless, reactions cannot be understood as uniform across stakeholder communities.

Conclusion

Efforts on the part of leading figures in Mexico to boycott future Wal-Mart stores are gaining momentum due mostly to Internet-based petitions and editorial polemics in left-leaning newspapers. The trend is to highlight the horrific working conditions (including sexual abuse of women) within factories that produce goods for Wal-Mart. By pointing out the destructive patterns emerging from the marriage of neoliberalism and corporate greed, commentators track the spatial contours of these practices and stress how the effects are overwhelmingly felt in developing areas precisely because such places are viewed as more easily exploited (see, e.g., Ribeiro 2004; López y Rivas 2004). The increased attention brought about by the Teotihuacán location has helped to mark Wal-Mart as "an economic disease" rather than a business (quoted in López y Rivas 2004: 1). Outrage and cartoonish characterizations of evil global pillagers versus humble traditional peoples must be nuanced and tempered by the interpretations of the multifaceted and often contradictory communities that are most affected. It is this balance that makes Wal-Mart an intriguing case study.

We have provided a brief insight into the sociospatial politics and a sampling of the on-the-ground realities and reactions to Wal-Mart in Teotihuacán in the state of Mexico. Our hope is that we have shown the complexities embedded within the power relationships across and among diverse sectors when confronted with the presence of a transnational corporation. Such studies are increasingly necessary considering the proliferation of multinational organizations that travel along a north-south trajectory. More investigation is needed into the ways in which global processes, when grounded in place, coalesce with existing economic, political, and cultural materialities. The controversy surrounding the Wal-Mart-owned Bodega Aurrerá in Teotihuacán is not over. After its October 2004 inauguration, it was revealed that several artifacts had been discovered during construction, including a pre-Hispanic altar. Perhaps as a response, the director of INAH in Mexico City resigned, as did the director of INAH for the state of Mexico.

Notes

1. Malinchismo is a distrust of native products with historical roots in the encounter between Cortez and La Malinche, Cortez's translator and guide. For more about malinchismo, see Octavio Paz.
2. For more on this historical and contemporary practice, see Riding 1985.
3. Non-union workers have been hired or appointed since the emergence of the PAN (President Fox's party) to the federal government and are for building the megastore in Teotihuacan. Unionized members began working at INAH prior to 2000 and uphold the laws of the INAH and are opposed to construction of the megastore.
4. For a sampling of these Web sites, see http://reclaimdemocracy.org/walmart/links.php, http://unionizewalmart. ws, www.sprawl-busters.com, and www.ufcw.org/espanol/asuntos_y_acciones/walmart/index.cfm.

Part V

Globalization

17

Global Production and Distribution: Wal-Mart's Global Logistics Empire (with Special Reference to the China/Southern California Connection)

Edna Bonacich and Jake B. Wilson

Every Day Low Prices Equals Minimum Margins and Maximum Returns

Wal-Mart is the biggest corporation in the United States and in the world in terms of revenues and number of employees. It keeps growing at a rapid pace, showing no sign of letting up. In the first decade of the twenty-first century it appears as if no other company has a chance of catching up to it (Useem 2003).

What is the secret of Wal-Mart's success? Its philosophy, first set in motion by its founder, Sam Walton, is to offer the lowest prices to its customers, thereby undercutting all of its competitors. Wal-Mart's basic approach is to minimize margins and maximize returns (i.e., it emphasizes the speed with which goods move through the store over the profit it makes per unit). How is this difficult task accomplished? The answer can be divided into three categories: internal processes, relational processes, and external processes.

Internal Processes

Wal-Mart manages to keep its prices low by keeping its own costs down. This is achieved by abstemious management practices (limiting lavish spending by managers) and by keeping down the wages of its workforce (called "associates" by the company). The low-wage policy is maintained by providing weak benefits (for example, relying on spouses' health care coverage) and by a fierce antiunionism. Wal-Mart has used every trick in the book, legal and illegal, to keep unions out. For this reason alone, it has become the prime enemy of the labor movement in the United States and elsewhere.

Relational Processes

Wal-Mart is noted for its logistics excellence. It has been a leader in revolutionizing logistics processes, creating a form of just-in-time (JIT) retailing by developing high-tech coordination with its suppliers. In part for this reason, and in part because of its sheer size and power, the company has gained a dominance over its suppliers, putting constant pressure on them to lower their prices, sometimes with the consequence of pushing them to move their production offshore to lower-wage countries such as China. Indeed, it helps to play a role in maintaining and perhaps even driving down the low labor standards of poor developing countries. In addition, the company puts pressure on its service providers, including transportation and warehousing companies. These relational processes also cut the company's costs, enabling it to offer lower prices.

External Processes

Wal-Mart uses its considerable power to pressure government for various favorable policies and advantages. Its campaign contributions show a heavy tilt toward Republicans. In the 2004 election, Wal-Mart gave over $2 million in campaign contributions, 80 percent of which went to Republicans. In contrast, Costco gave 98 percent of its $208,000 in contributions to Democrats. Wal-Mart was a latecomer to the lobbying game, but has now become an important lobbyist in Washington. At a local level it has promoted favorable referenda and sought subsidies from local jurisdictions. These kinds of activities are aimed at maintaining or developing a political climate that supports its expansion and low-price strategy.

Wal-Mart's cost-cutting policies have had widespread effects. The company has driven small businesses out of business, destroying Main Street in the words of some critics (e.g., Quinn 2000). It has forced its major competitors, the other giant retailers, to follow its example. It has helped shift the balance of power between producers and retailers in favor of retailers. Typically, one would expect that a company with this amount of power would begin to raise prices, but so far Wal-Mart has single-mindedly pursued its low-price approach, thereby playing an important role in keeping inflation in check. Wal-Mart justifies its practices, viewed by critics as ruthless, by claiming that it provides the vital service of lowering the cost of consumer goods for everyone.

While its claim to benefit consumers may be undeniable, criticisms can certainly be raised about the many other effects of the company's policies. One potent claim is that Wal-Mart is ratcheting down labor standards along with prices. It lowers labor standards for its own workers, forcing most of its competitors to lower their standards for retail workers; it forces down the labor standards of its suppliers; it promotes the flight of U.S. manufacturing to the poorest countries of the world; it weakens unions (thereby strengthening capital); and, in supporting Republicans, it promotes a neoliberal free market ideology that threatens to keep increasing social inequality both within and between countries. In other words, the lowering of consumer prices is elevated as the only important social good before which all other social goods must crumble.[1]

The low-price approach has, of course, not restricted the wealth of the company's owners. This wealth is mainly reflected in the value of company stock, which makes billionaires of the Walton family, five of whom are among the richest ten people in the United States. The Walton family owns 39 percent of the company's stock, worth about $90 billion. They are as rich as Bill Gates and Warren Buffett combined, and their fortune is equal to the gross domestic product of Singapore (Server 2004). The discrepancy between the amount of wealth that the Walton family commands, and the earnings (and living conditions) of workers who are employed in Wal-Mart's worldwide supply, distribution, and sales network, points out the underlying hypocrisy of the company's claim that it is a great beneficiary to society.

This chapter focuses on the second form of price reduction, namely, relational processes (or logistics), leaving internal and external processes to other authors. Our purpose is to examine Wal-Mart's logistics processes, with special focus on production in China and the importing of Asian goods through the ports of Los Angeles and Long Beach.

Logistics

Logistics has two related meanings. On one hand, it refers to transportation and warehousing, that is, the movement and storage of goods. The term is used not only in business but also for the supplying of armed forces, which face the challenge of keeping far-off troops fed, clothed, and armed.

A second, newer meaning of logistics has emerged, namely, management of the entire supply chain, from purchase of raw materials through sale of the final product, and back again for replenishment of goods as they are sold. This expansion of the concept is reflected in the Council of Logistics Management, which, on January 1, 2005, changed its name to the Council of Supply Chain Management Professionals. Transportation and warehousing certainly remain an important part of logistics, but they are now incorporated into a more holistic view of the process of production, distribution, and sales.

Wal-Mart is considered to be the leading corporation in terms of logistics innovation and efficiency. Indeed, many observers consider logistics to be the key to Wal-Mart's success. Top executives of the company often have a logistics background and have brought strong experience to this task. By mastering supply chain management and continually increasing its supply chain efficiency, Wal-Mart has made logistics a primary area for cost cutting.

The Logistics Revolution

Wal-Mart's logistics innovations are part of a broader shift in the way goods are produced and distributed, a shift that we term "the logistics revolution." Wal-Mart has been one of the leaders in this revolution, but it certainly cannot be seen as its main cause. The forces that have led to this shift are much larger than one company, no matter how big and powerful, having to do with the evolution of global capitalism as a whole. Wal-Mart is both a product of these changes and a creator of them.

The basic purpose of the logistics revolution has been to improve sales by getting a clearer command of what is actually selling. In so doing, firms avoid the twin dangers of producing too much of products that are not selling or too little of products in heavy demand. At the same time, piles of inventory can be avoided, as a smooth flow develops between demand and supply. A major tool for achieving this goal is the collecting of point-of-sale (POS) data, using bar coding. Information on what is actually selling is used to trigger new production, automatically in many cases. The information can be used to follow and predict buying patterns of specific demographics and to track regional differences. It allows industries to gain better command of micro markets.

The logistics revolution is described by industry as a paradigm shift—movement from "push" to "pull" production and distribution. The "push" system describes the way goods were produced before the logistics revolution. Production was dominated by large consumer goods manufacturers who had long production runs in order to gain efficiencies of scale and minimize unit costs. This system leads to production of inventory surpluses which are pushed out to retailers. Manufacturers used deals and promotions to get retailers to make large purchases well in advance of delivery. This pattern is still common in some industries, but is disappearing for most consumer goods (WERC 1994).

Under the "pull" system, consumer behavior is tracked by retailers, who transmit these preferences up the supply chain to producers. Manufacturers are required to meet short lead times, making it difficult for them to engage in mass production of identical items. They must produce smaller lots of greater numbers of specialized items in direct response to what is selling (WERC 1994). One important goal of the "pull" system is the reduction of inventory for all actors, so that unsold and unsellable goods do not accumulate in warehouses. This system has been called just-in-time (JIT) or "lean" retailing (Abernathy et al. 1999).

The pull system leads to efforts to integrate processes along the entire supply chain, rather than within organizations. The goal is to make the whole supply chain more efficient and to minimize total cost. Firms try to move beyond functional excellence of one part of the supply chain (e.g., warehousing) to integrated solutions that serve the whole chain (WERC 1994). Retailers, their suppliers, and transportation providers ideally form strategic partnerships, sharing information so that all participants are able to rapidly respond to shifts in demand. Making this happen is the job of logistics specialists or analysts (Bowersox, Closs, and Cooper 2002).

The logistics revolution entails the following features:

1. A shift in power from producers/manufacturers to retailers, and a rise in retailer power
2. Changes in the character of production
3. Changes in the distribution of freight
4. Implications for labor in production and distribution

Let us consider each of these briefly.

The Rise of Retailer Power

Having POS data as the driver of production puts power in the hands of retailers, especially big retailers, because they are at the end of the supply chain. They are in the position of telling manufacturers what to produce, when to produce it, and often for what price. This power shift is epitomized by the rise of Wal-Mart to the position of biggest company in the United States and the world in terms of revenue. Wal-Mart was the first retailer to achieve the number one position in the Fortune 500, surpassing General Motors and Exxon in 2001.

The size of giant retailers adds to their power, and the bigger they are the more power they are able to exert. They can offer take-it-or-leave-it deals to their vendors, who often have no option but to take it because of the volume involved and the dominance of a handful of retailers over whole industries.

Retailers are placing ever more stringent requirements on their providers. They insist on speed and perfection in deliveries, and fine their vendors for the tiniest error or delay. For example, retailers may specify that goods be delivered "store ready," with labels and packaging meeting the retailer's specifications. Given that most manufacturers are producing for multiple retailers, they are left with the headache of meeting each one's specific requirements (WERC 1994).

Changes in Production

Accompanying the logistics revolution has been a shift from what has been called Fordism, or mass production, to flexible specialization (Piore and Sabel 1986). The latter is linked to product proliferation. Basic, mass-produced items have been transformed into "fashion basics," that is, minor variations around a central theme, giving the consumer many more choices. This greater variety is then produced in response to an ever-changing demand (Abernathy et al. 1999).

Flexibility appears to have two related meanings. First, it means the ability to respond to shifting demand—in other words, to produce and deliver a much greater variety of fashion basics than was possible under a system of mass production with long runs of the same products. Second, it refers to flexible production schedules, or growth in contingency. In this meaning, goods are only produced on an as-needed basis. Contingent production takes the place of predictable production runs.

Flexible production is linked to outsourcing, or contracting out. A core firm (the "parent company") contracts out much of its production, rather than having it done in-house. It uses multiple contractors that produce only part of its wide array of products and services. These contractors can be employed, or not, as the need arises, and generally cannot count on a steady, predictable set of orders. The parent employs a changing network of contractors, depending on shifting demand. This network can be in constant flux, as some contractors are dropped from the roster and others are added. The contractors themselves may produce for several parent companies. The result is a set of overlapping and continually changing relationships.

Despite our use of the term "parent company" to designate the firm that sits at the top of the network, its outsourced producers are typically not subsidiaries. The parent usually has no ownership stake in its contractors (though there may be exceptions in some cases). The typical relationship is at arm's length, allowing the parent the supreme flexibility of terminating the relationship at any time with minimal cost.

Flexible production is linked to offshore production. Once core firms began to outsource their production, there was no need to keep it close by. Contracting out freed them to scour the world for the best deals they could find. They could seek out the cheapest labor, working under the most oppressed conditions. Globalization became a partner of flexible production. This pattern has been associated with the rise of global sweatshops (Varley 1998) and what has been called "the race to the bottom" in terms of labor standards, as poor, developing countries have vied for production contracts by offering promises of low-cost, compliant labor. Needless to say, the rise in offshore production is linked to the decline of manufacturing jobs in the United States, a loss estimated at about 3 million jobs since 2000.

The relationship between retailers and their suppliers can be seen as a variant on the contracting relationship, as big, powerful retailers become more involved in production of the goods they sell. Retailers are playing an important role in the shift to offshore production. They set up buying offices around the developing world, and procure goods made to their specifications (Gereffi 1994). The producers of these goods may be "independent" companies, but they are fully dependent on the design and merchandising of U.S. (and other developed-world) retailers. Producers exist in response to retailer demand. Sometimes it may be possible for them to break out of this dependent role, but a huge amount of production occurs on these terms.

Changes in Freight Movement

Global production networks require more efficient logistics (meaning production planning and freight transportation). It is necessary to coordinate complex, sprawling, ever-changing supply networks. Goods need to be moved quickly and accurately, at low cost, over great distances. This kind of coordination has depended upon evolving information and communications technology.

A very important innovation was the development of containerization, starting in the 1970s. Containers allow for intermodal transportation (movement of goods between ship, rail, and truck without having to unload and reload the cargo). A container can be packed at a factory in Asia and unpacked when it arrives at a warehouse in Chicago.

Development of intermodalism is a critical element in the emergence of southern California as a major global gateway to Asia for the United States. Before containers, freight bound from Asia to the East and Midwest, still the most important economic regions of the country, had to pass through the Panama Canal to be discharged at East Coast ports. Intermodalism allowed containers to be unloaded on the West Coast and sent by rail (called "land bridge") to the East. This was quicker than the canal and opened the possibility of almost limitless growth in trade. The canal imposes a limit on container ship size, whereas intermodalism imposes no such limitation.

Consequently, vessels that ply the Pacific have become larger and larger, with no limit in sight. The ports of Los Angeles and Long Beach now handle about 43 percent of the nation's imports, dealing with 24,000 containers a day or 62 percent of all shipments to West Coast ports from Asia (Gimbel 2004).

The Impact on Labor

The logistics revolution and the rise of retailer power have had a major impact on labor in both production and distribution. The rise in outsourcing means there are layers of intermediaries between the "parent company" and its "employees." Although workers of these outsourced entities are not strictly employees of the parent, in reality their fate is often a direct product of the parent's actions. Not only can the parent cause them to lose their jobs by shifting production away from their direct employer, but the parent can also set the terms of their employment.

Flexibility (contingency) works well for the retailer but makes life more difficult for the outsourced producers and service providers. In turn, this makes life more difficult for employees of these entities, who face increased contingency in the form of piece rates, temporary and part-time positions, independent contracting, and so on. These irregular forms of employment have grown enormously in the United States as a concomitant of the logistics revolution. Contingent workers often suffer from a host of ills, including not only irregular work but also low pay and an absence of benefits. Big, stable companies (common under the "push" system) lend themselves to unionization. Contingent relations make unionizing much more difficult. With contingent connections, the parent can effectively shut out unionization by shifting work to contractors or regions or countries where they will not have to deal with "labor problems."

The contracting-out system makes both the direct employer (the contractor) and the geographical jurisdictions that house contractors fiercely antiunion. Contractors know that if a union manages to establish itself in their factory (or among their transportation workers), the parent companies will shun them and drive them out of business. Therefore, contractors are highly motivated to keep unions out—by legal or illegal methods. Similarly, regions, export-processing zones (EPZs), and entire countries face the same basic logic: if organized labor becomes a force that can improve wages, benefits, and working conditions, industry will flee the territory. Workers will have won hollow rights without jobs. Some countries, such as Mexico and China, have state-recognized unions, which participate in curbing the rise of labor standards and set another layer of constraint on worker protest and demand for change. Others set up legal and political restraints on unionism, including tolerating murder of labor leaders.

The weakening of unions is also clearly linked to a change in regulatory regime in the developed world, from the welfare state of the post–World War II period to the neoliberalism that began to take over in the mid-1970s and that has been imposed on most of the developing world. The welfare state fits well with the push production model, whereas neoliberalism, with its promotion of the free market as the primary regulatory mechanism, fits well with flexible production and distribution.

Weakened unions have a direct relationship to increasing social, economic, and political inequality. Increased inequality is patently evident throughout the world, both within and between countries. Capital is able to act in its own interests without much serious opposition. While unions are not the only important opposition to the unchecked growth of capitalist power, they are certainly an essential part of any oppositional coalition. Their weakening hurts the entire society.

The rise in contingent employment relations and the weakening of unions lead to the lowering of labor standards. Workers in the global consumer goods industries find themselves generally working for long hours, low pay, and with poor health and safety protections. Who is responsible for deteriorating labor standards in much of the world? The beauty of contingent relations is that the ultimate perpetrator, retailers who engage in arm's-length relations with their suppliers and contractors, can deny responsibility for labor conditions in their supply chain. Their defense is simple: "They are separate companies. We don't run their businesses for them. If they oppress their workers, it is not our fault." Absent from their model of the world is any acknowledgment of the power retailers exercise to create lowered or bottom-level labor standards.

Focusing on logistics labor (transportation and warehousing), in particular, statistics show that U.S. logistics costs have declined significantly since the early 1980s. They have dropped from around 14.5 percent of GDP in 1982 to 8.5 percent in 2003 (Wilson 2004). The logistics industry prides itself that the reason for this shift lies in all the efficiency gains of the logistics revolution. Inventory costs have been cut, and so have costs connected with most of the modes of freight transportation. Yet we can ask: How much have these gains been made at the cost of workers? How much of this reduction is a product of the shift to contingent employment relations and to the weakening of unions?

Wal-Mart's Logistics System

Wal-Mart has been a leader in changing the way goods are delivered to retailers and, in the process, the way goods are produced. The company has been a major innovator in the area of developing partnerships with its major suppliers. The prime example that is frequently touted is Procter and Gamble. Wal-Mart uses its satellite system and a program called Retail Link to share POS data with its suppliers so they know which of their products are moving and can plan production accordingly. Sometimes Wal-Mart lets the supplier take full responsibility for replenishment orders. This saves the company the expense of placing purchase orders and allows for a much smoother flow between sales and orders. This kind of partnership is a major gain for supply chain efficiency, and Wal-Mart has been rightly praised for it. Other companies have copied the practice, but Wal-Mart remains the most successful firm in this regard (see Bonacich 2005). Some argue that Wal-Mart's major suppliers have benefited from this approach and have grown along with the company (Morgan Stanley 2004). But there is an uglier side to this story, as Wal-Mart is in a position to exercise considerable power over its vendors. Wal-Mart tells its suppliers what it wants, and they jump through hoops to provide it.

The power of Wal-Mart lies not only in its control of POS data but also in its semi-monopsonistic position in a number of industries. In the United States as a whole, Wal-Mart accounts for about 7 percent of retail sales, which can hardly be seen as a monopsony. However, in its five most productive states apart from Arkansas, where it reigns, the company captures close to 20 percent of retail sales (Morgan Stanley 2004: 13). Wal-Mart dominates certain commodities, especially those that fit its model of "low margin, high turn." The company controls 10 percent of the U.S. apparel market, 13 percent of consumer electronics, 16 percent of food and drug, and 21 percent of toys, while home improvement and automotive occupy a smaller but rising share (Morgan Stanley 2004: 14). Procter and Gamble sells 17 percent of its goods to Wal-Mart (Boyle 2003).

While JIT retailing certainly benefits retailers, there is some question regarding its effects on their suppliers. Frequently the time allotted for an order from Wal-Mart to be filled is too short for the goods to be produced from scratch. The result is that manufacturers sometimes find inventory expense pushed back onto them. What appears to be an overall supply chain saving in practice turns out to be a retailer saving at the expense of the manufacturer.

Another criticism of JIT retailing arises regarding the retailer's payment pattern. The term "Bank of Wal-Mart" was used to describe this by a logistics specialist, Jon DeCesare. Wal-Mart will buy goods using "terms," such as paying for them thirty days after delivery. Because Wal-Mart tries to get the goods delivered at the last minute, they can be sold long before the thirty days are up. Yet Wal-Mart holds on to the money for the full thirty days, drawing interest on it all the while. This leads some manufacturers to feel resentful.

A criticism also arises from the steamship lines, as represented by Jay Winters, who was then chair of the Steamship Association of Southern California. The problem is that retailing of the kinds of consumer goods that Wal-Mart sells is a very seasonal business, with much of it piling up at the end of the year for back-to-school and Christmas. The steamship companies that carry the goods produced in Asia have highly expensive fixed assets in their ships, which ideally would sail on a regular basis all year long. JIT retailing is decidedly not in their interest.

Putting Demands on Suppliers to Cut Costs

A key aspect of Wal-Mart's relationships with its suppliers (and service providers) concerns its demand that suppliers keep cutting their costs. Some of this cost cutting has led to more efficient operations and the cutting out of unnecessary middlemen. However, at some point all the excess fluff has been cut out of a business, and you start reaching the bone.

Lehman (2004), previously a store manager for Wal-Mart, reports that the company wants to look into the books of its suppliers, examining their cost of production, packaging, shipping, and so on. Then Wal-Mart invites the supplier to meet with its buyers, asking it to sell the same merchandise at reduced cost, citing the areas (including wages) where it deems excesses exist. Lehman views the term *partnership* with sarcasm, pointing to the arrogance that lies behind it. In Lehman's words: "It's a ruthless situation, because the buyer already knows before that vendor walks in there how much your cost of production is, how much your cost of raw material is. So you're transparent. You're naked in front of that buyer."

There are many stories about the effects of this policy on suppliers (Fishman 2003; Bonacich 2005). Vendors may appeal to Wal-Mart that they cannot cut prices any further without ceasing to make a profit, but Wal-Mart appears to be heartless when it comes to such appeals. Some companies have found themselves forced to move off-shore (to China, for example) in order to meet Wal-Mart's stringent demands.

While much of the cost-cutting pressure falls on the shoulders of production workers, Wal-Mart also insists on various logistics practices that can be costly for its suppliers while saving money for Wal-Mart. Note how Lehman's (2004) description of negotiations with suppliers also includes logistics:

> It's very one-sided. There is no negotiation.... The manufacturer walks into ... these little cubicles ... sits down with the buyer, and the buyer brings up last year's cost and says, "We want to buy this much more this year, but we want you to manufacture for this much less and sell it to us and cut your lead time in half, cut your shipping cost in half, ship it to us on prepackaged displays instead of cartons."

So pressure is put on the logistics aspect as well.

A classic example of this is RFID (radio-frequency identification). Wal-Mart is pushing for its top suppliers to move beyond conventional bar coding to this new (and unproven) technology. RFID tags and readers are very expensive to install, and a standardized form of the technology has yet to emerge from the pack of those who are producing it, so a heavy investment in the wrong form may end up a costly mistake. Moreover, in interviewing one of Wal-Mart's suppliers, the firm's logistics manager pointed out that his company cannot see any benefits to itself from installing it—only Wal-Mart will be in a better position to track its products more thoroughly. Boyle (2003) of *Fortune* reports that one analyst estimates Wal-Mart will save about $8 billion a year by using RFID, while a typical consumer products supplier will spend between $13 million and $23 million to install it.

According to a reporter for the *Journal of Commerce:*

> Like it or not, many suppliers are scrambling to meet the mandate by two of the world's largest buyers—Wal-Mart and the Department of Defense—that they start attaching radio-frequency identification tags to their shipments next year [2005].... There is little doubt that over the long term, RFID can revolutionize the way companies manage their supply chains and even revolutionize their business processes. But a few problems stand in the way, such as the cost of RFID tags, conflicting standards and the lack of time to re-engineer business processes to justify the investment.... Suppliers will not see any return on the investment they'll have to make in order to comply with Wal-Mart's requirements, beyond the fact that they will keep Wal-Mart as a big customer. (Leach 2004 p 12–13)

Pushing Production Offshore

The growth of China as the manufacturing center of the world has played a critical role in the shift to offshore production, and we can only anticipate a strong upward trend in this development. China's exports to the United States grew by approximately

17 percent per year over the last three years. Wal-Mart imported approximately $15 billion worth of goods from China in 2003, and it alone accounted for almost 11 percent of U.S. imports from China (Useem 2004). This figure has risen to $18 billion in 2004 (Schafer 2004). Faced with pressure to constantly lower prices, some U.S. manufacturers come to the conclusion that they can no longer make goods in the United States at the prices Wal-Mart is insisting on. So they close U.S. factories and move to China or Mexico or Central America (Cleeland, Iritani, and Marshall 2003; Lehman 2004).

One can ask why U.S. manufacturers put up with this kind of pressure. Here is where Wal-Mart's quasi-monopsony becomes important. Suppliers find themselves too dependent on Wal-Mart, with no other outlet offering them remotely the same volume. In Lehman's (2004) words, suppliers reason: "We can't get out of bed with Wal-Mart now. We've been in bed too long. We have nobody else to sell our merchandise to that matters anymore."

Global Sourcing

Most focus on Wal-Mart's international activities concerns expansion of its stores. For example, in a special issue of *DSN Retailing Today*, focusing on Wal-Mart International, forty-eight pages out of fifty deal with the stores. Two pages are devoted to global procurement (Troy 2004). This is the aspect of Wal-Mart's global empire that we are most interested in.

The home office of Wal-Mart Global Procurement is in Shenzhen, China. Before 2002, Wal-Mart worked through a Hong Kong–based third party that handled its imports. The company also had an internal group known as Global Sourcing, which sought out regional and global opportunities, and often worked with the third party. In early 2002, Wal-Mart terminated its relationship and brought its import business in-house, setting up offices in Shenzhen. Global Sourcing also was absorbed by this new group. By the end of 2004, Global Procurement employed 1,200 people, most based at the Shenzhen headquarters. The company also has a network of over two dozen field offices in other countries and oversees the sourcing of products from 5,000 factories in sixty-five countries (Troy 2004). The company moved its sourcing functions in Taiwan, including apparel, shoes, groceries, and hard goods, to Shenzhen. By early 2004 Wal-Mart had two sourcing centers in China, one in Shenzhen and the other in Shanghai (Morgan Stanley 2004: 19).[2] According to Troy (2004 p. 27–28), "Aside from reducing sourcing costs by eliminating layers of middlemen, bringing the global procurement function in-house has given Wal-Mart greater oversight of the suppliers it sources products from and the factories they use."

An analyst for the investment company Morgan Stanley (2004: 19) states that Wal-Mart's product sourcing can be divided into two areas: general merchandise (including apparel) and food. At the time of the analysis, almost all the food products Wal-Mart sold were sourced domestically, though the company was planning to move much of this segment of the business offshore soon. Global procurement accounted for 15–20 percent of general merchandise products, a percentage the company planned to increase.

Wal-Mart's experience was that global sourcing lowered merchandise costs by 10–20 percent. The top fifteen supplying countries, in alphabetical order, were Bangladesh, Brazil, China, Guatemala, Honduras, Hong Kong, India, Indonesia, Malaysia, Pakistan, Philippines, South Korea, Sri Lanka, Taiwan, and Thailand. These countries accounted for 95 percent of Wal-Mart's direct import volume. China is by far the largest source, accounting for about 50 percent of direct imports. Still, in early 2004 it accounted for less than 10 percent of total company purchases (Morgan Stanley 2004: 19).

The importance of retailing in global production is shown in imports. Every year the *Journal of Commerce* develops a report of the top importers to the United States. It measures this by number of containers (TEUs, or 20-foot equivalent units). This is a measure of volume rather than tonnage or value. A rough estimate of tonnage can be made from the fact that each 40-foot container (FEU) carries an average of 30 tons of goods. Missing from this source are air freight and cross-border imports. Air freight represents a significant portion of the value of imports but accounts for a small proportion of the volume. In reality, the vast majority of manufactured imports arrive via ocean carriers, and most of these are now container vessels.

The *Journal of Commerce* lists the top one hundred importers. In 2002, thirty-two were retailers. The top three are Wal-Mart, which brings in 291,000 TEUs, followed by Home Depot, with 182,000 TEUs, and Target, with 173,100 TEUs. Among the top twenty are also Lowe's, Payless ShoeSource, Pier 1 Imports, Kmart, Big Lots, and Ikea (*Journal of Commerce* April 28, 2003: 18A). The top three retailers account for almost 40 percent of the TEUs imported by the top twenty importers. As can be seen, Wal-Mart towers above all others.

Imports by the retailers measured by *Journal of Commerce* do not include the imports of their vendors. Thus Mattel, the toy manufacturer, imported 43,700 TEUs in 2002, a large proportion of which went to its primary retailer, Wal-Mart. The actual number of imports sold by retailers is thus far larger than these statistics would indicate.

Production and Procurement in China

About half of the $18 billion worth of goods brought into the U.S. by Wal-Mart in 2004 were directly imported by the company, while the remaining half came indirectly through Wal-Mart's suppliers (Dobson 2004).[3] Wal-Mart sources such an immense amount of Chinese-made products that if it were a country, Wal-Mart would be China's eighth largest trading partner and its sixth largest export market after Germany (Schafer 2004). These numbers are expected to continue to rise as Wal-Mart's sourcing in China is projected to reach $25–$30 billion within the next five years (Hua 2004). Wal-Mart's immense volume of Chinese imports brings with it an enormous amount of power over the Chinese economy. Needless to say, Wal-Mart is not just a passive recipient of Chinese-produced goods but an active producer of those goods. The company is a major actor in China not only as an expanding retailer power but perhaps more importantly as a shaper of production.

There are a number of reasons that explain Wal-Mart's success in China, ranging from its relentless control of the supply chain to its constant search for the cheapest suppliers.

Former store manager Lehman (2004) reports that the pressure to cut production and shipping costs is just as intense in China as in the United States. The "natural" cheapness of Chinese production is not enough for Wal-Mart. The company puts pressure on already poor conditions to lower them still further (see also Goodman and Pan 2004).

As reported above, in 2002 Wal-Mart Global Procurement was established in China. Wal-Mart Global Procurement (or the "negotiations center," as it is commonly referred to in the industry) is the backbone behind Wal-Mart's grip over China's supply chain (Schafer 2004). On a daily basis, Wal-Mart's procurement staff members are constantly making deals with hundreds of Chinese manufacturers in order to produce goods tailored to Wal-Mart's own stringent specifications, including pricing, quality assurance, efficiency, and delivery. For many Wal-Mart suppliers entering the negotiations center, the experience is a painful one. If particular suppliers' goods are not maintaining Wal-Mart's specified sales levels, the suppliers are immediately shown the door, unless they have utilized Wal-Mart's computer software to examine the market situation at hand and can propose alternatives. In the negotiations center, supply deals are made, or terminated, in a heartbeat (Schafer 2004). Many Chinese contractors have been required by Wal-Mart to send their representatives to intensive training seminars at Wal-Mart's procurement center to learn how to integrate Wal-Mart's proprietary software, further emphasizing Wal-Mart's control over the production process and its suppliers. This also places Wal-Mart clients at the mercy of the giant retailer.

Wal-Mart is also known to demand that its suppliers change their bookkeeping systems and improve their logistics to meet rigid delivery schedules while maintaining the lowest price margins. In exchange for Wal-Mart contracts, Chinese companies are often required to open up their books to Wal-Mart and cut prices where necessary if Wal-Mart decides the supplier's profit margins are too large (Jubak 2004). Wal-Mart demands rock-bottom prices and forces its clients to cut costs in order to remain in contention for export orders.

For example, Ching Hai is a contract manufacturer that produces juicers, fans, and toasters for some of the largest retailers, with Wal-Mart as its biggest client. Over the last decade, the average wholesale price for Ching Hai's products has almost halved, from $7 to $4, in order to continue doing business with Wal-Mart (Wonacott 2003). Wal-Mart's Chinese producers have to find ways to lower their costs, which often leads to further exploiting their labor force. Wal-Mart's control too often translates into low labor standards for workers, who are usually economically oppressed women who have moved from rural areas to find work:

> Ching Hai manager, David Liu, has cut his labor force in half, to 1,500 workers, even while maintaining the same level of orders. The company's starting salary of about $32 a month is some 40 percent less than the local minimum wage. Many workers put in 18-hour days with minimal training and constant pressure to boost output. Despite the cost cutting, Mr. Liu says Ching Hai is just barely profitable, although he declines to provide any figures. (Wonacott 2003)

Ching Hai has been investigated for its high rate of workplace accidents, presumably because of the intense pressure placed on the supplier to increase production output (Wonacott 2003).

Wal-Mart directly sources products from suppliers in various regions of China, but its presence is most extensive in southern China. Wal-Mart's presence in Shenzhen has undoubtedly influenced the port's rise to its current position as the fourth largest port in the world. Wal-Mart's gigantic warehouse at the Shenzhen port serves as the major distribution center for its Chinese procurements, with its distribution center in Tianjin following closely behind in significance. Wal-Mart's reliance on its distribution centers, such as the one in Shenzhen, and its (contracted) back-haul trucking system allows the giant retailer to have significant control over the distribution chain (Huffman 2003). However, Wal-Mart is certainly gaining ground in other parts of China's northern and eastern regions. For instance, market insiders have indicated Wal-Mart's interest in acquiring a 340,000-square-meter (3,659,730-square-foot) warehouse at a logistics park in the Bonded Area of Shanghai Waigaoqiao, which would surely increase Wal-Mart's sourcing abilities in China (Jingjin 2004). According to a reporter for the *China Business Review:*

> Wal-Mart has used case studies of fragmented transportation and distribution to educate its suppliers to help them streamline their operations and reduce costs—to the benefit of both parties. Sometimes these issues require company participation in the debate for liberalization and standardization. As a result, Wal-Mart has become heavily involved in government relations and has participated in these debates by talking directly with Chinese government officials at both local and national levels and through trade groups in both the United States and China. To overcome the difficulties of distribution and supply chain management in China, supply chain managers will have to be creative and persevere to achieve success in a market that will be central to them and their customers in the twenty-first century. (Huffman 2003)

In sum, Wal-Mart is far from a passive recipient of Chinese-produced goods, taking advantage of the low wages that are prevalent in a newly developing country with a large, untapped, labor supply. Rather, it is playing a role in keeping labor standards in China as low as they can be pushed.

Wal-Mart and the Ports of Southern California

As stated above, Wal-Mart is by far the largest importer of goods to the United States by marine transportation. This makes Wal-Mart the largest user of the ports as well as of the entire intermodal freight transportation system, with consequences throughout.

In October 2004, in anticipation of the Christmas season, a major jam developed at the ports of Los Angeles and Long Beach. Ninety-four ships were stuck outside the ports waiting to enter. All the logistics systems were overwhelmed: there was a shortage of longshore workers, the railroads could not handle the flood of cargo, and truck drivers were quitting because of long, unpaid waits in line (Gimbel 2004).

A key to this jam was the behavior of Wal-Mart. In August 2004 Wal-Mart called a meeting in Long Beach of railroads, truckers, warehouse operators, and third-party logistics providers and announced that it would push more containerized goods through the southern California ports during the months of September and October than it had ever done before during peak season. Writing in early September, Mongelluzzo noted:

> Wal-Mart's decision to ship most of its peak-season cargo in two months rather than spreading it out over the late summer and fall will ripple through the international supply chain, affecting shipping lines, ports, warehouses, distribution centers, and inland transportation providers. (Mongelluzzo 2004 p. 22)

The expectation was that Wal-Mart would ship at least 50,000 FEUs in each of the two months, and maybe as many as 63,000 per month.

> To tighten its supply chain and minimize inventory-carrying costs, Wal-Mart has negotiated with factories in Asia to hold the cargo until September.... Putting off inventory-carrying costs is not a new concept. Many retailers have been gravitating in that direction. No other retailer, however, operates on the scale of Wal-Mart.... Wal-Mart's surge in volume will tax the resources of an intermodal transportation chain that already is struggling with tight capacity. (Mongelluzzo 2004 p. 24)

This prediction proved all too true. Because capacity was squeezed, steamship companies were able to impose peak-season surcharges of up to $400 per container, which smaller shippers would have to pay but larger shippers (including Wal-Mart) could avoid. Wal-Mart's decision to narrow its window of importing was subsidized, in a sense, by a tax on its smaller competitors.

Gimbel describes the impact on manufacturers who are importing goods from China:

> Take K. C. McCarthy, the supply-chain manager of Topco Sales, a cosmetic company. He thought he would be saving substantial sums of money by manufacturing his goods in China this year, but instead he's had to get some of his products out of Los Angeles on planes to get them to retailers like Target and Wal-Mart on time. (If he misses a deadline, he can suffer fines called chargebacks or, worse, lose his contract altogether.) The cost differences are staggering. A 40-foot container costs about $900 to ship from Los Angeles to Houston by train.... Putting that same "can" on a truck raises the price to more than $4,000. Air freight for 22 tons of cargo? Try about $40,000. There go your profits and then some. "The big guys don't care," Morales says. "They say 'get it here or else.'" (Gimbel 2004 p. 162–170)

Putting Demands on Logistics Providers

Just as Wal-Mart puts demands for cost-cutting on its suppliers, it also puts pressure on its logistics providers. The most notorious case was its involvement in the West Coast ports lockout of longshore workers in 2002. The contract between the Pacific Maritime Association (PMA), the organization of steamship lines and port terminal operators who employ the longshore workers, which oversees the contract, wanted to win some concessions from the powerful International Longshore and Warehouse Union (ILWU). Normally the contract renewal process is conducted by these two parties, but in 2002 a new actor entered the arena, the West Coast Waterfront Coalition (WCWC).

While the details surrounding the formation of this organization may be complex, the basic story is that Wal-Mart was a leader in this organization and used its considerable clout to try to intervene in the contract negotiations. At one point, someone from Wal-Mart called President George W. Bush in an effort to get him to force the ILWU back to work (even though the union had been locked out rather than striking). Even though it failed to break the union because of some tactical mistakes, it is clear that Wal-Mart hoped to reconstruct the waterfront in its own image.

The complaints of logistics providers against Wal-Mart are less well documented than the grievances of suppliers, but they are equally vivid. The company gets called the 800-pound gorilla for throwing its weight around to get what it wants. For example, one trucking company reported to me that they would never work with "people like that" because they are too heavy-handed and show no mercy for the survival of the company. Another example came from a director of one of their distribution centers, who found himself under such pressure that he was beginning to suffer heart symptoms. He felt that no matter what he did, it was never good enough. The Wal-Mart "suits" would descend on the distribution center only to criticize and place more stringent demands.

Certainly more research needs to be done on this aspect of their business. Our main point is that there is a neglected problem here, which is symptomatic of the general approach of this company. Because it has so much purchasing power, it can bully its service providers as well as its suppliers. The resulting degradation extends far beyond its own employees. Wal-Mart's effects are felt not only by its 1.4 million associates but by surrounding circles of firms that work for Wal-Mart. One might counter that if they don't like it, they shouldn't work for Wal-Mart. Unfortunately, in too many cases they have little option. Wal-Mart is too big to be avoided.

Conclusions

Much of the research and anger devoted to Wal-Mart focuses on its stores and their impact on store employees and the surrounding communities. But there is another entire level at which Wal-Mart's power and arrogance are felt, namely, its local and global procurement and logistics providers and their workers. Wal-Mart is building an empire of suppliers and distribution providers that all operate under its rules. Prices for consumers are undeniably pushed down as a consequence, but at what cost to all these other actors, who are themselves consumers and who must struggle harder to earn a living? While the interests of consumers are pitted against those of producers and transportation providers, the owners of Wal-Mart grow richer and richer at the expense of the majority of the population.

Notes

1. This value is enshrined in U.S. antitrust law, which sees the primary purpose of the law to be the protection of consumers from anticompetitive behavior. There is no concern with the problem of monopsony (or the power of the buyer over suppliers). In his letter introducing the agency, the chairman of the Federal Trade Commission (FTC) used the word *consumer* five times in the first six sentences but never mentions suppliers (Morgan Stanley 2004: 28). See also Useem 2004.
2. Wal-Mart believes that India will become a significant source for offshore procurement and will be second to China within a decade (Morgan Stanley 2004: 19).
3. For a similar analysis of production and procurement, updated here, see Bonacich and Wilson 2005.

18

ASDA: Wal-Mart in the United Kingdom

Steve Burt and Leigh Sparks

Introduction

In June 1999, Wal-Mart intervened spectacularly in an agreed merger between ASDA and Kingfisher by paying $10.72 billion (£6.7 billion) to buy ASDA (the number three British food retailer) outright. Reactions to this takeover were often hyperbolic (see the review in Whysall 2001); this was the death knell of British retailing and the salvation of British consumers through massive price reductions. Wal-Mart had been widely predicted to enter the United Kingdom, but the intervention in an agreed merger was a surprise, although ASDA was seen as the best fit for Wal-Mart (Arnold and Fernie 1999, 2000; Hallsworth 1999). Whatever views were held about the likely impact, Wal-Mart's purchase of ASDA was a landmark in its internationalization and possibly in the globalization of retailing generally. Until then Wal-Mart had really been a minor international retailer outside of the United States and its own "backyard" of Mexico and Canada. As Burt and Sparks show in their chapter in this volume, Wal-Mart's internationalization beyond North America for most of the 1990s could best be considered as opportunistic flag planting. The takeover of ASDA, however, marked a large-scale strategic investment in one of the major retail economies of the world. The success or failure of this move, particularly given the mixed reaction to the company's comparatively small-scale purchases in Germany in 1997 and 1998, would go a long way in ascertaining if Wal-Mart's business model could work in the (arguably) tougher Western European markets.

The takeover of ASDA was not uncontested either within or outside Wal-Mart. Within the business, Bob Martin, head of the International Division at that time, promptly resigned, suggesting divisions within the company over the takeover itself and the way it was conducted, although this was denied at the time by all concerned. Externally, the takeover prompted Carrefour and Promodès to merge in France to produce a stronger "national champion." In the United Kingdom, Tesco, the market leader, promised a hard fight for market share.

This chapter considers the extent to which Wal-Mart has made a success of its takeover of ASDA (Figure 18.1). First, we cover the background to ASDA—some of the details leading up to the takeover and the significance of ASDA to Wal-Mart.

Figure 18.1   An ASDA Wal-Mart supercenter in the United Kingdom.

Second, a consideration of the changes that have occurred to ASDA since the take-over is presented. Third is a review of the impact of these changes. This is undertaken at two levels: some of the emerging U.K. research on the effectiveness of the "market spoiler" impact of Wal-Mart on consumers is considered (Arnold, Handelman, and Tigert 1998), then an examination of the macro figures and market performance data, particularly comparing ASDA to the two other leading U.K. competitors, Tesco and Sainsbury, is presented. The fourth main section examines some of the recent events in the U.K. market and the ways in which ASDA and Wal-Mart have reacted to the challenges they have increasingly come to face. Finally some conclusions are drawn.

ASDA: Origins, Growth, Decline, Turnaround, and Takeover

The ASDA that Wal-Mart purchased was founded in the mid-1960s, although its origins can be traced back to the 1920s, when Hindells Dairy Farms Limited (a group of Yorkshire farmers) began to develop wholesale and retail outlets for its milk and milk products. In the 1930s and 1940s, other businesses were acquired, including a bakery and a pork butchery firm. In 1949, Associated Dairies and Farm Stores (Leeds) Ltd. brought all of these businesses together. By 1960 a chain of approximately 150 small shops had been established to sell the company's own products. In 1963 the company's name was abbreviated to Associated Dairies Ltd.

By the early 1960s Associated Dairies' small shops were being affected by the growth of multiple chains in the grocery business. In 1965 the company was approached by a local butcher, Peter Asquith, who had formulated the idea of selling a full range of grocery items at discounted prices in what had formerly been a local cinema. This proposal seemed a way of refocusing on the grocery sector through the competitive advantages of low price and large scale. ASDA was able to apply new price-cutting techniques stimulated by the recent abolition of resale price maintenance.

In 1966 ASDA acquired an 80 percent share (later increased to full ownership) in the GEM discount stores at Leeds, Preston, and West Bridgford, Nottingham, having been approached by the American owners, who were anxious to quit British retailing because of consistent losses. Although these stores had an average floor space of 58,000 square feet (at a time when the average supermarket operated from no more than 4,000 square feet), they cannot properly be described as superstores or hypermarkets, as they were somewhat unconventional (Whysall 2005). These GEM stores provided ASDA management with further invaluable experience in volume trading. ASDA's small stores were disposed of and new large stores opened.

ASDA had a number of advantages over its main grocery rivals. During the turbulent and inflation-riven trading times of the 1970s it had no inheritance of smaller, unprofitable shops causing distribution problems and tying up management skills and much-needed capital. Also, its larger stores allowed it to experiment with new ways of using backroom and sales space. The relative uniformity of the large stores allowed ASDA to enforce a policy of standard pricing across the chain, thus saving management resources and also acting as a major promotional device.

ASDA, from its base in Leeds (in the north of England), found a large and profitable market in the northern England metropolitan districts, where supermarket penetration by southern-England-based multiples, such as Tesco and Sainsbury, was limited. From these urban areas ASDA expanded gradually into Scotland, Wales, and the southwest of England; again, these were areas where the general quality of grocery retailing was quite poor (Jones 1981; Davies and Sparks 1986).

However, with all its advantages (compared to some of its rivals), and despite its impressive growth in terms of sales floor space and number of superstores, by the early 1980s ASDA had some problems. Out-of-town superstore growth was being held up by land use planning restrictions, which slowed down new store openings. In particular, it faced increasing levels of cost and competition as it attempted to move into the more profitable and populous southeast of England. In addition, ASDA was very proud of the fact that it did not have the large management infrastructure of other retailers. Yet the inability of managers to accept delegation and participation was threatening to halt the pace of the company's growth. Further, ASDA, despite spending considerably (when it could) on new store capital expenditure, was a cash-generating business, and the cash pile needed a home.

A merger/takeover between ASDA and MFI (a major flat-pack furniture retailer) was announced in 1985, as the result of a prolonged but secret series of meetings between the companies (see Davies and Sparks 1986). The stock market was far from convinced, arguing that there was little to be gained from increased buying power, store rationalization, or any of the other "traditional" benefits of takeover. As Seth and Randall (1999: 81) comment, the merger "had little real industrial synergy and was another triumph of investment banking rather than a brilliant strategic move." Given current predilections for general merchandisers such as Wal-Mart and hypermarkets (large stores with over 50,000 square feet of sales area, selling food and nonfood items) such as those operated by Tesco, a more charitable view might be that this merger was considerably premature and that continuing planning constraints for large out-of-town stores reduced the synergetic possibilities. However one looks at it, though, the merger was a drain on resources (including management), and in 1987 a management buyout brought divorce from MFI.

In hindsight, the merger with MFI was an indication that ASDA had lost its way. This was allied to a number of emerging problems. The business had too little store space, and often it was found in the "wrong" part of the country (northern England). ASDA had not invested in central distribution or in retail branding (private label), both of which had given significant advantages to competitors. Additionally, ASDA's low price position had been somewhat lost as it focused on profits (not consumers), and prices drifted upward. The most serious long-term problem—the lack of space—was "solved" by purchasing sixty stores from Gateway in 1989 at the (perceived) very high price of $1,148 million (£700 million). The high price paid and the need to make a return on this space, together with the eventual major investments in centralized distribution and retail branding, overloaded the business and management. ASDA became even more uncompetitive and was in dire trouble by 1991. There was a real danger of debt default. After a series of profit warnings and a share price collapse, there was a shareholder revolt and the management team left.

This history of ASDA is, as will be seen, crucially important to the Wal-Mart story. In 1991 a new chief executive, Archie Norman, and a new marketing director, Allan Leighton, took over. They set out to refocus and rebuild ASDA as an organization and as a brand. By succeeding, they created a classic turnaround story. At the heart of this turnaround was a conscious imitation and series of borrowings from Wal-Mart (for example, everyday low prices [EDLP], price rollbacks, "huddles," greeters, and the "smiley"). When Archie Norman left for politics in 1996–97, Allan Leighton took over as CEO and the turnaround process continued. Figure 18.2 pictures the business process, but in addition there was a huge cultural change in the organization as communications were opened up and "colleagues" were encouraged to be entrepreneurial and customer-focused and to celebrate achievements. All this was designed to create a new price-led, customer-centered, colleague-driven superstore/hypermarket value business. Success came quickly: ASDA became "the best operator of value for money, fresh food, and clothing superstores in Britain" (Seth and Randall 1999 p. 92). The mention of clothing is important. One of ASDA's few successful innovations of the 1980s was the introduction of the George clothing brand. Recruited after a boardroom coup in Next (a leading clothing retailer in the United Kingdom), George Davies set about creating a value-conscious "fast fashion" clothing brand for ASDA. This, in the long run, proved enormously successful, with brand sales of over $1.5 billion (£1 billion) per annum by the early 2000s.

One of the key issues for ASDA was a lack of investment in new stores. With high debts in the early 1990s, store development finance was slashed and even store development sites with planning permission were sold to rivals to raise money. The turnaround focused on existing stores primarily, so ASDA's store numbers and floor space began to fall behind the competition. In addition, from the mid-1990s the planning

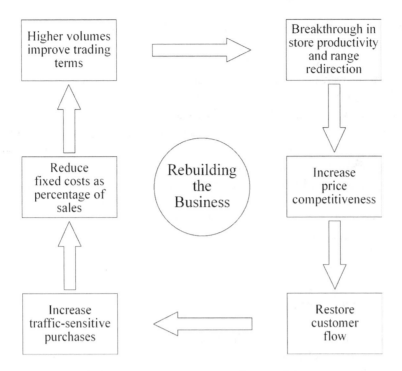

Figure 18.2   The ASDA Virtuous Circle. Source: Adapted from Seth and Randall (1999: 89).

regime turned increasingly against large and out-of-town superstore development, restricting site availability even further. In 1997, secret merger talks with Safeway (the number-four food retailer) were mounted, collapsing as the talks became public and differences over the merger came to light (including whether the competition authorities would allow it). A revitalized ASDA had forced prices down in the market and had developed a strong operational culture, both of which owed much to its copying of Wal-Mart. However, scale and floor space expansion remained a problem. It is in this context that ASDA looked to merge with Kingfisher (a leading nonfood retailer) before Wal-Mart interrupted the agreed deal.

The other important context of the mid-1990s in the United Kingdom was a massive government-encouraged campaign over high retail prices. "Rip-off Britain" was a slogan pioneered by politicians, the media, and others from 1995 onward (see Burt and Sparks 1997). It culminated in a major competition authority investigation of the multiple-retailer supermarket sector (Competition Commission 2000). By this time, however, the fallacy of international price comparisons was becoming more clear (Competition Commission 2000; Sparks 2002). The continued price pressure, inaugurated by ASDA and followed by Tesco, had in any case combined to bring much-reduced food price inflation (even deflation in some years) to the United Kingdom. ASDA, by pushing an EDLP policy borrowed from Wal-Mart and by drawing attention to low prices and a colleague-focused culture, had transformed the market. Tesco realized the price pressure ASDA was building and began to price-match ASDA (although at a slightly higher price point), whereas Sainsbury continued to increase prices (Burt and Sparks 2003). If ASDA could obtain more sales space, it would be able to inflict more price pressure on the sector. In essence, ASDA tried to mimic the Wal-Mart "market spoiler" effect (Arnold, Handelman, and Tigert 1998). When Wal-Mart took it over, the general view, therefore, was that ASDA was "Wal-Mart-ready" (Whysall 2001; Burt and Sparks 2001).

As Fernie and Arnold (2002) note, ASDA was the best strategic fit for Wal-Mart in the United Kingdom, due to its high average store size, high proportion of non-food items, and overt cultural, pricing, and promotional borrowings from Wal-Mart. For the price of $10.72 billion (£6.7 billion), Wal-Mart obtained the number-three food retailer in the United Kingdom, with almost 230 large (in British terms) super-stores and hypermarkets, totaling 9.6 million square feet of sales space and taking in $12.8 billion (£8.0 billion) per annum in sales. Because it was focused mainly on food retailing, its nonfood range was somewhat weaker, although within this the George clothing brand was increasingly strong.

What Wal-Mart Did to ASDA

ASDA was Wal-Mart's first really big international expansion. To a considerable extent, if Wal-Mart's global ambitions were to have credibility, then it had to suc-ceed. There is a symbolic issue here, as well as a real difference compared to the other internationalizations of the 1990s (Burt and Sparks, this volume). That the purchase appears to have been controversial within the company simply demonstrates the high stakes involved. ASDA has had to provide a return for the purchase price, and Wal-Mart has moved to improve its performance. Four elements of this are consid-ered below, following the discussion outlined in Burt and Sparks (2001): store portfo-lio, efficiencies, suppliers, and merchandise.

Store Portfolio

The ASDA store portfolio at takeover was a mix of the old and the new. While it had received investment in the late 1990s by ASDA, including some store openings, a considerable proportion of the portfolio was both dated and belonged formerly to another weaker chain (Gateway). Store investment had not been a priority for ASDA in the debt-ridden early 1990s, following the hiatus of the ASDA-MFI merger and the Gateway purchase. The store portfolio also remained spatially biased away from the important market of the south of England (Langston, Clarke, and Clarke 1997). Probably the initial biggest opportunity for Wal-Mart was the potential conversion in many stores of gross space to sales floor space. Despite the size of the store portfolio on acquisition (about 9.8 million sales square feet), Wal-Mart needed to expand both sales floor space (as opposed to "back-room space") and total floor space (for all stores in the chain) to gain sales volume to allow its nonfood expertise to be introduced and to impact the competition.

Three main methods were used to expand floor space. First, reconstruction of the supply and distribution channel allowed for changes to the internal store floor space. The ratio of sales floor space to gross floor space in ASDA's stores at takeover was approximately 52.5 percent to 47.5 percent. The other leading food chains operated on an average of between 52 and 59 percent sales space. At Wal-Mart in the United States, the overall figure was 84 percent. By improving the supply systems and reexamining the layout and operations at the store, considerable sales floor space was created from gross and underemployed space. Given that ASDA stores were already substantially bigger than those of the competition, this was a major benefit.

Second, the opportunity was taken at some stores to expand the physical store space itself. As stores were renewed and redeveloped, opportunities were taken where possible to expand the size of the "box." In some cases this enabled the store to be redeveloped and opened as an ASDA/Wal-Mart Supercentre (a larger hypermarket with more nonfood space and service areas than the standard ASDA store). In addition, ASDA began to exploit a loophole in the land use planning system whereby a mezzanine development within a store was classified as an interior alteration and was thus not subject to planning permission (Warren 2005). ASDA, like other retailers, quickly realized that in some stores the sales floor space could be considerably expanded through the introduction of a mezzanine floor. While not the preferred solution (as it leads to two-story stores), mezzanines do allow floor space growth in an otherwise restricted market. So concerned has the government become at the prevalence of mezzanine development that in 2005 it moved to close this planning loophole by requiring planning permission for them.

The third element of store portfolio development has been the most difficult and is the most controversial. Wal-Mart has sought to expand the actual number of stores in the chain. Some organic growth has been possible (twenty-nine stores opened between 2000 and 2003, with twenty-four outstanding planning consents [Competition Commission 2003]). This space, however, has not necessarily been in the chain's preferred locations, and some of these are replacement stores. In particular, ASDA has found planning permissions hard to obtain in London, the southeast of England, and East Anglia, all areas where the chain is underrepresented for historical reasons. Planning permissions generally and for extensions specifically have become more problematic, under revised and stricter government interpretations of national planning policies (Wrigley 1998; Pal et al. 2001; Guy 2003; ODPM 2004; Scottish Executive 2004; Wood, Lowe, and Wrigley 2006). ASDA's floor space growth has thus been restricted by the U.K. land-use planning system. The CEO of ASDA commented, "What is frustrating is that we cannot get new sites. We have a business model that works. There is demand out there. But we cannot get planning consents" (*Sunday Times* 2004: 11).

It is likely that planning legislation would have to be changed to allow expansion at the rate Wal-Mart would ideally wish. It is difficult to believe this will occur, for both political and economic reasons. There has been a considerable struggle within government between those with a belief in the need for more stores (to increase competitive and productivity levels and reduce prices) and others who point to the damage such a policy relaxation could wreak on existing towns and on the social costs of such a change (see Hallsworth and Clarke 2001; Sparks 2005; Department of Trade and Industry 2004; Reynolds et al. 2005). The current view is to tighten rather than relax planning restrictions. The competition authorities, however, have become more interventionist in retail takeovers and the sales of stores among chains.

The other, quicker method of increasing the store portfolio is by acquisition. Many rumors have circulated that ASDA would attempt to purchase either a food chain or a nonfood chain. In 2002 the company entered the bidding war for Safeway (the number-four food retailer), after Morrisons (the number-five food retailer) had made an agreed offer. After an investigation by the Competition Commission (2003), Morrisons was allowed to purchase Safeway, subject to selling off some of the newly acquired stores. ASDA was prohibited by the Competition Commission from buying Safeway on the grounds of too great a reduction in competition and thus potential adverse effects on consumers and prices. The Competition Commission controversially argued that ASDA's aggressive price cutting would not be financially rational in such a situation and would not be sustainable. This refusal to allow ASDA's bid was a grievous blow to ASDA, as it effectively fossilized a view that there must be four main competitors in the superstore market. With the problems in getting new store planning permissions, this decision effectively forces the competition to be between existing stores and any stores that could be developed through outstanding planning permissions (of which ASDA has fewer than the main competition). ASDA did purchase twelve stores in Northern Ireland from Morrisons (as that company retreated to core business after the Safeway takeover), which were its first in that area, but that was scant consolation for not acquiring Safeway. Rumors still abound that ASDA may well look to buy a nonfood retailer to expand into that market. In the case of nonfood stores, some may also have open planning consents, and thus conversion to food or to a supercenter format may be easier.

Efficiencies

Wal-Mart's revamping of ASDA has produced efficiencies in the business. Wal-Mart has taken opportunities to reformat the distribution operation. These have brought benefits in effectiveness and allowed new enhanced volumes to be handled. Similarly, the introduction of the Wal-Mart information technology systems to ASDA has made it more efficient. With better systems and distribution allied to an enhanced merchandise mix and store use intensification, the cost base has been driven down and productivity has been increased. In essence, ASDA has become a better retailer, increasing store productivity and continuing to lead on prices.

Suppliers

Unlike the previous two elements, which have been essentially internal and have had few outside implications beyond any impact on competition, Wal-Mart has also had an impact on ASDA's suppliers. Suppliers have been subjected to the Wal-Mart vendor process. Some have been replaced as the merchandise mix has changed. Multinational suppliers have seen their position strengthened through their existing Wal-Mart arrangements and changes that have brought purchasing for all of Wal-Mart together, including a revamp of ASDA's retailer branding across Europe (IGD 2004). ASDA has followed the competition in adopting a trilevel retailer product brand strategy, encompassing ASDA Extra Special, ASDA, and ASDA Smart Price. Currently over 40 percent of sales are accounted for by these brands. The pressure on suppliers to reduce prices and costs has been immense: "ASDA told us that most of the investments it had made in price reductions had been funded by suppliers" (Competition Commission 2003: para. 2.270). This is exacerbated by the ability of Wal-Mart to buy in huge volumes from countries such as China, where nonfood quotas have effectively been removed. Nonfood and clothing products have had their entry prices in ASDA stores reduced remarkably. In that respect, Wal-Mart and cheaper prices have spelled bad news for some British suppliers, who already thought that they were getting a raw deal. There have been continued mutterings from suppliers for all of the major chains about the practices of buyers. Despite pleas for examples from the competition authorities, breaches of the new Code of Conduct for supplier-retailer relations have not been reported to them.

There is one area where Wal-Mart has had a particular effect on the business and its pricing. The George clothing line was already a successful clothing brand in its own right. Wal-Mart has put more emphasis on George, and not only in the United Kingdom—it is now in Wal-Mart stores in seven countries. As a result of adding George to Wal-Mart stores in other countries and expanding its scale in the United Kingdom, often through sharp price reductions for products due to Wal-Mart's chain buying, this operation has grown considerably. The George brand has been subdivided in the United Kingdom into George Collection, George, and George Essentials to reflect various price and value points. Stand-alone George stores have been introduced on high streets as a trial, although there are only about ten at present and recent reports suggest a pause to consider their contribution.

Merchandise Mix

Finally, the merchandise mix in stores has changed. Much has been said in the press about the scope of Wal-Mart to bring lower prices and to affect competition (Whysall 2001). This is undoubtedly true, but the strength of Wal-Mart is away from the core ASDA food business. Service areas have been expanded considerably in the ASDA stores and supercenters. Wal-Mart's impact has been felt on many nonfood sectors, and in particular retailers in sectors as diverse as pharmacy, film processing, and clothing. The "soft underbelly" of British retailing has been less Tesco and Sainsbury and more Boots and BhS, for example. As former chief executive Allan Leighton indicated, many ASDA food prices were already at U.S. levels, and the ASDA food offerings and processes were better than their counterparts in Wal-Mart, but in nonfood items (including health and beauty) there was massive scope for price reductions, range extensions, and enhanced coherence (*In Business,* BBC Radio 4, September 27, 1999). The introduction of a strong, cheap nonfood merchandise mix and sharp reductions on existing nonfood items brought customers to the stores. The start of this process was seen in the July 2000 reopening of the ASDA at Bristol Patchway as an ASDA/Wal-Mart Supercentre. As *Retail Week* reported:

> Rival retailers ... should look ... at the quantum leap in ranging and presentational standards across the nonfood departments; cards, books, office supplies, DIY, consumer electronics, toys, housewares, optical and pharmacy in addition of course to George. This is the real challenge that Wal-Mart poses. (*Retail Week* 2000: 8)

Such supercentres have been at the forefront of Wal-Mart's restructuring of ASDA and as much as possible of the new and redeveloped floor space for ASDA has been in this form. There are now more than twenty such supercentres, but as noted earlier, obtaining planning permission remains a problem. As nonfood sections are shown to work in ASDA/Wal-Mart Supercentres, they have been inserted into existing ASDA stores. Such has been the success in nonfood that ASDA has been also trialing ASDA Living stores, which are nonfood-only stores in retail parks. These have begun to prove successful, and a rollout plan has been put in place. This has raised the pressure on a range of nonfood retailers often found in such parks and has even forced Tesco into trialing its own nonfood Tesco Homeplus stores.

By April 2005, ASDA had 283 stores in the United Kingdom, containing a total of 12.687 million square feet of sales space. Of these stores there were 6 George stores, 2 Living stores, 19 ASDA/Wal-Mart Supercentres, and 256 ASDA superstores (IGD 2005). The supercenters on average are more than twice the size of the company's standard stores (89,500 versus 42,300 square feet), with much of this additional floor space given over to nonfood merchandise (including George) and service areas (such as pharmacies, photo centers, opticians, and jewelry).

In the initial period after the takeover and as the Wal-Martization of ASDA was put into place, Wal-Mart saw ASDA as a "model acquisition" and claimed that it was producing desired returns. It is certainly the core of the International Division's retail sales volumes (in fiscal year 2004 ASDA contributed 46 percent of the sales) and the substantial majority of its profits. ASDA has real significance for Wal-Mart. However, these changes have not come without cost. High-profile departure of senior executives such as Allan Leighton and George Davies have been followed by comparatively frequent changes to board and senior managers. Some of these have been done to shore up Wal-Mart in other countries (Germany, Canada), and some moves appear to have been made in order to transfer expertise around the organization internationally. Nonetheless, there has been perhaps less management stability than might have been expected. This pattern has continued with the resignation of CEO Tony De Nunzio in March 2005.

Impact of the Changes

Wal-Mart has undoubtedly placed its mark on ASDA. Some of this is visible in the development of ASDA/Wal-Mart Supercentres and the strapline "ASDA—part of the Wal-Mart family." Some of it is invisible, as technology and distribution changes reorganize ASDA's operations. This section looks at the impact of changes through research into the reactions of consumers and the business performance of ASDA.

Consumers

Since the takeover in 1999, the United Kingdom has seen price deflation in food and a variety of price skirmishes among the leading retailers. Price pressure would appear to have mounted in the United Kingdom. Safeway has been the major casualty, although Sainsbury has also suffered. But there has been limited research until recently on consumer reactions to ASDA under Wal-Mart's stewardship. Academic conference presentations (Fernie et al. 2005; Pioch, Fernie, and Arnold 2005) have begun to reveal outcomes of work in the newer Wal-Mart markets of the United Kingdom, Germany, and China, targeted at replicating earlier work by Arnold (Arnold, Handelman, and Tigert 1998). Through employee and customer surveys between 2001 and 2003 at new ASDA Wal-Mart Supercenters at Manchester and Livingston, the impacts of Wal-Mart have been initially assessed. The employee research (Fernie et al. 2005) notes that ASDA looked and operated like Wal-Mart prior to takeover and employees had adjusted well. The researchers did note some concerns over responsibility, pay, and incentives, but broadly new practices were introduced easily.

Research on consumers shows that price had increased in importance for consumers and that ASDA was outperforming its competitors on store patronage norms. Particular ASDA strengths were in value prices, selection, environment, and service, details reinforced by rankings in the trade press and elsewhere (IGD 2005). Pioch, Fernie, and Arnold (2005: 11) remark on "ASDA Wal-Mart's high performance on value prices, which suggests that their EDLP strategy and constant downward pressure on prices through their high profile roll back campaigns is making an impact on store patronage norms." In short, the authors found that ASDA was generating a "market spoiler" effect, as Wal-Mart had in North America (Arnold, Handelman, and Tigert 1998). Price had become more significant to U.K. customers, and they were willing to go out of their way to ASDA, as ASDA Wal-Mart most clearly matched their needs. This accords with Taylor Nelson Sofres data reported by the Competition Commission (2003), that in the year to March 2003, ASDA almost doubled the proportion of its consumers from the AB social classes (from 8 to 15 percent). This suggests an increasing and wider concern about prices in the United Kingdom.

There is, however, a problem with this conclusion. The market share and business performance evidence (see below) suggests that the market leader, Tesco, has outperformed ASDA. If Tesco is pulling away from ASDA, why did this not show up in the consumer work? A consideration of the consumer research suggests that it has taken place in catchments where Tesco is underrepresented. As such, these conclusions on consumer reactions to ASDA Wal-Mart need to be treated with some caution. There may also be issues of timing, as the research was undertaken in 2002–2003, when ASDA was most impacted by the Wal-Mart technological introductions.

Business Performance

There is no doubt that Wal-Mart has had an impact on ASDA, the market, and consumers. It is the extent of the impact that is open to question. Sales and profit have

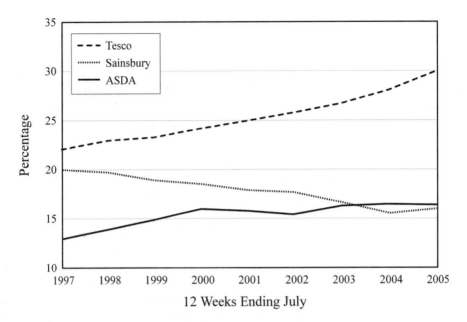

Figure 18.3   U.K. Grocery Market Shares, 1997–2005. Note: 2001 is estimated. *Source:* Press reports on TNS Superpanel.

risen since the takeover by Wal-Mart, although perhaps more in the former than in the latter. This increase in sales volume has enabled ASDA to take over the number-two spot in the U.K. grocery rankings from Sainsbury. Figure 18.3 shows the way in which ASDA caught up and then overtook Sainsbury. The figure, however, also shows two other things. The recent momentum for ASDA has slowed. This might help explain the consumer findings above, as the slowing in growth postdates the consumer survey work. Also, Tesco has continued to power ahead, widening the gap between itself and ASDA. Some of Tesco's growth has been achieved by (controversial) takeovers in the convenience store market, but it is clear that its multiformat, multibrand offerings have proved a huge success with consumers.

The extent of this outperformance by Tesco over ASDA is shown in Table 18.1. The differences between the two businesses over the last five years are clear. While sales growth is similar, profit has not been as successfully generated by ASDA. Even though

TABLE 18.1   United Kingdom Comparative Performance January 2000–January 2005

Percentage Change	Tesco	Sainsbury	ASDA
Sales	61.5	20.7	58.3
Operating profit	70.6	−38.0	52.8
U.K. operating margin	5.1	−47.6	−4.0
Space productivity	12.3	−19.5	21.6
Capital expenditure	69.0	23.6	11.7
Sales area	50.9	40.2	30.8

Source: IGD 2005.

TABLE 18.2   ASDA and Tesco Hypermarket and Superstore Sales Floor Space, January 2005

	Number of Stores	Total Square Feet	Average Square Feet per Store
ASDA Wal-Mart Supercentre	19	1,699,700	89,457
Tesco Extra Hypermarket	100	6,982,000	69,820
ASDA superstore	256	10,815,800	42,249
Tesco superstore	446	13,900,000	31,200

Source: IGD 2005.

ASDA has increased its sales space productivity faster than Tesco, it still remains below Tesco's level. The figures on sales area growth show that Tesco has added more space than ASDA. It has also spent considerably more in capital expenditure terms, probably because Tesco has a higher proportion of new space and new stores in its mix. ASDA has increased existing store space but has struggled to add new stores to its portfolio. In the five years since acquisition, fewer than fifty stores have been added. ASDA has focused its attention in store terms on developing ASDA Wal-Mart Supercentres, which are among the larger stores in the United Kingdom, but these have been matched by the Tesco Extra hypermarket format, of which there are over a hundred in the United Kingdom. The core of the portfolio remains the ASDA superstore, but expansion of this base other than by store purchases (e.g., the twelve stores acquired in Northern Ireland from Morrisons) has been difficult. The result is that despite having larger stores on average, ASDA has far less total hypermarket and superstore floor space than Tesco (Table 18.2). Table 18.1 also shows, however, the degree to which ASDA has in turn outperformed Sainsbury.

The conclusion in terms of business performance might be that after takeover ASDA took the obvious steps, enhanced efficiencies in the business, and obtained good growth from the business for a few years. In the last couple of years, however, this growth has slowed as the lack of new store space and Tesco's stronger performance have begun to take their toll. ASDA has been stymied by the lack of store investment dating back to the 1980s, reinforced by the financial crisis of the early 1990s. With a smaller land bank (*Retail Week* 2005a) and planning permission pipeline than Tesco, the potential to close the gap may be limited. *Retail Week* also estimates that Tesco has 70 percent of all U.K. retail land bank sites, though as Tesco points out:

> In the 1980s and 1990s, Tesco took the decision to invest in new stores, while other supermarkets halted expansion and concentrated on other areas of the business. ASDA even sold several of its sites to Tesco, so our strong position is a result of company decisions made several years ago. (*Retail Week* 2005b: 39)

This explains ASDA's keenness to take over Safeway. By failing to be allowed to take over Safeway, ASDA has effectively been forced into a subservient market position. The dominant chain (Tesco) has successfully defended itself (Burt and Sparks 2003).

Recent Events: Reacting to Adversity

> In the United Kingdom, the ASDA acquisition has been much more successful.... . ASDA was
> a good strategic fit for Wal-Mart. It already had the largest stores in the United Kingdom with
> a retail proposition not dissimilar from that of Wal-Mart—low prices, large assortment, good
> customer service and a strong non-food offer. In terms of organizational structure, ASDA
> had already incorporated Wal-Martian principles into the corporate culture.... . Wal-Mart
> has been fine-tuning the retail proposition, logistical support and the organizational cul-
> ture. The "market spoiler" effect has occurred in the United Kingdom with a much stronger
> emphasis on lower prices than in 1999. (Fernie *et al.* 2005: 10–11)

Recent events, however, hint at a story different from the one told in the quotation above and suggest that ASDA is an organization under some stress. In March
2005, the chief executive, Tony De Nunzio, left suddenly to head up the private Dutch
retailer Vendex. He claimed he needed new challenges, and by joining a private company he would gain the opportunity for an equity stake in the company, from which
he would benefit significantly later if the company went public. Others, however, felt
that he was paying the penalty for failing to close the market share gap on Tesco and
that the Wal-Mart board expected more from ASDA.

De Nunzio's replacement as chief executive was chief operating officer Andy Bond.
Previously the head of the George brand, Bond was clearly a rising star, though this
latest promotion was perhaps earlier than even he expected. One of Bond's first
announcements, however, was of about 1,200 job cuts as part of a review of staffing
levels. These job cuts included 185 at the head office, 15 at the George main office, and
4 or 5 management positions in every store. Bond's comment that "whilst it's the right
thing to do for our business, we say goodbye to some great colleagues this week and
I thank them for all they have done for ASDA" no doubt made the people whose jobs
were cut feel a lot better (BBC News 2005a). These job cuts followed admissions that
ASDA would miss its profit targets and that sales growth was slowing.

More signs of stress came in the summer of 2005 when new price promotional
items and signage began to appear in ASDA stores. Though it was a longtime advocate of EDLP (and the only major U.K. retailer with a national pricing policy), ASDA
moved to try to develop some promotional excitement in the stores for consumers.
This departure from its EDLP strategic position, however, much presented as an
"extra" for consumers (and named EDLP+), ran the risk of confusion. More price
problems also emerged through the ruling by the Advertising Standards Authority
(ASA), following a complaint by Tesco, that ASDA's price claim in various advertisements that it was "officially Britain's lowest-priced supermarket" was misleading.
Tesco had complained that both the use of the word *officially* and the claim itself were
flawed, being based on a trade magazine's (*The Grocer*) basket of thirty-three items.
While the "Grocer 33" is a recognized basket and survey, the ASA ruled that it is not
"official" (i.e., governmental), is too limited to reflect the product range in supermarkets, and excluded low-price discounter companies. ASA told ASDA to stop making
the claim.

No doubt a little irritated by this, ASDA reported Goldman Sachs to the Financial
Services Authority (FSA), complaining about the analysts' report that said Tesco was
beating ASDA on price. In a scathing observation in *Retail Week* (the main retail
magazine in the United Kingdom) the deputy editor noted:

> Whether [ASDA] is right or wrong to feel aggrieved, the direct approach to the FSA smacks of an attempt to limit comment and perhaps intimidate other brokers who may make unflattering comparisons with Tesco. If ASDA is worried that it is misunderstood in the City, then it should ensure financial connections are well informed, rather than running screaming to the regulator. Then it should take criticism on the chin and get on with serving shoppers. (*Retail Week* 2005b: 7)

One might even suspect that Tesco has got ASDA Wal-Mart worried. In late summer, and without even the merest hint of irony, Lee Scott, CEO of Wal-Mart, called on the British government to investigate Tesco because it was "dominating" the sector (BBC News 2005b). He was reported as saying that the government had to investigate Tesco's continuing domination because it was so difficult for rivals to try to catch up. This line has subsequently been repeated by Andy Bond, who stated:

> One of the unintended consequences of the planning rules is that it is unlikely the competitive landscape will be defined by competitive advantage. It is defined by who has got the land. I would not want to be judged as wanting something uncompetitive but there is a fundamental economic point. Maybe someone should be looking at this in terms of market share and customer choice. (quoted in Butler 2005)

This is grist for the mill of those who would like to see Tesco "cut down to size," but this jumping on a bandwagon smacks a little of desperation. What if the positions were reversed? Can you imagine Wal-Mart's reaction if it held 30 percent of the U.K. grocery market and Tesco (with 17 percent) had called for it to be cut down to size?

Most recently, the press has reported that 40 percent of ASDA staff do not shop with ASDA despite a 10 percent staff discount. ASDA disputes the level of "outshopping," but an internal investigation is apparently under way. However, and perhaps as another sign of cost pressures, the staff discount (20 percent) for Christmas has been halved to 10 percent, apparently to "protect profits" (Clement 2005). Further accusations about pressures on staff have also recently surfaced (Macalister 2005; War on Want/GMB 2005).

These signals and events suggest that ASDA is currently in an uncomfortable position. After initially getting a boost from Wal-Mart's investment and systems, the momentum has stalled. Tesco has proved itself to be a strong competitor. There are even signs of some resurgence of Sainsbury, which could push ASDA down to third place in the grocery market in the United Kingdom. Foiled from buying Safeway by the Competition Commission and the government, stymied in new large-scale store development by tight planning regulations, being forbidden to add more space through mezzanine floors as that planning loophole gets closed, and constrained by its overriding focus on a single store format, ASDA has only limited opportunities to outcompete its main competitors. As it stands, ASDA has to focus on its existing stores and limited new developments and hope that it can put its "market spoiler" effect into stronger practice. But without a strong store expansion plan in key locations this is difficult. The price emphasis might also provide a stronger entry into consumer's minds for Lidl, Aldi, and Netto, the limited-line hard-discount chains, all of which plan to expand strongly in the United Kingdom. ASDA's only other hope is that the government does listen to the many voices criticizing the scale of Tesco. It would take quite a reversal of policy. But would ASDA be the winner in this? In the short term ASDA is in quite an awkward position, and it will be a long, tough battle to get to the number-one spot in the United Kingdom. Can Wal-Mart really be fully content with the progress of its biggest and highest-profile investment in Western Europe? The boys from Bentonville may not be best pleased.

Conclusions

ASDA is not a retailer in commercial trouble in the sense that many other leading retailers have been (e.g., Wrigley and Currah 2003; Mellahi, Jackson, and Sparks 2002). It remains a strong performer, and there can be no doubt that its contribution to Wal-Mart's International Division is significant. The question, however, is whether this was what was envisaged when Wal-Mart bought ASDA in 1999. Wal-Mart has improved ASDA in terms of its performance, building on a model that had copied Wal-Mart for some years. Some of the expertise that ASDA had in terms of George and food retailing has been transferred to other countries in the Wal-Mart empire. ASDA has benefited from operational efficiencies, technological development, and the massive buying power that Wal-Mart can bring, particularly in nonfood. Despite all of this, however, ASDA has not been able to close the gap on market leader Tesco, and it has been reduced to calling for Tesco to be cut down to size. In that respect it is fair to ask what has gone wrong.

The key factor is one that has dogged ASDA for over a quarter of a century. Its northern England roots and its difficulties in getting the right amount of sales floor space in the right places at a fast enough pace have constrained its expansion plans time and again. The financial crisis of the 1980s and early 1990s saw ASDA effectively forced out of new store development for some time. As a consequence, it has always had trouble expanding as much as it would like. With a land use planning regime that has turned strongly against large out-of-town stores such as those favored by ASDA, store development has been less than would have been imagined by Wal-Mart in 1999. Space has proved to be the final frontier for Wal-Mart, one that has been unconquerable thus far. Without a change in land use planning (perhaps focusing on consumer choice and not purely on floor space amounts in a catchment), a greater willingness to change the store formats used by ASDA (a new small ASDA Essentials format is coming in 2006), or a forced breakup of Tesco, it is hard to see how the gap to Tesco can be bridged.

The is why the bid for Safeway was so significant. A combined ASDA/Safeway in 2003 would have been a close number two to Tesco in grocery but bigger than Tesco in terms of all revenue (Competition Commission 2003). In addition, and critical for the market spoiler effect, the ASDA/Safeway combination would have directly confronted Tesco in over 64 percent of Tesco's store catchments, as opposed to only 42 percent with a direct ASDA-to-Tesco confrontation. If regulators wanted a strong competitor to Tesco, then allowing Morrisons, not ASDA, to buy Safeway was not the best way to go about it, as was predicted (Burt and Sparks 2003).

Even with a positive consumer reaction, there may simply not be a dense enough store network to bridge the gap. Tesco could of course stumble or be "cut down to size," or there could be a consumer reaction to its seeming ubiquity and ever-increasing market share. Even if this occurs, will ASDA, if it fails to obtain new space, be the beneficiary, or will it be more-nimble competitors? Perhaps Wal-Mart might decide that there is not much more it can do in the United Kingdom and instead focus its investment and management attention on the emerging large markets of Asia, particularly China. Perhaps there are also bigger pickings to be had in Central and South America, where recent purchases have been made (Burt and Sparks, this volume). While Wal-Mart regularly makes positive noises about further investment in Europe, it is unlikely to be allowed to buy a food retailer in the United Kingdom.

Was this predictable? One issue in the Wal-Mart takeover of ASDA received considerable press attention in 1999 and has been picked up by academics and others (Hallsworth and Clarke 2001; Whysall 2001; Burt and Sparks 2001). Rumors about a meeting between Wal-Mart and British prime minister Tony Blair began to surface in mid-April 1999, prior to the Wal-Mart takeover of ASDA. Over time, various reports about the meeting have circulated in the British press, making a variety of claims about those present, its origins and timing, and what was discussed.

After initial stonewalling, some details have emerged. In answer to a parliamentary question in May 1999, the prime minister indicated the meeting was "about a month ago." However, in response to another parliamentary question in April 2001, the prime minister refused to reveal the exact date. The most detailed press report of the meeting claims that Bob Martin (then president and chief executive officer of Wal-Mart's International Division) and Prime Minister Tony Blair talked face-to-face in late February 1999 (i.e., a few months prior to the Wal-Mart bid for ASDA) (Walters and Moss, 1999). The prime minister refused to reveal the attendees at the meeting in an answer to a parliamentary question in June 1999. A spokesman for the prime minister's office (unnamed in the British press but identified as Peter Wilkinson in the Arkansas press) stated:

> He [Bob Martin] was coming through Europe at the time and requested a *short courtesy call* with the Prime Minister. My understanding is that it was *a brief exchange of views* on the economic situation, both here and wider, and *no concrete business* was discussed. (Little 1999, emphasis added)

The prime minister described it as "a short courtesy call at his [the Wal-Mart representative's] request" in his answer to a parliamentary question in May 1999.

The meeting is of interest because of the topics that might have been discussed (Hallsworth and Clarke 2001; Burt and Sparks 2001). Questions raised in Parliament have contended that issues such as the relaxation of land use planning and the takeover of a British company must have been discussed. The prime minister is on record at the time as desiring greater competition and lower prices in the United Kingdom, and many commentators describe grave fears about the relaxation of planning at this time (see Hallsworth and Clarke 2001; Hallsworth and Evers 2002). Indeed, the Select Committee on the Environment, Transport, and Regional Affairs specifically examined the issue of Wal-Mart's takeover of ASDA and the possible discussion of planning issues at the Martin/Blair meeting. The committee chairwoman stated: "We were given straightforward assurances that planning was not discussed. We must accept the evidence and we don't assume people are lying" (Brown 2000).

Under the new (introduced January 1, 2005) Freedom of Information Act, the minutes of the meeting are potentially available. Following a formal request by Leigh Sparks, however, the Cabinet Office claimed that release would be "prejudicial to the effective conduct of public affairs," and refused the formal release request (this decision is being appealed to the Information Commissioner):

> The information we hold in relation to your request is exempt under Section 35(1)(a) because it relates to the *formulation or development of government policy*. This exemption is subject to the balance of the public interest. We have concluded that it is not in the public interest to release this information as advice should be broadly based and there may be a deterrent effect on external aspects or stakeholders who might be reluctant to provide advice in the future because it might be disclosed. (Cabinet Office 2005, emphasis added)

So the prime minister met a Wal-Mart executive not for some courtesy call or social visit, lasting an hour while sherry was sipped, but rather for a meeting on the formulation and development of government policy.

The curiosity in this is that Bob Martin does not seem to have been involved in the actual takeover itself. He resigned as soon as the deal went through, and press reports say that not only was he not involved in it, he was against it (see Whysall 2001). Maybe he saw that while the British government would want Wal-Mart in the U.K. market, the land use planning system was not going to be overturned in Wal-Mart's favor. ASDA/Wal-Mart has been able to exploit loopholes, produce efficiencies, and engineer an expansion of its floor space, but it has been refused permission to buy Safeway and has found the competition for space tough and the planning regime strengthened. Perhaps Tony Blair failed to deliver any promises discussed in 1999, or perhaps Wal-Mart back in Bentonville and those not in the meeting didn't want to hear a negative message. Either way, ASDA currently remains a long way from being number one in grocery retailing in the United Kingdom.

Wal-Mart's presence in the United Kingdom, ASDA, is not in the same problematic position as Wal-Mart in Germany. It is, however, constrained by the land use planning system and by the activities of at least one very good competitor. Perhaps the main lesson from the United Kingdom is that strong retailers can resist Wal-Mart, particularly when aspects of the free market system (the freedom to develop new stores in the United Kingdom) are denied to it.

Postscript

In May 2006, the U.K. Office of Fair Trading ordered a market investigation by the Competition Commission into grocery retailing, citing particular concerns over planning restrictions, land-banks, and aspects of pricing. While responding to the investigation will cost ASDA considerable money and management time, potential outcomes include restrictions on Tesco or even forced site or store sales by Tesco. ASDA described the investigation as unnecessary, but welcomed the focus on planning and local monopolies. Perhaps there may be some light at the end of the tunnel, after all.

19

Challenges Facing Wal-Mart in the German Market

Susan Christopherson

Introduction

In 2003, Wal-Mart continued its reign as the world's largest corporation, with sales of $259 billion. Wal-Mart's revenues grew by more than $100 billion between 1997 and 2002, and the value of its stock increased 400 percent. In the United States alone, Wal-Mart employs over 1 million people, making it the country's largest employer. To maintain and increase its high stock value, which in 2002 was 42 times earnings, Wal-Mart has undertaken an aggressive plan to go global with the Wal-Mart concept. Wal-Mart has succeeded in transplanting its cost- and logistics-driven model to Canada and Mexico, which in 2001 composed the lion's share of the 17 percent of Wal-Mart's total profits obtained from non-U.S. operations. Despite its mammoth size and technical prowess, however, Wal-Mart is having difficulty building successful operations in Europe, particularly in Germany, where after four years of significant investment, Wal-Mart cannot foresee a profit.

The literature on the internationalization of retailing provides considerable insight into Wal-Mart's difficulties in Germany, enumerating the problems Wal-Mart has faced in implementing its international expansion strategy. Behind this list of problems, however, is a broader story about national differences in economic policy that raises questions about the concept of globalization itself.

Wal-Mart is, as Alexander and Myers (2000) have described, an "ethnocentric" retailer. Its enormous success can be traced to effective firm strategies in a global marketplace but also to the evolution of its concept under the rules that govern firm investment in the United States. While there are many individual features of this governance regime, they can be encompassed in one concept: the ability to continually experiment to find the optimal ways to reduce costs and increase profits. A major portion of the cost of this experimentation is borne outside the firm, by the workforce, and by the communities in which Wal-Mart locates.

In contrast with the United States, the institutions and practices that make up German market governance discourage experimentation and redistribution of risks from firm to labor or communities. Despite its risks and experimentation-averse positions, Germany has sustained a highly competitive retail market and low prices.

So the story of Wal-Mart in Germany ultimately raises questions of market governance alternatives.

A first reaction that is in line with how the business press has covered Wal-Mart's move into the country might be to focus on the nation's characteristics, assuming that Germany is not only "rigid" but an exception; that the market regime of the United States is more flexible and adaptable and thus more easily implanted in other economies. A close look at the Wal-Mart case, however, points out the fact that there is no completely adaptable regime—flexibility in one dimension is balanced by rigidity in another. Thus, global implants always involve a compromise, and the U.S. regime, as much as any other, has rigidities that limit the internationalization of its corporate concepts and firms. While Germany may be an exceptional case, we can still learn about the potential limits of U.S.-style globalization by focusing on the stand-off between the Wal-Mart concept and German economic policy.

The Case: Wal-Mart Confronts Germany

Wal-Mart is a retail phenomenon because of a set of characteristics that define its retail concept. The most important of these is "everyday low prices," which are achieved by economies of scale, purchasing power over suppliers, and a highly efficient sales forecasting and replenishment system that incorporates state-of-the-art information processing and supply chain logistics systems (Fernie and Arnold 2002). Although Wal-Mart has cultivated a community-friendly image, its economic size and power means it wields great power over the small communities where it invests (and disinvests) (Store Wars 2001). Wal-Mart is also famously antiunion, and one important dimension of its ability to keep profits high and prices low is a personnel policy that keeps the number of employees receiving health benefits to a minimum and emphasizes the use of a demand-driven part-time workforce.[1]

Analysts of international retailing have examined the expansion experience of U.S. retailers, including Wal-Mart (Alexander and Myers 2000; Fernie and Arnold 2002; Sternquist 1997; and Vida 2000), and the logistics supply model that has come to be associated with "Wal-Martization" (Christopher 2000). These analyses shed light on how Wal-Mart's strategy compares with those of other international retailers and on the potential contradictions between the Wal-Mart model and the requirements for success in a retail market such as Germany. Among the key features of Wal-Mart's global expansion strategy is its desire "to be the McDonald's of retailing and to stamp its brand on every store" (Fernie and Arnold 2002 p. 423). Alexander and Myers (2000) and Vida (2000) note that Wal-Mart favors repeating its successful U.S. strategy (branding, regional distribution centers, highly centralized operational control) in markets that are similar to the United States, such as Canada and Mexico, rather than adapting its strategy to a multiplicity of international market conditions. Significantly, Vida (2000) notes Wal-Mart's desire to enter international markets under a full-control strategy that is more generally characteristic of U.S. retail expansion. Wal-Mart's success in the United States has been enabled by a high degree of corporate control over all dimensions of the distribution and retailing process and vertical organization of supply chains. This command-and-control orientation is echoed in the work on Wal-Mart-style logistics.

Christopher (1998), for example, in arguing for what are essentially Wal-Mart–style logistics and information processing as "best practice," suggests that the types of applications considered and adopted will differ depending on the significance of (1) reduction of input cost through competitive bidding, (2) assurance of input quality, (3) assured flow relative to demand, (4) ability to respond rapidly to unexpected market shifts, and (5) the need for complex coordination of inputs in conjunction with projects or virtual firms.

Even within its own terms, this description of best practice evinces contradictions, for example, emphasizing information sharing and cooperation with subcontractors as a mark of success in some instances while pointing to centralization of control in the lead firm as critical to success in others. In the case of Wal-Mart, however, the origins of its success in a vertically oriented command-and-control process are quite clear. This rigidity of the Wal-Mart corporate model (and generally that of the United States) is one of the factors that makes adaptation to a multiplicity of international market situations problematic.

In the late 1990s, Wal-Mart entered the German market as a part of its international expansion strategy. Wal-Mart intended to generate one-third of its profits outside the United States by 2005, so Germany is a critical market to enter and (Wal-Mart hopes) to dominate. Germany accounts for fully 15 percent of Europe's $2 trillion retail market.

In the United States, Wal-Mart has expanded primarily by building new stores in rural and suburban areas. In its international expansions, however, the discount retailer has relied more on takeovers of already existing chains because of regulations governing new facilities and in order to move to scale very quickly. In this respect, Wal-Mart faced some serious obstacles in entering the German market. German companies tend to be privately held, relying on self-investment (rather than public capital markets) for capital. Because the leading major chains in Germany are privately held, there were no opportunities for hostile takeovers as there would be in Anglo-American markets. Wal-Mart was forced to purchase chains to enter the market, and it could only get two relatively weak chains, Interspar and Wertkauf, which together placed Wal-Mart in approximately eleventh place in overall retail sales. The German food retailing market is, however, highly concentrated, so the top five chains account for nearly 80 percent of overall sales. Thus, Wal-Mart began from a relatively weak position. Wal-Mart's strategy, in addition to pursuing one of the bigger privately held chains, Metro (thus far unsuccessfully), was to implement its major competitive device—cutthroat competition—over prices. Wal-Mart hoped to use this strategy to make up for its lack of an embedded network of neighborhood retail establishments and to weaken competitors so they could be acquired.

The chains Wal-Mart acquired were unionized by the major German commercial workers unions, HBV and DAG, and each had an operative works council with elected personnel representatives. Works councils, or within-firm consultative councils of elected workers' representatives, are a key feature of the German economy. However, Wal-Mart's U.S. managers, unfamiliar with the central role played by the works councils, have consulted them only sporadically, thus contravening a taken-for-granted feature of management practice in Germany.

Although Wal-Mart has paid its German workforce 3 percent above the collectively bargained scale, the company refused to adopt German collective agreements (Gewerkschaft HBV 2000). And in a development that demonstrates the coordination underlying German employer-employee relations, German Wal-Mart workers picketed the stores in July 2000 to force the company to join the employers' association and abide by collective agreements (Gewerkschaft HBV 2000).

The story of Wal-Mart in Germany suggests that despite their power, scale of operations, and experience, multinational retailers still face significant problems in using a strategy that is eminently successful in one economy, such as predatory pricing in the United States, and transferring it to a differently regulated economy (Langer Atem 2001).

It is, however, not only the regulatory environment and the interests behind it that make it difficult to transfer the Anglo-American model of lean retailing. It is also the kind and quality of relationships among firms that supply the distribution center it acquired and, apparently, an inability to recruit labor to operate the facility. According to articles in *Wirtschaftswoche*, a German weekly economics magazine, expediters delivering products to the distribution center had to wait hours to unload their cargo and, by comparison with the smooth efficiency that characterizes its U.S. operations, Wal-Mart Germany had difficulty keeping its networks of stores adequately supplied, especially with fresh produce (UNI 2000a).

By 2001, Wal-Mart Germany was the focus of concerted attacks in the press by unions, the employer or trade association membership, and farmers, all of whom attacked the company's pricing strategy. This occurred in an economy in which price competition among retailers is hot and taken for granted.

What was potentially more significant, however, was that Wal-Mart's shareholders began to lose patience for Germany to produce a profit in the short-term. Wal-Mart has had significant losses, over $200 million every year it has operated in the German markets. The higher-than-expected costs of renovating existing stores and the aggressive stance of the competition, which is using all of its institutional resources, including unions, to halt Wal-Mart's expansion, have discouraged investors (Greimel 2001). Wal-Mart is slowing down considerably and may pull out of the German market altogether.

The Limits to Best Practice in International Investment

Wal-Mart is touted as an exemplar of best practice because of its ability to continuously reduce costs through management of suppliers, use of logistics technology, and labor policies. What the best-practice literature typically neglects, however, is the institutional context within which technologies and firm strategies are introduced and applied. Particular choices of what to do and how to do it are influenced, if not determined, by the rules that define what constitutes success (e.g., rapidly increasing shareholder value or return on investment versus capturing market share over time). They are also influenced by regulation in areas such as labor market policy, competition, and intellectual property, and by the capacity of the state or states to set standards that enable effective integration of production, transport, and distribution.

As with lean production, there is an interesting debate over whether, and in what ways, lean retailing will be implemented globally. This debate has broad significance because it touches on the question of how economic interests respond to exogenous change in sectors that are more porous and open to global influences than are the core sectors in an economy. Within this debate, national differences in market governance have important implications for the strategies of individual firms and for the interactions of firms in networks—the processes at the center of the lean retailing revolution. So to understand Wal-Mart's resources as it moves to invest internationally, as well as the barriers to its investment methods in Germany, we need to refer to the institutional contexts within which U.S. and German firms develop their strategic capacities.

Varieties of Capitalism, Convergence, and Hybridization?

The literature describing and analyzing varieties of capitalism provides a starting point for discussions of continuing differences among advanced capitalist economies. To begin, the "varieties of capitalism" perspective is rooted in the idea that national political and economic institutions, and the power and agency they construct, have a profound bearing on how private sector and state actors try to shape national and global institutions in a global economy. Or, according to Regini (2000: 8), "preexisting institutions play a key role in shaping responses to exogenous factors by acting as a filter or intervening variable between external pressures and the responses to them." Thus, a crucial, and continuing, difference among capitalist regimes lies in the way in which economic activities are controlled and coordinated.

One major criticism of the "varieties of capitalism" approaches is that they deal almost exclusively in ideal types and neglect both differentiated trends within a type and the interplay of political forces that influence national regulation and, ultimately, firm strategies. In response to these critiques, a more nuanced approach to analyzing national institutional differences has emerged. Regini (2000: 9), for example, while rejecting crude versions of convergence, also points out general tendencies toward decentralization of collective bargaining and labor market deregulation. He suggests that we need a wider set of hypotheses about actors' behaviors because agents of change, including trade associations and governments, act pragmatically: "they concentrate on the policy areas in which they encounter less resistance or which they consider to be more vital to the interests they represent ... they take only a partial account of the context in which they operate and even less of the abstract need to provide consistent responses in the various policy areas."

Exemplifying this more politically nuanced type of analysis, Kathleen Thelen argues that the conventional explanations of union power do not explain the reluctance of German employers to opt out of traditional bargaining institutions. She suggests that employer interest in predictability and protection from wage disputes, rather than union strength, accounts for the stability of the system thus far (Thelen and Kume 1999; Thelen 2000).

Most analyses of Wal-Mart's difficulties point to German "inflexibility" as the explanation for Wal-Mart's failures. A careful look at the reasons behind Wal-Mart's recent failure, however, indicates that it cannot be explained by what might be considered obvious—Germany's regulated economy and the power of organized labor. In fact, the German food retailing market has many features in common with those in so-called merchant economies such as the United States. So a more complex story must be told—one that pays attention to the interplay of internal forces attempting to influence the future of industrial relations and interfirm competition in the sector in Germany as well as to more mundane considerations such as organizational scale. In fact, the story of how Wal-Mart has attempted to enter the German market but has faced barriers in realizing the benefits of its management and technological assets raises questions about its U.S. "ethnocentricity."

The Context for Lean Retailing in the United States

Market Governance and the Functioning of Firm Networks

Like lean production, lean retailing is not only about what happens inside a firm but also about the nature and content of relationships among firms—suppliers and manufacturers, retailers and distributors. These relationships are influenced by the incentives faced by the firms as individual entities and by the network. In some important respect, lean retailing competition is among supply networks rather than among firms. So the type and quality of governance of firm networks makes a difference as to the form lean retailing will take.

Despite its paeans to flat hierarchies, lean retailing in the merchant mode is best described in terms of a virtual, vertically integrated firm (Christopher 1998). It is organized vertically to enable the retailer to assess the market for subcontractors and to contract with those offering the lowest price. Lean retailing in a coordinated economy may likely follow the pattern of manufacturing, using horizontal, cooperative firm networks to expand market penetration across European countries (Christopherson 2000). Scale and complexity can come in the form of multicountry markets rather than sheer firm or establishment size.

In merchant regimes dominated by firms with short investment return horizons, decision-making authority in firm networks is centralized so that lead firm executives can move very swiftly to respond to changes in customer demand and enter and exit new markets rapidly (Christopherson 2000). Case studies from the food and apparel industries in the United States demonstrate that one of the key uses of information technology applications is to concentrate information at the executive level of the lead retail firm (Christopher 1998).

Particularly in the United States, emphasis is on the use of logistics applications to facilitate subcontracting as many aspects of the production, distribution, and retailing process as possible, in order to redistribute risk downward and allow for rapid market response to unpredictable consumer markets.

An Import-Oriented, Retailer-Dominated Market

Process innovation in the United States and in other merchant economies has been very strong in final customer-oriented industries, including applications associated with e-commerce. That logistics-based applications have been pioneered and rapidly adopted in U.S. retail firms is consonant with the position of retailers in the market as a whole. Large retailers have been active in using their market and political power to influence regulation in the transport industry (to reduce their costs) and in trade policy (to increase their scope of action in the import arena).

In these import-oriented economies, retailers use international commodity sub-contracting to substantially increase firm profits. The scale of the U.S. retail market and the increasing dominance of the market by fewer retailers gives these retailers significant bargaining power with commodity producers.

Market Composition

Because of its immigration policies and high degree of income inequality, the United States has a more diverse customer market than other industrialized countries. While this differentiated market may have only a minor impact in the automobile industry (or for most capital goods, for that matter), it has a significant impact in the markets for daily necessities, such as clothing and food, and for entertainment products. These industries have been leaders in adopting practices that allow rapid responses to changes in fashion and total demand.

Regulatory Environment

The regulatory environment in the United States has encouraged increasing firm size and market dominance in the retail sector (large firms with many establishments) and increasing competition and deunionization of the critical transport sector (Belzer 2000).

At the local scale, U.S. tax policy and economic development incentives in combination with limited land use controls have favored "gorilla retailing"—encouraging very large-scale retailers who offer goods at very low prices. These big-box retailers include Wal-Mart and other discounters, book stores (such as Barnes and Noble or Borders), and home improvement centers (such as Home Depot or Lowe's). While retailers with very large-scale establishments exist in Europe (for example, IKEA), they have not entered as many geographic markets as in the United States. Wal-Mart, for example has 2,500 stores in the United States.

Labor Market and Employment Practices

The U.S. (and U.K.) approaches to lean retailing rest on the ability to use a very large contingent workforce, particularly in part-time jobs. As in lean production in manufacturing, employers have been able to restructure work along the production chain, for example, eliminating skilled craft jobs, such as those of butchers and bakers, and replacing them with less skilled and nonunionized service workers. Technology has been used to circumvent a lack of skilled labor, even extending to basic literacy.

Wal-Mart, the largest private employer in the United States, with over 1 million employees, is a model for the approaches to personnel management in lean retailing. The store chain pays its sales staff slightly above minimum wage, but because such a high proportion of the workforce is part-time, only 40 percent of Wal-Mart's employees are covered by the chain's health insurance package. This compares with a national average of 47 percent covered by employer health insurance in wholesale and retail jobs (UFCW 2000).

Wal-Mart is aggressively anti-union. One strategy the U.S. United Food and Commercial Workers used to encourage unionization was to organize meat cutters, who because of their skills were more susceptible to organization. Wal-Mart then eliminated meat cutter jobs in many of its stores, turning to prepackaged meat products. The company has also issued a fifty-six-page booklet called "Manager's Toolbox to Remaining Union Free." The rationale for Wal-Mart's policies is the flexibility and low operating costs required to compete on the basis of product cost.

The approaches used in Wal-Mart-style lean retailing have contributed to a bifurcation of the workforce and a disruption of formerly accessible career hierarchies. With the organizational changes associated with lean retailing, we also see significant shifts in power associated with those who control information about end markets and associated skills and job content. Whereas midlevel managers and buyers were once an important source of information on customer demand, that information is now provided by point-of-sale data. The availability of point-of-sale data and customer order information transforms the role of the midlevel product manager from that of an information holder to one that is more interpretive, problem-solving, and entrepreneurial. The food store product manager is, for example, evaluated on his or her ability to successfully introduce new high value-added products in cooperation with manufacturing suppliers rather than as a basic information keeper. The manager may also have more prerogatives and incentives to determine working conditions at the establishment level.

Historically, the U.S. food retailing industry was unusual in providing a fairly straightforward career path from bagger to cashier to department manager to store manager and then chain executive. Progress along this path depended primarily on firm-specific knowledge and could be followed without an advanced degree. Food retail chain executives are still notable for having a lower level of formal education than executives in other industries.

The technological demands associated with lean retailing are changing this picture. Retailers, as well as their suppliers, are facing a people problem all along the supply chain. With no career development or training programs, and because of the lack of glamour associated with basic industries (such as food and apparel), firms have been unable to attract or retain the managerial and technical labor they need to make lean retailing work.

An observer of the skills market in logistics and lean retailing in the United States and U.K. makes this assessment:

So far the industry's response has been more damaging than helpful. A "beggar my neighbor" policy of poaching has tended to drive salary levels up but without improving the attraction of the industry. The industry's customers have hardly helped either. Cut-throat rates leave little margin for training budgets. Moving contracts from firm to firm makes career development and long term human resource planning an impossibility. And, while there are plenty of penalties for failure, the industry has found, or is allowed, few opportunities for rewarding success. (*Logistics Europe* 2001: 7)

The context that has shaped lean retailing in merchant economies has provided firms with the ability to innovate and to move in and out of markets depending on their short-term profitability. Lean retailing, however, like lean production, can be adapted under different circumstances. In Germany, a changing but still distinctive institutional context will influence the adoption of lean retailing and how it is put into practice.

The Context for Lean Retailing in Germany

The German retailing sectors, especially food retailing, are a different world from that of the coordinated high-price, high-wage manufacturing sectors that have defined the modern German economy. Food retailing in Germany is very price-competitive and profit margins are as low as they are in the United States (that is, typically under 3 percent). This compares with profits of 6 percent or more in the United Kingdom, which has historically been less price-competitive (Lewis 2001).

Germans are accustomed to shopping at so-called hard discounters, such as Aldi, which operate out of small-scale establishments, providing a narrow range of goods with special offers each week and no customer service. The week Wal-Mart opened in Berlin, the Aldi across the street from the new superstore was offering for only 34 cents the same bread that Wal-Mart was selling for $1.13.

The German food industry, including food retailing, has lower levels of unionization than the core export manufacturing sectors, and the unions are not as powerful. In addition, while trade associations are major players in regulating the industry, they are also experiencing the trends that Thelen (2000) describes in the manufacturing industries. Membership has become less cohesive, and smaller employers are frequently at odds with larger players over how the industry should be regulated.

At the same time, many of the same processes that are transforming retailing in the United States are present in Germany. Concentration has occurred in retail sectors and is especially striking in the food retailing industry. Chain stores and large retail facilities account for an increasing proportion of sales, while the number of small retailers is declining. The German market, however, has also become more complex because of the economic consequences of unification. West German cities retain land use controls that protect smaller-scale inner-city retailers. These retailers maintain a dense network of establishments. In East Germany, retailers established larger-scale American-style retail establishments in the fast-growing urban periphery even before suburbanization started, encouraged by a deteriorated central city environment and unresolved property issues. Very small, in-town establishments (one-third the size of West German food stores) were not able to compete and have disappeared.

Germany has also developed successful shopping centers and is following many U.S. retailing trends including the development of factory outlet stores. As in the United States, shopping is becoming more important as a leisure activity.

As sales floor size grew in the 1990s, sales per square meter declined 10 percent. Restructuring of the industry toward bigger enterprises in a more concentrated market has produced a decline in retail employment of approximately 4 percent per year. The major German commercial workers union (HBV) estimates that 80,000 full-time jobs have been lost in the 1990s (UNI 2000b).

Like its counterparts in other industrialized countries, the German retail sector is a major employer of women, especially in part-time work. As the sector has been deregulated, the employment of women has increased to fill an expanded number of part-time jobs.

As Regini (2000) notes, deregulation of the labor force has occurred across Europe, including in Germany. The lower level of labor protections (particularly in sectors such as trucking and retail, historically peripheral to Germany's core industrial strengths) enabled German retailers to pursue their own version of price competition long before Wal-Mart came on the scene.

These common features, however, exist within an economy with a considerably different market governance structure than that in the United States (and Anglo-American economies in general). This market governance regime is frequently described as "coordinated" because it is based on continuing negotiation among the social partners—private enterprises, labor represented by powerful unions, and government. In Germany, labor, especially in the manufacturing sectors, exerts considerable influence over a wide range of public policies.

So if we look at the conditions shaping the development of retailing in Germany, we also find a different set of underlying conditions and incentives.

A "Patient Capital" Coordinated Market Governance Regime

In general, coordinated economies have been slower to utilize the logistics applications focused on cutting costs through subcontracting. In coordinated economies, such as Germany, there is greater relative emphasis on using logistics applications to ensure flow relative to demand and to ensure input quality. Both of these are related to the importance of customer service, whether the customer is the retailer or manufacturer.

Although a third-party logistics provision is increasing in Germany, logistics activities (and its associated knowledge) are more likely to be carried out within the firm of the commodity producer. In part, this is a reflection of the service dimension embedded in German manufacturing, whose history is one of technical innovation and a reputation for consistent high quality produced by close relations with both customers and suppliers. While third-party logistics providers exist in Germany, they primarily meet limited strategic needs. A study of German production networks indicated that informal exchange of technical knowledge was perceived as the most important mode of cooperation between firms and their customers. This was particularly evident in the major German exporting industries: fabricated metals processing, machinery, motor vehicles, and technical services. While manufacturing practices regarding logistics are not followed in the same way in German lean retailing, there is a greater tendency to see logistics suppliers as strategic partners rather than as subcontractor-service providers.

An Export-Oriented Manufacturing-Dominated Market

In contrast with the United States and United Kingdom, Germany is an exporting economy with a strong, sophisticated manufacturing base. The development of an advanced logistics infrastructure in Germany (ahead of other European economies) was driven by the need of its manufacturers to move their goods into an international market. Political influence in Germany is disproportionately held by manufacturers and manufacturing unions, especially IG Metall. Together, they influence trade policy to favor manufacturers rather than retailers.

What this means in practice is more emphasis on building a national and European infrastructure, both physical and regulatory, that will encourage the easy flow of exports.

Regulatory Environment

The German retail market is less open to competitive incursion because of its strong firm networks and the local neighborhood scale of operation, at least in the higher-income Western part of the country. While the market may be technically open, regulation of land use along with other scale-sensitive regulations favor existing firm networks. The influence of local regulation on competition was evident in the failure of Wal-Mart (see below). The impasse suggests an entry barrier to firms that need to operate at a large scale to achieve bargaining power with manufacturing subcontractors, but for whom their scale is a barrier to entry into the highest-density urban markets. They may find it easier to move into the suburbs and eastern German greenfields than into the high-density urban centers.

Labor Market and Employment

As Streeck (1996) describes in his comparison of Japanese lean production and the limits to its application in Germany, the German employment system has distinctive characteristics that shape the way technology is introduced and adopted. As in Japan, the United States has a weak occupational tradition. Even with traditional crafts, such as meat cutting and baking, there has been a long-term trend to provide standard packaged goods through mass production. The exception to this trend is the specialized boutique butcher or baker who serves the upper end of the food retail market.

As Streeck indicates, an occupation is not a job. A job belongs to an employer, and an occupation belongs to an employee—or better, employees belong to occupations, and occupations belong to the society that defines and redefines them (Streeck 1996: 145). German education and training systems continue to adhere to the principle that individuals should operate in the workforce with standardized and certified occupational qualifications. Much of the training for occupations takes place in the workplace and in the context of a presumed career development path. In retail, two paths are available to students, one in sales and one in business administration.

It is important to note, however, that with increasing employment in commercial and other services (and with increasing feminization of the workforce) the traditional concept of *Beruf*, or occupation, is changing in Germany. In some industries and employment categories it is being replaced by the concept of "competence," closer to that of the generally skilled worker who can fill a number of medium-skilled positions.

Importantly, coordination problems among workers, such as those that would develop with the introduction of lean retailing, have typically been dealt with by the development of new training programs. When tasks arise, such as those involved with the introduction of new technology, they give rise to the creation of new skilled occupations defined so that their areas of competence overlap with those of workers performing adjacent tasks (Streeck 1996: 147).

In a coordinated/manufacturing economy, such as Germany, the role of midlevel managers in retail is changing, but more slowly. They continue to hold information about customers and suppliers. The skills required of midlevel managers in a German retail firm may thus be different from those in U.S. or U.K. retail firms. German managers, for example, do not have as many prerogatives available to them in affecting the conditions of work in the establishment. There also may be a different balance between entrepreneurial skills and firm-specific knowledge, with the latter more emphasized in the German context.

In addition to the occupational skills system, the industrial relations system also provides for methods of adaptation to new technology that are absent in the Anglo-American merchant economies, particularly the United States. Unions independent of any particular workplace have the research capacity and political influence to shape the development of new occupations through political pressure for training programs and career paths as well as to protect traditional skilled craft occupations, which might be displaced by lean retailing. The consequences of the distinctive features of German market governance are manifested in the difficulties Wal-Mart is having in establishing its retail model in the country.

Conclusions: Not "If" But "In What Way"

What can differences between German and U.S. market governance regimes tell us about the possibilities for adoption of U.S.-style lean retailing in different economies? Examined at face value, the lean-retailing best practice model builds on supply chain management strategies that have transformed high-end manufacturing industries, but is distinguishable in several important respects:

- It is driven by customer information. Because retailers hold customer information through point-of-sale data, retailers drive the restructuring process.
- It is serving as a vehicle to transform traditional, low-technology manufacturing industries (such as food processing and apparel manufacture) by forcing suppliers to adopt new practices to avoid being left to absorb costs that have been redistributed downward (Abernathy et al. 2000).
- Its applications are dependent on numerical labor flexibility, using overtime and short hours in response to unexpected changes in demand at the level of the retailer and short production cycles at the supplier level. Deregulation of the transport industry and of the retail sector has played a major role in the types of restructuring options available.

Looked at from a different perspective, however, lean retailing is also an ideological model, that is, it incorporates particular ideas about what exists and what is good. For example, in Christopher (1998), a key text in lean retailing, the only differences worth noting are cultural differences in commodity preferences. Some people prefer top-loading washing machines, while others prefer the front-loading kind. Some people eat more meat; others eat less. The assumption is that these differences can be solved by technical strategies, such as postponing production until it is based on actually existing demand.

Given that lean retailing methods depend on labor markets with a high degree of labor flexibility and require strong influence on trade regulation and work organization by retailers, there is surprisingly little discussion of politics or institutions as a context for lean retailing. When institutions do enter, they are perceived as barriers to best practice. So, retail is expected (à la staged economic development models) to move through a series of stages from "traditional retailing," with low market concentration and segmentation of retail formats, to the "highest" and "best" form, advanced retailing, characterized by a high degree of market concentration, segmentation, capitalization, supply chain integration, and use of information technology.

What is interesting (and ideological) about the lean retailing model is that it conveys that bigger is better. The possibility of alternative mixes, such as smaller-scale establishments with sophisticated supply chain management, is not considered, although that combination exists in one of the "advanced" retailing countries, Germany.

One could suggest, therefore, that the lean retailing model and its stages derive from a particular vision of the economic and political context necessary for efficient and competitive retailing.

As in lean production, variants of lean retailing will be adopted by firms internationally. The particular form in which they will be adopted, however, will be influenced, if not determined, by the institutional and regulatory context. If we are to understand how this technology will affect retailing in different political and economic contexts, we need to move beyond both idealized models of capitalist economies and ideological models of lean retailing.

The comparison of developments in the retail sectors of the United States and Germany tells us that globalization of technology via multinational firms is neither easy nor straightforward. The very basis for success in one market may be inappropriate to competitive conditions in another.

Of course, there are different capacities and styles. With respect to lean production, U.S. firms are using logistics applications in manufacturing in ways that emphasize control and coordination of cross-national production networks, just as they are in retailing. In another common pattern, they are rapidly applying efficient customer response strategies in retail so as to respond to rapid changes in market demand and further commoditize the retailer-customer relationship through control of point-of-sale information.

Manufacturing-oriented German firms are using logistics applications to expand the market for their products and, in conjunction with their European partners, to develop a high-quality transportation and communications infrastructure that can withstand economic assaults from firms (in Anglo-American economies) that shy away from long-term responsibility for physical assets (Plehwe 2000).

In addition, home country constraints arising from corporate governance regimes may clash with management objectives to internationalize. The impatience of Wal-Mart's stockholders may foreclose entry into the largest European food retailing market.

At the same time, corporate governance rules in the host country may constrain the use of the full range of strategies a firm may wish to use to enter a market. The private ownership of Wal-Mart's major competitors prevents the use of takeover strategies that would be available in the United States.

Finally, a comparison indicates that lean retailing is no more likely to be universally adopted in its U.S./Wal-Mart form than lean production was in its Japanese form (Streeck 1996). Instead what is more likely is adaptation to existing market governance institutions (Dörrenbächer et al. 2000; Katz and Darbishire 2000).

Acknowledgment

Research for this paper was supported by a visiting fellowship from the Wissenschaftszentrum, Berlin.

Note

1. In recent years, antagonism to Wal-Mart's profit strategies and personnel policies has produced an active anti-Wal-Mart movement in the United States.

20

The Myth of Wal-Martization: Retail Globalization and Local Competition in Japan and Germany

Yuko Aoyama and Guido Schwarz

Introduction

Is Wal-Mart taking over the world? With so much unfavorable press generated in the past few years in the United States over Wal-Mart's labor practices and competition strategies to drive out local independent retailers, its globalization strategies have come under scrutiny. Wal-Mart has been far more successful in globalizing its sourcing activities than globalizing its retail operations. In this chapter, Wal-Mart's challenges in Japan and Germany are analyzed, and the role of local regulations and consumer behavior in retail globalization is explored.

Wal-Mart's initial expansion into overseas markets began with North America, first with acquisition of a chain in Mexico in 1991, followed by expansion into Puerto Rico in 1992 and acquisition of a chain in Canada in 1994 (refer to Table 2.1). In 1995 Wal-Mart entered Latin America by opening stores in Argentina and Brazil. In the following year it expanded to Asia through joint ventures in China and a licensing agreement in Indonesia that was subsequently terminated. In 1997 Wal-Mart entered Europe through acquisition in Germany, followed by an acquisition in the United Kingdom two years later. Wal-Mart also expanded in Asia, opening stores in South Korea in 1998 and Japan in 2002. In sum, in 2005 Wal-Mart operated a total of 1,620 stores in eight countries in addition to Puerto Rico (excluding minority stakes in Seiyu Japan), and roughly half of the entries into those countries were made through acquisition.

In this chapter we will first examine the prevailing theories of retail globalization by analyzing the strategies adopted by Wal-Mart in Japanese and German retail markets, particularly with respect to local competition, regulations, and consumer preferences. We conclude that successful retail globalization is synonymous with retail localization, and entry of foreign retailers does not necessarily result in market standardization across international borders. These findings question the notion of market convergence as a process of globalization.

Retail Globalization, Local Competition

Until recently, the retail sector has been understood as activities that are localized and small-business-based (Akehurst and Alexander 1996). Globalization of retailing is a relatively new phenomenon, and expansions have generally been limited to neighboring countries. Wal-Mart, which has been regarded as one of the instigators of globalization among large retailers, also began investing internationally by first entering Mexico. The major driving forces behind retail globalization include the emergence of common markets (particularly the European Union), maturity of the retail sector in many of the advanced industrialized economies (particularly Western Europe), and competitive pressures (both from domestic market players as well as from competitors aggressively globalizing their operations).

Retail globalization has been largely driven by a series of "push" factors. While many retailers consider globalization a necessary strategy for expansion, challenges in successful retail globalization are well recognized by the retailers themselves as well as by financial institutions (Palmer and Quinn 2001). On one hand, foreign entry into the retail sector does stimulate the domestic market, providing impetus for innovation and achieving higher efficiency. On the other hand, success by foreign retailers is far from guaranteed. As a result, globalization is generally regarded by retailers as a strategy for diversification and hedging of risks through involvement of multiple markets.

Wrigley and Currah (2004) argued that retailers face a distinctive organizational challenge because the "distribution-based" nature of their business requires them to embed themselves in the markets and local cultures of consumption to a far greater degree than "production-based" firms. Many marketing strategies successful in home markets are often nontransferable due to their context-specific nature. Scale economies is insufficient as a rational for retail globalization, as successful products often vary across societies. Furthermore, foreign retailers face significant disadvantages in understanding local market trends, yet face the same set of restrictions local retailers face, which range from regulation to transportation infrastructure. Wal-Mart's early lessons from Argentina and Brazil suggested cultural and market infrastructural differences (Friedland and Lee 1997; Burt and Sparks 2001). As of 2003, only a handful of retailers have successfully expanded their operations internationally: IKEA (Sweden), Marks & Spencer (United Kingdom), Toys 'R Us (United States), Metro (Germany), and Carrefour (France) maintain operations in more than twenty countries (Futagami 2003).

Today, significant variations exist across societies in the structure of the retail sector, and the strength of each retail category is determined by the competitive forces in the domestic market. Organization of the retail sector has traditionally been viewed as driven largely by two variables: economic factors, such as income and related standards of living (e.g., household automobile ownership), and settlement patterns (population growth and density) (Russel 1957; Ferber 1958; Hall, Knapp, and Winsten 1961; Arndt 1972; Rosenbloom 1975; Takeuchi and Bucklin 1977). These factors in turn shape competition in the retail sector, resulting in emergence of various retail categories. For example, Aoyama (2001a) discussed the relationship between urban density and retail category, comparing the strength of warehouse clubs and supercenters in the United States vis-à-vis neighborhood convenience stores in Japan. U.S. consumers are willing to travel extra distance for low prices. The average travel distance for warehouse membership clubs is 13 miles, which is significantly longer than the average distance traveled to traditional supermarkets, at 1 to 2 miles (Cotter, Arnold, and Tigert 1992). During the ten-year period between 1992 and 2002, warehouse clubs and superstores grew almost fivefold in the number of establishments, over sixfold in sales, and were by far the fastest-growing retail category in the United States. Price Club, founded in San Diego in 1976, was merged with Washington-based Costco in June 1993, and together they control 231 stores worldwide with 13.5 million members. Wal-Mart Supercenters in the United States more than doubled from 682 in 1999 to 1,471 stores in 2003. Combined with Wal-Mart discount stores and Neighborhood Markets, Wal-Mart operates more than 3,000 stores, in addition to 538 Sam's Club stores (Wal-Mart 2004).

Regulatory framework is another major factor that shapes domestic competition in the retail sector (McCraw and O'Brien 1986; Tamura 1986; Maruyama 1993; Hancock 1993; Heshiki 1996). Regulatory environment is increasingly recognized as an important element of consumption, along with its contribution to shaping the patterns and practices of the retailing system (Marsden and Wrigley 1995; Wrigley 1992; Wrigley, Lowe, and Currah 2002). The influence of regulation on consumption is particularly relevant for Germany and Japan, where the state has historically and generally been highly interventionist.

How do Wal-Mart's successful strategies, developed in the United States for American consumers, translate to the German and Japanese markets? In the following sections, we analyze the challenges faced by Wal-Mart and other foreign retailers in Germany and Japan. Particular foci will include local competition, regulations, and consumer behavior.

Wal-Mart in Germany

Germany was the first European market for Wal-Mart. In 1997, Wal-Mart purchased the Wertkauf chain, a privately held firm with 21 stores (mostly in Western Germany), annual sales of $1.4 billion, and 6,000 employees, for $880 million (Gerhard and Hahn 2005; Gotterbarm 2004; Zellner et al. 2001; O'Connor 1998; Tomkins 1997). A year later, Wal-Mart purchased Interspar and its 74 stores for $650 million. Unlike the Wetkauf chain, which was composed of profitable stores of roughly uniform size and style appropriate for a supercenter, Interspar was struggling financially and included stores of various sizes. Although the intention was to instantaneously gain a significant presence through acquisition, the initial entry was hampered by the challenge of managing the merger of two very different retail chains with aging facilities. It has been rumored that Wal-Mart intended but failed to purchase two additional existing chains, which would have provided the necessary scale economies and presence in the market. Thus, unlike the case of the United Kingdom, where Wal-Mart purchased a profitable and growing chain (ASDA), in Germany from the outset Wal-Mart was faced with significant investment for renovation and rebranding, in addition to

Figure 20.1 Wal-Mart Supercenter in Wurzburg, Germany. The store has been renovated to Wal-Mart colors and styles. (Photo by Guido Schwarz.)

entering an entirely new and unfamiliar market. It was estimated that upgrading and integrating in 1998 resulted in $200 million in losses (Zeller 2001).

In 2005, Wal-Mart ranked a distant twelfth among all retailers in Germany. Considering only food, Wal-Mart Germany was ranked 10th in 2003 while more recent data are no longer available for Wal-Mart's food sales. The figures suggest that Wal-Mart is no longer among the top 10 food retailers in Germany (Table 20.1). Even in the supercenter category, in which Wal-Mart dominates in the United States, Wal-Mart ranked only fourth both in terms of the number of stores as well as in sales. Today, more than seven years after entering the market, Wal-Mart has yet to turn a profit in Germany. Despite periodic announcements of positive progress in cash flow and returns on investment (Wal-Mart Germany 2004), the year 2004 has likely ended with another loss for Wal-Mart in Germany (Ronke 2005). Wal-Mart is struggling in the face of fierce competition from domestic retailers. As of today, Wal-Mart is the only major foreign food retailer in the German market.

As a result of lackluster performance since its entry, skepticism is high for the future of Wal-Mart in Germany. Some analysts believe that Wal-Mart "mistakenly came to Germany and compounded that felony by buying the wrong retailers and mishandling their transformation and Americanization" (MMR 2004).

Wal-Mart's Challenges in Germany I: Demise of the German Retail Sector

Saturation of the German retail sector is a frequently cited reason for the lack of success by Wal-Mart Germany. Indeed, the decade of the 1990s was widely known

TABLE 20.1   Top 10 Food Retailers in Germany, 2005

Rank	Company	Food Sales (US Billion $)
1	Edeka Group	38.8
2	Rewe Zentral AG	27.9
3	Schwarz Group	23.1
4	Aldi Group	21.8
5	Metro Group	16.4
6	Tengelmann Group	10.2
7	Lekkerland GmbH	7.7
8	Schlecker	6.5
9	Norma	2.9
10	dm-Drogeriemarkt	2.7
	Wal-Mart Germany	3.3*

* Wal-Mart data is estimated and includes all of its sales (food and non-food)

Source: Trade Dimensions/M+M Eurodata 2006, Lebensmittel Zeitung, http://www.lz-net.de/rankings/handeldeutschland/pages/show.prl?id=162

TABLE 20.2   Major Retail Sector Trends in Germany, 1994–2001

	Number of Firms			Sales (in million €)			Number of Employees		
	1994	2001	Change	1994	2001	Change	1994	2001	Change
Specialized food stores	38,160	29,406	−22.9%	14,007	12,532	−10.5%	183,400	147,812	−19.4%
Food supermarkets	29,971	24,540	−18.1%	102,205	113,120	10.7%	637,700	687,151	7.8%
Variety and department stores	3,076	3,149	2.3%	20,763	18,122	−12.7%	196,200	154,549	−21.2%
Drugstores, pharmacies, and medical equipment stores	25,037	24,109	−3.7%	25,954	36,211	39.5%	237,400	269,914	13.7%
Specialized (nonfood) stores	172,516	139,412	−19.2%	116,008	112,764	−2.8%	1,232,900	1,099,811	−10.8%
Nonstore retailers	57,258	34,771	−39.2%	33,807	33,285	−1.5%	229,100	175,118	−23.6%
Total retail	329,851	258,507	−21.6%	313,225	326,542	4.2%	2,724,800	2,542,226	−6.7%

Source: Lambertz 2002; Statistisches Bundesamt 1997, 2002.

as the worst time in history for retail trade in Germany. As shown in Table 20.2, the number of retail businesses in Germany declined across the board, and total retail sales contracted 0.3 percent in nominal prices between 1994 and 1999, although they recovered somewhat thereafter, making the total sales growth 4.3 percent between 1994 and 2001. The downward trend continued for employment in the retail sector, decreasing to -6.7 percent since 1994. The combined effects of ongoing restructuring and consolidation due to intensified European Union–wide competition and sluggish domestic growth were cited as the reasons behind the decline. However, a closer look at the data shows that during the decade of overall decline, two retail categories fared better than the rest: food supermarkets and drugstores.[1] Since this is the sector that Wal-Mart competes in, the macroeconomic environment cannot be solely responsible for Wal-Mart's sluggish performance in Germany.

Wal-Mart's lack of success in Germany is instead attributed to the profound differences in Germany's retail environment that are related to the locational strategies and the regulatory environment. Wal-Mart stores in Germany focus on food retailing (50–60 percent of revenue in Germany, as opposed to 40 percent in the United States) and less on the nonfood discount items typical of U.S. Wal-Mart stores (Gotterbarm 2004). This means Wal-Mart in Germany is heavily exposed to the competitive pressures of food retailing, a sector that is particularly cutthroat in Germany. Domestic competitors, such as Aldi and Lidl, have already negotiated rock-bottom prices from suppliers and are known to command significant power in determining prices. Yet German retailers remain relatively unsophisticated when it comes to product variety, customer service, and efficiency. The combination of price-conscious consumers and inefficiency among domestic competitors made the German market seem ideal for Wal-Mart's first experiment in the European market.

Domestic competitors mounted a significant counterattack to Wal-Mart's entry into the German market. Metro, for example, reportedly dispatched executives to the first Wal-Mart store in Dortmund on its opening day and compiled information on product variety, prices, and customer service (Kitoh 2003). In response, Metro renovated its Real chains, devised a new tricolor logo similar to that of Wal-Mart, changed the store opening hours to match those of Wal-Mart, and initiated new advertising campaigns with the slogans "Honestly Low Prices" and "Permanently Reasonable" to counteract Wal-Mart's emphasis on everyday low prices. Other domestic competitors such as Aldi and Lidl followed suit and were able to match Wal-Mart's prices with a more traditional German retailing strategy: weekly sale of a limited selection of items and advertising in a flyer. In response, Wal-Mart was forced to review its trademark pricing policy and began emphasizing its weekly limited-time sales items under the label "Save Even More." However, general consensus of the German consumers today is that Wal-Mart prices are neither necessarily nor significantly cheaper than those of their competitors.

Domestic competitors also focused on other aspects of retailing traditionally considered weak in German retailing. Metro revamped its customer service training and introduced a $3 cash-back guarantee if the wait at the cashier is longer than five minutes. Metro also purchased domestic chains Allkauf and Kriegbaum to ensure scale economies and improve efficiency. Other domestic chains, such as Aldi, Rewe, and Edeka, closed smaller stores, opened larger ones, and centralized the supply chain to better negotiate more bulk discounts from manufacturers. Spar Handels reduced prices up to 20 percent on a thousand items, and Rewe focused on devising a twenty-seven-point strategy for better customer service in addition to granting store managers more autonomy for product selection (Kitoh 2003). In the meantime, Wal-Mart initiatives were met with strong resistance. One such initiative was to take greater control over distribution. In Germany, manufacturers traditionally have their own distribution system, and retailers and suppliers are in adversarial relationships. Wal-Mart insisted on building its own distribution center, managing the supply chain, and implementing its proprietary "Retail-Link" system to develop partnerships with key suppliers (JCMRI 2002). However, Wal-Mart Germany today still lacks the size and market share to make these systems pay off the initial costs. Thus, Wal-Mart's entry served as a catalyst for domestic food supermarket chains to make significant improvements in their efficiency. Domestic competitors' effectiveness, however, eroded the impacts of any new strategies Wal-Mart introduced to the German market.

Wal-Mart's Challenges in Germany II: Land Use, Competition, and Labor Regulations

Germany's stringent regulations on retail sector activities gave Wal-Mart little freedom to exercise various strategies that have been successfully employed in the United States. Germany's competition laws originated as a response to large-scale retailers, particularly department stores, beginning in the late nineteenth century (Gellately 1974: 41). The Gesetz gegen den unlauteren Wettbewerb, a 1909 law against unfair competition, prohibits general price reductions on a retailer's products, in effect outlawing storewide sales and leaving retailers only the weekly flyer with featured products as a marketing tool (Reichsgesetzblatt 1909; Gellately 1974: 127). Under this law, price reductions for apparel, textiles, shoes, and sporting goods are allowed only for the two-week period starting on the last Monday of January and July (the winter and summer clearance sales), on a retailer's twenty-fifth business anniversary, and with permission under extraordinary circumstances (liquidation, fire, or flood damage). The giveaway regulation of 1932, which prohibited retailers from offering additional items or services with the purchase of another product, eliminated marketing strategies popular in the U.S., such as buy-one-get-one-free offers or free gifts with purchase (Reichsgesetzblatt 1932). The rebate law of 1933 expanded the restrictions by prohibiting monetary rebates as well as volume discounts and discounts above 3 percent of the price (Reichsgesetzblatt 1933). This meant that neither store/manufacturer discount coupons nor targeted promotions for frequent buyers are used in Germany.

The remarkable aspects of these regulations is not only their highly restrictive nature but also the fact that they survived to the early twenty-first century and were strictly enforced. Typically 20,000 cases were brought before courts annually by the Center for the Fight Against Unfair Competition, charging retailers with infringing on some of these regulations (Ronke and de Paoli 2002). Foreign retailers faced particular difficulties, as many of the marketing strategies they employed at home were illegal in Germany. American Express, for example, was prevented from offering customers frequent flyer miles, and Lands' End, an American catalog company, was deterred from printing its money-back guarantee in its catalogues, as the German court interpreted such a policy as a "free gift."

The recent relaxation of various retail regulations therefore marks a significant change. The giveaway regulation and the rebate law were abolished in August 2001 (Bundesregierung 2001), and competition laws are also under consideration (Bundesministerium der Justiz 2003). This shift was the result of globalization and technological advancement in the retail sector, prompted primarily by three external pressures on the industry. First, the mandate of the European Union (EU) to standardize certain retail regulations across member countries has put pressures on lawmakers to reassess the century-old regulations. The German competition policy did not harmonize with those of the EU until the mid-1990s after being challenged by the EU Commission (Eyre and Lodge 2000).

Second, the onset of e-commerce with its border-crossing market access provided an additional incentive for the retail sector to offer concessions to changes that were otherwise unwelcome by small retailers and labor unions. These trends toward deregulation, however, do not by any means suggest that government interventions no longer occur in the German retail sector. In 2000, for example, the German Cartel Office accused Wal-Mart, along with its competitors Aldi-Nord and Lidl, of engaging in the practice of dumping (selling below cost) milk, butter, and a few other grocery items. This means Wal-Mart cannot use the practice of loss leaders, a tactic widely adopted by its stores in the United States and Britain, to outcompete other retailers.

The German labor law that regulated store hours was one of the most restrictive in the EU until 2001. The Store-Closing Act, enacted in 1956 to restrict store hours, was regarded as a victory by the Mittelstand (small and medium-sized business) against competition from large-scale retailers. The Mittelstand viewed longer store hours as giving advantages to large retailers while posing a significant burden on small retailers in paying wages for extra hours. Changes in the law in 1996 extended store closing times from 6:30 p.m. to 8:00 p.m. on weekdays and from 1:00 p.m. to 4:00 p.m. on most Saturdays. The much-anticipated increase in store revenue did not materialize, however, and many smaller stores have again cut back their hours (Economist 1997). Hours were further extended in 2003 to 8:00 p.m. on Saturdays, with one work-free Saturday per month guaranteed for employees, yet Sunday and holiday closures remain mandatory. Lack of freedom in setting store hours is therefore yet another lost opportunity for Wal-Mart to exercise differentiation in the German market. In addition, Wal-Mart's practices met with significant resistance from labor unions representing workers in chains purchased by Wal-Mart. Disagreements between Wal-Mart and labor unions contributed to delays in renovation as well as various changes implemented by Wal-Mart, particularly in the first two years of its operation (Kitoh 2003).

Finally, Germany's stringent land use policy has prevented Wal-Mart's practice of low-cost location strategy. Germany's land use policy has been highly effective in preserving traditional urban commercial districts and has limited U.S.-style sprawl in favor of preserving open space while placing high barriers to building new suburban shopping malls. Comprehensive regional planning has a long tradition in Germany and is based on the federal spatial planning law (Bundesgesetzblatt 1997), which in turn mandates all states (*Länder*) to develop comprehensive state development programs. At the regional level, spatial planning must be based on the principles of Christaller's central place theory, with states designating the centrality of each municipality. Infrastructure and services, including retail, must be concentrated in central places, aimed at ensuring that the entire country is equitably supplied with goods and social services (Vielberth 1995). Local zoning maps must be approved by the states and will often be rejected or modified. In addition, individual large-scale retail projects above a certain threshold are subject to independent approval by the state spatial planning authority to test for conformity with the state development plan. The Bavarian state development plan, for instance, specifies that such projects must be accessible by public transit and be located adjacent to existing dense urban development. In addition, greenfield sites can be approved only if the municipality proves there are no adequate integrated locations in its territory, the site does not pose a significant threat to downtown retailing in surrounding centers of a higher hierarchy, and the ministers of the environment and interior give joint approval (Bayerisches Staatsministerium für Landesentwicklung und Umweltfragen 2005: 36–37). The law also specifies ceilings on regional purchasing power that may be tapped by large-scale retail projects, and the authorities routinely limit the floor space of stores accordingly. Only the downtown cores of designated large centers (Oberzentren) carry no restrictions on the types or sizes of stores. As a result, locating supercenter-size stores in low-order rural centers, as Wal-Mart frequently does in the United States, is therefore expressly prevented in Germany. Medium-scale centers are permitted a consecutively broader range of stores with larger trading floors, but the type of store operated by Wal-Mart is permitted only in the largest urban areas. These laws place significant limitations on Wal-Mart's locational strategy in Germany, which explains Wal-Mart's decision to enter Germany through the acquisition of an existing chain.

Wal-Mart in Japan

While no clear judgment has been made, the performance of Wal-Mart in Japan has so far been a disappointment. Wal-Mart entered the Japanese market in 2002 through a minority stake in an existing chain, Seiyu, adopting a strategy of keeping a low profile from Japanese consumers by making no visible changes in storefront design and product variety. It has been widely speculated that this strategy, as well as the much-delayed entry to the Japanese market, were direct outcomes of its failure in the German market. So far, changes Wal-Mart implemented in Japan are exclusively in the area of back-end operations. Yet its financial performance has been less than notable, and given the most recent reports from the Japanese media showing a pessimistic outlook, Wal-Mart's strategies are treated with mild skepticism in Japan today.

Wal-Mart's first experience with the Japanese market was an experiment conducted in 1994 through a major domestic chain, Ito-Yokado. Ito-Yokado sold Wal-Mart private brands including ketchup, snacks, and casual apparel, but the experiment was terminated within a year, accomplishing only half the sales target (JCMRI 2002). After briefly considering purchase of a small retail chain facing bankruptcy in 2001, Wal-Mart eventually formed a strategic alliance with Sumitomo Trading and

Figure 20.2 Seiyu in Saitama, Japan. Wal-Mart Japan keeps the appearance of the domestic chain it purchased as is. The store is four stories above ground, with a basement dedicated to groceries. (Photo by Gozo Aoyama.)

Figure 20.3 Seiyu in Saitama, Japan: storefront. The same Seiyu store in Saitama, Japan also features Starbucks (left) and KFC (right) on the first floor on both sides of its entrance. (Photo by Gozo Aoyama.)

TABLE 20.3   Top 4 Food Supermarkets in Japan: Midyear Report, 2003

Rank	Supermarket	Revenue (in ¥ million)	Profits (in ¥ million)	Revenue (in $ million*)	Profits (in $ million*)
1	Aeon	853,572	9,045	7,221	76
2	Ito-Yokado	737,789	15,312	6,242	130
3	Daiei	708,943	5,153	5,998	44
4	Seiyu	381,829	−3,436	3,230	−29

* In 2005 USD.
Source: Mizuho Bank 2004.

purchased a 34 percent share of Seiyu in 2002, with the option of increasing its share to 50.1 percent by the end of 2005 and to 66.7 percent by the end of 2007. At the time of purchase, Seiyu was Japan's fourth-largest retailer and had more than 200 super-market-category stores nationwide. However, Seiyu lagged far behind the top three retailers, which had double to triple the size of revenue, and was the only retailer operating at a loss (Table 20.3). In mid-2004, Seiyu yielded profits for the first time since Wal-Mart took over, but it also reported a 3.5 percent decline in revenue from the previous year (*Nikkei Net* 2004). Most recently, Seiyu announced a downgrade of their revenue projection for the second time in the past fiscal year, which led to widespread speculations about the negative impacts of Wal-Mart-initiated strategies at Seiyu. In July 2005, Seiyu's CEO was forced to resign without completing his term, still a rare occurrence in Japan's corporate world. By mid-2005 Seiyu's stock price, which doubled immediately after the announcement of Wal-Mart's involvement, had plummeted to a third of its peak in 2002.

Wal-Mart has so far implemented two major changes in Seiyu's operations. The first change was much-needed downsizing, which was executed through the voluntary early retirement of 1,600 Seiyu employees, or 25 percent of its total full-time workers. Wal-Mart also has plans to increase the share of part-time workers to 85 percent of its total employees in the near future (Tsukiizumi 2004). As exemplified by the case of Renault's takeover of Nissan, Japan's firms often avoid implementing major restructuring schemes and let their foreign partners bear the burden of making difficult decisions, particularly downsizing. The second change involved implementation of information technology in supply chain management. By the end of 2003, all Seiyu stores were connected to Wal-Mart's Retail Link system, with 600 suppliers in Japan signed onto the network. Seiyu also introduced new supplier-retailer relations in Japan by implementing the Joint Business Plan System, which allows Seiyu and suppliers to jointly set targets for sales, profits, and inventory. So far, seventy-three suppliers have signed on to be part of this service (*Gekiryu* 2005). While voluntary retirement has helped Seiyu cut significant costs, introduction of the new supply chain system has placed significant burden on the stores' part-time employees.

Major challenges for Wal-Mart in Japan reflect two factors. First, Wal-Mart entered the category of retailing known in Japan as "general supermarkets," which is becoming rapidly obsolete in Japan's retail sector. Today, general supermarkets face increasing competition from convenience stores, co-ops, and specialized supermarket chains. Second, foreign retailers in the past have faced particular difficulties in implementing strategies that have been successful elsewhere. They face challenges on two fronts: knowledge of local consumer preferences and long-standing practices in the distribution sector.

Challenges for Wal-Mart in Japan I: The Demise of General Supermarkets

Part of the success of Wal-Mart Supercenters in the United States is the combination of non-food and food categories of retailing, which was somewhat innovative in the American market. In the case of Japan, however, general supermarkets already combine nonfood and food items, thereby reducing the novelty of the supercenter approach to size only. As a retail category, general supermarkets are becoming increasingly obsolete and have been experiencing a decline in both the number of establishments and in sales. *Gekiryu,* a major industry magazine for the retail sector, reported that the situation of the general supermarket category is "dire" and 2005 may become the year when its performance may "make or break" this category of retailing (*Gekiryu* 2005).

General supermarkets in Japan were modeled after those in the United States. They were introduced to Japanese consumers in the 1950s, and phenomenal nationwide growth followed in the 1960s and the 1970s. General supermarkets grew at the expense of department stores, which were under legal restrictions by the Large-Scale Retail Law of 1973. This law was enacted to restrict activities of large-scale retailers in order to protect small retailers and sustain urban retail centers. It restricted opening hours for most large-scale grocery stores at the national level and regulated the entry of large retailers at the regional level by restricting the floor size of new entrants (see McCraw and O'Brien 1986; Hancock 1993). A symbolic event occurred in 1972 when Daiei, one of the pioneers of general supermarkets, exceeded the revenue of Mitsukoshi, a highly reputable, major department store chain. As general supermarkets incorporated ever greater varieties of product lines and also upgraded them, general supermarkets have effectively come to function as pseudo department stores in Japan. Simultaneously, however, general supermarkets have been gradually losing their raison d'être in Japan's retail sector. The recent bankruptcies of major supermarket chains such as Nagasakiya and Maikaru, as well as Daiei, which is currently under bankruptcy protection, reflect this tendency. The industry blames fierce competition and deflation.

Their demise is in part explained by the fact that the strategy they developed in the 1980s—attracting customers with groceries and selling them highly profitable apparel—proved ineffective in the face of rising competition from specialized retailers focusing on discount clothing, drugstore items, or electronics and other electrical household appliances. Specialized (nonfood) supermarkets recorded the fastest growth in the 1990s in Japan's retail sector, with growth of 179 percent in sales between 1991 and 2002. General supermarkets declined 0.9 percent in the number of establishments and grew a meager 0.2 percent in sales during the same period.

In response, general supermarket chain Ito-Yokado is gradually shifting its focus on the up-market segment of apparel, and using team merchandising, a strategy similar to that of Wal-Mart (i.e., abandoning traditionally strong relationships with wholesalers and teaming up with manufacturers for product development). Seiyu is introducing low-priced Wal-Mart items and is competing based on prices. So far, however, neither has produced significant results. Ito-Yokado has been unable to completely abandon its relationship with wholesalers, while Seiyu's low-cost approach has only reinforced the view among consumers that their stores offer low-quality products.

Significant competition on food items is also emerging from home delivery services run by regional co-ops. A survey in 2000 showed 43.3 percent of households surveyed used some kind of home delivery service, and 27 percent of them used weekly home delivery (AFC 2000). Regional co-ops have grown phenomenally since the 1970s, with an established reputation for providing safe and quality alternatives to conventional processed food. Co-ops now boast a 45 percent share in home delivery food services in Japan (Fuji Keizai 2003). Co-ops cater to the growing segment of Japan's consumers today who are particularly concerned with imported produce grown with heavy use of fertilizers and pesticides and are willing to pay a premium for regionally grown (often organic or low-fertilizer-use) produce, or processed food with few additives. Mislabeling food products (both intentional and unintentional) has caused numerous scandals in Japan's retail and agro-food sectors in the recent past, including a well-known incident of meat mislabeling by a Seiyu store shortly before Wal-Mart's takeover. Thus, without proper marketing, a simplistic, low-cost approach can potentially add to consumers' growing suspicions.

Challenges for Wal-Mart in Japan II: Regulations and Localization

Similar to Germany, foreign retailers in general have not performed well in the Japanese market. The first foreign involvement with Japan's retail sector began with Sumitomo Trading announcing an alliance with Safeway in 1962. This was subsequently canceled upon huge protests by the Japan Retail Trade Association, which primarily comprises independent small- and medium-sized retailers. In 1975, for the first time, the retail sector was excluded from the list of sectors that come under trade restrictions, and this theoretically opened up the retail sector for foreign entry. However, this did not immediately translate into an increase in foreign investment, in part due to complex distribution systems and in part due to high property values in Japan (Nippon Kogyo Ginko 2002). As a result, foreign entry in the Japanese retail sector was spearheaded by European luxury brands with their own product lines, such as Chanel (France, 1980), Versace (Italy, 1981), Louis Vuitton (France, 1981), and Hermès (France, 1981). In the early 1990s, the Large-Scale Retail Law became a target of criticism by the U.S. government, and was viewed as "structural impediments" for international trade. The Japanese government responded by relaxing the law gradually in the early 1990s and finally eliminating it in 2000. The Large-Scale Retail Law was replaced by the Large-Scale Retail Location Law, in which control was shifted from the central government to the prefecture level, and the objective was shifted from industry (i.e., protection of small and medium-sized retailers) to land use (i.e., protection and promotion of retail corridors). In addition, while the new law eradicated the size limitation and store hours regulations, it introduced new requirements for environmental impacts, including parking, noise pollution, and waste disposal. Deregulations led to the growth of suburban malls from 16 percent of the total greenfield development in 1971–75 to 44 percent in 1996–98 (Mizuho Bank 2004).

These changes in the legal environment, as well as the decline of property values after the end of the "bubble" economy of the late 1980s, finally captured interests of foreign retailers, such as Virgin Megastore (joint venture, U.K., 1990), The Body Shop (U.K., 1990), Toys "R" Us (U.S., 1991), and Disney Store (U.S., 1992). Foreign grocery and supermarket chains did not enter the Japanese market until 1995. Aside from Wal-Mart's participation in the Seiyu chain, foreign firms with a presence in Japan in the general supermarket category are limited to small-scale operations such as Costco (U.S., 1999, five stores) and Metro (Germany, joint venture with Marubeni Trading, 2002, one store). We have yet to see the outcome of Tesco's purchase of C Two-Network in 2003, a convenience store chain with 78 stores in the Tokyo area. Tesco can potentially use the chain as a springboard for building bigger outlets (Rowley 2004).

Divestments from Japan's retail sector are not uncommon. Past examples include Sports Authority (U.S., 1996, with 49 percent interest by JUSCO, Japan's major supermarket chain owned by AEON, which subsequently took over the entire operation), OfficeMax (U.S., 1997–99, joint venture), Footlocker (U.S., 1997–2000), and J. C. Penney (U.S., 1998–99). In the supermarket category, Daily Farm, a Hong Kong retailer, set up a joint venture with Seiyu and opened four stores in Japan but was forced into closure due to lackluster sales in 1998. Carrefour, which was the largest foreign investor in the retail sector in the recent past, with eight greenfield sites beginning 2000, announced in March 2005 what is effectively a divestment, agreeing to sell all its stocks to AEON, a major domestic chain. Lackluster performance in France prompted the firm to reconsider some of its international operations, and Carrefour Japan has operated at a loss since its initial investment. Also, Carrefour's focus in Asia is rapidly shifting to China, where it has already established a solid track record as the number one foreign retailer.

The experience of Carrefour in many ways is typical of foreign retailers in Japan's food retailing sector. Carrefour was facing the problem of "branding," a particularly complex issue in the Japanese market (Jacobson 2002). A survey of consumers at Carrefour showed that the firm needs to resolve the gap between consumer expectation and their product offerings (Nippon Kogyo Ginko 2002). In spite of Carrefour's initial intentions, even on the first day of business at its Makuhari store, domestic chains in the neighborhood were able to undercut many of Carrefour's prices, which effectively prevented consumers from equating Carrefour with price competitiveness. Furthermore, few Japanese consumers expected to purchase price-competitive, day-to-day food items by entering a Carrefour store. Rather, with their previous experience being largely shaped by other French retailers in Japan (Chanel, Louis Vuitton, and Hermès), consumers expected Carrefour to offer a distinct experience of shopping at a foreign (and in particular French) store. Carrefour responded by altering its strategies, adding 150 private-brand food items to the existing 120 sold in Japan as well as prepared food that was "French home-style." Carrefour also organized special events such as tastings of French wines and a sweepstakes for a trip to Paris, and conducted a limited-quantity sale of luxury leather items from Louis Vuitton and

Hermès. Carrefour remodeled its first store in Makuhari, Chiba, hired core executives from the now-defunct Daiei chain and others, and was rapidly developing its model of retailing in Japan. Yet there was a persistent rumor of divestment for at least a year before its sellout to AEON.

Wal-Mart in Japan has experienced a reverse problem that arises from branding. While Japanese consumers at Seiyu stores had not noticed price changes in the food category, they recognized lower prices offered in the apparel category since Wal-Mart's entry. These lower prices have not translated into growth, however, as Wal-Mart products are viewed as cheap and low-quality (*Asahi Shimbun* 2005; *Shukan Daiyamondo* 2005). Not only has Wal-Mart been unable to establish a distinctive identity for its apparel products, but its low-cost, low-quality approach, which reduced the per-unit price of clothing sold in Seiyu as much as 26 percent in a single quarter, ruined a highly profitable apparel segment and has been blamed for Seiyu's most recent poor performance. Competition from specialty private-label apparel firms such as Uniqlo, known for quality casual clothing with direct factory links in China, constitute formidable competition for Wal-Mart's low-end apparel products. Furthermore, popular 100-yen store chains (equivalent of a dollar store) run by two major firms, Daiso and Kyankyan, also increasingly capture market share of household items and consumer nondurables.

Japan's typical urban consumers shop in smaller quantities and more frequently than their American counterparts. Since consumers are more likely to walk or bicycle to a nearby grocery store or drop by a store after work en route from a nearby train or subway station, occupying strategic urban locations is the single most important factor for successful retail performance in Japan. Lack of storage space provided no incentive for customers to shop at large-volume discount stores, popular in the United States. Because Japanese consumers are known to be far more willing to trade after-sale service, convenience, and proximity for a higher price when compared with American consumers (McCraw and O'Brien 1986; Goldman 1991; Hancock 1993), some question the effectiveness of Wal-Mart's fundamentally scale-economy-driven approach in Japan. As the examples of convenience stores have shown, successful retailing in Japan takes advantage of the locational premium and logistical efficiency particular to densely populated urban areas (Aoyama 2001b). Japan's operating costs remain high even after the bursting of the real estate bubble, which requires significant adjustments to Wal-Mart's strategies. In comparison to its U.S. counterparts, Wal-Mart's operating cost is estimated to be five times greater in Japan in terms of property cost, three times greater in terms of operating cost per store, and twice as high in terms of constructing new buildings (JCMRI 2002). However, domestic competitors are moving toward the supercenter approach to counteract competition from new Wal-Mart stores. AEON Group claims it will have built 100 Wal-Mart-style supercenters in suburban areas by the end of 2005, up from the current 4, and Beisia Group hopes to open 75 supercenters by the end of 2005. It is unclear, however, whether this strategy will prove to be successful. Ito-Yokado, for example, has decided to not take this approach, and is instead beefing up its information technology system.

Others argue that Wal-Mart represents nonurban, down-to-earth, basic American values and lifestyles, which are not well suited for the Japanese market (Shimada

2003). Cultural aspects of retail strategies are often neglected but may prove to be critical for success in the retail sector. Similar to the case of Germany, Seiyu briefly adopted Wal-Mart's "everyday low price" approach without notable success, as Japanese consumers prefer special prices and limited-time sales. In an attempt to lure back customers, Seiyu is reverting to the traditional method of flyers announcing limited-time sales. In the food category, the fast-growing segment is prepared food for take-out, which ranges from sushi, tempura, and salads to desserts. Department stores and general supermarket chains are both active in Japan's prepared food market. This is not an area that Wal-Mart has much experience in, and besides, it requires an in-depth understanding of local cultures.

Finally, similar to the case of Germany, foreign retailers also face difficulties in changing distribution practices. Wal-Mart, Carrefour, and Costco had difficulties convincing manufacturers to sell directly to them, in part due to their new status, and in part due to the lack of economies of scale. Traditionally, Japan's manufacturers dictated the behavior of wholesalers, which in turn governed the behavior of retailers. Retailers effectively represented the interest of the manufacturer, rather than that of consumers (Tsukiizumi 2004). Furthermore, retailers were often protected from financial risks by wholesalers and manufacturers through a number of distinctive market practices (such as rebates), and manufacturers and wholesalers controlled prices by enforcing districting and exclusive dealerships. Because wholesalers dictated retailers' behavior and sanctioned those who broke exclusive distribution rights, Japan's retail sector faced an added disincentive to support a new retail category, including diversification of distribution networks and supplying multiple categories of retailers.[2] This form of closed-network distribution, which dominated the Japanese market, provided significant barriers to new retailer entry. For foreign retailers, Japan's complex retail and distribution system has long been inaccessible, so much so that the U.S. government considered it a nontariff barrier and a structural impediment for U.S.-Japan trade.

In a bold move, Seiyu recently severed ties with its third largest wholesaler, Ryoshoku, which has been its supplier for more than forty years. While Seiyu's business with Ryoshoku is about a quarter of that of its largest wholesaler, Kokubu, Seiyu is one of Ryoshoku's top ten customers. It has been widely speculated that Ryoshoku's high-cost investment to achieve high-quality service became inconsistent with Wal-Mart's drive for cost reduction at Seiyu stores (*Nikkei BP* 2004). While Seiyu intends to negotiate directly with manufacturers, industry insiders suggest that it is highly unlikely for Seiyu to achieve a dramatic price reduction for food items it sells, given the current state of Japan's manufacturers and their distribution networks (*Shukan Daiyamondo* 2005). Given its declining share, Seiyu will unlikely be able to convince manufacturers and wholesalers to come to the negotiation table for further volume discounts.

Conclusions

In the retail sector, successful globalization necessitates in-depth localization of storefront operations, product categories, and distribution practices. In the case of Germany, Wal-Mart entered a market that had already achieved a low-cost, low-margin environment. Furthermore, domestic competitors successfully reorganized their operations in time to counteract competitive pressures from Wal-Mart. In the case of Japan, Wal-Mart's limited involvement and the strategy to maintain the Seiyu store-front has had mixed results. Learning from the experience in Germany, Wal-Mart's strategy in Japan so far has been balanced with taking advantage of Seiyu's strength in local market knowledge and bringing in Wal-Mart's expertise in supply chain management. The real impact of Wal-Mart in these markets is the acceleration of already ongoing retail restructuring and further efficiency building.

In addition to the differences in regulations and local competition, demand structure may also have played a role in Wal-Mart's performance. The relatively small share of low-income households in Japan and Germany, as opposed to the United States and the United Kingdom, also means a smaller size of the target market for Wal-Mart's low-end products (JCMRI 2002). Mature markets dominated by the middle class with significant competition in the domestic retail market means that consumers are not only price-conscious but also discriminating in terms of quality, and the drive to reduce costs further is often met with complex challenges.

One of Wal-Mart's major impacts in the retail sector is "destabilization," in which the combined effects of price cutting and economies of scale overwhelm the existing retail sector, or at the very least work as a catalyst for major changes there (Burt and Sparks 2001). Such destabilization and its impacts on competitors and communities have not been felt in either Germany or Japan due to Wal-Mart's limited involvement at this stage. Because Wal-Mart cannot readily implement the same labor practices, locational strategies, and distribution system used in its U.S. operation elsewhere, the firm needs to devise a different set of strategies that are market-specific. Once Wal-Mart enters a foreign market, it is faced with the same constraints local competitors face, and *must* develop successful retailing strategies in spite of its lack of local knowledge. Because of this formidable challenge, it is unlikely that Wal-Mart, or any other single retailer, will successfully dominate the world in the near future. It will take standardization of various institutional fronts, including local zoning laws and labor regulations, as well as consumer tastes and preferences.

Acknowledgment

This work was in part supported by the Henry J. Leir Faculty Fellowship provided by the Ridgefield Foundation.

Notes

1. The expansion of drugstores was fueled by both the highly regulated, small-business-dominated pharmacy sector and large drugstore chains. Both profited from increased consumer spending on health and wellness products, with pharmacies benefiting from prescription drug sales. The emergence of large drugstore chains such as Müller, selling a variety of personal care and household items, also explains part of this growth, which successfully captured sales from the variety and department store category, as well as other specialized nonfood stores.
2. Retail trade experts argue that Japan's sectoral division of power is characterized by the dominance of manufacturers, and the wholesalers and the retailers are regarded simply as the distribution arm of the manufacturers.

21

Penetrating the Great Wall, Conquering the Middle Kingdom: Wal-Mart in China

Shuguang Wang and Yongchang Zhang

Introduction

Of the nine foreign markets that Wal-Mart has penetrated, China is perhaps the most challenging. Being the only non-GATT/non-WTO (General Agreement on Tariffs and Trade/World Trade Organization) country among the nine, China retained a great wall of barriers to the entry and expansion of Wal-Mart. In its first four years after entry in 1996, Wal-Mart was able to open merely six stores in three cities. By the end of 2004, it operated only 42 outlets in the vast country of 1.3 billion consumers, compared with 241 units in Canada and 671 in Mexico (Wal-Mart International 2005). While Wal-Mart is prudent in exploiting this culturally dissimilar market, its growth has been much slower than it desires, constrained mainly by slow-paced retail deregulation on the part of the Chinese government. Nonetheless, Wal-Mart is determined to conquer the Middle Kingdom (the name of China in Chinese). Its experience in China presents an interesting case study of the retail internationalization process.

Retail Internationalization

Retail internationalization is, in essence, a process of transforming retail capital across national borders.

To begin with, the international operation of retailers is motivated either by saturation of the domestic market or by a strategic need to secure first-mover advantages in a new market (Yip 1989, 1992; Akehurst and Alexander 1995; Simpson and Thorpe 1999; Alexander and Myers 2000). While the number and variety of forms of these operations have increased since the early 1990s and international retailing has now become a larger and larger component of retail activity in many countries (Dawson 1994; Simmons and Kamikihara 1999), only firms that have adequate resources in administration as well as research and development and have achieved high operational efficiency are likely to succeed in expanding into foreign markets (Elango

1999). To use the terminology of regulationist theories, these firms have entered a new regime of accumulation—flexible accumulation—in response to the opportunities created by new production, transportation, and communication technologies (Knox, Agnew, and McCarthy 2003). Wal-Mart, Carrefour, Metro AG, and Ikea are among such successful international retailers.

As Dawson (1994: 268) correctly points out, "any move towards multi-store operation has to acknowledge that culture varies through space." This is especially true when retailers transform retail capital across international borders. According to the location advantages theory (Dunning 1988; Pelligrini 1991) and the stages theory (Dupuis and Prime 1996), firms initially choose markets that have the least physical and cultural distances to minimize cost and degree of uncertainty about sourcing and operation (Whitehead 1992). As a firm gains more experience, it enters markets with greater physical or cultural distances, but also with great potential profitability (Erramilli 1991; Vida and Fairhurst 1998). This explains why Wal-Mart began its international operation in U.S. neighbors Mexico and Canada. More recently, major international retailers have increasingly turned their attention to the "emerging markets" in Asia and Latin America, which offer the attractions of potentially rapid economic development and rising levels of affluence and consumer spending, combined with low levels of penetration of Western forms of retailing and associated distribution systems (Wrigley 2000). China is the largest emerging market in the world.

Once a target market is selected, the international retailer considers a suitable entry mode and path. Entry mode is defined as forms of capital participation (or transformation) in international businesses (Sun 1999). Retailers seeking entry into a foreign market can take the mode of either wholly owned subsidiaries or joint ventures. Each mode has relative advantages and limitations (Anderson 1993; Sternquist 1997; Sun 1999). In wholly owned subsidiaries, firms can impose their own operating methods with little friction, but they may also face higher risks. In joint ventures, local partners allow foreign retailers to connect with the host government and compatible organizations to gain strategic advantages in activities such as obtaining business licenses and development permits, as well as in sourcing and logistics. They can also be relied upon for their expertise in exploring domestic markets and managing the local workforce. Both entry modes can be realized through two possible paths: greenfield development or acquisition of local firms (Vida and Fairhurst 1998). Usually, a firm chooses the most suitable entry mode and path to either minimize transaction cost or best overcome barriers, but its choice may also be constrained by regulations of the host country. For Wal-Mart, this is perhaps more evident in China than in any other foreign market it has entered.

Of equal importance, an international retailer chooses a suitable format to ground its retail capital. As a general rule, for a format to be successful, it must serve the market better than competing formats. A firm may also need to modify a standard format in a foreign market, as many expansion failures result from an attempt to force standardized formats into a variable or unsuitable commercial environment (Simmons, Jones, and Yeats 1998). A particular format must be supported not only by the right location but also by available and affordable real estate. As well, it depends on the settlement patterns of the local market and the embedded transportation system. Together, they manifest the spatial outcomes of retail capital transformation.

Retail internationalization is a cultural affair (Shackleton 1996). Whatever format is chosen, international retailers must adapt their products to differing regional tastes and needs and provide local content in their commercial offerings, while at the same time surrounding those offerings with contextual values desired by local consumers (Crawford 2001). After a business goes into operation, the foreign retailer periodically evaluates its firm's performance in the local market. Depending on the evaluation results, the firm, again, may make varying decisions: to replicate the business at different locations, to expand in a different format, or to withdraw from the foreign market (as did the Dutch firm Royal Ahold from China in 2001).

Using this process of retail internationalization as a convenient framework, this chapter reconstructs the Wal-Mart experience in China. First, we present an overview of progressive deregulations in China's retail sector. This is the necessary context for our Wal-Mart study because the Wal-Mart experience has largely been dictated by this deregulation process. Next, we examine Wal-Mart's entry mode and expansion patterns in China, including the spatial outcomes of its retail capital transformation. In the third part, we explore how Wal-Mart executes its business strategy to overcome political and cultural barriers in its efforts to conquer the vast but highly guarded consumer market. Wherever appropriate, references are made to other international retailers, especially Carrefour and Metro AG, for comparison.

Retail Deregulation in China: The Political Context

After economic reform began to bring improved income to its ordinary citizens in the mid-1980s, China became a dream market for international retailers. However, China did not allow foreign retail operations until 1992, nearly ten years after its manufacturing and agricultural sectors were opened to foreign direct investment. Since then, China has made a series of policy changes to gradually open its consumer market to international retailers. The changes were made in large part to fulfill its commitments to the international community as China was bidding for a WTO membership. The entire process is marked by four distinctive phases of retail deregulation.

Phase One: 1992–1995

In July 1992, China designated six cities and five special economic zones (SEZs) to experiment with opening its retail market to foreign capital. The six cities were Beijing, Shanghai, Tianjin, Guangzhou, Dalian, and Qingdao. The five SEZs are Shenzhen, Zhuhai, Shantou, Xiamen, and Hainan. All are located in the eastern coastal region. To control the experiment process effectively, the Chinese government cautiously imposed a series of restrictions on the entry and operation of foreign retailers, ranging from geographical limitations to restrictions on capital participation, business format, and sourcing (Editorial Board 1997). For example, only the eleven designated cities and SEZs were allowed to participate in the experiment, and each of them was permitted to host only one or two foreign retailers (including those based in Hong Kong, Taiwan, and Macao, which were treated as foreign investors by the Chinese government). The entry of foreign retailers had to be approved by the state government; local governments were prohibited from admitting foreign retailers independently. Approved foreign retailers had to operate in joint ventures with at least one Chinese partner; whole foreign ownership was prohibited. In joint ventures, foreign investors' stake had to be less than 50 percent. With regard to format, joint ventures were strictly limited to single-store retailing; retail chains and wholesaling were prohibited. While foreign retailers were allowed to import certain types of merchandise for retailing, total import could not exceed 30 percent of their total sales, meaning that at least 70 percent of the merchandise had to be purchased from local manufacturers and suppliers.

With designation of the eleven cities and SEZs for the experiment, the state government approved fifteen foreign retailers, including Wal-Mart, to establish joint ventures in China.

Phase Two: 1995–1999

In October 1995, the state government took the second step to opening its retail sector, but only slightly wider. This time, it authorized Beijing to experiment with expanding joint ventures from single-store operations to retail chains. It also allowed the expansion of foreign participation from retailing to wholesaling, and from general merchandise to food products. Two international retailers were subsequently approved to form chains in Beijing: Japan's Ito-Yokado and the Netherlands' Makro. As a measure of precaution, the state government still insisted that partnership with Chinese retailers was mandatory, and these Chinese partners had to have a controlling ownership.

Phase Three: 1999–2004

To speed up its negotiations with the WTO, in June 1999 the state government made its third major move with further and more significant deregulations (State Economic and Trade Commission and Ministry of Foreign Trade 1999). The experiment was expanded geographically to include all provincial capitals. Total foreign ownership was still prohibited, but majority ownership was allowed in retail chains that purchased large quantities of domestically made products and exported these products through their own distribution channels. While all joint ventures became allowed to engage in wholesaling as well as retailing, more stringent criteria were set forth for the selection of foreign retailers and Chinese partners (Wang 2003). In correspondence with the country's newly devised national strategy of "developing the west," preferential treatments were offered to joint ventures that were willing to set up business operations in western China.

The new policies were aimed at raising the entry bar and selecting only large international retailers as future entrants. These policies were expected to bring needed capital, information technology, merchandising techniques, and managerial knowledge to China. At the same time, the new policies were meant to ensure that only the large domestic retailers with adequate resources and experiences could become partners. This would raise the level of participation by Chinese retailers in business decision making, so their role in joint ventures would not be reduced to that of liaison or messenger between the foreign retailer and the government.

Phase Four: 2004 Onward

After fifteen years of prolonged negotiation and numerous concessions, China was finally admitted to the WTO in 2001. This required that China remove all the remaining trade barriers and open its retail market completely within a period of three years. To fulfill its obligations, in April 2004 the state government announced its latest policy changes with regard to FDI in commercial sectors (including retailing), marking the end of the twelve-year experiment. The latest policies, released by the Ministry of Commerce in its Document No. 8 of 2004 (Ministry of Commerce 2004), lifted virtually all remaining restrictions and promised a fully open and fair retail market to international retailers. Effective December 11, 2004, foreign retailers are permitted to establish business operations, both retailing and wholesaling, anywhere in China. As well, foreign retailers and investors are permitted to operate wholly owned retail enterprises as well as joint ventures in China. In addition to in-store retailing, other forms of business are now permitted, including selling goods via television, telephone, mail, Internet, and vending machines. With the exception of large wholly owned and foreign-controlled joint ventures, provincial governments are now delegated the authority to approve future entrants or opening of new outlets in their respective jurisdictions.

These policies are particularly welcomed by big international chains, but they have also opened up new areas of business for smaller companies that did not qualify to compete under the 1999 laws. With the removal of unconventional barriers, China shifted to regulating foreign retailers by legal means commonly acceptable to WTO members. For example, the Ministry of Commerce, in the same year, issued two related documents. The first, Document No. 180 of 2004, requires that all municipalities make their own bylaws in regard to commercial facility development, and that the bylaws be compatible with the municipal general plan. The second, Document No. 390 of 2004, provides standard definitions of the various retail formats and types of facilities. Municipalities across the country are expected to follow these standards in developing their own bylaws. The new policies stipulate that future retail establishments must conform to municipal plans and local land use bylaws. Large facilities that are 10,000 square meters in size or more (most foreign operations are in this category) must also go through the public hearing process. Pertinent government officials, industry leaders, interested retailers, and representatives of potentially affected communities are invited to comment on business proposals. Enterprises with foreign investment must also pass annual inspections with audited financial reports. Those that fail to pass will not be allowed to open new stores, and may even be ordered to close their existing operations.

Entry, Expansion, and Spatial Outcomes

Within the political context of retail deregulations, we now examine how Wal-Mart has evolved in China over time and space. As mentioned earlier in this chapter, Wal-Mart was among the first fifteen foreign retailers approved by the state government in 1992 to set up an operation in China. It was also the only one from the Western Hemisphere; the other fourteen were from Asia: Japan (4), Singapore (1), Malaysia (1), Thailand (1), and Hong Kong (7). In the words of China's chief negotiator with the WTO, Yongtu Long, Wal-Mart was in fact invited to China by the Chinese government (Lin and Sun 2004). This should have given Wal-Mart a huge first-mover advantage over its principal European competitors, Carrefour and Metro AG.

Soon after state approval, Wal-Mart established and registered a subsidiary, Wal-Mart China Co. Ltd., in Hong Kong to prepare for its entry. The subsidiary was created with Ekchor, a Thailand distribution company, as a minor partner through which initial contacts with local governments and business partners were made.

Despite the tremendous market opportunities, retail regulations in China were very restrictive, the distribution system chaotic, and the retail channels fragmented (Chan et al. 1997). Like all other foreign retailers, Wal-Mart was looking for "islands of prosperity," or plum markets with affluent consumers, to ground its first retail capital. At first, it targeted Shanghai as the beachhead for its landing. This was not surprising because, with the establishment of the Pudong New Area in the early 1990s and the restoration of the historical role of the Bund, Shanghai was emerging to become an international financial and trade center. While the Shanghai government welcomed Wal-Mart, negotiations failed for undisclosed reasons. This cost Wal-Mart one of the largest and the wealthiest consumer markets in China until 2005.

Its next choice was Shenzhen in south China, which was also an ideal market for Wal-Mart investment. As the first SEZ of the country and the harbinger of China's economic reform, Shenzhen was a city of immigrants from all over the country. Its population was relatively young and well educated. Wages and salaries were categorically higher than most other cities, yielding an affluent consumer market. As a new city, Shenzhen's distribution system was underdeveloped, with no real competitors. For example, none of the country's top 100 retailers in 1995 was based in Shenzhen (Cai 1997). The city's outward-looking policies and more transparent regulations, together with high government efficiency, created a favorable business environment for foreign investment. Equally important, the many factories that had already been established with foreign investment in the SEZ could be easily recruited to supply Wal-Mart stores with brand-name and quality merchandise. All in all, Shenzhen was viewed to have a shorter business distance for Wal-Mart to overcome than most other Chinese cities.

Unlike its entry into Canada and Germany by means of acquisition and merger, Wal-Mart entered China through joint ventures (Wal-Mart International 2005a and b). This was not a choice but rather was dictated by state regulations of the time. Wal-Mart decided to test the Shenzhen market with two contemporary formats: the supercenter and Sam's Club. Both were unique among the fifteen state-approved foreign retailers, as the other fourteen focused on high-end department stores. There were two strategic considerations for introducing these two particular formats. First, the supercenter—a combination of a discount department store and a supermarket—provides a one-stop shopping opportunity for ordinary Chinese citizens looking for mass consumer goods, and such shopping opportunities were very rare in China in the late 1990s. Second, Sam's Club, many of whose paid members were small retailers and corporate consumers, would allow Wal-Mart to bypass government restrictions on wholesaling.

However, Wal-Mart did not open any store until 1996. It waited until China began to experiment with foreign operation of retail chains, wholesaling, and food retailing. Although the experiment was at that time limited to Beijing, Wal-Mart foresaw the possibility of extending the experiment to other cities. After four years of preparation and waiting, it opened its first two outlets in the summer of 1996: a supercenter and a Sam's Club. Their grand opening was painted as a huge success, with each store reporting sales of more than $250,000 (RMB 2 million) on their first business day (Zhao 2003). Also dictated by the state regulations that prohibited foreign retailers from operating chains (except the Japanese Ito-Yokado and the Dutch Makro in Beijing), Wal-Mart had to have two different local partners: Shenzhen International Trust and Investment Corporation (SZITIC) for its supercenter, and Shenzhen SEZ Development Corporation for its Sam's Club. Because both local partners were city-government-controlled entities, the two joint ventures were soon merged into one single enterprise. It must be pointed out that Wal-Mart never agreed to a minority ownership arrangement in its joint ventures. Of the $8 million (RMB 64 million) registered capital, Wal-Mart invested 70 percent, and its local partner was limited to 30 percent, far less than the state requirement of 51 percent.

Its subsequent expansion was tentative and slow-paced, also due to state-imposed restrictions. In the next three years (1997–99), Wal-Mart opened only four more stores, all supercenters: one in Dongguan, two in Shenzhen, and one in Kunming (Figure 21.1). Two important observations are noted here. First, Dongguan, a second-tier city in Guangdong province, about 60 miles (100 km) northwest of Shenzhen, was not among the experimental cities. There is no report that the Dongguan operation was approved by the state government, and it is possible that Wal-Mart was testing the seriousness of the state restrictions. Second, Wal-Mart chose the city of Kunming in southwest China's Yunnan province as its first step in expansion outside Guangdong province. This happened somewhat incidentally. In 1998, a local retailer in Kunming, Daguan Shopping City, had just built a mammoth commercial complex of 210,000 square meters, with half of the floor space planned for retail use. Daguan was searching for an anchor and invited Wal-Mart to move in, knowing that both the provincial and municipal governments would approve the entry for sure. After three visits to the city and the site by Wal-Mart China's president, Joe Hatfield, and with Daguan doing all the public relations work plus offering significant concessions, Wal-Mart opened a supercenter in the complex in 1999 (Zhao 2003). This nonetheless marked a different growth trajectory from those of Carrefour and Metro, both of which focused on large cities in the eastern coastal region.

After 1999, when China expanded its experiment to include all provincial capitals, Wal-Mart stepped up its expansion accordingly. In 2000, it opened five supercenters, including one in the city of Dalian, in northeast China. In 2001, it relocated its global purchasing center from Hong Kong to Shenzhen. With that move, Wal-Mart increased

Figure 21.1   Wal-Mart host cities in China, September 2005.

its direct purchasing substantially and, at the same time, reduced indirect purchasing through its intermediary agents to improve profit margins. After 2001, when China became a full member of the WTO and promised to remove all remaining barriers in three years, Wal-Mart expansion accelerated in both number of new openings and geographical coverage. By September 2005, Wal-Mart had opened 47 stores in twenty-three cities (see Figure 21.1). Of the 47 stores, 41 are supercenters, 3 are Sam's Clubs, and 2 are Neighborhood Markets. Its typical supercenters and Sam's Clubs range from 12,000 square meters to 20,000 square meters in floor space, carrying 20,000 or more stock keeping units (SKUs). All but one of the twenty-three host cities are either experimental cities or provincial capitals. This geographical distribution signifies that Wal-Mart has largely followed Chinese laws during its expansion. Yet, this has also cost Wal-Mart many opportunities in other parts of the country. Both Table 21.1 and Figure 21.2 compare Wal-Mart with its two principal international rivals: Carrefour and Metro AG. The former entered China in 1995, the latter in 1996, and neither had state approval at the time of entry. Instead, they sought and obtained permission from local governments who were not content with the strict state control. These local governments complained that selection of the first fifteen foreign retailers simply wasted government quotas because what China really needed were large retailers from North America and Europe. Many local governments were therefore eager to admit foreign retailers independently, despite high political risks.

TABLE 21.1   Comparison of Wal-Mart with Carrefour and Metro AG

	Wal-Mart	Carrefour	Metro AG
Year of entry	1996	1995	1996
Entry was approved by state government	Yes	No	No
Format	Supercenter Membership club Neighborhood Market	Hypermarket (i.e., supercenter)	Membership club
Procurement (2003)	$15 billion	$2.15 billion	$2.46 billion
Retail sales (2003)	$910 million	$1,600 million	$660 million
No. of outlets (Sept. 2005)	47 (in 23 cities)	63 (in 25 cities)	25 (in 21cities)
Location of HQ office	Shenzhen	Shanghai	Shanghai

Sources: Cao 2004; Yang et al. 2004.

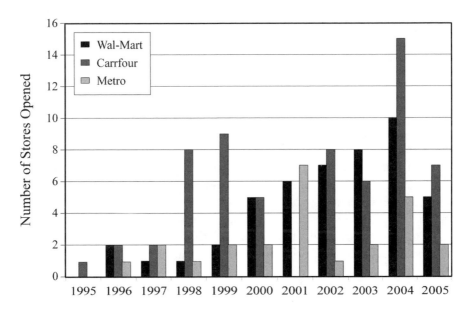

Figure 21.2   Comparison of Wal-Mart, Carrefour, and Metro AG in store openings, 1995–September 2005.

Because the state government permitted foreign firms to provide management services to domestic retailers in the early 1990s, Carrefour smartly teamed with Chinese company Zhongchuang Commerce to establish a business management firm (named Carrefour-Zhongchuang Business Management). This same firm then created a retail subsidiary, with Carrefour holding controlling shares. While the retail subsidiary was registered under the name of Zhongchuang Commerce exclusively, it was actually operated by Carrefour and sold the Carrefour brand (Chen 2004). This allowed Carrefour to effectively bypass state restrictions. In 1995, Carrefour opened its first hypermarket (the Carrefour version of supercenters) in Beijing. Shortly after, it negotiated and obtained approval from other local governments to open stores in Shanghai, Shenzhen, and a number of other cities. In 1999, Carrefour established its China headquarters (HQ) office in Shanghai and entered a new partnership with the Shanghai-based Lianhua Group, the largest domestic supermarket chain in China. It also established a global purchasing center in Shanghai. By September 2005, Carrefour had opened sixty-three hypermarkets in China (twenty-two more than Wal-Mart with its supercenters). Carrefour expanded much more aggressively than did Wal-Mart. It not only opened stores without state approval but also maintained controlling stakes in all its joint ventures. It even opened three wholly owned stores in northeast China (Chen 2004). Its aggressiveness and disregard for Chinese laws irritated the state government so much that it admonished Carrefour in 2001 by suspending any further expansion, which brought Carrefour's CEO to Beijing to apologize in person. Only after Carrefour restructured its operations by reducing ownership to 65 percent and transferring the rest to its Chinese partners was it allowed to resume opening new stores. While the admonishment delayed its plan of opening ten new stores in one year, the state government did not order the closure of any of its existing stores. This allowed Carrefour to retain its leading position over Wal-Mart. For example, Carrefour operates hypermarkets in twelve cities where there is no Wal-Mart supercenter as of yet. In comparison, Wal-Mart has entered only eight cities that have no Carrefour presence yet.

Metro AG opened its first China store in Shanghai in 1996 (in partnership with the local Jinjiang Group). Unlike Wal-Mart and Carrefour, Metro focused exclusively on the format of warehouse membership club, open only to registered members, mostly corporate consumers and small retailers. Until 1999, Metro's operation was limited to Shanghai and the neighboring Jiangsu and Zhejiang provinces, while awaiting state approval. In 2000, the state government retroactively recognized Metro as a "legitimate" corporate citizen and gave it permission to establish chain operations in any of the experimental cities (Shanghai Almanac Compilation Committee 2001). Seizing this opportunity, Metro opened seven stores in 2001 alone (see Figure 21.2). By September 2005, Metro operated a total of twenty-five membership clubs in twenty-one cities. This undoubtedly made the entry of Sam's Club in these cities difficult. So far, Metro does not have a store in Beijing. This may well explain why Wal-Mart rushed to open a Sam's Club in Beijing ahead of its planned supercenters, a first-mover opportunity that it could not afford to lose again.

In fact, Wal-Mart has never given up its hope to enter the large cities of Shanghai and Beijing. In October 2002, after patient negotiations with both the state and Shanghai governments, Wal-Mart finally obtained permission to enter Shanghai. This was achieved through establishing a new division—the East China Wal-Mart Store Ltd.—in partnership with the Beijing-based China International Trust & Investment Corporation (Shanghai Almanac Compilation Committee 2003). The new division is based in Shanghai and is to oversee Wal-Mart expansion in the Yangtze River delta region. With the formation of the new division, Wal-Mart was given the green light to open three supercenters in Shanghai. In return, Wal-Mart agreed to establish both a branch of its Global Purchasing Center and a distribution center in Shanghai to help local manufacturers export and to procure merchandise for its future stores in the Yangtze River delta region. For various reasons, but at least partly due to its loss of first-mover opportunities to Carrefour and Metro, only one of the three announced stores in Shanghai has opened (Figure 21.3).

Figure 21.3   Inside view of the first Wal-Mart store in Shanghai. The two-story supercenter opened July 2005 in the Pudong New Area, carries 20,000 stock keeping units, and has 550 associates working in the store to help the shopping crowd.

Indeed, after many years of delay, its entry in Shanghai has become much more difficult and costly. First, the retail market has become congested. Both Carrefour and Metro have already established a strong presence in Shanghai, with the former now operating eight hypermarkets and the latter four membership clubs. Ekchor Lotus, a Thai retailer, has opened another thirteen supercenters in Shanghai. Furthermore, three domestic retail chains (Lianhuan, Huanlian, and NGS) have emerged as strong competitors; together, they provide another thirty or so hypermarkets within the city limits (Shanghai Commerce Information Center and Sona Consulting Ltd. 2003). The existing hypermarkets have preempted Wal-Mart in many premium locations. Second, the price of land and commercial real estate in Shanghai have soared in the past five to six years (Li 2004). For reference, new apartments around the Wal-Mart store in Pudong (Figure 21.4) now sell for $1,100 per square foot (RMB 9,000 per square meter), 50 percent higher than five to six years ago (Shanghai Commerce Information Center 2004a). As Chan and colleagues (1997) point out, first movers are likely to be rewarded with good sites at favorable rents and the ability to cement local relationships that latecomers will find tough to replicate. Third, to further rationalize the spatial distribution of large retail facilities, the Shanghai government, for the first time in 2002, introduced the practice of holding public hearings into its planning and approval process. All future developments of hypermarkets and supermarkets must go through this process (Wang and Zhang 2005).

Figure 21.4   New apartments around the Wal-Mart store in Pudong, Shanghai. It is reported that these apartments now sell for RMB 9,000 ($1,100) per square meter.

Similar difficulties were encountered in Beijing. While Carrefour was suspended from expansion in 2001, Wal-Mart won approval from both the state and the local government to open five stores in Beijing—a stronghold of Carrefour (Kynge and Young 2001). To date, however, only two of the five (a Sam's Club and a supercenter) have opened, suggesting its difficulty in finding suitable locations and obtaining profitable real estate for its planned supercenters. In fact, when Wal-Mart announced its plans, Beijing was already served by four Carrefour hypermarkets, two (Dutch) Makro membership clubs, and three other membership clubs operated by Price-Smart, an American company.

Figure 21.5 illustrates the current organizational structure of Wal-Mart operations in China. Its retail business is now operated with two domestic partners, but the two divisions have recently been brought under one umbrella: Wal-Mart (China) Investment Co. Ltd., a wholly owned Wal-Mart subsidiary created in 2003. This is undoubtedly a strategic move to further consolidate business decision-making powers in its own hands. Wal-Mart now commands the operation of its forty-seven units from six focal points: Shenzhen for south China; Kunming for southwest China; Dalian for northeast China; Tianjin for north China; Wuhan for central China, and Shanghai for east China. In addition to retailing and merchandise procurement, Wal-Mart operates a wholly owned business consulting firm. This firm was created in 1996, but little is known about its impact.

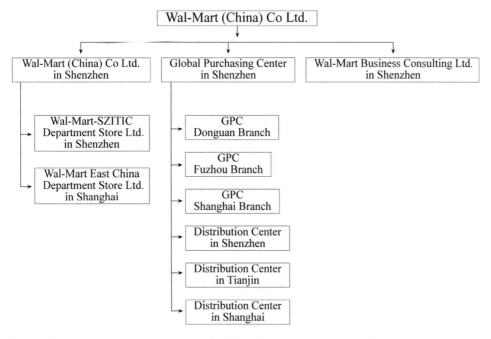

Figure 21.5   Organizational structure of Wal-Mart operations in China.

In 2003, the Wal-Mart China stores sold $731 million (RMB 5.85 billion) of merchandise (Zhang and Wang 2004), accounting for 1.9 percent of Wal-Mart International's total sales in that year. Still, Wal-Mart retail operations in China have not yet been able to make a profit. According to the China Chamber of Commerce, Wal-Mart had a negative balance of $30 million (RMB 240 million) in 2002, and $500,000 (RMB 4 million) in 2003 (*International Financial Post* 2004).

Executing Business Strategy

There is no question that Wal-Mart represents a new retail concept in China. When a retailer transplants a new concept to a foreign country, it inevitably has to adapt to the local market to make its offerings truly relevant not only to the consumer but also to the local cultural and political systems (Koopman 2000). In the case of Wal-Mart in China, this means the retailer must overcome significant business distances (cultural, political, and physical) in adapting to the local market and developing an effective delivery system. In this section, we look into various roadblocks Wal-Mart faces in doing business in China and how it overcomes these obstacles to execute its business strategy.

Grounding of Capital with Low Sunk Costs

The retail profit formula includes many factors. One of them is access to premium business locations and prime real estate in the chosen market. According to retail analysts, this factor plays a determinant role in the value chain for most retailers (Koopman 2000).

At home in the United States, Wal-Mart customarily acquires land at strategically selected locations and builds its own stores. This is known as greenfield development (Simmons and Graff 1998). In China, where all land is owned by the state and users can only lease the land from the state or local government, the risk for foreign retailers to build self-owned stores is unpredictable. Instead of investing in brick-and-mortar structures, Wal-Mart chose to lease properties from either local retailers or domestic real estate developers to minimize "sunk costs," defined as costs a firm commits to a particular use (in this case, commercial real estate) and are not recoverable upon exit (Mata 1991). Local developers usually have various forms of connection with government departments and state-owned banks, and are often able to obtain land at premium locations and loans at reasonable costs. This also frees Wal-Mart from the burden of land lease negotiation and property construction, so it can focus on its core business—retailing of goods to consumers.

Wal-Mart has been relying on two major Chinese developers to provide business premises: Shenzhen International Trust and Investment Corporation (SZITIC) and Wanda Group. SZITIC is Wal-Mart's longtime partner in China. Most supercenters in Shenzhen are constructed and owned by SZITIC and are leased to the Wal-Mart joint venture. To facilitate Wal-Mart's expanding further and faster, SZITIC in 2002 created a subsidiary named SZITIC Commercial Property Development Ltd., whose main purpose is to locate sites, obtain land use rights, and develop retail premises in different cities to accommodate Wal-Mart's retail operations. In 2004, it broke ground in Shenzhen to build a new facility of 200,000 square meters to house Wal-Mart's Asia and China headquarters and a new Sam's Club (*Shenzhen Economic Daily* 2004). To beef up its financial capability, SZITIC Commercial Property Development Ltd. in late 2004 entered a joint venture with Singapore's largest real estate corporation, Capital Land Group. The two parties announced plans to raise new capital through Hong Kong's stock exchange.

The Wanda Group, whose core business is in property development, is based in Dalian, Liaoning province, in northeast China. In addition to commercial properties, Wanda develops large-scale housing projects, and often combines the two types of development on the same tract of land. A number of international chains have entered agreements with Wanda to lease commercial spaces from its properties. Besides Wal-Mart, they include the German OBI, Malaysia's Parkson, and America's KFC, Pizza Hut, and Time Warner. At present, ten Wal-Mart supercenters are operated in Wanda-built shopping centers, with six more to open in the near future (in Beijing, Harbin, Ningbo, Shanghai, Wuhan, and Xi'an). Because Wanda centers are all constructed in high-density, built-up areas with a multistory structure (usually four or five stories high), Wal-Mart has to modify its format accordingly: its food department is usually operated on the second floor and the general merchandise department on the third. The first floor is typically leased to small independent retailers and fast-food venders. The upper floors are occupied by large-space users such as furniture stores and movie theaters.

In addition to SZITIC and Wanda, Wal-Mart leases premises from other developers. In Kunming, it operates in a facility developed and owned by its local partner,

Daguan Commercial City. In Dalian, one of its stores is located in a building owned by Dalian Friendship Group (Zhao 2003). In Shanghai, its first store opened in the summer of 2005 in a freestanding facility leased from You-you Group. In Beijing, Wal-Mart signed a leasing agreement with a local developer, Huayuan Group, for its first supercenter in the city. The lease has a fifteen-year life, with an option for Wal-Mart to renew it for another fifteen years (Shanghai Commerce Information Center 2004b).

It is not clear how Carrefour obtains commercial property in Chinese cities. Metro certainly employs a different approach from that of Wal-Mart. To control leasing costs and reduce reliance on Chinese developers, Metro created its own property development arm independent of its joint venture with Shanghai Jinjiang Group. This subsidiary is responsible for locating sites, negotiating land leases, and building stores (Lu 2000). It is also possible that Metro made this decision due to its difficulties in obtaining suitable premises from local developers. Its warehouse-style retail outlets typically require a one-floor configuration surrounded by spacious parking lots. Perhaps few Chinese developers are willing to invest in this exclusive type of structure for fear of heavy sunk costs.

Merchandise Procurement and Sourcing

For any international retailer, the next important task, after retail spaces are constructed or leased, is to secure supplies of merchandise for its local retail outlets. In both the United States and Canada, a large proportion of the merchandise that Wal-Mart stores carry is imported. Yet, it would not be feasible to fill its China stores with imports for several reasons. First, imports, despite high quality, are often too expensive for local consumers. Second, consumers purchase goods that have not only practical utility but also complex cultural meanings (Foord et al. 1996). Not surprisingly, Wal-Mart purchases 95 percent of the merchandise it sells in its China stores from local suppliers, plus much more for export. In fact, both state and local governments value Wal-Mart's contribution to exports of Chinese products far more than the number of jobs it creates through its retail stores and the amount of corporate taxes it pays.

Wal-Mart began purchasing merchandise from China in the 1980s. Until the late 1990s, all its purchases were made through intermediary companies. After it moved its Global Purchasing Center to Shenzhen in 2001, it established three branches in Dongguan, Fuzhou, and Shanghai. Consequently, both its direct and total purchases increased steadily. In 2001, its total purchase in China was $10 billion. This went up to $18 billion in 2004, an increase of 80 percent in just three years.

Presently, Wal-Mart deals with thousands of Chinese suppliers (Wal-Mart China 2005). Yet becoming a Wal-Mart supplier is not easy. According to Paul J. Kelly, a merchandise distribution consultant with Silvermine Consulting Group in the United States (Liu 2004), Wal-Mart suppliers must meet all of the following expectations: be committed to constantly improving production efficiency and reducing costs, be willing to invest in development of creative and exclusive products that can bring added value to Wal-Mart, and be willing to disclose its financial books to Wal-Mart.

In December 2004, Wal-Mart held one of its many supplier fairs in Hangzhou, Zhe-jiang province. The fair attracted 266 interested producers who were eager to have their products sold on Wal-Mart store shelves, but after a thirty-minute screening interview for each, two-thirds of them were eliminated on site. Only 96 were invited to send samples to Wal-Mart's purchasing center in Shenzhen for further evalua-tion (*Golden Times* 2004), but more could be eliminated after that. In addition to the usual questions about financial status, production capacity, industrial certification, and delivery lead time, Wal-Mart asks other questions that most Chinese suppli-ers said they had never heard before. For example, Wal-Mart asks whether factory employees are required to work overtime and about the ratio of green space to build-ings at a factory. Wal-Mart wants to avoid dealing with suppliers that may drag it into social issues such as exploitation of workers and sweatshop working conditions. Once selected, manufactures must make required changes to meet the stringent demands of Wal-Mart and must be prepared for unannounced inspections.

Besides its purchasing centers, Wal-Mart has built three distribution centers, one each in Shenzhen, Tianjin, and Shanghai, to supply its stores in China. Because the stores are spread widely among twenty-three cities, with twelve cities having only one store, the distribution centers cannot yet operate to their full capacity. Most mer-chandise is still shipped to its stores directly from suppliers. According to a Wal-Mart China executive in charge of distribution, the difficulties are manifold (Tu 2004). Without its own truck fleet, Wal-Mart relies on local trucking companies for deliv-ery. Yet, large trailers are still rare in China, and local governments often impose restrictions on out-of-province trucks to protect the interest of their own trucking companies. Moreover, because most Chinese suppliers do not have electronic data interchange (EDI) systems, few are known to be on Wal-Mart's Retail Link program. Therefore, Wal-Mart can hardly speak "one language" with its local suppliers. Nor do trucking companies have the kind of information systems that enable them to moni-tor and track the flow of goods. All these frictions contribute to higher merchandise costs for Wal-Mart and affect its fast expansion in China.

This problem is not unique to Wal-Mart, though. Other international retailers face the same difficulties. To compensate for the "lost profits" in merchandise dis-tribution, some foreign retailers turned to squeezing suppliers by imposing a variety of fees, including a store entrance fee and a promotion fee. Carrefour was the most notorious (Zheng 2003). Wal-Mart claims it does not levy such fees. However, during an interview in Shenzhen in 2004, the authors of this chapter were told by the owner of a small trading firm that when she approached Wal-Mart and proposed to supply Wal-Mart stores with mutton, she was told that her firm would have to pay RMB 5,000 (about $630) for an entrance fee, and RMB 3,000–5,000 ($375–630) on each of the major national holidays to sponsor storewide promotions. In its early years of operation, Wal-Mart was well known for paying its suppliers in a short period of time, three to seven days, and with cash. More recently, it is reported that Wal-Mart has extended its payment period to two months (Wang 2004). These reports suggest that Wal-Mart has been changing its practice of dealing with suppliers in order to keep its "everyday low prices" and maintain its competitive edge over other foreign retailers.

Fostering a Positive Corporate Image

At a European Day of Commerce conference in 2001, the president and CEO of the Dutch firm Royal Ahold stressed the importance of companies' social reputations: "We see consumers and consumer groups who increasingly make their choices, positively and negatively, based on the social reputations of companies. And we see governments looking to hold companies accountable for their behaviors everywhere in the world" (Crawford 2001). Wal-Mart's top brass certainly know very well the importance of developing and maintaining good relations with the various levels of government in China, and they have been making concerted efforts to foster a positive corporate image as an "outstanding corporate citizen."

Since becoming Wal-Mart CEO in 2000, Lee Scott has paid five visits to China to meet with high-ranking officials, including the head of state (Che 2002). At every occasion, Scott repeats the message that Wal-Mart contributes to China's economic development in five significant ways: (1) it purchases large quantities of goods from local producers and supports export; (2) it creates jobs and pays corporate taxes to government coffers; (3) it shares consumer feedback information with producers and helps them develop new products and improve product quality; (4) it introduces advanced retail techniques and experience to promote Chinese retail industry standards and development; and (5) it will contribute to development of China's west through investment in new stores.

In March 2004, Wal-Mart held its board of directors meeting in Shenzhen, with twelve of its fourteen board members present. This was the first time its decision-approving body held its annual meeting in Asia. The meeting was to showcase, symbolically, Wal-Mart's seriousness about expanding investment in China. The chair of the board, Robert Walton, also took the opportunity to emphasize, through local media, that China is very important to Wal-Mart both as a consumer market and as a source of commodity supplies.

Wal-Mart plays a corporate slogan for the same purpose: "Work with the community; pay back to the community." Each time it opens a new store, Wal-Mart announces at the grand opening ceremony a donation to charitable organizations or communities to "help neighborhood, support education, care for children, and protect environment" (Wal-Mart China 2004a). The donations range from RMB 100,000 to 200,000 ($12,500–25,000). Between 1996 and 2003, it donated a total of RMB 9.3 million ($1.2 million). In November 2004, it made another donation of $1 million (RMB 8 million) to China's Tsinghua University to help establish the Center for the Study of Retailing, with Lee Scott presenting the check to the university in person (Ma 2004).

Apparently its public relations efforts have worked in its favor, and possibly contributed to its sales performance as well. In 2003, Wal-Mart was selected by consumers in Shenzhen as their most favored retail store. In the same year, it was rated one of the most respected enterprises in a national survey conducted jointly by Peking University and *Economic Observer* (a Chinese newspaper). In June 2004, it was elected to receive the Best Community Service of Guangming Charity Award by *Guangming Daily*, another national newspaper (Wal-Mart China 2003 and 2004b). Despite the fact that Wal-Mart has always maintained a majority ownership in its joint ventures, it was never admonished by the state government, as was Carrefour.

While making every effort to cooperate with the Chinese government for political support, Wal-Mart has shied away from the government request that it establish workers' unions in its China stores. On October 26, 2004, the Standing Committee of the Chinese Parliament had to name Wal-Mart publicly (along with Kodak, Samsung, and a few other foreign corporations) for denying the formation of workers' unions. On the same day, the All China Federation of Trade Unions threatened to take Wal-Mart to court if it did not change its stand (Yang and Ma 2004). In response, Wal-Mart argued, correctly, that there were no unions in its China stores simply because employees had not requested that one be formed (McGregor 2004). In the same response, Wal-Mart insisted it is in full compliance with China's Trade Union Law, which states that establishing a union is a voluntary action of the employees (Shanghai Commerce Information Center 2004c). Indeed, the unionization drive was initiated not by store workers themselves but by government-controlled unions at the national, provincial, and municipal levels. The government request is rather ironic. In state-owned enterprises, workers' unions are management-controlled puppets, which hardly represent the independent interests of workers. When millions of workers were laid off or forced to take early retirement in the name of economic restructuring, there was no report that any union ever represented them to negotiate with the management for a satisfactory settlement, despite the fact that many workers subsequently fell into financial difficulties. In China, working in a Wal-Mart store is considered a good job by many local employees. The wage, albeit low by Western standards, is usually slightly higher than the average paid by domestic retailers. So "wage depression" has not happened, and there have been no reports of exploitation and labor disputes in any Wal-Mart store in China.

Because the Chinese government cannot install a Communist Party Committee in a foreign company, as it does in all state-owned enterprises, a workers' union can be used as a convenient instrument for the Communist Party to control workers, or as a government-installed watchdog in Wal-Mart (and other foreign operations). Forcing establishment of unions in foreign companies is also a means of levying extra "taxes." According to Chinese law, a worker needs to pay only 0.5 percent of his/her wages to the union for membership dues, but the employer must pay 2 percent of the total wages of all workers to the local branch of All China Federation of Trade Unions, regardless of the number of workers choosing to join the union (Li and Liu 2004).

Nonetheless, Wal-Mart did not insist on its global nonunion policy in China. This represents a huge concession on the part of Wal-Mart to the Chinese government, given that it still adamantly prohibits unions in its U.S. and Canadian stores and has lately announced the closure of its first unionized store in Québec, Canada, due to fear of domino effects across its North America operation (Flavelle 2005a).

While Wal-Mart, since entry, has tried to adhere to the letter of the Chinese laws, it has also paid a price for being a good corporate citizen. In addition to losing first-mover opportunities to Carrefour in a number of key cities including Beijing, Shanghai, and Guangzhou, there have been other frustrations. One example is its lack of success in introducing gift cards in its China stores. The gift card is a common means of business transaction in the Western retail system, and Wal-Mart sells it in all its stores in North America. When the gift card was introduced in China by some foreign retailers, it was quickly banned by the state government for two reasons. First, as the state government reasons, if a retailer becomes bankrupt after selling many cards and before the cards are redeemed, consumers are victimized. This is a valid concern because in the still volatile retail sector in China, the bankruptcy rate of retailers has been high. Even the American company PriceSmart closed all its operations in China in late 2004. Second, and more important to the Chinese government, gift cards could be abused and lead to corruption. For instance, some government agencies and state enterprises were reported to have purchased gift cards in large numbers and given them to officials and managers as well as other employees as a disguised form of bonus. This form of bonus evades state tax and is difficult for the government to monitor. While Wal-Mart refrained from selling gift cards, it is frustrated by the fact that some other foreign retailers and many domestic retailers have been quietly selling them without respect for the law. Wal-Mart has been lobbying the Chinese government to relinquish the law, but to no avail. In a recent report, Wal-Mart was found, in one of its supercenters in Shenyang (the Pengli store), selling merchandise to customers who paid with Wal-Mart-issued gift cards (Yang and Li 2005). The gift cards were sold not to individual customers at the store but to corporate consumers during the busiest shopping season, prior to the Chinese New Year. The gift cards, most of which have a face value of RMB 100 (about $12), can be used only once. If the merchandise presented to the cashier is less than the value of the card, the customer does not receive cash as change. Instead, the customer receives cooking oil and other staples at the store's discretion (Yang and Li 2005). This suggests that Wal-Mart's patience with the Chinese law has been stretched to the limit.

Conclusions

While Wal-Mart still derives 85 percent of its profit from its stores in the United States (Hays 2004), it has by and large saturated its home country's rural regions, and its expansion into metropolitan cities has often met strong community resistance—as has happened in New York, Chicago, and Los Angeles (Olive 2004; Greenhouse 2005). Growth abroad is therefore increasingly important to Wal-Mart, and it has been making persistent pushes into China, the largest emerging market in the world. Yet this study illustrates that penetrating and conquering the China market have not been easy. In implementing its business strategy, Wal-Mart must overcome both political and cultural obstacles, which requires considerable adaptation and compromise on its part.

First of all, Wal-Mart had to enter China through joint ventures, and it was required to have only a minority ownership. While local partners were, and still are, helpful in assisting Wal-Mart in penetrating the culturally dissimilar market, the restriction to minority ownership was too much for Wal-Mart to swallow. It must also have been difficult for Wal-Mart to develop and implement a national growth plan with two local partners (see Figure 21.5). This has never been a preferred business model. Not surprisingly, as soon as the restrictions were lifted, Wal-Mart moved quickly to consolidate the power of decision making into its own hands and toward a true national chain. In fact, Wal-Mart has been in effective charge of sales and distribution, because neither Chinese partner is a retailer and Wal-Mart always retains controlling shares in its joint ventures. On the other hand, this may also be a reason why Wal-Mart has not been competing well with Carrefour, whose principal Chinese partner is one of the largest domestic retailers.

In its home country, Wal-Mart evolved by starting in smaller cities and expanding into larger urban centers, a growth trajectory described as "bottom-up diffusion" within the settlement hierarchy. In China, however, it only made sense to have taken the opposite, top-down approach. It made a single point entry (in Shenzhen) and then fanned out slowly. Almost all of its forty-seven stores opened in large cities, which are also priority markets in China. As it becomes more established in each city and builds the necessary organizational and logistics capacities, mature strategies seeking market domination similar to those used in the home country are to be applied. This has already happened in Shenzhen, where Wal-Mart has established itself as a dominant player with eight supercenters, one Sam's Club, and two Neighborhood Markets. Elsewhere, however, the same success is far from being accomplished. In each of the other twenty-two cities where it has established a presence, Wal-Mart has only one to three stores. This makes it very difficult for its distribution centers to support the scattered stores efficiently; one of its competitive advantages in logistics is therefore lost in China.

Rightly, Wal-Mart never attempted to introduce the discount department store format to China, where plenty of department stores already exist. Many department stores started as upscale emporiums in the early 1990s during the country's first retail boom but had to be downgraded to discount outlets due to loss of market shares to the newly emerged specialty stores and hypermarkets. Of the three formats that Wal-Mart has introduced into China, the supercenter, which offers a wide assortment of consumer goods to mass consumers at competitive prices, proves to serve the local market better than Sam's Club and the Neighborhood Markets. The supercenter has to be modified to suit the local environment, but the two-floor configuration has not deterred shoppers. So far, Wal-Mart has opened only three Sam's Clubs in the whole country, suggesting that this format may not be viable in the China market. While each city has numerous small retailers, it is not clear whether Sam's Club is their preferred "supplier" and if purchasing from Sam's Club would leave them with a reasonable profit margin. For individual consumers, real savings from shopping at a Sam's Club would be achieved by purchasing in bulk. Yet, due to the lack of private automobiles and shortages of living spaces, few shoppers can carry multiple shopping bags or have space at home for a second refrigerator or freezer to store bulk purchases of groceries. There are already signs of the lack of market support for membership clubs. One of the three Wal-Mart stores in Kunming was launched as a Sam's Club but had to be converted to a supercenter shortly thereafter. The Dutch Makro has had great difficulty expanding in this format. It entered Beijing in 1997 but was able to expand in the city with only one other store in seven years. It opened a store in Shenyang in May 2004 but had to shut it down permanently less than ten months later (Du 2005). PriceSmart closed its entire operation (with thirteen membership clubs) in China in late 2004. The only chain that seems to be still expanding is the German Metro AG.

The Wal-Mart experience also shows that in the post-entry phase, foreign retailers must continue engaging themselves in the political process of the host country, even though this may require some measure of humility. In the past eight years, Wal-Mart limited itself to opening stores only in the cities permitted by the state government. It bowed to Chinese law in allowing workers' unions to be formed in its China stores. The existence of workers' unions in its China stores may not be detrimental to the stores' economic viability, but "the Wal-Mart announcement surprised union officials in the United States and Canada, many of whom are still battling with Wal-Mart over the formation of unions" (Barboza 2004). Since then, workers in its Québec stores stepped up their push to form independent unions, and Wal-Mart workers in Windsor, Ontario, are trying for the second time to form a union (Flavelle 2005b). This ripple effect brings a new challenge to Wal-Mart. After all, a global company such as Wal-Mart is expected to have a set of consistent standards across its global operations.

To date, Wal-Mart has neither closed nor relocated any stores in China. In prospect, there is still plenty of room for Wal-Mart to grow. As a matter of fact, its geographical diffusion to secondary tier cities and western cities has just begun. These cities in general are receptive to Wal-Mart, where community resistance is unlikely. All Wal-Mart needs is a patient plan to unlock the value in the vast China market.

22

Consuming Wal-Mart: A Case Study in Shenzhen

Lucia Lo and Lu Wang, with Wei Li

Introduction

Twenty-five years ago China embarked on one of the most unprecedented economic reforms in human history. The transformation from a planned economy to a market-oriented one has huge social and economic consequences, one of which is the freedom to purchase and consume in the open market. The economic reforms, normalization of international trade relations, and opening to the outside world have led to a remarkable growth in gross national product and a much expanded retail sector. Despite some institutional obstacles and social and cultural barriers, a large number of foreign retailers such as Wal-Mart, Carrefour, Metro, KFC, and Cartier have succeeded in entering China (Davies 1994; Zhang and Kapur 1995; Child and Stewart 1997; Cui and Liu 2000; Wong and Yu 2003). Meanwhile, driven by the forces of modernization as well as increased foreign competition, the Chinese domestic retail sector has also undergone dramatic restructuring (Nilsson and McNiel 1994; Wang and Jones 2001). New retail formats and retailing concepts such as chain stores, supermarkets, and shopping malls have been adopted in many Chinese cities. As global marketers and international retailers of all stripes are looking for a slice of the Chinese market, few studies attend to how retail modernization and the presence of international retailers change Chinese shopping behavior or how Chinese consumers respond to the expanded and modernized retail sector (see Sin and Ho 2001 for a review of consumer research development in greater China).

This study focuses on the consumer side, with Wal-Mart as a case study. Wal-Mart is arguably the most aggressive international retailer. It entered China in 1996 with its first retail outlet in Shenzhen, one of the first five Chinese special economic zones established in the 1980s to direct foreign investment. By the end of 2004, Shenzhen hosted one Sam's Club, eight Wal-Mart Supercenters, and two Wal-Mart Neighborhood Markets. The presence of Wal-Mart in China is felt most strongly in this border city. Similar to many other Chinese cities, Shenzhen's retail sector has experienced two interlocking processes during the last decade—the entry of global retailers such as Wal-Mart and the modernization of domestic retailers, both bringing dramatic changes to the consumption experience of the local Chinese. The objective of this chapter is to explore the change and adaptation of Chinese in the city of Shenzhen in response to the entry of Wal-Mart. Using grocery retailing as an example, we specifically examine three areas of change and adaptation: first, consumer attitudes toward the new retail format that Wal-Mart brings to China; second, the ways in which residents in Shenzhen choose between Wal-Mart and the competing domestic stores for various grocery and sundry items; and third, the perception of Wal-Mart as a carrier of Western culture.

Retail Internationalization and Consumer Acculturation

The global expansion of international retailers such as Wal-Mart, Carrefour, and Metro has profound impacts on the (re)distribution of retail capital (Wrigley 2002), inter-firm relationships in a global economy (Dicken 2003), and local culture and lifestyle (Jackson 2004). Much of the existing work on retail internationalization in the area of management and business is "firm-centric" (Coe 2004), with attention focused on international retail activities and strategies, and conceptualization of the retail internationalization process (McGoldrick and Daview 1995; Alexander 1997; Alexander and Myers 2000). In geography, the focus has been on the spatial and temporal fluctuation of the globalization of retailing (Coe 2004), retail internationalization and regulation (Wrigley 2002), and the retail structure of emerging markets such as China and Mexico as a result of the expansion of global retailers (Wang 2003; Wang and Jones 2002). Despite useful insights into the retail internationalization process, management/business and geography literatures have revolved around the supply side—major retailers and big players—with little emphasis on the demand side, in particular, consumers in a culture that receives the expansion of international retail capital.

We believe consumers are not passive receivers of changes brought by retail internationalization. Local consumption influences the retail internationalization process, and the expansion of retail operations internationally in turn changes local consumption patterns and consumer culture. With McDonald's and Coca-Cola often cited as examples, the literature has characterized globalization as oppositions between homogenization that leads to cultural universalization and indigenization that produces local differences (Peet 1989; Knox 1995; Classen 1996; Watson 1998). This has implications for understanding the impact of global retailers on local consumption, as internationalization of retailing is a key aspect of contemporary globalization. Focusing on smaller retailers such as Cadbury's, Jackson (2004) examines local consumption in a globalizing world and suggests that retailers adapt their global brands to a variety of local conditions by culturally modifying their marketing strategies and changing some aspects of their product (for example, taste, to suit local consumer preference). This suggests business practices are culturally and socially embedded (Mitchell 1995). However, the extant literature on globalization has paid limited attention to how locals in emerging markets receive foreign retailers; even with the vast business literature on McDonaldization and Coca-colonization, the emphasis has been on the retailers' localization strategies rather than consumer reaction.

It follows that consumer acculturation can be seen as an important aspect of how consumers in a regional culture respond to the emergence and expansion of international retailers. Consumer acculturation refers to the general process of movement and adaptation to the consumer cultural environment by people from another culture (Penaloza 1994). When foreign retailers such as Wal-Mart enter a different culture and sell an alternative concept or format—the Western one—consumer acculturation is expected to occur, and people may choose to accept and patronize or reject and bypass foreign retail businesses. Here it is important to conceptualize Wal-Mart stores as distinct shopping venues in the city with some cultural meanings. In the literature, shopping places are often considered as manipulated, instrumented, and contested social and cultural spaces (Zukin 1995, 1998). Compared to a local store, a Wal-Mart in China may be perceived by locals in relation to its Western cultural ambience, nontraditional architectural style (for example, the big-box style of Sam's Club stores), nontraditional product assortments and goods display, new marketing concepts, and services unavailable at other local stores (for example, its refund policy). In addition to purchasing from foreign retailers, people are also likely "consuming" those new shopping spaces through experiencing a new cultural atmosphere that reflects Western lifestyles and culture. Thus, when facing both foreign retailers and local businesses, some consumers may be more acculturated in shopping at foreign retailers than others.

The interpretation of consumer acculturation is closely related to the cultural interpretation of consumption. A growing body of work in geography sees consumption as far removed from an isolated and momentary act of purchase, and more of a social-cultural process (Jackson and Holbrook 1995; Jackson 2002; Dwyer and Jackson 2003; Miller et al. 1998; Gregson 1995; Glennie and Thrift 1996; Crang 1996; Gregson, Crewe, and Brooks 2002), and store choice is more based on "questions of image and identity rather than narrow economically driven criteria" (Crewe and Lowe 1995). Closely related to this social-cultural perspective of consumption is the debate on the social use of consumption and shopping spaces, such as malls, in contemporary cities (Goss 1993; Michell 1995; Jackson 1998; Miller et al. 1998; Erkip 2003; Vanderbeck 2000; Wang and Lo 2006). Despite the apparent private ownership of many urban shopping places, they are open to the public and have become important parts of the social world of groups such as seniors, young people, and ethnic minorities. The nature and usage of shopping places as "public" spaces is particularly interesting to look at in this study, as China's rapid economic development and urbanization have greatly reduced the available urban public space (such as public squares and city parks), with some being privatized and converted to other uses to generate higher economic returns, leaving its citizens with limited open space beyond home and work.

Foreign retailers such as Wal-Mart often stand out in local urban landscapes because of their large store size and nontraditional marketing strategies, which likely attract local residents for purposes other than shopping. In this regard, the cultural perspective on consumption and consumption spaces provides useful insights into local consumer reaction to entrant foreign retailers. However, the cultural approach to consumption cannot be detached from the traditional economic analysis of consumption. As any shopping in space incurs travel and expenditure, economic considerations are valid in any study of consumer behavior. In the case of foreign expansion into China, foreign retailers are often associated with larger floor area and greater product variety when compared to local ones. In this regard, we believe that a proper departure point is to consider both the economy and culture in examining local consumption in the context of retail internationalization.

Shenzhen and Its Wal-Mart Stores

Compared to Beijing or Shanghai, Shenzhen may not be the most well-known Chinese city to the Western world, but it certainly has experienced the most dramatic socio-economic change during the last two decades or so in China. It is a brand-new city that has emerged on the lands of a fishing village. Located in the south of Guangdong province, Shenzhen borders Hong Kong, the hub of the Asian-Pacific's finance, trade, transportation, and service industries. Historically, Shenzhen and Hong Kong were both parts of the Xin An county of Guangdong province. For more than 150 years they have been separated by a border, the result of Hong Kong being a British colony. The border remains even though Hong Kong was returned to China in 1997, reflecting the "one country, two systems" motto galvanized by Deng Xiaoping (Wang 2000). Before 1978, Shenzhen was only a small fishing village with a population of 10,000. By 2000, Shenzhen had become a modern city with 7 million permanent residents and close to 1 million temporary residents (Chan 2003).[1]

In China, the rapid development of Shenzhen is often termed the "miracle of Shenzhen." As one of the first five Chinese special economic zones (SEZs) established in the post-Mao era, Shenzhen was able to attract foreign direct investment under a rigid planned and state-controlled communist economy. Since 1982, investment from Hong Kong, Taiwan, Southeast Asia, Europe, and North America has been flooding into Shenzhen in areas such as manufacturing, high technology, and finance. The economic opportunities in Shenzhen also attracted a large number of young Chinese from other provinces to participate in a variety of jobs, ranging from white-collar jobs in foreign insurance companies and local real estate offices to working in the city's manufacturing and construction sectors. High technology, finance, and logistics are the city's three major industries. Before the mid-1990s, retailing was not a particularly strong sector. The impetus for change started in 1992 when the Chinese government opened six Chinese cities and the five SEZs to direct investment from foreign retail operators. The vast urban population base, increasing wealth of the population, and proximity of the city to Hong Kong (and thus relatively easy access to modern products and new information) made Shenzhen an excellent opportunity for Western retailers to penetrate the local market.

Wal-Mart first came to China in 1996 by opening a Sam's Club and establishing its China headquarters in Shenzhen. Since then, Wal-Mart has opened eight supercenters and two Neighborhood Markets in the city. These represent 22 percent of China's Wal-Mart Supercenters, 33 percent of China's Sam's Clubs, and 100 percent of China's Wal-Mart Neighborhood Markets. Figure 22.1 shows their locations in Shenzhen, which is made up of eight districts. It should be noted that of the eight districts, Nanshan, Futian, Luohu, and Yantian make up the SEZ, which enjoys some

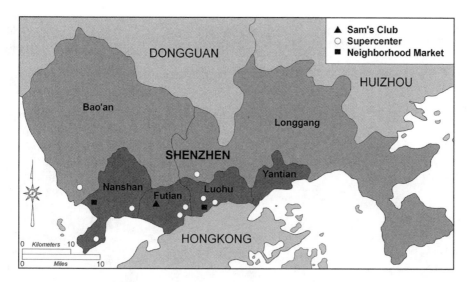

Figure 22.1   Wal-Mart stores in Shenzhen, China.

Figure 22.2   Sam's Club in China.

favorable policies in receiving foreign direct investment, and Bao'an and Longgang are outside the SEZ. The first Wal-Mart stores were established inside the SEZ in Luohu and Futian, and the latest, added in 2004, are in Bao'an and Longgang.

A look at Shenzhen's Sam's Club from its parking lot does not reveal its China location (Figure 22.2). Rather, it looks like any Sam's Club in North America. Located in

Figure 22.3 Neighborhood Market in China.

a newly urbanized area, this 20,000-square-meter facility is most accessible to high-income earners who own a car. Compared to Sam's Club, however, most Wal-Mart Supercenters in Shenzhen are not freestanding. Some sit in busy commercial areas to capture pedestrian traffic to adjacent international retailers (such as Carrefour), local department stores, or shopping plazas; some chose to locate right in residential areas where high population density is ensured by high-rise apartments and condominiums, Shenzhen's typical housing forms for urban workers. In Shenzhen, six out of eight Wal-Mart Supercenters are found inside residential or office high-rises (refer to Figure 21.4). They typically occupy the first three stories of the building, with their floor space ranging anywhere between 12,000 and 18,000 square meters. Open long hours, they provide the neighboring community with great shopping convenience. The two Neighborhood Markets are located in busy urban cores with high pedestrian traffic (Figure 22.3). Functioning like a neighborhood supermarket, they are much smaller in size than the supercenters and occupy either a basement or ground-floor location.

A Mixed Approach

We used a combination of methods to attain our goals. They included field visits, focus group discussions, and a questionnaire survey. Our research process started with focus groups; the aim was to explore some general issues related to local consumption patterns, shopping experience with foreign retailers, and attitudes toward Wal-Mart in China. The focus groups informed the questionnaire design. The field visit allowed one of the authors to have a taste of Wal-Mart in Shenzhen, especially in comparison to the local domestic stores. Fieldwork covered all three types of Wal-Mart stores, traditional markets, small neighborhood grocery stores, and large local domestic supermarket chains such as Ren Ren Le, which have a format similar to Wal-Mart Supercenters. Finally, the questionnaire survey conducted in Shenzhen collected a wide range of quantitative information on Chinese consumers' shopping behavior, their attitudes toward Wal-Mart, and the choice they made between Wal-Mart, the competing domestic supermarkets, and the traditional markets still widely available in the city. By providing a rich source of qualitative and quantitative information, these methods complement each other in our study of Shenzhen's Wal-Marts. We discuss below in more detail our focus groups and questionnaire survey.

Focus Groups

Two focus groups were conducted in the summer of 2004. For reasons of expedience, these two focus groups interviewed current and former residents of Shenzhen who were living in Toronto, Canada, at the time of the research, either temporarily or permanently. The decision to conduct the focus groups in Toronto (where the first two authors were based) instead of having someone in Shenzhen conduct the discussions and transcribe for us was based on the importance of having the researcher moderate the discussion to allow flexibility in exploring relevant issues and to facilitate understanding of qualitative information based on rich and detailed firsthand conversations.

The four participants in the first focus group are officials from the Shenzhen municipal government who were visiting the University of Toronto for a short period of time. They represent those with a high income and high educational background. Their work experience with the Shenzhen government enriched our understanding of the city's view on Wal-Mart's entry. The second focus group interviewed seven Chinese who have immigrated from Shenzhen to Canada within the last couple of years. The conversation with this group was particularly interesting, as all participants had exposure to Wal-Mart in both Canada and China and were able to compare various aspects of Wal-Mart in two different cultures.

Questionnaire Survey

Based on our literature review and the focus group discussions, a questionnaire was constructed to probe the attitude of Shenzhen's residents toward shopping, their patronage of Wal-Mart relative to the competing domestic supermarkets and the traditional market forms, and their general view of Wal-Mart. With the help of a local market research company, a survey was completed over three days toward the end of November 2004. Interview posts were simultaneously set up in three central locations: two within the SEZ in Luohu and Futian, and one outside the SEZ in Bao'an, where the latest Wal-Mart Supercenter was recently opened. Pedestrians and passersby in the surrounding area were randomly intercepted and screened before they were invited to the interviewers. This method was deemed appropriate given the constraints in time and budget, although it did not produce a completely random probability sample. In total, 216 interviews were completed, with all respondents permanent residents of Shenzhen who have full or partial decision-making power over their grocery and sundry lists and have shopped at supermarkets. These 216 individuals cover all six districts in Shenzhen, with about 65 percent residing within the SEZ and 35 percent outside the SEZ.

Of all, only four have never shopped at Wal-Mart because the Wal-Mart locations are either too far from where they live or are not known to them. Unlike our focus group participants, who are/were the well educated and well-heeled of Shenzhen, those who responded to the survey represent a cross-section of Shenzhen's residents. There are slightly more women than men (58 percent versus 42 percent), and the majority (over 70 percent) are both young (below twenty-six years of age) and single. They came from all parts of China and have been living in Shenzhen for an average of less than six years. About 63 percent of them do not have a postsecondary education, but only 15 percent make less than $375 (RMB 3,000) per month. This composition reflects the largely migrant population of one of the most urbanized and industrialized cities of China and is quite representative of its local populace.

Observations from Focus Groups and Field Visits

Localization of Wal-Mart

The literature suggests that globalization fosters similarity in material culture, institutions, and lifestyle, on one hand, and leads to differential identities and experiences in response to local circumstances, on the other hand (Knox 1995). In a similar vein, the internationalization of Wal-Mart contributes to Shenzhen a globalizing retailing tendency and a retail landscape familiar to the Western world. At the same time, Wal-Mart quickly domesticates itself and adapts its "global" name to local conditions by creating new forms of marketing, diversifying its product variety, and incorporating Chinese business practices.

In all Shenzhen Wal-Mart stores visited, the operational format is quite different from those we experience in Canada. Whereas in China the dominant format is the supercenter (a combination of a supermarket and a discount department store), in Canada most Wal-Marts are discount department stores. Thus, in China, Wal-Mart puts a great deal of emphasis on grocery retailing and devotes considerable space to the grocery section. The range of grocery products and business practices are similar to the local supermarkets in Shenzhen or China per se. There is a large live fish section, a huge meat counter with butcher blocks, and a barbeque food section, as is common in all Chinese supermarkets both inside and outside China. While the Japanese model of supplying ready-to-eat hot food was first adopted by the domestic supermarkets, Wal-Mart not only takes that in completely but also makes it larger and more prominent. Some foods are freshly prepared just behind the counter. A noon visit found it rather like a fast-food counter in our own North American shopping malls, with several dozen people—students, office workers, parents with young children—lined up to place their order, which was quickly filled in a Styrofoam box. Many took their boxes outside the store and enjoyed their meal at picnic tables under the shade of large umbrellas. Others carried them in Wal-Mart plastic bags, walking toward home or the office.

In terms of merchandise mix, similar to Wal-Mart stores in North America, where most products are made in China, the majority of goods in Shenzhen's Wal-Marts are from China. However, the mix of goods and the selection of brands differ greatly from what is available in Wal-Mart stores in North America. For instance, there are a number of brands of soy sauce in both Wal-Marts and Sam's Clubs. The Wal-Marts in Shenzhen also sell a number of middle- to high-end electronic products such as plasma televisions and digital cameras, in contrast to their sister North American stores, which generally offer choices of low-end electronic products.

This localization strategy of Wal-Mart provoked much interest among participants in the focus groups. Most recognized and appreciated how Wal-Mart articulates to suit local social, economic, and cultural contexts. They mentioned little consumer resistance in consuming Wal-Mart. They appreciated the emphasis on grocery retailing. In Chinese culture, eating and fine cuisine are important elements of daily life, and Chinese cooking emphasizes using the freshest possible ingredients (Veeck 2004). The old but still much-quoted saying "Food is the first necessity of the people" is still very relevant in this Chinese city marked by growth, prosperity, and affluence. Grocery shopping plays an important role in getting the freshest and best product for preparing high-quality food. Jing mentioned how cheap groceries attract consumers to shopping at Wal-Mart.

> I think they attract people by setting the prices of some vegetables really low … look, 10 cents for a big bag of carrots and 5 cents for a bag of bok choy. Who wouldn't want to buy them? … Then you go to the store, get these bargains, and you stay more and buy more.

The Meanings of Shopping at Wal-Mart

Most participants mentioned the desirable shopping environment provided by Wal-Mart stores in Shenzhen, as well as the high quality of goods and services. Compared to most local markets and supermarkets, Wal-Mart stores are spacious, clean, and air-conditioned, and their refund policy is exceptional. Some even said that although the Wal-Mart store is a little far away, they still go there because of the positive attributes they see in the store.

Visits to Wal-Mart are not entirely due to rational considerations. Some are imbued with social meanings. For Lin, who lives in a high-density residential area, her everyday after-dinner stroll takes places in a nearby Wal-Mart Supercenter.

> I go to Wal-Mart almost every day. We live in a high-rise and we are surrounded by other high-rises; there are not many public places we can go to. So we [she and her daughter] usually take a walk to Wal-Mart after dinner and spend some time in the store… . They stay open late… . [smile] The Wal-Mart store is like a leisure place for us.

The scarcity of, and thus the need for, public space is common for urban residents living in many rapidly developing Chinese cities. The generally large floor area of

Wal-Mart stores and their residential location offers locals a convenient social space for daily hanging out. Their air-conditioning is another attraction for people living in this tropical city. As Ming commented,

> They [Wal-Mart stores] are big, clean, nice, and cool. You know Shenzhen is hot all year round. Wal-Mart is the most comfortable place I can find in the city. Even if I don't buy, I still go and walk around the store.

Consuming a New Culture

It has been recognized that consumption and shopping are utterly tethered to culture (Slater 2003; Jackson 2002). Even grocery shopping, a most mundane and taken-for-granted activity, is practiced with social and cultural meanings (Wang and Lo 2006). In Shenzhen, the name "Wal-Mart" not only represents large supercenters providing shopping convenience but to some extent is associated with a new culture that Wal-Mart brings to the city. Before Wal-Mart opened its first store (Sam's Club) in Shenzhen in 1996, a sense of "Western imagination" was sparked. In the media, Wal-Mart was often described as the world's biggest retailer, symbolizing modern retailing, Western culture, and American values. This is evident from the preopening sale of memberships in Sam's Club. Li, a reporter for *Shenzhen Business Weekly* before he joined the Shenzhen municipal government, mentioned the massive reporting on Wal-Mart in almost all media outlets shortly after the city granted entry to Wal-Mart.

> At that time Wal-Mart got a lot of publicity from the media ... the largest retailer in the world with a car park as big as an airport and a spacious shopping area. People got hooked up with these nice images of Wal-Mart long before it actually came to the city.

Apart from the media, influences from Western colleagues and prior exposure to stories about Wal-Mart collectively constructed a unique identity for Wal-Mart before people in Shenzhen had any direct experience with the retailer. This identity is associated with a new Western culture that finally has a chance to sink into China. Roy, who worked for a U.S. company in Shenzhen before immigrating to Toronto, said:

> My white colleagues [from the United States] were so excited—"Wal-Mart is coming to town!"—and got their membership cards long before the new store was even built. I was curious about this American retailer that made my colleagues so excited. So I also bought a membership almost a year before the store opened.

And Ming, who claims herself a "loyal customer of Sam's Club," relayed:

> I read the book about how Sam Walton started and succeeded in business.... . I knew their story.... . So when I heard that Sam's Cub was coming [to Shenzhen], I immediately got a membership card.

However, the progression from imagining Wal-Mart that sells an alternative lifestyle to actually consuming Wal-Mart can be less than exciting. For one, the practice of checking purchase receipts at the exit of Sam's Club is considered "insulting" and "offensive" in a Chinese culture, and it has repelled some from shopping there. This led Wal-Mart to modify its business practice, and now it is up to the shoppers to show their receipts at the exit of the store. For another, "spacious air-conditioned shopping area," "big car park," and "nice warranty and refund policy" construe the positive images of Wal-Mart. The "new" cultural experience is countered, however, by the general lack of access to a car and the arrival of the modern supermarket before Wal-Mart came along. Our focus group participants greatly appreciated Wal-Mart Supercenters and Sam's Club, but they also said that two or three years before Wal-Mart entered Shenzhen in 1996, domestic supermarkets and warehouse stores such as Wan Jia were already operating in Shenzhen.[2] Some had already "got used to" these new retail formats. So when Wal-Mart came, some felt "less excited," although Wal-Mart generally outperformed its local competitors in size and service.

Observations from the Questionnaire Survey

View of Wal-Mart

All except two respondents were familiar with the big-box/warehouse shopping format introduced to China in the early 1990s. Like most of our focus group participants, they showed a favorable attitude toward Wal-Mart. While about one-fifth retained their neutrality, over 60 percent considered Wal-Mart the most successful retailer in Shenzhen. They said that Wal-Mart raises the service quality and the standard of retail operation in Shenzhen, and that it operates very efficiently. They also believe that Wal-Mart's retail format has had tremendous impact on Shenzhen's retail industry; its range of goods suits local consumer needs and increases consumer product knowledge.

The survey echoes the focus groups when it comes to whether Wal-Mart produces a new cultural experience among Shenzhen's residents. While 20 percent disagreed, about 50 percent of our respondents found shopping at Wal-Mart provides a new cultural experience. They liked browsing around Wal-Mart even when there is no specific shopping need.

While only two of our respondents have traveled outside China, their proximity to Hong Kong and wide use of the Internet in urban China have exposed many of them to information and knowledge of Western cultures and practices. The majority recognized Wal-Mart as the world's largest and most successful retailer, and about half believed in Wal-Mart as a symbol of globalization and modernization. However, due largely to Wal-Mart's localization strategy, less than a third considered shopping in Wal-Mart stores analogous to shopping in the United States, though a slightly higher percentage found Wal-Mart symbolic of the United States. We should, however, qualify that the Shenzhen residents we interviewed are ambivalent about Western culture. Slightly more expressed interest than disinterest in Western culture; similar percentages said that the United States would be, or would not be, their first destination if they have a chance to travel outside China.

People's Choice: Wal-Mart versus Others

Wal-Mart was founded on three principles developed by its founder Sam Walton. One of them is "service to the customer": the customer is the boss, and everything possible is done to make shopping at Wal-Mart and Sam's Club a friendly, pleasant experience. Wal-Mart China widely advertises the "ten-foot attitude" and the "satisfaction guaranteed" refund and exchange policy which are quite novel to consumers in China. The "ten-foot attitude" means whenever associates come within 10 feet of a customer, they will look them in the eye, greet them and ask if they can help them. The refund and exchange policy allows customers to be fully confident of Wal-Mart and Sam's Club's merchandise and quality (Wal-Mart China 2005).

Indeed, of the 212 respondents who had shopped at Wal-Mart, 99 percent considered its service very good or good, although most did not feel like they were "the boss" when they shopped at Wal-Mart. In addition, of the 119 respondents who had experience with its refund policy, only 10 disliked it. This implies that these principles are working well, at least in Shenzhen.

Compared to another international retailer, Carrefour, which has a noticeable presence in China as well as in Shenzhen, 56 percent were definite that Wal-Mart provided better service. This percentage is even higher when comparisons were made to the modernized domestic supermarket (71 percent) and the traditional market (91 percent) sectors. The same can be said of product variety and shopping environment. On the price front, opinions were more varied. Despite its "everyday low prices" slogan, only about 66 percent agreed that Wal-Mart has better prices compared to Carrefour. In addition, only 10 percent agreed that Wal-Mart beats Carrefour in price as well as store attributes. A similar percentage also disagreed that prices at Wal-Mart are more competitive than prices in domestic markets or traditional markets.

Entry of Wal-Mart has altered the balance of power in Shenzhen's grocery retail scene. Before its arrival, people mostly purchased their groceries from either domestic chains (44 percent) or traditional markets (54 percent). At the time of the survey, 24 percent of grocery trips made by our respondents were to Wal-Mart, 30 percent to domestic supermarkets, and 46 percent to traditional markets. As we also observe a significant negative correlation between frequency of visits to Wal-Mart stores and frequency of visits to domestic supermarkets, these figures tell us that Wal-Mart gains primarily at the expense of domestic supermarkets. They do not reveal the respective market shares among various store types (Wal-Mart, domestic supermarkets, and traditional markets), however, and our survey did not explore this issue.

Unlike North America, where grocery shopping is a weekly event for most people, making multiple grocery trips on a weekly basis is not uncommon among the residents of Shenzhen. Approximately 30 percent of our respondents visited Wal-Mart at least twice a week. This percentage increases to 45 percent for domestic supermarkets and 60 percent for traditional markets. That more people made more frequent visits to traditional markets and domestic supermarkets can be explained by the relative availability of these stores as well as what people want to buy from each of these store types.

Compared to eleven Wal-Mart stores, there are at least thirty-three other supermarkets (more if different branches of a chain are counted) and ninety-six traditional

TABLE 22.1   Percentage Visiting Each Store Type in Relation to Store Availability

	Wal-Mart (N = 212)	Domestic Supermarket (N = 216)	Traditional Market (N = 212)
Number of stores	11	33+	96+
Average walk time to closest store (in minutes)	29.7	19.7	13.4
Frequency of visit			
Every day	8.0	9.7	23.6
Twice a week	22.2	35.6	35.2
Once a week	31.1	28.2	17.1
Once every 2 weeks	15.6	12.0	4.6
Once every month	7.5	1.9	3.7
Once every 2 months	4.7	2.3	1.9
Once every 3 to 12 months	2.4	1.9	2.8
Not fixed	8.5	8.3	11.1

Source: Authors' survey.

markets in Shenzhen, as named by the survey respondents. A trip to a Wal-Mart store is less convenient than a trip to any other place where groceries are sold. As they reported, it took them an average of thirteen minutes to walk to the closest traditional market, twenty minutes to the closest domestic supermarket, and thirty minutes to the closest Wal-Mart.

Table 22.1 shows the relative frequency of visiting the various store types. A quarter of our sample shopped at traditional markets on a daily basis, whereas less than 10 percent would visit a supermarket on a daily basis. This cannot be explained by the convenience factor alone. We need to look at where people purchase what and how culture determines that. Generally we can classify the grocery retail sector into two forms: the traditional market format and the modern supermarket format. While some people bought the same product item from both the traditional market and the modern supermarket, the modern supermarket is preferred to the traditional market in all product categories except live poultry. The traditional market still plays a significant role in providing residents with fish, vegetables, and maybe meat. But it definitely cannot compete with the modern supermarket in dairy products, beverages, snacks, household cleaning items, and personal hygiene products.

The modern supermarket appeared in China before Wal-Mart came along. Wal-Mart Supercenters are larger than most domestic supermarkets. This, in conjunction with other factors, has made Wal-Mart very competitive. As Figure 22.4 shows, Wal-Mart is the preferred choice for eight of the fifteen product categories, including personal hygiene products and food items that are ready for immediate consumption (i.e. cooked meat, canned and frozen food, milk and other dairy products, bread and cereals, snacks, water and other beverages, and condiments). With respect to food items that require preparation before consumption, meat and poultry

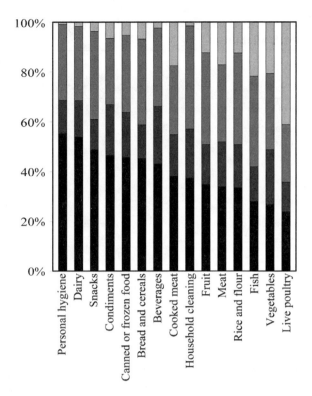

Figure 22.4   Preference of purchasing various items from Wal-Mart and domestic super-markets. Note: black indicates percent of persons who prefer purchasing at Wal-Mart as com-pared with other stores (the lighter shades).

were purchased at similar frequencies from Wal-Mart and domestic stores. All oth-ers, such as vegetables, fish, rice, and flour, were obtained slightly more frequently from the domestic stores.

While the modern sector and the traditional sector serve different functions in terms of grocery and sundry purchases, there are obvious reasons why people shop at different places. Store attributes, perceived or actual, play an important role in the choice of stores. Price and convenience appear to be among the main divides between the traditional and the modern retail formats. Overall, traditional markets are preferred for their lower prices and convenient locations, and complaints about supermarkets are primarily due to their higher prices and fewer (hence inconvenient) locations. In a similar vein, supermarkets are praised for their pleasant shopping environment, high quality of goods, and the large variety of product items they offer, whereas there are real concerns about traditional markets' wet floors, untidy layout, and lower quality of goods, ranging from canned and frozen goods and dairy prod-ucts to personal hygiene and household cleaning items sold. Figure 22.5 provides in greater detail the reasons given by our survey respondents regarding why they shopped or did not shop at various store types. Compared to the domestic stores, Wal-Mart is seen as providing better quality, greater variety, and a more pleasant shopping environment, but selling at higher prices and being less accessible. These findings echo what our focus group participants said.

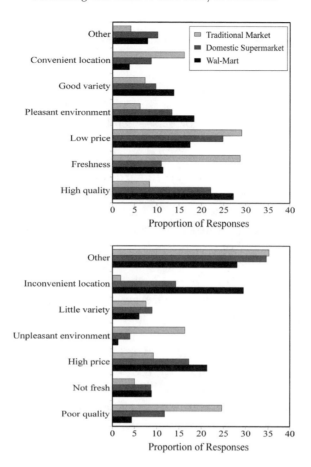

Figure 22.5   Reasons for buying (top) and not buying (bottom) from Wal-Mart, domestic supermarkets, and traditional markets.

Conclusions

This study explores an important aspect of retail internationalization—how the locals adapt—through a case study of Wal-Mart's expansion into China. As mentioned earlier, the internationalization of retailing is a cultural affair, and business practices are culturally and socially embedded. To succeed, international retailers must adapt to local tastes and needs. Wal-Mart has won the heart of the Chinese by not transplanting its North American standard and by localizing its offerings. Participants in our focus groups, especially those who have lived in Toronto for several years and have traveled back and forth between Shenzhen and Toronto after they immigrated to Canada, attested to this. They saw the Wal-Marts in China as more upscale. They commended the clean and tidy displays and the high quality of goods. They enjoyed the cooked food and the wide range of snacks the stores offer. In contrast, they perceived Wal-Marts in Canada as "dirty and messy," always with "things on the floor." Unlike the Japanese-brand televisions and digital cameras that fill the floor in Shenzhen's Wal-Mart stores, goods sold in Wal-Mart Canada were considered of lower quality. For instance:

> The Wal-Mart here [in Canada] is much worse [than in Shenzhen]. In Shenzhen it feels like I
> am a middle or upper class shopping in Wal-Mart, but here [in Canada] I feel like an under-
> class when stepping into the store.

Between China and Canada, it is obvious that Wal-Mart has employed different
entry strategies, targeting at different consumer cohorts in the two countries.

Selling through three different formats—membership warehouses, supercenters,
and supermarkets—in Shenzhen, Wal-Mart undoubtedly represents a new retail
concept in China. To some extent this concept, coupled with its operational efficiency,
has transformed the local retail culture. In particular, the supercenter format—putting a discount department store and a supermarket under the same roof—has been
copied by some of the larger domestic retailers such as Ren Ren Le. And in part,
Wal-Mart's format has contributed to the acculturation of local consumers on the
meaning of shopping and shopping places.

The impact of Wal-Mart on local consumption is not strictly a cultural phenomenon.
Economics matters. Compared to domestic stores, modern or traditional, Wal-Mart
is deemed better for its high-quality service, great product variety, and spacious and
pleasant environment, although its price is not the most competitive and its locations
are not the most convenient. Except for live poultry, live fish, and fresh vegetables,
the consumption of which is very much dictated by traditional Chinese customs and
values, Shenzhen's residents prefer either Wal-Mart or domestic supermarkets for a
whole range of sundries and food items that are ready for immediate consumption.
It is fair to say that the entry of Wal-Mart has altered the balance of power in Shenzhen's grocery retail sector. Whereas most people purchased their groceries from
domestic chains and traditional markets before, now a quarter of all grocery trips
go to Wal-Mart stores. Domestic supermarkets, particularly the smaller ones, are at
a disadvantage. While they are more accessible, as shopping habits change and consumer preferences vary, economic rationalization coupled with acculturation traits
will have significant implication on their maintenance if they do not adapt, adjust, or
reposition their management and business practices. Similarly, what is observed in
this study also has implications for Wal-Mart's China strategy as the Chinese society
changes in the heaving process of urban and economic development.

Notes

1. The statistics on Shenzhen's population vary in different sources. In the 2001 Shenzhen Statistical Yearbook,
   the 2000 year-end population total for Shenzhen is 1.25 million, which excluded many people without a
   local residence card (*hukou*). A more accurate number of Shenzhen's population comes from the Chinese
   census. As of November 1, 2000, Shenzhen had a permanent population (*changzhu renkou*) of 7 million,
   which includes those without a local residence card (*hukou*) but who have stayed in the city for more than
   six months, plus a temporary population (*zanzhu renkou*) of 923,619 (Chan 2003).
2. From the early 1990s on, foreign supermarket and hypermarket chains such as Carrefour and Metro have
   been actively tapping the Chinese urban market (Wang and Jones 2002). Meanwhile, local supermarkets emerged and have grown dramatically in response to the increasing consumer needs. In Shenzhen,
   Wal-Mart is the first foreign supercenter, but not the first store with a modern retailing concept. Influenced
   by retail changes in other Chinese cities, local supermarkets and warehouse-type stores (*cangchu*) began to
   operate in Shenzhen around 1993, bringing a whole new shopping experience to people in the city.

23

Supermarkets and the (M)art of *Ling Shou*

Chris Webster

Introduction

Ling shou is Chinese for retailing, and retailing is shorthand for the body of knowledge and skills that mediate between suppliers and customers. Since the 1989 reforms that heralded the end of the centrally planned era, the art of retailing in China has had to be rediscovered. Foreign direct investment by global chains such as Wal-Mart plays an important role in demonstrating to consumers the advantages of modern retailing technology and in developing the local knowledge and skills needed for its wider dissemination. This is the premise of this chapter. The resumption of capitalist-led economic organization in China after a gap of half a century has meant that all kinds of economic organizational and institutional forms have had to face step-change adaptation or wholesale replacement. Rather than attempt to document this change in any detail, I use the chapter to reflect on some of the economic advantages of modern supermarket technology. These are particularly apparent in the context of China. In so doing I touch on a behavioral explanation for the global spread of Wal-Mart and its competitors, and emphasize its positive impact on local retail practices. The two main sections focus on key qualities of supermarkets that have contributed to their success: global sourcing and economies of scale, and standardization and consumer search-cost reduction. A final section concludes by noting that Wal-Mart's family-like human resource strategy is not at all dissimilar to the institutions of China's former work units.

Wal-Mart has forty Chinese stores. Figure 23.1 shows one in a giant Filipino-owned shopping mall in the coastal city of Xiamen in Fujian province. Until 2004, the Beijing government closely controlled the number of foreign-owned retailers, opening its doors only to those with global sales of over $2 billion and limiting the list of cities in which they could operate. On this basis, Wal-Mart entered China in 1996, joining German giant Metro and the French chain Carrefour. It has managed to plant thirty-seven Wal-Mart stores, three Sam's Clubs, and two Neighborhood Markets in fifteen cities since then (2004 figures). In these stores it employs approximately 20,000 people and captures an estimated 1 percent of the $550 billion domestic retail market. Supplying the stores is a network of approximately 10,000 businesses, mostly

Figure 23.1   Wal-Mart in a giant mall in the city of Xiamen. (Photo by Chris Webster, February 2005.)

small and medium sized and most of them not among the 5,000 or so larger enterprises that have formed supply alliances for Wal-Mart's U.S. and other international operations (Jiang 2004; Schafer 2005).

Global Sourcing and Economies of Scale

The *Book of Guan Zi*, written in the fourth century BC in China, offers an Eastern version of Adam Smith's "invisible hand" in its chapter "Jin Zang":

> It is human nature not to refrain from going after profit and to keep away from danger when either of them is in sight. Where profit is anticipated, traders will quicken their pace day and night and make light of travelling over a thousand li [miles] to get it. When gain is expected from the water, fishermen will go out to the sea thousands of fathoms deep, sail against the tide and venture on a dangerous voyage of hundreds of li for nights on end…. They will go forward with nobody's push and come along with nobody's pull, and the ruler has no worries or troubles while the people get rich spontaneously. He will be like a bird hatching eggs, sitting there easily and silently, expecting fledglings to come out.

"Profit" in *Guan Zi* refers generally to interest, benefit, or the economist's general notion of welfare. The principal point being made is that the human drive to be fruitful is a reliable device for those vested with the responsibility of governing society toward greater prosperity—something governments at all levels in China are actively relearning. The illustration used to make the point in the excerpt above also nicely demonstrates the timelessness of global sourcing.

China has embraced capitalism, as economist Stephen Cheung predicted it would (Cheung 1982). The information costs of governing a centrally coordinated economy proved too high, and the Communist Party has happily turned the task of allocating productive resources over to capitalist entrepreneurs—including entrepreneurial local governments whose revenue-seeking behavior often scarcely distinguishes them from private firms. Far from representing some extreme exotic economic form, Wal-Mart enters China as a kind of supermodel—a role model honed to perfection in the art of selling. From its Chinese headquarters in the boom city of Shenzhen across the old border with Hong Kong, the company's executives travel to give well-attended lectures on the art of efficient retailing and welcome a constant stream of awed visitors. China is interested in foreign investors that can teach it super-growth business technology. Playing to this role, the company has just invested $1 million to fund China's first institute for retail research at Beijing's elite Tsinghua University.

The Chinese retail chain Wumei is open about copying Wal-Mart technology. According to a spokesman quoted in a *Newsweek* article, Wumei has adapted its management practices, customer services, and supplier relations in the light of lessons learned from Wal-Mart. Among other innovations, the company has copied Wal-Mart's Sam's Club membership-based store model (there are currently three Sam's Clubs in China, including the only Wal-Mart store in Beijing) (Schafer 2004).

It is worth considering in a little more detail the makeup of this supermodel—in particular, the extraordinary global pattern of decentralized economic cooperative acts that make possible an enterprise such as Wal-Mart. Contrasting this with China's former attempts to organize production (including distribution and retailing) by fiat and centralized control is awe-inspiring and shows the organizing power of the market compared with that of government. The Wal-Marts of this world should be understood for what they are: organizations that do something so apparently right that they grow, seemingly without limit, by consensual contract. They connect countless numbers of individuals through organized trade to the mutual benefit of at least the vast majority, if not all. The value of stock procured by Wal-Mart in China in 2004 was in the region of $18 billion—a figure that grew by 10 percent annually in the previous two years (Jiang 2004). Channeled through 5,000 or so local supply partner firms, this stock found its way to customers in 4,900 stores in ten countries through the intermediating skills of 1.3 million employees. The scope for a single firm to do this on such a scale is daunting because of the power that firm acquires. But this is a risk—addressed by other chapters in this volume—associated with an activity (buying and selling) that succeeds only because it meets the needs of those who buy and sell. There are always risks associated with populist innovations.

Consider the nature of urbanization. Supermarkets are a quintessentially urban phenomenon. Urbanization is a process of spatial concentration and economic specialization. More precisely, it is a process of knowledge diversification and deepening interdependence between individuals. Cities grow as people and firms with specialized knowledge locate themselves near others who have complementary knowledge. Cities are a type of social order that reduce distance-related and other transaction costs, such as the costs of searching for partners with whom to exchange knowledge (see next section). At early and intermediate stages of urbanization, as in China currently, rural migrants travel to cities with little more wealth than the right to their own labor. They seek others who value their laboring, petty-trading, and other skills and who can combine these with managerial, entrepreneurial, and capital management know-how. Farmers and fishermen negotiate contracts with urban firms that can combine agricultural knowledge with the knowledge of other individuals who know how to process, package, market, and retail. Individuals trained as accountants sell their knowledge to supermarket firms that also purchase the knowledge of those who can construct buildings, provide electricity, write signs, make stock-taking ledgers, and manufacture pencils.

Even something as simple as a pencil requires the combination of knowledge from millions of individuals spread across the globe. A team of the best scientists in the world, using their efforts alone without the assistance of others, may not be able to make a single pencil in their lifetime.

> Actually, millions of human beings have a hand in my creation, no one of whom even knows more than a very few of the others. Now, you may say that I go too far in relating the picker of a coffee berry in far-off Brazil and food growers elsewhere to my creation; that this is an extreme position. I shall stand by my claim. There isn't a single person in all these millions, including the president of the pencil company, who contributes more than a tiny, infinitesimal bit of knowledge. From the standpoint of know-how, the only difference between the miner of graphite in Ceylon and the logger in Oregon is in the type of know-how. Neither the miner not the logger can be dispensed with, any more than the chemist at the factory or the worker in the oil field—paraffin being a by-product of petroleum.
>
> Here is an astounding fact: Neither the worker in the oil field nor the chemist nor the digger of graphite or clay nor anyone who mans or makes the ships or trains or trucks nor the one who runs the machine that does the knurling on my bit of metal nor the president of the company performs his singular task because he wants me. Each one wants me less, perhaps, than does a child in the first grade. Indeed, there are some among this vast multitude who never saw a pencil nor would they know how to use one. Their motivation is other than me. Perhaps it is something like this: Each of these millions sees that he can thus exchange his tiny know-how for the goods and services he needs or wants. I may or may not be among these items. (Read 1958)

The complexity of making a pencil is much lower than making a supermarket frozen display cabinet or supermarket trolley or building a retail chain, but the idea is the same. Without cooperation, almost no object of consumption we take for granted can ever come into existence. Global retail chains such as Wal-Mart are truly astounding examples of organized voluntary human cooperation.

It is instructive to think about the different kinds of cooperation such chains organize. First, at the buying end, under the discipline of competition, supermarket chains spend resources actively searching for new products and suppliers. They offer far-flung producers, who can meet certain standards, the chance of premium prices for exacting overseas customers. They offer local producers mass markets, saving them costly investments in looking for customers on their own. They offer producers sophisticated real-time market information about product type and quality, such as the shape of cucumbers or varieties of apple customers prefer in a particular market. It is unthinkable that growers of avocados in Egypt or Malaysia could ever develop knowledge about the shade, texture, size and ripeness preferred by customers in Shanghai but for the intermediation of a company that specializes in transferring such knowledge.

Second, at the selling end, supermarket chains "pile them high" with scientific attention to detail and variously combining quantity, price, and variety (quality). They bring together all manner of skills to create optimally configured shopping environments. The increasing size of supermarkets is of interest in this respect. There are two important explanations: economies of scale in production and economies of search in consumption. The first supposes that increasing store size is driven by the pursuit of lower fixed costs, the second that it is driven by pursuit of greater customer convenience. There are very few studies that compare the two explanations systematically. Zhuang, Zhou, and Hernon (2002) is a Chinese example of the kind of study found in the economies-of-scale literature, showing that store size has a positive effect on efficiency in Chinese department stores. A rare example of a study that examines the alternative explanation is an important paper on the evolution of retail format by Paul Messinger and Chakravarthi Narasimhan (1997). In it, they dismiss the idea that one-stop shopping is driven principally by economies of scale or the opportunity to sell higher-margin goods (gains in economies of scale are typically exhausted beyond 10,000 square feet). Instead, they give evidence from time series analysis of aggregate U.S. retailing data for a twenty-six-year period, suggesting that one-stop shopping is a response to the rising demand for time-saving convenience. They estimate that the time saved by consumers in using supermarkets is equal to approximately 2.2 percent of grocery expenditures over the study period. The time-saving hypothesis is intuitively appealing—one-stop shops save search time in the routine tasks of shopping. So citizens with an eye to the value of their own time vote with their feet and use them.

If this is a fundamental explanation in the success of the large-store format and chains that have mastered the art of organizing them, then it is of interest to ask where store sizes might end up. This is reminiscent of the English Nobel prize-winning economist Ronald Coase's question, posed when still an undergraduate at the London School of Economics: what are the natural boundaries of firm size (Coase 1937)? He first asked why firms exist, and gave the answer in terms of transaction costs. Firms exist when it is cheaper to exchange resources (including knowledge and labor) by organization and centrally planned fiat than via market transactions. The latter include the costs of searching for partners with whom to transact, and making and policing contracts. It would be prohibitively costly for someone with comprehensive retailing knowledge and wanting to organize a supermarket to contract separately with buyers, accountants, stockists, check-out workers, cleaners, owners of a building, and so on. It is much more convenient for them all to become part of a unified legal entity—to pool their respective rights over various factors of production—and be organized by hierarchy and rule rather than market and price. This led Coase to ask a second question: why is society therefore not one large firm? China's centrally planned era offers a practical answer: it would be too costly to organize by rule and fiat. The theoretical answer is that at some point the cost savings of organizing cooperation by unified ownership is outweighed by the costs of doing so. Firms can become too large. When they do, they will become uncompetitive and may break up, lose markets, or die. Spin-off companies form to perform specialist inputs more efficiently, and leaner firms take market share. Wal-Mart's relentless growth, like Microsoft's, is of great interest to theorists of the firm.

Wal-Mart and its rivals are still on the increase in terms of size of company, number of markets served, and size of stores. Following Beijing's liberalization of the rules governing foreign retailers, Wal-Mart plans to open thousands of new stores to capture an increasing percentage of the Chinese domestic retail market, which is predicted to grow to between $2 trillion and $4 trillion in the next twenty years. The signs are that many of these stores will be superstores—with rumors of Wal-Mart executives eyeing massive warehouses in Shanghai and elsewhere (Pun 2004). Store sizes may have stopped growing or shrunk in countries where government regulations limit land supply, but the secular technological trend is expansionist. Regulations notwithstanding, the answer to the store size question must probably be that—unconstrained, and with local institutions and land supply permitting—retailing companies would evolve to replicate the normal urban retail function. This has happened in malls, which now offer private versions of the high street in nearly every city on the globe. Supermarkets are going the same way, experimentally bringing different complementary activities under one roof. When an ancillary activity proves to be a successful complement with cost advantages, it may be brought under unified ownership too. Unified ownership may not follow, but the chain may still command the power to organize its own version of the private high street. The make-or-buy decision (vertically integrate or remain independent), as Oliver Williamson has shown, depends on the frequency of transactions between two firms, among other factors (Williamson 1985). If the frequency is great, then two firms may merge to save transaction costs. If a firm is merely a complementary retail or service activity, it may be most efficient to rent it space. On the other hand, if customers would find it more convenient to put produce from such an outlet in the same basket as their groceries, then the activity may well be brought in-house. Thus dry cleaners and restaurants are likely to be offered rental space in the mall section of supermarket sheds, but pharmacies, newspaper, card, and flower shops are likely to be given space on the shop floor and subsumed under unified ownership and control. It is customer convenience that most likely determines the shape of business expansion on the retail floor. Outside the retail floor, the cluster of commercial activities attracted onto one site will be limited by site availability, customer search costs (which may become too high with too much quantity and variety), and the ability to manage a cluster of retailing outlets (which is a different business than managing a cluster of products). If the risks of doing the latter become great, for example, because of the cost of managing externalities such as traffic congestion, litter and crime, then this might be a limiting factor. On the other hand, externalities are more easily controlled under a unified ownership structure (Nelson 1999), and from this point of view, shopping malls are in principle more sustainable and efficient than traditional shopping streets.

Wal-Mart enters China at a time of expanding car ownership, personal wealth, consumerism, and rapidly increasing value of personal time. There is nothing about modern supermarkets that is ill-adapted to the conditions in modern China. On the contrary, the country started its current phase of development with such a paucity of appropriate institutions and organizations that there is still huge scope for catch-up and a thirst for know-how. One specific lesson being learned from foreign retailers is that in an ultracompetitive market, a winning strategy is to find ever more effective ways of lowering consumers' transaction costs—specifically by making it easier for shoppers to search for familiar and new products.

Standardization and Search Costs

To the Western eye, trained by perpetual highly sophisticated adaptations in retail technology, many Chinese stores are confusing. Take a walk down Shanghai's Nanjing Road shopping thoroughfare and the signs are hard to read—in all senses. The massive buildings with anonymous but idiosyncratic forms could be office buildings, hotels, conference centers, warehouses, malls, or department stores. Many are, in fact, stores of one kind or another—and it is not easy to immediately categorize the types. The closest analogy to a Western milieu is perhaps a street full of large independents such as Britain's Selfridges and Harrods, but without the uniform conventions of ground-floor window displays and cosmetic stands glimpsed through revolving doors. Inside the buildings there is similar idiosyncrasy. An escalator might surprisingly present itself to the left or right of the main entrance, running up the inside of the building's front wall, with no clue in the otherwise empty ground floor lobby as to what may be beyond the doors—a sales floor, a restaurant, or a car park, perhaps.

Diversity in design and labeling is also apparent in hotels. This is true of the external design of hotels in all cities of Asia that grew up in the frenzy of the 1980s and 1990s. Capital that was more abundant than skills in the construction industry gave young architects fresh out of college the job of designing city skylines. In China, local governments of all sizes—municipal, district, street office—and the former *dan wei* or work units joined the fray and invested in real estate projects in and out of their own territory. One of the sparkling new hotel towers in Shanghai's Pudong district carries the name of a "rural" district within the boundary of the city of Shenzhen, Wal-Mart's home in China, over a thousand miles to the south. Within the Bao'an district of Shenzhen, the eight towns and 113 villages became rich in the early days of the reforms by speculatively converting collective farm land into industrial workshop space and worker dormitories rented largely to Hong Kong manufacturers. By the end of 1997, in Bao'an's Shajing town alone, for example, approximately 4 million square meters of industrial workshop space and 1.5 million square meters of worker dormitories had been constructed, accommodating more than 800 firms with an annual output in 1997 of approximately 3.2 billion yuan ($364 million) (Webster et al. 2005). All this is co-owned by twenty-six villages within the town's territory, which are organized as a single villager committee with more than 26,000 members. Many such collectives have organized themselves as shareholder companies and have engaged in major speculative investments out of territory.

It is the idiosyncratic nature of the investment sector that must partly account for the lack of standardization of many investment projects. Major international investors have a script to read from, and the brand names and high-profile projects using foreign design teams tend to look much more familiar and are more homogeneous within their kind. Local investors in hotels or retailing malls do not need to pay too much attention to the fine art of those trades, however. At double-digit annual growth, they are guaranteed a return in a few short years. The Bao'an Hotel in Shanghai has luxurious rooms, but its lobby looks like a cross between an ancient grand hotel, a nightclub, and a cheap shopping arcade, with some very strange features that will register awkwardly with the all-important discerning business travelers.

Standardization is important for several reasons. Transactions of all kinds require that buyers and sellers outlay certain costs in searching for each other. Search costs are a particular kind of transaction cost—the nonprice costs of making an exchange. Sellers need to find buyers who want their products and services, and buyers need to find sellers. Standardization lowers search costs.

Competition between firms supplying goods and services forces them to outlay costs in the search for new information about the wants of their customers. Supermarkets invest huge amounts in acquiring this information and respond with new and improved processes and products, which become standardized within a chain. Standardization means consumers can be sure of the quality and range of goods and services and where to find goods in a shop, whatever branch they visit. Talking to customers of China's Wal-Mart stores, it seems clear that they are first and foremost attracted by the reliability of quality rather than low prices.

Competition among consumers causes them to outlay costs in seeking products that better satisfy their preferences—including trying out new shops, products, and services and visiting branches not normally patronized. Without competing consumers, suppliers would not incur costs in process or product innovation. Without competing suppliers, consumers would not incur costs in seeking the best retail outlet, hotel, dentist, restaurant, or car mechanic. Competition among suppliers acts as a discipline, therefore, keeping them actively reconfiguring their resources to better meet consumers' wants. The discipline is good for consumers but costly to suppliers, who in a competitive market have to bear a share of the costs of seeking buyers. Conversely, competition among consumers is costly for them but good for suppliers since it saves suppliers search costs. Competition therefore has the effect of distributing search costs between suppliers and consumers. Where demand is slack, sellers incur a greater share of the search costs in seeking buyers—supermarkets putting on special promotions and advertising more widely, for example. When it is strong, sellers can rely on buyers to assume more of the costs of discovering goods.

Search costs vary considerably between products. For nonstandard products or "experience goods"—goods such as package holidays and homes, the true value of which is learned only through consumption—the information costs to buyers are potentially high. This is because the product is actually a complex bundle of attributes, each one of which may contribute independently or interactively to a buyer's enjoyment. Comparing two homes, office buildings, or holidays is a nontrivial, multicriteria evaluation problem because there are many points for and against each option. As a result, sellers of "experience goods" have an incentive to bear some of the search costs. They can generally produce information about their products at lower cost than can buyers. They can subsidize buyers' search costs as a competitive strategy. With some products the information costs to buyers may be too great and a market may not develop without producers investing heavily in advertising, product packaging, and branding—all strategies that lower buyers' search costs. By contrast, standardized goods, such as groceries, audio equipment, and new cars, require much less information before a buyer is able to form a view about value. There is less intrinsic need for suppliers to have to assume search costs, and buyers will generally outlay more of the search costs for these "search goods." However, in these very competitive markets, suppliers may use competition strategies that effectively offer consumers savings on search costs. Like experienced good providers, they do this by standardizing and bundling. Supermarkets offer a standardized experience so that repetitive shopping trips become increasingly efficient. They bundle different goods under one roof to reduce trips and increase choice; they standardize layout to make the shopping experience familiar. The multipurposing of trips and the choices themselves become objects of familiarity—attributes of shopping that are expected and planned for and thus sources of time economy. Search costs are therefore a function of standardization and familiarity. In fact, it is familiarity that lowers search costs. Familiarity increases with standardization—hence the success of franchised burger businesses, package holiday operators, branded high-street fashion, and branded supermarket chains.

In the 1990s, when foreign supermarket stores started to appear in China, Chinese people couldn't believe that it was possible to shop by selecting your own basket of produce and taking it to a checkout counter. Early local innovators such as the Shanghai chain Lian Hua picked up the basic technology and quickly outcompeted more traditional forms of retailing, spreading throughout the country. The traditional server-counter technology remains but is under threat. Similarly, no retailer could imagine a standardized negotiation process with suppliers that involved supplier representatives queuing up for a delicatessen-counter style ticket to enter the "negotiations room" in Wal-Mart's Shenzhen headquarters (Schafer 2005). The Chinese government has opened up the field for Wal-Mart stores. These will be accompanied by new Metro and Carrefour stores and the most recent arrival, the Thai chain Lotus, in partnership with the British market leader Tesco. The effect is a rapid dissemination of standardized processes and products. The scope for local adaptation would seem to be surprisingly small. Modern convenience shoppers in Chinese cities want the same thing as their counterparts in other cities around the world: choice, quality, and value for money at the greatest convenience possible. And apparently Chinese suppliers are willing to learn the painful lessons required to deliver these conveniences. Years of experiments by shopping psychologists, store designers, product buyers, advertisers, accountants, and managers have produced generic formulae that are apparently bedding down as well in Guangzhou as in Glasgow or Gloucester, Massachusetts. The foreign supermarkets generally locate in the dense suburbs of China's big cities. Wal-Marts in China tend to be more of an urban phenomenon than their rural and suburban-sprawl counterparts in the United States. By and large, however, they perform the same function there as they do in Western cities. They carry locally sourced as well as exotic produce and cater to a mix of incomes. More than 70 percent of products on sale in Chinese Wal-Mart stores are made in China (Jiang 2004). The stores that have been in operation for some years have gradually increased the proportion of locally sourced produce by reproducing local versions of supply chain management systems and related knowledge and skills and by replacing exotic and more expensive sources. Above all, they are efficient selling machines, and they are transforming the shopping business practices *(ling shou ye)* of the Chinese, just as they have done so successfully with those of Western nations.

Dan Wei, Wal-Mart's Way, and the Chinese Way

I conclude with two final points: the first about Wal-Mart's particular approach to organizing retailing and the second, more substantial, about the Chinese government's approach to organizing retailing.

Much has been made of Wal-Mart's practices in respect of labor rights, and the company has recently hit back with counterclaims that emphasize the package of benefits it offers its "partner" employees. Among all the major chains, Wal-Mart's "family feel" human resource strategy is likely to be particularly appealing to the Chinese. Until the early 1990s, most of the Chinese economy was organized by the *dan wei.* It is a misconception that the state organized production and consumption centrally in the communist era. It did so via decentralized semiautonomous production organizations, which received funds from and paid revenue or surplus back to particular central government departments. These can be thought of economically as joint production-consumption clubs. A university, steel factory, food distribution agency, or department store would each be organized as a *dan wei.* Each would have its own structures of control and governance and, if large enough, would provide housing, schools and other benefits to its workers. Many residual features remain of China's collectives. The majority of city dwellers still live in neighborhoods provided by their former *dan wei,* and their welfare is as likely to come from the residual agencies (for example, a factory enterprise's real estate department now turned semiprivate property management company) as from local government. During the 1990s, many former *dan wei* offered workers a share of their former assets by giving them the right to buy their apartments or by distributing ownership shares (the latter also happened in Mongolia in a big way after the Soviet collapse). The idea, therefore, of a capitalist company that has a benevolent policy toward its workers—calling them associates, giving them share options, paying their health insurance, and so on—is likely to go down well with a Chinese workforce still feeling a little insecure in the absence of a strong state. The Wal-Mart-style set of rights—to welfare and a share in the enterprise—may well be more important to Chinese employers than any union rights now on offer after Wal-Mart's recent landmark decision to allow unions at its Chinese stores.

The Chinese government knew what it was doing when it made a few carefully negotiated concessions to foreign retailers in the 1990s. Forty Wal-Marts have hardly scratched the surface of the domestic market, with supermarket sales in China growing at 30–40 percent per year (Hu et al. 2004). The trade diversion impact of the early entry foreign stores on existing local stores has been much less than predicted. Much greater will have been the learning effect as local entrepreneurs observe and copy. Local Chinese retail chains are now in a good shape to compete in other lucrative markets such as South Korea. In the city of Xiamen in Fujian province, many Chinese versions of Western-style supermarkets, DIY, electrical, and local stores have opened in recent years. The city's Metro supermarket is located in a cluster of new local stores. Not far away a new electrical-goods supermarket has opened directly opposite Wal-Mart and draws on the latter's customers and retailing technology. It is owned by a local entrepreneur. How long China's trade walls can last is not clear, but the Chinese are fast enough learners to make haste in catching up while the protected space lasts. And since so many of the sources supplying the world's Wal-Marts and other stores lie in their territory, it might be expected that the retail sector has a big role to play in building up the crucial domestic demand base that China will need to sustain its economic growth into the future.

Conclusions

As with everything else about China at the moment, retail research is a wide-open field. The new Wal-Mart-sponsored unit at Tsinghua University will help give this focus and respectability. Staying with the themes in this chapter, there is a variety of questions that may be asked with respect to innovation diffusion, knowledge specialization, supply-chain evolution, store size, and competition. One of the most interesting things to ask about China, rather than about some other foreign footfall of Wal-Mart and the other multinational merchants, is what patterns of spatial and organizational order in the retail sector will emerge in the absence of the kinds of regulative controls that typically influence this order in the advanced economies. Urban government is being reinvented in China, and municipal, district, and street office agencies are in open competition with each other for footloose investment. They also compete as investors and land developers, as I have illustrated, and as regulators. At the national level, there is no modern tradition of managing competition in a market economy. The Chinese Ministry of Commerce has only just announced (in 2005) its intention to issue antitrust laws. These are intended in particular to help develop foreign trade, but they will inevitably have consequences for the development of domestic trade, including retailing. In this laboratory of relatively unconstrained entrepreneurialism and rapidly evolving public and private institutions, it is of great interest to observe how the retail sector takes shape. How large will stores grow in those cities that do not seek to control size? How will market structure develop? Will dominant giants emerge in this free-for-all, or will weak regulation make it easier for new entrants to challenge larger and less flexible chains? How will market structure play out in spatial terms? Will greater competition lead to more clustering of retailing, with attendant influences on the growth of subcenters and the shape of cities? In cities where large retailers dominate, will they seek to carve up the spatial markets to avoid price-based competition (the so-called Bertrand problem)? Chinese urban planners are used to planning by design, public investment, and edict. Most have yet to fully realize the unyielding power of spontaneous economic transactions in shaping cities. With the door now much wider open to foreign supermarkets, Wal-Mart will participate even more profoundly in China's search for an efficient retailing sector. It will be interesting to see what it makes of the opportunity.

Acknowledgment

I am grateful to Yanjiang Zhao and staff at the Xiamen Planning Bureau for providing statistics on stores in Xiamen.

24

Globalization of Food Retailing and the Consequences of Wal-Martization in Mexico

James J. Biles

Introduction

The impact of Wal-Mart on its competitors, suppliers, employees, and the communities where it locates has received considerable attention in the United States for more than a decade. Only recently, however, have social scientists turned their attention to the international dimensions of Wal-Mart's emergence as the world's largest corporation. To date, the majority of international research has been carried out in Europe. Perhaps the two best-known case studies are Wal-Mart's foray into Germany and its takeover of the British retailer ASDA in 1999 (Hallsworth and Evers 2002; Christopherson 2001; Burt and Sparks 2001).

This chapter places Wal-Mart's emergence as an international retailer into the broader context of the globalization of retailing and focuses on its impacts in Mexico, a less developed country, and its first and perhaps most successful international market. More specifically, this study reveals how Wal-Mart's dominance of the Mexican retail sector has transformed the practices of domestic supermarket chains, modified supply chain relationships with food producers, brought about opportunities and challenges for small-scale farmers, and generated uncertainty for the country's informal economy.

The remainder of this chapter is organized into six parts. The following section places Wal-Mart's international expansion into the broader context of the globalization of retailing. Subsequently, the emergence of Wal-Mart as the world's largest food retailer is sketched out. The third section assesses Wal-Mart's expansion into Mexican retailing. The next section discusses how Wal-Mart's dominance of Mexican retailing has transformed domestic supermarket chains. Then the potential consequences of the Wal-Martization of Mexican retailing for supermarket chains, food producers, small-scale farmers, and the country's informal economy are explored. The last part of this paper reviews the implications of the Wal-Martization of food retailing in Mexico and identifies opportunities for additional research.

Globalization of Food Retailing

The international expansion of Wal-Mart and its emergence as the world's largest food retailer must be understood as part of a broader process of the globalization of retailing that began in the 1980s and gathered momentum during the 1990s. Like all processes of globalization, the dual forces of policy and technology have facilitated the transformation of food retailing on a global scale in ways that profoundly affect the livelihoods of producers, consumers, and retailers in distant places.

In general, the 1990s were characterized by the triumph of free markets as nations adopted neoliberal economic reforms almost universally and removed barriers to trade and capital flows. The United States, for example, dismantled a set of regulatory barriers that had been imposed in the 1930s to preclude the concentration of market share among national supermarket chains, leading to widespread consolidation of food retailers (Wrigley 2002). In the case of Mexico specifically, the 1990s were marked by the inception of the North American Free Trade Agreement (NAFTA), which not only removed trade barriers but also facilitated the large-scale entry of international retail chains.

Globalization of retailing has also been facilitated by the application of information technologies and development of centralized accounting, purchasing, distribution, and logistics operations that have allowed large food retailers to achieve economies of scale and advantages over smaller firms (Wrigley 2002). Application of information management technology is exemplified by the adoption of just-in-time practices, in which retailers collect real-time point-of-sale data that are shared with key suppliers to achieve more efficient procurement systems and reduce warehousing and transaction costs (Christopherson 2001). One, perhaps unintended, consequence of retailers' use of information technologies has been a profound shift in market power, which has allowed supermarket chains to exert greater control over the activities of multinational food producers and other suppliers (Busch and Bain 2004).

The globalization of retailing has resulted in rapid proliferation of supermarkets throughout Latin America, where multinational food retailers such as Wal-Mart, Carrefour, and Ahold led investment during the late 1990s (Reardon and Berdegué 2002). Supermarkets have increased their market share in Latin America from between 10 and 20 percent of all food sales to more than 50 percent in less than two decades (Dugger 2004; Reardon and Berdegué 2002). In the largest countries of Latin America, such as Argentina, Brazil, Colombia, and Venezuela, international food retailers routinely figure among the top four or five supermarket chains. In Mexico the number of supermarkets nearly doubled between 1990 and 2000 to more than 1,000, and national and international supermarket chains now account for 50 percent of retail food sales (Chávez 2002; Reardon and Berdegué 2002). In general, the entry of international food retailers and the rapid growth of supermarkets in Latin America has followed a traditional hierarchical diffusion process, spreading from capital cities to intermediate and smaller cities and from niche markets in upper-income areas to middle- and working-class populations (Schwentesius and Gómez 2002).

Emergence of Wal-Mart as an International Food Retailer

The early 1990s was a momentous time for Wal-Mart in at least two respects. It was at this time that the company adopted the supercenter as its dominant retail format, moving away from its traditional discount store format (Wrigley 2002). In 1990 discount stores made up about 90 percent of Wal-Mart's retail portfolio; by 2005 supercenters accounted for slightly less than half of all stores in the United States and a significant share of its outlets abroad (Burt and Sparks 2001; Wal-Mart Stores 2005). The shift toward the supercenter, in which food sales account for a large amount of floor space and a significant share of revenue (30 to 40 percent), also signified a diversification strategy and explicit commitment to food retailing (Wrigley 2002). By 2000 Wal-Mart had become the largest food retailer in the United States (and the world). Since 2003 food sales have accounted for more than 25 percent of the firm's total revenue (Wal-Mart Stores 2005; Wrigley 2002).

The early 1990s also marked Wal-Mart's initial foray into international retailing—a joint venture with Mexican retail conglomerate CIFRA in 1991. Wal-Mart has subsequently established fully owned subsidiaries or joint ventures in eight other countries (Argentina, Brazil, Canada, China, Germany, Japan, South Korea, and United Kingdom), as well as Puerto Rico. The firm currently operates almost 2,000 retail outlets in these locations, employing more than 400,000 people (Wal-Mart Stores 2005). In Mexico and elsewhere, Wal-Mart has typically initiated operations by entering into joint ventures with domestic retail firms. Wal-Mart takes advantage of these partnerships to introduce its own retail formats and to learn the intricacies of new international markets. Although this model has proved successful in some cases (such as Mexico), it has not achieved comparable results in countries such as Germany and Japan (*Economist* 2005).

Wal-Mart increasingly relies on international sales, and the supercenter format and food sales have played an important role in the company's international success (Burt and Sparks 2001). Wal-Mart's international operations are its fastest-growing division, accounting for almost 20 percent of revenue and growing consistently at between 10 and 15 percent annually (refer to Figure 3.1). According to one retail trade publication (Masters 2004), Wal-Mart hopes to increase its international presence to one-third of total revenue. Currently, 80 percent of Wal-Mart's international sales are concentrated in Britain, Canada, and Mexico (Masters 2004). Wal-Mart's Mexican operations account for about 25 percent of total international revenue and are growing more rapidly than in the nine other countries (including the United States) where the firm operates (Dolan 2003). In Mexico, food sales alone make up more than 50 percent of its total revenue (Chávez 2002).

Structure of the Food Retailing Sector in Mexico

Prior to Wal-Mart's arrival, the Mexican food retailing sector had passed through two distinct stages (Schwentesius and Gómez 2002). The first supermarkets appeared in Mexico's largest cities during the period following World War II. This system of regional supermarket monopolies remained intact until the 1980s, when Mexico's entry into the General Agreement on Tariffs and Trade resulted in widespread consolidation, the emergence of national supermarket chains, and the initial partnerships with international retailers (Schwentesius and Gómez 2002). At the time of Wal-Mart's arrival in the early 1990s, Mexico's food retailing sector comprised a handful of national supermarket chains and several large regional food retailers that primarily served upper- and middle-income households in the country's largest urban areas, particularly in close proximity to Mexico City and northern border states (Chávez 2002). The largest Mexican supermarket chain at that time was Gigante, with approximately 150 locations, mostly in central Mexico (Harris 1995).

In the early 1990s, responding to saturated home markets, and in anticipation of the inception of the North American Free Trade Agreement (NAFTA), several large international retailers, including Carrefour, Ahold, and Wal-Mart, formed joint ventures and strategic alliances with Mexican firms (Morais 2004; Chávez 2002). The scale of internationalization in Mexican retail trade is revealed by the enormous increase in foreign direct investment (FDI) that has occurred during the past fifteen years. In the 1980s, FDI in the Mexican retail sector averaged about $130 million annually, representing only 6 percent of total foreign investment. Since Wal-Mart's initial entry into Mexico in 1991, foreign investment in retail has increased nearly tenfold to an average of more than $1.2 billion a year, 11 percent of total FDI.

The entry of international firms has brought about a process of expansion and consolidation among Mexican food retailers. As in other areas of Latin America, expansion has occurred as supermarket chains increasingly located in different parts of the country and in intermediate and smaller cities. Consolidation has occurred as national and regional retailers ceased operations or merged with international and national chains (Schwentesius and Gómez 2002). Patterns of supermarket expansion and consolidation are clearly displayed in the location of major supermarket chains in the city of Mérida, the retail hub of the Yucatán Peninsula in southeastern Mexico, as of early 2005 (Figure 24.1). Before 1990 the city was served almost exclusively by a handful of regional supermarket chains. Several of these regional chains have lost market share during the past decade, and the only remaining major regional food retailer, Super Maz, merged with Gigante in 2003.

Between 1990 and 2000, at least six new supermarkets were built, primarily by national and international retailers and mostly as anchor stores in shopping centers within or in close proximity to affluent and middle-class neighborhoods. The most dramatic changes in supermarket location have taken place since 2000. The six supermarkets built during this time serve much more diverse populations. Most of these new stores are located in outlying middle-income or working-class neighborhoods; the majority are stand-alone stores serving neighborhoods that have historically lacked easy access to major supermarkets chains. Notwithstanding the impressive expansion of supermarkets in Mérida in recent years, the densely populated (and poor) southern part of the city continues to lack a major supermarket chain.

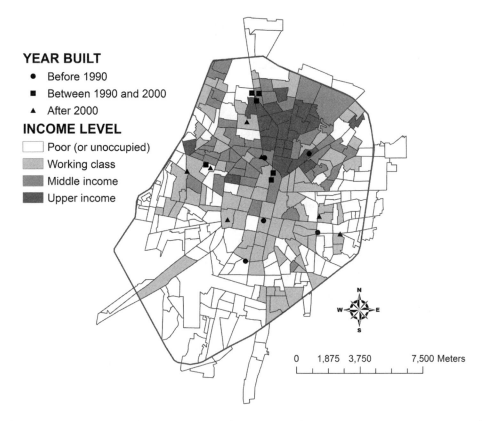

Figure 24.1   Location of major supermarkets in Mérida, Mexico. *Source:* Company Web sites.

Wal-Mart's Impact on Mexican Retailing

Wal-Mart pursued a three-stage expansion strategy in Mexico (Dolan 2003). As mentioned above, the firm entered into a partnership with domestic retail conglomerate CIFRA in 1991. Initially Wal-Mart held a 50 percent share in this joint venture, which it employed to launch its Sam's Club and Wal-Mart Supercenter retail formats in Mexico. In 1997 Wal-Mart acquired the majority stake in CIFRA and in 2000 changed its name to Wal-Mart de México (Walmex). As of early 2005 the firm operates 63 Sam's Club and 89 Wal-Mart supercenters, as well as the department store Suburbia (50) and the Aurrerá (165) and Superama (48) supermarkets, which target working-class and middle-/upper-income customers, respectively, and more than 280 Vips restaurants (Wal-Mart de México 2005).

Wal-Mart operates ten distribution centers that channel goods to its supermarkets throughout Mexico. According to Dolan (2003), the firm is debt-free because its inventory averages thirty-five days from initial procurement to sale and it employs a forty-five-day accounts payable system. Wal-Mart has also established a procurement office in Mexico and organized a group of 200 domestic suppliers that have the potential to export to the United States (Dolan 2003). The U.S. parent company owns more than 60 percent of its subsidiary's stock. The remainder is traded publicly on the

TABLE 24.1   Four Largest Food Retailers in Mexico

Retailer	Number of Outlets	Sales, 2003 (billions of $ U.S.)	Profits, 2003 (millions of $ U.S.)
Wal-Mart de México	699	$11.7	$585
Organización Soriana	162	$3.2	$144
Controladora Comercial Mexicana	225	$3.1	$93
Grupo Gigante	298	$2.8	$34

Source: Morais 2004; company Web sites.

Mexican stock exchange, making Walmex the country's second-largest corporation after Telmex, the national telephone company (Lee 2003).

Wal-Mart currently employs more than 112,000 people in Mexico, making it the country's largest private employer (Wal-Mart de México 2005; Weiner 2003). Its total sales for the 2005 fiscal year were more than $13 billion, which is equivalent to 2 percent of Mexico's GDP and 12.5 percent of all formal sector retail trade in Mexico (Wal-Mart de México 2005). Wal-Mart alone accounts for 30 percent of all supermarket sales in Mexico (Weiner 2003). As shown in Table 24.1, Wal-Mart now controls 55 percent of total sales among Mexico's four largest retailers, which make up 80 percent of the country's formal food retail sector (Morais 2004). The average Wal-Mart Supercenter in Mexico sells about 80,000 different products; the total number of stock keeping units (SKUs) sold by Wal-Mart de México stood at nearly 140,000 by early 2004 (Castillo 2004a).

The location of Wal-Mart's retail operations in Mexico clearly reflects the general hierarchical diffusion pattern of supermarket expansion in Latin America. Figure 24.2 displays the location of Wal-Mart de México's three main food retail formats. Fully one-half of these stores are concentrated in central Mexico, within 250 kilometers of

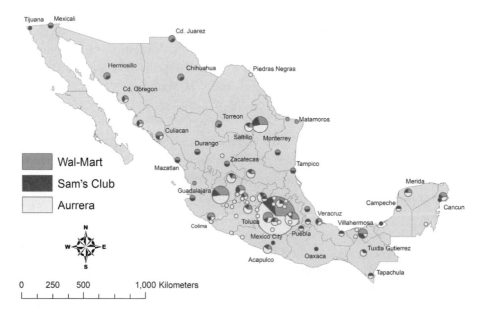

Figure 24.2   Location of Wal-Mart, Sam's Club, and Aurrerá stores in Mexico, April 2005. *Source:* Wal-Mart de México 2005.

Mexico City. Although Wal-Mart operates in only seventy-eight cities throughout the country, its retail strategy allows the firm to reach a potential market of almost 70 million Mexicans, representing two-thirds of the population (and an even greater share of disposable income). In addition, while the majority of Aurrerá stores are located in Mexico City, the map reveals that Wal-Mart increasingly employs this retail format to reach consumers in intermediate and smaller cities, particularly in the central and southern parts of the country.

The rapid proliferation of Wal-Mart and its unprecedented success have provoked widespread consolidation among food retailers in Mexico, particularly among regional supermarket chains and international firms with smaller operations. To a certain extent consolidation of the Mexican food retailing sector has followed a similar path to that of the United States in the 1990s, which transformed a group of major regional supermarket chains into a national food retailing system (Wrigley 2002). As mentioned above, national food retailer Gigante acquired Super Maz, an important regional supermarket chain, in 2003 as part of its expansion strategy in the southern part of the country. In addition, smaller international retailers have found it difficult to compete with Wal-Mart and large domestic chains, primarily due to a lack of distribution centers. Interestingly, national supermarket chains (rather than Wal-Mart) have rushed to acquire their foreign competitors. For example, in 2003 Comercial Mexicana purchased Auchan México, a subsidiary of a French retail chain with stores in fourteen countries (Lee 2003). In early 2005, Chedraui, a major regional retailer in the southern part of the country, acquired Carrefour's Mexican operations (twenty-nine stores). This merger reflects Chedraui's strategy to transform itself into a national chain and Carrefour's decision to withdraw from countries (including Japan as well as Mexico) where it is not among the top three retailers (*Economist* 2005).

The globalization of food retailing in Mexico differs from the experience of other Latin American countries in one fundamental way. Notwithstanding the presence of some smaller international chains, such as HEB Supermarkets in northern Mexico, and a handful of joint ventures with foreign retailers, consolidation has essentially left Wal-Mart the sole major international retailer in Mexico. Its decision to withdraw from Mexico's national association of department and self-service stores (ANTAD) in 2002 provides additional evidence of dominance of retail trade (Castillo 2004b). Given its market power and impact on its domestic competitors, it is not an exaggeration to speak of the Wal-Martization, rather than globalization, of retailing in Mexico.

In spite of its rapid proliferation in Mexico, Wal-Mart's expansion has not been entirely unfettered, particularly in the past year. The company's plans to build a 72,000-square-foot (6,689 square-meter) Aurrerá grocery store in close proximity to the Teotihuacán archaeological site in central Mexico created an enormous uproar in 2004 (McKinley 2004). Despite protests by local community groups and national and international media attention, the store opened to a brisk business in November 2004 (Ross 2005). In Mérida, however, a group of concerned citizens was able to stave off an effort by Wal-Mart to build a supercenter in their upscale neighborhood in late 2004. Despite a feasibility study carried out by Wal-Mart, the Mexican federal court system upheld the city's decision to prohibit construction of a large retail outlet in a primarily residential zone (Casares 2004). Although this defeat represents the first time Wal-Mart has failed to open a planned store in Mexico, the firm merely decided to move construction to a less controversial site near the city's *periférico* ring road a couple of kilometers from the original location.

Wal-Martization of Mexican Food Retailing

The Wal-Martization of retailing has transformed the operations of supermarket chains in Mexico in a variety of ways. Two of the most significant changes, the transformation of supply chain relationships and procurement practices and the propensity of domestic supermarket chains to emulate Wal-Mart, are highlighted quite succinctly by an article entitled "Beneficia a 15 mil yucatecos un convenio," which appeared in *Diario de Yucatán* in December 2004 (Domínguez 2004), and is translated here:

Agreement Benefits 15,000 Yucatecans

Fifteen thousand small-scale farmers will benefit from an agreement signed this past Tuesday in Mexico City between the supermarket chain Wal-Mart and the National Federation of Small-scale Farmers [in Spanish, CNC].

The state representative of farmers, Jorge Carlos Berlín Montero, indicated that the agreement will commence in January when Yucatecan producers begin delivering their crops to the firm.

"The huge advantage of this agreement," he added, "is that in addition to providing a guaranteed market, it also eliminates intermediaries because the producers will deal directly with representatives of Wal-Mart."

Other chains, such as Soriana and Gigante, have shown an interest in signing similar agreements with similar benefits for small-scale farmers.

The representative revealed that local CNC members could sell 60 tons of maradol papaya, 8 to 10 tons of habanero chili peppers, 200 twenty-kilo crates of squash, 400 crates of cucumbers, and 500 crates of tomatoes, chaya, seasonal fruits, honey, and other products each week.

According to the article, 15,000 small producers of papaya, squash, chile peppers, cucumbers, tomatoes, honey, and other products in the state of Yucatán in southeastern Mexico stood to benefit from an agreement between Wal-Mart and a national organization of campesinos (small-scale farmers) to sell produce directly to the supermarket chain. The purported goal of the agreement was to provide campesinos with a secure market for their production and to avoid wholesalers and brokers, who generally benefit disproportionately from distributing produce to supermarket chains.

The agreement to obtain fruit and vegetables directly from small-scale growers emphasizes the extent to which Wal-Mart has transformed the procurement systems of supermarket chains, particularly with respect to fresh produce and other unprocessed perishable commodities (such as seafood) that are sold directly to consumers. Prior to the Wal-Martization of food retailing in Mexico, supermarket chains relied heavily on the national wholesale market (CEDA) in Mexico City, as well as a small group of wholesalers who controlled the distribution of the majority of a wide variety of fruits and vegetables. The CEDA system allowed retailers to obtain large volumes of high-quality produce on a consistent basis; partnerships with the largest wholesalers reduced transaction costs by providing supermarkets with large volumes of fruit and vegetables at favorable prices (Schwentesius and Gómez 2002).

The globalization of food retailing has forced supermarket chains to cut costs, ensure consistent volume and quality, and provide a greater diversity of products. In addition, retailers have had to respond to changing tastes and greater preference for fresh produce and unprocessed food products. Cutting costs is achieved by improving logistics, increasing the scale and volume of production, and working with suppliers that have the capacity to provide large volumes of high-quality produce on a regular basis (Schwentesius and Gómez 2002). Although the CEDA system and key wholesalers continue to provide a large share of fresh produce, food retailers have adopted more diversified procurement systems, including establishment of their own distribution centers and directly contracting with growers (Reardon and Berdegué 2002; Schwentesius and Gómez 2002).

Distribution centers allow supermarket chains to achieve economies of scale, reduce intermediation costs, and facilitate more efficient inventory management and application of just-in-time practices (Schwentesius and Gómez 2002). Direct procurement may take place through individual stores or through distribution centers (Reardon and Berdegué 2002); information technologies allow supermarket chains to coordinate contracts with growers and consolidate purchases, which results in savings of 10 to 20 percent on costs from wholesalers. Direct procurement, however, is possible only among the largest chains and in the case of the most commonly consumed produce (Reardon and Berdegué 2002; Schwentesius and Gómez 2002).

The *Diario de Yucatán* article also mentions that domestic supermarket chains (Soriana and Gigante) have demonstrated an interest in entering into similar agreements, under the same terms, with small growers. This brief note confirms the research of Chávez (2002), who asserts that Mexican food retailers are increasingly emulating the business practices of Wal-Mart. Numerous examples of copycatting on the part of domestic supermarket chains may be identified. For example, Mexican retailers have expanded to other regions of the country, imitated Wal-Mart's procurement practices, implemented centralized information systems, integrated their logistics operations, and established their own distribution centers. In addition, domestic supermarket chains have adopted the supercenter as the dominant retail format.

Wal-Martization has also transformed the operations of Mexican food retailers in numerous other ways. In order to reduce costs and exert greater control over their supply chains, the country's three largest domestic supermarket chains formed Sinergia, a bulk purchasing consortium, in 2004 (Castillo 2004a). This move to coordinate purchasing mirrors the response of U.S. supermarket chains to Wal-Mart's entry into food retailing in the early 1990s (Wrigley 2002). The formation of Sinergia was protested by a group of Wal-Mart's preferred multinational food producers, including Coca-Cola, Procter and Gamble, and Philip Morris, which feared that domestic retailers would collude to fix prices through large-scale purchases. Sinergia now coordinates about 30 percent of purchasing on behalf of Soriana, Comercial Mexicana, and Gigante, all from a limited number of Mexican suppliers (Castillo 2004b).

Although Wal-Mart has been one of the driving forces in the globalization of food retailing during the past decade, the company has adapted its business practices in order to succeed in Mexico (and elsewhere). For example, Wal-Mart tweaked its retail model by retaining CIFRA's multiple formats and local names. In addition, the firm pursued a clearly segmented market strategy, using different retail formats to target different customers (Dolan 2003). During its first decade in Mexico, Wal-Mart focused primarily on expanding its supercenter and Sam's Club retail formats, explicitly targeting upper- and middle-class consumers. Its recent expansion strategy, however, has depended more heavily on its Aurrerá retail format. In general, Aurrerá stores carry fewer products than supercenters and Sam's Clubs, and they target poorer and working-class shoppers. This tactic of downscaling, which contrasts sharply with Wal-Mart's recent efforts to appeal to more affluent customers in the United States, has proved so successful that the company has followed a similar strategy in Brazil and other countries (Dolan 2003).

Domestic food retailers have also responded to Wal-Mart's presence and the globalization of retailing by developing their own "indigenous" strategies. Soriana, for example, has been Wal-Mart's most successful domestic competitor in spite of its purchasing and cost disadvantages. Unlike other domestic chains, Soriana has completely avoided partnerships with international retailers and focuses on its core food retailing formats (rather than restaurants and specialty retail stores). The firm's success derives from targeting "Mexican" tastes and offering middle-class customers a shopping experience different from those of Wal-Mart and other national retailers (Morais 2004; Chávez 2002). Yet another example is provided by Gigante, which has become an international retailer by establishing ten supermarkets in southern California, primarily serving markets with large populations of Mexican immigrants and Mexican Americans.

Implications of the Wal-Martization of Food Retailing in Mexico

As the previous section indicates, Mexican supermarket chains have responded to the globalization of food retailing and the emergence of Wal-Mart as the world's dominant retailer by adopting some of its business practices in hopes of achieving the economies of scale needed to remain competitive. In other instances, domestic firms have devised their own solutions, such as supply chain cooperation and the introduction of marketing strategies that highlight differences with Wal-Mart. With respect to food producers, the balance of power has shifted toward large supermarket chains during the past decade due to the application of information technology and the use of point-of-sale data to control and coordinate the activities of suppliers (Busch and Bain 2004). Multinational food producers, however, continue to offer brand-name goods that consumers purchase in large quantities. Consequently, food retailers such as Wal-Mart increasingly share information and coordinate supply chain operations with dominant multinational food manufacturers in order to keep inventories stable and reduce costs (Masters 2004). Notwithstanding partnerships with large food producers, major supermarket chains exert substantial pressure on suppliers to reduce costs and improve profit margins, as demonstrated by Wal-Mart de México's decision to remove Danone yogurt from its shelves for several months in 2003 due to a dispute over pricing (Busch and Bain 2004).

In the case of small-scale farmers and Mexico's informal economy, the implications of the Wal-Martization of food retailing are somewhat less certain. As discussed in the previous section, large supermarket chains have adopted more diverse procurement practices, including directly contracting with growers. At the same time, international food retailers have also imposed strict quality and certification standards, required suppliers to refrigerate shipments to minimize spoilage, and implemented commercial accounting practices that pay suppliers within seven to forty-five days of delivery (Reardon and Berdegué 2002). Although large supermarket chains generally pay higher prices to growers than wholesalers, small producers in developing countries frequently lack the institutional, technological, and infrastructural capabilities to respond to retailers' procurement requirements (Busch and Bain 2004). As a consequence, the transformation of supply chain relationships has eliminated all but the largest, most well-financed producers and impels small-scale farmers either to group together in cooperatives or to sell directly to intermediaries (Schwentesius and Gómez 2002).

Schwentesius and Gómez (2002) offer a revealing case study of the difficulties that confront small farmers who wish to obtain better prices by exporting their output or selling directly to large supermarket chains. In the southern state of Oaxaca small-scale lime producers formed a cooperative of more than 200 members with more than 800 hectares. With the assistance of an extension agent, producers were initially able to sell more than 40 percent of their harvest directly to supermarkets, which paid considerably higher prices than wholesalers. However, supermarket chains required lime producers to transport and refrigerate their shipments (the cooperative lacked refrigerated vehicles) and made payment more than a month after delivery of goods. By the following year, the organization had fallen into debt and disarray, as the cooperative did not have the working capital to cover the costs of production, packing, distribution, and credit. In addition, local intermediaries circumvented the cooperative by paying slightly higher than wholesale prices to individual producers. Unlike supermarket chains, however, wholesalers provided their own transportation and paid farmers on the spot (Schwentesius and Gómez 2002).

Indeed, although supermarket chains now control and coordinate supply chains in the food retail sector, the linkages of most small-scale agricultural producers in Mexico have changed very little in the past decade. During the 1990s, when large food producers controlled supply chains, small growers generally sold their output to brokers, who distributed produce to the national wholesale market or national and international food producers. Currently, the majority of small-scale producers sell their crops to the same brokers, who are now linked to national and international supermarket chains as well as the national wholesale market or national and international food producers (Steffen and Echánove 2003).

Theoretically, the expansion of international and domestic supermarket chains should also displace Mexico's enormous informal retail sector, with estimated annual sales of more than $100 billion, representing about 6 percent of the county's gross domestic product (GDP) (Wright 2001). In addition to large self-service and convenience store chains, the Mexican retail sector comprises public and itinerant markets, street vendors, mom-and-pop and corner stores, and specialized retailers (Schwentesius and Gómez 2002). With the exception of large national and regional chains and some specialized retailers, however, the majority of retailers operate (at least to some degree) within the informal economy. Consequently, as much as one-third of all retail sales in Mexico occurs outside the formal economy (Wright 2001).

In theory, the globalization of retailing permits large chains to provide consumers with a greater variety of products at lower prices than smaller competitors. As a consequence, consolidation should take place as larger retailers displace smaller firms. As discussed above, substantial consolidation has taken place within Mexico's formal retail sector. However, there is no evidence that globalization of retailing has reduced the size of Mexico's informal economy. In fact, what little research exists suggests that informal retailers may have several important competitive advantages over large retail chains. On one hand, street vendors and itinerant markets are able to charge lower prices than supermarkets precisely because they operate outside the formal economy and avoid taxes and other costs associated with carrying out business. Small informal retailers can also locate in dense urban locations (barrios), where large-scale retail outlets cannot. In addition, some informal retailers identify opportunities in peripheral locations (both geographically and economically) that lack the infrastructure required by supermarket chains. Informal retailers also compete successfully by offering their customers short-term credit and access to products that are unavailable in large retail chains (Reardon and Berdegué 2002). Furthermore, with respect to fresh produce, research by Schwentesius and Gómez (2002) confirms that public markets routinely offer a greater variety of fruit and vegetables than supermarket chains.

Ultimately the most important factor favoring the persistence of informal food retailing in Mexico is poverty. As long as a large share of the population remains unemployed or underemployed and two-thirds of households control less than 20 percent of disposable income, the informal economy will continue to be an important vehicle for creating jobs and providing a large share of Mexico's population with access to relatively inexpensive food products.

Conclusions

The globalization of retailing has clearly brought about changes in supply chain relationships between supermarket chains, food producers, growers, and consumers. In the case of Mexico, Wal-Mart has transformed the country's food retailing landscape almost single-handedly. Since its arrival in 1991, the number of supermarkets has grown rapidly as domestic firms, primarily, have increased the scale and scope of their operations to compete more successfully. As a consequence, consumers throughout the country have access to more supermarkets and a greater variety of products than ever before.

Theoretically, the globalization of retail trade benefits all: consumers benefit from lower prices, suppliers increase efficiency and quality, and retail chains improve the quality of their services (*Economist* 2004). In the real world, however, things are never quite that simple; the Wal-Martization of retailing in Mexico has obviously generated winners and losers. Unfortunately, the proliferation of Wal-Mart in Mexico has also produced a great deal of controversy and rhetoric, but very little meaningful research.

Based on the cursory assessment of the Wal-Martization of food retailing in the preceding pages, several potential research areas may be identified. Although domestic supermarket chains have apparently adopted many of Wal-Mart's business practices, no research exists as to the extent of Wal-Martization among Mexican retailers. Furthermore, given the preference of large supermarket chains to coordinate supply chain activities with multinational food manufacturers, little is known about relationships between these retailers and domestic food producers. As discussed above, small-scale growers often lack the resources to build and sustain linkages with large supermarket chains. However, production of many types of fresh fruit and vegetables is not prone to economies of scale, and small growers, technically, should be able to compete with larger processors. Notwithstanding the seminal work of Schwentesius and Gómez (2002) reviewed in this study, additional investigation and fieldwork are needed to determine which products offer small-scale farmers opportunities to reach national and international food retailers directly and which regions of Mexico stand to benefit (and lose) from the transformation of procurement practices among supermarket chains. Although globalization purportedly benefits consumers with lower prices and greater variety, the Wal-Martization of food retailing in Mexico has shifted a large share of market power to a small group of supermarket chains. Given this increasingly oligopolistic market structure, additional research is also needed to determine the extent to which consumers actually benefit (through lower prices) from the transformation of the food retailing sector. Finally, Mexico's informal economy offers food retailers much potential for growth, and supermarket chains have responded with marketing and advertising strategies to undermine public markets and small corner stores. Lacking, however, is an assessment of changes in consumers' shopping habits and an estimate of the impact of the Wal-Martization of food retailing on the informal economy.

Wal-Mart's impact in Mexico should not be underestimated. In slightly more than a decade the firm has become the country's most important retailer and largest private employer. In a given year the average Mexican household visits a Wal-Mart store more than twenty times, spending about $500 annually. The firm's influence undeniably extends to domestic supermarket chains and the retail trade sector as a whole. Given the sheer magnitude of Wal-Mart's footprint in Mexico, some observers have taken the transformation of the country's retail sector for granted. However, as this study reveals, the Wal-Martization of retail trade in Mexico may have profound consequences for supermarket chains, food producers, small-scale agriculture, consumers, and the country's informal economy.

25

Wal-Mart Goes South: Sizing Up the Chain's Mexican Success Story

Chris Tilly

Pyramids versus Discounts

In November 2004, global headlines trumpeted a bitter conflict over the opening of a Wal-Mart store in Mexico. Wal-Mart was on the verge of launching a store in Teotihuacán, just north of Mexico City. The site was about a mile from a huge pre-Aztec temple complex including the majestic Pyramid of the Sun, larger than Egypt's Great Pyramid. Mexican activists denounced the desecration of Mexico's archaeological heritage by the retail giant from the north, and began a hunger strike. Wal-Mart and its critics conducted a noisy debate. But a few weeks later, the struggle was over: the Wal-Mart opened (Case 2004; Cevallos 2004; Ross 2005).

The Teotihuacán brouhaha highlights several important facts about the Mexican retail world and Wal-Mart's place within it. To begin, this was far from Wal-Mart's first foray into Mexico. Wal-Mart entered the Mexican market in 1991. As of Wal-Mex's 2005 annual report, it was not only Mexico's largest retailer but also Mexico's biggest private employer, with over 124,000 employees spread across 783 retail units, including restaurants (Wal-Mart de México 2006). Only a minority of these units carry the familiar Wal-Mart or Sam's Club labels; most operate under brand names from the Mexican retail group CIFRA, which Wal-Mart acquired in 1997. In fact, the Wal-Mart that opened in Teotihuacán is an Aurrerá superstore, CIFRA's flagship brand.

Another important fact is that Wal-Mart critics actually advanced three distinct arguments against the store in Teotihuacán. One argument focuses on the impact on Mexico's historical patrimony. The temple complex was part of what was, in its time, the largest city in the world. A giant store located in this larger archaeological zone inevitably destroyed artifacts and erased a part of the historical record. Moreover, the critics maintained, this symbol of crass consumerism by its very presence connotes disrespect for Mexico's heritage. Second, critics objected specifically to a U.S.-owned company erecting a store so close to a monument to Mexico's greatness. They portrayed Wal-Mart's spread as an assault on Mexican economic sovereignty. Third, local merchants expressed a narrower complaint: Wal-Mart will put them out of business. "They're going to destroy us," said cosmetics saleswoman Stephanie

Gleason González. "The people here are going to go from business owners to employees" (Hawley 2004). In short, it is not just reverence for the past but economic self-
interest that fuels Mexican anti-Wal-Mart sentiment.

An additional fact: it was not Wal-Mart that introduced retailing to Teotihuacán.
The locale where Wal-Mart built its store was in fact already a cluttered commercial
area, including "a hotel, a small Ford Motor Co. dealership, an electronics retailer
and a mattress store"; this helps explain the vocal protests from existing retail establishments (Case 2004). Even within the enclosed archaeological site itself, visitors
to the Pyramid of the Sun are accosted by souvenir stand proprietors and roving
vendors hawking trinkets. The broader point is that retail activity is ubiquitous in
Mexico, especially in urban areas such as Teotihuacán. Chain stores, corner stores,
market stalls, and street vendors permeate every neighborhood; Wal-Mart is a recent
addition to this bustle of selling activity.

Finally, Mexicans' response to the Teotihuacán Aurrerá, and to Wal-Mart in general, is deeply ambivalent—just as the response in the United States has been (Featherstone 2005; Goodwin 2004). Wal-Mart opponents mounted their hunger strike, but
when the store opened, consumers flooded in to shop. "Almost everybody is in favor
of the store because it has more products at lower prices," shopper Evangelina Enciso
told a reporter. "We also need the jobs" (Case 2004). Many (perhaps most) Mexicans
agree that Wal-Mart is "a threat to sovereignty," in the words of a headline in the
daily *La Jornada* (González Amador 2004), but this did not prevent them from giving
Wal-Mart 140 billion pesos (about $12.7 billion) in sales in 2004.

In the shadow of Wal-Mart's Teotihuacán branch, this chapter takes up four questions. How did we get here—that is, what is the recent history of Mexican retailing
leading up to Wal-Mart's leap into the Mexican market? To what extent has Wal-Mart
exported its U.S. model to Mexico? What are the key limits on Wal-Mart's success in
Mexico? And what will determine the future direction of retailing in Mexico—and,
by extension, in Latin America and perhaps other parts of the world as well?

How We Got Here: A Selective History of Mexican Retail

Foreign investment in the retail sector is nothing new in Mexico. Immigrants have
started most of the notable retail chains in Mexico. French traders established the two
leading department store chains, Puerto de Liverpool and Palacio de Hierro, in the
late nineteenth century (Buchenau 2004; Bunker 2003; Mulder 2002). In the second
half of the twentieth century, Spaniards founded the major Mexican grocery chains,
including CIFRA, the chain Wal-Mart acquired. Anticipating Wal-Mart by nearly
fifty years, Sears entered the Mexican market in 1947 and became a trusted brand.
As an aside, Sears de México struggled in the 1990s and finally sold its stores and
name to a Mexican company in 1997. Ironically, that Mexican company is Sanborns,
a chain of department stores and restaurants founded in 1903 by migrants from the
United States to Mexico but now owned by the richest man in Mexico, Carlos Slim
(and featuring Mexican cuisine served by waitresses in traditional Mexican dress).
U.S. convenience store titan 7-Eleven began opening Mexican branches in 1971 and
had over 550 stores in Mexico in mid-2005 (7-Eleven 2005, 7-Eleven Mexico 2005).

Nor did Wal-Mart introduce the hypermarket—a big-box store combining groceries with other merchandise lines—to Mexico. Given Mexican retailers' links to capital in Europe (where the hypermarket was invented), some of them had hypermarkets in place by the early 1980s. In contrast, Wal-Mart did not establish its first U.S. supercenter—Wal-Mart's name for the hypermarket format—until 1988 (The Wal-Mart Story 2005).

But Wal-Mart's step into Mexico was nonetheless a bellwether for a new wave of retail globalization. Wal-Mart, along with its U.S. and European counterparts, encountered increasingly saturated home markets over the 1980s and 1990s (Wrigley 2002; Hoover's Online 2000). At the same time, the global spread of free trade agreements—the North American Free Trade Agreement (NAFTA), which took effect in 1994, was an early one—created newly hospitable environments for companies seeking to expand globally. NAFTA, like other such agreements, barred restrictions on foreign business ownership. It also lowered trade barriers—a tremendous boon to global retailers that have built competitive advantage with large-scale, integrated systems of purchasing and distribution of merchandise.

As already noted, Wal-Mart began doing business in Mexico in 1991, as NAFTA headed for adoption. Wal-Mart started out with a joint venture with CIFRA, Mexico's largest retailer, to operate Sam's Club warehouse stores in Mexico. Sam's Club flourished in Mexico, and the two partners expanded the collaboration. In 1994, as Mexico experienced a profound economic crisis, including a cataclysmic devaluation of the peso, observers questioned the wisdom of Wal-Mart's venture. But in 1997, when Wal-Mart saw the Mexican economy beginning to recover while the peso remained low in dollar terms, they seized the chance to purchase a majority share of CIFRA at an exchange-rate-depressed price, forming Wal-Mart de México (Walmex for short). Wal-Mart then bankrolled an aggressive expansion, more than doubling its sales (in amounts adjusted for inflation) between 1997 and 2003 (Álvarez 2005c).

Wal-Mart was not alone in seeing the opportunity afforded by NAFTA. French grocery giants Carrefour (the world's second-largest retailer) and Auchan followed Wal-Mart, as did J. C. Penney department stores, Texas-based grocer HEB, and the Spanish apparel retailer Inditex, among others. Meanwhile, Mexican retailers numbers two, three, and four (Gigante, Comercial Mexicana, and Soriana), spurred by the appearance of foreign entrants, also made concerted efforts to expand beyond their regional origins (Schwentesius and Gómez 2002).

A Model Exported?

How much of the model born in Bentonville has Wal-Mart exported to Mexico? The model has five main elements.

1. *Everyday low prices (EDLP)*. Wal-Mart offers ongoing low prices rather than periodic discounts. In Walmex's early years, EDLP was not a viable competitive strategy. High inflation meant that prices changed rapidly, obscuring price differences between merchants. But by the late 1990s, Mexico had stabilized inflation. Wal-Mart rolled out EDLP to its Mexican stores with much fanfare in 1999–2000 and posted price comparisons with their competitors (*DSN* 2001; Luhnow 2001).

The price comparisons got Walmex tossed out of Mexico's National Association of Supermarkets and Department Stores (ANTAD) in 2002, but the company has stuck with the pricing strategy.

The EDLP policy and the aggressive use of price comparisons should not be taken to mean that the "Blue Giant" charges lower prices on all items than do other stores. Mexico's Attorney General for Consumers conducts periodic, extensive price surveys on hundreds of items in Mexico's three largest cities. Results in 2005 showed that Wal-Mart had the lowest price for between 3 and 18 percent of items (depending on the city); however, Wal-Mart had the highest price for between 4 and 7 percent of the items (Álvarez 2005c). This appears to echo Wal-Mart's U.S. practice of offering staggeringly low prices on a small number of highly visible items while charging more normal prices on much of its merchandise (*Frontline* 2004).

2. *Highly automated inventory management.* Walmex has implemented the same automated system in place in the United States. In fact, in the early years, the computerized inventory system caused problems in the hands of Mexican managers unfamiliar with it. According to *Wall Street Journal* reporter David Luhnow, Wal-Mart's "first Mexican stores carried many items Mexicans rarely used: ice skates, riding lawn mowers, fishing tackle—even clay pigeons for skeet shooting. Hapless local managers would radically discount the pigeons to get rid of them, only to have automated inventory systems linked to Wal-Mart's corporate headquarters in Bentonville, Ark., order a fresh batch" (Luhnow 2001). Walmex has worked out those bugs and by 2004 had twelve distribution centers operating in Mexico (Velasco 2004). With NAFTA reducing the costs and delays of shipping merchandise across the border, Wal-Mart has linked its Mexican distribution system to its U.S. one.

3. *Pressure on suppliers for price reductions.* Wal-Mart's beating down of supplier prices, even to the point of driving vendors into bankruptcy, is legendary (Fishman 2003). Walmex plays the same game, whether pooling its buying power with the rest of Wal-Mart or acting on its own. According to an unhappy executive of a small Mexican clothing manufacturer I will call Ropinta:

> Wal-Mart has driven many suppliers out of business. Wal-Mart maintains its profit margin.... They never reduce *their* margin. They *do* pass on savings in price, but at the expense of the manufacturer. You can increase efficiency a certain amount, but ... For example, they may tell you, "We're going to sell shirts at a discount of 40 percent—you, the manufacturer, have to cut your price 40 percent." So the consumer benefits, but they're driving out of business the manufacturers that provide *jobs.*

Raúl Alejandro Padilla, the head of Mexico's confederation of local chambers of commerce for retail and services, agreed, stating that Wal-Mart "makes demands on its suppliers to such an extent, and punishes them by requiring discounts for displays, promotions, and shelf placement, all of which implies a large sacrifice of profit margins by those selling to Wal-Mart, to the point where the opening of new branches is practically 100 percent financed by the costs borne by its suppliers" (Maldonado 2005).

As in the United States, Wal-Mart de México pursues lower prices by sourcing from low-wage countries, especially China. Cédric Durand reported that Walmex imported more than half the value of its merchandise in 2002–2003 (Durand 2005).

4. *Elaborate systems and rules for employees.* Executives and managers in other Mexican retail chains whom I interviewed were in awe of Wal-Mart's detailed specification

of management and job procedures. These include rallying employees each morning with the famous Wal-Mart cheer. After finding that Mexican staff disliked belting out a translation of the English version, the company adopted a local variant: "Chee-kee-tee-boom-a-la-beem-boom-bah, Wal-Mart, Wal-Mart, rah-rah-rah!"(Luhnow 2001). Walmex also promulgated Wal-Mart's "ten-foot rule" (directing employees to greet and offer help to any customer coming within ten feet), translated, of course, into a "three-meter rule." Beyond these widely known guidelines, Walmex spells out in detail how to carry out virtually every activity in the store. As an executive of another chain put it, "There's a sign on the Wal-Mart headquarters [in Bentonville] saying 'Ordinary people coming into a company to do extraordinary things.' … With the right systems, training, and tools, ordinary people *can* do extraordinary things." Of course, we should not exaggerate Wal-Mart's ability to micromanage its employees, either in the United States or in Mexico. In my experience shopping in many Mexican Wal-Mart affiliates in 2004, it was rare that stepping within three meters of an employee prompted a greeting.

5. *Low wages and union avoidance.* Here Walmex's practice deviates from that of its northern parent. Wal-Mart in the United States has developed a reputation for paying low wages even by the low-wage retail industry's standards. Headquarters distributes a union-busting manual to all managers, and when meat cutters at one store nonetheless managed to vote in a union, Wal-Mart responded by shutting down that meat-cutting department two weeks later (Featherstone 2004b). Similarly, when workers at a store in Jonquière, Québec, voted to join a union, Wal-Mart shuttered the store (Geller 2005). Wal-Mart de México follows a somewhat different path—but only somewhat. Walmex stores, like virtually all other large chain stores in Mexico, have union contracts.[1] However, as Mexican economists Alfonso Bouzas and Mario Vega have argued, these are largely "protection contracts," protecting the employers from more militant unions in return for union dues, while offering relatively minimal provisions to the workers (Bouzas and Vega 1999). A former executive at one major chain confirmed this:

> In Mexico you can have a union which is a paper union. It's really *not* something. But you'd rather have it because if you don't have it, then you get another union coming in and when you get two unions fighting, then you're in trouble. So you do have a union but in the past as I'm sure today, whenever we have problems in a store, we notify the six or ten individuals who are starting to really try to make a union, we'll just get rid of them. But yes, you do have legally a document whereby you say that your union is such and such, and really it's a white-paper type of deal. It's not only in retailing, but in retailing, it's particularly the way.

In the unionized chains, I found that workers were most often unaware there was a union, and if they were aware, they had very little contact with union representatives.

In terms of salaries, Walmex is not a low-paying retailer. Based on union contracts from the cities of Guadalajara and León, Wal-Mart offers pay levels comparable or superior to those in other chains. Other useful comparisons are Mexico's minimum daily salary, which was $3.98 (43.73 pesos) in Guadalajara and $3.83 (42.11 pesos) in León in 2004 (Secretaría del Trabajo y Previsión Social 2004), and the national average of daily compensation in retail, which I estimate at $6.00 (66 pesos) in 2003, far below the economy-wide average of $14.55 (160 pesos). Wal-Mart exceeds these yardsticks as well—though not by much. To get a sense of the purchasing power of

TABLE 25.1   Wal-Mart Benefits Compared to Those in Other Chains, 2004

	Wal-Mart (Léon, Guadalajara)	Comercial Mexicana (Léon)	Comercial Mexicana (Guadalajara)	Soriana (Léon)	Gigante (Guadalajara)
Days of pay in year-end bonus (aguinaldo)	30	30	30	30	30
Vacation days after 2 years	8	8	8	8	10
Vacation pay as percentage of regular pay	25%	25%	30%	25–30% after 2 years	50%
Pension plan beyond social security	No	No	No	No	Yes

Source: Collective bargaining contracts from the Juntas Locales de Conciliación y Arbitraje (Local Labor Relations Commissions), Guadalajara and León.

the salaries, in January 2005, urban supermarket customers at Wal-Mart stores in Mexico City and Tehuacán, Puebla, were paying about 73 cents (8 pesos) for a kilo of rice, 82 cents (9 pesos) for a kilo of beans, $1.55 (17 pesos) for a liter of corn oil, and $2.82 (31 pesos) for a gallon of pasteurized milk.

In fringe benefits, Wal-Mart de México lags somewhat behind other chains (Table 25.1). Walmex offers a year-end bonus of double the amount required by law, but otherwise offers only benefits required by Mexico's national labor law. Comercial Mexicana (in Guadalajara), Soriana, and Gigante all offer somewhat more generous packages. Gigante stands out, providing more vacation days, double the vacation pay, and its own pension plan. But with that exception, Wal-Mart compensation does not appear far out of step with other chains. Moreover, given high employee turnover rates in retail, differences in vacation times and pension plans for senior employees will affect only a small proportion of the retail workforce. Supermarket staff turnover was estimated at 30 percent in the third trimester of 2004, implying an annual turnover rate of 120 percent (ANTAD 2005).

In the United States, Wal-Mart faces litigation for forcing large numbers of workers to work extra hours "off the clock" (a charge the company denies) (Featherstone 2005). On this dimension, Wal-Mart de México appears to be in step with its parent's alleged misdeeds. A cashier at a Wal-Mart-owned Aurrerá store reported:

> They only pay when you work a full [additional] hour. And only when it's authorized by the manager or assistant manager. If not, they don't pay me for the hour. [Interviewer: And do you usually get that authorization?] No.

Working extra time is sufficiently common that she described one eight-hour shift (her shift fluctuates weekly), including a one-hour meal break, as "from 1:00 to 10:00 or 10:30." On this score, Walmex is in step not only with Wal-Mart in the United States but also with other Mexican retailers. Workers at several other chains told me of having to work added hours without pay as well.

In summary, Wal-Mart de México is replicating most of the competitive strategies of Wal-Mart in the United States, but not all. After some initial delays, Walmex instituted a low-price policy, a high-tech distribution system, a strategy of squeezing suppliers, and closely specified operational procedures. In regard to compensation and unions, Walmex, like its U.S. counterpart, pays low wages, offers few benefits beyond those required by law, avoids "real" unions, and pushes workers to do extra, unpaid work. But while these workforce policies put Wal-Mart outside the mainstream of U.S. retailers, creating one source of competitive advantage via cost savings, they situate Walmex squarely within the Mexican retail mainstream.

Successes and Limits of the Wal-Mart Model in Mexico

Wal-Mart has, without a doubt, achieved tremendous success in Mexico. Walmex grew far more rapidly than its rivals, its 2002 sales outstripping the combined total sales of its three nearest competitors, Soriana, Comercial Mexicana, and Gigante. Perhaps even more striking, following the 1995 economic crisis Wal-Mart exceeded its 1994 peak by 1998, whereas its three competitors still had not returned to their 1994 level even by 2003.

Walmex's success is particularly notable in comparison with the fortunes of other major NAFTA-era retail entrants from abroad. Many of these other transnationals have since fled, and Wal-Mart's store count dwarfs that of almost all that remain (Table 25.2). The one partial exception is 7-Eleven, but a convenience store has one-twentieth the employment of a superstore, and within the convenience store niche 7-Eleven is swamped by Mexican competitor OXXO. Thus, Wal-Mart's success does not reflect general success by U.S. or multinational companies in Mexico; rather, it appears to be distinctive.

Nonetheless, Wal-Mart's triumphant foray into Mexico is beginning to encounter its limits. Two principal frictions threaten to impede the growth of the Blue Giant. For one thing, Mexico's other major retail chains have, with varying degrees of success, striven to imitate the Wal-Mart model (Tilly forthcoming). Wal-Mart's three major Mexican competitors all now offer some version of everyday low prices, have begun

TABLE 25.2 Wal-Mart and Other Recent International Retail Entrants in Mexico

Chain	Country	Format	Year Entered	Mexican Stores in July 2005
Wal-Mart	U.S.	Self-service	1991	729 (388 grocery stores)
7-Eleven	U.S.	Convenience	1971	More than 550 (compare OXXO with 3,466)
Auchan	France	Self-service	1997	Exited in 2003 with 5 stores
Carrefour	France	Self-service	1994	Exited in 2005 with 31 stores
HEB	U.S.	Self-service	1997	21
Inditex (Zara)	Spain	Department	1992	108
J. C. Penney	U.S.	Department	1995	Sold its 6 stores to Grupo Sanborns in 2003

Sources: Number of stores and related information from company Web sites. Year of entry from Schwentesius and Gómez 2002, except 7-Eleven, Inditex, and J. C. Penney from company Web sites.

to implement Wal-Mart-style automated distribution systems, are demanding steep discounts from their suppliers, and are more carefully specifying operating procedures. Comercial Mexicana and Soriana, in particular, aggressively publicize price differences with Wal-Mart. "In terms of service, prices, assortment, they're all pretty much the same," commented a Guadalajara cab driver.[2] *Christian Science Monitor* reporter Ken Bensinger likewise observed, "In reality ... prices for common groceries are essentially identical at Wal-Mart's competitors" (Bensinger 2005). The net result is that Wal-Mart's share of sales among the top five Mexican retailers leveled off beginning in 2002 (El Universal 2005).

A second factor threatening Walmex's juggernaut is the country's growing income polarization. Robert Buchanan, an analyst at NatWest Securities, commented: "Mexico is a land of haves and have-nots. It's a poor bet for an American broad-lines retailer that is mostly aimed at the middle class" (Seckler and Ramey 1997). As unlikely as it might appear to U.S. consumers, according to *DSN Retailing Today*, "for the average Mexican consumer a trip to a Wal-Mart supercenter is a high-end experience" (Braine 2004). For Mexican consumers, alternatives include public markets, corner stores, and informal street markets, all of which offer lower prices than Wal-Mart on at least some items. As repeated economic crises hammered Mexico in the 1990s and the early 2000s, the percentage of Mexicans who stated a preference for shopping in a supermarket—any supermarket—tumbled from 75 percent in 1993 to 56 percent in 2000 (Schwentesius and Gómez 2002) and further down to 34 percent in 2003 (Rodríguez and Reider 2004). Neither Wal-Mart nor any of its three major competitors has attained the level of sales per employee that they enjoyed in the mid-1990s. In addition to shifting consumer preferences, the downward trend in sales per employee presumably reflects the saturation of major geographic markets, a topic to which I will return. Walmex (along with its competitors) has grown sales not by attracting more shoppers to existing stores but by adding to the number of stores.

Indeed, though Wal-Mart has enjoyed a decade and a half of success in Mexico, there is considerable evidence that this winning streak has been based in part by exceptional circumstances. As one department store executive commented, "They bought the business [CIFRA] that was already the leader." This gave them a significant advantage over French global grocers Carrefour and Auchan, who pursued partnerships with Gigante and Comercial Mexicana, respectively—joint ventures that soon stumbled due to their limited capacity in the early 1990s (Álvarez 2005a).

Wal-Mart has not enjoyed such good fortune in the other two Latin American countries it has entered. Historian Julio Moreno characterized Wal-Mart's success in Brazil as modest and its experience in Argentina as "disastrous" (Moreno 2004)—although it is important to add that subsequent to Moreno's 2004 article, Wal-Mart vaulted from sixth to third place among Brazilian retailers by purchasing a leading chain, demonstrating the advantage of deep pockets. Even within Mexico, Wal-Mart has struggled to gain a foothold in the affluent north, where Soriana and Texan grocer HEB had already built up a loyal customer base by the time Wal-Mart arrived (Hanrath 2002).

The Future of Retailing—and Wal-Mart—in Mexico

The future of retailing in Mexico depends principally on three factors. First, the strategies adopted by leading companies, including Wal-Mart, will be critically important. Second, a number of dimensions of Mexican public policy will shape retail. Third, and perhaps hardest to predict, the path of Mexico's future economic development will dictate the range of possible outcomes in retailing as in other sectors.

At one level, the question of strategy simply involves enumerating the game plans of the major and emerging players. Wal-Mart's pattern is well established: grow fast, reap economies of scale, and use low prices to elbow aside competitors. Wal-Mart's three major competitors in Mexico (Soriana, Comercial Mexicana, and Gigante) are all using more or less the same strategy, although Soriana and Comercial Mexicana have recently begun to more actively woo a high-end clientele with fancy food offerings (Bensinger 2005). Of the three Walmex rivals, Soriana is pursuing the most distinctive path. Unlike Gigante and Comercial Mexicana, whose store locations are centered in Mexico City like Wal-Mart's, Soriana has built a strong regional base in the north and only gradually expanded to other parts of the country. Soriana also has a reputation for catering more to Mexican tastes, for maintaining strong supplier relationships (including some self-owned farms) that help in securing fresh, high-quality produce, and for making major investments in training that have allowed it to reduce personnel turnover (Chávez 2002; Morais 2004). Not coincidentally, Soriana has grown more rapidly than its counterparts, though starting from a smaller base. Between 1992 and 2003, Soriana's sales grew by 160 percent, outpacing even Walmex. Sales at Comercial Mexicana and Gigante sputtered by comparison, growing 40 percent and 17 percent, respectively.

There is much speculation about the possibility of mergers and acquisitions among Mexico's three second-tier retailers. The three formed a buying consortium dubbed Sinergia (Synergy) in 2004, in an attempt to match the Blue Giant's buying power (Castillo 2005). Executives I interviewed widely viewed Gigante as overextended from excessively rapid growth, and potentially ripe for takeover. As José Luis Álvarez has pointed out, Wal-Mart would gain little from acquiring Gigante, since their stores occupy similar regional footprints, but Soriana could potentially gain much (Álvarez 2005c).

Another wild card in Mexico is Texas-based grocer HEB. While a late entrant (1997) compared to others, and a slow store builder (currently with twenty-one Mexican stores), HEB has attracted a loyal following in the north—as it has in Texas—by combining EDLP with attractive store formats and high-quality meats and produce, and in the last year has begun a push into other regions of the country. Finally, the Chedraui chain, based in the southeast of Mexico, which has generally been discounted as a major competitor, made an unexpected bid for growth in 2005 by purchasing French retail Carrefour's thirty-one Mexican stores. The resulting total of ninety-five stores positions it close behind Soriana, and Grupo Financiero Imbursa, the holding company of Carlos Slim, Mexico's richest man, financed the sale (Castro 2005).

A second dimension of strategy, beyond this set of general plans of attack, is the prospect for expansion into geographic areas not currently served by any of the major self-service stores. Comparison with Wal-Mart in the United States is instructive. In the United States, the next major frontier for Wal-Mart is older, larger cities, particularly in the Northeast and Great Lakes regions. In its attempts to open stores in New York, Chicago, and Los Angeles, Wal-Mart has encountered political resistance, limited land availability, and entrenched competitors. One solution has been to expand use of the Neighborhood Market format, which has a smaller footprint.

In Mexico, Wal-Mart, along with its competitors, has filtered from the largest cities to smaller regional centers. Walmex "has told investors that it would like eventually to have a presence in each of approximately 180 towns with more than 50,000 residents in which it does not yet operate," according to *DSN Retailing Today* (Braine 2004). Forty percent of Walmex's grocery stores are still located in Mexico City and neighboring Mexico state, densely populated areas containing only 22 percent of the country's population in 2000 (Wal-Mart de México 2005; Álvarez 2005b). A significant challenge faces Walmex (and, for that matter, any of the large self-service retailers) in the quest to serve smaller cities, especially ones with lower-income populations. Wal-Mart reaps economies of scale from both the size of the entire system and the size of individual stores. Further expansion will heighten system-wide scale economies, but less dense and less affluent areas are less capable of supporting Wal-Mart's standard-issue superstores. In response, Walmex has begun to roll out smaller Mi Bodega stores (*Latin America News Digest* 2004; Braine 2004).

But the shift to smaller-format stores pits Walmex directly against a powerful competitor, FEMSA, the huge business group that produces Tecate beer, distributes Coca-Cola products in Mexico, and operates almost 3,500 OXXO convenience stores. About a year before Walmex started sizing stores down, FEMSA began sizing them up, launching the Bara (short for *barato*, meaning "inexpensive") chain of no-frills supermarkets. FEMSA guards operating details closely, but the sizzling pace at which it has added OXXO stores in the past suggests that it could ramp up the Bara chain rapidly. FEMSA's extensive retail experience, deep pockets, and political connections render it a formidable rival.

Mexican Public Policy and Walmex

Setting the context for all of these strategic moves and countermoves is a set of public policies. One potentially important change would be the extension of Mexico's value-added tax (VAT) to foods, a reform long sought by the Fox administration to broaden the nation's tax base. A broader VAT would doubtless be met with widespread evasion. When I asked the proprietor of several small clothing stores (clothing is already covered by the VAT) for a sales figure, he explained that the sales he reports to the government are only half of his actual sales, and added, "There's not a single business in Mexico that operates paying taxes according to what the law says." However, given its high profile, Wal-Mart is poorly positioned to avoid taxes. According to the McKinsey Global Institute, in Brazil the presence of a broad VAT, which domestic retailers can avoid but Wal-Mart cannot, constitutes a key competitive disadvantage for Wal-Mart (McKinsey Global Institute 2003).

A second critically important policy arena is Mexican antitrust law. For all practical purposes, Mexico's Federal Competition Commission has applied a double standard, leaving Wal-Mart untouched while stalling the formation of the Sinergia purchasing consortium for months, despite the fact that Sinergia is smaller than Walmex (Mireles 2005). Mexican business associations have increasingly clamored for what some press accounts have called "anti-Wal-Mart laws." The head of the national confederation of retail and service chambers of commerce, for example, recently spoke of "the need for both federal and state legislation to regulate the penetration of this business in the Mexican economy" (Maldonado 2005). The Fox government remains officially committed to the free trade policies of its predecessors, but Fox or the next president (to be elected in 2006) may well bow to populist pressures and alter the rules of the game to the Blue Giant's disadvantage.

Another important policy consideration is the extent to which the Mexican government will reduce its support and tolerance of more informal retail channels. Mexico's state governments organized expansion of the *tianguis* street markets beginning in the 1980s, through programs such as the state of Michoacán's "Combating the High Cost of Living," aimed at job creation and reduction of food prices (Government of the State of Michoacán 2004). Virtually all levels of government have placed little emphasis on enforcing laws (tax, licensure, even copyright and brand protection) that might restrict the growth of informal commerce—such enforcement would block a critical employment safety valve as well as cutting off consumer access to inexpensive goods. Indeed, cases when government *has* taken action against informal commerce (as when Mexico City mayor and 2006 presidential hopeful Andrés Manuel López Obrador cleared street vendors out of the capital city's historic center) are noteworthy precisely because they are exceptional. Nonetheless, ANTAD, the powerful national retailers' federation, is lobbying hard for government action against the informal fringe. The slogan of the federation's 2004 conference, at which President Vicente Fox gave the keynote address, was "Legal commerce—building Mexico!" Large retail chains have already rolled out their own economic strategy against the informal sector, providing vouchers usable only at a specific retail company (called *vales de despensa*) to their own employees, and promoting them as a benefit to be offered by other large employers.

A final policy question mark is the exchange rate. Many analysts, such as economist Enrique Dussel, argue that the peso is significantly overvalued, making eventual devaluation inevitable (Dussel 2004). A substantial devaluation would decrease overall consumer purchasing power and diminish the price advantage of import-intensive retailers, both potentially slowing Walmex's expansion. (As with the 1994 devaluation, it would also have the countervailing effect of reducing dollar-denominated purchase prices of Mexican companies and land to U.S.-based Wal-Mart.)

Ultimately, Mexico's future pattern of development will fix the limits of Walmex's growth. If, as seems likely, Mexico's economy continues to polarize incomes and impoverish a growing proportion of the population, Wal-Mart's strategy targeting sales to a broad working and middle class will hit natural limits. At the same time, sluggish employment growth will drive more job seekers into informal retail and make cracking down on informal vendors politically unpalatable, boosting Wal-Mart's low-end competitors in the informal sector. Ironically, Wal-Mart's competitive strategies (which are also those of its imitators) themselves contribute to the economic conditions that may ultimately undermine the company. Decreasing retail staffing via technological efficiencies, offering low wages, pressing for cost reductions to the point of crippling some suppliers, and sourcing from abroad all feed a cycle of slow growth and unequal incomes.

Mexico's economic trajectory is a matter not simply of luck but also of public policy—in this case, macroeconomic policy much broader in scope than the specific laws affecting the retail industry. And herein lies another irony. The neoliberal, free-trade approach pursued steadily by Mexican presidents beginning with Carlos Salinas (1988–94) opened the door to Wal-Mart, removing restrictions on foreign ownership of Mexican businesses and allowing importation of the low-priced goods that fuel Wal-Mart's everyday low prices. But over the long haul, neoliberal policies have not brought Mexico sustained growth or broadly shared prosperity—and the resulting economic stagnation threatens Wal-Mart's prospects for growth.

Overall, Wal-Mart appears likely to continue to occupy the dominant position in Mexico's competitive terrain for the foreseeable future. No other retailer in the country has a strategy that appears adequate to match Wal-Mart's scale or geographic scope within the short or middle term. Mergers of two or more major rivals, or years of rapid growth by a smaller challenger, could create a contender of similar weight, but what seems more likely is that competitors will carve out niches among particular customer segments—in the north, in smaller cities, among richer or poorer customers. A dramatic policy turn—not to be ruled out in Mexico, where exuberant populism and pervasive corporate influence are both entrenched elements of the political landscape—could tip the scales toward or away from Wal-Mart's retail model. But again, the factor most likely to box Wal-Mart in is neither corporate strategy nor specific public policies regulating the retail sector. It is the unhealthy trend in Mexico's economy—a trend to which Wal-Mart and its business model have themselves contributed significantly.

Acknowledgment

I thank the Rockefeller Foundation, the Fulbright–Garcia Robles Fellowship Program, and the University of Massachusetts, Lowell, for financial support. José Luis Álvarez, Patricia Jiménez de Greiff, and Beth O'Donnell provided outstanding research assistance.

Notes

1. No publicly available data shows which companies are unionized. However, I reviewed union contracts on file with the local labor relations commissions in Mexico City and León. I also conducted interviews at eleven Mexican supermarket and department store chains (along with dozens of smaller retailers). Based on these sources of information, I conclude that virtually all chains are unionized, including Walmex, which is represented in the union contracts in all three cities.
2. A research assistant and I conducted thirty-eight short interviews with consumers about where they like to shop for food and clothing, supplemented by field observation of a variety of retail settings. The interviews were conducted in 2003–2004 in seven Mexican states and the Federal District (the capital region that includes Mexico City).

Bibliography

Chapter 1

Allen, Michael (1986) *Anglia, Prefect, Popular: From Ford Eight to 105E*. Croydon: Motor Racing Publications.

Blouet, Brian W. (1987) *Halford Mackinder: A Biography*. College Station: Texas A&M University Press.

———, ed. (2005) *Global Geostrategy: Mackinder and the Defence of the West*. London: Frank Cass.

Chaudhuri, K. N. (1978) *The Trading World of Asia and the English East India Company 1660-1760*. Cambridge: Cambridge University Press.

Dymock, Eric (1999) *The Vauxhall File: All Models since 1903*. Sutton Veny, Wiltshire: Dove.

Furber, Holden (1976) *Rival Empires of Trade in the Orient, 1600-1800*. Minneapolis: University of Minnesota Press.

Hayes, Tracey (2004) "Karl Haushofer and His Impact on the German-Japanese Alliance." M.S. thesis, Department of Geography, Texas A&M University.

Hays, Constance (2004) "International Business: From Bentonville to Beijing and Beyond." *New York Times*, December 6.

Hugill, Peter J. (1988) "Technology Diffusion in the World Automobile Industry, 1885-1985." Pp. 110-42 in Peter Hugill and Bruce Dickson, eds., *The Transfer and Transformation of Ideas and Material Culture*. College Station: Texas A&M University.

——— (1993) *World Trade since 1431: Geography, Technology, and Capitalism*. Baltimore: Johns Hopkins University Press.

——— (2005) "Trading States, Territorial States, and Technology: Mackinder's Contribution to the Discourse on States and Polities." Pp. 107-24 in B. W. Blouet, ed., *Halford Mackinder: A Biography*. College Station: Texas A&M University Press.

Hugill, Peter J., and D. Bruce Dickson, eds. (1988) *The Transfer and Transformation of Ideas and Material Culture*. College Station: Texas A&M University Press.

Irwin, John (1955) "Indian Textile Trade in the Seventeenth Century. (1) Western India." *Journal of Indian Textile History* 1; 4-30.

——— (1956) "Indian Textile Trade in the Seventeenth Century. (2) Coromandel Coast." *Journal of Indian Textile History* 2: 24-42.

——— (1957) "Indian Textile Trade in the Seventeenth Century. (3) Bengal." *Journal of Indian Textile History* 3: 58-74.

Kagan, Robert (2003) *Of Paradise and Power: America and Europe in the New World Order*. New York: Knopf.

Kristol, William, and Robert Kagan (1996) "Toward a neo-Reaganite Foreign Policy." *Foreign Affairs* 75, 4: 18-32.

Kupchan, Charles A. (2003) *The End of the American Era: U.S. Foreign Policy and the Geopolitics of the Twenty-First Century*. New York: Knopf.

Mackinder, Halford J. (1902) *Britain and the British Seas*. London: Heinemann.

——— (1904) "The Geographical Pivot of History." *The Geographical Journal* 23: 421-44.

——— (1919) *Democratic Ideas and Reality: A Study in the Politics of Reconstruction*. Reprint: New York: Henry Holt, 1942.

Maddison, Angus (1995) *Monitoring the World Economy 1820-1992*. Paris: OECD.

——— (2001) *The World Economy: A Millennial Perspective*. Paris: OECD.

——— (2003) *The World Economy: Historical Statistics*. Paris: OECD.

Nichols, John P. (1973) *Skyline Queen and Merchant Prince: The Woolworth Story*. New York: Trident.

Norbye, Jan P. (1992) *Opel Astra*. Milano: Automobilia.

Olive, David (2004) "Hitting the Wall." *Toronto Star*, August 29, 2004.

Philips, Cyril H. (1961) *The East India Company, 1784-1834*. Second Edition. Manchester: Manchester University Press.

Sloan, Alfred P., Jr. (1964) *My Years With General Motors*. Garden City, NY: Doubleday.
Spykman, Nicholas (1942) *America's Strategy in World Politics: The United States and the Balance of Power*. New York: Harcourt Brace.
Sutherland, Lucy S. (1952) *The East India Company in Eighteenth Century Politics*. Oxford: Clarendon Press.
Talton, Jon (2004) "We're to Blame for Wal-Mart's Grip." *The Arizona Republic*, November 18, 2004.
Taylor, Peter J., and Colin Flint (2000) *Political Geography: World-Economy, Nation-State and Locality*, 4th ed. Englewood Cliffs, NJ: Prentice Hall.
Whittlesey, Derwent (1943) "Haushofer: The Geopolitician." Pp. 388–411 in Edward Meade Earle, ed., *Makers of Modern Strategy. Military Thought from Machiavelli to Hitler*. Princeton: Princeton University Press.
Wilkins, Mira, and Frank Ernest Hill (1964) *American Business Abroad: Ford on Six Continents*. Detroit: Wayne State University Press.
Winkler, John K. (1940) *Five and Ten: The Fabulous Life of F. W. Woolworth*. New York: Robert McBride.
Woolworth, F. W. and Co. (1954) *Woolworth's First 75 Years: The Story of Everybody's Store*. New York: Woolworth.

Chapter 2

Anonymous (2004) "Taking on Sprawl-Mart." *Multinational Monitor*, 30–34.
Barnes, N. G., A. Connell, L. Hermenegildo, and L. Mattson (1996) "Regional Differences in the Economic Impact of Wal-Mart." *Business Horizons* 39, 4: 21–25.
Basker, E. (2005) "Job Creation or Destruction? Labor Market Effects of Wal-Mart Expansion." *The Review of Economics and Statistics* 87, 1: 174–83.
Beaver, W. (2005) "Battling Wal-Mart: How Communities Can Respond." *Business and Society Review* 110 (2): 159–69.
Christaller, W. (1966) *Central Places in Southern Germany*. Trans. C. W. Baskin. Englewood Cliffs, NJ: Prentice-Hall.
Edwards, Thomas (2001) "Corporate Nations: The Emergence of New Sovereignties." In L. Leinbach and S. Brunn, eds., *World of E-Commerce*. New York: Wiley.
Flint, Robert (2004) "How Wal-Mart Treads Heavily In Foreign-Exchange Forest." *Wall Street Journal*, November 17.
Gerhard, U., and B. Hahn. 2005. "Wal-Mart and Aldi: Two Retail Giants in Germany." *GeoJournal* 62: 15–26.
Graff, T. (1998) "The Locations of Wal-Mart and Kmart Supercenters: Contrasting Corporate Strategies." *Professional Geographer* 50, 1: 46–57.
Graff, T., and D. Ashton (1994) "Spatial Diffusion of Wal-Mart: Contagious and Reverse Hierarchical Elements." *Professional Geographer* 46, 1: 19–29.
Gunyon, Janet (2005) "Fortune Global 500." *Fortune*, July 25, 97–102.
Hjelt, Paola (2002) "Fortune Global 500." *Fortune*, July 22, 144–47.
Holmes, Thomas (2005) "The Diffusion of Wal-Mart and Economies of Density." Federal Reserve Bank of Minneapolis and National Bureau of Economic Research, July. Available at www.nber.org/~confer/2005/si2005/io/holmes.pdf.
International Monetary Fund (2005) *World Economic Outlook Database*. Available at www.imf.org/external/pubs/ft/weo/2005/02/index.htm, accessed September 27, 2005.
Kroll, Luisa, and Lea Goldman (2005) "The World's Billionaires." *Forbes*, March 10.
Lösch, A. (1954) *The Economics of Location*. Trans W. H. Woglom. New Haven: Yale University Press.
——— (1975) "The Nature of Economic Regions." In John Friedmann and William Alonso, eds., *Regional Policy: Readings in Theory and Applications*. Cambridge, MA: MIT Press.
Peterson, M., and J. E. McGee (2000) "Survivors of 'W-day': An Assessment of the Impact of Wal-Mart's Invasion of Small Town Retailing Communities." *International Journal of Retail and Distribution Management* 28, 4/5: 170–80.
Reuters (2005) "Wal-Mart Stores Inc.: Company Description." Available at www.investor.reuters.com/business/BusCompanyFullDesc.aspx?ticker=WMT.N&target=%2fbusiness%2fbuscompany%2fbuscompfake%2fbuscompdescr, accessed September 29, 2005.
Stone, K. (1995) "Impact of Wal-Mart Stores on Iowa Communities: 1983–93." *Economic Development Review*, spring: 60–69.
Wal-Mart (2005a) "Wal-Mart Stores, Inc. at a Glance." Available at www.walmartstores.com/wmstore/wmstores/HomePage.jsp, accessed September 27, 2005.
——— (2005b) "Annual Report." Available at http://library.corporate-ir.net/library/11/112/112761/items/146737/Wal-Mart_final.pdf, accessed September 27, 2005.

Chapter 3

Aggarwal, R. (2001) "Viewpoint: Value-Added Annual Shareholders Meetings: Reflections on People's Capitalism at Wal-Mart." *Journal of Retailing and Consumer Services* 8: 347–49.

Arnold, S. J. (1998) "Why Is Wal-Mart the World's Largest Retailer, and Can the Reasons for Its Success Be Applied in Europe?" Pp. 29–40 in Enrique Ortega Martinez, Ladislao González Ruiz, and Enrique Pérez del Campo, eds., *Forum International Sobre, Las Ciencias, Las Técnicas y el Arte Aplicadas al Marketing, Academia y Profesión, Ponencias Academicas.* Sección de Comercialización e Investigación de Mercados, Facultad de CC.EE. Universiada Complutense de Madrid.

Arnold, S. J., and J. Fernie (1999) "Wal-Mart into the UK." *Journal of Enterprising Culture* 7: 407–16.

——— (2000) "Wal-Mart in Europe: Prospects for the UK." *International Marketing Review* 17: 416–32.

Arnold, S. J., J. Handelman, and D. J. Tigert (1998) "The Impact of a Market Spoiler on Consumer Preference Structures (or, What Happens When Wal-Mart Comes to Town)." *Journal of Retailing and Consumer Services* 5: 1–13.

Arnold, S. J., R. V. Kozinets, and J. M. Handelman (2001) "Hometown Ideology and Retailer Legitimation: The Institutional Semiotics of Wal-Mart Flyers." *Journal of Retailing* 77: 243–71.

Arnold, S. J., and M. N. Luthra (2000), "Market Entry Effects of Large Format Retailers: A Stakeholder Analysis." *International Journal of Retail and Distribution Management* 28: 139–54.

Au-Yeung, A. Y. S. (2003) "International Transfer of Retail Know-How through Foreign Direct Investment from Europe to China." Pp. 136–54 in J. A. Dawson, M. Mukoyama, S. C. Choi, and R. Larke, eds., *The Internationalization of Retailing in Asia.* London: Routledge Curzon.

Barnes, N. G., A. Connell, L. Hermenengildo, and L. Mattson (1996) "Regional Differences in the Impact of Wal-Mart." *Business Horizons* 39: 21–26.

Basker, E. (2005) "Job Creation or Destruction? Labor-Market Effects of Wal-Mart Expansion." *Review of Economics and Statistics* 87.

Benoit, W. L., and B. Davies (1996) "*Dateline NBC*'s Persuasive Attack on Wal-Mart." *Communication Quarterly* 44: 463–77.

Berggoetz, R., and M. Laue (2004) "Wal-Mart's Entry into the German Market: An Intercultural Perspective." Pp. 265–69 in J. Reynolds and C. Cuthbertson, eds., *Retail Strategy: View from the Bridge.* Oxford: Elsevier Butterworth-Heinemann.

Bloom, P. N., and V. G. Perry (2001) "Retailer Power and Supplier Welfare: The Case of Wal-Mart." *Journal of Retailing* 77: 379–96.

Boudreaux, D. (1996) "Predatory Pricing in the Retail Trade: The Wal-Mart Case." Chapter 10 in M. B. Coate and A. N. Kleit, eds., *The Economics of the Anti-Trust Process.* Topics in Regulatory Economics and Policy, 22. Boston: Kluwer.

Boyd, D. (1997) "From 'Mom and Pop' to Wal-Mart: The Impact of the Consumer Goods Pricing Act of 1975 on the Retail Sector in the United States." *Journal of Economic Issues* 31: 223–32.

Brennan, D. P., and L. Lundsten (2000) "Impact of Large Discount Stores on Small US Towns." *International Journal of Retail and Distribution Management* 28: 155–61.

Burt, S. L., and L. Sparks (2001) "The Implications of Wal-Mart's Takeover of ASDA." *Environment and Planning A* 33: 1463–87.

——— (2003) "Power and Competition in the UK Retail Grocery Market." *British Journal of Management* 14: 237–54.

Choi, S. C. (2003) "Moves into the Korean Market by Global Retailers and the Response of Local Retailers: Lessons for the Japanese Retailing Sector?" Pp. 49–66 in J. A. Dawson, M. Mukoyama, S. C. Choi, and R. Larke, eds., *The Internationalization of Retailing in Asia.* London: Routledge Curzon.

Christopherson, S. (2001) "Can Walmartization Be Stopped? Barriers to the Globalization of Retailing" Department of TK, Clark University. Available at www.clarku.edu/leir/christopherson.htm, accessed December 21, 2004.

Christopherson, S., and Lillie, N. (2005) "Neither Global nor Standard: Corporate Strategies in the New Era of Labor Standards." *Environment and Planning A* 37: 1919–38.

Coe, N. M. (2004) "The Internationalization/Globalization of Retailing: Towards an Economic-Geographic Research Agenda." *Environment and Planning A* 36: 1571–94.

Colla, E., and M. Dupuis (2002) "Research and Managerial Issues on Global Retail Competition: Carrefour/Wal-Mart." *International Journal of Retail and Distribution Management* 30: 103–111.

Currah, A., and N. Wrigley (2004) "Networks of Organizational Learning and Adaptation in Retail TNCs." *Global Networks* 4: 1–23.

da Rocha, A., and L. A. Dib (2002) "The Entry of Wal-Mart in Brazil and the Competitive Responses of Multinational and Domestic Firms." *International Journal of Retail and Distribution Management* 30: 61–73.

Davidson, S. M., and A. Rummel (2000) "Retail Changes Associated with Wal-Mart's Entry into Maine." *International Journal of Retail and Distribution Management* 28: 162–69.

Dawson, J. A. (1994) "Internationalization of Retail Operations." *Journal of Marketing Management* 10: 267–82.

——— (2003) "Towards a Model of the Impacts of Retail Internationalization." Pp. 189–209 in J. A. Dawson, M. Mukoyama, S. C. Choi, and R. Larke, eds., *The Internationalization of Retailing in Asia.* London: Routledge Curzon.

Deloitte Research (2003) *Retail Tsunami? Wal-Mart Comes to Japan.* Available at www.de.com/research, accessed January 3, TK.

DSN Retailing Today (2004) "Wal-Mart International." Special Report. *DSN Retailing Today* 43, 23: 20–79.

Dube, A., and K. Jacobs (2004) "Hidden Costs of Wal-Mart Jobs." University of California, Berkeley, Labor Center Briefing Paper, August.

Dunnett, A. J., and S. J. Arnold (1999) "Falling Prices, Rising Morale: The Impact of Organisational Culture on Customer Satisfaction at Wal-Mart." Paper presented at Academy of Marketing Doctoral Colloquium, Stirling, July.

Evans, W., and P. Barbiero (1999) "Foreign Retailers in Canada." CSCA Research Report 1999-11. Toronto: Ryerson Polytechnic University.

Featherstone, L. (2004) *Selling Women Short: The Landmark Battle for Workers' Rights at Wal-Mart.* New York: Basic Books.

Fernie, J., and S. J. Arnold (2002) "Wal-Mart in Europe: Prospects for Germany, the UK and France." *International Journal of Retail and Distribution Management* 30: 92–102.

Fox, M. A. (2005) "Market Power in Music Retailing: The Case of Wal-Mart." *Popular Music and Society* 28: 501–19.

Franklin, A. W. (2001) "The Impact of Wal-Mart Supercenters on Supermarket Concentration in US Metropolitan Area." *Agribusiness* 17: 105–14.

Goetz, S. J., and H. Swaminathan (2004) "Wal-Mart and County Wide Poverty." AERS Staff Paper 371, Pennsylvania State University, October 18. Available at http://cecd.aers.psu.edu/pubs/PovertyResearchWM.pdf.

Graff, T. O. (1998) "The Locations of Wal-Mart and K-Mart Supercenters: Contrasting Corporate Strategies." *Professional Geographer* 150: 46–57.

Graff, T. O., and D. Ashton (1993) "Spatial Diffusion of Wal-Mart: Contagious and Reverse Diffusion Elements." *Professional Geographer* 46: 19–29.

Halebsky, S. (2004) "Superstores and the Politics of Retail Development." *City & Community* 3: 115–34.

Hallsworth, A. (1999) "Waiting for Wal-Mart?" *Environment and Planning A* 31: 1331–36.

Hallsworth, A., and L. Clarke (2001) "Further Reflections on the Arrival of Wal-Mart in the United Kingdom." *Environment and Planning A* 33: 1709–16.

Hallsworth, A., and D. Evers (2002) "The Steady Advance of Wal-Mart across Europe and Changing Government Attitudes towards Planning and Competition." *Environment and Planning C* 20: 297–309.

Han, D., I.-W. G. Kwon, M. Bae, and H. Sung (2002) "Supply Chain Integration in Developing Countries for Foreign Retailers in Korea: Wal-Mart Experience." *Computers & Industrial Engineering* 43: 111–21.

Jinglun Han (2003) "The Reform of the Distribution System in China: Opening the System to the Outside World." Pp. 155–68 in J. A. Dawson, M. Mukoyama, S. C. Choi, and R. Larke, eds., *The Internationalization of Retailing in Asia.* London: Routledge Curzon.

Hawker, N. (1996) "Wal-Mart and the Divergence of State and Predatory Pricing Law." *Journal of Public Policy and Marketing* 15, 141–47.

Hemphill, T. A. (2005) "Rejuvenating Wal-Mart's reputation." *Business Horizons* 48: 11–21.

Hicks, M. J., and K. L. Wilburn (2001) "The Regional Impact of Wal-Mart Entrance: A Panel Study of the Retail Trade Sector in West Virginia." *Review of Regional Studies* 31: 305–13.

Huffman, T. P. (2003) "Wal-Mart in China: Challenges Facing a Foreign Retailer's Supply Chain." *China Business Review,* September–October, 18–22.

IGD (Institute of Grocery Distribution) (2004) *Wal-Mart: Delivering Global Growth.* Watford: Institute of Grocery Distribution.

——— (2003) *The Wal-Mart Report.* Watford: Institute of Grocery Distribution.

Jacques, P., R. Thomas, D. Foster, J. McCann, and M. Tunno (2003) "Wal-Mart or World-Mart? A Teaching Case Study." *Review of Radical Political Economics* 35: 513–33.

Khanna, N., and S. Tice (2000) "Strategic Responses of Incumbents to New Entry: The Effect of Ownership Structure, Capital Structure and Focus." *Review of Financial Studies* 13: 749–79.

Knorr, A., and A. Arndt (2003) "Why Did Wal-Mart Fail in Germany?" Institute for World Economics and International Management Working Paper 24, Universitat Bremen. Available at www.iwim.uni-bremen.de/publikationen/pdf/w024.pdf.

Kotabe, M., K. G. de Godoy, and M. Salzstein (1997) "Wal-Mart Operations in Brazil." Available at www.wiley.com/college/kotabe/walmart.html, accessed January 5, 2005.

M&M Planet Retail (2004) "Where Next for Wal-Mart." *M&M Planet Retail Global Retail Bulletin* 130: 16–18.

Mattera, P., and A. Purinton. (2004) *Shopping for Subsidies: How Wal-Mart Uses Taxpayer Money to Finance Its Never-Ending Growth.* Washington: Good Jobs First.

McCune, J. (1994) "In the shadow of Wal-Mart." *Management Review* 83: 10–16.

McGee, J. E. (1996) "When Wal-Mart Comes to Town: A Look at How Local Merchants Respond to the Retailing Giant's Arrival." *Journal of Business and Entrepreneurship* 8: 43–52.

McKinsey and Co. (2002) "The Wal-Mart Effect." *McKinsey Quarterly* 1. Available at www.mckinseyquarterly.com, accessed January 10, 2005.

Norman, A. (1999) *Slam-Dunking Wal-Mart.* New York: Raphel Marketing.

——— (2004) *The Case Against Wal-Mart.* New York: Raphel Marketing.

O'Higgins, E. R. E., and J. R. Weigel (2002) "Has Sam's Magic Passed Its Sell-By Date?" *Business Strategy Review* 13, 3: 52–61.

Ortega, B. (1998) *In Sam We Trust: The Untold Story of Sam Walton and How Wal-Mart is Devouring America.* New York: Random House.

——— (1999) "Organizing Wal-Mart: An Anti-Union Company Beats Labor." *WorkingUSA* 2, 5: 41–53.

Peterson, M., and J. E. McGee (2000) "Survivors of 'W-day': An Assessment of the Impact of Wal-Mart's Invasion of Small Town Retailing Communities." *International Journal of Retail and Distribution Management* 28: 170–80.

Porter, D., and C. L. Mirsk (2002) *Megamall on the Hudson: Planning, Wal-Mart and Grassroots Resistance.* Victoria, Canada: Trafford Publishing.

Quinn, B. (1996) *How Wal-Mart Is Destroying America.* Berkeley: Ten Speed Press.

Schneider, M. J. (1998) "The Wal-Mart Annual Meeting: From Small-town America to a Global Corporate Culture." *Human Organization* 57: 292–99.

Seiders, K., and D. J. Tigert (2000) "The Impact of Supercenters on Traditional Food Retailers in Four Markets." *International Journal of Retail and Distribution Management* 28: 181–93.

Simmons, J. (2001) "The Economic Impact of Wal-Mart stores." CSCA Research Report 2001-12, Ryerson Polytechnic University, Toronto.

Simmons, J., and T. O. Graff (1998) "Wal-Mart Comes to Canada." CSCA Research Report 1998-9, Ryerson Polytechnic University, Toronto.

Slater, R. (2003) *The Wal-Mart Decade.* New York: Portfolio Books.

Stone, K. E. (1995) "Impact of Wal-Mart Stores and Other Mass Merchandisers in Iowa 1983–1993." *Economic Development Review* 13: 60–69.

Trimble, V. H. (1990) *Sam Walton: The Inside Story of America's Richest Man.* New York: Dutton.

Udell, G. G., and L. S. Pettijohn (1991) "A Retailer's View of Industrial Innovation: An Interview with David Glass, President and CEO of Wal-Mart Stores, Inc." *Journal of Product Innovation Management* 8: 231–39.

Upbin, B. (2004) "Wall-to-Wall Wal-Mart." *Forbes,* April 12. Available at http://www.forbes.com/free_forbes/2004/0412/076.html.

Vance, S. S., and R. V. Scott (1992) *Wal-Mart: History of Sam Walton's Retail Phenomenon.* New York: Twayne Publishers.

Vias, A. C. (2004) "Bigger Stores, More Stores or No Stores: Paths of Retail Restructuring in Rural America." *Journal of Rural Studies* 20: 303–18.

Walton, S. (1992) *Sam Walton: Made in America—My Story.* With J. Huey. New York: Bantam Books.

Wang, S. (2003) "Internationalization of Retailing in China." Pp. 114–35 in J. A. Dawson, M. Mukoyama, S. C. Choi, and R. Larke, eds., *The Internationalization of Retailing in Asia.* London: Routledge Curzon.

Whysall, P. (2002) "Wal-Mart's Takeover of Asda: What the Papers Said." *British Food Journal* 103: 729–43.

Wrigley, N. (2000) "The Globalization of Retail Capital: Themes for Economic Geography." Pp. 292–313 in G. L. Clark, M. P. Feldman, and M. S. Gertler, eds., *The Oxford Handbook of Economic Geography.* Oxford: Oxford University Press.

——— (2002) "Transforming the Corporate Landscape of US Food Retailing: Market Power, Financial Reengineering and Regulation." *Tijdschrift voor Economische en Sociale Geografie* 93: 62–82.

Wrigley, N., and Currah, A. (2003) "The Stresses of Retail Internationalization: Lessons from Royal Ahold's Experience in Latin America." *International Review of Retail, Distribution and Consumer Research* 13: 221–43.

Chapter 4

Bodenman, John (2000) "Firm Characteristics and Location: The Case of the Institutional Investment Advisory Industry in the United States, 1983–1996." *Papers in Regional Science* 79: 33–56.

Carlton, David, and Peter Coclanis (1989) "Capital Mobilization and Southern Industry, 1880–1905: The Case of the Carolina Piedmont." *Journal of Economic History* 49: 73–94.

Graff, Thomas O., and David Ashton (1993) "Spatial Diffusion of Wal-Mart: Contagious and Reverse Hierarchical Elements." *The Professional Geographer* 46: 19–29.

Graves, William (2002) "Corporate Command Status in the Nonmetropolitan South, 1990–2001." *Southeastern Geographer* 42: 302–10.

——— (2003) "Financing Flexibility in a Global Market: The Metropolitan Distribution of Equity Investment." *Urban Geography* 24: 611–35.

Green, Milford (1995) "A Geography of U.S. Institutional Investment." *Urban Geography* 16: 46–69.

Hartshorn, Truman A., and Susan M. Walcott (2000) "The Three Georgias: Emerging Realignments at the Dawn of the New Millennium." *Southeastern Geographer* 48: 127–50.

Johnson, Merril L. (1997) "To Restructure or Not to Restructure: Contemplations on Postwar Industrial Geography in the U.S. South." *Southeastern Geographer* 38, 162–92.

Lundegaard, Karen (1999) "Research Triangle Firm Faces Quandary of Its Age." *Wall Street Journal,* November 3.

Lyson, Thomas A. (1989) *Two Sides to the Sunbelt: The Growing Divergence between the Rural and Urban South.* New York: Oxford University Press.

Meyer, Judith, and Lawrence Brown (1979) "Diffusion Agency Establishment: The Case of Friendly Ice Cream and Public-Sector Diffusion Processes." *Socio-Economic Planning Sciences* 13: 241–49.

Thaler, Richard H. (1993) *Advances in Behavioral Finance.* New York: Russell Sage Foundation.

Vance, Sandra, and Roy Scott (1994) *Wal-Mart: A History of Sam Walton's Retail Phenomenon.* New York: Twayne.

——— (1992) "Sam Walton and Wal-Mart Stores, Inc.: A Study in Modern Southern Entrepreneurship." *The Journal of Southern History* 58: 231–52.

Walton, Sam (1992) *Sam Walton: Made in America.* New York: Doubleday.

Zook, Matt A. (2004) "The Knowledge Brokers: Venture Capitalists, Tacit Knowledge and Regional Development." *International Journal of Urban and Regional Research* 28: 621–41.

——— (2002) "Grounded Capital: Venture Financing and the Geography of the Internet Industry, 1994–2000." *Journal of Economic Geography* 2: 151–77.

Chapter 5

Albright, Mark (2003) "Super Marketing at Wal-Mart." *St. Petersburg Times,* October 19. Available at www.sptimes.com/2003/10/19/Tampabay/Super_marketing-at-wa.shtml, accessed November 27, 2004.

BEA (Bureau of Economic Analysis) (2004) *Regional Economic Accounts, CA1–3, Local Area Personal Income* (Washington: U.S. Department of Commerce). Available at www.bea.doc.gov/bea/regional/reis/scb.cfm, accessed November 17.

Franklin, Andrew W. (2001) "The Impact of Wal-Mart Supercenters on Supermarket Concentration in U.S. Metropolitan Areas." *Agribusiness* 17: 105–14.

Frontline (2004) "Is Wal-Mart Good for America? Secrets: Where in the World Is Wal-Mart?" PBS documenatry, October 16. Available at http://pbs.org/wgbh/pages/frontline/shows/walmart/secrets/where.html, accessed October 23, 2004.

Graff, Thomas O. (1998) "The Location of Wal-Mart and Kmart Superstores: Contrasting Corporate Strategies." *The Professional Geographer* 50: 46–57.

Graff, Thomas O., and Dub Ashton (1994) "Spatial Diffusion of Wal-Mart: Contagious and Reverse Hierarchical Elements." *The Professional Geographer* 46: 19–29.

Halkias, Maria (2004) "Wal-Mart Leads D-FW Grocery Sales." *Dallas Morning News,* February 5. Available at www.walmartaction1099.org/articles/2_5_04.pdf, accessed October 27, 2004.

Lilien, G. L., and P. Kotler (1983) *Marketing Decision Making: A Model-Building Approach.* New York: Harper and Row.

Lilien, G. L., and A. Rao (1976) "A Model for Allocating Retail Outlet Building Resources Across Market Areas." *Operations Research* 24: 1–14.

Mahajan, V., S. Sharma, and R. Kerin (1988) "Assessing Market Penetration Opportunities and Saturation Potential for Multi-Store, Multi-Market Retailers." *Journal of Retailing* 64: 315–33.

Trade Dimensions International, Inc. (2004a) *2005 Marketing Guidebook.* Wilton, CT: Trade Dimensions International.

—— (2004b) *Market Scope 2004: The Desktop Guide to Supermarket Share*. Wilton, CT: Trade Dimensions International.

U.S. Census Bureau (2003) *Statistical Abstract of the United States,* Washington, D.C.: U.S. Government Printing Office.

Wrigley, Neil (2002) "Transforming the Corporate Landscape of US Food Retailing: Market Power, Financial Re-engineering, and Regulation." *Tijdschrift voor Economische en Sociale Geografie* 93: 62–82.

Chapter 6

Bailey, Jim (2002) "Wal-Mart's Application for Liquor License Tabled Pending Legal Opinion." *Sawyer County Record,* March 27.

Bascom, Johnathan (2001) "'Energizing' Rural Space: The Representation of Countryside Culture as an Economic Development Strategy." *Journal of Cultural Geography* 19, 1: 53–73.

Beaumont, Constance E., and Leslie Tucker (2002) "Big-Box Sprawl (and How to Control It)." *Municipal Lawyer* 43, 2: 7–9, 30–31.

Benton, James E. (2002) "Wal-Mart's Not Totally to Blame." *Sawyer County Record,* November 7.

Boettcher, Terrell (2002) "Wal-Mart Super Center Opens Doors in Hayward." *Sawyer County Record*, February 26.

Broman, Andrew (2004a) "Wal-Mart Looks to Build Supercenter in Ashland." *The Daily Press*, September 23.

—— (2004b) "Proposal to Block Traffic Noise, Light from Wal-Mart Denied." *The Daily Press,* November 18.

—— (2004c) "Group Examines Wal-Mart's Practices." *The Daily Press*, December 2.

Civic Economics (2002) "Economic Impact Analysis: A Case Study: Local Merchants vs. Chain Retailers." Prepared by Civic Economics, December. Available at www.shopaustin.org/documents/Lamar_Retail_Analysis_December.pdf, accessed January 26, 2005.

Clute, Margaret (2001) "Wal-Mart Could Provide Opportunities." *Sawyer County Record*, February 6.

Dube, Arindrajit, and Ken Jacobs (2004) "Hidden Cost of Wal-Mart Jobs: Use of Safety Net Programs by Wal-Mart Workers in California." Briefing Paper Series, University of California, Berkeley, Labor Center.

ERS (2003) "Rural-Urban Continuum Codes." USDA-Economic Research Service. Available at www.ers.usda.gov/briefing/rurality/urbaninf, accessed August 22, 2004.

Forum (2004) Archived forums. Available at www.ashlandwi.com/dailypress/search.pdp, sponsored by AshlandWI.com, accessed January 12, 2005.

Friends of Wisconsin (2005) "Wal-Mart in Wisconsin." Available at www.1kfriends.org/benchmarks_project/infrastructure/Wal-Marts.htm, accessed January 15, 2005.

Fuguitt, Glenn V., and James J. Zuiches (1975) "Residential preferences and population distribution." *Demography* 12, 3: 491–504.

Furuseth, Owen (1992) "Countryside in Revolt: Rural Response to a Proposed Hazardous Waste Facility." Pp. 159–77 in A. W. Gilz, ed., *Restructuring the Countryside: Environmental Policy in Practice.* Avebury: Ashgate Publishing.

—— (1998) "Service Provision and Social Deprivation." Pp. 233–56 in Brian Ilbery, ed., *The Geography of Rural Change.* UK: Addison Wesley Longman. Reading, Mass.

Galston, William A., and Karen J. Baehler (1995) *Rural Development in the United States: Connecting Theory, Practice and Possibilities.* Washington, D.C.: Island Press.

Goss, Jon (1993) "The 'Magic of the Mall': An Analysis of Form, Function, and Meaning in the Contemporary Retail Built Environment." *Annals of the Association of American Geographers* 83, 1: 18–47.

Graff, Thomas O. (1998) "The Locations of Wal-Mart and Kmart Supercenters: Contrasting Corporate Strategies." *The Professional Geographer* 50, 1: 46–57.

Graff, Thomas O., and Dub Ashton (1994) "Spatial Diffusion of Wal-Mart: Contagious and Reverse Hierarchical Elements." *The Professional Geographer* 46, 1: 19–29.

Hagan, Jim (2001) "Wal-Mart in Hayward Is a Bad Idea." *Sawyer County Record,* February 6.

Halfacree, Keith (1993) "Locality and Social Representation: Space, Discourse and Alternative Definitions of the Rural." *Journal of Rural Studies* 9: 23–37.

Hanson, Hans (2003) "Business Trends across Northern Wisconsin." In *Let's Talk Business: Ideas for Expanding Retail Services in Your Community,* no. 86.

Hulsey, Brett, and Erin Burg (2005) "Protect Your Job and Community from Big Box Sprawl." Available at wisconsin.sierraclub.org, accessed January 15.

Ilbery, Brian (1998) "Dimensions of Rural Change." Pp. 1–10 in Brian Ilbery, ed., *The Geography of Rural Change.* UK: Addison Wesley Longman. Reading, Mass.

Jakle, John A. (1999) "America's Small Town/Big City Dialectic." *Journal of Cultural Geography* 18, 2: 1–27.

Johnson, Kenneth (1999) "The Rural Rebound." Reports on America. Population Reference Bureau, Washington, D.C.

Little, J., and P. Austin (1996) "Women and the Rural Idyll." *Journal of Rural Studies* 12: 101–11.

McCourt, Jeff, Doug Hoffer, Stephanie Greenwood, and Alyssa Talanker (2004) "Shopping for Subsidies: How Wal-Mart Uses Taxpayer Money to Finance Its Never Ending Growth." Good Jobs First, Washington, D.C., May.

McCune, Jenny C. (1994) "In the Shadow of Wal-Mart." *Management Review,* December, 10–16.

Miller, George (2004) "Everyday Low Wages: The Hidden Price We All Pay for Wal-Mart." Report by the Democratic staff of the Committee on Education and the Workforce, U.S. House of Representatives, Washington, D.C., February 16.

Mitchell, Clare J. A. (1998) "Entrepreneurialism, Commodification and Creative Destruction: A Model of Post-Modern Community Development." *Journal of Rural Studies* 14, 3: 273–86.

Mokhiber, Russell, and Robert Weissman (1998) "Wal-Mart and the Strip-Mining of America: Focus on the Corporation." *Multinational Monitor,* November 9. Available at www.rtmark.com/more/walmart.html, accessed January 14.

Morand, J. T. (2001a) "Business Community Concerned about Possible Wal-Mart Store." *Sawyer County Record,* January 30.

——— (2001b) "Wal-Mart Applies to Build Near Wetlands." *Sawyer County Record.* February 8.

——— (2001c) "Wal-Mart Closes on Hayward Property: Feelings Are Mixed about Chain 'Super Center.'" *Sawyer County Record,* June 5.

——— (2001d) "Developing Strategies Is Key to Competing against Wal-Mart: Retailers Could Face Negative Impact if They Don't." *Sawyer County Record,* October 2.

——— (2001e) "UW-Extension Offers Tips to Survive Wal-Mart in Hayward." *Sawyer County Record,* October 30.

——— (2001f) "What Will Wal-Mart Do to Hayward? A Tale of Two Cities with Big Discount Chain." *Sawyer County Record,* November 19.

——— (2001g) "Wal-Mart Reveals Plans for Hayward Store to Open in Spring 2002." *Sawyer County Record,* June 12.

Murdoch, Jonathan, and Terry Marsden (1994) *Reconstituting Rurality.* London: UCL Press.

Pedersen, Karla (2002) "Wal-Mart Supercenter Opens in Hayward." *Sawyer County Record,* February 22.

Peled, Micha X. (2001) *Store Wars: When Wal-Mart Comes to Town.* Bullfrog Films, Oley, Pennsylvania.

Rowles, Graham D., and John F. Watkins (1993) "Elderly Migration and Development in Small Communities." *Growth and Change* 24: 509–38.

Rudzitis, Gundars (1999) "Amenities Increasingly Draw People to the Rural West." *Rural Development Perspectives* 14, 2: 9–13.

Solomon, Alan (1997) "The Best Little Town in the Midwest: After 6 Weeks, 8,000 Miles and 139 Towns, This Is the Place." *Chicago Tribune,* August 3.

Speich, Steven (2001) "Wal-Mart Is Wal-Mart." *Sawyer County Record,* February 14.

Stockinger, Darlene (2001) "Glad to See Wal-Mart." *Sawyer County Record,* June 12.

Stone, Kenneth E. (1995) "Impact of Wal-Mart Stores on Iowa Communities: 1983–1993." *Economic Development Review,* spring, 60–69.

Tonts, Matthew, and Shane Greive (2002) "Commodification and Creative Destruction in the Australian Rural Landscape: The Case of Bridgetown, Western Australia." *Australian Geographical Studies* 40, 1: 58–70.

U.S. Census Bureau (1990) "Census Fact Finder." Available at www.census.gov, accessed February 20, 2005.

——— (2000a) "Census Fact Finder." Available at www.census.gov, accessed February 20, 2005.

——— (2000b) "Zip Code Business Patterns." U.S. Census Bureau, Washington, D.C.

Wal-Mart Stores 2006. Earnings and Dividends page, article entitled "Wal-Mart Reports Record Sales and Earnings for 4th Quarter 2006". http://walmartstores.com/GlobalWMStoresWeb/navigate.do?catg=561&contId=6057

——— (2005) "New Store Locator, 2004–2005." Available at www.walmartfacts.com/community, article. aspx?id=210 accessed January 25, 2005.

Wal-Mart Watch (2005) www.walmartwatch.com/locator, accessed January 25.

Wisconsin Sierra Club (2004) "Big Box Sprawl Costs Jobs and Threatens Communities with More Flooding, Traffic, Air, Water Pollution." Available at wisconsin.sierraclub.org, accessed January 10, 2005.

Zimmerman, Ann, and Laura Stevens (2005) "Attention, Shoppers: Bored College Kids Competing in Aisle 6." *Wall Street Journal,* February 23.

Chapter 7

Arnold, S. J., and E. Fischer (1994) "Hermeneutics and Consumer Research." *Journal of Consumer Research* 21, 1: 55–70.

Brown, A. (1995) *Organisational Culture.* London: Pitman Publishing.

Cialdini, R. B. (1993) *Influence: Science and Practice*, 3rd edition. New York: HarperCollins College Publishers.

Hamper, B. (1991) *Rivethead: Tales from the Assembly Line*. New York: Warner Books.

Meyer, J. P., and N. J. Allen (1997) *Commitment in the Workplace: Theory, Research, and Application*. Thousand Oaks, CA.: Sage Publications.

Miklas, S., with S. J. Arnold (1999) "The Extraordinary Self: Gothic Culture and the Construction of the Self." *Journal of Marketing Management* 15, 6: 563–76.

Robinson, S. L. (1995) "Violation of Psychological Contracts: Impact on Employee Attitudes." Pp. 91–108 in L. E. Tetrick and J. Barling, eds., *Changing Employment Relations: Behavioural and Social Perspectives*. Washington, D.C.: American Psychological Association.

Schein, E. H. (1990) "Organizational Culture." *American Psychologist* 45, 2: 109–19.

Schouten, J. W., and J. H. McAlexander (1995) "Subcultures of Consumption: An Ethnography of the New Bikers." *Journal of Consumer Research* 22, 1: 43–61.

Van Maanen, J., and S. R. Barley (1985) "Cultural Organisation: Fragments of a Theory." Pp. 31–53 in P. J. Frost et al., eds., *Organisational Culture*. Beverly Hills, Calif.: Sage Publications.

Wal-Mart (2004). www.walmartfacts.com/newsdesk/Wal-Mart-fact-sheets.aspx#a125, accessed January 17, 2005.

Walton, S., with J. Huey (1992) *Sam Walton: Made in America*. New York: Bantam Books.

Workman, J. P., Jr. (1993) "Marketing's Limited Role in New Product Development in One Computer Systems Firm." *Journal of Marketing Research* 30, 4: 405–21.

Chapter 8

Bendick, Marc, Jr. (2003) "The Representation of Women in Store Management at Wal-Mart Stores, Inc." January.

Bernhardt, Annette, and Laura Dresser (2002) "Why Privatizing Government Services Would Hurt Women Workers." Institute for Women's Policy Research, April.

Bielby, William T. (2003) "Expert Report of William T. Bielby," *Betty Dukes et. al. v. Wal-Mart Stores, Inc.*, February.

Democratic Staff of the Committee on Education and the Workforce (2004). Report, February 16.

Drogin, Richard (2003) "Statistical Analysis of Gender Patterns in Wal-Mart Workforce." February.

Ehrenreich, Barbara (2001) *Nickle and Dimed*. New York: Henry Holt.

Greenhouse, Stephen (2002) "Suits Say Wal-Mart Forces Workers to Toil of the Clock." *New York Times,* June 25.

Kim, Marlene (2000) "Women Paid Low Wages: Who They Are and Where They Work." *Monthly Labor Review* 123: 9.

Lovell, Vicky, Xue Song, and April Shaw (2002) "The Benefits of Unionization for Workers in the Retail Food Industry." Institute for Women's Policy Research.

McCall, William (2002) "Jury Rules Wal-Mart Didn't Pay OT." Associated Press, December 20.

McKinsey and Co. (2002) The Report found that between 1995 and 1999, led by Wal-Mart, the productivity growth of America's retail industry was the highest of any U.S. industry during that time.

National Labor Committee for Worker and Human Rights (2003) "Wal-Mart's Toys of Misery." Available at www. nlcnet.org/campaigns/china, accessed May 15.

Ortega, Bob (1998) *In Sam We Trust: The Untold Story of Sam Walton and How Wal-Mart Is Devouring America.* New York. Random House.

Walton, Sam, with John Huey (1992) *Made in America*. New York: Bantam.

Xinhua News Agency (2003) "Wal-Mart Boosts Win-Win Cooperation with China's Manufacturers." February 2.

Chapter 9

Adamy, Janet (2003) "Wal-Mart's Benefits Come under Fire." *Contra Costa Times*, October 19.

Aglietta, Michel (1979) *A Theory of Capitalist Regulation: The U.S. Experience*. London: New Left Books.

Arndorfer, James B. (2003) "Unions Put Squeeze on Wal-Mart." *Crain's Chicago Business*, July 7.

Associated Press (2005) "Breakaway Unions Set to Go After Wal-Mart." *Los Angeles Times*, September 28.

Bair, Jennifer, and Gary Gereffi (2001) "Local Clusters in Global Chains: The Causes and Consequences of Export Dynamism in Torreón's Blue Jeans Industry." *World Development* 29, 11: 1885–903.

Barboza, David (2004) "Chinese Union Gives Labor a Little Victory." *New York Times*, November 25.

Bernstein, Aaron (2005) "A Stepped Up Assault on Wal-Mart." *Business Week*, October 20.

Bernstein, Sam (2005) "Against the Wal-Martization of America: Lessons for the Labor Movement from the ILWU and UFCW in California." *Yale Journal of Sociology*, fall.

Bhushan, Ratna (2005) "Wal-Mart to Step Up Sourcing from India." *Times of India Mumbai*, September 27.

BLS (Bureau of Labor Statistics) (2004) *Occupational Outlook Handbook 2004–2005 Edition*. Available at www.bls. gov/oco/home.htm.

Bonacich, Edna, with Khaleelah Hardie (2005) "Wal-Mart and the Logistics Revolution." In Nelson Lichtenstein, ed., *Wal-Mart: Template for 21st Century Capitalism?* New York: New Press.

Borda, Deborah (2003) "What Wal-Mart Women Want." *Ms. Magazine*, fall.

Callahan, Patricia, and Ann Zimmerman (2003) "Wal-Mart, After Remaking Discount Retailing, Now Nation's Largest Grocery Chain." *Wall Street Journal*, May 31.

Candaele, Kelly, and Peter Dreier (2003) "A Watershed Strike." *The Nation*, October 23 (Web only).

CBS (Congressional Budget Office) (2004) "What Accounts for the Decline in Manufacturing Employment?" Economic and Budget Issue Brief, February 18. Available at www.cbo.gov/showdoc.cfm?index=5078&sequence=0.

Cleeland, Nancy, and Abigail Goldman (2003) "Grocery Unions Battle to Stop Invasion of the Giant Stores." *Los Angeles Times*, November 25.

Coodin, Freda (2003) "Longshore Union Calls It a Win." *Labor Notes*, January. Available at www.labornotes.org/archives/2003/01/b.html.

Dube, Arindajit, and Ken Jacobs (2004) "Hidden Cost of Wal-Mart Jobs." University of California, Berkeley, Labor Center Briefing Paper Series, August 2. Available at http://laborcenter.berkeley.edu/lowwage/walmart.pdf.

Ehrenreich, Barbara (2001) *Nickle and Dimed: On (Not) Getting By in America*. New York: Henry Holt.

Fantasia, Rick, and Kim Voss (2004) *Hard Work: Remaking the American Labor Movement*. Berkeley: University of California Press.

Featherstone, Liza (2004) *Selling Women Short: The Landmark Battle for Workers' Rights at Wal-Mart*. New York: Basic Books.

——— (2005) "Wal-Mart's P.R. War." *Salon*, August 2.

Goodman, Amy (2004) "Will the AFL-CIO Split? A Debate on the Future of Organized Labor." Interview on radio program *Democracy Now*, December 9. Transcript available at www.democracynow.org.

Greenhouse, Steven (2005a) "Wal-Mart to Pay U.S. $11 Million In Lawsuit on Immigrant Workers." *New York Times*, March 19.

——— (2005b) "Can't Wal-Mart, a Retail Behemoth, Pay More?" *New York Times*, May 4.

——— (2005c) "At a Small Shop in Colorado, Wal-Mart Beats a Union Once More." *New York Times*, February 26.

Harrison, Bennett, and Barry Bluestone (1989) *The Great U-Turn: Corporate Restructuring and the Polarizing of America*. New York: Basic Books.

Holmes, S. and Zellner, W. (2004) "The Costco Way: Higher Wages Mean Higher Profits, But Try Telling Wall Street." *Business Week*, April 12.

Jiang Jingjing (2004) "Wal-Mart's China Inventory to Hit US$18b this year." *China Business Weekly*, November 29.

Joyce, Amy (2005) "Logging on with a New Campaign." *Washington Post*, May 31.

Lan Xinzhen (2005) "Wal-Mart Presence." *Beijing Review*, August 2.

LeDuff, Charlie, and Steven Greenhouse (2004) "Grocery Workers Relieved, if Not Happy, at Strike's End." *New York Times*, February 27.

Leonard, Christopher (2005) "Potent Wal-Mart Watch Shadows Retailer." *Arkansas Democrat Gazette*, June 5.

Lichtenstein, Nelson, ed. (2005) *Wal-Mart: Template for 21st Century Capitalism?* New York: New Press.

Maher, Kris (2005) "Breakaway Coalition of Unions Lays Out Strategy for Organizing." *Wall Street Journal*, September 28.

Marglin, Stephen, and Juliet B. Schor (1992) *The Golden Age of Capitalism: Reinterpreting the Postwar Experience*. New York: Oxford.

Moberg, David (2005) "Can't Workers of the World Unite?" *The Nation*, February 24.

Mongelluzzo, Bill (2005) "ILWU Sets New West Coast Targets; Union Sees Import Distribution Centers Ripe for Organizing." *Journal of Commerce Online*, May 24.

Murray, Alan (2005) "Labor Tries Political Tack Against Wal-Mart." *Wall Street Journal*, August 10.

Peltz, James F. (2003) "Wall Street is Chains' Not-So-Silent Partner." *Los Angeles Times*, December 22.

Said, Carolyn (2004) "State to File Antitrust Suit in Grocery Strike." *San Francisco Chronicle*, January 31.

Serwer, Andy, Kate Bonamici, and Corey Hajim (2005) "Bruised in Bentonville." *Fortune*, April 18.

Shaiken, Harley (2003) "Grocery Strike Animates Unions." *Los Angeles Times*, December 5.

Struck, Doug (2005) "Wal-Mart Leaves Bitter Chill: Quebec Store Closes After Vote to Unionize." *Washington Post*, April 14.

Tatge, Martk (2003) "As A Grocer, Wal-Mart Is No Category Killer." *Forbes*, June 30.

Tirschwell, Peter M. (2004) "Demanding. Exacting. Uncompromising. Retailers Raise the Bar on Logistics Performance." *Journal of Commerce*, January 19–25.

Uthappa, Renuka N. (2003) "Union Pulls Pickets at Ralph's: Grocery Workers Fight Health Cuts and Job Loss to Vendors." *Labor Notes*, December.

Wall Street Journal (2002) "Taft-Hartley, Victorious." *Wall Street Journal* editorial, November 26.

Chapter 11

Arnold, Stephen J. (2003) "Retail Store Patronage in the U.S., Canada, and Mexico: An Institutional Theory Perspective." Pp. 50–55 in Joel R. Evans, ed., *Retailing 2003: Strategic Planning in Uncertain Times, Proceedings of the Seventh Triennial National Retailing Conference.* Columbus, Ohio: The Academy of Marketing Science and The American Collegiate Retailing Association.

Arnold, Stephen J., and J. Fernie (2000) "Wal-Mart in Europe: Prospects for the UK." *International Marketing Review* 17, 4/5: 416–32.

Arnold, Stephen J., Robert V. Kozinets, and Jay M. Handelman (2001) "Hometown Ideology and Retailer Legitimation: The Institutional Semiotics of Wal-Mart Flyers." *Journal of Retailing* 77: 243–71.

Bottomore, T. B. (1965) *Classes in Modern Society.* London: Allen & Unwin.

Burt, Steve, and Leigh Sparks (2001) "The Implications of Wal-Mart's Takeover of ASDA." *Environment and Planning A* 33, 8: 1463–87.

Chen, M. (1995) *Asian Management Systems: Chinese, Japanese and Korea.* New York: Routledge.

Cui, Gen, and Qiming Liu (2001) "Emerging Market Segments in a Traditional Economy: A Study of Urban Consumers in China." *Journal of International Marketing* 9: 84–106.

DiMaggio, Paul J., and Walter W. Powell (1983) "The Iron Cage Revisited: Institutional Isomorphism and Collective Rationality in Organizational Fields." *American Sociological Review* 48, April: 147–60.

Fernie, John, and Stephen J. Arnold (2002) "Wal-Mart in Europe: Prospects for Germany, the UK and France." *International Journal of Retail and Distribution Management* 30, 2: 92–102.

Fiske, Alan P. (1992) "The Four Elementary Forms of Sociality: Framework for a Unified Theory of Social Relations." *Psychological Review* 99: 689–723.

Floum, J. R. (1994) "Counterfeiting in the People's Republic of China." *Journal of World Trade* 28.

Hwang, K. K. (1987) "Face and Favor: The Chinese Power Game." *American Journal of Sociology* 92: 944–74.

Jakobson, Roman (1985) "Linguistics and Poetics." Pp. 147–75 in Robert E. Innis, ed., *Semiotics: An Introductory Anthology.* Bloomington: Indiana University Press.

Knorr, Andreas, and Andreas Arndt (2003) "Why Did Wal-Mart Fail in Germany?" Institute for World Economics and International Management, Universität Bremen.

Lawes, Eachel (2002) "Demystifying Semiotics: Some Key Questions Answered." *International Journal of Market Research* 44, 3: 251–64.

Lodge, G. C., and E. F. Vogel (1987). *Ideology and National Competitiveness.* Boston: Harvard Business School Press.

Meyer, John W., and Brian Rowan (1977) "Institutionalized Organizations: Formal Structure as Myth and Ceremony." *American Journal of Sociology* 83, 2: 340–63.

OECD (Organization for Economic Co-operation and Development) (2002) *OECD Employment Outlook.* Paris: OECD.

Peltz, J.F. (2002) "Wal Street is Chains' Not-So-Silent Partner." *Los Angeles Times,* December 22.

Peerenboom, R. (1995) "Truthful Touting." *China Business Review* 22: 26.

Ralston, D. A., D. J. Gustafson, F. M. Cheung, and R. H. Terpstra (1993) "Differences in Managerial Values: A Study of U.S., Hong Kong and PRC Managers." *Journal of International Business Studies* 24: 249–75.

Smith, P. B., S. Dugan, and F. Trompenaars. (1996) "National Culture and Managerial Values: A Dimensional Analysis across 43 Nations." *Journal of Cross-Cultural Psychology* 27: 231–64.

Solon, G. (2004) "A Model of Intergenerational Mobility Variation over Time and Place." Pp. 38–47 in M. Corak, ed., *Generational Income Mobility in North America and Europe.* Cambridge: Cambridge University Press.

Suchman, Mark C. (1995) "Managing Legitimacy: Strategic and Institutional Approaches." *Academy of Management Review* 20, July: 571–610.

Vanneman, R. (1980) "U.S. and British Perception of Class." *American Journal of Sociology* 85: 769–90.

Yang, M. M. (1994) *Gifts, Favors, and Banquets: The Art of Social Relationships in China.* Ithaca, NY: Cornell University Press.

Zucker, Lynne G. (1987) "Institutional Theories of Organization." *Annual Review of Sociology* 13: 443–64.

Chapter 12

Adams, D. (2003) "How DUMB Do They Think We Are?" Menopause and Women's Health Information. Available at www.minniepauz.com/celebritymeno.html, accessed November 2, 2005.

Barbaro, M. (2005) "A New Weapon for Wal-Mart: A War Room." *New York Times,* November 1, 2005.

Baudrillard, J. (1988) *America.* New York: Verso.

———— (1998) *The Consumer Society: Myths and Structures.* Thousand Oaks, CA: Sage.

Bell, D., and G. Valentine (1997) *Consuming Geographies: We Are Where We Eat.* London: Routledge.

Bhatnagar, P. (2005) "Lookin' for a Cheap Date? Try Wal-Mart." CNNMoney, April 15. Available at http://money.cnn.com/2005/04/07/news/fortune500/walmart_dating.

Bianco, A. (2003) "Is Wal-Mart Too Powerful?" *Business Week,* October 6.

The Boxtank: A Collaborative on Urbanism and Retailing (2004) "Walmartbox." Available at www.theboxtank.com/walmartbox/2004/06/wm_hosts_bubble.html.

Brundage, S. (2002) "The Games Wal-Mart Doesn't Play." Wired.com, December 2. Available at www.wired.com/news/games/0,2101,55955,00.html.

Buck-Morss, S. (1989) *The Dialectics of Seeing: Walter Benjamin and the Arcades Project.* Cambridge: MIT Press.

Charette, Mark. (1998) "Kathie Lee, Wal-Mart, Fail to Deliver." *Swarthmore College Phoenix,* October 23. Available at www.sccs.swarthmore.edu/org/phoenix/1998/1998-10-23/9.html.

Circle Racing Online (2005) "NASCAR: Doin' It for Dad at Wal Mart." Available at www.circleracingonline.com/cronews/ovaloffice_i_4.html.

Clarke, D. (2000) "Space, Knowledge and Consumption." In J. Bryons, P. Daniels, N. Henry, and J. Pollard, eds., *Knowledge, Space, Economy.* London: Routledge.

Clarke, D., and M. Purvis (1994) "Dialectics, Difference, and the Geographies of Consumption." *Environment and Planning A* 26: 1091–109.

Cohen, M. (1989) "Walter Benjamin's Phantasmagoria." *New German Critique* 48: 87–107.

Consumers Union (2002) "Megastore Ratings." *Consumer Reports* 2001 Annual Questionnaire of Readers.

Cramer, James (2004) "Wal-Mart Gives False Economic Tell." http://www.thestreet.com/_tcs/money/JamesCramer/10196305.html. Nov. 2.

Crewe, L., and M. Lowe (1995) "Gap on the Map? Towards a Geography of Consumption and Identity." *Environment and Planning A* 27: 1877–89.

Dailycut.blogspot.com (2005). Available at http://dailycut.blogspot.com/2005/01/bingo.html, accessed November 2.

Featherstone, L. (2002) "Wal-Mart Values." *The Nation.* Available at http://thenation.com, accessed post November 26.

Fine, B. (1995) "From Political Economy to Consumption." In D. Miller, ed., *Acknowledging Consumption.* New York: Routledge.

Fishman, C. (2003) "The Wal-Mart You Don't Know." *Fast Company* 77: 68.

French, Anita (2004) "Wal-Mart Upgrading Its In-Store TV Network." *Morning News* (Springdale, AR), October 13.

Gale Group (2004) "Wal-Mart Reshapes Consumers, Brands and Packaging: The King Retailer Champions Low Prices, but It Needs National Brands to Make Consumers Feels 'Good' about Shopping Its Stores." *Business and Management Practices* 8, 3: 6.

Gereffi, G., and M. Korzeniewicz, eds. (1994) *Commodity Chains and Global Capitalism.* Westport, CT: Greenwood Press.

Goss, J. (1993) "The Magic of the Mall: An Analysis of Form, Function, and Meaning in the Contemporary Retail Built Environment." *Annals of the Association of American Geographers* 83: 18–47.

——— (1999) "Once upon a Time in the Commodity World: An Unofficial Guide to the Mall of America." *Annals of the Association of American Geographers* 98: 45–75.

Graff, T. (1994) "Spatial Diffusion of Wal-Mart: Contagious and Reverse Hierarchical Elements." *Professional Geographer* 46: 19–29.

——— (1998) "The Locations of Wal-Mart and Kmart Supercenters: Contrasting Corporate Strategies." *Professional Geographer* 50: 46–58.

Greenhouse, Steven (2004) "Wal-Mart, a Nation unto Itself." *New York Times,* April 17.

Gregory, D. (1994) *Geographical Imaginations.* Oxford: Blackwell.

Hajewski, D. (2002) "Customers Seem to Rank Value over Convenience." *Milwaukee Journal Sentinel,* June 12.

Hall, S. (2004) "Wal-Mart Nixes Stewart's 'America.'" Eonline. Available at www.eonline.com/News/Items.

Hallsworth, A. (1992) *The New Geography of Consumer Spending: A Political Economy Approach.* London: Belhaven.

Hartwick, E. (2000) "Towards a Geographical Politics of Consumption." *Environment and Planning A* 32: 1177–92.

Hays, C. (2005) "Wal-Mart Is Upgrading Its Vast In-Store Television Network." *New York Times,* February 21.

Holbrook, M. and E. Hirschman (1982) "The Experiential Aspects of Consumption: Consumer Fantasies, Feelings, and Fun." *Journal of Consumer Research* 9: 132–40.

Hopkins, J. (1990) "West Edmonton Mall: Landscapes of Myth and Elsewhereness." *Canadian Geographer* 30: 2–17.

Katz, Rachel (2005) "Wal-Mart Starts Advertising Campaign to Counter Criticism." Bloomberg.com Financial News, January 13. Available at www.bloomberg.com/apps/news?pid=10000103&sid=aS40y4zL4Bik&refer=us.

King, B. (2003) "NASCAR Plans Toy Races for Wal-Mart Fan Days." *Sports Business Journal,* December 15, 2003. Available at www.sportsbusinessjournal.com/index.cfm?fuseaction=page.feature&featureId=1076.

Kowinski, W. (1985) *The Malling of America: An Inside Look at the Great Consumer Paradise.* New York: William Morrow.

Magical Mountain News (2005) "Wal-Mart Welcomes Disney to Wonderful World of Retailing." Online newsletter of the Walt Disney Corporation. Available at www.magicalmountain.net/WDWNewsDetail.

Marx, K. (1976) *Capital*, vol. 1. New York: Vintage Books.

Murray, J., and J. Ozanne (1991) "The Critical Imagination: Emancipatory Interests in Consumer Research." *Journal of Consumer Research* 18: 129–44.

National Labor Committee (2000) "Made in China: The Role of U.S. Companies in Denying Human and Worker Rights." Available at www.nlcnet.org/campaigns/archive/chinareport/walmart.shtml, accessed November 2.

Noe, H. (2005) "A Walk through the New Wal-Mart." *Daily Cardinal,* February 25. Available at www.dailycardinal.com/news/2005/02/25/Features.

Norman, A. (1999) *Slam-Dunking Wal-Mart.* Atlantic City, NJ: Raphel Marketing.

Owens, D. (1996) "David vs. Wal-Mart." *Hartfort Courant,* March 17.

PBS (Public Broadcasting Service) (2005) "Store Wars: When Wal-Mart Comes to Town." Available at www.pbs.org/itvs/storewars/stores3_2.html.

Peet, R. (1998) *Modern Geographical Thought.* Oxford: Blackwell.

Quinn, B. (2000) *How Wal-Mart is Destroying America (and the World).* Berkeley: Ten Speed Press.

Relph, E. (1976) *Place and Placelessness.* London: Pion.

Ritzer, G. (2000) *The McDonaldization of Society.* Thousand Oaks, CA: Pine Forge Press.

Savage, M. (2000) "Walter Benjamin's Urban Thought: A Critical Analysis." In M. Crang and N. Thrift, eds., *Thinking Space.* London: Routledge.

Southern Poverty Law Center (2004) "Selling Extremism." Intelligence Report, Winter 2004. Available at www.splcenter.org/intel/intelreport/article.jsp?aid=514.

Stalk, G., and R. Lachenauer (2004) "Playing Hardball with Wal-Mart." *Forbes,* October 10. Available at www.forbes.com/global/2004/1018/026_print.html.

Thompson, C., W. Locander, and H. Pollio (1989) "Putting Consumer Experience Back into Consumer Research: The Philosophy and Method of Existential-Phenomenology." *Journal of Consumer Research* 16: 133–46.

—— (1990) "The Lived Meaning of Free Choice: An Existential-Phenomenological Description of Everyday Consumer Experiences of Contemporary Married Women." *Journal of Consumer Research* 17: 346–61.

Tuan, Y.-F. (1976) "Humanistic Geography." *Annals of the Association of American Geographers* 66: 266–76.

—— (1977) *Space and Place: The Perspective of Experience.* Minneapolis: University of Minnesota Press.

Valentine, G. (1999) "A Corporeal Geography of Consumption." *Environment and Planning D: Society and Space* 17: 329–41.

Vance, S., and R. Scott (1992) "Sam Walton and Wal-Mart Stores, Inc.: A Study in Modern Southern Entrepreneurship." *Journal of Southern History* 58: 231–52.

—— (1994) *Wal-Mart: A History of Sam Walton's Retail Phenomenon.* New York: Twayne Publishers.

Wal-Mart (2004) "2004 Annual Report to Shareholders." Available at www.walmartfacts.com/newsdesk/article.aspx?id=738, accessed November 3.

—— (2005) "2005 Annual Report to Shareholders." Available at www.walmartfacts.com/newsdesk/article.aspx?id=1078, accessed November 3.

Wal-Mart Korea (2004) "Retailers Introduced 'Retailtainment.'" February 12, 2004. Available at http://walmartkorea.com/en/wmnews/pr/wm_news_pr040212.htm, accessed November 3.

Warf, B. (1986) "Ideology, Everyday Life, and Emancipatory Phenomenology." *Antipode* 18: 268–83.

Zap2it (2004) "ABC Soap Helps Make Wal-Mart Stink." http://tvzap2it.com/tveditorial/tve_main/1,1002,271%7C88839%7C1%7C,00.html.

Zimmerman, A., and L. Stevens (2005) "Wal-Mart's Late Hours, Size Draw Students for Games; Scavenger Hunt, Anyone?" *Wall Street Journal,* February 23.

Chapter 13

Aitken, Stuart C., and Leo Zonn (1994) *Place, Power, Situation, and Spectacle: A Geography of Film.* Lanham, Md.: Rowman & Littlefield.

Arnold, S. J., R. V. Kozinets, and J. M. Handelman (2001) "Hometown Ideology and Retailer Legitimation: The Institutional Semiotics of Wal-Mart Flyers." *Journal of Retailing* 77, 2: 243–71.

Bai, Matt (2005) "'King of the Hill' Democrats." *New York Times,* June 26, 15.

Buckley, Neil (2004) "What Does the Giant Retailer Demand from Suppliers in Exchange for Precious Space on Its Miles of Shelves?" *Financial Times,* July 7, 8.

Bunnell, T. (2004) "Re-viewing the Entrapment Controversy: Megaprojection, (Mis)representation and Postcolonial Performance." *GeoJournal* 59, 4: 297–305.

Dixon, D., and J. Grimes (2004) "Capitalism, Masculinity and Whiteness in the Dialectical Landscape: The Case of Tarzan and the Tycoon." *GeoJournal* 59, 4: 265–75.

Fiske, Jonathan (2000) "Audiencing." Pp. 189–98 in Norman K. Denzin and Yvonna S. Lincoln, eds., *Handbook of Qualitative Research*, 2nd edition. Thousand Oaks, Calif.: Sage.

Graff, T. O., and D. Ashton (1994) "Spatial Diffusion of Wal-Mart—Contagious and Reverse Hierarchical Elements." *The Professional Geographer* 46, 1: 19–29.

Harpo Productions, Inc. (2005) "Billie Letts book, 'Where the Heart Is.'" Available at www.oprah.com/obc/pastbooks/billie_letts/obc_pb_19981207.jhtml, accessed October 21, 2005.

JibJab Media, Inc. (2005) Web site. Available at www.jibjab.com/Home.aspx, accessed October 21, 2005.

Kabel, Marcus (2005) "Wal-Mart to Toughen Overseas Standards," Associated Press, October 20.

Kaplan, Paul (2004) "Battles over Wal-Mart Stir Passions." *Atlanta Journal-Constitution*, December 27.

Letts, Billie (2000) *Where the Heart Is*. New York: Warner Books.

Lewis, Peirce (1979) "Axioms for Reading the Landscape: Some Guides to the American Scene." Pp. 11–32 in Donald Meinig, ed., *The Interpretation of Ordinary Landscapes: Geographical Essays*. New York: Oxford University Press.

Lukinbeal, C. (2004) "The Map That Precedes the Territory: An Introduction to Essays in Cinematic Geography." *GeoJournal* 59, 4: 247–51.

Melanie (2005) "Fox Jams JibJab Video about Outsourcing into a (Wal-Mart) Box," October 16, 2005. Available at www.newshounds.us/2005/10/14/fox_jams_jibjab_video_about_outsourcing_into_a_walmart_box.php, accessed October 22, 2005.

Mitchell, D. (2003) "Cultural Landscapes: Just Landscapes or Landscapes of Justice?" *Progress in Human Geography* 27, 6: 787–96.

Ritzer, George (1998) *The McDonaldization Thesis: Explorations and Extensions*. Thousand Oaks, Calif.: Sage.

——— (2004) *The McDonaldization of Society*. Rev. ed. Thousand Oaks, Calif.: Pine Forge Press.

Rose, Gillian (2001) *Visual Methodologies: An Introduction to the Interpretation of Visual Methods*. London: Sage.

Smith, Benjamin (2004) "Kentucky Fried Regionalism and the Commercial Imaginary of Harland Sanders." Paper presented at the Association of American Geographers annual meeting, Philadelphia, March.

Zimmerman, Amy (2000) "When Art Imitates Wal-Mart, It Gives the Company Jitters." *Wall Street Journal*, June 27.

Chapter 14

Blum, Debra (1999) "New Studies Provide Insight into Why Companies Give and Who Benefits." *Chronicle of Philanthropy* 11, 18.

——— (2000) "9 of 10 Companies Have Charity Marketing Deals." *Chronicle of Philanthropy* 12, 17.

——— (2001) "New Reports Focus on Business Social Investment and Corporate Citizenship." *Chronicle of Philanthropy* 13, 19.

Boyd, David W. (1997) "From 'Mom and Pop' to Wal-Mart: The Impact of the Consumer Goods Pricing Act of 1975 on the Retail Sector in the United States." *Journal of Economic Issues* 31: 223–32.

Burress, Charles (2004) "Wal-Mart Foes Detail Costs to Community; Public Subsidizes Workers, Study Says," *San Francisco Chronicle*, February 17.

CMR/TNS Media Intelligence (2004) *Ad$pender*. New York.

Demko, Paul (1998) "Americans Place High Value on Non-Cash Corporate Gifts." *Chronicle of Philanthropy* 10, 29.

Giving USA (2004) "The Annual Report on Philanthropy for the Year 2003." AAFRC Trust for Philanthropy, New York.

Gong, Hongmian (1997) "Location Analysis of Business and Professional Services in U.S. Metropolitan Areas, 1977–1992." Ph.D. dissertation, Department of Geography, University of Georgia.

Graff, Thomas O. (1998) "The Locations of Wal-Mart and Kmart Supercenters: Contrasting Corporate Strategies." *The Professional Geographer* 50: 46–57.

Graff, Thomas O., and Dub Ashton (1993) "Spatial Diffusion of Wal-Mart: Contagious and Reverse Hierarchical Elements." *The Professional Geographer* 46: 17–29.

MRI (Mediamark Research Incorporated) (2004) *Doublebase National Study*. New York: MRI.

Peterson, Mark, and Jeffrey E. McGee (2000) "Survivors of 'W-Day': An Assessment of the Impact of Wal-Mart's Invasion of Small Town Retailing Communities." *International Journal of Retail and Distribution Management* 28, 4/5: 170–80.

Speer, Tibbett (1994) "Where Will Wal-Mart Strike Next?" *American Demographics* 16: 11–12.

Swanson, Al (2004) "Analysis: Wal-Mart's Growing Pains." United Press International, July 6.

Vias, Alexander C. (2004) "Bigger Stores, More Stores, or No Stores: Paths of Retail Restructuring in Rural Amer
ica." *Journal of Rural Studies* 20: 303–18.

Walton, Sam (1992) *Made in America*. New York: Doubleday.

Chapter 15

Albright, S. (2005) "The Politics of Red, Wal-Mart, and Blue." *St. Petersburg Times*, April 10.

Barone, M. (1990) *Our Country*. New York: Free Press.

Berry, B. J. L., and F. E. Horton (1970) *Geographic Perspectives on Urban Systems*. Englewood Cliffs, N.J.:
Prentice-Hall.

Christaller, W. (1966) *Central Places in Southern Germany*. Translated by C. W. Baskin. Englewood Cliffs,
N.J.: Prentice-Hall.

CNNMoney (2005) "Wal-Mart Looks to Get Even Bigger." Available at http://money.cnn.com/2005/10/25/news/
fortune500/walmart_expansion.reut/index.htm, October 25.

Hofstadter, R. (1961) *The Age of Reform*. New York: Random House.

Hopkins, J. (2004) "Wal-Mart Heirs Pour Riches Into Education Reform." *USA Today*, March 11.

National Center for Charitable Statistics (2005) "Profiles of Individual Charitable Contributions by State, 2003."
Available at http://nccsdataweb.urban.org/kbfiles/680/Charitable%20Giving%202003%20complete.pdf.

Roberts, R. S., F. M. Ufkes, and F. M. Shelley (1990) "Populism and Agrarian Ideology: The 1982 Nebraska Corporate Farming Referendum." Pp. 153–75 in R. J. Johnston, F. M. Shelley, and P. J. Taylor, eds., *Developments
in Electoral Geography*. London: Routledge.

Shelley, F. M. (1993) "Political Culture and the Contemporary Restructuring of the American Great Plains."
Pp. 241–50 in M. D. Nellis, ed., *Proceedings: International Symposium on Contemporary Agriculture and
Rural Land Use*. Manhattan: Kansas State University.

Chapter 16

Amador Tello, Judith, and Columba Vertiz (2004) "La Larga Noche Teotihuacana." *Proceso*, October 17, 76–79.

Amin, Ash (2002) "Spatialities of Globalization." *Environment and Planning A* 34: 385–99.

Aridjis, Homero, and Francisco Toledo (2004) "Letter to the President." *La Jornada,* October 10.

——— (2004) "Carta de Mas de 60 Intellectuales." *El Financiero*, October 20.

Babb, Sarah (2001) *Managing Mexico*. Princeton: Princeton University Press.

Barajas, L. F., and E. Zamora (2002) "Nuevas Formas y viejos valores: urbanizaciones cerradas de lujo en Guadalajara."
In L.F. Barajas, ed., *Latinoamerica: paises abiertos ciudades cerradas*. Universidad de Guadalajara. UNESCO.

Bellinghausen, Hermann (2004) "Manual Antisindicalista de Wal-Mart." *La Jornada*, October 16.

Bravo Beristain, Francisco (2005). *La Construccion de Wal-Mart en Teotihuacan*. México, D.F.: Editorial Praxis.

Camp, Roderic (1989) *Some Interpretations of the Mexican System: Politics in Mexico*. New York: Oxford University Press.

Cano, Araceli (2004) "Fin a la Polemica: Abren Bodega Aurrera Teotihuacan." *El Financiero*, November 5.

Castells, M. (1989) *The Informational City: Information Technology, Economic Restructuring, and the Urban-
Regional Process*. New York: Blackwell.

Castillo, Ana (2000) *La Diosa de las Americas: Escritos Sobre la Virgen de Guadalupe/Writings on the Virge of
Guadalupe*. New York: Random House.

Castillo Mireles, Ricardo (2005) "Across the Border: Taking It to the Competition Mexican Style." *Logistics Today*,
December 2004.

Castillo Peraza, Carlos (2000) "Un llamado a Wal-Mart." *Proceso*. August 13, 2000.

Cornelius, W. (1992) "The Politics and Economics of Reforming the *Ejido* Sector in Mexico: An Overview and
Research Agenda." *LASA Forum* 23, 3: 3–10.

Cross, John C. (1998) *Informal Politics: Street Vendors and the State in Mexico City*. Stanford: Stanford University Press.

Dávila, Israel, and Silvia Chávez (2004) "Marcha atras en la construccion de Wal-Mart en Teotihuacan." *La Jornada,* October 2.

Davis, Diane E. (1994) *Urban Leviathan: Mexico City in the Twentieth Century*. Philadelphia: Temple University Press.

Dezalay, Yves, and Bryant Garth (2002) *The Internationalization of the Palace Wars: Lawyers, Economists, and the
Contest to Transform Latin American States*. Chicago: University of Chicago Press.

García Hernández, Arturo (2004) "Crece riesgo de destrucción del patrimonio cultural." *La Jornada,* October 25.

Herzog, Lawrence (1990) *Where North Meets South: Space and Politics along the U.S. Mexico Border.* Albuquerque: University of New Mexico Press.

LaBotz, Dan (1995) *Democracy in Mexico.* New York: Lighting Source Incorporated.

López Reyes, Carolina, and Olivia Casco Alva (2002) "Analisis territorial de los centros commerciales Wal-Mart." Master's thesis, UNAM, Mexico.

López y Rivas, Gilberto (2004) "Boicot a Wal-Mart." *La Jornada,* October 22.

Malkin, Elisabeth (2004) "Mexican Retailers Unite Against Wal-Mart." *New York Times,* July 9.

Marrero Ruiz, Carmelo (2002) "Wal-Mart: La invasion planetaria." Available at www.lafogata.org, accessed October 25, 2005.

Middlebrook, K. (2002) "Party Politics and Democratization in Mexico: The Partido Accion Nacional in Comparative Perspective." Pp. 3–46 in K. Middlebrook, ed., *Party Politics and the Struggle for Democracy in Mexico.* San Diego: Center for US-Mexican Studies.

Morais, Richard (2004) "One Hot Tamale." *Forbes,* December 20.

OECD (Organisation for Economic Co-operation and Development) (2005) "Economic Survey of Mexico 2005: Economic Performance and Key Challenges." Available at www.oecd.org.document, accessed October 20, 2005.

Ribeiro, Sylvia (2005) "Teotihuacán y la verdadera cara de Wal-Mart." Available at www.ecoportal.net/content/view/full/35154, accessed on September 14, 2005.

Riding, Alan (1985) *Distant Neighbors: A Portrait of the Mexicans.* New York: Random House.

Salinas, Javier, and René Ramón (2004) "Inminente apertura del centro comercial Wal-Mart en Teotihuacán." *La Jornada,* October 22.

Salinas Cesareo, Javier (2004). "Policías y opositores al Wal-Mart se enfrentaron en Teotihuacán." *La Jornada,* December 3.

Sassen, S. (1996) *Losing Control? Sovereignty in an Age of Globalization.* New York: Columbia University Press.

Slater, Robert (2004) *The Wal-Mart Triumph: Inside the World's #1 Company.* New York: Penguin USA.

Soderquist, Don (2005). *The Wal-Mart Way: The Inside Story of the Success of the World's Largest Company.* Nashville, TN: Nelson Business.

Wal-Mart de Mexico (2000) *International Competitive Benchmarks and Financial Gap Analysis.* San Diego, CA. Icon Group International Inc.

Warren, Chris (2005) "Meet the Corporation." *Sierra,* September/October, 34.

Chapter 17

Abernathy, Frederick H., John T. Dunlop, Janice Hammond, and David Weil (1999) *A Stitch in Time: Lean Retailing and the Transformation of Manufacturing—Lessons from the Apparel and Textile Industries.* New York: Oxford University Press.

Bonacich, Edna (2005) "Wal-Mart and the Logistics Revolution." In Nelson Lichtenstein, ed., *Wal-Mart: A Template for the 21st Century?* New York: New Press.

Bonacich, Edna, and Jake B. Wilson (2005) "Wal-Mart's Global Production and Distribution System." *New Labor Forum* 14, 2, summer.

Bowersox, Donald J., David J. Closs, and M. Bixby Cooper (2002) *Supply Chain Logistics Management.* Boston: McGraw-Hill.

Boyle, Matthew (2003) "Wal-Mart Keeps the Change: Suppliers Pay for New Technology, but Bentonville Really Benefits." *Fortune,* October 26.

Brown, A. (2000) "MP challenges Blair over Wal-Mart Talks. Press Association 11 January 2000.

Cleeland, Nancy, Evelyn Iritani, and Tyler Marshall (2003) "Scouring the Globe to Give Shoppers an $8.63 Polo Shirt." *Los Angeles Times,* November 24.

Dobson, Hugo (2004) "The World's Biggest Retailer Is Defying Its Critics by Continuing to Grow Vigorously." *The Economist,* April 15.

Fishman, Charles (2003) "The Wal-Mart You Don't Know: Why Low Prices Have a High Cost." *Fast Company,* 77 68–80.

Flint, Robert (2004) "How Wal-Mart Treads Heavily in Foreign-Exchange Forest." *Wall Street Journal,* November 17.

Gereffi, Gary (1994) "The Organization of Buyer-Driven Global Commodity Chains: How U.S. Retailers Shape Overseas Production Networks." In Gary Gereffi and Miguel Korzeniewicz, eds., *Commodity Chains and Global Capitalism.* Westport, CT: Praeger.

Gilman, Hank (2004). "The Most Underrated CEO Ever." *Fortune,* March 21.

Gimbel, Barney (2004) "Yule Log Jam." *Fortune,* December 13, 162–70.

Goodman, Peter S., and Philip Pan (2004). "Wal-Mart and China Leading the Race to the Bottom: Chinese Workers Pay for Wal-Mart's Low Prices; Retailer Squeezes Its Asian Suppliers to Cut Costs." *Washington Post*, February 8.

Hua, Vanessa (2004) "Wal-Mart's China Operation a Study in Contrasts: Workers at Many Factories That Supply Goods to the Stores Can't Afford to Shop There." *San Francisco Chronicle*, December 29.

Huffman, Ted P. (2003) "Wal-Mart in China: Challenges Facing a Foreign Retailer's Supply Chain." *China Business Review*, 18–22.

Jiang Jingjing (2004) "Wal-Mart's China Inventory to Hit US$18b This Year." *China Business Daily*, November 30.

Journal of Commerce (2003) April 28, 18A.

Jubak, Jim (2004) "3 Big Threats to China's Economic Miracle." MSN Money, Jubak's Journal, May 7. Available at http://moneycentral.msn.com/content/P82353.asp.

Leach, Peter T. (2004) "Ready for RFID? Wal-Mart, Military Aren't Waiting for the Technology to Be Perfected." *Journal of Commerce*, October 18, 12–14.

Lehman, Jon (2004) Interviews for *Frontline*: "Is Wal-Mart Good for America?" June 4 and October 7, www.pbs.org.

Mongelluzzo, Bill (2004) "Here Comes Wal-Mart: The Nation's Largest Retailer Asks Logistics Providers to Prepare for a Busy Two Months." *Journal of Commerce*, September 6, 22–24.

Morgan Stanley (2004) *Wal-Mart*. February 12.

Piore, Michael, and Charles Sabel (1986) *The Second Industrial Divide: Possibilities for Prosperity*. New York: Basic Books.

Quinn, Bill (2000) *How Wal-Mart Is Destroying America (and the World), and What You Can Do About It*. Berkeley: Ten Speed Press.

Schafer, Sarah (2004) "A Welcome to Wal-Mart." *Newsweek*, December 20.

Server, Andrew (2004) "The Waltons: Inside America's Richest Family." *Fortune*, November 15, 86–116.

Troy, Mike (2004) "Global Procurement: In-sourcing the Role of the Middleman." *DSN Retailing Today*, December 13, 27–28.

Useem, Jerry (2003) "How Could Wal-Mart Fall from No. 1." *Fortune*, April 14, 87–90.

—— (2004) "Should We Admire Wal-Mart?" *Fortune,* February 23.

Varley, Pamela, ed. (1998) *The Sweatshop Quandary: Corporate Responsibility on the Global Frontier*. Wahsington, D.C.: Investor Responsibility Research Center.

WERC (Warehousing Education and Research Council) (1994) *The Mass Merchant Distribution Channel: Challenges and Opportunities*. Oak Brook, Ill.: WERC.

Wilson, Rosalyn (2004) *15th Annual State of Logistics Report: Globalization*. Oak Park, Ill.: Council of Logistics Management.

Wonacott, Peter (2003). "Wilting Plants: Behind China's Export Boom, Heated Battle Among Factories; As Wal-Mart, Others Demand Lowest Prices, Managers Scramble to Slash Costs; Rising Concerns About Safety." *Wall Street Journal*, November 13.

Chapter 18

Arnold, S. J., and J. Fernie (1999) "Wal-Mart into the UK." *Journal of Enterprising Culture* 7: 407–16.

—— (2000) "Wal-Mart in Europe: Prospects for the UK." *International Marketing Review* 17: 416–32.

Arnold, S. J., J. Handelman, and D. J. Tigert (1998) "The Impact of a Market Spoiler on Consumer Preference Structures (or, What Happens When Wal-Mart Comes to Town)." *Journal of Retailing and Consumer Services* 5: 1–13.

BBC (2005a) "ASDA Planning to Shed 1,000 Jobs." *BBC News Online*, July 5, 2005. Available at http://news.bbc.co.uk/1/hi/business/4651305.stm, accessed October 14, 2005.

—— (2005b) "Wal-Mart Calls for Tesco Inquiry." *BBC News Online*, August 28, 2005. Available at http://news.bbc.co.uk/1/hi/business/4192746.stm, accessed October 14.

Brown, A. (2000) MP Challenges Blair over Wal-Mart Talks. Press Association 11 January.

Burt, S. L., and L. Sparks (1997) "Performance in Food Retailing: A Cross-National Consideration and Comparison of Retail Margins." *British Journal of Management* 8: 133–50.

—— (2001) "The Implications of Wal-Mart's Takeover of ASDA." *Environment and Planning A* 33: 1463–87.

—— (2003) "Power and Competition in the UK Retail Grocery Market." *British Journal of Management* 14: 237–54.

Butler, Sarah (2005) "ASDA Boss Fights for Business on New Battlefields." *The Times,* October 5.

Cabinet Office (2005) Letter to Leigh Sparks in response to formal FOI request, March 1.

Clement, Barrie (2005) "ASDA Investigates Why Staff Shop Elsewhere." *Independent*, October 10.

Competition Commission (2000) *Supermarkets: A Report on the Supply of Groceries from Multiple Stores in the United Kingdom.* Cm 4882, 3 vols. London: HMSO.

——— (2003) *Safeway plc and ASDA Group Limited (owned by Wal-Mart Stores Inc); Wm Morrison Supermarkets plc; J Sainsbury plc; and Tesco plc: A Report on the Mergers in Contemplation.* London: HMSO.

Davies, B. K., and L. Sparks (1986) "ASDA-MFI: The Superstore and the Flat-Pack." *International Journal of Retailing* 1: 55–78.

Department of Trade and Industry (2004) *The Retail Strategy Group—Driving Change.* London: Department of Trade and Industry. Available at www.dti.gov.uk/sectors_retail.html.

Fernie, J., and S. J. Arnold (2002) "Wal-Mart in Europe: Prospects for Germany, the UK and France." *International Journal of Retail and Distribution Management* 30, 2: 92–102.

Fernie, J., B. Hahn, U. Gerhard, E. Pioch, and S. J. Arnold (2005) "A Tale of Two Markets: Wal-Mart in the UK and Germany." Paper presented at the 13th International EAERCD Conference on Research in the Distributive Trades, Lund University, June 29–July 1.

Guy, C. M. (2003) "Is Retail Planning Policy Effective? The Case of Very Large Store Development in the UK." *Planning Theory and Practice* 3: 319–30.

Hallsworth, A. (1999) "Waiting for Wal-Mart?" *Environment and Planning A* 31: 1331–36.

Hallsworth, A., and I. Clarke (2001) "Further Reflections on the Arrival of Wal-Mart in the United Kingdom." *Environment and Planning A* 33: 1709–16.

Hallsworth, A., and D. Evers (2002) "The Steady Advance of Wal-Mart across Europe and Changing Government Attitudes towards Planning and Competition." *Environment and Planning C* 20: 297–309.

IGD (Institute of Grocery Distribution) (2005) *Grocery Retailing 2005.* Watford: Institute of Grocery Distribution.

——— (2004) *Wal-Mart: Delivering Global Growth.* Watford: Institute of Grocery Distribution.

Jones, P. (1982) "Retail Innovation and Diffusion—the Spread of ASDA Stores." *Geoforum* 13: 39–43.

Langston, P., G. P. Clarke, and D. B. Clarke (1997) "Retail Saturation, Retail Location and Retail Competition: An Analysis of British Grocery Retailing." *Environment and Planning A* 29: 77–104.

Little, A. (1999) Blair Meets Wal-Mart Chief. Press Association, 22 April.

Macalister, Terry (2005) "ASDA Attacked over Employees' Rights." *Guardian,* October 17.

Mellahi, K., T. P. Jackson, and L. Sparks (2002) "An Exploratory Study of Failure in Successful Organizations: The Case of Marks and Spencer." *British Journal of Management* 13: 15–29.

ODPM (Office of the Deputy Prime Minister) (2004) *A Policy Evaluation of the Effectiveness of PPG6.* London: ODPM.

Pal, J., D. Bennison, I. M. Clarke, and J. Byrom (2001) "Power, Policy Networks and Planning: The Involvement of Major Grocery Retailers in the Formulation of Planning Policy Guidance Note 6 since 1988." *International Review of Retail, Distribution and Consumer Research* 11: 225–46.

Pioch, E., J. Fernie, and S. J. Arnold (2005) "Challenges of Organizations in Global Markets." Paper presented at the British Academy of Management Conference, Said Business School, Oxford, September 13–15.

Retail Week (2000) "Grocers Have More to Fear than Price." July 28, 8.

——— (2005) "ASDA on the Offensive." September 23, 7.

——— (2005) "Lord of the Land." October 7, 38–39.

Reynolds, J., E. Howard, D. Dragun, B. Rosewell, and P. Ormerod. (2005) "Assessing the Productivity of the UK Retail Sector." *International Review of Retail, Distribution and Consumer Research* 15: 237–80.

Scottish Executive (2004) *The Effectiveness of NPPG8: Town Centres and Retailing.* Edinburgh: Scottish Executive.

Seth, A., and G. Randall (1999) *The Grocers.* London: Kogan Page.

Sparks, L. (2002) "The Findings Have Surprised Some Shoppers." *International Journal of Retail and Distribution Management* 30: 126–33.

——— (2005) "Editorial. Special Issue: Assessing Retail Productivity." *International Review of Retail, Distribution and Consumer Research* 15: 227–36.

Sunday Times (2004) "ASDA without Food Looks like a Winning Formula." October 17.

Walters S. and V. Moss (1999) Tony Blair, Wal-Mart and Now the Hillary Clinton Connection: Why the "Most Profitable No. 10 Chat in History May Bring a Giant American Stores Company to Britain. *Mail* on Sunday, 20 June 1999, p. 32–33.

War on Want/GMB, "ASDA Wal-Mart: The Alternative Report." London: War on Want (2005). Available at www.waronwant.org/?lid=8247, accessed October 17.

Warren, R. (2005) "Mezzanine Floor Outbreak—a Practical Reality." *Journal of Planning and Environment Law,* 156–58.

Whysall, P. (2001) "Wal-Mart's takeover of ASDA: What the Papers Said." *British Food Journal* 103: 729–43.

——— (2005) "GEM, 1964–1966: Britain's First Out-of-Town Retailer." *International Review of Retail, Distribution and Consumer Research* 15: 111–24.

Wood, S., M. Lowe, and N. Wrigley (2006) "Life after PPG6—Recent UK Food Retailer Responses to Planning Regulation Tightening." *International Review of Retail, Distribution and Consumer Research* 16.

Wrigley, N. (1998) "PPG6 and the Contemporary UK Food Store Development Dynamic." *British Food Journal* 100: 154–61.

Wrigley, N., and A. Currah (2003) "The Stresses of Retail Internationalization: Lessons from Royal Ahold's Experiences in Latin America." *International Review of Retail, Distribution and Consumer Research* 13: 221–43.

Chapter 19

Abernathy, F., J. Dunlop, J. Hammond, and D. Weil (2000) "Retailing and Supply Chains in the Information Age." *Technology in Society* 22: 5–31.

Alexander, N., and H. Myers (2000) "The Retail Internationalization Process." *International Marketing Review* 17, 4: 334–53.

Belzer, M. (2000) *Sweatshops on Wheels*. New York: Oxford University Press.

Christopher, M. (1998) *Logistics and Supply Chain Management*. London: Financial Times/Prentice Hall.

——— (2000) "The Agile Supply Chain." *Industrial Marketing Management* 29, 1: 37–44.

Christopherson, S. (1996) "The Production of Consumption: Retail Restructuring and Labor Demand in the U.S.A." In N. Wrigley and M. Lowe, eds., *Retailing, Consumption and Capital: Toward the New Retailing Geography*. London: Longman.

——— (2001) "Lean retailing in marketliberalen und koordinierten Wirtschaften" (Lean retailing in liberal market and coordinated economies). In H. Rudolph, ed., *Aldi oder Arkaden? Unternehmen und Arbeit im europaischen Einzelhande*. Berlin: Edition Sigma.

——— (2000) "Rules as Resources: How Market Governance Regimes Influence Firm Networks." In T. Barnes and M. Gertler, eds., *New Models in Industrial Geography*. New York: Routledge.

Dörrenbächer, C., M. Fichter, L. Neumann, A. Toth, and M. Wortmann (2000) "Transformation and Foreign Direct Investment: Observations on Path Dependency, Hybridization, and Model Transfer at the Enterprise Level." *Transfer* 6, 3: 434–49.

Fernie, J., and S. J. Arnold (2002) "Wal-Mart in Europe: Prospects for Germany, the UK and France." *International Journal of Retail Distribution and Management* 30, 2: 92–102.

Food Marketing Institute (1997) *Annual Report*. FMI: Washington, D.C.

"Germany Stymies Wal-Mart" (2000) *Detroit News,* October 29.

Gewerkschaft HBV (2000) "Tarifsituation bei Wal-Mart, Wir Bleiben Am Ball" (labor union pamphlet, Berlin).

Greimel, H. (2001) "Wal-Mart Scraps German Expansion." Associated Press, April 20.

Hector, B. (1998) "Handelsketten wollen neue Wege mit der Spedition Lagerlogistik." *Sonderbeilage der DVZ* 21, 3: 14–16.

Hollingsworth, J. R., and R. Boyer (1997) *Contemporary Capitalism: The Embeddedness of Institutions*. Cambridge: Cambridge University Press.

Kahn, B. E., and L. McAlister (1997) *Grocery Revolution*. Menlo Park: Addison Wesley.

Katz, H., and O. Darbishire (2000) *Converging Divergences*. Ithaca: Cornell University Press.

Kinsey, J., B. Senauer, R. King, and P. Phumpiu (1996) "Changes in Retail Food Delivery: Signals for Producers, Processors, and Distributors." Working Paper 96-03. Retail Food Industry Center, St. Paul.

"Langer Atem" (2001) *Wirtschaftswoche,* May 17, 82–86.

Lewis, C. (2001) "Muscling In." *Logistics Europe* 9, 3: 22–24.

Logistics Europe (2001) "The People Problem" (editorial). April, 7.

National Retail Federation (1998) *Annual Report*. Washington, D.C.: NRF.

Plehwe, D. (2000) "Why and How Do National Monopolies Go Global?" Research Series, FS 199-102. Wissenschaftszentrtum, Berlin.

Plunkett, J. (1997) *Plunkett's Retail Industry Almanac*. Galveston, Tex.: J. Plunkett.

Regini, M. (2000) "Between Deregulation and Social Pacts: The Responses of European Economies to Globalization." *Politics and Society* 28, 1: 5–34.

Sternquist, B. (1997) "International Expansion of US Realtors." *International Journal of Retail Distribution and Management* 25, 8/9: 262–68.

"Store Wars: When Walmart Comes to Town" (2001) Documentary film by Bullfrog films, produced in association with the Independent Television Service, with funding provided by the Corporation for Public Broadcasting, www.bullfrogfilms.com/catalog/store.html.

Streeck, W. (1996) "Lean Production in the German Automobile Industry: A Test Case for Convergence Theory" Pp. 138–70 in S. Berger and R. Dore, eds., *National Diversity and Global Capitalism*. Ithaca: Cornell University Press.

Thelen, K. (2000) "Why German Employers Cannot Bring Themselves to Dismantle the German Model." In Torben Iverson, Jonas Pontusson, and David Soskice, eds., *Unions, Employers, and Central Banks: Wage Bargaining and Macro-Economic Regimes in an Integrating Europe*. New York: Cambridge University Press.

Thelen, K., and I. Kume (1999) "The Effects of Globalization on Labor Revisited: Lessons from Germany and Japan." *Politics and Society* 27, 4: 476–504.

Union-Network.org (2000). Available at http://union-network.org/unisite/sectors.

UFCW (United Food and Commercial Workers) (2000). "Wal-Martization of Health Care." http://www.ufcw.org/issues_and_actions/walmart_workers_campaign_info/facts_and_figures/walmartonbenefits

UNI (2000a) "Wal-Mart in Germany is Not Doing Well: European Commerce Workers Don't Want to be Low-Paid Cheerleaders, Unions Say." 7 March 2000. http://www.union-network.org/unisite/sectors/commerce/multinationals/Wal-Mart_not_doing_well_in_Germany.htm

UNI (2000b) "Wal-Mart Continues its Price War in Britain and Germany—Unions Warn of Job and Wage Loses." 19 July 2000. http://www.union-network.org/UNIsite/Sectors/Commerce/Multinationals/Wal-Mart_price_wars.htm

Vida, I. (2000) "An Empirical Inquiry into International Expansion of US Retailers." *International Marketing Review* 17, 4: 454–75.

Chapter 20

AFC (Agriculture, Forestry, Fishery and Finance Corporation) (2000) "Katei ni okeru shokuseikatsu ni kansuru chosa." AFC, Tokyo, August 2000. Available at www.afc.go.jp/your-field/investigate/pdf/shohi-h12–01.pdf, accessed January 9, 2005.

Akehurst, G., and N. Alexander, eds. (1996) *The Internationalisation of Retailing*, London: Frank Cass.

Aoyama, Y. (2001a) "Structural Foundations for Electronic Commerce: A Comparative Organization of Retail Trade in Japan and the United States." *Urban Geography* 22, 2: 130–53.

——— (2001b) "Information Society, Japanese Style: Corner Stores as Hubs for E-commerce Access." Pp. 109–28 in T. R. Leinbach and S. D. Brunn, eds., *Worlds of Electronic Commerce*. Chichester: John Wiley.

Arndt, J. (1972) "Temporal Lags in Comparative Retailing." *Journal of Marketing* 36, October: 40–45.

Asahi Shimbun (2005) "Warumato ryu seiyu saiken michikewashi." February 15.

Bayerisches Staatsministerium für Landesentwicklung und Umweltfragen (2005) *Landesentwicklungsprogramm*. Munich. Available at www.umweltministerium.bayern.de/bereiche/entwick/bereiche/instrume/lep.htm, accessed January 31, 2005.

Bundesministerium der Justiz (Federal Ministry of Justice) (2003). *Referentenentwurf zur Reform des Gesetzes gegen den unlauteren Wettbewerb* (Secretary's draft of a reform of the law against unfair competition). Available at www.bmj.bund.de/images/11548.pdf, accessed January 23, 2005.

Bundesregierung (Federal Government) (2003) *Rabattgesetz und Zugabeverordnung werden abgeschafft* (Rebate law and giveaway regulation will be abolished), July 13. Available at www.bundesregierung.de/artikel,-26160/Rabattgesetz-und-Zugabeverordn.htm, accessed January 23, 2005.

Burt, S., and L. Sparks (2001) "The Implications of Wal-Mart's Takeover of ASDA." *Environment and Planning A* 33: 1463–87.

Cotter, T., S. J. Arnold, and D. Tigert (1992) "Warehouse Membership Clubs in North America." *Discount Merchandiser* 32, November: 42–47.

The Economist (1997) "Service with a Snarl: Longer Retail Hours in Germany Deemed a Failure." *The Economist*, November 8, 78.

Eyre, S., and M. Lodge (2000) "National Tunes and a European Melody? Competition Law Reform in the UK and Germany." *Journal of European Public Policy* 7, 1: 63–80.

Ferber, R. (1958) "Variations in retail sales between cities." *Journal of Marketing* 23, January: 295–303.

Friedland, J., and L. Lee (1997) "Foreign Aisles: The Wal-Mart Way Sometimes Gets Lost In Translation Overseas: Chain Changes Some Tactics to Meet Local Tastes." *Wall Street Journal*, October 8, A1.

Fuji Keizai (2003) "Shin takuhai food sabisu shijo no tenbo 2003" (Prospects for home delivery food service: new 2003 edition). Fuji Keizai, Tokyo. Available at www.group.fuji-keizai.co.jp/press/pdf/030711_03014.pdf, accessed January 10, 2005.

Futagami, Y. (2003) "Oushu kouri-gyo no sekai senryaku." Report of a speech given at International Distribution Institute, Tokyo, on October 13. Available at www.asyura2.com/0403/hasan35/msg/247.html, accessed December 16, 2004.

Gekiryu Magazine (2005) "Ote Supa: Shosha fuzai no gyotai fukkatsu ni kakeru sankyo no soryokusen" (Large general supermarket retailers: all-out-war among the three top retailers to revamp the retail category without winners). February, 20–21.

Gellately, R. (1974) *The Politics of Economic Despair: Shopkeepers and German Politics 1890–1914*. London: Sage.

Gerhard, U., and B. Hahn (2005) "Wal-Mart and Aldi: Two Retail Giants in Germany." *GeoJournal* 62, 1–2: 15–26.

Goldman, A. (1991) "Japan Distribution System: Institutional Structure, Internal Political Economy, and Modernization." *Journal of Retailing* 67, summer: 154–83.

Gotterbarm, C. (2004) *US-amerikanische Einzelhandelsunternehmen in Deutschland: Fakten, Trends und Theorien Städte* (US-American retail corporations in Germany: facts, trends and theories). Geographische Handelsforschung 9. Passau: L.I.S. Verlag.

Hall, M., J. Knapp, and C. Winsten (1961) *Distribution in Great Britain and North America: A Study in Structure and Productivity*. London: Oxford University Press.

Hancock, R. J. (1993) "Grocers Against the State: The Politics of Retail Food Distribution in the United States and Japan." Ph.D. dissertation, Department of Political Science, Stanford University.

Heshiki, T. (1996) "Environment and Retail Structure: A Cross-Sectional and Trend Analysis between the United States and Japan." Ph.D. dissertation, Department of Business Administration, Drexel University.

Jacobson, G. (2002) "Wal-Mart in Japan." *MMR,* April 22, 21–23.

JCMRI (Japan Consumer Marketing Research Institute) (2002) "Wal-Mart no nihon shinshutsu senryaku wo yomu" (Analysis of Wal-Mart's expansion strategy in Japan). Tokyo: JCMRI. Available at www.jmrlsi.co.jp/menu/case/lead/2002/walmart_1.html, accessed on April 21, 2004.

Kitoh, T. (2003) "Doitsu kourigyo warumato to kaku tatakaeri." Roland and Berger Strategic Consulting, Tokyo. Available at www.rolandberger.co.jp/pdf/rb_press/public/RB_article10.pdf, accessed April 21, 2004.

Lindblad, Cristina, ed. (2001) "Attention, Bargain Hunters." In "International Outlook" section, *BusinessWeek,* July 16, 53.

Marsden, T., and N. Wrigley (1995) "Regulation, retailing, consumption." *Environment and Planning A* 27: 1899–912.

Maruyama, M. (1993) "The Structure and Performance of the Japanese Distribution System." In M. Czinkota and M. Kotabe, eds., *The Japanese Distribution System*. Chicago: Probus.

McCraw, T. K., and P. A. O'Brien (1986) "Production and Distribution: Competition Policy and Industry Structure." Pp. 77–116 in T. K. McCraw, ed., *America Versus Japan: A Comparative Study*. Cambridge, Mass.: Harvard Business School Press.

Ministry of Economy, Trade and Industry (1997) Retail Census. Government of Japan.

——— (2002) Retail Census. Government of Japan.

Mizuho Bank (Mizuho Corporate Bank Industry Research Department) (2004) "Tokushu: 2004 nendo no nihon sangyo doukou, Kouri" (Special issue: dynamics of the Japanese industries in fiscal year 2004: the retail sector). *Mizuho Sangyo Chosa* 14, 13: 120–35.

MMR (2004) "Wal-Mart and the Americanization of German Retailing." *MMR,* July 26, 17.

Nikkei BP (2004) "Seiyu ga torihiki kitta tsuyoi oroshi: Wal-Mart shudo kosuto sakugensaku." *Nikkei BP.* Available at http://bizns.nikkeibp.co.jp/cgi-bin/search/wcs-bun.cgi?ID=307399&FORM=biztechnews, accessed January 8, 2005.

Nikkei Net (2004) "Seiyu no 6gatsu chukanki kosuto sakugen de 5-oku en no keijo kuroji ni" (Cost reduction yielded ¥5-oku yen profits for the month of June for Seiyu). *Nikkei Net.* August 18. Available at http://company.nikkei.co.jp/special/sp016/index.cfm?newsId=d2d1801d18&newsDate=20040818, accessed on January 8, 2005.

Nippon Kogyo Ginko (Industrial Bank of Japan) (2002) "Gurobaru kyoso jidai ni okeru wagakuni kouri kigyo no seicho senryaku" (Growth strategies of the domestic retail firms in the age of global competition). *Kogin Chosa* 308, 3: 59–130.

O'Connor, R. (1998) "Target Europe: Wal-Mart Sets up Beachhead in Germany." *Chain Store Age,* March, 55–60.

Palmer, K., and B. Quinn (2001) "The Strategic Role of Investment Banks in the Retailer Internationalisation Process: Is This Venture Marketing?" *European Journal of Marketing* 37, 10: 1391–408.

Raumordnungsgesetz (1997). In Bundesgesetzblatt I: 2081–102. Available at http://jurcom5.juris.de/bundesrecht/rog/gesamt.pdf, accessed April 23, 2004.

Reichsgesetzblatt (1909). "Gesetz gegen den unlauteren Wettbewerb" (Law against unfair competition), June 7, p. 499, June 7. Available at http://transpatent.com/gesetze/uwg.html, accessed December 15, 2004.

——— (1932) "Zugabeverordnung" (Giveaway regulation). In Reichsgesetzblatt I, p. 121, March 9. Available at http://transpatent.com/gesetze/zugabev.html, accessed April 23, 2004.

——— (1933) "Gesetz über Preisnachlässe" (Rebate law) (1933). In Reichsgesetzblatt 1933 I, p. 1011, November 25. Available at http://transpatent.com/gesetze/rabattg.html, accessed December 15, 2004.

Ronke, C. (2005) "Wal-Mart spürt Trendwende in Deutschland" (Wal-Mart perceives a reversal of the trend in Germany). *Financial Times Deutschland*, February 18, 6.

Ronke, C., and N. de Paoli (2002) "C&A entfacht Streit um Wettbewerbsrecht" (C&A triggers battle about competition legislation). *Financial Times Deutschland*, June 1. Available at www.ftd.de/ub/di/8180604.html?nv=hptn, accessed January 7, 2005.

Rosenbloom, B. (1975) "Distance and Number of Retail Stores: Land Area as a Proxy for Distance." *Journal of the Academy of Marketing Science* 3: 200–4.

Rowley, I. (2004) "Can Wal-Mart Woo Japan? Early Signs at Its Seiyu Chain Suggest the Retailer's Model May Work." *Business Week*, May 10, 18.

Russel, V. K. (1957) "The Relationship between Income and Retail Sales in Local Areas." *Journal of Marketing* 22, January: 329–32.

Shimada, Y. (2003) *Wal-Mart wa hontou ni kyoi ka* (Is Wal-Mart really a threat?). Tokyo: Daiamondosha.

Shukan Daiyamondo (2005) "Seiyu." February 12, 100–3.

Takeuchi, H., and L. P. Bucklin (1977) "Productivity in Retailing: Retail Structure and Public Policy." *Journal of Retailing* 53: 35–46.

Tamura, M. (1986) *Nihon-gata ryutsu shisutemu* (The Japanese system of distribution), Tokyo: Chikura Shobo.

Tomkins, R. (1997) "Wal-Mart Comes Shopping in Europe." *Financial Times* (London), December 21, 15.

Trade Dimensions/M+M Eurodata (2005) Racher Press research. *Lebensmittel Zeitung*, www.lz-net.de/companies/rankings/pages/show.prl?id=162.

Tsukiizumi, H. (2004) *Yokuwakaru ryutsu gyokai* (Understanding the distribution sector). Tokyo: Nippon Jitsu-gyo Shuppansha.

Vielberth, H. (1995) "Retail Planning Policy in Germany." In R. L. Davies, ed., *Retail Planning Policies in Western Europe*. London and New York: Routledge.

Wal-Mart (2004) *Annual Report 2004*. Available at http://media.corporate-ir.net/media_files/irol/11/112761/reports/wmt_040704.pdf.

Wal-Mart Germany (2004) "Wal-Mart sieht sich gestärkt durch anhaltende Rabattschlachten im Einzelhandel" (Wal-Mart sees itself strengthened through continuing rebate wars in retailing). Press release, Wuppertal, February 19.

Wrigley, N. (1992) "Antitrust Regulation and the Restructuring of Grocery Retailing in Britain and the USA." *Environment and Planning A* 24: 727–49.

Wrigley, N., and A. D. Currah (2004) "Networks of Organizational Learning and Adaptation in Retail TNCs." *Global Networks* 4: 1–23.

Wrigley, N., M. Lowe, and A. Currah (2002) "Retailing and E-tailing." *Urban Geography* 23, 2: 180–97.

Zellner, W., K. Schmidt, M. Ihlwan, and H. Dawley (2001) "How Well Does Wal-Mart Travel?" *Business Week*, September 3, 82.

Chapter 21

Akehurst, Gary, and Nicholas Alexander (1995) "Developing a Framework for the Study of the Internationalisation of Retailing." *The Service Industries Journal* 15: 204–10.

Alexander, Nicholas, and Hayley Myers (2000) "The Retail Internationalisation Process." *International Marketing Review* 17: 334–53.

Anderson, Otto (1993) "On the Internationalisation Process of Firms: A Critical Analysis." *Journal of International Business Studies* 2: 209–31.

Barboza, David (2004) "Wal-Mart Bows to Trade Unions at Stores in China." *New York Times*, November 24.

Cai, Z. (1997) "The Rise of Wal-Mart in China." *Science and Technology Think Tank* 11: 13–15.

Cao, Derong (2004) "Speech on Opening of China's Commercial Sector to FDI." *Shanghai Commerce News*. Available at www.commerce.sh.cn.

Chan, Wing-Kwong, et al. (1997) "China's Retail Markets Are Evolving More Quickly than Companies Anticipate." *The McKinsey Quarterly* 2: 206–11.

Che, Yuming (2002) "President Jiang Zemin Receives Wal-Mart CEO." *People's Daily* (overseas edition), October 9.

Chen, Guang (2004) *Carrefour Strategies*, Guangzhou: *South China Daily* Publishing House.

Crawford, Fred (2001) "Business without Borders." *Chain Store Age* 12: 86–96.

Dawson, John A. (1994) "Internationalisation of Retailing Operations." *Journal of Marketing Management* 10: 267–82.

Du, Yiming (2005) "Makro Is Closing Its Store in Shenyang." *Shenyang Daily*, February 21.

Dunning, J. H. (1988) *International Production and the Multinational Enterprise*. London: Allen and Unwin.

Dupuis, Marc, and Nathalie Prime (1996). "Business Distance and Global Retailing: A Model for Analysis of Key Success/Failure Factors." *International Journal of Retail and Distribution Management* 24: 30–38.

Economic Observer (2005) "Zhongxin-Taifu Purchases 35% Ownership of Wal-Mart East China Co. Ltd." February 17.

Editorial Board (1997) "An Overview of Regulations on Foreign Investment in Retailing in China." *Science and Technology Think Tank* 11: 4–6.

Elango, B. (1999) "An Empirical Examination of the Influence of Industry and Firm Drivers on the Rate of Internationalisation by Firms." *Journal of International Management* 4: 201–21.

Erramilli, M. Krishna (1991) "The Experience Factor in Foreign Market Entry Behaviour of Service Firms." *Journal of International Business Studies* 3: 479–501.

Flavelle, Dana (2005a) "Wal-Mart to Close Union Store." *Toronto Star*, February 10, D1.

———— (2005b) "Wal-Mart Workers in Windsor Seek Union, Again." *Toronto Star*, March 2, C5.

Foord, Jo, et al. (1996) "The Changing Place of Retailer-Supplier Relations in British Retailing." Pp. 68–89 in N. Wrigley and M. Lowe, eds., *Retailing, Consumption and Capital: Towards the New Retail Geography*. Essex, England: Longman Group Ltd.

Golden Times (2004) "Wal-Mart Recruit Suppliers in Zhejiang, Only One Third Pass Screening." December 20.

Greenhouse, Steven (2005) "Developer Drops Plan for City's First Wal-Mart." *New York Times*, February 24.

Hays, Constance L. (2004) "From Bentonville to Beijing and Beyond." *New York Times*, December 6.

International Financial Post (2004) "China's Retail Sector Now Completely Opens to Foreign Retailers, Competitions Are Expected to Intensify in 2005." December 23.

Knox, Paul, John Agnew, and Linda McCarthy (2003) *The Geography of the World Economy*, 4th ed. London: Hodder Arnold.

Koopman, John C. (2000) "Successful Global Retailers a Rare Breed." *Canadian Manager*, spring, 22–28.

Kynge, James, and Edward Young (2001) "Wal-Mart Gets Go-ahead to Open Stores in Beijing: Good Year for Retailer: U.S. Company's Fortunes Rise While Rival Carrefour's Fall." *Financial Post (National Post)*, November 8.

Li Mingwei (2004) "Property Rent at Premium Business Location in Shanghai Is Soaring: Department Stores Are Doomed to Suffer." *People's Daily* (overseas edition), March 15.

Li Youjun and Liu Xiaolin (2004) "Why Do Foreign Companies Refuse Formation of Workers Union?" *People's Daily* (overseas edition), December 3.

Lin Xiaoli and Li Sun (2004) "Wal-Mart Was Introduced in China by Us." *Guangzhou Daily*, December 11.

Liu Renhui (2004) "Which Suppliers Should Do Business with Wal-Mart?" *Financial Times*, May 9.

Lu Guoman (2000) "Speech at the Forum on Retail Chain Development." *Supplementary Papers Presented at the Second Forum on Chain Store Development in China*, Beijing: China Chain Store and Franchise Association.

Ma Xiaosen (2004) "Lee Scott: Wal-Mart Will Not Operate Wholly-Owned Stores in China." *Beijing Morning News*, November 3.

Mata, J. (1991) "Sunk Costs and Entry by Small and Large Plants." Pp. 49–62 in P. A. Geroski and J. Schwalback, eds., *Entry and Market Contestability and International Comparison*. Oxford: Blackwell.

McGregor, Richard (2004) "Wal-Mart Compliant with China's Trade Union Laws." *National Post*, November 24.

Ministry of Commerce (2004) *Policies Governing Foreign Investment in the Commercial Sector*. Beijing.

Olive, David (2004) "Hitting the Wall." *Toronto Star*, August 29.

Pelligrini, L. (1991) "The Internationalisation of Retailing, 1992 Europe." *Journal of Marketing Channels* 2: 3–27.

Shackleton, Ruth (1996) "Retailer Internationalization; A Culturally Constructed Phenomenon." Pp. 37–56 in N. Wrigley and M. Lowe, eds., *Retailing, Consumption and Capital: Towards the New Retail Geography*. Essex, England: Longman Group Ltd.

Shanghai Almanac Compilation Committee (2001) *Shanghai Almanac 2001*. Shanghai: Shanghai Almanac Publisher.

———— (2003) *Shanghai Almanac 2003*. Shanghai: Shanghai Almanac Publisher.

Shanghai Commerce Information Center (2004a) "Wal-Mart Is Quietly Developing Its Pudong Store; Its Two Other Stores in Shanghai Delayed." *Shanghai Commerce News*. Available at www.commerce.sh.cn.

———— (2004b) "Wal-Mart Signs Contract with Huayuan Group to Open a Supercenter in Beijing's Zhong-guan-cun." *Shanghai Commerce News*. Available at www.commerce.sh.cn.

———— (2004c) "Lee Scott Responds to Questions about the Union Issue in China." *Shanghai Commerce News*. Available at www.commerce.sh.cn.

Shanghai Commerce Information Center and Sona Consulting Ltd (2003). *The White Book of Shanghai's Retail Development*. Shanghai: Shanghai Commerce Information Center.

Shenzhen Economic Daily (2004) "Wal-Mart's Asia HQ Office Will Have a New Home in Shenzhen." October 27.

Simmons, Jim, Ken Jones, and Maurice Yeats (1998) "The Need for International Comparisons of Commercial Structure and Change." *Progress in Planning* 4: 207–16.

Simmons, Jim, and Tom Graff (1998) "Wal-Mart Comes to Canada." Research Report 9, Center for the Study of Commercial Activity, Ryerson Polytechnic University, Toronto.

Simmons, Jim, and Shizue Kamikihara (1999) "The Internationalisation of Commercial Activities in Canada," Research Report 7. Center for the Study of Commercial Activity, Ryerson Polytechnic University, Toronto.

Simpson, Eithel, and Dayle I. Thorpe (1999) "A Special Store's Perspective on Retail Internationalisation: A Case Study." *Journal of Retailing and Consumer Services* 6: 45–53.

The South Daily (2004) "Wal-Mart Massive Purchases in China Cause Chain Effects." November 18.

State Economic and Trade Commission and Ministry of Foreign Trade (1999) "Interim Stipulations for Foreign-Invested Commercial Enterprises." *Essays on Commerce Economy* 5: 38–40.

Sternquist, Brenda (1997) "International Expansion of US Retailers." *International Journal of Retail and Distribution Management* 8: 262–68.

Sun Haishun (1999) "Entry Modes of Multinational Corporations into China's Market: A Socioeconomic Analysis." *International Journal of Social Economics* 26: 642–59.

Tu Jianlu (2004) "Wal-Mart's Secret of Everyday Low Price." *Beijing Commence Times*, March 19.

Vida, Irena, and Ann Fairhurst (1998) "International Expansion of Retail Firms: A Theoretical Approach for Future Investigations." *Journal of Retailing and Consumer Services* 5: 143–51.

Wal-Mart China (2003) Wal-Mart Awarded "2002 Most Favorite Stores in Shenzhen." http://www.wal-martchina.com/english/news/2003040402.htm

Wal-Mart China (2004a) Wal-Mart Supercenter Qianjin Square Store Opens Wal-Mart Donated Again for Shanhe Hope School in Changchu http://www.wal-martChina.com/english/news/20040402.htm

Wal-Mart China (2004b) Wal-Mart China Awarded Outstanding Social Welfare Contribution. http://www.wal-martchina.com/english/news/20040601.htm

Wal-Mart China (2005) http://www.wal-martChina.com/english/index.htm

Wal-Mart International (2005a) Canada Fact Sheet http://walmartstores.com/GlobalWMStoresWeb/navigate.do?catg=374

Wal-Mart International (2005b) Germany Fact Sheet http://walmartstores.com/GlobalWMStoresWeb/navigate.do?catg=376

Wanda Group (2005) www.wanda.com.cn.

Wang Shuguang (2003) "Internationalization of Retailing in China." Pp. 114–35 in J. Dawson, M. Mukoyama, S. C. Choi and R. Larke, eds., *Internationalization of Retailing in Asia*. London: Routledge Curzon.

Wang Shuguang and Zhang Yongchang (2005) "The New Retail Geography of Shanghai." *Growth and Change* 1: 16–48.

Wang Xiaoming (2004) *Wa-Mart's 44 Secrets for Becoming a Retail Empire.* Beijing: Jiuzhou Publishing House.

Whitehead, Maureen B. (1992) "Internationalisation of Retailing: Developing New Perspectives." *European Journal of Marketing* 8–9: 74–79.

Wrigley, N. (2000) "The Globalisation of Retail Capital: Themes for Economic Geography." In Gordon Clark, Meric Gertler and Maryann Feldman, eds., *Handbook of Economic Geography*. London: Oxford University.

Yang Fang and Li Yan (2005) "Wal-Mart Broke Its Promise and Issued Gift Cards." *Huanshang Morning News*, January 31.

Yang Kairan and Ma Meifang (2004) "The Issue of Union Flares Up, Wal-Mart CEO Comes to Rescue." *Capital Times*, November 3.

Yang Lihong et al. (2004) "International Retail Giants Compete to Invest in China to Capitalize on a Completely Open Market." *China Business News*, November 15.

Yip, George S. (1989) "Global Strategy … in a World of Nations?" *Sloan Management Review* 1: 29–41.

——— (1992) *Total Global Strategy: Managing for Worldwide Competitive Advantage* Englewood Cliffs, N.J.: Prentice Hall.

Zhang Yi and Wang Yu (2004) "China's Retail Sector Is to Open Further to FDI." *People's Daily* (overseas edition), March 18.

Zhao Haifeng (2003) *Wal-Mart's Way of Doing Business,* Beijing: Economics and Technology Publisher.

Zheng Chunping (2003) "Suppliers of Toasted Nuts and Melon Seeds in Shanghai 'Toast' Carrefour." *People's Daily* (overseas edition), July 7.

Chapter 22

Alexander, N. (1997) *International Retailing*. Blackwell: Oxford.

Alexander, N., and H. Myers (2000) "The Retail Internationalization Process." *International Marketing Review* 17: 334–53.

Chan, K. W. (2003) "Chinese Census 2000: New Opportunities and Challenges." *The China Review* 3, 2: 1–12.

Child, J., and S. Stewart (1997) "Regional Differences in China and Their Implications for Sino-Foreign Joint Ventures." *Journal of General Management* 23, 2: 65–84.

Classen, C. (1996) "Sugar Cane, Coca-Cola and Hypermarkets: Consumption and Surrealism in the Argentine Northwest." Pp. 39–54 in D. Howes, ed., *Cross-Cultural Consumption: Global Markets, Local Realities.*

Coe, N. M. (2004) "The Internationalization/Globalization of Retailing: Toward an Economic-Geographical Research Agenda." *Environment and Planning A* 36: 1571–94.

Crang, P. (1996) "Displacement, Consumption and Identity." *Environment and Planning A* 28: 47–67.

Crewe, L. (2003) "Geographies of Retailing and Consumption: Markets in Motion." *Progress in Human Geography* 27, 3: 352–262.

Crewe, L., and M. Lowe (1995) "Gap on the Map? Toward a Geography of Consumption and Identity." *Environment and Planning A* 27: 1877–98.

Cui, G. and Liu, Q. (2000) "Regional Market Segments of China: Opportunities and Barriers in a Big Emerging Market," *Journal of Consumer Marketing*, 17(1):55–72.

Davies, K. (1994) "Foreign Investment in the Retail Sector of the People's Republic of China." *Columbia Journal of World Business* 29, 2: 56–69.

Dicken, P. (2003) *Global Shift,* 4th ed. London: Sage.

Dwyer, C., and P. Jackson (2003) "Commodifying Difference: Selling EASTern Fashion." *Environment and Planning D* 21: 269–91.

Erkip, F. (2003) "The Shopping Mall as an Emergent Public Space in Turkey." *Environment and Planning A* 35: 1073–93.

Glennie, P., and N. Thrift (1996) "Consumers, Identities, and Consumption Spaces in Early-Modern England." *Environment and Planning A* 28: 25–45.

Goss, J. (1993) "The Magic of the Mall." *Annals of the Association of American Geographers* 83: 18–47.

Gregson, N. (1995) "And Now It's All Consumption?" *Progress in Human Geography* 19: 135–44.

Gregson, N., L. Crewe, and K. Brooks (2002) "Shopping, Space, and Practice." *Environment and Planning D: Society and Space* 20: 597–617.

Jackson, P. (1998) "Domesticating the Street: The Contested Spaces of the High Street and the Mall." Pp. 176–91 in N. Fyfe, ed., *Images of the Street: Representation, Experience and Control in Public Space.* London: Routledge.

——— (2002) "Commercial Cultures: Transcending the Cultural and the Economic." *Progress in Human Geography* 26, 1: 3–18.

——— (2004) "Local Consumption Cultures in a Globalizing World." *Transactions IBG* 29: 165–78.

Jackson, P., and B. Holbrook (1995) "Multiple Meanings: Shopping and the Cultural Politics of Identity." *Environment and Planning A* 27: 1913–30.

Knox, P. (1995) "World Cities and the Organization of Global Space." Pp. 232–47 in R. J. Johnston et al., eds., *Geographies of Global Change: Remapping the World in the Late Twentieth Century* Blackwell, Cambridge, Mass.

McGoldrick, P. J., and G. Daview, eds. (1995) *International Retailing: Trends and Strategies.* London: Pitman.

Michell, D. (1995) "The End of Public Space? People's Park, Definition of the Public, and Democracy." *Annals of the Association of American Geographers* 85: 108–33.

Miller, D., P. Jackson, N. Thrift, B. Holbrook, and M. Rowlands (1998) *Shopping Place and Identity.* London: Routledge.

Mitchell, K. (1995) "Flexible Circulation in the Pacific Rim: Capitalisms in Cultural Context." *Economic Geography* 71, 4: 364–82.

Nilsson, K., and T. McNiel (1994) "A Retail Explosion." *China Business Review* 21, 6: 38.

Peet, R. (1989) "World Capitalism and the Destruction of Regional Cultures." Pp. 175–99 in R. J. Johnston and P. Taylor, eds., *A World in Crisis,* 2nd edition.

Penaloza, L. (1994) "Atravesando Fronteras/Border Crossings: A Critical Ethnographic Exploration of the Consumer Acculturation of Mexican Immigrants," *Journal of Consumer Research*, 22(1): 32–55.

Penazola, L. (1994) "Exploration of the Consumer Acculturation of Mexican Immigrants." *Journal of Consumer Research* 21, 1: 32–54.

Sin, L. Y. M. and S. C. Ho (2001) "An Assessment of Theoretical and Methodological Development in Consumer Research in Greater China: 1979-1997." *Asia Pacific Journal of Marketing and Logistics* 13, 1: 3–42.

Slater, D. (2003) "Cultures of Consumption." Pp. 147–64 in K. Anderson, M. Domosh, S. Pile, and N. Thrift, eds., *Handbook of Cultural Geography.* London: Sage.

Vanderbeck, R. M. (2000) "That's the Only Place Where You Can Hang Out: Urban Young People and the Space of the Mall." *Urban Geography* 21, 1: 5–25.

Veeck, A. (2004) "Changing Tastes: The Adoption of New Food Choices in Post-Reform China." *Journal of Business Research* 55, 8: 1–15.

Wal-Mart China (2005) "The Wal-Mart Culture." Available at www.Wal-Martchina.com/english/walmart/culture.htm, accessed March 9, 2005.

Wang, D. (2000) "Hong Konger's Cross-Border Consumption and Shopping in Shenzhen: Patterns and Motivations." *Journal of Retailing and Consumer Services* 11: 149–59.

Wang, L., and L. Lo (2006) "Immigrant Grocery Shopping Behavior: Ethnic Identity versus Accessibility." *Environment and Planning A* (forthcoming).

Wang, S. (2003) "Internationalization of Retailing in China." Pp. 114–35 in J. Dawson, M. Mukoyama, S. C. Choi, and R. Larke, eds., *Internationalization of Retailing in Asia*. London: Routledge Curzon.

Wang, S., and K. Jones (2001) "China's Retail Sector in Transition." *Asian Geographer* 20 (1–2): 25–51.

——— (2002) "Retail Structure of Beijing." *Environment and Planning A* 34: 1785–808.

Watson, J. L. (1998) "Introduction: Transnationalism, Localization, and Fast Foods in East Asia." Pp. 1–38 in J. L. Watson, ed., *Golden Arches East: McDonald's in East Asia*.

Wong, G. K. M., and L. Yu (2003) "Consumers' Perception of Store Image of Joint Venture Shopping Centers: First-Tier versus Second-Tier Cities in China." *Journal of Retailing and Consumer Services* 10, 2: 61–70.

Wrigley, N. (2002) "The Globalization of Retail Capital: Themes for Economic Geography." Pp. 292–313 in G. L. Clark, M. P. Feldman, and M. S. Gertler, eds., *The Oxford Handbook of Economic Geography*. Oxford: Oxford University Press.

Zhang, J., and A. Kapur (1995) "China: Poised for Retail Explosion." *Global Retailing* 71, 1: 10–15.

Zukin, S. (1995) *Cities of Culture*. Cambridge, MA : Blackwell.

——— (1998) "Urban Lifestyle: Diversity and Standardization in Spaces of Consumption." *Urban Studies* 35, 5: 825–39.

Chapter 23

Cheung, S. N. S. (1982) *Will China Go Capitalist?* London: Institute of Economic Affairs.

Coase, R. H. (1937) "The Nature of the Firm." *Economica* 4, 16: 386–405.

Friedman, M., and R. Friedman (1990) *Free to Choose: A Personal Statement*. London: Harcourt Brace.

Hu, D., T. Reardon, S. Rozelle, P. Timmer, and H. Wang (2004) "The Emergence of Supermarkets with Chinese Characteristics: Challenges and Opportunities for China's Agricultural Development." *Development Policy Review* 22, 5: 557–86.

Hu, J. (1988) *A Concise History of Chinese Economic Thought*. Beijing: Foreign Languages Press.

Jiang, Jinqjing (2004) "Walmart's China Inventoty to Hit US$ 18b in 2004." *China Daily,* November 29. Available at www.chinadaily.com.cn/english/doc/2004-11/29, accessed February 20, 2005.

Messinger, P. R., and C. Narasimhan (1997) "A Model of Retail Formats Based on Consumer' Economizing on Shopping Time." *Marketing Science* 16, 1: 1–23.

Nelson, R. H. (1999) "Privatizing the Neighbourhood: A Proposal to Replace Zoning with Private Collective Property Rights to Existing Neighbourhoods." *George Mason Law Review* 7, 4: 827–80.

Pun, P. (2004) "Wal-Mart Juggernaut Roars Ahead in China." *The Standard*, November 22, 2004. Available at www.thestandard.com.hk/news_detail_frame.cfm?articleid=52383&intcatid=1, accessed February 21, 2005.

Schafer, S. (2004) "A Welcome to Walmart." *Newsweek* International Edition, December 20. Available at www.msnbc.msn.com/id/6700787site/newsweek, accessed February 20, 2005.

Webster, C., F. Wu, and Z. Zhao (2005) "China's modern gated cities." In G. Glasze, C. Webster, and K. Frantz, eds., *Private Cities: Global and Local Perspectives*. London: Routledge.

Webster, C. J., and L. W. C. Lai (2003) *Property Rights, Planning and Markets: Managing Spontaneous Cities*. Cheltenham, UK: Edward Elgar.

Williamson, O. E. (1985) *The Economic Institutions of Capitalism*. New York: Free Press.

Zhuang, G., N. Zhou, and N. C. Hernon Jr. (2002) "Scale Economies of Department Stores in the People's Republic of China." *The International Review of Retail, Distribution and Consumer Research* 12, 1: 3–12.

Chapter 24

Burt, S., and L. Sparks (2001) "The Implications of Wal-Mart's Takeover of ASDA." *Environment and Planning A* 33: 1463–87.

Busch, L., and C. Bain (2004) "New! Improved? The Transformation of the Global Agrifood System." *Rural Sociology* 69, 3: 321–46.

Casares, H. (2004) "Fallo Judicial contra Wal Mart." *Diario de Yucatán*, October 19.

Castillo, R. (2004a) "Wal-Mart Stirs Up Mexico's Retail Landscape." *Logistics Today*, April, 11.
——— (2004b) "Taking It to the Competition, Mexican Style." *Logistics Today*, December, 10.
Chávez, M. (2002) "The Transformation of Mexican Retailing with NAFTA." *Development Policy Review* 20, 4: 503–13.
Christopherson, S. (2001) "Can Wal-Martization Be Stopped? Barriers to the Globalization of Retailing." Paper presented at the Leir Initiative on the Geographies of Global Economic Change, Clark Universty, Worcester, Mass., October 13.
Dolan C. and Humphrey, J. (2004) Changing Governance Patterns in the Trade in Fresh Vegetables between Africa and the United Kingdom" *Environment and Planning A* 36(3), 491–506.
Domínguez Massa, D. (2004) "Beneficia a 15,000 Yucatecos un Convenio." *Diario de Yucatán,* December 10.
Dugger, C. (2004) "Survival of the Biggest: Supermarket Giants Crush Central American Farmers." *New York Times*, December 28.
The Economist (2004) "How Big Can It Grow?" *The Economist*, April 17.
——— (2005) "Growing Pains." April 14.
Hallsworth, A., and D. Evers (2002) "The Steady Advance of Wal-Mart across Europe and Changing Government Attitudes towards Planning and Competition." *Environment and Planning C* 20: 297–309.
Harris, R. J. (1995) "Apparel Retailing in Mexico." *Textile Outlook International,* May 1995, 89–112.
INEGI (Instituto Nacional de Estadistica, Geographica e Informatica) (2005) Banco de Informacion Economica. Available at http://dgcnesyp.inegi.gob.mx, accessed May 31.
Lee, M. (2003) "Retail Giant Grows in Stature." *Business Mexico*, March, 36–37.
Masters, G. (2004) "Wal-Mart's Global Challenge." *Retail Merchandiser*, May, 26–27.
McKinley, J. C. (2004) "No, the Conquistadors Are Not Back. It's Just Wal-Mart." *New York Times*, September 28.
Morais, R. C. (2004) "One Hot Tamale." *Forbes* 174, 13, 137–47, Dec. 20.
Reardon, T., and J. A. Berdegué (2002) "The Rapid Rise of Supermarkets in Latin America: Challenges and Opportunities for Development." *Development Policy Review* 20, 4: 371–88.
Ross, J. (2005) "Teoti-Wal-Mart." *The Progressive,* March, 28–30.
Schwentesius, R., and M. A. Gómez (2002) "Supermarkets in Mexico: Impacts on Horticultural Systems." *Development Policy Review* 20, 4: 487–502.
Steffen, C., and F. Echánove (2003) "Efectos de las Políticas de Ajuste Estructural en los Productos de Granos y Hortalizas de Guanajuato." Universidad Autónoma Metropolitana, Mexico City.
Wal-Mart (2005) Annual Report to U.S. Securities and Exchange Commission (Form 10–K). January 31.
Wal-Mart de México (2005) Informe Annual 2004. Available at www.walmartmexico.com.mx/informe2004.pdf, accessed May 15.
Weiner, T. (2003) "Wal-Mart Invades and Mexico Gladly Surrenders." *New York Times*, December 6.
Wright, J. (2001) "For Sale." *Business Mexico* 10, 12: 32–37.
Wrigley, N. (2002) "Transforming the Corporate Landscape of US Food Retailing: Market Power, Financial Re-Engineering and Regulation." *Tijdschrift voor Econonische en Sociale Geografie* 93, 1: 62–82.

Chapter 25

7-Eleven Mexico (2005) Corporate website, "Quienes somos" page. http://www.7-eleven.com.mx/7-Eleven_Quienes_somos/7-eleven_quienes_somos.htm,
7-Eleven (2006) Corporate website, "International licensing" page. http://www.7-eleven.com/about/globalsites.asp.
Álvarez, José Luis (2005a) "Participación extranjera en el autoservicio mexicano: El efecto Wal-Mart." *Economía Informa*, forthcoming.
——— (2005b) "Wal-Mart Expansion in Mexico, 1999–2004." Department of Regional Economic and Social Development, University of Massachusetts, Lowell.
——— (2005c) "Four Companies: FDI Effects on Mexican Retail." Master's thesis, Department of Regional Economic and Social Development, University of Massachusetts, Lowell.
ANTAD (Asociacion Nacional de Tiendas de Autoservicio y Departamentales) (2005) Available at www.antad.org.mx, accessed January 2005.
Bensinger, Ken (2005) "Like the U.S., Mexico Feels Wal-Mart Era." *Christian Science Monitor*, March 15.
Bouzas, José Alfonso and Mario Vega (1999) "Condiciones de trabajo y relaciones laborales en las tiendas de autoservicio del D.F.: el caso de Gigante." Pp. 453–84 in Enrique de la Garza and José Alfonso Bouzas, eds., *Cambios en las Relaciones Laborales: Enfoque Sectoral y Regional,* vol. 2. México, DF: Universidad Nacional Autónoma de México, Instituto de Investigaciones Económicas.

Braine, Theresa (2004) "Good Things in Mexico Come in Small Formats." *DSN Retailing Today,* December 13, 43–44.

Buchenau, Jürgen (2004) *Tools of Progress: A German Merchant Family in Mexico City, 1865–Present.* Albuquerque: University of New Mexico Press.

Bunker, Steve (2003) "Business Most Unusual: The Business Practices and Pitfalls of the Palacio de Hierro in Porfirian Mexico." Paper presented at the Latin American Studies Association annual meeting, March 27–29, Dallas.

Case, Brendan (2004) "Millions of consumers welcome Wal-Mart to Mexico. *Dallas Morning News*, November 10.

Castillo Mireles, Ricardo (2005) "Across the Border: Taking It to the Competition, Mexican Style." *Logistics Today*, February.

Castro, Raúl (2005) "Entra Chedraui a puntos de venta de Carrefour." *Milenio Diario*, May 11.

Cevallos, Diego (2004) "Wal-Mart, the Pyramids' New Neighbour." Inter Press Service, September 4.

Chávez, Manuel (2002) "The Transformation of Mexican Retailing with NAFTA." *Development Policy Review* 20, 4: 371–88.

DSN Retailing Today (2001) "Wal-Mart International: Resilience and Format Diversity Keep First International Entry *Excelente*." June 1, 26.

Durand, Cédric (2005) "Externalities from FDI in the Mexican Self-Service Retailing Sector." Departamento de Economía, UNAM, Mexico City, February.

Dussel Peters, Enrique. 2004. *Efectos de la apertura comercial en el empleo y el mercado laboral de México y sus diferencias con Argentina y Brasil (1990–2003).* Employment Strategy Documents 2004/10, Internacional Labour Office, Geneva, Switzerland.

Featherstone, Liza (2004a) *Selling Women Short: The Landmark Battle for Workers' Rights at Wal-Mart.* New York: Basic Books.

——— (2004b) "Will Labor Take the Wal-Mart Challenge?" *The Nation*, June 28.

——— (2005) "Down and Out in Discount America." *The Nation*, January 3.

Fishman, Charles (2003) "The Wal-Mart You Don't Know." *Fast Company,* December, 68.

Frontline (2004) "Is Wal-Mart Good for America?" Public Broadcasting Service, November.

Geller, Adam (2005) "Wal-Mart to Close Store That's About to Unionize." Associated Press, February 10.

González Amador, Roberto (2004) "Riesgo para la soberanía, el poder de Wal-Mart en el mercado mexicano." *La Jornada*, July 8.

Goodwin, Neva (2004) "What Does the Wal-Mart Model Tell Us about the Globalized Economy?" Global Development and Environment Institute, Tufts University, Medford, Mass., December.

Government of the State of Michoacán (2004) "Por su contenido social, se buscará fortalecer el Programa de Lucha contra la Carestía en el Estado." Press release. August 30. Available at www.michoacan.gob.mx/noticias/ impresion.php?idsesion=b47f679c47d6ee5be680c8e3ed9b1773.

Hanrath, Alexander (2002) "Mexican Stores Wilt in the Face of US Group's Onslaught." *Financial Times*, August 14, 21.

Hawley, Chris (2004) "Wal-Mart vs. Pyramids." *Arizona Republic*, November 2.

Hoover's Online (2000). "Retail and Wholesale Industry Snapshot." Available at www.hoovers.com/industry/ snapshot/0,2204,37,00.html, accessed April 2000.

Latin America News Digest (2004) "Walmex Launches New Store Brand." November 9.

Luhnow, David (2001) "Crossover Success: How NAFTA Helped Wal-Mart Reshape the Mexican Market." *Wall Street Journal*, August 31.

Maldonado, Salvador Y. (2005) "La Concanaco insistirá en las leyes anti Wal-Mart." *Milenio Diario*, May 13.

McKinsey Global Institute (2003) *New Horizons: Multinational Company Investment in Developing Economies.* October. Available at www.mckinsey.com/mgi/publications/newhorizons/index.asp.

Mireles Castillo, Ricardo (2005) "To Combat Wal-Mart's Entry into the Market, Mexican Supermarkets Have Changed Their Supply Chains." *Logistics Today*, www.logisticstoday.com. February.

Morais, Richard C. (2004) "One Hot Tamale." *Forbes*, December 20.

Moreno, Julio (2004) "Wal-Mart y la diplomacia económica en América Latina." *Foreign Affairs en Español*, April-June.

Mulder, Nanno (2002) *Economic Performance in the Americas: The Role of the Service Sector in Brazil, Mexico and the USA.* Cheltenham, UK: Edward Elgar.

Rodríguez, Rogelio, and Ian Reider (2004) "Tendencias en México: Actitudes del consumidor y el supermercado." Presentation at the XXI Convención del Asociación Nacional de Tiendas de Autoservicio y Departamentales, March 12–15, Guadalajara, Jalisco.

Ross, John (2005) "Teoti-Wal-Mart." *The Progressive*, March. Available at www.progressive.org/march05/teoti0305. html.

Schwentesius, Rita, and Manuel Ángel Gómez (2002) "The Rise of Supermarkets in Mexico: Impacts on Horticulture Chains." *Development Policy Review* 20, 4: 487–502.

Seckler, Valerie, and Joanna Ramey (1997) "Sears Unloading Bulk of Mexican Business, Said to Eye Eaton's." *Women's Wear Daily*, April 3, 1–2.

Secretaría del Trabajo y Previsión Social (2004) "Salarios mínimos vigentes a partir del 1o. de enero 2004." Available at www.stps.gob.mx, accessed March 2005.

Tilly, Chris (forthcoming) "Wal-Mart in Mexico: The Limits of Growth." In Nelson Lichtenstein, ed., *Wal-Mart: The Face of 21st Century Capitalism*. New York: New Press.

El Universal/Mexico News (2005) "New Head Named for Wal-Mart in Mexico." January 8.

Velasco, Carlos (2004) "Firma Wal-Mart convenio con campesinos." *El Universal* online, December 7. Available at www.eluniversal.com.mx.

Wal-Mart (2005) corporate web site, "The Wal-Mart Story" page, http://walmartstores.com/globalwmstoresweb/navigate.do?catg=5

Wal-Mart de Mexico (2005) corporate web page, "Distribucion geografica" http://www.walmartmexico.com.mx/acerca.html?id=48.619811137149306.

Wal-Mart de Mexico (2006) corporate web page 2006 Annual Report. http://www.walmartmexico.com.mx/files/2005informeanual.pdf.

Wrigley, Neil (2002) "Transforming the Corporate Landscape of US Food Retailing: Market Power, Financial Re-engineering, and Regulation." *Tijdschrift voor Economische en Sociale Geografie* 93, 1: 62–82.

Contributors

Yuko Aoyama is associate professor in the Department of Geography, Clark University. Her research interests are global economic change, technological innovation, and industrial organization.

Stephen J. Arnold is professor emeritus in the School of Business at Queen's University, Kingston, Ontario. His research interest is the globalization of retail.

Jennifer Bair is assistant professor of sociology at Yale University. Her research interests include globalization, labor, and development in Latin America.

Holly Barcus is assistant professor in the Department of Geography, Macalester College. Her major research interests are in rural geography, population geography, and GIS.

Sam Bernstein is a recent graduate of Yale University with a B.A. in sociology. His research interests include social movements, labor, and class theory.

James J. Biles is an assistant professor in the Department of Geography, Indiana University. His research interests are regional development and globalization in Latin America.

Edna Bonacich is professor of sociology and ethnic studies at the University of California, Riverside. Her research interests are social inequality, race, class, and labor.

Alecia M. Brettschneider is a Ph.D. student at Texas State University—San Marcos. Her research interests include urban geography, population geography, and GIS.

Nailin Bu is an associate professor of international relations at Queen's University School of Business, Queen's University, Kingston. Her research interests are in cross-cultural management and business and management in China.

Steve Burt is professor of retail marketing at the University of Stirling. His research interests are in retail internationalization, retail branding, and comparative retailing.

Thomas Chapman is a Ph.D. student in the Department of Geography, Florida State University, Tallahassee. His research interests are social theory, geographies of human rights and social justice, and political identities.

Susan Christopherson is professor in the Department of City and Regional Planning at Cornell University. Her research interests are labor markets, media studies, market governance, and European studies.

Lisa De Chano is assistant professor of geography at Western Michigan University. Her major research interests are environmental geography, natural hazards and hazard perception, environmental education, and the geography of sport.

A. Jane Dunnett is assistant professor of marketing in the Faculty of Business Administration at the University of New Brunswick. Her research interests include retailing, organizational culture, and the dynamics of consumer choice.

Ulrike Gerhard is *doctor habilitation* in the Geographisches Institut at the Universität Wurzburg, Wurzburg. His research interests are in retail geography, urban geography, North America, and Germany.

Mark Graham is a Ph.D. student in the Department of Geography at the University of Kentucky. His research interests are cyberspace, economic geography, and local economic development.

William Graves is assistant professor of geography and John H. Biggs Faculty Fellow at the University of North Carolina at Charlotte. His research interests are the geography of finance and urban change in the U.S. South.

Peter Hugill is professor of geography in the Bush School International Affairs Program at Texas A and M University, College Station. His major research interests are the historical, political, and cultural geography of the world economy.

Wei Li is an associate professor in the Asian Pacific American Studies Program and the Department of Geography at Arizona State University. Her research interests are urban ethnicity and ethnic geography, immigration and integration, the financial sector, and minority community development.

Lucia Lo is an associate professor in the Department of Geography at York University. Her research interests are immigrant settlement and integration; culture, ethnicity, and consumer behavior; and ethnic economy.

Dennis Lord is professor emeritus, Department of Geography, University of North Carolina, Charlotte, where he taught for thirty-five years. His major interests include retail location analysis, trade area assessment, store sales forecasting methods, and retail saturation.

Elke Pioch is senior lecturer in the Department of Retail Management at Manchester Metropolitan University. Her research interests are retail internationalization and retail change, employment issues in retailing, and consumption studies.

Adrienne M. Proffer is an M.A. candidate in the Department of Geography at the University of Oklahoma. Her research interests include ecotourism and small-town revitalization in the United States.

Ellen Rosen is a sociologist and professor emeritus at Nicholas College. Her research interests include women and the workplace, sex discrimination, and corporate globalization's impacts on women in the labor force.

Guido Schwarz is a Ph.D. candidate in the Department of Geography, Clark University. His interests are economic geography of logistics and transportation, retail trade, and location and simulation modeling.

Fred Shelley is professor and chair of the Department of Geography, University of Oklahoma. His research interests include political geography, electoral geography, and the cultural geography of North America.

Ben Smith is a Ph.D. student in the Department of Geography, University of Kentucky. His major interests are in landscape, cultural economy, and the Persian Gulf.

Leigh Sparks is professor of retail studies at the University of Stirling. His research interests are in spatial-structural change in retail systems.

Zhengxin Sun is a Ph.D. student in the School of Business at Queen's University, Kingston. His interests include retail globalization, consumers' participation in services, and the marketing of technology.

Chris Tilly is University Professor of Regional Economics and Social Development at the University of Massachusetts, Lowell. His research interests are low-wage work, income distribution, and regional development in the United States and Mexico.

Lea VanderVelde is Josephine Witte Professor of Law at the University of Iowa. Her research is in the areas of labor and property rights and the nature of legal change over time. She draws inspiration from social and legal history, cross-cultural observation, and legal realism. Her current interests include modern slavery, labor migration, and globalization.

Yanga Villagómez Velázquez is a researcher at El Colegio de Michoacán, México, where he studies communal land holdings, such as *ejidos* and *propiedades de bienes y comunales.* He also studies water rights in rural communities, peasants and the socioeconomic development process of globalization, and hydroagricultural politics and their impacts on the natural environment.

David Walker is a Ph.D. student in the Department of Geography, University of Kentucky. His major interests incorporate a theoretical approach to urbanization and spaces of resistance, neoliberalization, and the restructuring of urban spaces vis-à-vis race/gender and identity within the milieu of Mexican cities.

Margath Walker is a Ph.D. student in the Department of Geography, University of Kentucky. Her major interests are at the intersection of critical border theory, discursive construction of the "nation," and gender in Latin America.

Lu Wang is an assistant professor in the Department of Geography, Queen's University, Kingston. Her research interests are in consumption, culture and identities; economic geography; ethnicity, immigration, and ethnic economies; transnationalism; and retail internationalization and cultural globalization.

Shuguang Wang is associate professor and chair in the Department of Geography, Ryerson University. His major research interests are the internationalization of retailing and the geography of retailing.

Barney Warf is professor and chair of the Department of Geography, Florida State University, Tallahassee. His major research interests are social theory and the political economy of services.

Chris Webster is professor of urban planning at Cardiff University and also an honorary professor in the Department of Construction and Real Estate at Hong Kong University. His major research interests are in the economies of cities, city planning, and the spatial complexities in urban systems.

Jake Wilson is a Ph.D. student in the Department of Sociology at the University of California, Riverside. His interests are race, class, labor, and masculinities.

Yougchang Zhang is a lecturer in the Department of Geography, East China Normal University. His research interests are economic geography and the geography of retailing in China.

Matthew Zook is an assistant professor in the Department of Geography, University of Kentucky. His major research interests include e-commerce, the geographies of cyberspace, and the interaction between technological, spatial, and organizational structures in the economy.

Index